GRAPHICS TECHNOLOGY

James H. Earle

Texas A&M University

ADDISON-WESLEY PUBLISHING COMPANY

Reading, Massachusetts • Menlo Park, California • New York
Don Mills, Ontario • Wokingham, England • Amsterdam • Bonn
Sydney • Singapore • Tokyo • Madrid • San Juan • Milan • Paris

Dedicated to Theresa Earle

Sponsoring Editor	Denise Descoteaux/Stuart Johnson
Production Supervisor	Juliet Silveri
Production Packaging Services	Sandra Rigney
Copyeditor/Proofreader	Joyce Grandy
Dummier	Julia Fair/Sandra Rigney
Art Coordinator	Alena Konecny
Cover Designer	Eileen Hoff
Manufacturing Manager	Roy Logan

Library of Congress Cataloging-in-Publication Data

Earle, James H.

  Graphics technology / James H. Earle.
     p.   cm.
  Includes index.
  ISBN 0-201-51650-0
  1. Engineering graphics.   I. Title.
  T353.E35   1995
  604.2--dc20

                                                        94-41524
                                                          CIP

4 5 6 7 8 9 10 -DOC- 00 99

Preface

Graphics Technology covers the principles of engineering graphics and graphical problem solving for courses in two- and four-year programs. Its content is based on the needs of industry and is presented in a classroom-tested format that is as functional and understandable as possible.

Content

The major areas of engineering graphics that this text presents are:

- working drawings
- descriptive geometry
- computer graphics
- introductory design
- specialty areas
- communications in general

Knowledge of all of these areas is important to the career of the engineer, technologist, and technician.

The principles of working drawing preparation are based on the ANSI standards, and include dimensioning, tolerances, welding, and material specifications. Descriptive geometry principles are covered to aid three-dimensional problem solving and spatial analysis.

Chapter 30 gives an overview of two- and three-dimensional computer graphics. Introductory design is covered in Chapter 2, along with design problems that can be assigned as projects. Specialty areas of pipe drawing, electronic drawing, technical illustration, data analysis, and nomography are included to broaden the students' understanding of graphics technology.

Format Features

Graphics Technology has been designed to be as teachable as possible by including a number of features that make teaching easy for the teacher and learning easy for the student. These features are especially useful when students are working and studying on their own without the help of their teacher.

Features that help this learning transfer include:

- A second color which highlights steps in the solution

- Clear, teachable examples that assist with visualization

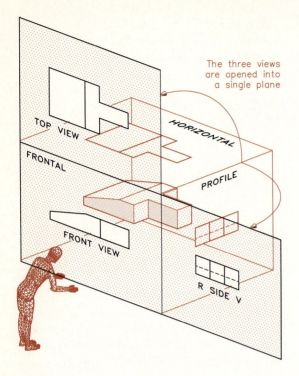

The three views are opened into a single plane

- Key points noted on the illustrations
- Human figures that show viewpoints

Line of sight is parallel to the FRP & perpendicular to the inclined plane

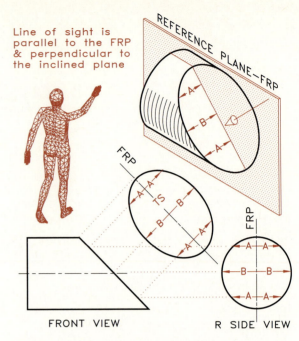

- Industrial examples which make problems meaningful

- Problems and examples that are presented using step-by-step illustrations

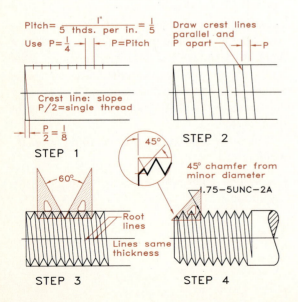

A Career Reference Book

Some material in this book may not be covered in the course for which it is used due to time limitation or the emphasis of the course by the instructor. Because the course may be the only graphics course that a student will encounter, this book should be retained for reference.

An engineering drawing is not just a document that is essential for a project to become a reality; it is a legal contract. As such its preparation must adhere to strict standards and be as clearly prepared as possible. Students can use this book as a reference throughout their professional careers.

A Learning System

This book can be used in combination with the supplements listed inside the back cover to create a complete teaching system.

Textbook Problems   Over 500 problems are available to aid the student in mastering important concepts.

Problem Manuals   Nineteen problem books and guides (with outlines, problem solutions, tests, and test solutions) are available for use with this book, and new problem books will be introduced in the future. Fifteen of the manuals include computer graphics versions of the exercises on the backs of the problem sheets, allowing the student to find the solution to each problem by both computer and pencil.

Acknowledgments

We are grateful for the assistance of many who have influenced the development of this volume. Numerous industries have furnished photographs, drawings, and applications that have been acknowledged in the corresponding legends. The Engineering Design Graphics staff of Texas A&M University have been helpful in making suggestions for this book. Professor Tom Pollock provided valuable information on various metals in Chapter 12.

We are indebted to Neal Alen, Rodger Payne, and Jimm Meloy of AutoDesk, Inc. for their assistance with AutoCAD®. We appreciate the assistance of Karen Kershaw of MegaCADD, Inc. David Ratner of Biomechanics Corporation was helpful in providing HUMANCAD® software.

We are appreciative of the many institutions that have thought enough of our publications to adopt them for classroom use. It is an honor for one's work to be accepted by colleagues. We are hopeful that this textbook will fill the needs of engineering and technology programs. As always, comments and suggestions for improvement and revision of this book will be appreciated.

College Station, Texas   *Jim Earle*

Brief Contents

Contents

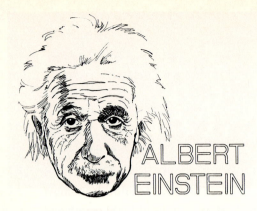

Figure 1.2 Albert Einstein: "Imagination is more important than knowledge."

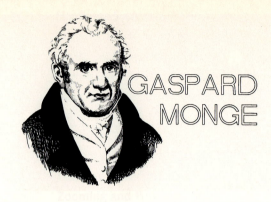

Figure 1.3 Gaspard Monge was the "father of descriptive geometry."

Descriptive Geometry

Gaspard Monge (1746–1818), the "father of descriptive geometry" **(Fig. 1.3)**, used graphical methods to solve design problems related to fortifications and battlements while a military student in France. His headmaster scolded him for not using the usual long, tedious mathematical process. Only after lengthy explanations and demonstrations of his technique was he able to convince the faculty that graphical methods (now called descriptive geometry) produced solutions in less time.

Descriptive geometry was such an improvement over mathematical methods that it was kept as a military secret for fifteen years before the authorities allowed it to be taught as part of the civilian curriculum. Monge went on to become a scientific and mathematical aide to Napoleon.

Descriptive geometry is the projection of three-dimensional figures on the two-dimensional plane of paper in a manner that allows geometric manipulations to determine lengths, angles, shapes, and other geometric information about the figures.

1.3 Technological Advances

Many of the technological advances of the twentieth century are engineering achievements. Since

TECHNOLOGICAL ADVANCES OF THE TWENTIETH CENTURY

TECHNOLOGICAL ADVANCEMENTS OF THE 20TH CENTURY			
1900	Vacuum cleaner Airplane Dial telephone Light bulb Model T Ford	1950	A-bomb tests Optical fibers Soviet satellite Microchip
1910	Washing machine Refrigerator Wireless phone	1960	Commun. satellite Indus. robot Nuclear reactor Heart transplant Man on moon
1920	Radio broadcasts Telephone service 35mm camera Cartoons & sound	1970	Silicon chip Personal computer Videocassette record. Supersonic jet Neutron bomb
1930	Tape recorder Atom split Jet engine Television	1980	Stealth bomber Space shuttle Artificial heart Soviet space station

1940	Elect. computer
	Missile
	Transistor
	Microwave
	Polaroid camera
		1990	Computer voice
			  recognition
			Artificial intelligence
			Space-based
			  assembly plant

Figure 1.4 This chronology lists some of the significant technological advances of the twentieth century.

1900, technology has taken us from the horse-drawn carriage to the moon and back, and more advances are certain in the future.

Figure 1.4 shows a few of the many technological mileposts since 1900. It identifies products and processes that have provided millions of jobs

Figure 1.5 Technological and design team members, with their varying backgrounds and areas of expertise, must communicate and interact with each other. (Courtesy of Honeywell, Inc.)

and a better way of life for all. Other significant achievements were building a railroad from Nebraska to California that met at Promontory Point, Utah, in 1869 in less than four years; constructing the Empire State Building with 102 floors in a mere thirteen and a half months in 1931; and retooling industry in 1942 for World War II to produce 4.5 naval vessels, 3.7 cargo ships, 203 airplanes, and 6 tanks each day while supporting 15 million Americans in the armed forces.

1.4 The Technological and Design Team

Technology and design have become so broad and complex that teams of specialists rather than individuals undertake most projects (**Fig. 1.5**). Such teams usually consist of one or more scientists, engineers, technologists, technicians, and craftspeople, and may include designers and stylists (**Fig. 1.6**).

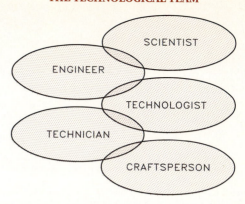

Figure 1.6 This ranking of the typical technological team is from the most theoretical level (scientists) to the least technical level (craftspeople).

Figure 1.7 This geologist is studying seismological charts to determine the likelihood of petroleum deposits. (Courtesy of Texas Eastern; photo by Bob Thigpen.)

Scientists

Scientists are researchers who seek to discover new laws and principles of nature through experimentation and scientific testing (**Fig. 1.7**). They are more concerned with the discovery of scientific principles than with the application of those principles to products and systems. Their discoveries may not find applications until years later.

Figure 1.8 These engineers are discussing geological data and area surveys to arrive at the best placement of exploratory oil wells. (Courtesy of Texas Eastern; photo by Bob Thigpen.)

Figure 1.9 Engineering technologists combine their knowledge of production techniques with the design talents of engineers to produce a product. (Courtesy of Omark Industries, Inc.)

Engineers

Engineers receive training in science, mathematics, and industrial processes to prepare them to apply the findings of the scientists (**Fig. 1.8**). Thus engineers are concerned with converting raw materials and power sources into needed products and services. **Creatively applying scientific principles to develop new products and systems is the design process, the engineer's primary function.** In general, engineers use known principles and available resources to achieve a practical end at a reasonable cost.

Technologists

Technologists obtain backgrounds in science, mathematics, and industrial processes. But, whereas engineers are responsible for analysis, overall design, and research, technologists are concerned with the application of engineering principles to planning, detail design, and production (**Fig. 1.9**). They also provide support and act as liaison between engineers and technicians.

Technicians

Technicians assist engineers and technologists at a less theoretical level than technologists and provide

Figure 1.10 This engineering technician performs laboratory tests as a member of the technological and design team. (Courtesy of Texas Eastern; photo by Bob Thigpen.)

liaison between technologists and craftspeople (**Fig. 1.10**). They have backgrounds in mathematics, drafting, computer programming, and materials testing. Their work varies from conducting

Figure 1.11 This craftsperson, a welder, is skilled in joining metal parts according to prescribed specifications. (Courtesy of Texas Eastern, *TE Today;* photo by Bob Thigpen.)

Figure 1.12 Thomas A. Edison essentially had no formal education, but he gave the world some of its most creative designs.

routine laboratory experiments to supervising craftspeople in manufacturing or construction.

Craftspeople

Craftspeople are responsible for implementing designs by fabricating them according to specifications. They may be machinists who make product parts or electricians who assemble electrical components. Their ability to produce a part according to design specifications is as necessary to the success of a project as engineers' ability to design it. Craftspeople include electricians, welders, machinists, fabricators, drafters, and members of many other occupational groups (**Fig. 1.11**).

Designers

Designers may be engineers, technologists, inventors, or industrial designers who have special talents for devising creative solutions. Designers do not necessarily have engineering backgrounds, especially in newer technologies where there is little design precedent. Thomas A. Edison (**Fig. 1.12**), for example, had little formal education, but he created some of the world's most significant inventions.

Figure 1.13 The stylist develops a product's outward appearance to make it as marketable as possible, as illustrated by this body design for GM's Ultralite, a concept car of the future. (Courtesy of General Motors Corporation.)

Stylists

Stylists are concerned with the appearance and market appeal of a product rather than its fundamental design (**Fig. 1.13**). They may design an automobile body or the exterior of an electric iron. Automobile stylists, for example, consider the car's appearance, driver's vision, passengers' enclosure, power unit's space requirement, and so on. However, they are not involved with the design of the car's internal mechanical functions, such as the engine, steering linkage, and brakes. Stylists must have a high degree of aesthetic awareness and an instinct for styling that appeals to the consumer.

1.5 Engineering Fields

All engineers specialize in one of two major areas: research engineering or design engineering. Research engineers conduct investigations and experiments in search of new ideas and engineering breakthroughs. On the other hand, design engineers are more concerned with the translation of research findings into workable applications.

Recent changes in engineering include the emergence of technologists and technicians and the growing number of women pursuing engineering careers. More than 15% of today's freshman engineering students are women; 15% of master's degrees and 10% of doctor's degrees in engineering are awarded to women.

1.6 Aerospace Engineering

Aerospace engineering has progressed from the Wright brothers' first flight at Kittyhawk, North Carolina, in 1903 to the penetration of outer space. It deals with all aspects (speeds and altitudes) of flight. Aerospace engineering assignments range from developing complex vehicles capable of traveling millions of miles into space to hover aircraft that can transport and position large construction components. In the space exploration branch of this profession, aerospace engineers work on all types of aircraft and spacecraft—missiles, rockets, propeller-driven planes, and jet-powered planes **(Fig. 1.14)**.

Second only to the auto industry in sales, the aerospace industry contributes immeasurably to national defense and the economy. Specialized areas include aerodynamics, structural design, instrumentation, propulsion systems, materials,

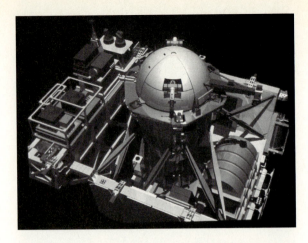

Figure 1.14 Aerospace engineers design and develop space systems such as this payload assembly. (Courtesy of Trilby Wallace, McDonnell Douglas; Kennedy Space Center, Florida; and Intergraph Corporation, Huntsville, Alabama.)

reliability testing, and production methods. The professional society for aerospace engineers is the American Institute of Aeronautics and Astronautics (AIAA).

1.7 Agricultural Engineering

Agricultural engineers are trained to serve the world's largest industry—agriculture—in which they deal with the production, processing, and handling of food and fiber.

Mechanical Power

Agricultural engineers who work with manufacturers of farm equipment are concerned with gasoline and diesel engine equipment, including pumps, irrigation machinery, and tractors. Machinery must be designed for the electrical curing of hay, milk and fruit processing, and heating environments for livestock and poultry. Today's farmer produces enough food for 120 people, whereas one hundred years ago a farmer was able to feed only 4 people.

Figure 1.15 Agricultural engineers of the future will design food production environments and systems for space settlements. (Courtesy of NASA.)

Farm Structures

The construction of barns, shelters, silos, granaries, processing centers, and other agricultural buildings requires specialists in agricultural engineering. They must understand heating, ventilation, and chemical changes that might affect the storage of crops.

Electrical Power

Agricultural engineers design electrical systems and select equipment that will operate efficiently and meet the requirements of many situations. They may serve as consultants or designers for manufacturers or processors of agricultural products.

Soil and Water Control

Agricultural engineers are responsible for devising systems to improve drainage and irrigation systems, resurface fields, and construct water reservoirs **(Fig. 1.15)**.

Characteristics

Most agricultural engineers are employed in private industry, especially by manufacturers of heavy farm equipment and specialized lines of field, barnyard, and household equipment; by electrical service companies; and by distributors of farm equipment and supplies. The professional society for agricultural engineers is the American Society for Agricultural Engineers (ASAE).

1.8 Chemical Engineering

Chemical engineering involves the design and selection of equipment used to process and manufacture large quantities of chemicals. Chemical engineers develop and design methods of transporting fluids through ducts and pipelines, transporting solid material through pipes or conveyors, transferring heat from one fluid or substance to another through plate or tube walls, absorbing gases by bubbling them through liquids, evaporating liquids to increase concentration of solutions, distilling mixed liquids to separate them, and handling many other chemical processes. Process control and instrumentation are important specialties in chemical engineering.

Chemical engineers often utilize chemical reactions of raw products, such as oxidation, hydrogenation, reduction, chlorination, nitration, sulfonation, pyrolysis, and polymerization, in their work **(Fig. 1.16)**. They develop and process chemicals such as acids, alkalies, salts, coal-tar products, dyes, synthetic chemicals, plastics, insecticides, and fungicides for industrial and domestic uses. Chemical engineers help develop drugs and medicines, cosmetics, explosives, ceramics, cements, paints, petroleum products, lubricants, synthetic fibers, rubber, and detergents.

Figure 1.16 The contributions of scientists, chemical engineers, petroleum engineers, structural engineers, and others are required in the construction and operation of refineries that produce the petroleum products and by-products vital to our economy. (Courtesy of Exxon Corporation.)

They also design equipment for food preparation and canning plants.

New fields requiring chemical engineers are nuclear sciences, rocket fuel development, and environmental pollution control. The professional society for chemical engineers is the American Institute of Chemical Engineers (AIChE).

1.9 Civil Engineering

Civil engineering, the oldest branch of engineering, is closely related to virtually all our daily activities. The buildings we live and work in, the transportation we use, the water we drink, and the drainage and sewage systems we rely on are all the results of civil engineering.

Construction

Civil engineers manage the workers, finances, and materials used on construction projects. **Structural engineers** design and supervise the construction of buildings, harbors, airfields, tunnels, bridges, stadiums, and other types of structures.

City Planning

Civil engineers working as city planners develop plans for the growth of cities and systems related to their operation. They are involved in street planning, zoning, residential subdivisions, and industrial site development.

Hydraulics

Civil engineers work with the behavior of water and other fluids from their conservation to their transportation. Civil engineers design wells, canals, dams, pipelines, flood control and drainage systems, and other methods of controlling and using those resources (**Fig. 1.17**).

Transportation

Civil engineers design and supervise construction, modification, and maintenance of railroad and mass transit systems. They design and supervise construction of airport runways, control towers, passenger and freight stations, and aircraft hangars. They are involved in all phases of developing the national systems and local networks of highways and interchanges for moving automobile traffic including the design of tunnels, culverts, and traffic control systems.

Sanitary Engineering

Civil engineers maintain public health by designing pipelines, treatment plants, and other facilities for water purification and water and air pollution control. They also are involved in solid waste disposal activities.

Other Areas of Specialization

Civil engineers are involved in **geotechnical engineering,** which deals with the study of soils. They also work in **environmental engineering,** which relates to all aspects of the environment and methods of preserving it.

Characteristics

Many civil engineers hold positions in administration and municipal management and are associated with federal, state, and local government

Figure 1.17 Civil, structural, hydraulic, mechanical, and electrical engineers work on projects such as the Morrow Point Dam in Colorado, which provides a water reserve and controls downstream flooding. (Courtesy of the U.S. Department of Interior.)

agencies and the construction industry. Many work as consulting engineers for architectural firms and independent consultants. The professional society for civil engineers is the American Society of Civil Engineers (ASCE). Founded in 1852, it is the oldest engineering society in the United States.

1.10 Electrical Engineering

Electrical engineers are concerned with **power**, which deals with providing the large amounts of energy required by cities and large industries, and **electronics**, which deals with the small amounts of power used for communications and automated operations that have become part of everyday life.

Power

Power generation, transmission, and distribution pose many electrical engineering problems from the design of generators for producing electricity to the development of transmission equipment. Power applications are quite numerous in homes for computers, washers, dryers, vacuum cleaners, and other appliances. Only about one-quarter of electric energy is consumed in the home. About half is used by industry for metal refining, heating, motor drives, welding, machinery controls, chemical processes, plating, and electrolysis. **Illumination** (lighting) is required in nearly every phase of modern life.

Electronics and Computers

Electronics and computers have contributed to the development of a gigantic industry that is the domain of electrical engineers. Used with industrial electronics (such as robotics), computers have changed industry's manufacturing and production processes, resulting in greater precision and less manual labor.

Communications applications are devoted to the improvement of radio, telephone, telegraph, and television systems, the nerve centers of most industrial operations (**Fig. 1.18**).

Instrumentation applies systems of electronic instruments to industrial processes. Electrical engineers make extensive use of the cathode-ray tube and the electronic amplifier in industry and nuclear reactors.

Military electronics encompasses most weapons and tactical systems ranging from the walkie-talkie to radar networks for detecting enemy aircraft. Remote-controlled electronic systems are used for navigation and interception of guided missiles.

Characteristics

There are currently more electrical engineers than any other type of engineer. The increasing need for electrical equipment, automation, and computerized systems is expected to sustain the rapid growth of this field. The professional society for

Figure 1.18 Electrical engineers in cooperation with aerospace engineers develop space outposts, such as this satellite for providing mobile voice and data services to customers beyond the range of standard cellular systems. (Courtesy of BCE, Inc.)

Figure 1.19 Industrial engineers design and lay out automatic conveyor systems such as those used at the Sara Lee plant. (Courtesy of Honeywell, Inc.)

electrical engineers is the Institute of Electrical and Electronic Engineers (IEEE). Founded in 1884, the IEEE is the world's largest professional society.

1.11 Industrial Engineering

Industrial engineering, one of the newer engineering fields, differs from other branches of engineering in that it relates primarily to people, their performance, and working conditions. Industrial engineers often manage people, machines, materials, methods, and money in the production and marketing of goods.

Industrial engineers may be responsible for plant layout, development of plant processes, or determination of operating standards that will improve the efficiency of a plant operation. They also design and supervise systems for improved safety of personnel and increased production at lower costs **(Fig. 1.19)**.

Areas of industrial engineering include management, plant design and engineering, electronic data processing, systems analysis and design, control of production and quality, performance standards and measurements, and research. Industrial engineers are increasingly involved in implementing automated production systems.

People-oriented areas include the development of wage incentive systems, job evaluation, work measurement, and environmental system design. Industrial engineers are often involved in management–labor agreements that affect operations and production.

More than two-thirds of all industrial engineers are employed in manufacturing industries. Others work for insurance companies, construction and mining firms, public utilities, large businesses, and government agencies. The professional society for industrial engineers is the American Institute of Industrial Engineers (AIIE), which was organized in 1948.

1.12 Mechanical Engineering

Mechanical engineering's major areas of specialization are power generation, transportation, manufacturing, power services, and atomic energy.

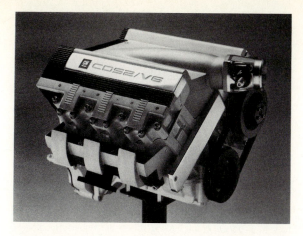

Figure 1.20 Mechanical engineers designed and supervised the building of this 3.0-liter, V-6, two-stroke automobile engine. (Courtesy of General Motors Corporation.)

Power Generation

Mechanical engineers develop and design prime movers (machines that convert natural energy into work) to power electric generators that produce electricity. They are involved in the design and operation of steam engines, turbines, internal combustion engines, and other prime movers **(Fig. 1.20).**

Transportation

Mechanical engineers participate in the design of trucks, buses, automobiles, locomotives, marine vessels, and aircraft. In aeronautics they develop aircraft engines, controls, and internal environmental systems. Mechanical engineers design marine vessels powered by steam, diesel, or gas-turbine engines, as well as power services throughout the vessels, such as lighting, water, refrigeration, and ventilation.

Manufacturing

Mechanical engineers design new products and the equipment and factories needed to manufacture them economically and at a uniformly high level of quality. The professional society for manufactur-

ing engineers is the Society of Manufacturing Engineers (SME).

Power Services

Mechanical engineers in this area must have a knowledge of pumps, ventilation equipment, fans, and compressors. They apply this knowledge to the development of methods for moving liquids and gases through pipelines and the design and installation of refrigeration systems, elevators, and escalators.

Nuclear Energy

Mechanical engineers develop and handle protective equipment and materials and assist in constructing nuclear reactors. The professional society for mechanical engineers is the American Society of Mechanical Engineers (ASME).

1.13 Mining and Metallurgical Engineering

Mining engineers are responsible for developing methods of extracting minerals from the earth and preparing them for use by manufacturing industries. Working with geologists to locate ore deposits, which are exploited through the construction of tunnels and underground operations or surface strip mining, mining engineers must understand safety, ventilation, water supply, and communications. Mining engineers who work at mining sites usually are employed near small, out-of-the-way communities, whereas those in research and consulting most often work in large urban areas.

The two main areas of metallurgical engineering are **extractive metallurgy,** the extraction of metal from raw ores to form pure metals, and **physical metallurgy,** the development of new products and alloys. The need to develop new lightweight, high-strength materials for spacecraft, jet aircraft, missiles, and satellites will require more metallurgical engineers in the future **(Fig. 1.21).** The professional society for mining and metallurgical engineers is the American Institute of Mining, Metallurgical, and Petroleum Engineering (AIME).

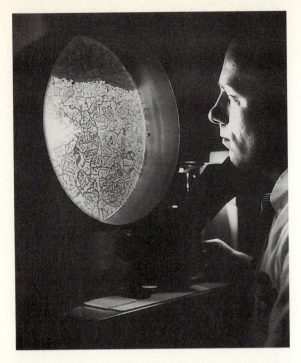

Figure 1.21 A metallograph shows the structure of an alloy that may be used in the construction of a refinery unit. Metallurgical engineers specially develop materials for specific applications for various industrial uses. (Courtesy of Exxon Corporation.)

Figure 1.22 Nuclear engineers will design the nuclear reactors to produce economically much of the electric power needed in the future.

ical or electric power is a major application of nuclear engineering (**Fig. 1.22**). In the production of electric power, nuclear energy is the fuel used to produce steam to drive turbine generators.

Most nuclear engineering training focuses on the design, construction, and operation of nuclear reactors. Other areas include the processing of nuclear fuels, thermonuclear engineering, and the use of various nuclear by-products. The professional society for nuclear engineers is the American Nuclear Society.

1.14 Nuclear Engineering

The earliest work in nuclear engineering involved military applications. Nuclear power for domestic needs was developed for a time, but the new emphasis in nuclear engineering is for medical applications.

Peaceful applications of nuclear engineering fall into two major areas: radiation and nuclear power reactors. **Radiation** is the propagation of energy through matter or space in the form of waves. In atomic physics, radiation includes fast-moving particles (alpha and beta rays, free neutrons, and so on), gamma rays, and X rays.

The use of **nuclear energy** to produce mechan-

1.15 Petroleum Engineering

The recovery of petroleum and natural gas is the primary concern of petroleum engineers, but they also develop methods for transporting and separating various petroleum products. They also are responsible for improving drilling equipment and ensuring its economical operation (**Fig. 1.23**). In exploring for petroleum, petroleum engineers are assisted by geologists and by instruments such as the airborne magnetometer, which indicates uplifts in the earth's subsurfaces that could hold oil or gas.

Petroleum engineers develop equipment to

Figure 1.23 Petroleum engineers supervise the operation of offshore platforms used in the exploration for oil. (Courtesy of Texas Eastern; photo by Bob Thigpen.)

Figure 1.24 This drafter is aided by a computer graphics system. (Courtesy of Hewlett-Packard.)

remove oil from the ground most efficiently and supervise oil-well drilling. They also design systems of pipes and pumps to transport oil to shipping points or to refineries. Development, design, and operation of petroleum processing facilities are done jointly with chemical engineers.

The Society of Petroleum Engineers (SPE) is a branch of AIME, which includes mining and metallurgical engineers and geologists.

1.16 Drafting

Drafters help engineers and designers select materials. They also prepare construction documents and specifications and translate designs into working drawings and technical illustrations. **Working drawings** are visual instructions for fabricating products and erecting structures in all fields of engineering. **Technical illustration,** the most artistic area of engineering design graphics, visually depicts projects and products for operations manuals and presentations.

In addition, drafters prepare maps, geological **sections,** and **plats** from data given them by engineers, geologists, and surveyors. These drawings show the locations of property lines, physical features, strata, rights-of-way, building sites, bridges, dams, mines, and utility lines.

The three levels of certification for drafters are drafters, design drafters, and engineering designers:

- **Drafters** are graduates of a two-year, post–high school curriculum in engineering design graphics.
- **Design drafters** complete two-year programs at an approved junior college or technical institute.
- **Engineering designers** are graduates of a four-year college course in engineering design graphics who can become certified as technologists.

Computer Graphics

Industry, in particular, is embracing computer graphics as a way to improve drafters' productivity. **However, the use of computer graphics systems does not lessen the need for a knowledge of graphics. The principles of graphics remain the same; only the medium—the computer—is different (Fig. 1.24).**

1. Write a report that outlines the specific duties of and relationships among the scientist, engineer, technologist, technician, craftsperson, designer, and stylist in an engineering field of your choice. For example, explain this relationship for an engineering team involved in an aspect of civil engineering. Your report should be supported by factual information obtained from interviews, brochures, or library references.

2. Investigate and write a report on the employment opportunities, job requirements, professional challenges, and activities of your chosen branch of engineering or technology. Illustrate this report with charts and graphs where possible for easy interpretation. Compare your personal abilities and interests with those required by the profession.

3. Arrange a personal interview with a practicing engineer, technologist, or technician in your field of interest. Discuss with that person the general duties and responsibilities of the position to gain a better understanding of this field. Summarize your interview in a written report.

4. Write to the professional society in your field of study for information about it. Prepare a notebook of these materials for easy reference. Include in the notebook a list of books that provide career information for that field.

Addresses of Professional Societies

Publications and information from these societies were used in preparing this chapter.

American Ceramic Society
65 Ceramic Drive, Columbus, OH 43214

The American Institute of Aeronautics and Astronautics
1290 Avenue of the Americas, New York, NY 10019

American Institute of Chemical Engineers
345 East 47th Street, New York, NY 10017

American Institute for Design and Drafting
3119 Price Road, Bartlesville, OK 74003

The American Institute of Industrial Engineers
345 East 47th Street, New York, NY 10017

American Institute of Mining, Metallurgical, and Petroleum Engineering
345 East 47th Street, New York, NY 10017

American Nuclear Society
244A East Ogden Avenue, Hinsdale, IL 60521

American Society of Agricultural Engineers
2950 Niles Road, St. Joseph, MI 49085

American Society of Civil Engineers
345 East 47th Street, New York, NY 10017

American Society for Engineering Education
11 DuPont Circle, Suite 200, Washington, DC 20036

American Society of Mechanical Engineers
345 East 47th Street, New York, NY 10017

The Institute of Electrical and Electronic Engineers
345 East 47th Street, New York, NY 10017

National Society of Professional Engineers
2029 K Street, N.W., Washington, DC 20006

Society of Petroleum Engineers (SPE)
P.O. Box 833836, Richardson, TX 75083

Society of Women Engineers
United Engineering Center, Room 305
345 East 47th Street, New York, NY 10017

2
The Design Process

2.1 Introduction

The design process is a way of devising innovative solutions to problems that will result in new products or systems. Engineering graphics and descriptive geometry are excellent tools for developing designs from initial concepts to final working drawings. Initially, a design consists of sketches and ultimately becomes precise detail drawings and specifications. They, in turn, become part of the contract documents for the parties involved in funding and constructing a project.

At first glance, the solution of a design problem may appear to involve merely the identification of a need and the application of effort toward its solution, but most engineering designs are more complex than that. The engineering and design efforts may be the easiest parts of a project.

For example, engineers who develop roadway systems must deal with constraints such as ordinances, historical data, human factors, social considerations, scientific principles, budgeting, and politics **(Fig. 2.1)**. Engineers can readily design driving surfaces, drainage systems, overpasses, and

ASPECTS OF ENGINEERING DESIGN

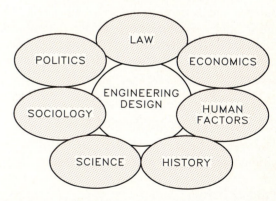

Figure 2.1 An engineering project may involve the interaction of people representing many professions and interests, with engineering design as the central function.

other components of the system. However, adherence to budgetary limitations is essential, and funding is closely related to politics.

Traffic laws, zoning ordinances, environmental impact statements, right-of-way acquisition, and

ASPECTS OF PRODUCT DESIGN

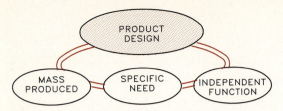

Figure 2.2 Product design seeks to develop a product that meets a specific need, that can function independently, and that can be mass produced.

ASPECTS OF PRODUCT DESIGN

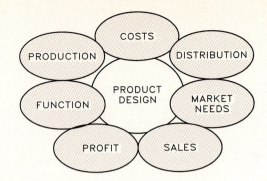

Figure 2.3 These factors affect product design.

liability clearances are legal aspects of roadway design that engineers must deal with. Past trends, historical data, human factors (including driver characteristics), and safety features affecting the function of the traffic system must be analyzed. Social problems may arise if proposed roadways will be heavily traveled and attract commercial development such as shopping centers, fast-food outlets, and service stations. Finally, designers must apply engineering principles developed through research and experience to obtain durable roads, economical bridges, and fully functional systems.

A RESIDENTIAL SYSTEM

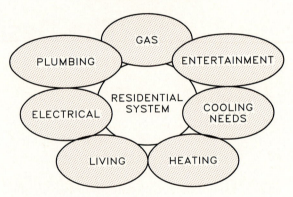

Figure 2.4 The typical residence is a system composed of many components and products.

2.2 Types of Design Problems

Most design problems fall into one of two categories: product design and systems design.

Product Design

Product design is the creation, testing, and manufacture of an item that usually will be mass produced, such as an appliance, a tool, or a toy (Fig. 2.2). In general, a product must have sufficiently broad appeal for meeting a specific need and performing an independent function to warrant its production in quantity. Designers of products must respond to current market needs, production costs, function, sales, distribution methods, and profit predictions **(Fig. 2.3)**.

Products can perform one or many functions. For instance, the primary function of an automobile is to provide transportation, but it also contains products that provide communications, illumination, comfort, and safety. Because it is mass produced for a large consumer market and can be purchased as a unit, the automobile is regarded as a product. However, because it consists of many products that perform various functions, the automobile also is a system.

Figure 2.5 The cart for carrying luggage in an airport terminal is a product and part of a system. (Courtesy of Smarte Carte.)

Figure 2.6 Luggage carts are dispensed from coin-operated centers at major entrances of an airport terminal. (Courtesy of Smarte Carte.)

Figure 2.7

A The coin-operated gate releases a cart to the customer. (Courtesy of Smarte Carte.)

B A vending machine makes change for $5, $10, and $20 bills and issues baggage cards that can be used at any other airport terminal having the same cart system. (Courtesy of Smarte Carte.)

Systems Design

Systems design combines products and their components into a unique arrangement and provides a method for their operation. A residential building is a system of products consisting of heating and cooling, plumbing, natural gas, electrical power, and others that together form the overall system (**Fig. 2.4**).

Systems Design Example

Suppose that you were carrying luggage to a faraway gate in an airport terminal. You would soon recognize the need for a luggage cart that you could use and then leave behind for others to use. If you have this need, then others do, too. You could design a cart like the one shown in **Fig. 2.5** to hold luggage—and even a child—and make it available to travelers. The cart is a product.

How could you profit from providing such a cart? First you would need a method of holding the carts and dispensing them to customers, such as the one shown in **Fig. 2.6**. You would also need a method for users to pay for cart rental, so you could design a coin-operated gate for releasing them (**Fig. 2.7A**).

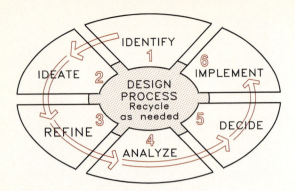

Figure 2.8 The design process consists of six steps. Each step can be repeated as necessary.

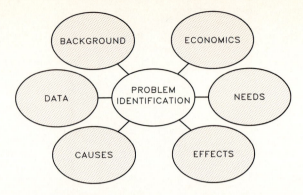

Figure 2.9 Problem identification requires that the designer accumulate as much information about a problem as possible before attempting a solution. The designer also should keep product marketing in mind.

For customer convenience you could provide a vending machine that will take bills both to make change and to issue cards entitling customers to multiple use of carts at this and other terminals (**Fig. 2.7B**). A mechanism to encourage customers to return carts to another, conveniently located dispensing unit would be helpful and efficient. A coin dispenser (see Fig. 2.6) that gives a partial refund on the rental fee to customers returning carts to a dispensing unit at their destination might work.

In combination, these products make up a system. Such a system of products is more valuable than the sum of the products alone.

2.3 The Design Process

Design is the process of creating a product or system to satisfy a set of requirements that has multiple solutions by using any available resources. In essentially all cases, the final design must be completed at a profit or within a budget.

The six steps of the design process (**Fig. 2.8**) are

1. problem identification,
2. preliminary ideas (ideation),
3. refinement,
4. analysis,
5. decision, and
6. implementation.

Designers should work sequentially from step to step but should review previous steps periodically and rework them if a new approach comes to mind during the process.

Problem Identification

Most engineering problems are not clearly defined at the outset and require identification before an attempt is made to solve them (**Fig. 2.9**). For example, air pollution is a concern, but we must identify its causes before we can solve the problem. Is it caused by automobiles, factories, atmospheric conditions that harbor impurities, or geographic features that trap impure atmospheres?

Another example is traffic congestion. When you enter a street where traffic is unusually congested, can you identify the reasons for the congestion? Are there too many cars? Are the signals poorly synchronized? Are there visual obstructions? Has an accident blocked traffic?

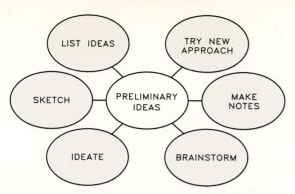

Figure 2.10 The designer develops preliminary ideas after completing the identification step. The designer should list and sketch all these ideas to have a broad selection to work from.

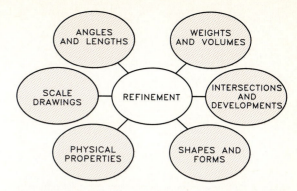

Figure 2.11 Refinement begins with the construction of scale drawings of the best preliminary ideas. Descriptive geometry and graphical methods are used to describe geometric characteristics.

Problem identification involves much more than simply stating, "We need to eliminate air pollution." We need data of several types: opinion surveys, historical records, personal observations, experimental data, and physical measurements from the field.

Preliminary Ideas

The second step of the design process is the development of as many ideas for problem solution as possible (**Fig. 2.10**). A brainstorming session is a good way to collect ideas that are bold, revolutionary, and even wild. Rough sketches, notes, and comments can capture and preserve preliminary ideas for futher refinement. The more ideas, the better at this stage.

Refinement

Next, several of the better preliminary ideas can be selected for refinement to determine their merits. Rough sketches should be converted to scale drawings for spatial analysis, determination of critical measurements, and calculation of areas and volumes affecting the design (**Fig. 2.11**). Descriptive geometry aids in determining spatial relationships, angles between planes, lengths of structural mem-

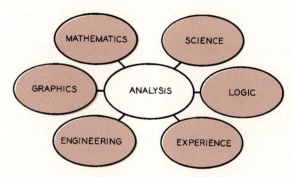

Figure 2.12 The designer should use all available methods, from science to technology to graphics to experience, to analyze designs.

bers, intersections of surfaces and planes, and other geometric relationships.

Analysis

Analysis is the step at which engineering and scientific principles are used most intensively to evaluate the best designs and compare their merits with respect to cost, strength, function, and market appeal (**Fig. 2.12**). Graphical methods play an

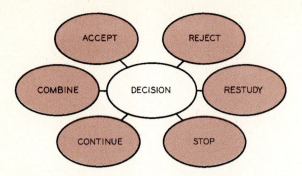

Figure 2.13 Decision involves selecting the best design or design features to be implemented. This step may require a compromise or a rejection of the proposed solution.

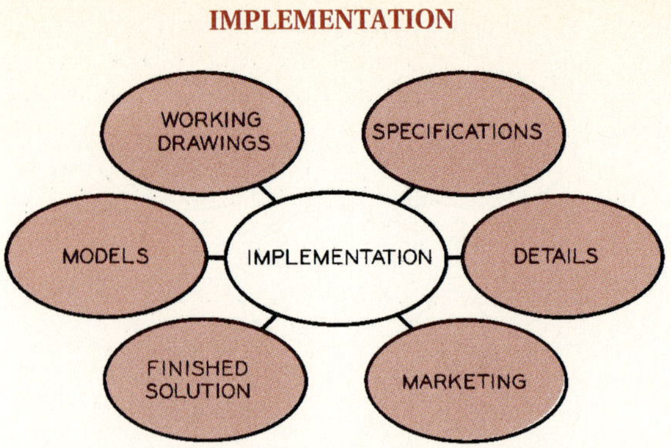

Figure 2.14 Implementation is the preparation of drawings and specifications from which the final product can be made. The product is produced and its marketing is begun.

important role in analysis. Data can be analyzed graphically, forces analyzed by graphical vectors, and empirical data can be analyzed, integrated, and differentiated by other graphical methods.

Decision

After analysis, a single design, which may be a compromise among several designs, is selected as the solution to the problem **(Fig. 2.13)**. The designer alone, or a team, may make the decision. The outstanding aspects of each design usually lend themselves to graphical comparisons of manufacturing costs, weights, operational characteristics, and other data essential in decision making.

Implementation

The final design must be described in detail in working drawings and specifications from which the project will be built, whether it is a computer chip or a suspension bridge **(Fig. 2.14)**. Workers must have precise instructions for the manufacture of each component, often measured within thousandths of an inch to ensure proper fabrication assembly. Working drawings must be sufficiently explicit to serve as part of the legal contract with the successful bidder on the job.

2.4 Design Worksheets

Designers must make numerous notes and sketches on worksheets throughout the design process. They serve to document what has been done and allow periodic review of earlier ideas to avoid overlooking previously identified concepts. Moreover, a written and visual record of design work helps establish ownership of patentable ideas.

The following materials aid in maintaining permanent records of design activities.

1. **Worksheets** (8½ by 11 inches). Sheets can be either grid-lined or plain and should be three-hole punched for a notebook or binder.

2. **Pencils.** A medium-grade pencil (F or HB) is adequate for most purposes.

3. **Binder or envelope.** Keep worksheets in a binder or envelope for reference.

2.5 Design Example: Exercise Bench

Design an exercise bench that can be used by those who lift weights for body fitness. This apparatus should be as versatile as possible and at the low end of the price range of exercise equipment.

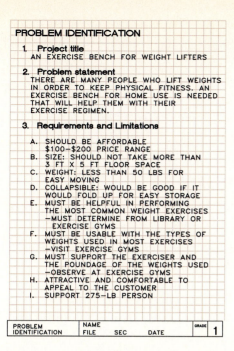

Figure 2.15 Part of the problem identification step is to give the project a title, to describe what the product will be used for, and to list basic requirements and limitations for the design.

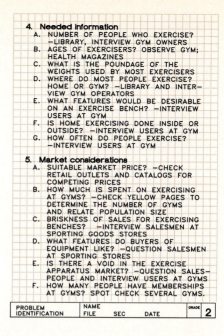

Figure 2.16 Continuation of problem identification for the exercise bench includes gathering information on market potential.

The contents of worksheets shown in **Figs. 2.15–2.18** identify the problem in a typical manner.

First, give the title of the project and a brief problem statement to describe the problem better. Then list requirements and limitations and add sketches as necessary. **You will have to list some requirements as questions for the time being, but in all cases make estimates and give sources for the answers (Fig. 2.15).** Make estimates as you go along; for example, it must cost between $100 and $200, it must weigh less than 50 pounds, and it must at least support a person weighing 250 pounds. Give estimates as ranges of prices or weights rather than exact numbers. Use catalogs offering similar products as sources for prices, weights, and sizes.

Next, make a list of the questions that need answers. **Follow each question with a source for its answer and give a preliminary answer.** How many people exercise? What are their ages? Do they buy exercise equipment? What are the most popular weight exercises? You may obtain this type of information from interviews, product catalogs, the library, and sporting-goods stores. Market considerations include the average income of a typical exerciser. How much does he or she spend on physical fitness per year? The opinions of sporting-goods dealers are helpful, and they should be able to direct you to other sources of information (**Fig. 2.16**).

Record the data that you gather by interviewing gym managers, looking at catalogs, and visiting sporting-goods stores to learn about the people who exercise and the equipment they use (**Fig. 2.17**). Determine the most popular weight exercises of those for whom this bench is to be designed by

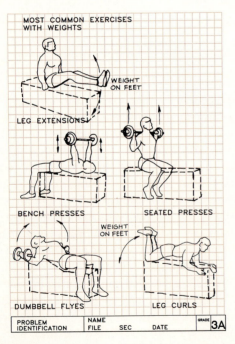

Figure 2.17 worksheet content:

```
PROBLEM IDENTIFICATION
A. CHECK YELLOW PAGES FOR GYMS
   -8 GYMS FOR POPULATION OF 100,000
   -ONE GYM PER 12,500 PEOPLE
B. GYM MEMBERSHIP FOR STILLMAN'S GYM
   YEAR     MEN      WOMEN
   1984     75       20
   1986     70       36
   1988     110      70
   1990     175      82
   1992     180      120
   1994     210      135

C. INTERVIEW RETAILERS OF EQUIPMENT
   -3 DEALERS POSITIVE ABOUT BENCH
   -2 DEALERS NEUTRAL
   -1 DEALER NEGATIVE ABOUT PROSPECTS

D. AGES OF EXERCISERS (BY OBSERVATION)
   -20% UNDER 20
   -40% BETWEEN 20 AND 30
   -30% BETWEEN 30 AND 50
   -10% OVER 50

E. PRICES AT STORES
   1. COMPLEX MULTI-USE        $1000
   2. MEDIUM-RANGE EQUIPMENT    700
   3. LIGHTWEIGHT BENCHES       130
   4. WEIGHTS                   100

F. TYPICAL BRANDS OF EQUIPMENT
   ON THE MARKET?
   1. WEIDER
   2. NAUTILUS
   3. BODY WONDERFUL
   4. HEALTH PLUS

PROBLEM          NAME                      GRADE
IDENTIFICATION   FILE    SEC    DATE          3
```

Figure 2.17 This worksheet shows the data collected for use in designing the exercise bench.

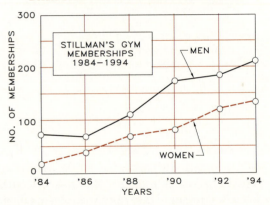

```
MOST COMMON EXERCISES
WITH WEIGHTS

                    WEIGHT
                    ON FEET
LEG EXTENSIONS

BENCH PRESSES          SEATED PRESSES

           WEIGHT
           ON FEET
DUMBBELL FLYES         LEG CURLS

PROBLEM          NAME                      GRADE
IDENTIFICATION   FILE    SEC    DATE         3A
```

Figure 2.18 These sketches are of the most popular weight exercises.

ECONOMIC ANALYSIS MODEL

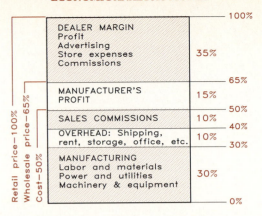

```
                                              100%
DEALER MARGIN
Profit
Advertising
Store expenses              35%
Commissions
                                               65%
MANUFACTURER'S              15%
PROFIT
                                               50%
SALES COMMISSIONS          10%
                                               40%
OVERHEAD: Shipping,        10%
rent, storage, office, etc.                    30%
MANUFACTURING
Labor and materials        30%
Power and utilities
Machinery & equipment
                                                0%
```

(left axis labels: Retail price—100% Wholesale price—65% Cost—50%)

Figure 2.19 This chart shows the breakdown of costs involved in the retail price of a product.

DATA GRAPHED FOR INTERPRETATION

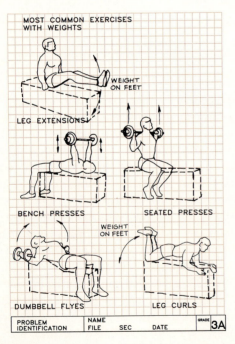

```
300

NO. OF MEMBERSHIPS

        STILLMAN'S GYM          MEN
        MEMBERSHIPS
        1984-1994
200

100
                               WOMEN

  0
   '84    '86    '88    '90    '92    '94
                  YEARS
```

Figure 2.20 This graph describes visually the trends in potential customers for the exercise apparatus.

surveying users, coaches, and sporting-goods outlets. Sketch those exercises on a worksheet (**Fig. 2.18**).

Think about costs and pricing the product even during problem identification. Figure 2.19 shows how products may be priced from wholesale to retail, but these percentages vary by product. For

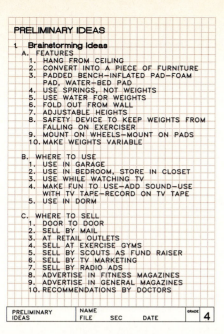

Figure 2.21 This worksheet contains a list of the brainstorming ideas for the exercise bench.

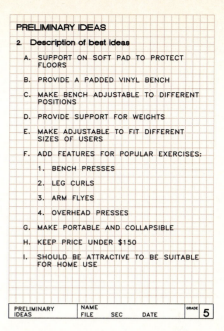

Figure 2.22 These are the best of the brainstorming ideas, selected and summarized from the first list.

instance, profit margins are smaller for food sales than furniture sales. If an item retails for $50, the production and overhead cost cannot be more than about $20 to maintain the necessary margins.

Data are easier to interpret if presented graphically (**Fig. 2.20**). Thorough problem identification includes graphs, sketches, and schematics that improve the communication of your findings.

Problem identification is not complete at this point. However, this example should give you a basic understanding of the process.

2.6 Preliminary Ideas: Exercise Bench

To continue our example of designing an exercise bench, recall that it is to be used by those who lift weights to maintain body fitness. This apparatus should be versatile and at the low end of the price range for exercise equipment.

List the brainstorming ideas obtained from a session with team members on a worksheet (**Fig. 2.21**). Then select the better ideas and list their features described on the worksheet (**Fig. 2.22**), even if they have more features than you could possibly use in a single design. The reason is to make sure that you do not forget or lose any.

Using rapid freehand techniques, such as orthographic views and three-dimensional pictorial sketches, sketch ideas on worksheets. Note on the drawings any ideas or questions that come to mind while you sketch.

In **Fig. 2.23**, note the adaptation of ideas from various types of benches and exercise techniques. A number identifies each idea. Another worksheet (**Fig. 2.24**) shows other ideas and modifications of previous ideas.

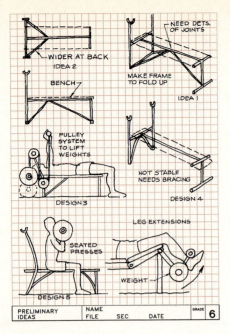

Figure 2.23 These sketches and notes illustrate preliminary ideas for the exercise bench.

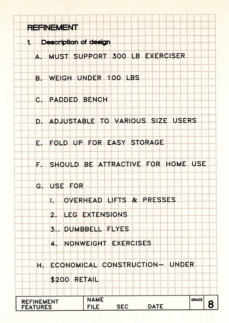

Figure 2.25 This list of desirable features is a refinement of the exercise bench.

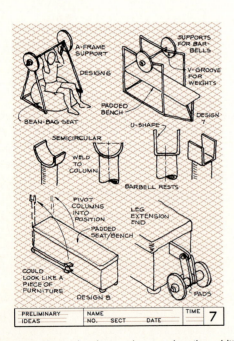

Figure 2.24 These sketches and notes describe additional design concepts for the exercise bench.

2.7 Refinement: Exercise Bench

Now, in this step, we refine the preliminary ideas for the exercise bench with instrument drawings.

First, list the features to be incorporated into the design on a worksheet (**Fig. 2.25**). Then refine a preliminary idea, say, idea 2 from Fig. 2.23 in an orthographic scale drawing of the seat (**Fig. 2.26**). Block in extruded parts, such as the framework members, to expedite the drawing process and omit unneeded hidden lines.

Refinement drawings must be drawn to scale. Use of instruments is important to portray precisely the design from which angles, lengths, shapes, and other geometric elements will be obtained. The drawing shows only overall dimensions, and several connecting joints are detailed to explain the design. **Figure 2.27** shows additional design features. These worksheets depict representative types of drawings required to refine a design; additional drawings would be required for a complete refinement of the design.

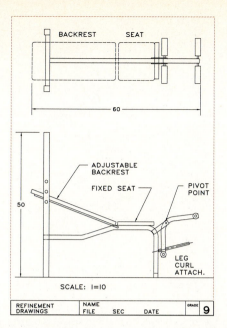

Figure 2.26 This refinement drawing of a preliminary idea for the exercise bench is a scale drawing, with only a few major dimensions shown.

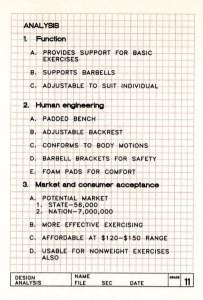

Figure 2.28 A worksheet containing an analysis of function, human engineering, and market considerations for the exercise bench.

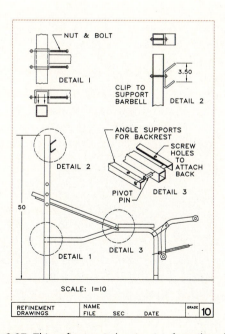

Figure 2.27 This refinement drawing is of another design concept for the exercise bench.

2.8 Analysis: Exercise Bench

The main areas of analysis listed on the worksheets in **Figs. 2.28–2.31** will assist you in analyzing the design. Additional worksheets and large sheet sizes for analysis drawings may be used if more space is needed.

Figure 2.31 shows how graphics is used to determine the range of positions of the backrest. Those positions affect the design of the angle-iron supports for the backrest and the locations of the semicircular holes in the angle irons for a range of settings of 30°.

The leg-exercising attachment at the end of the bench is designed to move through a 90° arc, which is sufficient for leg extensions. By determining the maximum loads on the backrest and the leg exerciser, you can select the member sizes and materials that provide the strength required. For further analysis, construct a model and test the design for suitability.

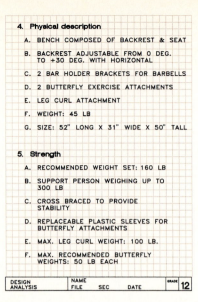

4. **Physical description**

   A. BENCH COMPOSED OF BACKREST & SEAT

   B. BACKREST ADJUSTABLE FROM 0 DEG. TO +30 DEG. WITH HORIZONTAL

   C. 2 BAR HOLDER BRACKETS FOR BARBELLS

   D. 2 BUTTERFLY EXERCISE ATTACHMENTS

   E. LEG CURL ATTACHMENT

   F. WEIGHT: 45 LB

   G. SIZE: 52" LONG X 31" WIDE X 50" TALL

5. **Strength**

   A. RECOMMENDED WEIGHT SET: 160 LB

   B. SUPPORT PERSON WEIGHING UP TO 300 LB

   C. CROSS BRACED TO PROVIDE STABILITY

   D. REPLACEABLE PLASTIC SLEEVES FOR BUTTERFLY ATTACHMENTS

   E. MAX. LEG CURL WEIGHT: 100 LB.

   F. MAX. RECOMMENDED BUTTERFLY WEIGHTS: 50 LB EACH

| DESIGN ANALYSIS | NAME FILE   SEC   DATE | GRADE 12 |

Figure 2.29 A worksheet giving the physical description and strength analysis for the exercise bench.

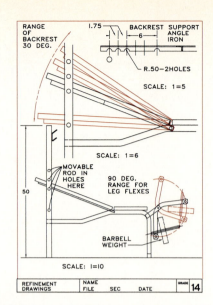

Figure 2.31 A worksheet that shows graphical analysis of the range of movements for the adjustable parts of the exercise bench.

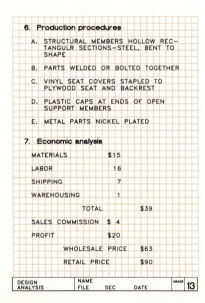

6. **Production procedures**

   A. STRUCTURAL MEMBERS HOLLOW REC-TANGULR SECTIONS—STEEL, BENT TO SHAPE

   B. PARTS WELDED OR BOLTED TOGETHER

   C. VINYL SEAT COVERS STAPLED TO PLYWOOD SEAT AND BACKREST

   D. PLASTIC CAPS AT ENDS OF OPEN SUPPORT MEMBERS

   E. METAL PARTS NICKEL PLATED

7. **Economic analysis**

MATERIALS	$15
LABOR	16
SHIPPING	7
WAREHOUSING	1
TOTAL	$39
SALES COMMISSION	$ 4
PROFIT	$20
WHOLESALE PRICE	$63
RETAIL PRICE	$90

| DESIGN ANALYSIS | NAME FILE   SEC   DATE | GRADE 13 |

Figure 2.30 A worksheet containing an analysis of the production procedures for and economics of the exercise bench.

Figure 2.32 A full-size model of the exercise bench is tested for function and acceptability.

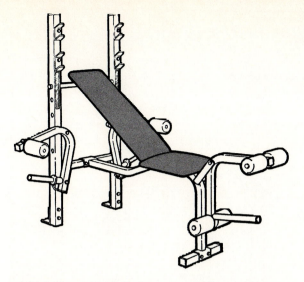

Figure 2.33 This catalog description gives the key features of the exercise bench: Weider® bench with butterfly attachment. It features no-pinch supports, multiposition padded back and leg lift, and tubular steel frame. Total weight capacity is 1000 lb; butterfly capacity, 50 lb; leg lift capacity, 65 lb; overall size, 58″ × 45″ × 41″; weight, 48 lb; and price, $89.99. (Courtesy of Sears, Roebuck and Company.)

DECISION

1. Decision for evaluation

DESIGN 1 A–FRAME

DESIGN 2 U–FRAME

DESIGN 3 2–COLUMN FRAME

DESIGN 4

DESIGN 5

MAX	FACTORS	1	2	3	4
3.0	FUNCTION	2.0	2.3	2.5	
2.0	HUMAN FACTORS	1.6	1.4	1.7	
0.5	MARKET ANALYSIS	0.4	0.4	0.4	
1.0	STRENGTH	1.0	1.0	1.0	
0.5	PRODUCTION EASE	0.3	0.2	0.4	
1.0	COST	0.7	0.6	0.8	
1.5	PROFITABILITY	1.1	1.0	1.3	
0.5	APPEARANCE	0.3	0.4	0.4	
10	TOTALS	7.4	7.3	8.5	

DESIGN DECISION | NAME FILE SEC DATE | GRADE 16

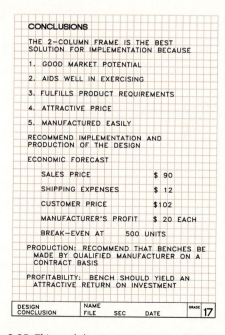

Figure 2.34 This worksheet shows the decision table used to evaluate the design alternatives for the exercise bench.

CONCLUSIONS

THE 2–COLUMN FRAME IS THE BEST SOLUTION FOR IMPLEMENTATION BECAUSE

1. GOOD MARKET POTENTIAL
2. AIDS WELL IN EXERCISING
3. FULFILLS PRODUCT REQUIREMENTS
4. ATTRACTIVE PRICE
5. MANUFACTURED EASILY

RECOMMEND IMPLEMENTATION AND PRODUCTION OF THE DESIGN

ECONOMIC FORECAST

SALES PRICE $ 90

SHIPPING EXPENSES $ 12

CUSTOMER PRICE $102

MANUFACTURER'S PROFIT $ 20 EACH

BREAK–EVEN AT 500 UNITS

PRODUCTION: RECOMMEND THAT BENCHES BE MADE BY QUALIFIED MANUFACTURER ON A CONTRACT BASIS

PROFITABILITY: BENCH SHOULD YIELD AN ATTRACTIVE RETURN ON INVESTMENT

DESIGN CONCLUSION | NAME FILE SEC DATE | GRADE 17

Figure 2.35 This worksheet summarizes the designer's conclusions about the best alternative and recommendations concerning the feasibility of implementing that design.

Figure 2.32 illustrates testing of a commercial version of the exercise bench to measure its functional features. The catalog description in **Fig. 2.33** lists the physical properties of the Weider® exercise bench to help the consumer understand its features.

2.9 Decision: Exercise Bench

A decision regarding the exercise bench is made at this point as the fifth step of the design process.

Decision Table

Use a table like the one shown in **Fig. 2.34** to compare designs, where each idea is listed and given a number for identification. Assign maximum values for each factor of analysis, based on your best judgment, so they total to ten points. Rate each

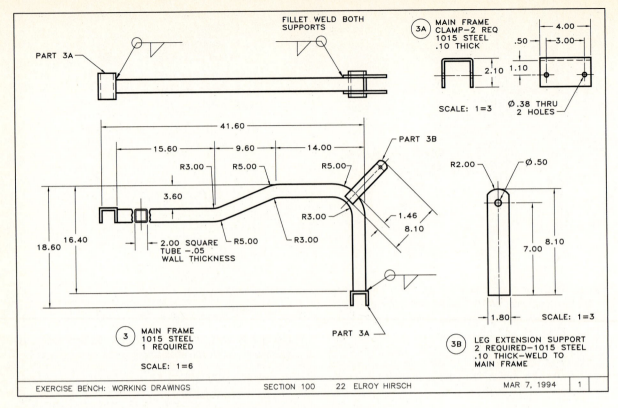

Figure 2.36 This working drawing depicts exercise bench parts (sheet 1 of 5).

factor for the competing designs by entering points for each.

Sum the columns of numbers to determine the total for each design and compare the scores of each design. Your instincts may disagree with the outcome of this numerical analysis. If so, have enough faith in your judgment to go with your intuition. **The scores from the decision table are meant to be a guide for you and not the absolute final word in your decision.**

Conclusion

After making a decision, state it and the reasons for it clearly (**Fig. 2.35**). Record any additional information, such as number to be produced initially, selling price per unit, profit per unit, estimated sales during the first year, break-even number, and the product's most marketable features, that will help you prepare your presentation.

If you believe that none of your designs are satisfactory, you should recommend that they not be implemented. **A negative recommendation is not a failure of the design process; it means only that your solutions developed so far are not feasible.** Going forward with an inadequate solution could cause both monetary losses and wasted effort.

2.10 Implementation: Exercise Bench

Implementation is the final step of the design process applied to the exercise bench.

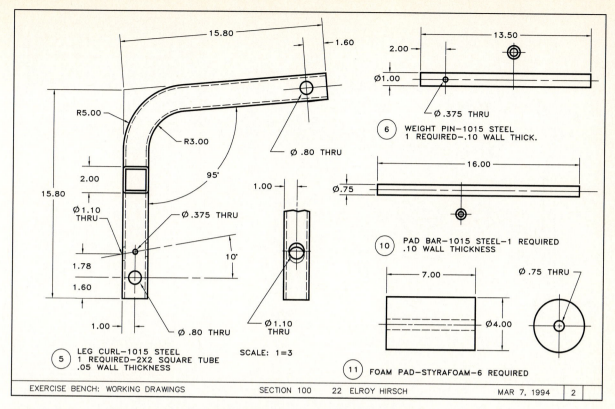

Figure 2.37 This working drawing depicts additional exercise bench parts (sheet 2 of 5).

Working Drawings

The two working drawings shown in **Figs. 2.36** and **2.37** depict some details of the exercise bench design. Additional working drawings are required to show the other parts of the bench, which are dimensioned in decimal inches. Standard parts to be purchased from suppliers are not drawn but are itemized on the drawing, given part numbers, and listed in the parts list on the assembly drawing.*

---

*This particular design was developed and patented and is marketed by Weider Health and Fitness, 2100 Erwin Street, Woodland Hills, CA 91367.

Assembly Drawing

Figure 2.38 shows an assembly drawing that illustrates how the parts are to be assembled after they have been made. The assembly is shown pictorially, with the different parts identified by numbered balloons attached to leaders. The parts list identifies each part by number and describes it generally.

Packaging

The Weider exercise bench is packaged in a corrugated cardboard box and weighs approximately 40 pounds. It is shipped unassembled so that it will fit into a smaller carton for ease of handling during shipment (**Fig. 2.39**).

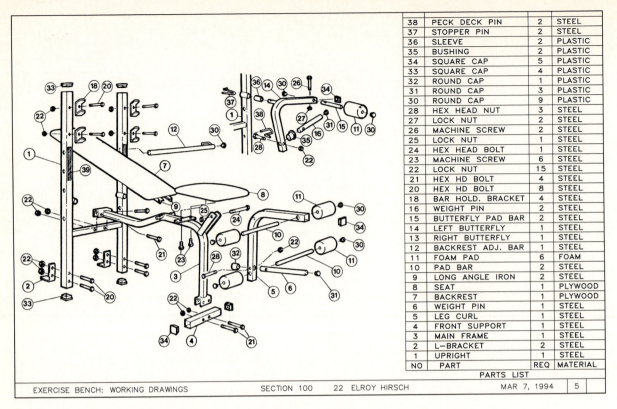

NO	PART	REQ	MATERIAL
38	PECK DECK PIN	2	STEEL
37	STOPPER PIN	2	STEEL
36	SLEEVE	2	PLASTIC
35	BUSHING	2	PLASTIC
34	SQUARE CAP	5	PLASTIC
33	SQUARE CAP	4	PLASTIC
32	ROUND CAP	1	PLASTIC
31	ROUND CAP	3	PLASTIC
30	ROUND CAP	9	PLASTIC
28	HEX HEAD NUT	3	STEEL
27	LOCK NUT	2	STEEL
26	MACHINE SCREW	2	STEEL
25	LOCK NUT	1	STEEL
24	HEX HEAD BOLT	1	STEEL
23	MACHINE SCREW	6	STEEL
22	LOCK NUT	15	STEEL
21	HEX HD BOLT	4	STEEL
20	HEX HD BOLT	8	STEEL
18	BAR HOLD. BRACKET	4	STEEL
16	WEIGHT PIN	2	STEEL
15	BUTTERFLY PAD BAR	2	STEEL
14	LEFT BUTTERFLY	1	STEEL
13	RIGHT BUTTERFLY	1	STEEL
12	BACKREST ADJ. BAR	1	STEEL
11	FOAM PAD	6	FOAM
10	PAD BAR	2	STEEL
9	LONG ANGLE IRON	2	STEEL
8	SEAT	1	PLYWOOD
7	BACKREST	1	PLYWOOD
6	WEIGHT PIN	1	STEEL
5	LEG CURL	1	STEEL
4	FRONT SUPPORT	1	STEEL
3	MAIN FRAME	1	STEEL
2	L–BRACKET	2	STEEL
1	UPRIGHT	1	STEEL
NO	PART	REQ	MATERIAL

PARTS LIST

| EXERCISE BENCH: WORKING DRAWINGS | SECTION 100 | 22 ELROY HIRSCH | MAR 7, 1994 | 5 |

Figure 2.38 This assembly drawing demonstrates how the parts of the Weider exercise bench design are to be assembled (sheet 5 of 5). (Courtesy of Weider Health and Fitness.)

Storage

An inventory of benches must be maintained to meet retailer demand. The need to hold inventory increases overhead costs for interest payments, warehouse rent, warehouse personnel, and loading equipment.

Shipping

Shipping costs for all types of carriers (rail, motor freight, air delivery, and mail services) must be evaluated. The shipping cost for a Weider bench with its accessories is $10–$15, depending on distance, when shipped one at a time by United Parcel Service. The cost per unit is about 50% less when units are shipped in bundles of ten to the same destination.

Prices

The retail price of the Weider bench is about $100. This type of product generally retails for about five or six times the cost of manufacturing them (materials and labor). Retailers receive approximately a 40% margin, distributors earn about 10%, and the remainder of the price represents advertising costs and the other miscellaneous costs mentioned previously. The consumer pays all of these costs (prorated to each exercise bench) as part of the purchase price.

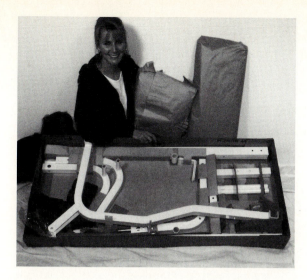

Figure 2.39 The exercise bench is packaged unassembled and flat for ease of packaging and handling during shipment.

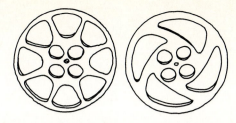

Figure 2.40 Problem 4. A typical movie projector reel and one allowing more finger room.

2.11 Design Problems

This section offers problems that are suitable for both individual assignments and team projects to provide experience in applying the methods of creative problem solving presented in this textbook. All new products begin with sketches at the preliminary idea step and end with working and assembly drawings at the implementation step.

Problem Specifications

An individual or team may be expected to complete any or all of the following tasks.

Short Problems (One or Two Work Hours)

1. Worksheets that record development of a design procedure.

2. Freehand sketches of the design intended for implementation.

3. Instrument drawings of the solution.

4. Pictorial sketches (or drawings made with instruments) illustrating the design.

5. Visual aids, flip charts, or other media for presentation to a group.

Short Design Problems

The following short design problems can be completed in less than two hours.

1. **Lamp bracket.** Design a simple bracket to attach a desk lamp to a vertical wall for reading in bed. It should be removable for use as a conventional desk lamp.

2. **Towel bar.** Design a towel bar for a kitchen or bathroom. Determine optimum size and consider styling, ease of use, and method of attachment.

3. **Pipe aligner for welding.** The initial requirement for joining pipes with a butt weld is to align the pipes. Design a device that will align 2-to-4-in.-diameter pipes for on-the-job welding.

4. **Film reel (Fig. 2.40).** The film reel used on projectors is difficult to thread because of limited working space. Redesign the typical 12-in.-diameter movie reel shown to allow more space for threading.

5. **Side-mounted mirror.** Design an improved side-mounted rearview mirror for an automobile. Consider aerodynamics, protection from inclement weather, visibility, and other factors.

Figure 2.41 Problem 15. A wall-mounted stool.

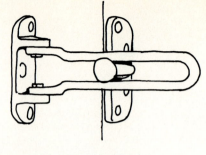

Figure 2.42 Problem 20. A door latch.

6. **Nail feeder.** Design a device that can be attached to a worker's chest for holding roofing nails and that will feed to the worker nails that are lined up and ready for removal and driving.

7. **Paint-can holder.** Paint cans held by their wire bails are difficult to hold and get paint brushes into. Design a holding device that can be attached and removed easily from a gallon-size paint can. Consider weight, grip, balance, and function.

8. **Self-holding hinge.** Design a hinge that will hold a door in a completely open position to prevent it from remaining slightly ajar.

9. **Audio cassette storage unit.** Design a storage unit for an automobile that will hold several audio cassettes, making them accessible to the driver but not to a thief.

10. **Slide projector elevator.** Design a device for raising a slide projector to the proper angle for projection on a screen. It may be part of the original projector or an accessory to be attached to existing projectors.

11. **Book holder 1.** Design a holder to support a book for reading in bed.

12. **Table leg design.** Do-it-yourselfers build a variety of tables using hollow doors or ply-wood for the tops and commercially available legs. Determine standard heights for various types of tables and design a family of legs that can be attached to table tops with screws.

13. **Boat rack.** Design an accessory that will enable one person to load a boat (ranging from 14 to 17 ft in length and weighing from 100 to 200 lb) on an automobile, secure it, and later remove it.

14. **Toothbrush holder.** Design a toothbrush holder for a cup and two toothbrushes that can be attached to a bathroom wall.

15. **Wall-mounted stool (Fig. 2.41).** Design a stool that can be attached to a wall and that will swing out of the way when it is not in use.

16. **Book holder 2.** Design a holder to support a textbook or reference book at a workstation for ease of reading and accessibility.

17. **Clothes hook.** Design a clothes hook that can be attached to a closet door for hanging clothes on.

18. **Hammock support.** Design a hammock support that will fold up and that will require minimal storage space.

19. **Door stop.** Design a door stop that can be attached to a wall or floor to prevent a door knob from hitting the wall.

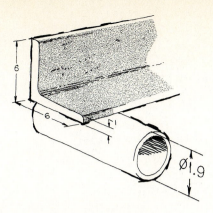

Figure 2.43 Problem 24. A pipe clamp.

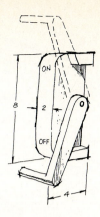

Figure 2.44 Problem 29. A safety lock.

20. Door latch (Fig. 2.42). Design a door latch that provides security to a home owner or an apartment dweller.

21. Cup dispenser. Design a dispenser that can be attached to a vertical wall to hold 2-in.-diameter paper cups that measure 6 in. in height when stacked together.

22. Drawer handle. Design a handle for a standard file cabinet drawer.

23. Paper dispenser. Design a dispenser that will hold a 6-×-24-in. roll of wrapping paper.

24. Pipe clamp (Fig. 2.43). A pipe with a 4-in. diameter must be supported by angles that are spaced 8 ft apart. Design a clamp that will support the pipe without drilling holes in the angles.

25. TV yoke. Design a yoke to hang from a classroom ceiling that will support a TV set and that will permit it to be adjusted for viewing from various parts of the room.

26. Flagpole socket. Design a flagpole socket that is to be attached to a vertical wall.

27. Cup holder. Design a holder that will support a soft-drink can or bottle in an automobile.

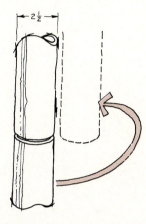

Figure 2.45 Problem 30. A tubular hinge.

28. Gate hinge. Design a hinge that can be attached to a 3-in.-diameter tubular post to support a 3-ft-wide wooden gate.

29. Safety lock (Fig. 2.44). Design a safety lock to hold a high-voltage power switch in the "off" and "on" positions to prevent an accident.

30. Tubular hinge (Fig. 2.45). Design a hinge for portable scaffolding that can be used to hinge 2.5-in. outside diameter, high-strength aluminum pipe in the manner shown.

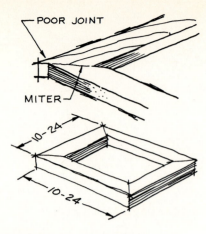

Figure 2.46 Problem 31. A miter fixture.

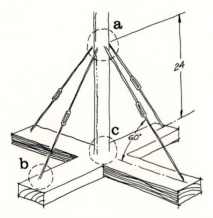

Figure 2.47 Problem 32. Base hardware for a volleyball net.

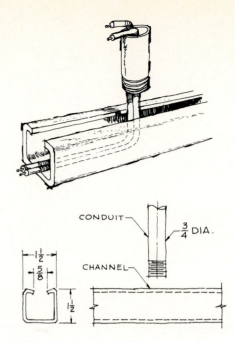

Figure 2.48 Problem 33. A conduit connector hanger.

31. **Miter jig (Fig. 2.46).** Design a jig for assembling mitered wooden frames at 90° angles. The stock used for the frames is rectangular in cross section, varying from 0.75 × 1.5 in. to 1.60 × 3.60 in. and in length from 10 to 24 in.

32. **Base hardware (Fig. 2.47).** Design the hardware needed for points *a, b,* and *c* on a standard volleyball net support. The 7-ft-tall pipes are attached to crossing 2-×-4-in. boards.

33. **Conduit connector hanger (Fig. 2.48).** Design an attachment for a 3/4-in. conduit to support a channel used as an adjustable raceway for electrical wiring.

34. **Fixture (Fig. 2.49).** Design a fixture for a small manufacturer that will permit sawing the corner of blocks as shown.

35. **Drum truck (Fig. 2.50).** Design a truck that can be used for handling 55-gal drums of turpentine (7.28 lb per gallon) one at a time. Drums are stored in a vertical position and used in a horizontal position. The truck should be useful in tipping a drum into a horizontal position (as shown), as well as for moving the drum.

Product Design Problems

Product design involves developing a device that will perform a specific function, be mass produced, and be sold to a large number of consumers.

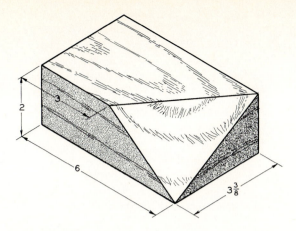

Figure 2.49 Problem 34. A fixture design for sawing a block at an angle.

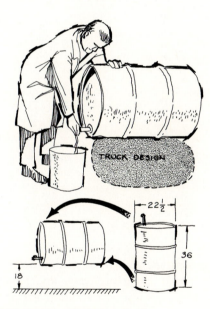

Figure 2.50 Problem 35. A drum truck.

36. **Hunting blind.** Design a portable hunting blind to house two hunters for hunting geese or ducks. It should be portable so that the two hunters can carry it.

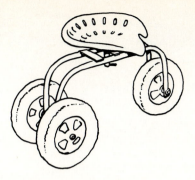

Figure 2.51 Problem 37. A garden seat.

Figure 2.52 Problem 39. A firewood caddy for hauling firewood.

37. **Garden seat (Fig. 2.51).** Design a mobile seat that can be used for work that requires much bending over, such as work in the garden.

38. **Writing table arm.** Design a writing table arm that can be attached to a folding chair.

39. **Firewood caddy (Fig. 2.52).** Design a cart that can be used for carrying firewood inside from the outdoors. It should be easy to handle when the user is climbing steps.

40. **Computer mount.** Design a device that can be clamped to a desk top for holding a computer, permitting it to be adjusted to various

Figure 2.53 Problem 41. A portable hauler.

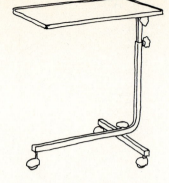

Figure 2.54 Problem 45. A hospital bed table.

Figure 2.55 Problem 49. A portable sawhorse.

positions while leaving the desk top free to work on.

41. **Portable hauler (Fig. 2.53).** Design a portable, collapsible hauler that can be used for various applications.

42. **Workers' stilts.** Design stilts to give workers access to an 8-ft high ceiling, permitting them to nail 4-×-8-ft ceiling panels into position.

43. **Pole-vault uprights.** Pole-vault uprights must be adjusted for each vaulter by moving them forward or backward 18 in. The crossbar must be replaced at heights of over 18 ft by using poles and ladders. Develop a more efficient set of uprights that can be readily adjusted and allow the crossbar to be replaced easily.

44. **Sportsman's chair.** Design a sportsman's chair that can be used for camping, for fishing from a bank or boat, at sporting events, and for other purposes.

45. **Bed table (Fig. 2.54).** Modify the design of a hospital table to permit it to be used for studying, computing, writing, and eating in bed.

46. **Bicycle child carrier.** Design a seat that can be used to carry a small child as a passenger on a bicycle.

47. **Car washer.** Design a garden-hose attachment that can apply water and agitation to wash a car. Suggest other applications for this device.

48. **Power lawn-fertilizer attachment.** The rotary power lawnmower emits a force caused by the rotating blades that might be used to distribute fertilizer during mowing. Design an attachment for a lawnmower that can be used in this manner.

Figure 2.56 Problem 51. A heavy-appliance mover.

49. **Sawhorse (Fig. 2.55).** Design a portable sawhorse for use in carpentry projects that folds up for easy storage. It should be about 36 in. long and 30 in. high.

50. **Projector cabinet.** Design a cabinet to serve as an end table or some other function while housing a slide projector and slide trays ready for use.

51. **Heavy-appliance mover (Fig. 2.56).** Design a device for moving large appliances—stoves, refrigerators, and washers—about the house for the purposes of rearranging, cleaning, and servicing them.

52. **Map holder.** Design a map holder to give the driver a view of the map in a convenient location in the car while driving. Provide a method of lighting the map that will not distract the driver.

53. **Stump remover.** Design an apparatus that can be attached to a car bumper to remove dead stumps by pushing or pulling.

54. **Gate opener.** An annoyance to farmers and ranchers is the necessity of opening and closing gates. Design a manually operated gate that could be opened and closed without the driver having to get out of the vehicle.

55. **Paint mixer.** Design a product for use at paint stores or by paint contractors to mix paint quickly in the store or on the job.

56. **Automobile coffee maker.** Design a device that will provide hot coffee from the dashboard of an automobile. Consider the method of changing and adding water, the spigot system, and similar details.

57. **Baby seat (cantilever).** Design a chair to support a child. It should attach to and be cantilevered from a standard table top. The chair also should be collapsible for ease of storage.

58. **Miniature-TV support.** Design a device that would support TV sets ranging in size from 6×6 in. to 7×7 in. for viewing from a bed. Provide adjustments on the device to allow positioning of the set.

59. **Panel applicator.** A worker applying $4\text{-}\times\text{-}8\text{-}$ft plasterboard to a ceiling needs a helper to hold the panel in place while she nails it. Design a device to hold the panel and eliminate the need for an assistant.

60. **Backpack.** Design a backpack that can be used for carrying camping supplies. Adapt the backpack to the human body for maximum comfort for extended periods of time. Suggest other uses for your design.

61. **Automobile controls.** Design driving controls that can be easily attached to the standard automobile to permit a car to be driven without using the legs.

62. **Bathing apparatus.** Design an apparatus that would help a wheelchair-bound person to get in and out of a bathtub without assistance from others.

63. **Adjustable TV base.** Design a base to support full-sized TV sets and allow maximum adjustment up and down and rotation about vertical and horizontal axes.

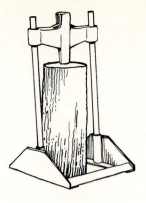

Figure 2.57 Problem 64. A log splitter.

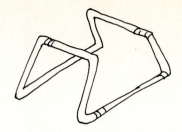

Figure 2.58 Problem 72. A push-up and sit-up exerciser.

64. **Log splitter (Fig. 2.57).** Design a device to aid in splitting logs for firewood.

65. **Projector cabinet.** Design a portable cabinet that can remain permanently in a classroom to house a slide projector and/or a movie projector in a ready-to-use position. It should provide both convenience and security from theft.

66. **Projector eraser.** Design a device to erase grease-pencil markings from the acetate roll of a specially equipped overhead projector as the acetate is cranked past the stage of the projector.

67. **Cement mixer.** Design a portable cement mixer that a home owner can operate manually. Such mixers are used only occasionally, so it also should be affordable to make it marketable.

68. **Boat trailer.** Design a trailer from which a boat hangs rather than riding on top of it so that the boat can be launched in very shallow water.

69. **Washing machine.** Design a manually operated washing machine. It may be considered an "undesign" of an electrically powered washing machine.

70. **Pickup truck hoist.** Design a lift that can be attached to the tailgate of a pickup truck for raising and lowering loads from the ground to the bed of the truck without a motor.

71. **Display booth.** Design a portable display booth for use behind or on an 8-ft-long table for displaying your company's name and product information. It must be collapsible so that it can be carried by one person as airplane luggage.

72. **Exerciser (Fig. 2.58).** Design a simple exercise device that can be used for doing push-ups and sit-ups and that would sell for about $20.

73. **Patio grill (Fig. 2.59).** Design a portable charcoal grill for cooking on the patio. Consider how it would be cleaned, stored, and used. Study competing products already on the market.

74. **Deer-hunting seat.** Design a deer-hunting seat that can be carried to the field and attached to a tree trunk.

Figure 2.59 Problem 73. A patio grill.

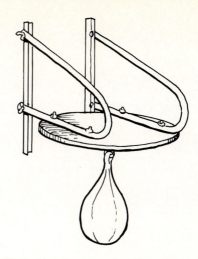

Figure 2.61 Problem 76. A punching bag platform.

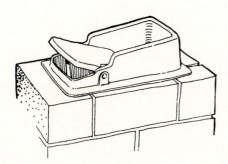

Figure 2.60 Problem 75. A chimney cover.

Figure 2.62 Problem 77. A shopping caddy.

75. **Chimney cover (Fig. 2.60).** Design a chimney cover that can be closed from inside the house for repelling rain and reducing temperature loss.

76. **Punching bag platform (Fig. 2.61).** Design a platform for a speed punching bag that is adjustable to various heights, is portable, and ships in a flat box.

77. **Shopping caddy (Fig. 2.62).** Design a portable lightweight caddy that a shopper can use for carrying parcels.

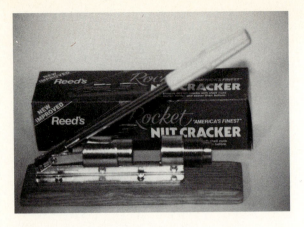

Figure 2.63 Problem 78. A nutcracker.

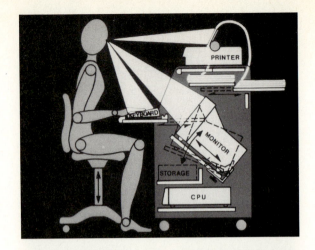

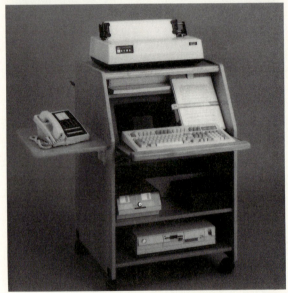

78. Nutcracker (Fig. 2.63). Design a nutcracker similar to the one shown.

79. Computer workstation. Figure 2.64 illustrates a unique design for a computer workstation that reduces user discomfort. Components of the computer system are positioned for greatest visibility and comfort. Design a similar workstation, using this example as a guide.

Figure 2.64 Problem 79. The Peanut Ultra View Workstation. (Courtesy of Continental Engineering Group, Inc.)

3

Drawing Instruments

3.1 Introduction

The preparation of technical drawings requires knowledge of and skill in the use of drafting instruments. Skill and productivity increase with practice. Even people with little artistic ability can produce professional technical drawings when they learn to use drawing instruments properly.

3.2 Drafting Media

Pencils

A good drawing begins with the correct pencil grade and its proper use. Pencil grades range from the hardest, 9H, to the softest, 7B (**Fig. 3.1**). The pencils in the medium-grade range, 4H–4B, are used most often for drafting work of the type covered in this textbook.

Figure 3.2A–C shows three standard pencils used for drawing. The leads used in the lead holder shown in Fig. 3.2A (the best all-around pencil of the three) are marked white at their ends. The fine-line leads used in the lead holder in Fig. 3.2B are

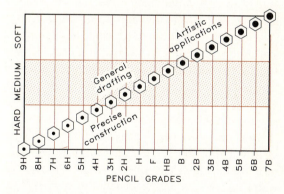

Figure 3.1 The hardest pencil lead is 9H, and the softest is 7B. The diameters of the hard leads are smaller than those of the soft leads.

more difficult to identify because their sizes are smaller and are not marked. A different fine-line holder must be used for each size of lead. The common sizes are 0.3 mm, 0.5 mm, and .007 mm, which are the diameters of the leads. A disadvan-

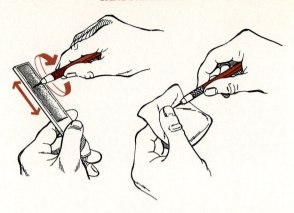

DRAFTING PENCILS

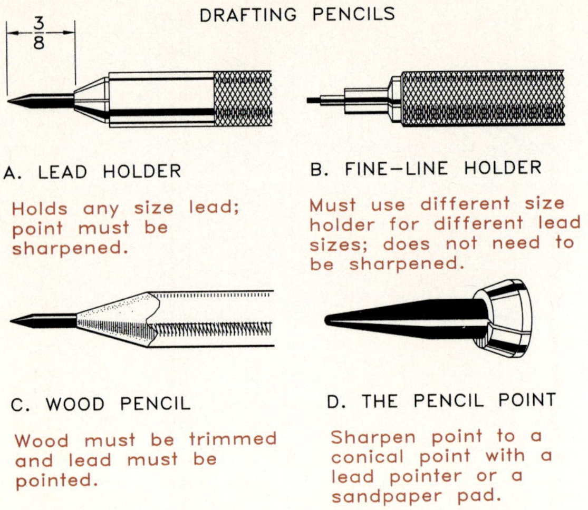

A. LEAD HOLDER

Holds any size lead; point must be sharpened.

B. FINE—LINE HOLDER

Must use different size holder for different lead sizes; does not need to be sharpened.

C. WOOD PENCIL

Wood must be trimmed and lead must be pointed.

D. THE PENCIL POINT

Sharpen point to a conical point with a lead pointer or a sandpaper pad.

Figure 3.2 Sharpen the drafting pencil to a tapered conical point (not a needle point) with a sandpaper pad or other type of sharpener.

Figure 3.3 Revolve the drafting pencil about its axis as you stroke the sandpaper pad to form a conical point. Wipe away the graphite from the sharpened point with a tissue.

Figure 3.4 A pencil pointer of this type is useful in sharpening pencils.

tage of the fine-line pencil is the tendency of the lead to snap off when you apply pressure to it.

Although you have to sharpen and point its lead, the wood pencil shown in Fig. 3.2C is very satisfactory for lettering and drawing. The grade of the lead appears clearly on one end of the pencil. Sharpen the opposite end of the pencil so the identity of the grade of lead will be retained.

You must sharpen a pencil point properly, as shown in **Fig. 3.2D**. You may do so with a small knife or a drafter's pencil sharpener, which removes the wood and leaves approximately 3/8 inch of lead exposed. You should then sharpen the point to a conical point with a sandpaper pad by stroking the sandpaper with the pencil point while revolving the pencil about its axis **(Fig. 3.3)**. Wipe excess graphite from the point with a cloth or tissue.

You also may use a pencil pointer **(Fig. 3.4)** to sharpen wood and mechanical pencils. Insert the pencil in the hole and revolve it to sharpen the lead. Other types of small hand-held point sharpeners also are available.

Pens and Ink

Unlike drawings made by pencil, drawings made in ink remain dark and distinct. Ink lines also reproduce better than pencil lines. India ink—a dense, black carbon ink that is much thicker and

INKING A PEN

Figure 3.5 Ink the pen between the nibs by using the spout on the ink bottle cap.

RULING A LINE

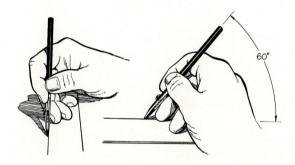

Figure 3.6 Hold the ruling pen in a plane perpendicular to the paper and at 60° to the drawing surface.

faster drying than fountain pen ink—is excellent for engineering drawings.

Ink the ruling pen by using the spout on the cap of the ink bottle (**Fig. 3.5**). Learning the proper amount of ink to apply to the nibs takes practice. When drawing horizontal lines, hold the ruling pen as you would hold a pencil (**Fig. 3.6**), maintaining a space between the nibs and straightedge.

An alternative type of pen is the technical ink pen (**Fig. 3.7**), which comes in sets with pen points of various sizes for drawing lines of differ-

INK PEN

Figure 3.7 The Rapidograph® is one type of technical ink pen.

DRAFTING SHEET SIZES

	ENGINEERS'	ARCHITECTS'		METRIC
A	11" X 8.5"	12" X 9"	A4	297 X 210
B	17" X 11"	18" X 12"	A3	420 X 297
C	22" X 17"	24" X 18"	A2	594 X 420
D	34" X 22"	36" X 24"	A1	841 X 594
E	44" X 34"	48" X 36"	A0	1189 X 841

Figure 3.8 Standard sheet sizes vary by purpose.

ent thicknesses. Lines drawn with this type of pen dry faster than those drawn with ruling pens because the ink is applied in a thinner layer.

Papers and Films

Sizes   Sheet sizes are specified by the letters A–E. These sizes (**Fig. 3.8**) are multiples of either the standard 8 1/2-×-11-inch sheet (used by engineers) or the 9-×-12-inch sheet (used by architects). The metric sizes (A4–A0) are equivalent to the 8 1/2-×-11-inch modular sizes.

Detail Paper   When drawings are not to be reproduced by the diazo or blue-line process, you may use an opaque paper, called **detail paper**, as the drawing surface. The higher the rag content (cotton additive) of the paper, the better is its quality and durability. You may draw preliminary layouts on detail paper and then trace them onto the final surface.

Tracing Paper Tracing paper or tracing vellum is a thin, translucent paper used for making detail drawings. This paper permits light to pass through it, allowing reproduction by the blue-line process. Tracing papers that yield the best reproductions are the most translucent ones. **Vellum** is a chemically treated tracing paper. The treatment improves its translucency, but vellum does not retain its original quality as long as do high-quality, untreated tracing papers.

Tracing Cloth Tracing cloth is a permanent drafting medium used for both ink and pencil drawings. It is made of cotton fabric that has been covered with a starch compound to provide a tough, erasable drafting surface that yields excellent blue-line reproductions. Tracing cloth does not change shape as much as tracing paper with variations in temperature and humidity. Repeated erasures do not damage the surface of tracing cloth, an especially important feature for ink drawings. An application of a coating of powder or pounce to absorb oily spots that may repel an ink line prepares tracing cloths for inking.

Polyester Film An excellent drafting surface is polyester film, which is available under several trade names such as **Mylar**. It is more transparent, stabler, and tougher than paper or cloth and is waterproof. Mylar film is used for both pencil and ink drawings. A plastic-lead pencil must be used with some films, whereas standard lead pencils may be used with others. Ink will not wash off with water and will not erase with a dry eraser; a dampened hand-held eraser is required.

When you use polyester film, draw on the matte surface according to the manufacturer's directions. Use a cleaning solution to prepare the surface for ink, such as removing spots that might not take ink properly.

3.3 Drafting Equipment

T-Square and Board

The T-square and drafting board are basic pieces of drafting equipment (**Fig. 3.9**). Always tape

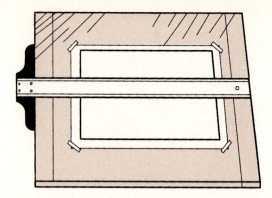

Figure 3.9 The T-square and drafting board are basic drafting tools.

drawing paper to the board parallel to the blade of the T-square. By holding its head against the edge of the drawing board, you may then move the T-square and draw parallel horizontal lines. Most small drafting boards are made of basswood, which is lightweight and strong. Standard board sizes are 12 × 14 inches, 15 × 20 inches, and 21 × 26 inches.

Drafting Machine

The T-square will always be used to some extent in industry and the classroom. However, most professional drafters prefer the mechanical drafting machine (**Fig. 3.10**), which is attached to the drawing table top and has fingertip controls for drawing lines at any angle.

Figure 3.11 shows a modern, fully equipped drafting station. Today, most offices are equipped with computer graphics stations, which have almost replaced manual equipment (**Fig. 3.12**).

Triangles

The two types of triangles used most often are the 45° triangle and the 30°–60° triangle. The 30°–60° triangle is specified by the longer of the two sides

DRAFTING MACHINE

Figure 3.10 The drafting machine often is used instead of the T-square and drafting board. (Courtesy of Keuffel & Esser Company.)

Figure 3.12 Many professional workstations are equipped with computer graphics equipment.

Figure 3.11 The professional drafter or engineer may work in this type of environment. (Courtesy of Martin Instrument Company.)

THE 30°–60° TRIANGLE

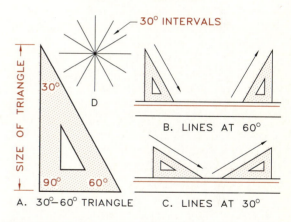

Figure 3.13 You may use a 30°–60° triangle to draw lines at 30° intervals throughout 360°.

adjacent to the 90° angle (**Fig. 3.13**). Standard sizes of 30°–60° triangles range in 2-inch intervals from 4 to 24 inches.

The 45° triangle is specified by the length of the sides adjacent to the 90° angle. These range in 2-inch intervals from 4 to 24 inches, but the 6-inch and 10-inch sizes are adequate for most classroom applications. **Figure 3.14** shows the various angles that you may draw with this triangle. By using the 45° and 30°–60° triangles in combination, you may draw angles at 15° intervals throughout 360° (**Fig. 3.15**).

45° TRIANGLE

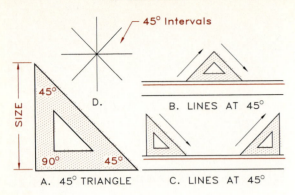

Figure 3.14 You may use a 45° triangle to draw lines at 45° intervals throughout 360°.

ANGLES DRAWN WITH TRIANGLES

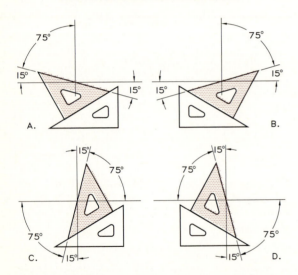

Figure 3.15 By using a 30°–60° triangle in combination with a 45° triangle, you may draw angles at 15° intervals.

Protractor

When drawing or measuring lines at angles other than multiples of 15°, use a protractor (**Fig. 3.16**). Protractors are available as semicircles (180°) or circles (360°). Adjustable triangles with movable edges that can be set at different angles with thumbscrews also are available.

THE PROTRACTOR

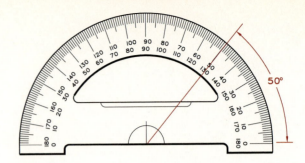

Figure 3.16 Use a semicircular protractor to measure angles.

DRAFTING INSTRUMENTS

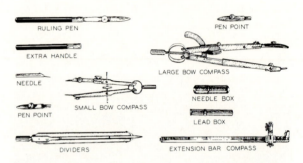

Figure 3.17 You may buy drafting instruments individually.

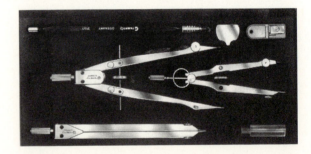

Figure 3.18 You also may buy instruments as a cased set. (Courtesy of Gramercy Guild.)

The Instrument Set

Figure 3.17 shows some of the basic drawing instruments. They are available individually or in cased sets, such as the one shown in **Fig. 3.18**.

USING THE COMPASS

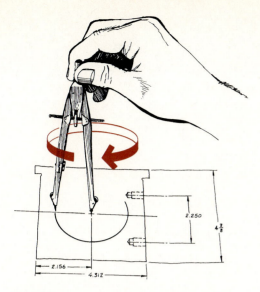

Figure 3.19 Use a compass for drawing circles.

SHARPENING THE COMPASS LEAD

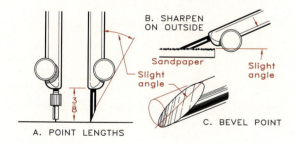

A. POINT LENGTHS

B. SHARPEN ON OUTSIDE

Sandpaper

Slight angle

Slight angle

C. BEVEL POINT

Figure 3.20
A Adjust the pencil point to be the same length as the compass point.
B Sharpen the lead from the outside with a sandpaper pad.
C Sharpen the lead to a beveled point.

Compass Use the compass to draw circles and arcs in pencil or ink **(Fig. 3.19)**. To draw circles well with a pencil compass, sharpen the lead on its outside with a sandpaper board **(Fig. 3.20)**. A bevel cut of this type gives the best point for drawing circles. You cannot draw a thick arc in pencil

SMALL BOW COMPASSES

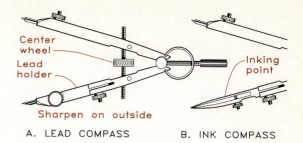

Center wheel

Lead holder

Sharpen on outside

A. LEAD COMPASS

Inking point

B. INK COMPASS

Figure 3.21 Use a small bow compass for drawing circles of up to 2-in. radius: (A) lead; (B) ink.

COMPASS EXTENSION

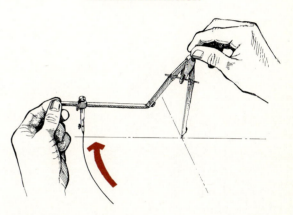

Figure 3.22 Use an extension bar with a bow compass to draw large arcs.

with a single sweep. **To thicken the pencil line of a circle, draw a series of thin concentric circles by adjusting the radius of the compass slightly.**

When setting the compass point in the drawing surface, insert it just enough for a firm set, not to the shoulder of the point. When the table top has a hard covering, place several sheets of paper under the drawing to provide a seat for the compass point.

Use a small bow compass **(Fig. 3.21)** to draw small circles of up to 2 inches in radius. For larger circles, use an extension bar to extend the range of the large bow compass **(Fig. 3.22)**. Use a beam compass **(Fig. 3.23)** to produce still larger circles.

BEAM COMPASS

Figure 3.23 Use a beam compass to draw large circles. Ink attachments also are available.

CIRCLES WITH A TEMPLATE

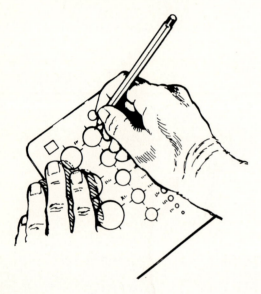

Figure 3.24 Circle templates are convenient for drawing small circles without a compass.

USING THE DIVIDERS

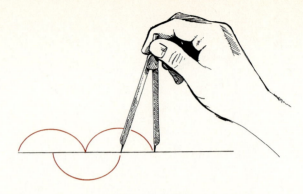

Figure 3.25 Use dividers to step off measurements.

TRANSFERRING DIMENSIONS

Figure 3.26 You may also use dividers to transfer dimensions from a scale to a drawing.

You may draw very small circles conveniently with a circle template aligned with the centerlines of the circles **(Fig. 3.24)**.

Dividers   The dividers look like a compass but do not have pencil or pen points. Use them for laying off and transferring dimensions onto a drawing. For example, you can step off equal divisions rapidly and accurately along a line **(Fig. 3.25)**. As

you make each measurement, the dividers' points make a slight impression mark in the drawing surface.

You may also use dividers to transfer dimensions from a scale to a drawing **(Fig. 3.26)** or to divide a line into a number of equal parts. Bow dividers **(Fig. 3.27)** are useful for transferring smaller dimensions, such as the spacing between lettering guidelines.

SMALL BOW DIVIDERS

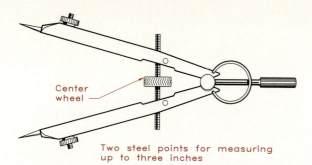

Center wheel

Two steel points for measuring up to three inches

Figure 3.27 Use a bow divider to transfer small dimensions, such as the spaces between guidelines for lettering.

PROPORTIONAL DIVIDERS

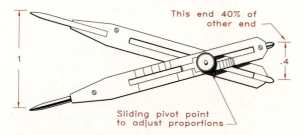

This end 40% of other end

Sliding pivot point to adjust proportions

Figure 3.28 Use a proportional divider to make measurements at one end that are proportional dimensions at the other end.

Proportional Dividers Proportional dividers allow transferral of dimensions from one scale to another. Moving the pivot point varies the ratio between the ends of the dividers (**Fig. 3.28**).

Templates

Various templates are available for use in drawing nuts and bolts, circles and ellipses, architectural symbols, and many other shapes. Templates work better when used with technical ink pens than with ruling pens.

ALPHABET OF LINES

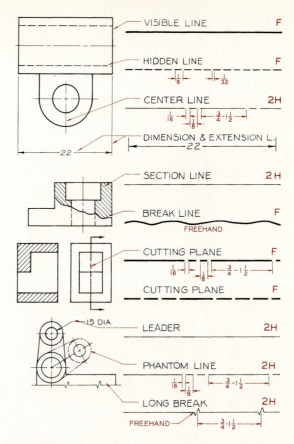

Figure 3.29 The alphabet of lines: Full-size lines and the pencil grades for drawing them appear in the right column.

3.4 Lines

The type of line produced by a pencil depends on the hardness of its lead, drawing surface, and your drawing technique. **Figure 3.29** shows examples of the standard lines, or **the alphabet of lines**, and the recommended pencils for drawing them, which vary somewhat with the drawing surface being used. Guidelines are light (just dark enough to be seen) and aid in lettering and laying out a drawing. A 2H or 4H pencil lead is recommended for drawing guidelines.

HORIZONTAL LINES

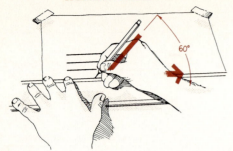

Figure 3.30 Draw horizontal lines along the upper edge of a straightedge while holding the pencil or pen in a plane perpendicular to the paper and at 60° to the surface.

ROTATION OF PENCIL

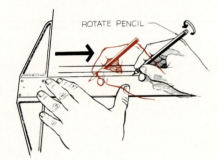

Figure 3.31 Rotate the pencil about its axis while drawing so that its point will wear evenly.

PENCIL POSITION

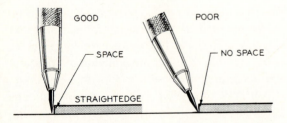

Figure 3.32 While drawing, hold the pencil or pen point in a plane perpendicular to the paper, leaving a space between the point and the straightedge.

VERTICAL LINES

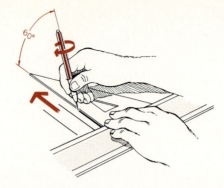

Figure 3.33 Draw vertical lines along the left side of a triangle (if you are right-handed) in an upward direction, holding the pencil or pen in a plane perpendicular to the paper and at 60° to the surface.

Horizontal Lines

To draw a horizontal line, use the upper edge of your horizontal straightedge and make strokes from left to right, if you are right-handed (**Fig. 3.30**), and from right to left if you are left-handed. Rotate the pencil about its axis so that its point will wear evenly (**Fig. 3.31**). Darken pencil lines by drawing over them with multiple strokes. For drawing the best line, leave a small space between the straightedge and the pencil or pen point (**Fig. 3.32**).

Vertical Lines

Use a triangle and a straightedge to draw vertical lines. Hold the straightedge firmly with one hand and position the triangle where needed and draw the vertical lines with the other hand (**Fig. 3.33**). Draw vertical lines upward along the left side of the triangle if you are right-handed and upward along the right side of the triangle if you are left-handed.

Parallel Lines

You may draw a series of lines parallel to a given line by using a triangle and straightedge (**Fig.**

DRAWING A PARALLEL LINE

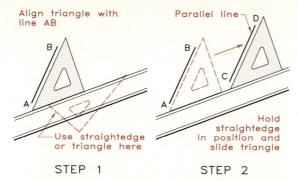

Align triangle with line AB

Use straightedge or triangle here

STEP 1

Parallel line

Hold straightedge in position and slide triangle

STEP 2

Figure 3.34 You may use a straightedge and a 45° triangle to draw a series of parallel lines. Hold the straightedge firmly in position and move the triangle into position to draw line CD.

DRAWING A PERPENDICULAR

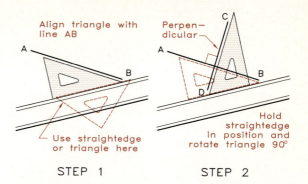

Align triangle with line AB

Use straightedge or triangle here

STEP 1

Perpen—dicular

Hold straightedge in position and rotate triangle 90°

STEP 2

Figure 3.35 You may use a 30°–60° triangle and a straightedge to construct a line perpendicular to line AB. Align the triangle with line AB and then rotate the triangle to draw line CD.

3.34). Place the 45° triangle parallel to the given line and hold it against the straightedge (which may be another triangle). By holding the straightedge in one position, you may move the triangle to various positions along the straightedge and draw parallel lines.

Perpendicular Lines

You may construct perpendicular lines by using either of the standard triangles. Use a 30°–60° triangle and a straightedge, or another triangle, to draw line CD perpendicular to line AB **(Fig. 3.35)**. Place one edge of the triangle parallel to line AB, with the straightedge in contact with the triangle (step 1). While holding the straightedge in place, rotate the triangle and move it to draw the perpendicular line CD (step 2).

Angular Lines

Figure 3.36 shows how to draw a 30° angle with a given line, AB, by using the 30°–60° triangle and another straightedge. You may use this same technique to draw angles of 60° and 45°.

DRAWING A 30° ANGLE

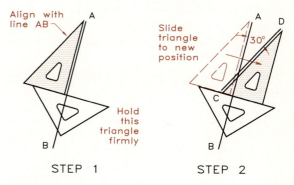

Align with line AB

Hold this triangle firmly

STEP 1

Slide triangle to new position

30°

STEP 2

Figure 3.36

Step 1 Hold the 30°–60° triangle in contact with a straightedge and align the triangle with line AB.

Step 2 Hold the straightedge in position and slide the triangle to where you want to draw the 30° line.

Irregular Curves

You have to draw curves that are not arcs with an irregular curve (sometimes called French curves). These plastic curves come in a variety of sizes and shapes, but the one shown in **Fig. 3.37** is typical.

USING THE IRREGULAR CURVE

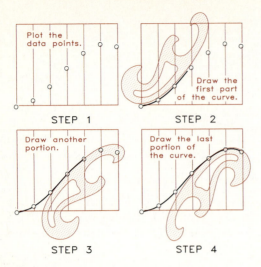

Figure 3.37

Step 1 Plot data points.

Step 2 Position the irregular curve to pass through as many points as possible and draw that portion of the curve.

Step 3 Reposition the irregular curve and draw another portion of the curve.

Step 4 Draw the last portion to complete the smooth curve.

Here, we used the irregular curve to connect a series of points to form a smooth curve.

Erasing Lines

Always use the softest eraser that will do a particular job. For example, do not use ink erasers to erase pencil lines because ink erasers are coarse and may damage the surface of the paper. When working in small areas, you should use an erasing shield to avoid accidentally erasing adjacent lines (**Fig. 3.38**). Follow all erasing by brushing away the "crumbs" with a dusting brush. Wiping the crumbs away with your hands will smudge the drawing. A cordless electric eraser (**Fig. 3.39**) accommodates several grades of erasers for erasing both pencil and ink lines.

ERASING SHIELD

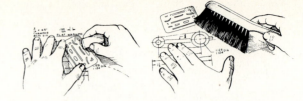

Figure 3.38 Use an erasing shield for erasing in tight spots. Use a brush, not your hand, to brush away the erasure crumbs.

ELECTRIC ERASER

Figure 3.39 This cordless electric eraser is typical of those used by professional drafters.

3.5 Measurement

Scales

All engineering drawings require the use of scales for measuring lengths and sizes. Scales may be flat or triangular and are made of wood, plastic, or metal. **Figure 3.40** shows triangular architects', engineers', and metric scales. Most scales are either 6 or 12 inches long.

Architects' Scale Drafters use the architects' scale to dimension and scale architectural features such as room-size, cabinets, plumbing, and electrical layouts. Most indoor measurements are made in feet and inches with an architects' scale. **Figure**

TYPES OF SCALES

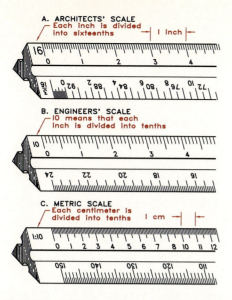

Figure 3.40 The architects' scale (A) measures in feet and inches. The engineers' scale (B) and the metric scale (C) are calibrated in decimal units.

ARCHITECTS' SCALE

BASIC FORM *SCALE:* $\frac{X}{X}$ *=1'–0*

— FROM END OF SCALE

TYPICAL SCALES

SCALE: FULL SIZE (USE 16–SCALE)

SCALE: HALF SIZE (USE 16–SCALE)

SCALE: 3=1'–0	*SCALE: $\frac{1}{4}$=1'–0*
SCALE: $1\frac{1}{2}$=1'–0	*SCALE: $\frac{3}{4}$=1'–0*
SCALE: $\frac{1}{2}$=1'–0	*SCALE: $\frac{3}{8}$=1'–0*
SCALE: $\frac{3}{16}$=1'–0	*SCALE: $\frac{1}{8}$=1'–0*
SCALE: $\frac{3}{32}$=1'–0	*SCALE: 1=1'–0*

Figure 3.41 Use this basic form to indicate the scale on a drawing made with an architects' scale.

3.41 shows how to indicate on a drawing the scale you are using. Place this scale designation in the title block or in a prominent location on the draw-

ARCHITECTURAL MEASUREMENTS

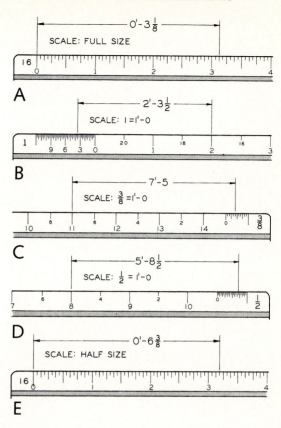

Figure 3.42 Lines measured with an architects' scale.

ing. Because dimensions measured with the architects' scale are in feet and inches, you should convert all dimensions to decimal equivalents (all feet or all inches) before making calculations.

Use the 16 scale for measuring full-size lines **(Fig. 3.42A)**. An inch on the 16 scale is divided into sixteenths to match the ruler used by carpenters. The measurement shown is 3 1/8". When the measurement is less than 1 ft, a zero may precede the inch measurements, with inch marks omitted, or 0'-3 1/8.

Figure 3.42B shows use of the 1 = 1'-0 scale to measure a line. Read the nearest whole foot (2 ft in this case) and then the remainder in inches from the end of the scale (3 1/2 in.) for a total of 2'-3 1/2.

MARKING MEASUREMENTS

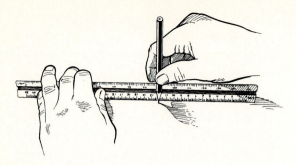

Figure 3.43 When marking off measurements along a scale, hold your pencil vertical for accuracy.

SPECIFYING FEET AND INCHES

Figure 3.44 Omit inch marks but show foot marks (according to current standards). When the inch measurement is less than a whole inch, use a leading zero.

Note that, at the end of each scale, a foot is divided into inches for use in measuring dimensions of less than a foot. The scale 1" = 1'-0 is the same as saying that 1 in. is equal to 12 in. or that the drawing is 1/12 the actual size of the object.

When you use the 3/8 = 1'-0 scale, 3/8 in. represents 12 in. on a drawing. Thus the line in **Fig. 3.42C** measures 7'-5. Similarly, at the 1/2 = 1'-0 scale, the line in **Fig. 3.42D** measures 5'-8 1/2.

To obtain a half-size measurement, divide the full-size measurement by 2 and draw it with the 16 scale. This scale is sometimes specified as scale: 6 = 12 (inch marks omitted). The line in **Fig. 3.42E** measures to be 0'-6 3/8.

ENGINEERS' SCALE

FROM END OF SCALE

BASIC FORM *SCALE: 1= XX*

EXAMPLE SCALES

10	*SCALE: 1=1'*	*SCALE: 1=1,000*
20	*SCALE: 1=200'*	*SCALE: 1=20 LB*
30	*SCALE: 1=3'*	*SCALE: 1=3,000'*
40	*SCALE: 1=4'*	*SCALE: 1=40'*
50	*SCALE: 1=50'*	*SCALE: 1=500'*
60	*SCALE: 1=6*	*SCALE: 1=0.6'*

Figure 3.45 Use this basic form to indicate the scale on a drawing made with an engineers' scale.

When marking measurements, hold your pencil or pen vertical for the greatest accuracy (**Fig. 3.43**). Specify dimensions in feet and inches as shown in **Fig. 3.44**, with fractions twice as tall as whole numerals.

Engineers' Scale On the engineers' scale, each inch is divided into multiples of 10. Because it is used for making drawings of outdoor projects—streets, structures, tracts of land, and other topographical features—it is sometimes called the civil engineers' scale.

With measurements already in decimal form, performing calculations is easy; there is no need to convert from one unit to another as when you use the architects' scale. **Figure 3.45** shows the form for specifying scales when using the engineers' scale. For example, scale: 1 = 10'.

Each end of the scale is labeled 10, 20, 30, and so on, which indicates the number of units per inch on the scale (Fig. 3.46). You may obtain many combinations simply by mentally moving the decimal places of a scale.

Figure 3.46A shows the use of the 10 scale to measure a line 32.0 ft long drawn at the scale of 1 = 10'. **Figure 3.46B** shows use of the 20 scale to

ENGINEERS' SCALES

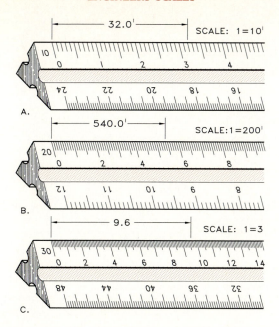

A.

B.

C.

Figure 3.46 Lines measured with an engineers' scale.

DECIMAL FRACTIONS

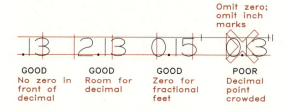

Figure 3.47 For decimal fractions in inches, omit leading zeros and inch marks. For feet, leave adequate space for decimal points between numbers and show foot marks.

measure a line 540.0 ft long drawn at a scale of 1 = 200'. **Figure 3.46C** shows use of the 30 scale to measure a line of 9.6 in. long at a scale of 1 = 3. **Figure 3.47** shows the proper format for indicating measurements in feet and inches.

ENGLISH UNITS

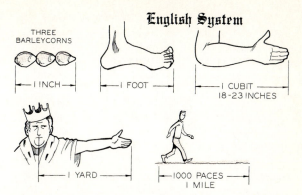

Figure 3.48 The units of the English system are based on arbitrary dimensions.

English System of Units

The English (Imperial) system of units has been used in the United States, Great Britain (until recently), and Canada since it was established. This system is based on arbitrary units (of length) of the inch, foot, cubit, yard, and mile **(Fig. 3.48)**. Because there is no common relationship among these units, calculations are cumbersome. For example, finding the area of a rectangle that measures 25 in. × 6 3/4 yd first requires conversion of one unit to the other.

Metric System (SI) of Units

France proposed the metric system in the fifteenth century. In 1793 the French National Assembly agreed that the meter (m) would be one ten-millionth of the meridian quadrant of the earth and fractions of the meter would be expressed as decimal fractions. An international commission officially adopted the metric system in 1875. Scientists later found a slight error in the first measurement of the meter, so the meter was redefined as being equal to 1,650,763.73 wavelengths of the orange-red light given off by krypton-86.

The worldwide organization responsible for promoting the metric system is the International

METRIC PREFIXES AND ABBREVIATIONS

Value		Prefix	Symbol	Pronunciation
1 000 000 = 10^6	=	Mega	M	"Megah"
1 000 = 10^3	=	Kilo	k	"Keylow"
100 = 10^2	=	Hecto	h	"Heck tow"
10 = 10^1	=	Deka	da	"Dekah"
1 =				
0.1 = 10^{-1}	=	Deci	d	"Des sigh"
0.01 = 10^{-2}	=	Centi	c	"Cen'—ti"
0.001 = 10^{-3}	=	Milli	m	"Mill lee"
0.000 001 = 10^{-6}	=	Micro	μ	"Microw"

Figure 3.49 These prefixes and abbreviations indicate decimal placement for SI measurements.

ENGLISH/METRIC CONVERSIONS

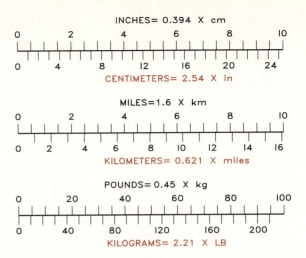

Figure 3.50 These scales show a comparison of the English system units with metric system units.

Standards Organization (ISO). It has endorsed the System International d'Unites (International System of Units), abbreviated SI.

Prefixes to SI units indicate placement of the decimal, as **Fig. 3.49** shows. **Figure 3.50** shows several comparisons of English and SI units.

Metric Scales
The basic metric unit of measurement for an engineering drawing is the millimeter (mm), which is one-thousandth of a meter, or one-tenth of a centimeter. Dimensions on a metric drawing are understood to be in millimeters unless otherwise specified.

The width of the fingernail of your index finger is a convenient way to approximate the dimension of one centimeter, or ten millimeters **(Fig. 3.51)**. Depicted in **Fig. 3.52** is the format for indicating metric scales on a drawing.

Decimal fractions are unnecessary on drawings dimensioned in millimeters. Thus dimensions usually are rounded off to whole numbers except for those measurements dimensioned with specified tolerances. For metric measurements of less than 1, a zero goes in front of the decimal. In the English system, the zero is omitted from measurements of less than an inch **(Fig. 3.53)**.

THE CENTIMETER

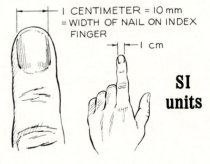

Figure 3.51 The nail width of your index finger is approximately equal to 1 centimeter, or 10 millimeters.

Metric scales are expressed as ratios: 1:20, 1:40, 1:100, 1:500, and so on. The scale ratios mean that one unit represents the number of units to the right of the colon. For example, 1:10 means that 1 mm equals 10 mm or 1 cm equals 10 cm or 1 m equals 10 m. The full-size metric scale **(Fig. 3.54)** shows the relationship between the metric units of the decime-

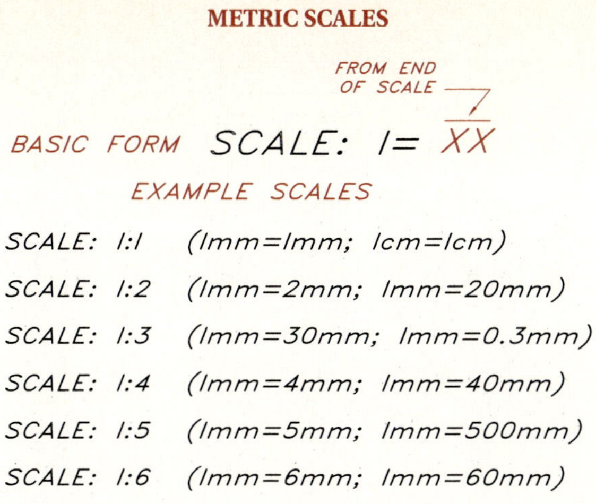

METRIC SCALES

EXAMPLE SCALES

SCALE: 1:1   *(1mm=1mm; 1cm=1cm)*

SCALE: 1:2   *(1mm=2mm; 1mm=20mm)*

SCALE: 1:3   *(1mm=30mm; 1mm=0.3mm)*

SCALE: 1:4   *(1mm=4mm; 1mm=40mm)*

SCALE: 1:5   *(1mm=5mm; 1mm=500mm)*

SCALE: 1:6   *(1mm=6mm; 1mm=60mm)*

Figure 3.52 Use this basic form to indicate the scale of a drawing made with a metric scale.

METRIC UNITS

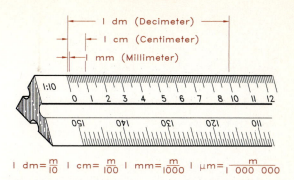

$$1 \text{ dm}=\frac{m}{10} \quad 1 \text{ cm}=\frac{m}{100} \quad 1 \text{ mm}=\frac{m}{1000} \quad 1 \text{ } \mu\text{m}=\frac{m}{1\,000\,000}$$

Figure 3.54 The decimeter is one tenth of a meter; the centimeter is one hundredth of a meter; a millimeter is one thousandth of a meter; and a micrometer is one millionth of a meter.

METRIC FRACTIONS

Figure 3.53 In the metric system, a zero precedes the decimal. Allow adequate space for it.

METRIC SCALES

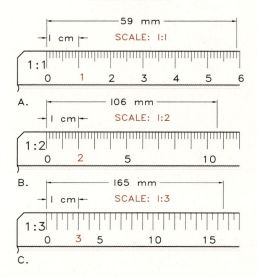

Figure 3.55 These lines are measured with a metric scale.

ter, centimeter, millimeter, and micrometer. The line shown in **Fig. 3.55A** measures 59 mm. Use the 1:2 scale when 1 mm represents 2 mm, 20 mm, 200 mm, and so on. The line shown in **Fig. 3.55B** measures 106 mm. **Figure 3.55C** shows a line measuring 165 mm, where 1 mm represents 3 mm.

Metric Symbols To indicate that drawings are in metric units, insert SI **(Fig. 3.56)** in or near the title block. The two views of the partial cone

denote whether the orthographic views were drawn in accordance with the U.S. system (third-angle projection) or the European system (first-angle projection).

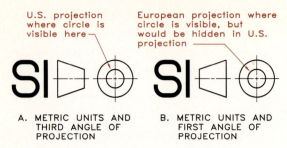

A. METRIC UNITS AND THIRD ANGLE OF PROJECTION

B. METRIC UNITS AND FIRST ANGLE OF PROJECTION

Figure 3.56 The large SI indicates that measurements are in metric units. The partial cones indicate whether the views are drawn in (A) the third-angle (U.S. system) or (B) the first-angle of projection (European system).

SI RULES

Omit commas and group into threes	I 000 000 GOOD	1,000,000 POOR
Use a raised dot for multiplication	N•M GOOD	NM POOR
Precede decimals with zeros	0.72 mm GOOD	.72 mm POOR
Methods of division	kg/m or GOOD	kg•m⁻¹ GOOD

Figure 3.57 Follow the general rules for showing SI units.

Expression of Metric Units **Figure 3.57** gives the general rules for expressing SI units. Do not use commas to separate digits in large numbers; instead, leave a space between them, as shown.

Scale Conversion
Appendix 2 gives factors for converting English to metric lengths and vice versa. For example, multiply decimal inches by 25.4 to obtain millimeters.

Multiply an architects' scale by 12 to convert it to an approximate metric scale. For example, Scale: 1/8 = 1'-0 is the same as 1/8 in. = 12 in. or 1 in. = 96 in.,

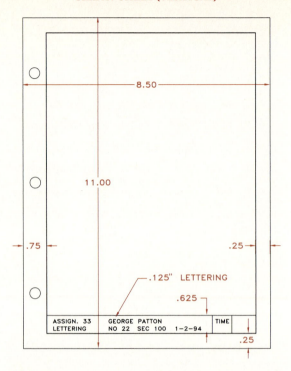

Figure 3.58 Use the format and title strip shown for a size AV sheet (8 1/2" × 11", vertical position) to present the solutions to problems at the end of each chapter.

which closely approximates the metric scale of 1:100. You cannot convert most metric scales exactly to English scales, but the metric scale of 1:60 does convert exactly to 1 = 5'.

3.6 Presentation of Drawings
The following formats are suggested for the presentation of drawings. The solutions to most problems may be drawn on 8 1/2-×-11-inch sheets with a title strip, as **Fig. 3.58** shows. When it is used vertically, we call this 8 1/2-×-11-inch sheet size AV throughout the rest of this textbook. When this sheet is used horizontally, as **Fig. 3.59** shows, we call it size AH.

Figure 3.59 shows the standard sizes of sheets, from size A through size E and an alternative title

SIZE AH SHEET (HORIZONTAL)

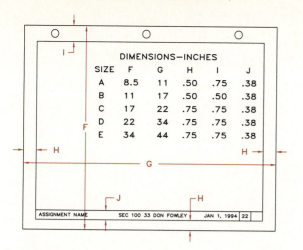

DIMENSIONS—INCHES

SIZE	F	G	H	I	J
A	8.5	11	.50	.75	.38
B	11	17	.50	.50	.38
C	17	22	.75	.75	.38
D	22	34	.75	.75	.38
E	34	44	.75	.75	.38

ASSIGNMENT NAME   SEC 100 33 DON FOWLEY   JAN 1, 1994 22

Figure 3.59 This format is for size AH sheet (11" × 8 1/2", horizontal position) and other sheet sizes. The numbers in columns A–E are the various layout dimensions.

PARTS LIST AND TITLE BLOCK

DRAWING TITLE			.38
BY: EDDIE CANTOR		SEC: 100	.38
DATE: 2–3–94		SHEET: I	.38
SCALE: FULL SIZE		OF I SHEETS	.38

← 5.00 APPROXIMATELY →

5	YOKE	3	CI	.38
4	HANDLE	1	CI	.38
3	COLLAR	2	STL	.38
2	SHAFT	2	STL	.38
I	BASE	1	CI	.38
NO	PART NAME	REQ	MATL	.38

Figure 3.60 You may use this title strip on sheet sizes B, C, D, and E instead of the one given in Fig. 3.58.

strip for sizes B, C, D, and E. Always use guidelines for lettering title strips.

Figure 3.60 shows a smaller title block and parts list, which go in the lower right-hand corner

of the sheet against the borders. When you use both on the same drawing, place the parts list directly above and in contact with the title block or title strip.

Problems

Problems 1–9 **(Figs. 3.61–3.63)**: Present your drawings on size AH paper, plain or with a printed grid, using the format shown in **Fig. 3.61**, in pencil or ink as assigned. Alternatively, you may present two half-size drawings per sheet on size AV paper, using the side of each square of a grid to represent .25 in., or 6 mm.

Problems 10–13 **(Figs. 3.64–3.67)**: Draw full-size views on size AH sheets and omit the dimensions.

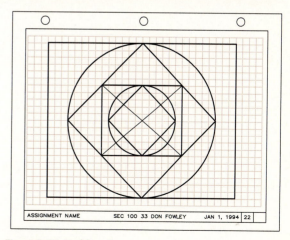

ASSIGNMENT NAME   SEC 100 33 DON FOWLEY   JAN 1, 1994 22

Figure 3.61 Problem 1.

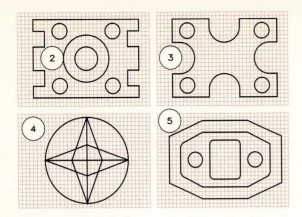

Figure 3.62 Problems 2–5.

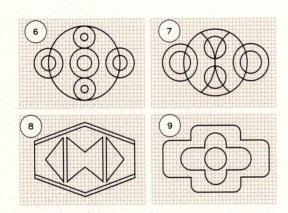

Figure 3.63 Problems 6–9.

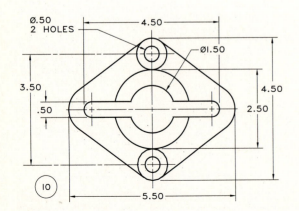

Figure 3.64 Problem 10.

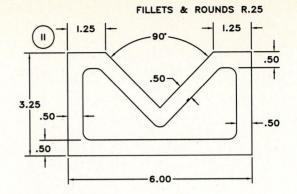

FILLETS & ROUNDS R.25

Figure 3.65 Problem 11.

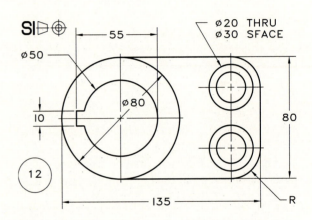

Figure 3.66 Problem 12.

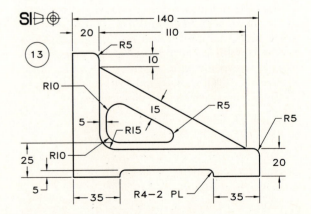

Figure 3.67 Problem 13.

4

Lettering

4.1 Introduction

Notes, dimensions, and specifications, which must be lettered, supplement all drawings. The ability to letter freehand is an important skill to develop because it affects the use and interpretation of drawings. It also displays an engineer's skill with graphics, and may be taken as an indication of professional competence.

4.2 Lettering Tools

The best pencils for lettering on most surfaces are the H, F, and HB grades, with an F grade pencil being the one most commonly used. Some papers and films are coarser than others and may require a harder pencil lead. To give the desired line width, round the point of the pencil slightly (**Fig. 4.1**), because a needle point will break off when you apply pressure.

While holding a pencil as shown in **Fig. 4.2**, revolve it slightly about its axis as you make

THE PENCIL POINT FOR LETTERING

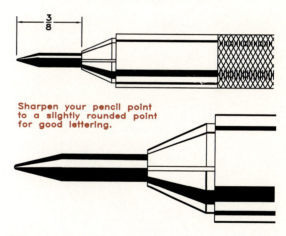

Sharpen your pencil point to a slightly rounded point for good lettering.

Figure 4.1 Good lettering begins with a properly sharpened pencil point. The F grade pencil is good for lettering.

strokes so that the lead will wear evenly. For good reproduction, bear down firmly to make letters black and bright with a single stroke. Prevent

PENCIL POSITION

Figure 4.2 Hold your pencil in a plane perpendicular to the paper and at 60° to the surface while lettering.

PROTECTIVE SHEET

Figure 4.3 Use a protective sheet under your hand to prevent smudges and work from a comfortable position for natural strokes.

smudging while lettering by placing a sheet of paper under your hand to protect the drawing **(Fig. 4.3)**.

GUIDELINES

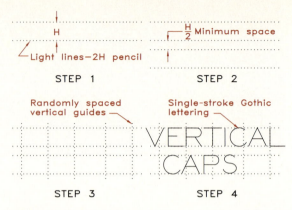

Figure 4.4 Use lettering guidelines in the following manner.

Step 1 Lay off letter heights, H, and draw light guidelines with a 2H pencil.

Step 2 Space lines no closer than H/2 apart.

Step 3 Draw vertical guidelines as light, thin, randomly spaced lines.

Step 4 Draw letters with single strokes using a medium-grade pencil: H, F, or HB. Do not erase the lightly drawn guidelines.

4.3 Guidelines

The most important rule of lettering is use guidelines at all times, whether you are lettering a paragraph or a single letter. Figure 4.4 shows how to draw and use guidelines. Use a sharp pencil in the 2H–4H grade range and draw light guidelines, just dark enough to be seen.

Most lettering on an engineering drawing is done with capital letters that are 1/8 inch (3 mm) high. The spacing between lines of lettering should be no closer than half the height of the capital letters, or 1/16 inch in this case.

Lettering Guides

Two instruments for drawing guidelines are the Braddock–Rowe lettering triangle and the Ames lettering instrument.

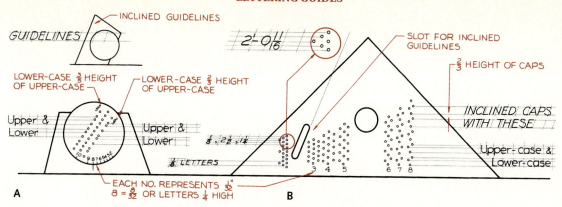

Figure 4.5

A The Ames lettering guide is used for drawing guidelines for lettering. Set the dial to the desired number of thirty-seconds of an inch for the height of uppercase letters.

B The Braddock–Rowe triangle also is used for drawing guidelines for lettering. The numbers near the guideline holes represent thirty-seconds of an inch.

The Braddock–Rowe triangle contains sets of holes for spacing guidelines (**Fig. 4.5B**). The numbers under each set of holes represent thirty-seconds of an inch. For example, the numeral 4 represents 4/32 inch or 1/8 inch for making uppercase (capital) letters. Some triangles have millimeter markings. Intermediate holes provide guidelines for lowercase letters, which are not as tall as capital letters (Fig. 4.6).

While holding a horizontal straightedge firmly in position, place the Braddock–Rowe triangle against its upper edge. Insert a sharp 2H pencil in the desired guideline hole to contact the drawing surface and guide the pencil point across the paper, drawing the guideline while the triangle slides along the straightedge. Repeat this procedure by moving the pencil point to each successive hole to draw other guidelines. Use the slanted slot in the triangle to draw guidelines, spaced randomly by eye, for inclined lettering.

The Ames lettering guide (**Fig. 4.5A**) is a similar device but has a circular dial for selecting proper guideline spacing. The numbers around the dial represent thirty-seconds of an inch. For example, the number 8 represents 8/32 inch, or

INCLINED AND VERTICAL GOTHIC

Figure 4.6 Use either vertical or inclined single-stroke Gothic lettering on engineering drawings.

guidelines for drawing capital letters that are 1/4 inch tall.

4.4 Freehand Gothic Lettering

The lettering recommended for engineering drawings is **single-stroke Gothic lettering**, so called because the letters are a variation of the Gothic

VERTICAL GOTHIC: UPPERCASE

ABCDEFG
HIJKLMN
OPQRSTU
VWXYZ&

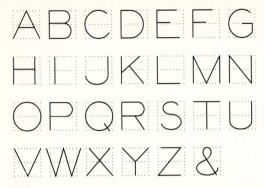

Figure .7 The alphabet is drawn here in single-stroke Gothic vertical uppercase letters. The letters are drawn inside a square to show their proportions.

COMMON ERRORS IN LETTERING

LETTERS POOR
A. LETTERS POORLY DONE
LETTERS THIN
B. STROKES TOO THIN
TOO HEAVY
C. STROKES TOO THICK
TOO LIGHT
D. BLACKER—BEAR DOWN WITH F PENCIL

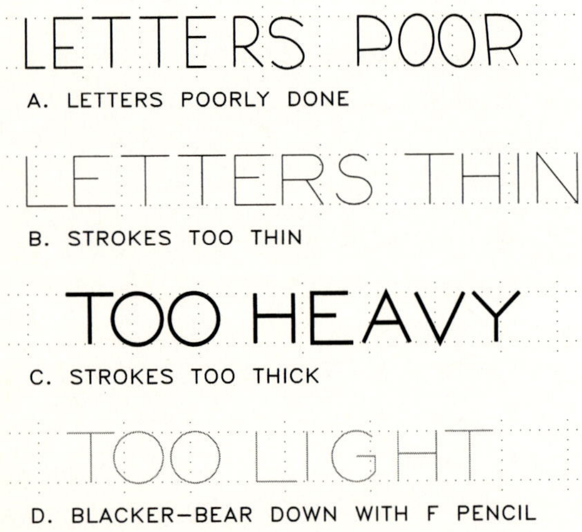

Figure 4.8 Avoid these errors in lettering.

style made with a series of single strokes. Gothic lettering may be vertical or inclined **(Fig. 4.6)**, but only one style or the other should be used on a single drawing.

VERTICAL GOTHIC: LOWERCASE

abcdefg
hijklm
nopqrst
uvwxyz

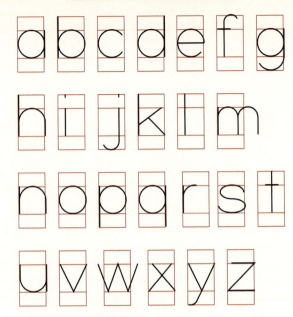

Figure 4.9 The alphabet is drawn here in single-stroke Gothic vertical lowercase letters.

Vertical Letters

Uppercase **Figure 4.7** shows the alphabet in the single-stroke Gothic uppercase (capital) letters. Each letter is drawn inside a square box of guidelines to show their correct proportions. Draw each straight line with a single stroke; for example, draw the letter A with three single strokes. Letters composed of curves can best be drawn in segments; for example, draw the letter O by joining two semicircles.

The shape (form) of each letter is important. Small wiggles in strokes will not detract from your lettering if the letter forms are correct. **Figure 4.8** shows common errors in lettering that you should avoid.

Lowercase **Figure 4.9** shows the alphabet in lowercase letters, which should be either two-thirds or three-fifths as tall as uppercase letters. Both

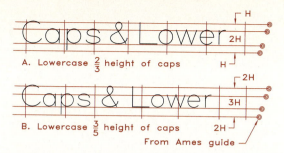

Figure 4.10 The ratio of lowercase letters to the uppercase letters should be either two-thirds (A) or three-fifths (B). The Ames guide has both ratios, but the Braddock–Rowe triangle has only the two-thirds ratio.

lowercase ratios are labeled on the Ames guide, but only the two-thirds ratio is available on the Braddock–Rowe triangle.

Some lowercase letters, such as the letter b, have ascenders that extend above the body of the letter; some, such as the letter p, have descenders that extend below the body. Ascenders and descenders should be equal in length.

The guidelines in Fig. 4.9 that form squares about the body of each letter are used to illustrate their proportions. Letters that have circular bodies may extend slightly beyond the sides of the guideline squares. **Figure 4.10** gives examples of capital and lowercase letters used together.

Numerals **Figure 4.11** shows vertical numerals for use with single-stroke Gothic lettering, with each number enclosed in a square box of guidelines. Numbers should be the same height as the capital letters being used, usually 1/8 inch high. The numeral 0 (zero) is an oval, whereas the letter O is a circle in vertical lettering.

Inclined Letters

Uppercase Inclined uppercase (capital) letters have the same heights and proportions as vertical

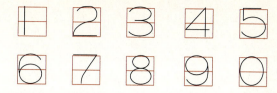

Figure 4.11 These numerals are used with single-stroke Gothic vertical letters.

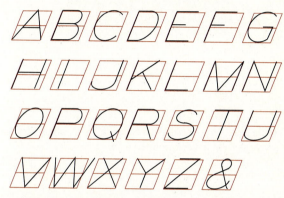

Figure 4.12 The alphabet is drawn here in single-stroke Gothic inclined uppercase letters.

letters; the only difference is their 68° inclination **(Fig. 4.12)**. You may draw guidelines for inclined lettering with both the Braddock–Rowe triangle and the Ames guide.

Lowercase Draw inclined lowercase letters in the same manner as vertical lowercase letters **(Fig. 4.13)**, but draw circular features as ovals (ellipses). The angle of inclination is 68°, the same as for uppercase letters.

Numerals **Figure 4.14** shows the form of inclined numerals to be used with inclined lettering. **Figure**

INCLINED GOTHIC: LOWERCASE

Figure 4.13 The alphabet is drawn here in single-stroke Gothic inclined lowercase letters.

INCLINED NUMERALS

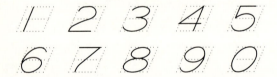

Figure 4.14 These numerals correspond to single-stroke Gothic inclined letters.

EXAMPLES OF NUMERALS

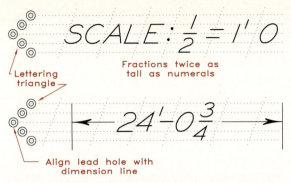

Figure 4.15 Make inclined common fractions twice as tall as single numerals. Omit inch marks.

GUIDELINES FOR FRACTIONS

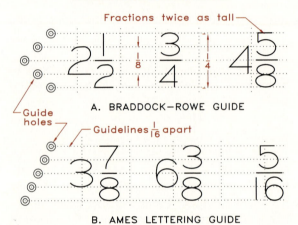

Figure 4.16 You may draw guidelines for common fractions, which should be twice as tall as single numerals, by using the (A) Braddock–Rowe triangle or the (B) Ames guide.

4.15 shows inclined letters and numbers in combination. **Figure 4.16** shows how to construct guidelines using the Braddock–Rowe triangle and the Ames lettering guide.

Spacing Numerals and Letters

Allow adequate space between numerals for the decimal point and fractions (**Fig. 4.17**). Avoid the errors of lettering numerals shown.

EXAMPLES OF FRACTIONS

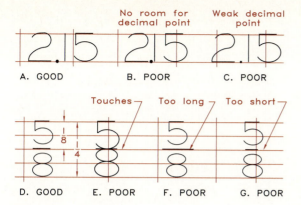

Figure 4.17 Avoid these errors in lettering.

SPACING OF LETTERS

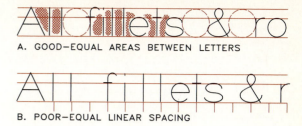

Figure 4.18 The areas between letters in a word should be approximately equal.

USING GUIDELINES

Figure 4.19 Always draw guidelines (vertical and horizontal) and use them whether you are lettering a paragraph or drawing a single letter.

Common fractions are twice as tall as single numerals (Fig. 4.17). Both the Braddock–Rowe triangle and the Ames guide have separate sets of holes, spaced 1/16 inch apart, for common fractions. The center guideline locates the fraction's crossbar.

When grouping letters to spell words, make the areas between the letters approximately equal for the most visually pleasing result (**Fig. 4.18**). **Figure 4.19** shows the incorrect use of guidelines and other violations of good lettering practice that you should avoid.

Problems

Present lettering problem solutions on size AH (11-×-8½-in.) paper, plain or with a grid, using the format shown in **Fig. 4.20**.

1. Practice drawing the alphabet in vertical uppercase letters, as shown in **Fig. 4.20**. Construct each letter three times: three A's, three B's, and so on. Use a medium-weight pencil—H, F, or HB.

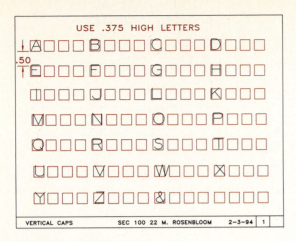

Figure 4.20 Problem 1.

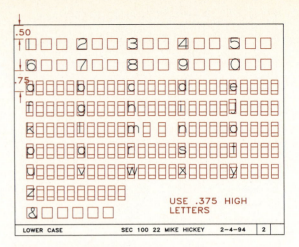

Figure 4.21 Problem 2.

2. Practice drawing vertical numerals and the alphabet in lowercase letters, as shown in **Fig. 4.21**. Construct each letter and numeral two times: two 1's, two 2's, two a's, two b's, and so on. Use a medium-weight pencil—H, F, or HB.

3. Practice drawing the alphabet in inclined uppercase letters, as shown in Fig. 4.12. Construct each letter three times. Use a medium-weight pencil—H, F, or HB.

4. Practice lettering the vertical numerals and the alphabet in lowercase letters, as shown in Figs. 4.11 and 4.9. Construct each letter two times. Use a medium-weight pencil—H, F, or HB.

5. Construct guidelines for $\frac{1}{8}$-in. capital letters starting $\frac{1}{4}$ in. from the top border. Each guideline should end $\frac{1}{2}$ in. from the left and right borders. Using these guidelines, letter the first paragraph of the text of this chapter. Use all vertical capitals. Spacing between the lines should be $\frac{1}{8}$ in.

6. Repeat Problem 5, but use all inclined capital letters. Use inclined guidelines to help you slant letters uniformly.

7. Repeat Problem 5, but use vertical capital and lowercase letters in combination. Capitalize only those words that are capitalized in the text.

8. Repeat Problem 5, but use inclined capital and lowercase letters in combination. Capitalize only those letters that are capitalized in the text.

Geometric Construction

5.1 Introduction

The solution of many graphical problems requires the use of geometry and geometric construction. Because mathematics was an outgrowth of graphical construction, the two areas are closely related. The proofs of many principles of plane geometry and trigonometry can be developed by using graphics. Moreover, graphical methods can be applied to solve some types of problems in algebra and arithmetic and virtually all types of problems in analytical geometry.

5.2 Angles

A fundamental application of geometric construction involves drawing lines at specified angles to each other. **Figure 5.1** gives names and definitions of various angles.

The unit of angular measurement is the degree, and a circle has 360 degrees. A degree (°) can be divided into 60 parts called minutes ('),

ANGLE DEFINITIONS

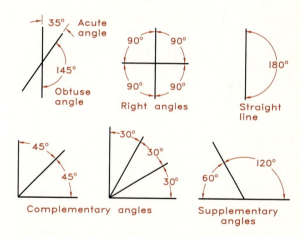

Figure 5.1 Standard angles and their names and definitions.

and a minute can be divided into 60 parts called seconds ("). An angle of 15°32'14" is an angle of 15 degrees, 32 minutes, and 14 seconds.

REGULAR POLYGONS

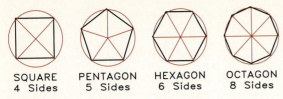

| SQUARE | PENTAGON | HEXAGON | OCTAGON |
| 4 Sides | 5 Sides | 6 Sides | 8 Sides |

Figure 5.2 Regular polygons can be inscribed in circles.

TYPES OF TRIANGLES

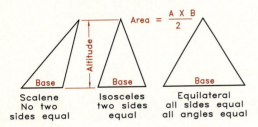

$$\text{Area} = \frac{A \times B}{2}$$

Scalene	Isosceles	Equilateral
No two	two sides	all sides equal
sides equal	equal	all angles equal

Figure 5.3 Types of triangles and their definitions.

QUADRILATERALS

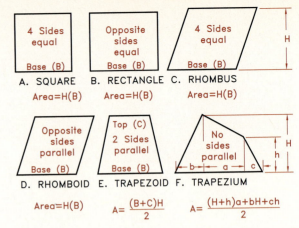

A. SQUARE	B. RECTANGLE	C. RHOMBUS
4 Sides equal	Opposite sides equal	4 Sides equal
Base (B)	Base (B)	Base (B)
Area=H(B)	Area=H(B)	Area=H(B)

D. RHOMBOID	E. TRAPEZOID	F. TRAPEZIUM
Opposite sides parallel	Top (C) 2 Sides parallel	No sides parallel
Base (B)	Base (B)	
Area=H(B)	$A = \dfrac{(B+C)H}{2}$	$A = \dfrac{(H+h)a + bH + ch}{2}$

Figure 5.4 Types of quadrilaterals, their definitions, and how to calculate their areas.

ELEMENTS OF CIRCLES

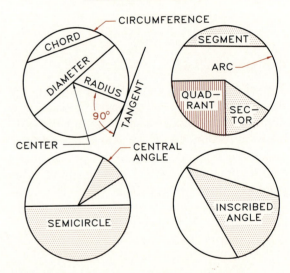

Figure 5.5 Elements of a circle and their definitions.

5.3 Polygons

A **polygon** is a multisided plane figure of any number of sides. If the sides of a polygon are equal in length, the polygon is a **regular polygon**. A regular polygon can be inscribed in a circle and all its corner points will lie on the circle (**Figure 5.2**). Other regular polygons not pictured are the heptagon (7 sides), the nonagon (9 sides), the decagon (10 sides), and the dodecagon (12 sides).

The sum of the angles inside any polygon (interior angles) is $S = (n - 2) \times 180°$, where n is the number of sides of the polygon.

Triangles

A **triangle** is a three-sided polygon. The four types of triangles are **scalene, isosceles, equilateral,** and **right** (**Fig. 5.3**). The sum of the interior angles of a triangle is always $180°$ $((3 - 2) \times 180°)$.

Quadrilaterals

A **quadrilateral** is a four-sided polygon of any shape. The sum of the interior angles of a quadri-

lateral is $360°$ $((4 - 2) \times 180°)$. **Figure 5.4** shows the various types of quadrilaterals and the equations for their areas.

5.4 Circles

Figure 5.5 gives the names of the elements of a circle that are used throughout this textbook. A

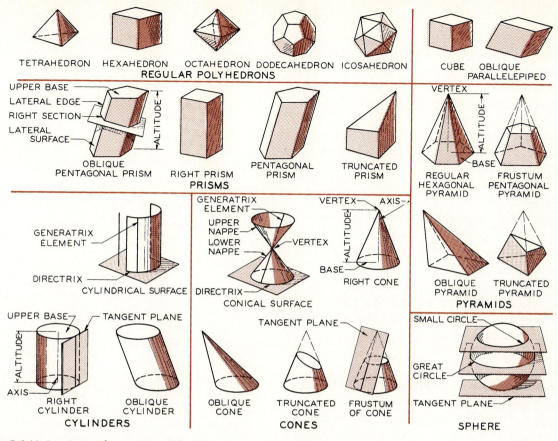

Figure 5.6 Various types of geometric solids, their names, and their elements.

circle is constructed by swinging a radius from a fixed point through 360°. The area of a circle equals πR^2.

5.5 Geometric Solids

Figure 5.6 shows the various types of solid geometric shapes and their names and definitions.

Polyhedra

A **polyhedron** is a multisided solid formed by intersecting planes. If its faces are regular polygons, it is a regular polyhedron. Five regular polyhedra are the **tetrahedron** (4 sides), the **hexahedron** (6 sides), the **octahedron** (8 sides), the **dodecahedron** (12 sides), and the **icosahedron** (20 sides).

Prisms

A **prism** has two parallel bases of equal shape connected by sides that are parallelograms. The line from the center of one base to the center of the other is the axis. If its axis is perpendicular to the bases, the prism is a right prism. If its axis is not perpendicular to the bases, the prism is an oblique prism. A prism that has been cut off to form a base not parallel to the other is a truncated prism. A **parallelepiped** is a prism with bases that are either rectangles or parallelograms.

Pyramids

A **pyramid** is a solid with a polygon as a base and triangular faces that converge at a vertex. The line from the vertex to the center of the base is the axis. If its axis is perpendicular to the base, the pyramid is a right pyramid. If its axis is not perpendicular to the base, the pyramid is an oblique pyramid. A truncated pyramid is called a **frustum** of a pyramid.

Cylinders

A **cylinder** is formed by a line or an element (called a *generatrix*) that moves about the circle while remaining parallel to its axis. The axis of a cylinder connects the centers of each end of a cylinder. If the axis is perpendicular to the bases, it is the altitude of a right cylinder. If the axis does not make a 90° angle with the base, the cylinder is an oblique cylinder.

Cones

A **cone** is formed by a generatrix, one end of which moves about the circular base while the other end remains at a fixed vertex. The line from the center of the base to the vertex is the axis. If its axis is perpendicular to the base, the cone is a right cone. A truncated cone is called a frustum of a cone.

Spheres

A **sphere** is generated by revolving a circle about one of its diameters to form a solid. The ends of the axis of revolution of the sphere are *poles*.

5.6 Constructing Polygons

A regular polygon (having equal sides) can be inscribed in or circumscribed about a circle. When it is inscribed, all corner points will lie on the circle (**Fig. 5.7**). For example, constructing a 10-sided polygon involves dividing the circle into 10 sectors and connecting the points to form the polygon.

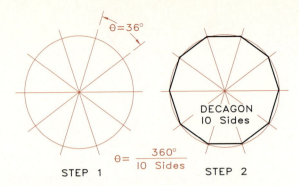

Figure 5.7 A regular polygon (sides of equal length):
Step 1 Divide circle into the required number of equal segments.
Step 2 Connect the segments where they intersect the circle.

TRIANGLE CONSTRUCTION

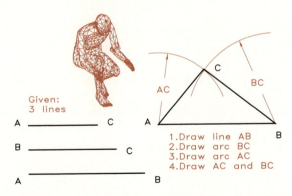

Figure 5.8 A triangle can be constructed from three given sides.

Triangles

When you know the lengths of all three sides of a triangle, you may construct it with a compass by *triangulation*, as **Fig. 5.8** shows. Any triangle inscribed in a semicircle, as **Fig. 5.9** shows, will be a right triangle.

RIGHT ANGLES: INSCRIBED IN A SEMICIRCLE

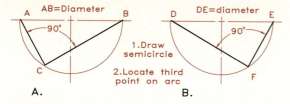

A.

B.

Figure 5.9 Any triangle inscribed in a semicircle is a right triangle.

HEXAGONS

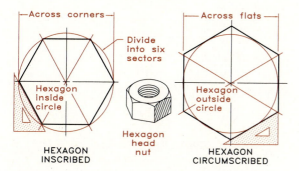

Figure 5.10 A hexagon can be inscribed in or circumscribed about a circle with a 30°–60° triangle.

OCTAGONS: CIRCLE METHOD

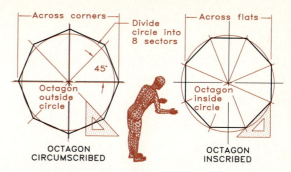

Figure 5.11 An octagon can be inscribed in or circumscribed about a circle with a 45° triangle.

OCTAGONS: SQUARE METHOD

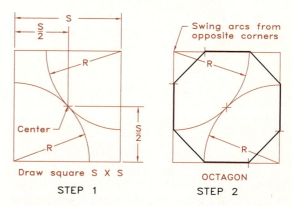

Figure 5.12 An octagon also can be constructed in a square.

Hexagons

The hexagon, a six-sided regular polygon, can be inscribed in or circumscribed about a circle (**Fig. 5.10**). Use a 30°–60° triangle to draw the hexagon. The circle represents the distance from corner to corner for an inscribed hexagon and from flat to flat for a circumscribed hexagon.

Octagons

The octagon, an eight-sided regular polygon, can be inscribed in or circumscribed about a circle (**Fig. 5.11**) or inscribed in a square (**Fig. 5.12**). Use a 45° triangle to draw the octagon in the first case

and a compass and straightedge in the second case.

Pentagons

The pentagon, a five-sided regular polygon, can be inscribed in or circumscribed about a circle. **Figure 5.13** shows another method of constructing a pentagon with a compass and straightedge.

PENTAGON: INSCRIBED

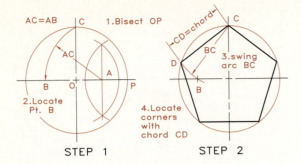

BISECTING A LINE

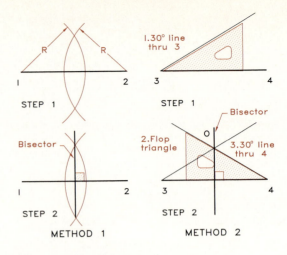

Figure 5.13 Constructing an inscribed pentagon:
Step 1 Bisect radius OP to locate point A. With A as the center and AC as the radius, locate point B on the diameter.

Step 2 With point C as the center and BC as the radius, locate point D. Use line CD as the chord to locate the other corners of the pentagon.

Figure 5.14 Bisecting a line:
Method 1 Use a compass and any radius.

Method 2 Use a standard triangle and a straightedge.

5.7 Bisecting Lines and Angles

Lines
Figure 5.14 shows two methods of finding the midpoint of a line. In the first method, a compass is used to construct a perpendicular bisector to a line. In the second method, a standard triangle and a straightedge are used.

Angles
You may bisect angles by using a compass and drawing three arcs, as shown in **Fig. 5.15**.

5.8 Revolution of Shapes

Figure 5.16 demonstrates how to rotate a triangle about point 1 of line 1–3. First rotate point 3 to its desired position (in this case vertically below point 1) with a compass. Then find point 2 by tri-

BISECTING AN ANGLE

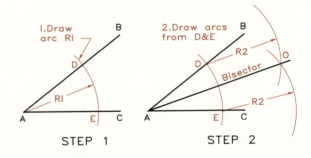

Figure 5.15 Bisecting an angle:
Step 1 Swing an arc of any radius R1 to locate points D and E.

Step 2 Draw equal arcs from D and E to locate point O. Line AO is the bisector of the angle.

angulation with arcs having radii 1–2 and 3–2. Use a straightedge to connect point 1 with new points 2 and 3 to complete the rotated view.

REVOLVING A FIGURE

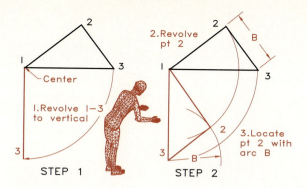

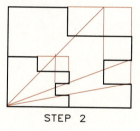

Figure 5.16 Revolving a figure:

Step 1 Revolve line 1–3 about point 1 with a compass.

Step 2 Locate point 2 by swinging arc 1–2 from point 1 and arc 3–2 from point 3.

ENLARGEMENT OF A FIGURE

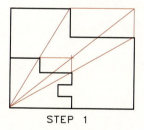

Figure 5.17 Enlarging a shape:

Step 1 To make a proportional enlargement, use a series of diagonals drawn through a single point, the lower left-hand corner in this case.

Step 2 Draw additional diagonals to locate the other features of the shape.

5.9 Enlargement and Reduction of Shapes

Figure 5.17 shows how to enlarge a shape by using a series of radial lines extending upward from its lower left corner. These lines pass through the corners of the shape and a rectangle drawn to enclose

DIVIDING A LINE

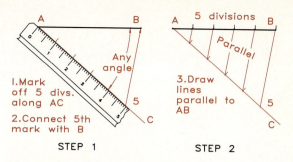

Figure 5.18 Dividing a line:

Step 1 To divide line AB into five equal lengths, lay off five equal divisions along line AC, and connect point 5 to end B with a construction line.

Step 2 Draw a series of five lines parallel to 5B to divide line AB.

it. Use a straightedge to connect the points that form the larger shape and rectangle, including the notches. The larger shape is proportional to the smaller shape. This method may also be used to reduce a larger shape.

5.10 Division of Lines

Dividing a line into several equal parts often is necessary. **Figure 5.18** shows the method used to solve this type of problem—in this case dividing line AB into five equal lengths.

The same principle applies to locating equally spaced lines on a graph (**Fig. 5.19**). Lay scales with the desired number of units (0 to 3 and 0 to 5, respectively) across the graph up and down and then left to right. Make marks at each whole unit and draw vertical and horizontal index lines through these points. These index lines are used to show data in a graph.

DIVIDING GRAPH AXES

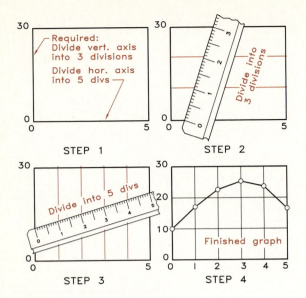

STEP 1

STEP 2

STEP 3

STEP 4

Figure 5.19 Dividing a space:
Step 1 Draw the outline of the graph.

Step 2 To divide the y axis into three equal segments, lay a scale having three units of measurement spanning the graph with the 0 and 3 located on the top and bottom lines. Make a mark at points 1 and 2 and draw horizontal lines through them.

Step 3 To divide the x axis into five equal segments, lay a scale having at least five units of measurement across the graph with the 0 and 5 on the left- and right-hand vertical lines. Make marks at points 1, 2, 3, and 4 and draw vertical lines through them.

Step 4 Plot the data points and draw the curve of the graph.

5.11 Arcs

Through Three Points

You may draw an arc through three points by connecting the points with two lines and drawing perpendicular bisectors through each line to locate the center of the circle at C **(Fig. 5.20)**. Draw the arc and lines AB and BD become chords of the arc.

ARC THROUGH THREE POINTS

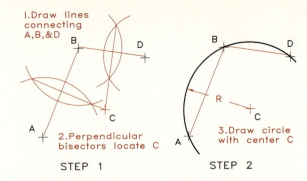

STEP 1

STEP 2

Figure 5.20 An arc through three points:
Step 1 Connect points A, B, and D with two lines and draw their perpendicular bisectors to intersect at the center, C.

Step 2 Using the center C, and the distance to the points as the radius, R, draw the arc through the points.

RECTIFYING AN ARC

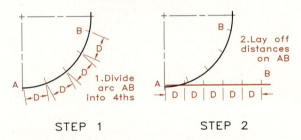

STEP 1

STEP 2

Figure 5.21 Rectifying an arc:
Step 1 Divide arc AB into a series of equal chords, D.

Step 2 Lay out the equal chords, D, along the tangent to the arc. The length of the arc is AB.

To find the center of a circle or an arc, reverse this process by drawing two chords that intersect at a point on the circumference and bisecting them. The perpendicular bisectors intersect at the center of the circle.

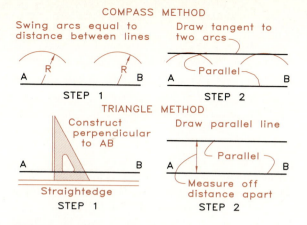

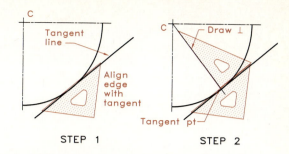

Figure 5.23 Locating a tangent point:

Step 1 Align a triangle with the tangent line while holding it against a firmly held straightedge.

Step 2 Hold the triangle in position, locate a second triangle perpendicular to it, and draw a line from the center to locate the tangent point.

Figure 5.22 Drawing parallel lines:

Compass Method

Step 1 Swing two arcs from line AB.

Step 2 Draw the parallel line tangent to the arcs.

Triangle Method

Step 1 Draw a line perpendicular to AB.

Step 2 Measure the desired distance, R, along the perpendicular and draw the parallel line through it.

Rectifying Arcs

Rectifying an arc means laying out its length along a straight line, as **Fig. 5.21** shows. You may also rectify an arc mathematically to check the accuracy of your construction. For example, because a circle has 360°, an arc of a 30° sector is one-twelfth of the full circumference. If the circumference of a circle is 12 inches, the rectified 30° arc would be 1 inch long.

5.12 Parallel Lines

You may draw one line parallel to another by using either method shown in **Fig. 5.22**. In the first method, use a compass and draw two arcs having radius R to locate a parallel line at the desired distance (R) from the first line. In the second method,

measure the desired perpendicular distance R from the first line, mark it, and draw the parallel line through it with your T-square or drafting machine.

5.13 Tangents

Points of Tangency

A **point of tangency** is the theoretical point at which a line joins an arc or two arcs join without crossing. **Figure 5.23** shows how to find the point of tangency with triangles by constructing a perpendicular line to the tangent line from the arc's center. **Figure 5.24** shows the conventional methods of marking points of tangency.

Line Tangent to an Arc

Figure 5.25 shows one way to find the point of tangency between a line drawn from point A and an arc. Connect point A to the arc's center and bisect line AC (step 1); swing an arc from point M through point C locating tangent point T (step 2);

MARKING TANGENT POINTS

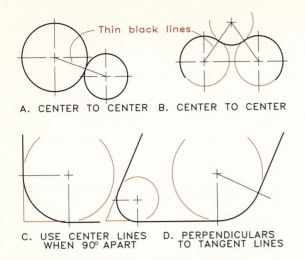

A. CENTER TO CENTER B. CENTER TO CENTER

C. USE CENTER LINES
   WHEN 90° APART

D. PERPENDICULARS
   TO TANGENT LINES

Figure 5.24 Use thin (construction) lines that extend from the centers slightly beyond the arcs to mark points of tangency.

LINE TANGENT TO AN ARC

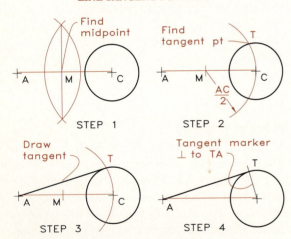

STEP 1   Find midpoint

STEP 2   Find tangent pt   T   AC/2

STEP 3   Draw tangent   T

STEP 4   Tangent marker ⊥ to TA   T

Figure 5.25 A line tangent to an arc from a point:

Step 1 Connect point A with center C and locate point M by bisecting AC.

Step 2 Using point M as the center and MC as the radius, locate point T on the arc.

Step 3 Draw the line from A to T that is tangent to the arc of point T.

Step 4 Draw the tangent marker perpendicular to line TA from the center past the arc.

LINE TANGENT TO AN ARC

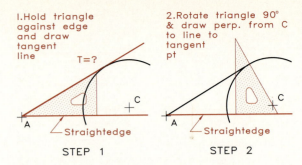

1. Hold triangle against edge and draw tangent line   T=?   A   Straightedge   STEP 1

2. Rotate triangle 90° & draw perp. from C to line to tangent pt   C   A   Straightedge   STEP 2

Figure 5.26 A tangent to an arc from a point:

Step 1 Hold a triangle against a straightedge and draw a line from point A that is tangent to the arc.

Step 2 Rotate your triangle 90° and locate the point of tangency by drawing a line through center C.

ARC THROUGH TWO POINTS

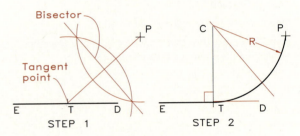

Bisector   P   Tangent point   E   T   D   STEP 1

C   R   P   E   T   D   STEP 2

Figure 5.27 An arc through two points:

Step 1 To draw an arc through point P that is tangent to line DE at point T, draw the perpendicular bisector of TP.

Step 2 Construct a perpendicular to line DE at point T to intersect the bisector at point C and draw the arc from C with radius CT.

draw the tangent to T (step 3); and mark the tangent point (step 4). The point of tangency may be found by using a triangle, as **Fig. 5.26** shows.

Arc Tangent to a Line from a Point

To construct an arc that is tangent to line DE at T and that passes through point P **(Fig. 5.27)**, draw

ARC THROUGH TWO POINTS

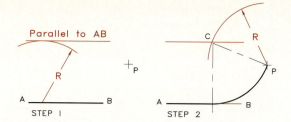

Figure 5.28 An arc tangent to a line through a point:
Step 1 When an arc is to be drawn tangent to line AB and through point P, first draw a line parallel to line AB and R distance from it.
Step 2 Draw an arc from point P with radius R to locate center C and draw the arc with radius R.

ARC TANGENT TO TWO LINES: ACUTE ANGLE

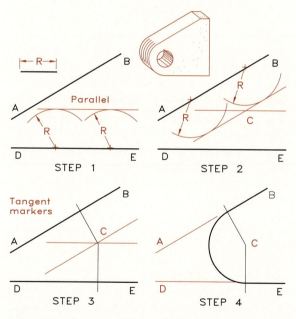

Figure 5.29 An arc tangent to lines making an acute angle:
Step 1 Construct a light line parallel to line DE with radius R.
Step 2 Draw a second light line parallel to and R distance from line AB to locate center C.
Step 3 Draw thin lines from center C perpendicular to lines AB and DE to locate the tangency points.
Step 4 Draw the tangent arc and darken your lines.

ARC TANGENT TO TWO LINES: OBTUSE ANGLE

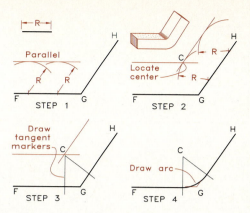

Figure 5.30 An arc tangent to lines making an obtuse angle:
Step 1 Using radius R, draw a light line parallel to line FG.
Step 2 Construct a light line parallel to line GH that is R distance from it to locate center C.
Step 3 Construct thin lines from center C perpendicular to lines FG and GH to locate the tangency points.
Step 4 Draw the tangent arc and darken your lines.

the perpendicular bisector of line TP. Draw a perpendicular to line DE at point T to locate the center at point C and swing an arc with radius OT. A similar problem (**Fig. 5.28**) requires drawing an arc of a given radius that is tangent to line AB and that passes through point P. An arc with its outer at C is tangent to the line.

Arc Tangent to Two Lines
Figure 5.29 shows how to construct an arc of a given radius tangent to two nonparallel lines that form an acute angle. The same steps apply to constructing an arc tangent to two lines that form an obtuse angle (**Fig. 5.30**). In both cases, the points

ARC TANGENT TO PERPENDICULAR LINES

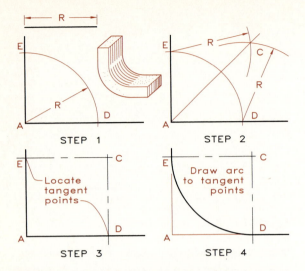

STEP 1 STEP 2

STEP 3 STEP 4

Figure 5.31 An arc tangent to perpendicular lines:
Step 1 Using radius R and center A, locate points D and E.
Step 2 Locate point C by swinging two arcs using radius R.
Step 3 Locate the tangent points with perpendiculars CE and CD.
Step 4 Draw the tangent arc and darken your lines.

ARC TANGENT TO LINE AND ARC

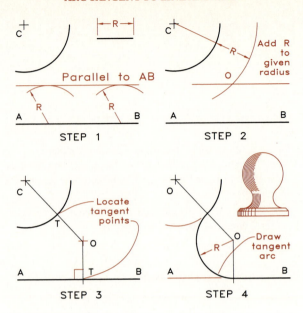

STEP 1 STEP 2

STEP 3 STEP 4

Figure 5.32 An arc tangent to an arc and a line:
Step 1 Draw a light line parallel to line AB that is R distance from it.

Step 2 Add radius R to the extended radius from center C. Swing the extended radius to locate the center, O.

Step 3 Draw lines OC and OT to locate the tangency points.

Step 4 Draw the tangent arc between the points of tangency with radius R and center O.

of tangency are located with lines drawn from the centers perpendicular and past the original lines. **Figure 5.31** shows a technique for finding an arc tangent to perpendicular lines only.

Arc Tangent to an Arc and a Line
Figure 5.32 shows the steps for constructing an arc tangent to an arc and a line. **Figure 5.33** shows a variation of this technique for an arc drawn tangent to a given arc and line with the arc reversed.

Arc Tangent to Two Arcs
Figure 5.34 shows how to draw an arc tangent to two arcs. Lines drawn between the centers locate the points of tangency. The resulting tangent arc is concave from the top. Drawing a convex arc tangent to the given arcs requires that its radius be greater than the radius of either of the given arcs, as shown in **Fig. 5.35**.

One variation of this problem (**Fig. 5.36**) is to

ARC TANGENT TO LINE AND ARC

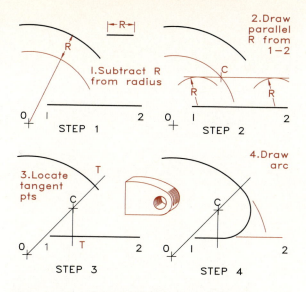

STEP 1

STEP 2

STEP 3

STEP 4

Figure 5.33 An arc tangent to an arc and a line:

Step 1 Subtract radius R from the radius through center O. Draw a concentric arc with this shortened radius.

Step 2 Draw a line parallel to line 1–2 and R distance from it to locate the center, C.

Step 3 Locate the tangency points with lines from O through C and from C perpendicular to line 1–2.

Step 4 Draw the tangent arc between the tangent points with radius R and center C.

ARC TANGENT TO TWO ARCS: CONCAVE

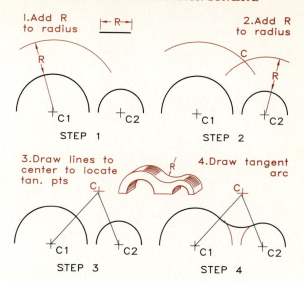

STEP 1

STEP 2

STEP 3

STEP 4

Figure 5.34 A concave arc tangent to two arcs:

Step 1 Extend the radius of one circle by adding the radius R to it. Use the extended radius to draw a concentric arc.

Step 2 Extend the radius of the other circle by adding radius R to it. Use this extended radius to construct an arc to locate center C.

Step 3 Connect center C with centers C1 and C2 with thin lines to locate the tangency points.

Step 4 Draw the tangent arc between the points of tangency using radius R and center C.

---

draw an arc of a given radius tangent to the top of one arc and the bottom of the other. Another **(Fig. 5.37)** is to draw an arc tangent to a circle and a larger arc.

Ogee Curves

The **ogee curve** is an S curve formed by tangent arcs. The ogee curve shown in **Fig. 5.38** is the result of constructing two arcs tangent to three

intersecting lines. **Figure 5.39** shows an unequal-arc ogee curve drawn to pass through points B, E, and C.

5.14 Conic Sections

Conic sections are plane figures that can be described both graphically and mathematically; they are formed by passing imaginary cutting planes through a right cone, as **Fig. 5.40** shows.

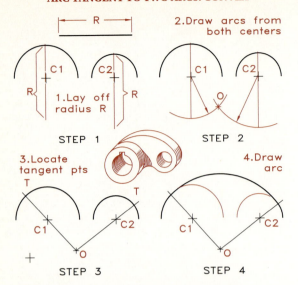

ARC TANGENT TO TWO ARCS: CONVEX

STEP 1

STEP 2
2.Draw arcs from both centers

1.Lay off radius R

STEP 3
3.Locate tangent pts

STEP 4
4.Draw arc

Figure 5.35 A convex arc tangent to two arcs:

Step 1 Extend the radius of each arc from the arc past its center and lay off radius R from the arcs along these lines.

Step 2 Use the distance from each center to the ends of the extended radii to swing arcs to locate center O.

Step 3 Draw thin lines from center O through centers C1 and C2 to locate the points of tangency.

Step 4 Draw the tangent arc between the tangent points using radius R and center O.

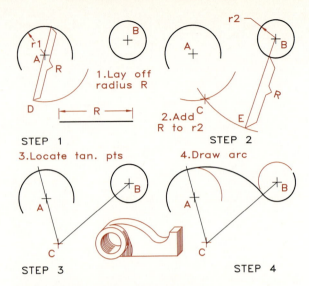

ARC TANGENT TO TWO CIRCLES

STEP 1
1.Lay off radius R

STEP 2
2.Add R to r2

STEP 3
3.Locate tan. pts

STEP 4
4.Draw arc

Figure 5.36 An arc tangent to two circles:

Step 1 Lay off radius R from the arc along an extended radius to locate point D.

Step 2 Extend the radius through center B and add radius R to it from point E. Use radius BE to locate center C.

Step 3 Draw thin lines from center C through centers A and B to locate the points of tangency.

Step 4 Draw the tangent arc between the tangent points using radius R and center C.

Ellipses

The **ellipse** is a conic section formed by passing a plane through a right cone at an angle (**Fig. 5.40B**). Mathematically, the ellipse is the path of a point that moves in such a way that the sum of the distances from two focal points is a constant. The largest diameter of an ellipse—the **major diameter**—is always the true length. The shortest diameter—the **minor diameter**—is perpendicular to the major diameter.

Revolving the edge view of a circle yields an ellipse (**Fig. 5.41**). The ellipse template shown in **Fig. 5.42** is used to draw the same ellipse. The angle between the line of sight and the edge of the circle is the angle of the ellipse template (or the

one closest to this size) that should be used. Ellipse templates are available in 5° intervals and in major diameter sizes that vary in increments of about 1/8 inch (**Fig. 5.43**).

You may construct an ellipse inside a rectangle or parallelogram by plotting a series of points to form the ellipse (**Fig. 5.44**). Two circles can be used to construct an ellipse by making the diameter of the large circle equal to the major diameter and the diameter of the small circle equal to the minor diameter (**Fig. 5.45**).

The mathematical equation of an ellipse is

$$\frac{x^2}{a^2}+\frac{y^2}{b^2}=1, \quad \text{where } a, b \neq 0.$$

ARC TANGENT TO TWO CIRCLES

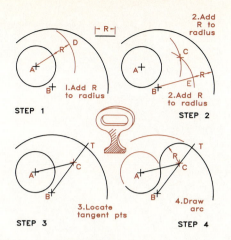

Figure 5.37 An arc tangent to two arcs:

Step 1 Add radius R to the radius from center A. Use radius AD to draw a concentric arc from center A.

Step 2 Subtract radius R from the radius through B. Use radius BE to draw an arc to locate center C.

Step 3 Draw thin lines to connect the centers and locate the points of tangency.

Step 4 Draw the tangent arc between the tangency points using radius R and center C.

AN OGEE CURVE

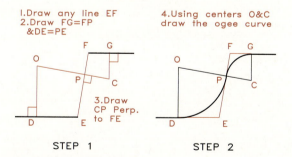

Figure 5.38 An ogee curve:

Step 1 To draw an ogee curve between two parallel lines, draw light line EF at any angle. Locate point P anywhere along EF. Find the tangent points by making FG equal to FP and DE equal to EP. Draw perpendiculars at G and D to intersect the perpendicular at O and C.

Step 2 Use radii CP and OP at centers O and C to draw two tangent arcs to complete the ogee curve.

OGEE CURVE: UNEQUAL ARCS

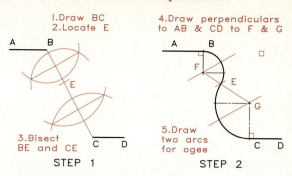

Figure 5.39 An unequal-arc ogee curve:

Step 1 Parallel lines are to be connected by an ogee curve passing through points B and C. Draw light line BC and select point E on it. Bisect BE and CE.

Step 2 Construct perpendiculars at points B and C to intersect the bisectors and locate centers F and G. Locate the points of tangency and draw the ogee curve using radii FB and GC.

CONIC SECTIONS

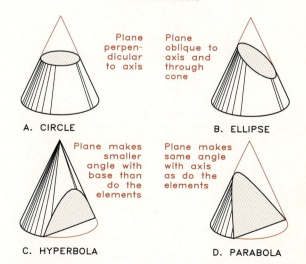

Figure 5.40 The conic sections are the (A) circle, (B) ellipse, (C) hyperbola, and (D) parabola. They are formed by passing cutting planes through a right cone.

ELLIPSES BY REVOLUTION

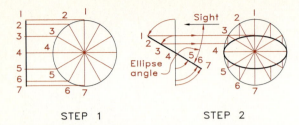

STEP 1   STEP 2

Figure 5.41 An ellipse by revolution:

Step 1 When the edge view of a circle is perpendicular to the projectors between its adjacent view, it appears as a circle. Mark equally spaced points around the circle's circumference and project them to the edge.

Step 2 Revolve the edge view of the circle and project the points to the circular view, which now appears as an ellipse. The points project vertically downward to their new positions.

ELLIPSE ANGLE

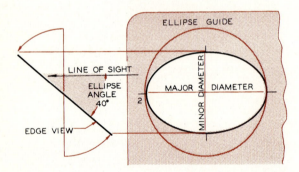

Figure 5.42 When the edge view of a circle is revolved so that the line of sight is not perpendicular to it, the circle appears as an ellipse. The angle between the line of sight and the edge view of the circle is the angle of the ellipse template.

Parabolas

The **parabola** is defined as a plane curve, each point of which is equidistant from a straight line (called a **directrix**) and a focal point. The parabola is the conic section formed when the cutting

ELLIPSE TEMPLATES

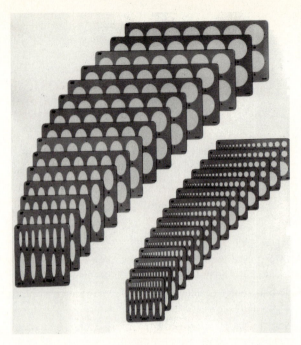

Figure 5.43 Ellipse templates are calibrated at 5° intervals from 15° to 60°. (Courtesy of Timely Products, Incorporated.)

ELLIPSE: PARALLELOGRAM METHOD

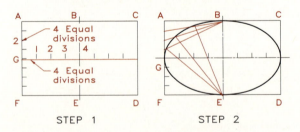

STEP 1   STEP 2

Figure 5.44 An ellipse by the parallelogram method:

Step 1 Draw an ellipse inside a rectangle or parallelogram by dividing the horizontal centerline into the same number of equal segments as the shorter sides, AF and CD.

Step 2 The method used to construct the curve is shown for one quadrant—sets of rays from E and B that intersect give the points on which to plot the curve.

ELLIPSE: CIRCLE METHOD

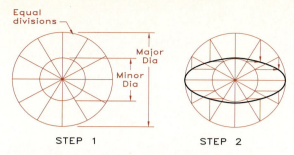

PARABOLA: TANGENT METHOD

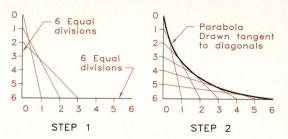

Figure 5.45 An ellipse by the circle method:

Step 1 Draw two concentric circles with the large one equal to the major diameter and the small one equal to the minor diameter. Divide them into equal sectors.

Step 2 Plot points on the ellipse by projecting downward from the large circle to intersect horizontal projectors drawn from the intersections on the small circle.

Figure 5.47 A parabola by the tangent method:

Step 1 Draw two thin lines at a convenient angle and divide each into the same number of segments. Connect the points with a series of diagonals.

Step 2 When finished, draw a smooth curve that is tangent to the diagonals.

PARABOLA: PARALLELOGRAM METHOD

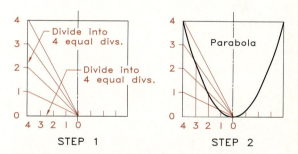

Figure 5.48 A parabola by the parallelogram method:

Step 1 Construct a parallelogram (shown here as a rectangle) to contain the parabola and locate its axis parallel to the sides through 0. Divide the sides into equal segments. Connect the segment division points to point 0.

Step 2 Construct lines parallel to the sides (vertical in this case) to locate points along the rays from 0 and draw a smooth curve through them.

PARABOLA: MATHEMATICAL METHOD

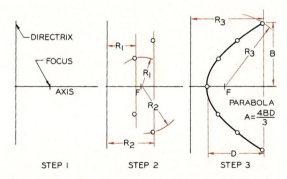

Figure 5.46 A parabola by the mathematical method:

Step 1 Draw an axis perpendicular to the directrix (a line). Choose a point for the focus, F.

Step 2 Use a series of selected radii to find points on the curve. For example, draw a line parallel to the directrix and R2 from it. Swing R2 from F to intersect the line and plot the point.

Step 3 Continue the process with a series of arcs of varying radii until you find an adequate number of points to complete the curve.

plane and an element on the cone's surface make the same angle with the cone's base (see Fig. 5.40D).

Figure 5.46 shows construction of a parabola from its mathematical definition. To draw a

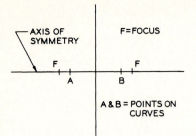

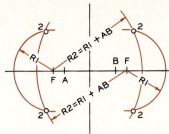

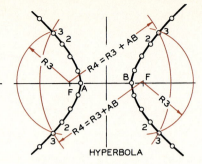

Figure 5.49 A hyperbola:

Step 1 Draw a perpendicular through the axis of symmetry. Locate focal points F equidistant from it on both sides. Locate points A and B equidistant from the perpendicular at a distance of your choosing, but between the focal points.

Step 2 Select radius R1 to draw arcs using focal points F as the centers. Add R1 to AB (the distance between the nearest points on the hyperbolas) to find R2. Draw arcs using radius R2 and the focal points as centers. The intersections of R1 and R2 establish points 2 on the hyperbola.

Step 3 Select other radii and add them to AB to locate additional points as in step 2. Draw a smooth curve through the points.

parabola geometrically, divide two perpendicular lines into the same number of equal segments, connect them as shown in **Fig. 5.47**, and draw a smooth curve through the plotted points. **Figure 5.48** shows a third method of drawing a parabola, which involves the use of a rectangle or parallelogram. The mathematical equation of the parabola is

$$y = ax^2 + bx + c, \quad \text{where } a \neq 0.$$

Hyperbolas

The **hyperbola** is a two-part conic section defined as the path of a point that moves in such a way that the difference of its distances from two focal points is a constant (see Fig. 5.40C). **Figure 5.49** shows construction of a hyperbola according to this definition.

Figure 5.50 shows a method of constructing a hyperbola by drawing perpendicular lines through point B to serve as asymptotes. The hyperbolic

EQUILATERAL HYPERBOLA

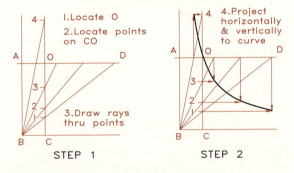

Figure 5.50 An equilateral hyperbola:

Step 1 Draw perpendiculars through B. Select any point as O and draw horizontal and vertical thin lines through O. Divide line CO into equal segments, and draw rays from B through them to horizontal line AD.

Step 2 Draw horizontal construction lines from the segment division points along line CO and project lines from AD vertically to points of intersection. Connect these points with a smooth curve.

SPIRAL

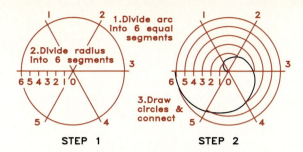

STEP 1   **STEP 2**

Figure 5.51 Constructing a spiral:

Step 1 Draw a circle and divide it into equal parts. Divide the radius into the same number of equal parts (six in this case).

Step 2 Begin inside and draw arc 0–1 to intersect radius 0–1. Then swing arc 0–2 to radius 0–2, and continue until you reach the last point, at 6, on the original circle, and connect the points.

HELIX

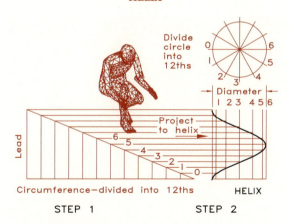

STEP 1   **STEP 2**

Figure 5.52 A cylindrical helix:

Step 1 Divide the top view of the cylinder into equal parts and project them to the front view. Lay out the circumference and the height (lead: pronounced leed) of the cylinder. Divide the circumference into the same number of equal parts by taking the measurements from the top view.

Step 2 Project the points along the inclined rise to their respective points on the diameter and connect them with a smooth curve.

CONICAL HELIX

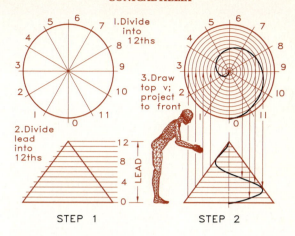

STEP 1   **STEP 2**

Figure 5.53 A conical helix:

Step 1 Divide the cone's base into equal parts. Pass a series of horizontal cutting planes through the front view of the cone. Use the same number as the number of divisions on the base (12 in this case).

Step 2 Project all the divisions along the front view of the cone to the line 3–9 and draw a series of arcs from the center to their respective radii in the top view and plot the points. Project the points to their respective cutting planes in the front view and connect them with a smooth curve.

curve comes closer and closer to the asymptotes as it is extended, but it never touches them.

5.15 Spirals

The **spiral** is a coil lying in a single plane that begins at a point and becomes larger as it travels around the origin. **Figure 5.51** shows the steps for constructing a spiral.

5.16 Helixes

The **helix** is a three-dimensional curve that coils around a cylinder or cone at a constant angle of inclination. Applications of helixes are corkscrews and the threads on a screw. **Figure 5.52** shows a helix constructed about a cylinder, and **Fig. 5.53** shows a helix constructed about a cone.

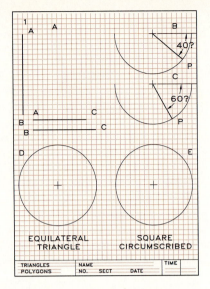

Figure 5.54 Problem 1(A–E). Basic constructions.

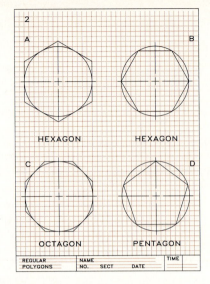

Figure 5.55 Problem 2(A–D). Constructions of regular polygons.

Present your solutions to these problems on size AV (8½-×-11-inch) paper similar in appearance to that shown in **Fig. 5.54**. The printed grid represents 0.20-in. intervals, so you can use your engineers' 10 scale to lay out the problems. By equating each grid interval to 5 mm, you also can use your full-sized metric scale to lay out and solve the problems. Show your construction and mark all points of tangency, as discussed in the chapter.

1. Basic constructions (**Fig. 5.54**)

    (A) Draw triangle ABC using the given sides.

 (B, C) Inscribe an angle in the semicircles with the vertexes at point P.

    (D) Inscribe a three-sided regular polygon inside the circle.

    (E) Circumscribe a four-sided regular polygon about the circle.

2. Construction of regular polygons (**Fig. 5.55**)

    (A) Circumscribe a hexagon about the circle.

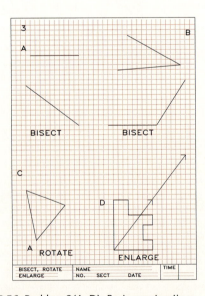

Figure 5.56 Problem 3(A–D). Basic constructions.

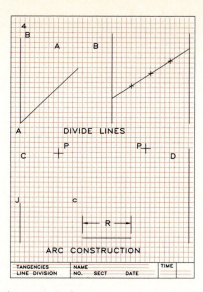

Figure 5.57 Problem 4(A–D). Tangency construction.

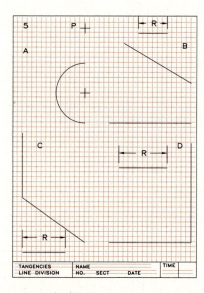

Figure 5.58 Problem 5(A–D). Tangency construction.

(B) Inscribe a hexagon in the circle.

(C) Circumscribe an octagon about the circle.

(D) Construct a pentagon inside the circle using the compass method.

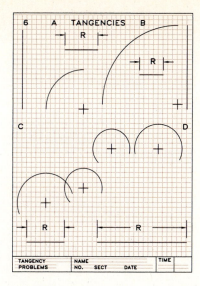

Figure 5.59 Problem 6(A–D). Tangency construction.

3. Basic constructions (**Fig. 5.56**)

    (A) Bisect the lines.

    (B) Bisect the angles.

    (C) Rotate the triangle 60° clockwise about point A.

    (D) Enlarge the given shape to the size indicated by the diagonal.

4. Line division and tangency construction (**Fig. 5.57**)

    (A) Divide line AB into seven equal parts. Draw a construction line through point A.

    (B) Divide the space between the two vertical lines into four equal segments. Draw three vertical lines at the division points that are equal in length to the given lines.

    (C) Construct an arc with radius R that is tangent to the line at J and that passes through point P.

    (D) Construct an arc with radius R that is tangent to the line and passes through point P.

5. Tangency construction (**Fig. 5.58**)

    (A) Construct a line from point P that is tangent to the semicircle. Locate the points of tangency. Use the compass method.

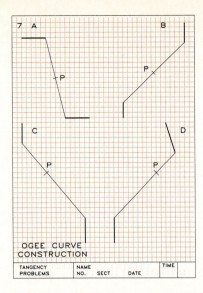

Figure 5.60 Problem 7(A–D). Ogee curve construction.

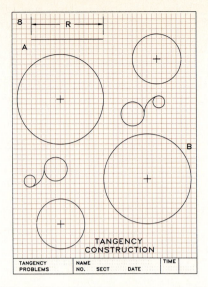

Figure 5.61 Problem 8(A, B). Tangency construction.

(B–D) Construct arcs with the given radii tangent to the lines.

6. Tangency construction (**Fig. 5.59**)

(A–D) Construct arcs that are tangent to the arcs or lines shown. The radii are given for each problem.

7. Ogee curve construction (**Fig. 5.60**)

(A–D) Construct ogee curves that connect the ends of the given lines and pass through point P.

8. Tangency construction (**Fig. 5.61**)

(A, B) Using the given radii, connect the circles with a tangent arc as indicated in the sketches.

9. Rectifying an arc and ellipse construction (**Fig. 5.62**)

(A, B) Rectify the arc along the given line by dividing the circumference into equal segments and laying them off with your dividers.

(C) Construct an ellipse inside the rectangular layout.

(D) Construct an ellipse inside the large circle. The small circle represents the minor diameter.

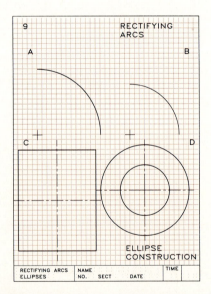

Figure 5.62 Problem 9(A–D). Rectifying an arc, ellipse construction.

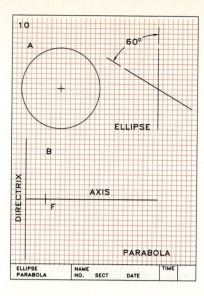

Figure 5.63 Problem 10(A, B). Ellipse and parabola construction.

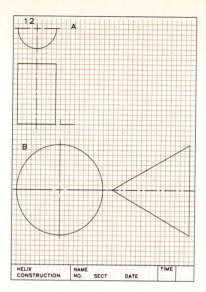

Figure 5.65 Problem 12(A, B). Helix construction.

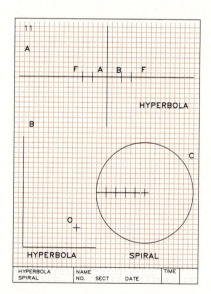

Figure 5.64 Problem 11(A–C). Hyperbola and spiral construction.

10. Ellipse and parabola construction (**Fig. 5.63**)

   (A) Construct an ellipse inside the circle when the edge view has been rotated as shown.

   (B) Using the focal point F and the directrix, plot and draw the parabola formed by these elements.

11. Hyperbola and spiral construction (**Fig. 5.64**)

   (A) Using the focal point F, points A and B on the curve, and the axis of symmetry, construct the hyperbola.

   (B) Construct a hyperbola that passes through O. The perpendicular lines are asymptotes.

   (C) Construct a spiral by using the four divisions marked along the radius.

12. Helix construction (**Fig. 5.65**)

   (A, B) Construct helixes that have a rise equal to the heights of the cylinder and cone. Show construction and the curve in all views.

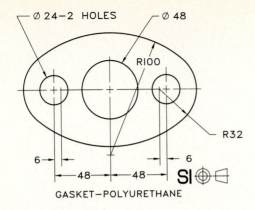

Ø 24–2 HOLES   Ø 48

R100

R32

6   6

48   48

SI ⊕ ⊏

GASKET–POLYURETHANE

Figure 5.66 Problem 13. Gasket.

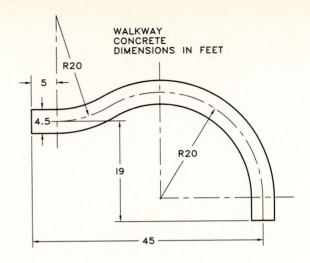

WALKWAY
CONCRETE
DIMENSIONS IN FEET

R20

5

4.5

19

R20

45

Figure 5.68 Problem 15. Road tangency.

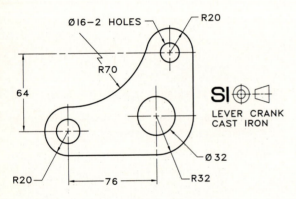

Ø16–2 HOLES   R20

R70

64

SI ⊕ ⊏

LEVER CRANK
CAST IRON

Ø 32

R20

76

R32

Figure 5.67 Problem 14. Lever crank.

13–22. Practical applications (Figs. 5.66–5.75). Construct the given shapes on size A sheets, one problem per sheet. Select the scale that will best fit the problem to the sheet. Mark all points of points of tangency and strive for good line quality.

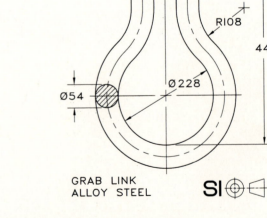

R

54

R108

444

Ø228

Ø54

GRAB LINK
ALLOY STEEL   SI ⊕ ⊏

Figure 5.69 Problem 16. Grab link.

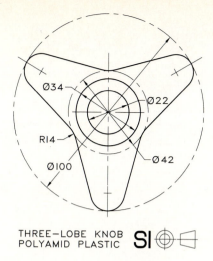

THREE-LOBE KNOB
POLYAMID PLASTIC

Figure 5.70 Problem 17. Three-lobe knob.

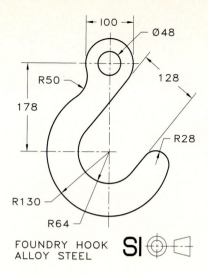

FOUNDRY HOOK
ALLOY STEEL

Figure 5.72 Problem 19. Foundry hook.

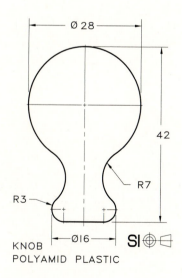

KNOB
POLYAMID PLASTIC

Figure 5.71 Problem 18. Knob.

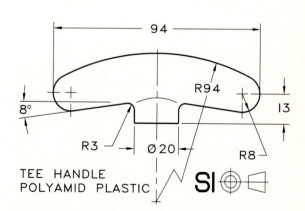

TEE HANDLE
POLYAMID PLASTIC

Figure 5.73 Problem 20. Tee handle.

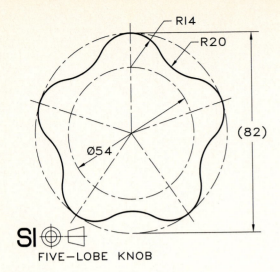

Figure 5.74 Problem 21. Five-lobe knob.

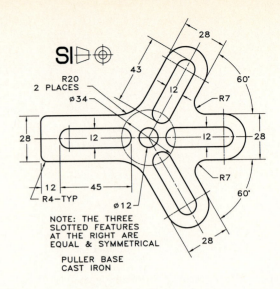

Figure 5.75 Problem 22. Puller base.

6

Orthographic Sketching

6.1 Introduction

Sketching is a rapid, freehand method of drawing rather than drawing with instruments. **Moreover, sketching is a thinking process as much as a method of communication.** Designers usually develop their ideas by making many sketches before arriving at the final solution.

Designers with sketching skills can use their sketches to assign the drafting of finished drawings to assistants. Without sketching skills, designers are unable to utilize their helpers effectively. Many new products and projects have begun as sketches made on the back of an envelope or on a napkin at a restaurant table. Sketching also helps to communicate on the job when words are inadequate. The ability to communicate by any means is a great asset, and sketching is one of the best ways to transmit ideas.

6.2 Shape Description

Although the angle bracket in **Fig. 6.1** is a simple three-dimensional object, describing it with

Figure 6.1 How can you sketch this angle bracket to convey its shape effectively?

words is difficult. Most untrained people would think that drawing it as a three-dimensional pictorial would be difficult. **To make drawing such**

95

VIEWPOINTS FOR A THREE-VIEW DRAWING

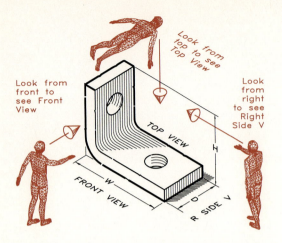

Figure 6.2 These positions give the viewpoints for three views of the angle bracket: top, front, and right side.

THREE-VIEW SKETCH

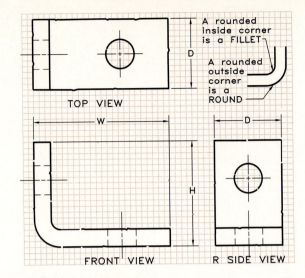

Figure 6.3 This sketch shows three orthographic views of the angle bracket.

POORLY POSITIONED VIEWS

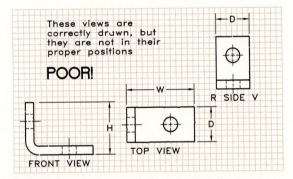

Figure 6.4 Views must be sketched in their standard orthographic positions. When they are incorrectly positioned as shown here, the object cannot be readily understood.

---

objects less difficult, engineers devised a standard system, called orthographic projection, for showing objects in different views.

In orthographic projection, separate views represent the object at 90° intervals as the viewer moves about it (**Fig. 6.2**). **Figure 6.3** shows two-dimensional views of the bracket from the front, top, and right side. The top view appears above the front view because both share the dimension of width. The side view appears to the right of the front view because both share the dimension of height.

The views of the bracket contain three types of lines: **visible lines, hidden lines,** and **centerlines.** Visible lines are the thickest. Thinner dashed lines, hidden lines, represent features that cannot be seen in a view. The thinnest lines are centerlines, or imaginary lines composed of long and short dashes to show the centers of arcs and axes of cylinders.

The space between views may vary, but the views must be positioned as shown here. This arrangement is logical, the views are easiest to

interpret in this order, and the drawing process is most efficient because the views project from each other. **Figure 6.4** illustrates the lack of clarity when views are incorrectly positioned, even though each view is properly drawn.

LINES FOR SKETCHING

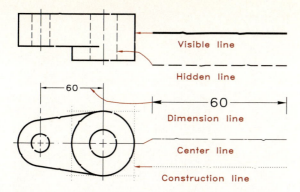

Figure 6.5 This series of lines comprises the alphabet of lines for sketching. The lines at the right are full size.

LINES FOR SKETCHING

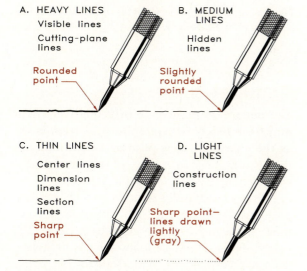

Figure 6.6 An F pencil is a good choice for all sketching lines if you sharpen it differently for varying line widths.

6.3 Sketching Techniques

You need to understand the application of line types used in sketching (freehand) orthographic views before continuing with the principles of projection. The so-called alphabet of lines for

GRID OVERLAY

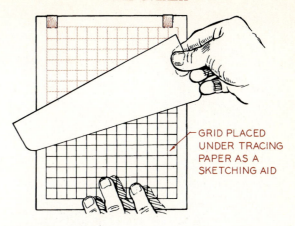

Figure 6.7 A grid placed under a sheet of tracing paper can aid you in freehand sketching.

sketching is presented in **Fig. 6.5**. All lines, except construction lines, should be black and dense. Recall that construction lines are drawn lightly so that they need not be erased. Using the proper widths of these lines is an important part of making good sketches.

Medium-weight pencils, such as H, F, or HB grades, are best for sketching the lines shown in Fig. 6.6. By sharpening the pencil point to match the desired line width, you may use the same grade of pencil for all these lines. Lines sketched freehand should have a freehand appearance; do not attempt to make them appear mechanical. Using a printed grid or laying translucent paper over a printed grid can aid your sketching technique (**Fig. 6.7**).

When you make a freehand sketch, lines will be vertical, horizontal, angular, and/or circular. By not taping your drawing to the table top, you can position the sheet for the most comfortable strokes, usually from left to right (**Fig. 6.8**). Examples of correctly sketched lines are contrasted with incorrectly sketched ones in **Fig. 6.9**.

STROKES FOR SKETCHING

HORIZONTAL LINES   VERTICAL LINES

ANGULAR LINES   CIRCLES AND ARCS

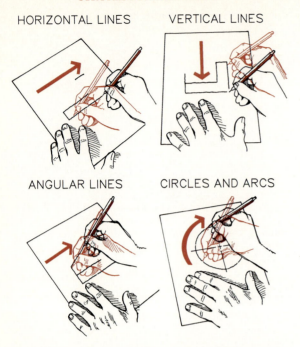

Figure 6.8 Sketch lines as shown here for the best results; rotate your sheet for comfortable sketching positions.

SKETCHING TECHNIQUE

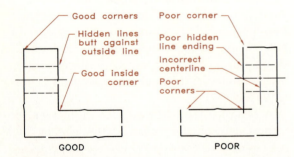

Good corners
Hidden lines butt against outside line
Good inside corner
GOOD

Poor corner
Poor hidden line ending
Incorrect centerline
Poor corners
POOR

Figure 6.9 For good sketches, follow the examples of good technique and avoid the common errors of poor technique shown.

SIX PRINCIPAL VIEWS

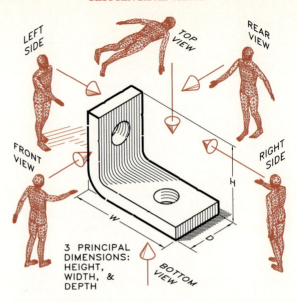

LEFT SIDE   TOP VIEW   REAR VIEW

FRONT VIEW

RIGHT SIDE

3 PRINCIPAL DIMENSIONS: HEIGHT, WIDTH, & DEPTH

BOTTOM VIEW

Figure 6.10 Six principal views of the angle bracket can be sketched from the viewpoints shown.

6.4 Six-View Sketching

The maximum number of principal views that may be drawn in orthographic projection is six, as the viewer changes position at 90° intervals (Fig. 6.10). In each view, two of the three dimensions of height, width, and depth are seen.

These views must be sketched in their standard positions (**Fig. 6.11**). The width dimension is common to the top, front, and bottom views. The height dimension is common to the right-side, front, left-side, and rear views. Note the simple but effective dimensioning of each view with two dimensions. Seldom is an object so complex that it requires six orthographic views.

6.5 Three-View Sketching

You can adequately describe most objects with three orthographic views—usually the top, front, and right-side views. **Figure 6.12** shows a typical

A SIX-VIEW SKETCH

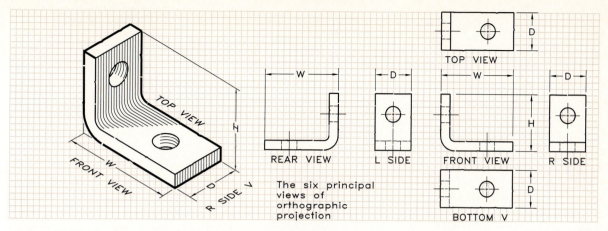

The six principal views of orthographic projection

Figure 6.11 This six-view sketch of the angle bracket shows the six principal views of orthographic projection. Note the placement of dimensions on the views.

STANDARD ARRANGEMENT

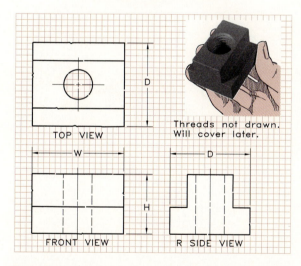

Threads not drawn. Will cover later.

Figure 6.12 This sketch shows the standard orthographic arrangement for three views of a jaw nut, with dimensions and labels.

three-view sketch of a T-block with height, width, and depth dimensions and the front, top, and right-side views labeled.

A PART TO SKETCH

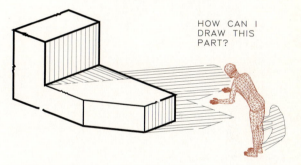

HOW CAN I DRAW THIS PART?

Figure 6.13 Sketches of three orthographic views describe this fixture block in Fig. 6.14.

The object shown in **Fig. 6.13** is represented by three orthographic views on a grid in **Fig. 6.14**. To obtain those views, first sketch the overall dimensions of the object, then sketch the slanted surface in the top view and project it to the other views. Finally, darken the lines; label the views; and letter the overall dimensions of height, width, and depth.

SKETCHING THREE VIEWS

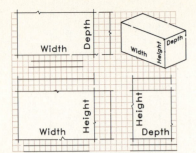

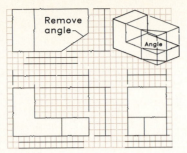

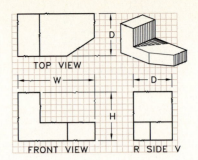

Figure 6.14 Three-view sketching:
Step 1 Block in the views with light construction lines that will not need to be erased. Allow proper spacing for labeling and dimensioning the views.

Step 2 Remove the notches and project from view to view.

Step 3 Check for correctness, darken the lines, and letter the labels and dimensions.

VIEW OF PLANS

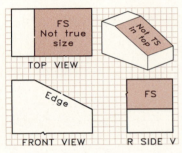

A. FORESHORTENED IN TOP

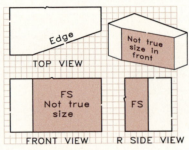

B. FORESHORTENED IN FRONT

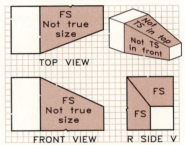

C. FORESHORTENED IN ALL

Figure 6.15 Views of planes:
A The plane appearing as an angular edge in the front view is foreshortened in the top and side views.

B The plane appearing as an angular edge in the top view is foreshortened in the front and side views.

C Two sloping planes appear foreshortened in the side view and each appears as an edge in either the top or the front view.

Slanted surfaces will appear as edges or fore-shortened (not-true-size) planes in the principal views of orthographic projection (**Fig. 6.15**). In **Fig. 6.15C**, two intersecting planes of the object slope in two directions; thus both appear foreshortened in the front, top, and right-side views.

A good way to learn orthographic projection is to construct a missing third view (the front view in **Fig. 6.16**) when two views are given. In **Fig. 6.17**, we construct the missing right-side view from the given top and front views. To obtain the depth dimension for the right-side view, transfer it from the top view with dividers; to obtain the height dimension, project it from the front view.

Figure 6.18 shows a fixture pad sketched in three views. The pad has a finished surface, indi-

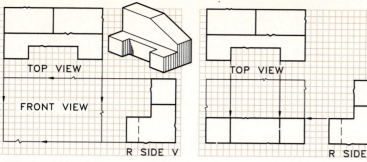

Figure 6.16 Sketching a missing front view:

Step 1 To sketch the front view, begin by blocking it in with light construction lines that will no need to be erased.

Step 2 Project the notch from the top view to the front view and sketch the lines as final lines.

Step 3 Project the ends of the angular notch from the top and right-side views, check the views, and darken the lines.

SKETCHING A MISSING SIDE VIEW

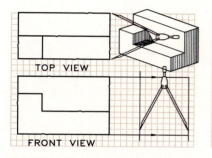

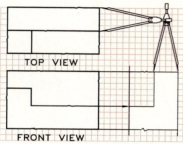

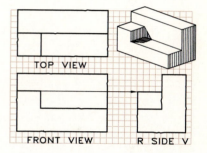

Figure 6.17 Sketching a missing side view:

Step 1 To find the right-side view, transfer the overall depth with dividers and project the height from the front view. Block in the view with light construction lines.

Step 2 Locate the notch in the side view with your dividers and project its base from the front view. Use light construction lines.

Step 3 Project the top of the notch from the front view, check for correctness, darken the lines, and label the views.

cated by "✔" marks in the two views where the surface appears as edges, and four counterbored holes. Dimension lines for the height, width, and depth labels should be spaced at least three letter heights from the views. For example, when you use 1/8-inch letters, position them at least 3/8-inch from the views.

Apply the finish mark symbol to the edge views of any finished surfaces, visible or hidden, to specify that the surface is to receive machining to make it smoother.

The surface in **Fig. 6.19** is being finished by grinding, which is one of many methods of smoothing a surface.

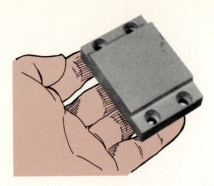

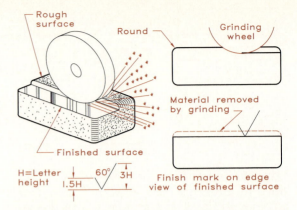

Figure 6.19 Place a finish mark on any edge view of a surface (visible or hidden) that has been (or is to be) smoothed by machining. Grinding is one of the methods used to finish a surface.

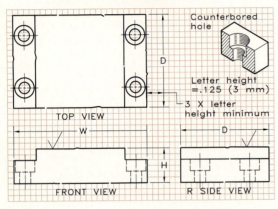

Figure 6.18 Three orthographic views adequately describe the rest pad. Space dimension lines at least three letter heights from the views. Finish marks (✔ marks) indicate that the top surface has been machined to a smooth finish. Counterbored holes allow bolt heads to be recessed.

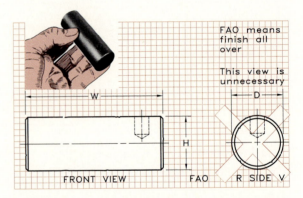

Figure 6.20 This pulley shaft is a typical cylindrical part that can be represented adequately by two views.

6.6 Circular Features

The pulley shaft depicted in **Fig. 6.20** in two views is composed of circular features. We enhanced these features by adding centerlines. **Figure 6.21** shows how to apply centerlines to indicate the center of the circular ends of a cylinder and its vertical axis. Perpendicular centerlines cross in circular views to locate the center of the circle and extend beyond the arc by about 1/8 inch. Centerlines consist of alternating long and short dashes, about 1 inch and 1/8 inch in length, respectively.

When centerlines coincide with visible or hidden lines, the centerline should be omitted because object lines are more important and centerlines are imaginary lines. **Figure 6.22** shows the precedence of lines.

BASICS OF CENTERLINES

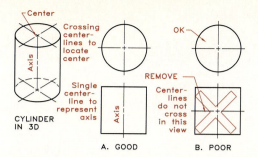

Figure 6.21 Centerlines identify the centers of circles and axes of cylinders. Centerlines cross only in the circular view and extend about ⅛ inch beyond the outside lines.

PRECEDENCE OF LINES

First priority: Visible lines
Second priority: Hidden lines
Third priority: Centerlines

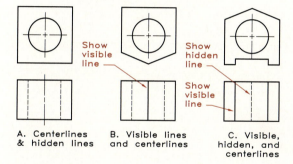

Figure 6.22 When visible lines coincide with hidden lines, show the visible lines. When hidden lines coincide with centerlines, show the hidden lines.

THE USE OF CENTERLINES

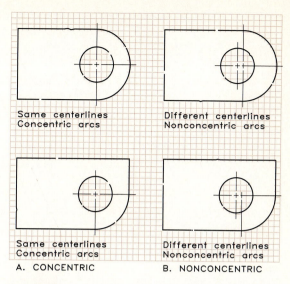

Figure 6.23

A Extend centerlines beyond the last arc that has the same center.

B Sketch separate centerlines when the arcs are not concentric.

RELATIVE LINE WEIGHTS

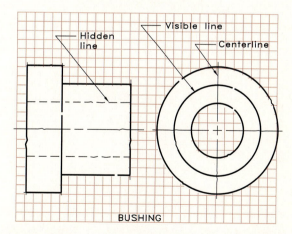

Figure 6.24 This orthographic sketch depicts the application of centerlines to concentric cylinders and the relative weights of various lines.

The centerlines shown in **Fig. 6.23** clarify whether the circles and arcs are concentric (share the same centers). **Figure 6.24** shows the correct manner of applying centerlines to orthographic views of an object composed of concentric cylinders.

SKETCHING CIRCLES

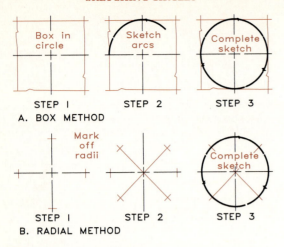

STEP 1   STEP 2   STEP 3
A. BOX METHOD

STEP 1   STEP 2   STEP 3
B. RADIAL METHOD

Figure 6.25 Sketching circles:

Box Method

Step 1 Using construction lines, block in the diameter of the circle about the centerlines.

Step 2 Sketch an arc tangent to the box through two tangent points.

Step 3 Complete the circle with other arcs.

Radial Method

Step 1 Mark off radii on the centerlines.

Step 2 Mark off radii on two construction lines drawn at 45°.

Step 3 Sketch the circles with arcs passing through the marked points.

CIRCULAR FEATURES

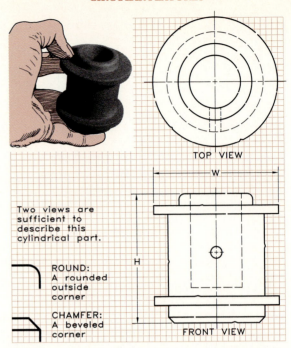

TOP VIEW

FRONT VIEW

Two views are sufficient to describe this cylindrical part.

ROUND:
A rounded outside corner

CHAMFER:
A beveled corner

Figure 6.27 Two orthographic views adequately describe this cylindrical pivot base.

CIRCULAR FEATURES

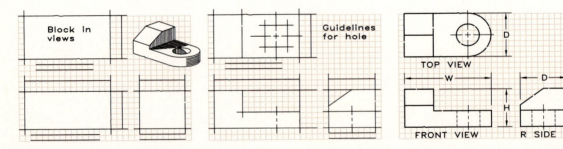

Figure 6.26 Sketching circular features in orthographic views:

Step 1 To sketch orthographic views of the part, begin by blocking in the overall dimensions with construction lines. Leave room for labels and dimensions.

Step 2 Construct the centerlines and the squares that block in the diameters of the circles. Find the slanted surface in the side view.

Step 3 Sketch the arcs, darken the lines, label the views, and show the dimensions W, D, and H.

OBLIQUE SKETCH

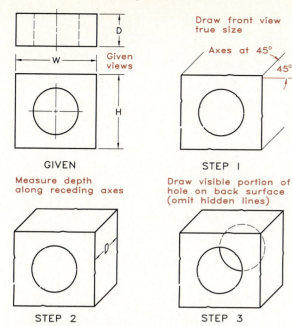

OBLIQUE SKETCHES WITH ARCS

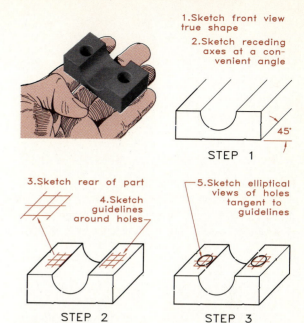

Figure 6.28 Sketching oblique pictorials:
Step 1 Sketch the front of the part as an orthographic front view. Sketch the receding lines at 45° to show the depth dimension.

Step 2 Measure the depth along the receding axes and sketch the back of the part.

Step 3 Locate the circle on the rear plane, show the visible portion of it, and omit the hidden lines.

Figure 6.29 Sketching arcs in oblique pictorials:
Step 1 Sketch the front view of the mounting bracket saddle as a true front view. Sketch the receding axes from each corner.

Step 2 Sketch the rear of the part by measuring its depth along the receding axes. Sketch guidelines about the holes on the upper planes.

Step 3 Sketch the circular features as ellipses on the upper planes tangent to the guidelines.

Sketching Circles

You may sketch circles by either of the methods shown in **Fig. 6.25**. Use light guidelines and dark centerlines to block in the circle. Drawing a freehand circle in one continuous arc is difficult, so draw short arcs with the help of the guidelines.

Figure 6.26 shows the steps involved in constructing three orthographic views of a part having circular features. **Figure 6.27** shows a typical part having circular features and two sketched views of it. Note the definitions of a **round** and a **chamfer**.

6.7 Oblique Pictorial Sketching

An **oblique pictorial** is a three-dimensional representation of an object's height, width, and depth. It approximates a photograph of an object, making the sketch easier to understand at a glance than orthographic views. Sketch the front of the object as a true-shape orthographic view (**Fig. 6.28**). Sketch the receding axes at an angle of between 20° and 60° oblique to the front view. Lay off the depth dimension as its true length along the receding axes. When the depth is true length, the oblique is a **cavalier oblique**.

ISOMETRIC SKETCH

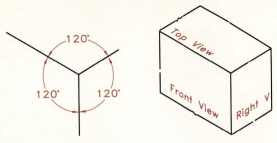

A. THE ISOMETRIC AXES

B. ISOMETRIC DRAWING

Figure 6.30 An isometric sketch:
A Begin an isometric pictorial by sketching three axes spaced 120° apart. One axis usually is vertical.

B Sketch the isometric shape parallel to the three axes and use its true measurements as the dimensions.

ISOMETRIC SKETCH

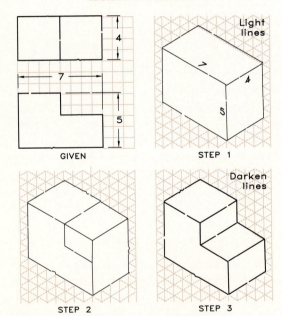

Figure 6.31 Sketching isometric pictorials:
Step 1 Use an isometric grid, transfer dimensions from the given views, and sketch a box having those dimensions.

Step 2 Locate the notch by measuring over four squares and down two squares, as shown in the orthographic views.

Step 3 Complete the pictorial by finishing the notch and darkening the lines.

ANGLES IN ISOMETRIC

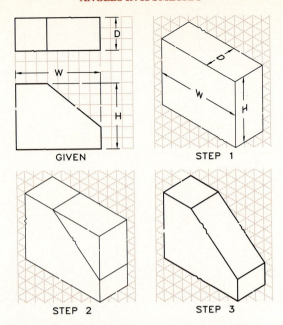

Figure 6.32 Sketching angles in isometric pictorials:
Step 1 Sketch a box from the overall dimensions given in the orthographic views.

Step 2 Angles cannot be measured with a protractor. Find each end of the angle with coordinates measured along the axes.

Step 3 Connect the ends of the angle and darken the lines.

The major advantage of an oblique pictorial is the ease of sketching circular features as circular arcs on the true-size front plane. **Figure 6.29** shows an oblique sketch of a shaft block. Circular features on the receding planes appear as ellipses, requiring slanted guidelines, as shown.

6.8 Isometric Pictorial Sketching

Another type of three-dimensional representation is the **isometric pictorial**, in which the axes make 120° angles with each other (**Fig. 6.30**). Specially printed isometric grids with lines intersecting at 60° angles make isometric sketching easier (**Fig. 6.31**).

DOUBLE ANGLES IN ISOMETRIC

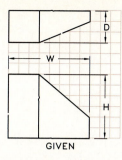

GIVEN

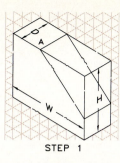

STEP 1

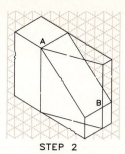

STEP 2

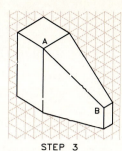

STEP 3

Figure 6.33 Sketching double angles in isometric pictorials:

Step 1 When part of an object has two sloping angles that intersect, begin by sketching the overall box and finding one of the angles.

Step 2 Find the second angle, which locates point B, the intersection line between the planes.

Step 3 Connect points A and B and darken the lines. Line AB is the line of intersection between the two sloping planes.

CIRCLES IN ISOMETRIC

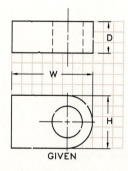

GIVEN

STEP 1

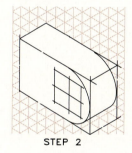

STEP 2

STEP 3

Figure 6.34 Sketching circles in isometric pictorials:

Step 1 Sketch a box using the overall dimensions given in the orthographic views. Sketch the centerlines and a rhombus of guidelines blocking in the

Step 2 Sketch the isometric arcs tangent to the box. These arcs are elliptical rather than circular.

Step 3 Sketch the hole and darken the lines. Hidden lines usually are omitted in isometric pictorial sketches.

Simply transfer the dimensions from the squares in the orthographic views to the isometric grid.

You cannot measure angles in isometric pictorials with a protractor; you must find them by connecting coordinates of the angle laid off along the isometric axes. In **Fig. 6.32**, locate the ends of the angular plane by using the coordinates for width and height. When a part has two sloping planes that intersect (**Fig. 6.33**), you have to sketch them one at a time to find point B. Line AB is found as the line of intersection between the planes.

ELLIPSES IN ISOMETRIC

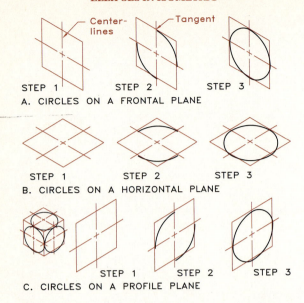

STEP 1 STEP 2 STEP 3
A. CIRCLES ON A FRONTAL PLANE

STEP 1 STEP 2 STEP 3
B. CIRCLES ON A HORIZONTAL PLANE

STEP 1 STEP 2 STEP 3
C. CIRCLES ON A PROFILE PLANE

Figure 6.35 Sketch circular features on the (A) frontal, (B) horizontal, and (C) profile plane of an isometric as ellipses:
Step 1 Lay out centerlines and guidelines.

Step 2 Sketch two arcs.

Step 3 Connect the ends of the arcs to complete the ellipses.

Circles in Isometric Pictorials

Circles appear as ellipses in isometric pictorials. When you sketch them, begin with their center-lines and construction lines enclosing their diameters, as shown in **Fig. 6.34**. The end of the block is semicircular in the front view, so its center must be equidistant from the top, bottom, and end of the front view. Circles and ellipses are easier to sketch if you use construction lines.

Figure 6.35 shows how to use centerlines and construction lines to draw ellipses in the three iso-metric planes: **frontal**, **horizontal**, and **profile** views. **Figure 6.36** shows an application of this technique to sketching a cylinder. Use this same technique to sketch an object having semicircular ends (**Fig. 6.37**). Hidden lines are visually omitted in isometric drawings.

CYLINDERS IN ISOMETRIC

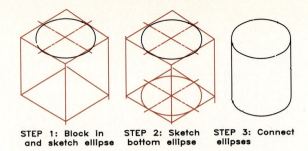

STEP 1: Block in and sketch ellipse   STEP 2: Sketch bottom ellipse   STEP 3: Connect ellipses

Figure 6.36 Sketching a cylinder as an isometric pictorial:
Step 1 Block in the cylinder and sketch the upper ellipse.

Step 2 Sketch the lower ellipse.

Step 3 Connect the ellipses with tangent lines and darken the lines.

ISOMETRIC SKETCH

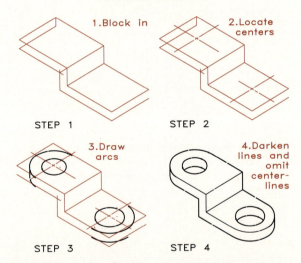

STEP 1   STEP 2

STEP 3   STEP 4

Figure 6.37 Sketching circular features in isometric pictorials:
Step 1 Block in the isometric shape of the object with light lines.

Step 2 Locate the centerlines of the holes and the rounded ends.

Step 3 Sketch the circular features of the ends of the part and the holes.

Step 4 Show the bottoms of the holes and darken the lines of all features.

Problems

Sketch your solutions to these problems on size A (8½-×-11-inch) paper, with or without a printed grid. **Figure 6.38** shows a format for this size sheet and a 0.20-in. grid (convertible to an approximate metric grid by equating each square to 5 mm). Execute all sketches and lettering by applying the principles covered in this chapter and Chapter 4. **Figures 6.39 and 6.40** contain the problems and instructions.

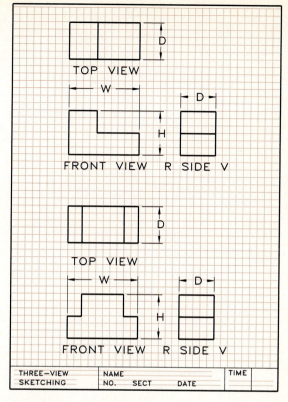

Figure 6.38 Use this layout of a size A sheet for sketching problems. You may sketch two problems on each sheet.

Figure 6.39 (A) Sketch top, front, and right-side views of the problems assigned, supplying lines that may be missing from all views. **(B)** Sketch obliques of the problems assigned. **(C)** Sketch isometrics of the problems assigned.

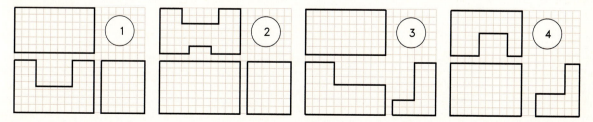

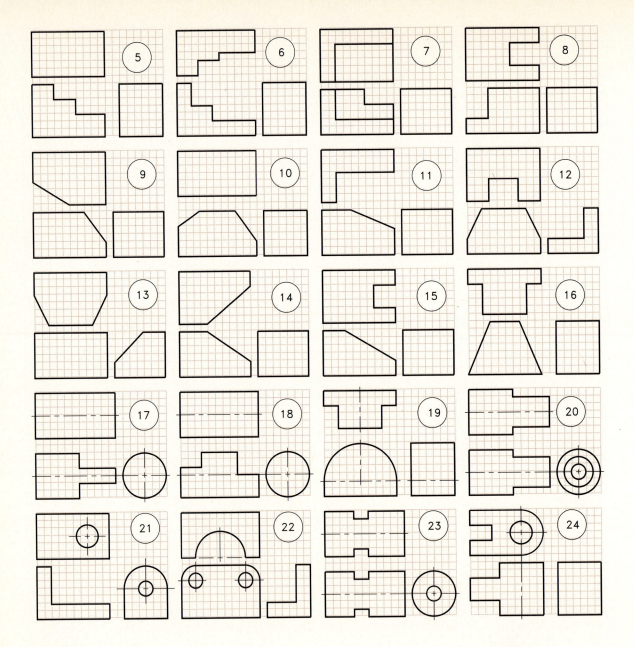

Figure 6.39 (continued)

Figure 6.40 Sketch the top, front, and right-side views of the problems assigned, two problems per sheet.

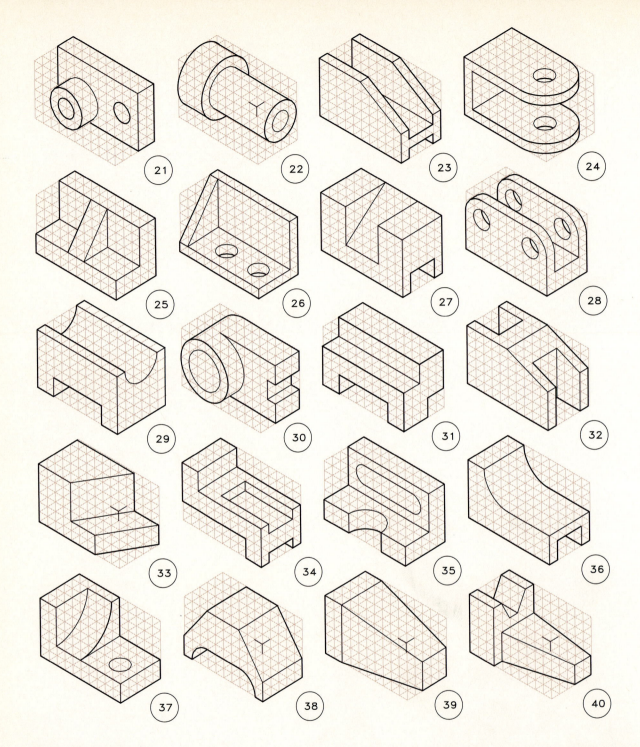

Figure 6.40 (continued)

7

Orthographic Drawing with Instruments

7.1 Introduction

In Chapter 6, you were introduced to orthographic projection by freehand sketching, which is an excellent way to develop a design concept. Now, you must convert these sketches into orthographic views drawn to scale with instruments (or by computer) to define your design more precisely. Then you will add dimensions, notes, and specifications to convert these drawings into working drawings from which the design will become a reality.

Orthographic drawings are three-dimensional objects represented by separate views arranged in a standard manner that are readily understood by the technological team. Because multiview drawings usually are executed with instruments and drafting aids, they are often called **mechanical drawings**. They are called **working drawings**, or **detail drawings**, when sufficient dimensions, notes, and specifications are added to enable the product to be manufactured or built from the drawings.

7.2 Orthographic Projection

An artist is likely to represent objects impressionistically, but the engineer must represent them precisely. Orthographic projection is used to prepare precise, scaled, and clearly presented drawings from which the project depicted can be built.

Orthographic projection is the system of drawing views of an object by projecting them perpendicularly onto projection planes with parallel projectors. **Figure 7.1** illustrates this concept of projection by imagining that the object is inside a glass box and three of its views are projected to planes of the box.

Figure 7.2 illustrates the principle of orthographic projection where the front view is projected perpendicularly onto a vertical projection plane, called the frontal plane, with parallel projectors. The projected front view is two dimensional because it has only width and height and lies in a single plane. Similarly, the top view is projected onto a horizontal projection plane, and the

THE GLASS-BOX APPROACH

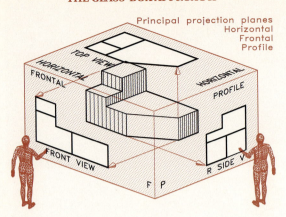

Principal projection planes
Horizontal
Frontal
Profile

Figure 7.1 Orthographic projection is the system of projecting views onto an imaginary glass box with parallel projectors to the three mutually perpendicular projection planes.

ORTHOGRAPHIC PROJECTION

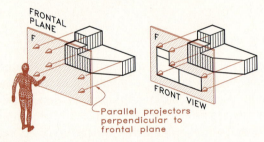

FRONTAL PLANE

Parallel projectors perpendicular to frontal plane

Figure 7.2 An orthographic view is found by projecting from the object to a projection plane with parallel projectors that are perpendicular to the projection plane.

GLASS-BOX THEORY

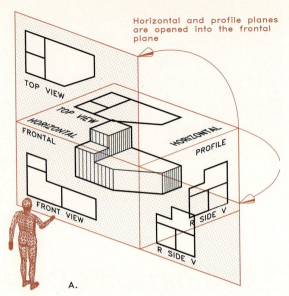

Horizontal and profile planes are opened into the frontal plane

A.

The standard arrangement of three orthographic views:
Top view above the front view
Right-side view right of the front view

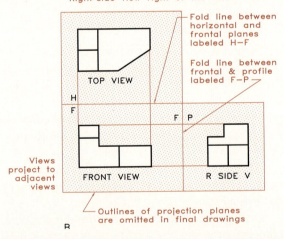

Fold line between horizontal and frontal planes labeled H–F

Fold line between frontal & profile labeled F–P

Views project to adjacent views

Outlines of projection planes are omitted in final drawings

B

Figure 7.3 When the imaginary glass box is opened into the plane of the drawing surface, the resulting orthographic views and associated labeling will appear as shown here.

side view is projected onto a second vertical projection plane.

Imagine that the box is opened into the plane of the drawing surface. **Figure 7.3A** illustrates how three planes of a glass box are opened into a single plane (**Fig. 7.3B**) to yield the standard positions for the three orthographic views. These views are the front, top, and right-side views.

The principal projection planes of orthographic projection are the horizontal (H), frontal

(F), and profile (P) planes. Views projected onto these principal planes are principal views. The dimensions used to give the sizes of principal views are height (H), width (W), and depth (D).

THE ALPHABET OF LINES

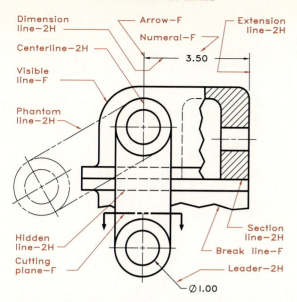

Figure 7.4 The alphabet of lines and recommended pencil grades for drawing orthographic views are shown here.

LINE WEIGHTS

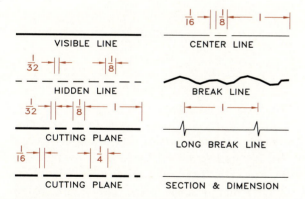

Figure 7.5 Full-size line weights recommended for drawing orthographic views are shown above.

7.3 Alphabet of Lines

Draw all orthographic views with dark and dense lines as if drawn with ink. Only the line widths should vary—except for guidelines and construction lines, which are drawn very lightly for layout

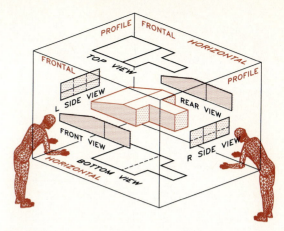

Figure 7.6 Six principal views of an object can be drawn in orthographic projection. Imagine that the object is in a glass box with the views projected onto its six planes.

and lettering. **Figure 7.4** gives examples of lines used in orthographic projection and the recommended pencil grades for them. The lengths of dashes in hidden lines and centerlines are drawn longer as a drawing's size increases. **Figure 7.5** further describes these lines.

7.4 Six-View Drawings

When you imagine that an object is inside a glass box, you will see two horizontal planes, two frontal planes, and two profile planes (**Fig. 7.6**). **Therefore the maximum number of principal views that can be used to represent an object is six.** The top and bottom views are projected onto horizontal planes, the front and rear views onto frontal planes, and the right- and left-side views onto profile planes.

To draw the six views on a sheet of paper, imagine the glass box is opened up into the plane of the drawing paper as shown in **Fig. 7.7**. Place the top view over and bottom view under the front view; place the right-side view to the right and the left-side view to the left of the front view; and place the rear view to the left of the left-side view.

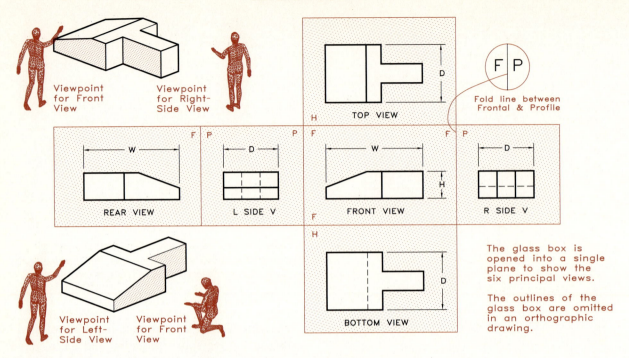

Figure 7.7 Opening the box into a single plane positions the six views as shown to describe the object.

7.5 Three-View Drawings

Projectors align the views both horizontally and vertically about the front view. Each side of the fold lines of the glass box is labeled H, F, or P (horizontal, frontal, or profile) to identify the projection planes on each side of the imaginary fold lines (Fig. 7.7).

Height (H), width (W), and depth (D), the three dimensions necessary to dimension an object, are shown in their recommended positions in Fig. 7.7. The standard arrangement of the six views allows the views to share dimensions by projection. For example, the height dimension, which is shown only once between the front and right-side views, applies to the four horizontally aligned views. The width dimension is placed between the top and front views, but applies to the bottom view also.

The most commonly used orthographic arrangement of views is the three-view drawing, consisting of front, top, and right-side views. Imagine that the views of the object are projected onto the planes of the glass box **(Fig. 7.8)** and the three planes are opened into a single plane, the frontal plane. **Figure 7.9** shows the resulting three-view drawing where the views are labeled and dimensioned with H, W, and D.

7.6 Arrangement of Views

Figure 7.10 shows the standard positions for a three-view drawing: The top and side views are projected from and aligned with the front view.

THE THREE-VIEW GLASS BOX

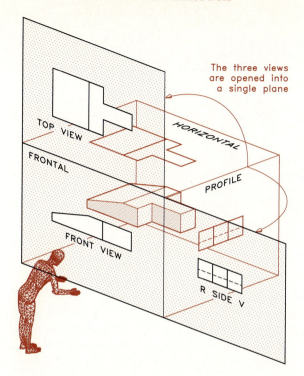

Figure 7.8 Three-view drawings are commonly used to describe small objects such as machine parts.

A THREE-VIEW DRAWING

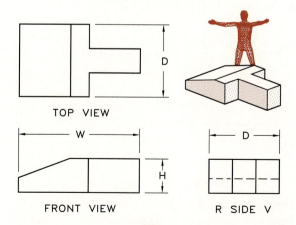

Figure 7.9 This three-view drawing depicts the object shown in Fig. 7.8.

ARRANGEMENT OF VIEWS

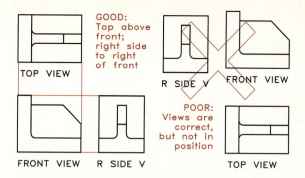

Figure 7.10 To be interpreted correctly, orthographic views must be arranged in their proper positions.

ALIGNMENT OF DIMENSIONS

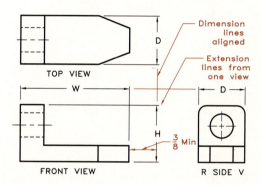

Figure 7.11 Dimension and extension lines used in three-view orthographic projection should be aligned. Draw extension lines from only one view when dimensions are placed between views.

Improperly arranged views that do not project from view to view are also shown. **Figure 7.11** illustrates the rules of projection and shows the proper alignment of dimensions. Orthographic projection shortens layout time, improves readability, and reduces the number of dimensions required because they are placed between and are shared by the views to which they apply.

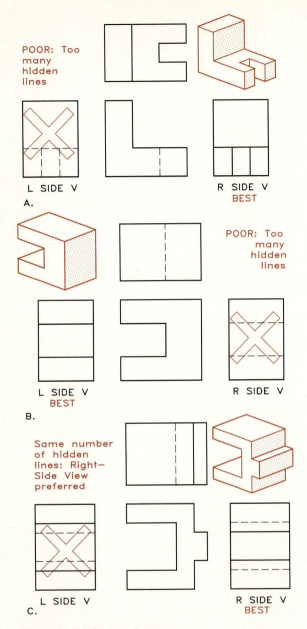

POOR: Too many hidden lines

L SIDE V

A.

R SIDE V
BEST

POOR: Too many hidden lines

L SIDE V
BEST

B.

R SIDE V

Same number of hidden lines: Right— Side View preferred

L SIDE V

C.

R SIDE V
BEST

Figure 7.12 Selection of views:

A Select the sequence of views with the fewest hidden lines.

B Select the left-side view because it has fewer hidden lines than the right-side view.

C When both views have an equal number of hidden lines, select the right-side view.

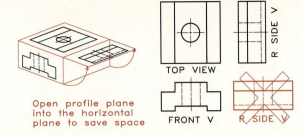

Open profile plane into the horizontal plane to save space

TOP VIEW

FRONT V

R SIDE V

R SIDE V

Figure 7.13 The side view can be projected from the top view instead of the front view. This alternative position saves space when the depth of an object is considerably greater than its height.

7.7 Selection of Views

Select the sequence of orthographic views with the fewest hidden lines. **Figure 7.12A** shows that the right-side view is preferable to the left-side view because it has fewer hidden lines. Although the three-view arrangement of top, front, and right-side views is more commonly used, the top, front, and left-side view arrangement is acceptable **(Fig. 7.12B)** if the left-side view has fewer hidden lines than the right-side view.

The most descriptive view usually is selected as the front view. If an object, such as a chair, has predefined views that people generally recognize as the front and top views, you should label the accepted front view as the orthographic front view.

Although the right-side view usually is placed to the right of the front view, the side view can be projected from the top view **(Fig. 7.13)**. This alternative position is advisable when the object has a much larger depth than height.

7.8 Line Techniques

Figure 7.14 illustrates techniques for handling most types of intersecting lines, hidden lines, and arcs in combination. Proper application of these principles improves the readability of orthographic drawings.

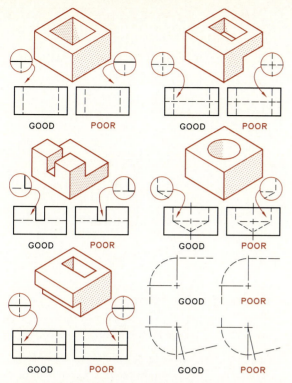

Figure 7.14 These drawings show proper intersections and other line techniques in orthographic views.

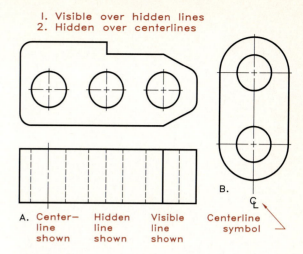

Figure 7.15 When lines coincide with each other, the more important lines take precedence (cover up) the other lines. The order of importance is: visible lines, hidden lines, and centerlines.

in the construction of the missing front view. Projecting points from the top and side views to the intersections of the projectors locates the object's front view.

7.10 Lines and Planes

A line can appear true length (TL), foreshortened (FS), or as a point (PT) in an orthographic view (Fig. 7.17). A line that appears true length is parallel to the reference line in the adjacent view. The reference line in these examples represents the fold line between the horizontal and frontal planes and therefore is labeled H-F. **A plane can appear true size (TS), foreshortened, or as an edge in orthographic projection (Fig. 7.17).**

Lines and planes that are true length or true size can be measured with a scale. Foreshortened lines and planes are not true length or true size and are less than full size.

Become familiar with the order of importance (precedence) of lines **(Fig. 7.15)**. **The most important line, the visible object line, is shown regardless of any other line lying behind it. Of next importance is the hidden line, which is more important than the centerline.**

7.9 Point Numbering

Some orthographic views are difficult to draw due to their complexity. By numbering the endpoints of the lines of the parts in each view as you construct it **(Fig. 7.16)**, the location of the object's features will be easier. For example, using numbers on the top and side views of this object aids

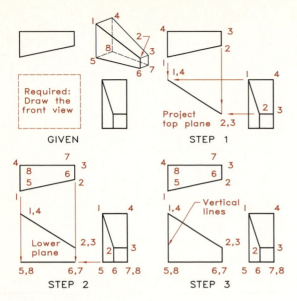

Figure 7.16 Point numbering:
Required Find the front view.

Step 1 Number the corners of plane 1–2–3–4 in the top and side views and project these points to the front view.

Step 2 Number the corners of plane 5–6–7–8 in the top and side views and project these points to the front view.

Step 3 Connect the numbered lines to complete the missing front view.

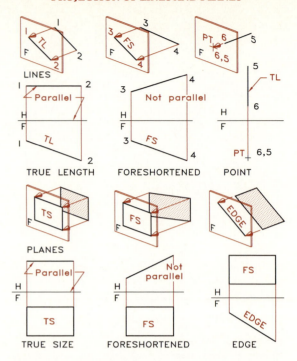

Figure 7.17 A line will appear in orthographic projection as true length, foreshortened, or as a point. A plane in orthographic projection appears as true size, foreshortened, or as an edge.

7.11 Views by Subtraction

Figure 7.18 illustrates how three views of a part are drawn by beginning with a block having the overall height, width, and depth of the finished part and removing volumes from it. This drawing procedure is similar to the steps of making the part in the shop.

7.12 Laying Out Three-View Drawings

The depth dimension applies to both the top and side views, but these views usually are positioned where depth does not project between them **(Fig. 7.19)**. The depth dimension can be transferred between the top and side views with dividers or by using a 45° line.

Layout Rules From the material presented so far, we can summarize the rules to be followed in drawing orthographic views:

1. **Draw orthographic views in their proper positions.**
2. **Select the most descriptive view as the front view, if the object does not have a predefined front view.**
3. **Select the sequence of views with the fewest hidden lines.**
4. **Label the views, for example, top view, front view, and right-side view.**
5. **Place dimensions between the views to which they apply.**

THREE VIEWS BY SUBTRACTION

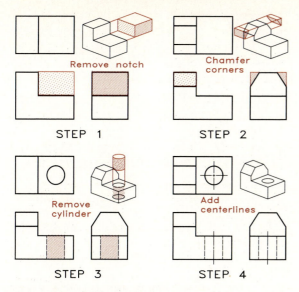

STEP 1

STEP 2

Remove notch

Chamfer corners

Remove cylinder

STEP 3

Add centerlines

STEP 4

Figure 7.18 Views by subtraction:

Step 1 Block in the views of the object using overall dimensions of H, W, and D. Create the notch by removing the block.

Step 2 Bevel the corners of the object by removing the triangular volumes.

Step 3 Form the hole by removing a cylindrical volume.

Step 4 Add centerlines to complete the views.

TRANSFERRING DEPTH

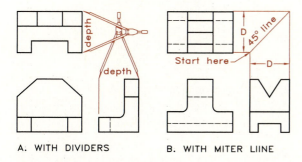

A. WITH DIVIDERS

B. WITH MITER LIINE

Figure 7.19

A Transfer the depth dimension to the side view with your dividers.

B Use a 45° miter line to transfer the depth dimension between the top and side views.

THREE-VIEW DRAWING

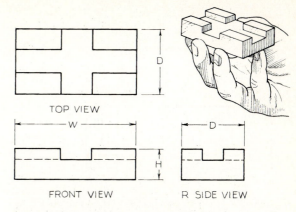

TOP VIEW

FRONT VIEW

R SIDE VIEW

Figure 7.20 This three-view drawing depicts an object that has only horizontal and vertical planes.

THREE-VIEW DRAWING

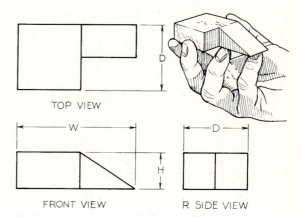

TOP VIEW

FRONT VIEW

R SIDE VIEW

Figure 7.21 This three-view drawing shows an object that has a sloping plane.

6. Use the proper alphabet of lines.
7. Leave adequate room between the views for labels and dimensions.
8. Draw the views necessary to describe a part. Sometimes fewer and more views are required.

Figures 7.20–7.24 show examples of three-view orthographic drawings of objects drawn by applying these rules.

THREE-VIEW DRAWING

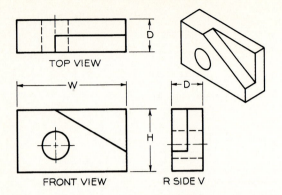

TOP VIEW

FRONT VIEW R SIDE V

Figure 7.22 This three-view drawing shows an object that has a sloping plane with a cylindrical hole through it.

THREE-VIEW DRAWING

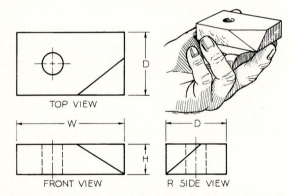

TOP VIEW

FRONT VIEW R SIDE VIEW

Figure 7.23 This three-view drawing depicts an object that has a plane with a compound slope.

THREE-VIEW DRAWING

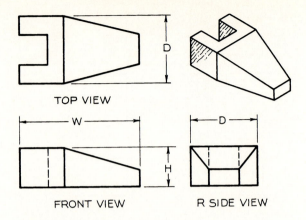

TOP VIEW

FRONT VIEW R SIDE VIEW

Figure 7.24 This three-view drawing shows an object that has planes with compound slopes.

TWO-VIEW ORTHOGRAPHIC DRAWINGS

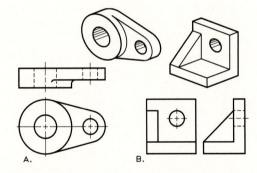

A. B.

Figure 7.25 These objects can be adequately described with two orthographic views.

7.13 Two-View Drawings

Economize on time and space by using only the views necessary to depict an object. **Figure 7.25** shows objects that require only two views. The fixture block in **Fig. 7.26** is another example of a part needing only two views to be adequately described.

7.14 One-View Drawings

Simple cylindrical parts and parts of a uniform thickness can be described by only one view as shown in **Fig. 7.27**. Supplementary notes clarify features that would have been shown in the omitted views. Diameters are labeled with diameter signs and thicknesses are noted.

7.15 Simplified and Removed Views

The right- and left-side views of the part in **Fig. 7.28** would be harder to interpret if all hidden lines were drawn by rigorously following the rules of orthographic projection. Simplified views in

TWO-VIEW DRAWING

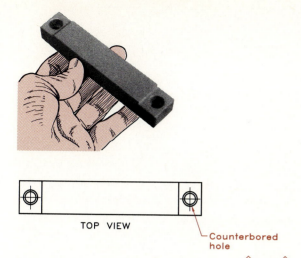

Figure 7.26 Two views adequately define this part.

ONE-VIEW DRAWING

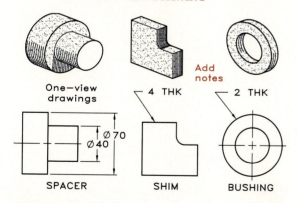

Figure 7.27 Objects that are cylindrical or of a uniform thickness can be described with only one orthographic view and supplementary notes.

SIMPLIFIED VIEWS

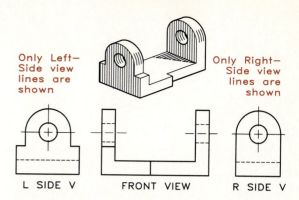

Figure 7.28 Use simplified views with unnecessary and confusing hidden lines omitted to improve clarity.

A REMOVED VIEW

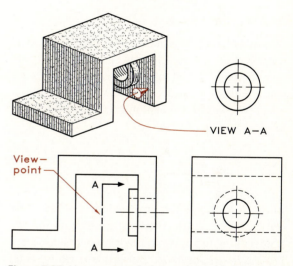

Figure 7.29 Use a removed view, indicated by the directional arrows, to show hard-to-see views in removed locations.

which confusing and unnecessary lines have been omitted are better and more readable.

When it is difficult to show a feature with a standard orthographic view because of its location, a **removed view** can be drawn (**Fig. 7.29**). The removed view, indicated by the directional arrows, is clearer when moved to an isolated position.

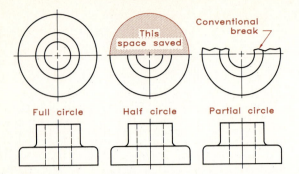

Figure 7.30 Save space and time by drawing the circular view of a cylindrical part as a partial view.

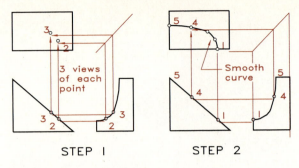

Figure 7.31 Curve plotting:

Step 1 Locate points 2 and 3 in the front and side views by projection. Project points 2 and 3 to the top view.

Step 2 Locate the remaining points in the three views and connect the points in the top view with a smooth curve.

7.16 Partial Views

Partial views of symmetrical or cylindrical parts may be used to save time and space. Omitting the rear of the circular top view in **Fig. 7.30** saves space without sacrificing clarity. To clarify that a part of the view has been omitted, a conventional break is used in the top view.

7.17 Curve Plotting

You may draw an irregular curve by following the rules of orthographic projection, as **Fig. 7.31** shows. Begin plotting by locating and numbering points along the curve in the front and side views. Project these points to the top view where each point is located and connect them with a smooth curve drawn using your irregular curve.

Figure 7.32 shows an ellipse plotted in the top view from front and side-view projections. The points on the curve should be numbered as they are transferred.

7.18 Conventional Practices

The readability of an orthographic view may be improved if the rules of projection are violated.

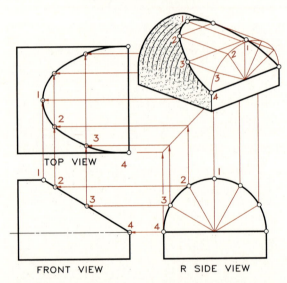

Figure 7.32 The ellipse in the top view was found by numbering points in the front and side views and then projecting them to the top view.

Violations of rules customarily made for the sake of clarity are called **conventional practices**.

Symmetrically spaced holes in a circular plate **(Fig. 7.33)** are drawn at their true radial distance

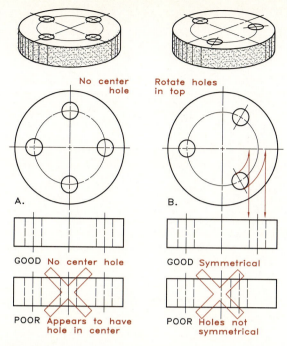

Figure 7.33

A Omit the center hole found by true projection that gives an impression that a hole passes through the center of the plate.

B Use a conventional view to show the holes located at their true radial distances from the center. They are imagined to be rotated to the centerline in the top view.

from the center of the plate in the front view as a conventional practice. Imagine that the holes are revolved to the centerline in the top view before projecting them to the front view.

This principle of revolution also applies to symmetrically positioned features such as ribs, webs, and the three lugs on the outside of the part shown in **Fig. 7.34**. **Figure 7.35** shows the applications of conventional practices to holes and ribs in combination.

Another conventional revolution is illustrated in **Fig. 7.36** where the front view of an inclined arm is revolved to a horizontal position so that it can be drawn true size in the top view. The

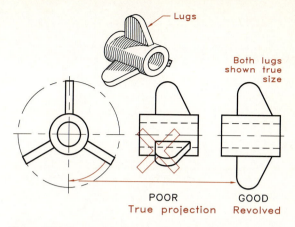

Figure 7.34 Symmetrically positioned external features, such as webs, ribs, and these lugs, are imagined to be revolved to their true-size positions for the best views.

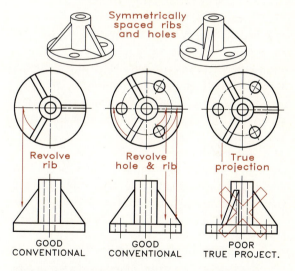

Figure 7.35 Conventional methods of revolving holes and ribs in combination improve clarity.

revolved arm in the front view is not drawn because the revolution is imaginary.

Figure 7.37 shows how to improve views of parts by conventional revolution. By revolving the

CONVENTIONAL REVOLUTION

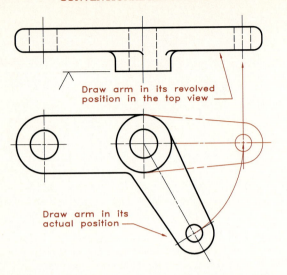

Draw arm in its revolved position in the top view

Draw arm in its actual position

Figure 7.36 The front view of the arm is imagined to be revolved so that its true length can be drawn in the top view. This is an accepted conventional practice.

SLOTS AND HOLES

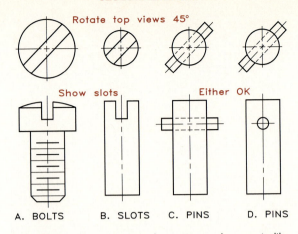

Rotate top views 45°

Show slots   Either OK

A. BOLTS   B. SLOTS   C. PINS   D. PINS

Figure 7.37 It is conventional practice to draw parts like these at 45° in the top view. Draw the front views with the slots and holes drawn true size.

top views of these parts 45°, slots and holes no longer coincide with the centerlines and can be seen more clearly. Draw the front views of the slots and holes true size by imagining that they have been revolved 45°.

Another type of conventional view is the true-size development of a curved sheet-metal part drawn as a flattened-out view (**Fig. 7.38**). The top view shows the part's curvature.

7.19 Conventional Intersections

In orthographic projection, lines are drawn to represent the intersections (joining lines) between planes of an object. Wherever planes intersect, forming a sharp edge, this line of intersection is projected to its adjacent view. **Figure 7.39** gives examples of views where lines are required and not required.

Figure 7.40 shows how to draw intersections between cylinders rather than plotting more com-

DEVELOPED VIEWS

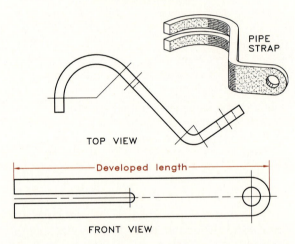

PIPE STRAP

TOP VIEW

Developed length

FRONT VIEW

Figure 7.38 It is conventional practice to use true-size developed (flattened-out) views of objects that have been made of bent sheet metal.

plex, orthographically correct lines of intersection. **Figures 7.40A** and **C** show conventional intersections, which means they are approximations drawn for ease of construction while being sufficiently representative of the object. **Figure 7.40B**

REPRESENTATION OF FEATURES

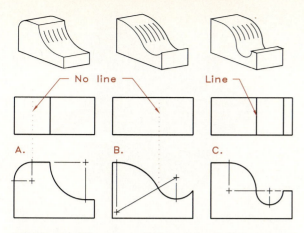

Figure 7.39 Object lines are drawn only where there are sharp intersections or where arcs are tangent at their centerlines, as shown in (C).

INTERSECTIONS: CYLINDERS

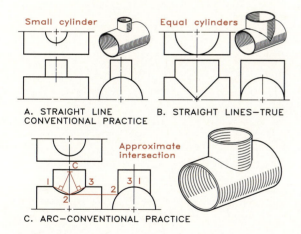

Figure 7.40

A and **C** Use these conventional methods of showing intersections between cylinders for ease of construction.

B This intersection is easy to draw and also is a true projection.

shows an easy-to-draw intersection between cylinders of equal diameters, and this is a true intersection as well. **Figures 7.41** and **7.42** show other cylindrical intersections, and **Fig. 7.43**

INTERSECTIONS: CYLINDERS AND PRISMS

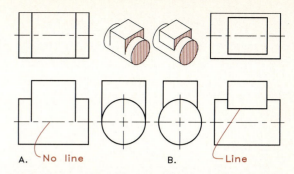

Figure 7.41 Conventional methods of drawing intersections between prisms and cylindrical shapes are easy to draw and are sufficiently clear.

INTERSECTIONS: RECTANGULAR SHAPES

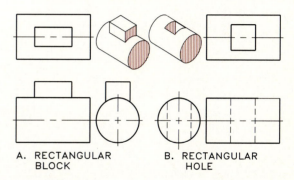

Figure 7.42 Conventional intersections between prisms and cylindrical shapes also are easy to draw and are sufficiently clear.

shows conventional practices for depicting intersections formed by holes in cylinders.

7.20 Fillets and Rounds

Fillets and rounds are rounded intersections between the planes of a part that are used on castings, such as the body of the Collet Index Fixture in **Fig. 7.44. A fillet is an inside rounding, and a round is an external rounding on a part.** The radii of fillets and rounds usually are small, about 1/4

HOLES IN CYLINDERS

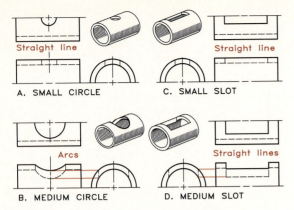

Straight line | Straight line
A. SMALL CIRCLE | C. SMALL SLOT

Arcs | Straight lines
B. MEDIUM CIRCLE | D. MEDIUM SLOT

Figure 7.43 Conventional methods of illustrating holes in cylinders are easy to draw and are sufficiently clear.

FILLETS AND ROUNDS

Figure 7.44 The edges of this Collet Index Fixture are rounded to form fillets and rounds. The surface of the casting is rough except where it has been machined. (Courtesy of Hardinge Brothers, Inc.)

FILLETS AND ROUNDS

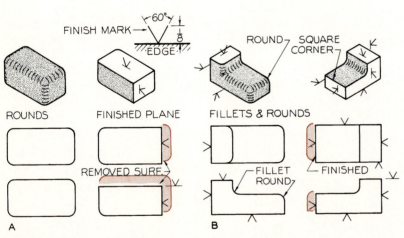

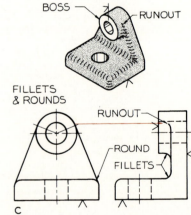

Figure 7.45 Fillets and rounds:
A Machining smooths (finishes) the surface of a casting and removes rounds, leaving square corners. A finish mark on an edge view of a surface indicates that it is to be finished.

B Fillets, rounded inside corners, and rounds, rounded outside corners, are removed when their surfaces are finished. The fillets can be seen only in the front view in this case.

C The views of an object with fillets and rounds must call attention to these features.

FINISH MARKS

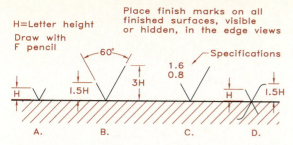

Figure 7.46 Any of these finish mark symbols are placed on all views of finished surfaces, whether hidden or visible.

FILLETS AND ROUNDS

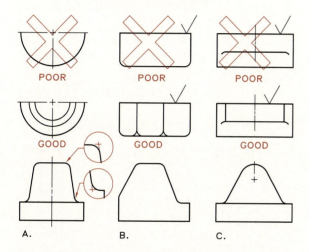

Figure 7.47 These examples show both poorly drawn and conventionally drawn fillets and rounds in orthographic views.

RUNOUTS

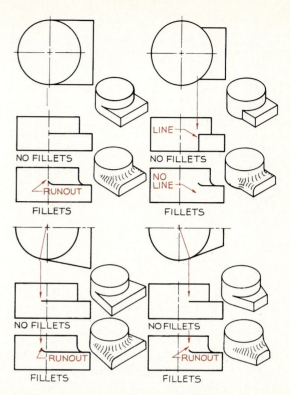

Figure 7.48 These examples show conventional ways of showing intersections between features of objects and runouts. Intersections with fillets have runouts drawn with a circle template.

inch. Fillets give added strength at inside corners, and rounds improve appearance and remove sharp edges.

A casting will have square corners only when its surface has been **finished**, which is the process of machining away part of the surface to a smooth finish **(Fig. 7.45)**. Indicate finished surfaces by placing a finish mark (V) on all edge views of fin-

ished surfaces whether the edges are visible or hidden. **Figure 7.46** shows four types of finish marks. A more detailed surface texture symbol is presented in Chapter 14.

Note in **Fig. 7.45C** that a boss is a raised cylindrical feature and that the curve formed by a fillet at its point of tangency is a **runout**. **Figure 7.47** illustrates several techniques for showing fillets and rounds on orthographic views with a circle template.

Figure 7.48 gives a comparison of intersections and runouts of parts with and without fillets and rounds. Large runouts are constructed as an

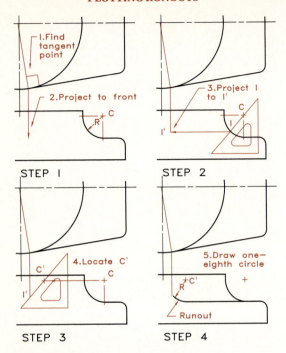

STEP 1

STEP 2

STEP 3

STEP 4

Figure 7.49 Plotting runouts:

Step 1 Find the point of tangency in the top view and project it to the front view.

Step 2 A 45° triangle is used to find point 1, which is projected to point 1'.

Step 3 Move the 45° triangle to locate point C', which is on the horizontal projector from center C.

Step 4 Use the radius of the fillet to draw the runout with C' as its center. The runout arc is equal to one-eighth of a circle.

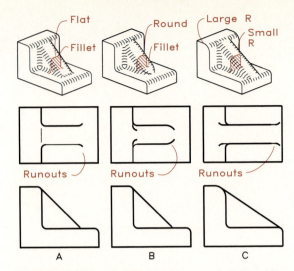

A   B   C

Figure 7.50 These drawings illustrate runouts for differently shaped ribs: (A) fillets, (B) equal rounded edges, and (C) unequal rounds.

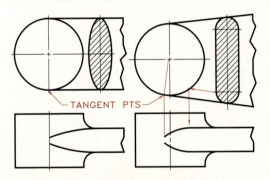

Figure 7.51 These drawings show conventional runouts for other differently shaped cross-sections.

eighth of a circle with a compass as shown in **Fig. 7.49**. Small runouts are drawn with a circle template. Runouts on orthographic views reveal much about the details of an object. For example, the runout in the top view of **Fig. 7.50A** tells us that the rib has rounded corners, whereas the top view of **Fig. 7.50B** tells us the rib is completely round. **Figures 7.51** and **7.52** illustrate other types of filleted and rounded intersections.

7.21 Left-Hand and Right-Hand Views

Two parts often are required that are "mirror images" of each other **(Fig. 7.53)**. Drawing time is reduced by drawing views of one of the parts and

RUNOUTS: ROUNDED FEATURES

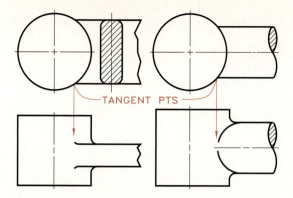

Figure 7.52 These drawings show conventional runouts for differently shaped cross-sections.

MIRROR-IMAGE PARTS

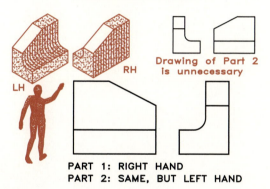

Figure 7.53 When left- and right-hand mirrored parts are needed, only one view is drawn and labeled. Indicate the other views by a note.

adding a note that the other matching part (mirrored part) has the same dimensions.

7.22 First-Angle Projection

The examples in this chapter are presented as third-angle projections, where the top view is placed over the front view and the right-side view is placed to the right of the front view, as shown in **Fig. 7.54**. This method is used in the United States,

THIRD-ANGLE PROJECTION: U.S. SYSTEM

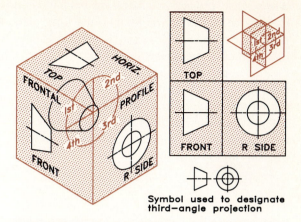

Figure 7.54 Third-angle projection is used for drawing orthographic views in the United States, Great Britain, and Canada. The top view is placed over the front view and the right-side view is placed to the right of the front view. The truncated cone is the symbol that designates third-angle projection.

FIRST-ANGLE PROJECTION: EUROPEAN SYSTEM

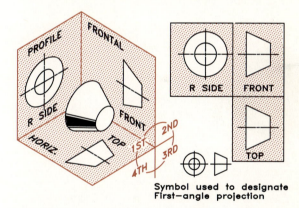

Figure 7.55 First-angle projection is used in most of the world. It shows the right-side view to the left of the front view and the top view under the front view. The truncated cone is the symbol that designates first-angle projection.

Great Britain, and Canada. Most of the rest of the world uses first-angle projection.

The first-angle system is illustrated in **Fig. 7.55**, in which an object is placed above the horizontal plane and in front of the frontal plane. When these projection planes are opened onto the surface of the drawing paper, the front view projects over the top view, and the right-side view to the left of the front view.

The angle of projection used in making a drawing is indicated by placing the symbol showing a truncated cone in or near the title block (**Fig. 7.56**). **When metric units of measurement are used, the SI symbol is given in combination with the cone on the drawing.**

THE SI SYMBOL

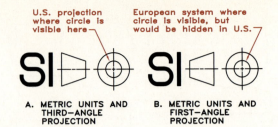

U.S. projection where circle is visible here

European system where circle is visible, but would be hidden in U.S.

A. METRIC UNITS AND THIRD—ANGLE PROJECTION

B. METRIC UNITS AND FIRST—ANGLE PROJECTION

Figure 7.56 These symbols are placed on drawings to specify first-angle or third-angle projection and metric units of measurement.

Problems

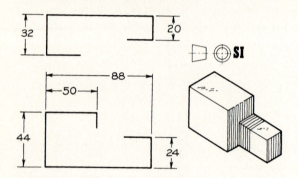

Figure 7.57 Problem 1. Guide block.

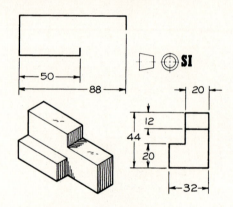

Figure 7.58 Problem 2. Double step.

Draw the following problems as orthographic views on size A or size B paper, one or two problems per sheet, as assigned by your instructor.

1–7. (Figs. 7.57–7.63) Draw the given views using the dimensions provided, and then construct the missing top, front, or right-side views.

8–17. (Figs. 7.64–7.73) Complete the three views of the objects. Each square grid is equal to 0.20 inch or 5 mm. Two problems can be placed on a size A sheet (AV format). Label the views and show the overall dimensions as W, D, and H.

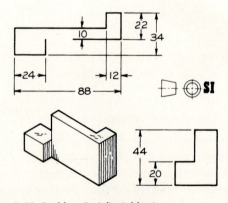

Figure 7.59 Problem 3. Adjustable stop.

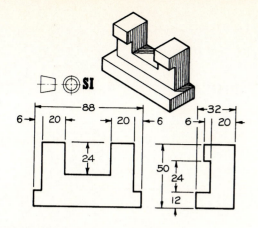

Figure 7.60 Problem 4. Lock catch.

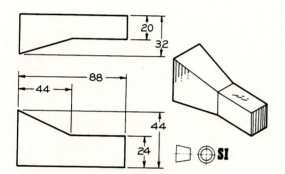

Figure 7.61 Problem 5. Two-way adjuster.

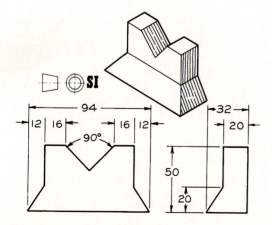

Figure 7.62 Problem 6. 90° Vee block.

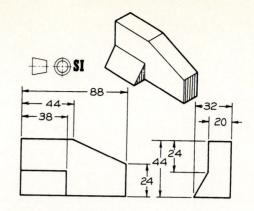

Figure 7.63 Problem 7. Filler.

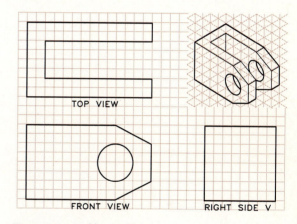

TOP VIEW

FRONT VIEW

RIGHT SIDE V

Figure 7.64 Problem 8. Clevis.

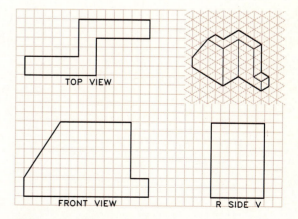

TOP VIEW

FRONT VIEW

R SIDE V

Figure 7.65 Problem 9. Corner box.

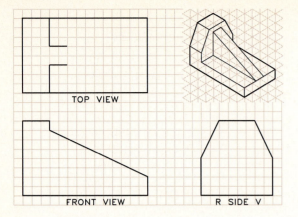

Figure 7.66 Problem 10. Angle block.

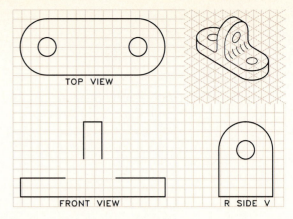

Figure 7.69 Problem 13. Pivot piece.

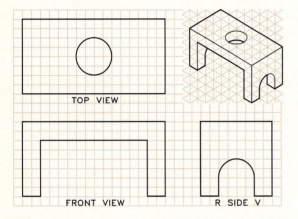

Figure 7.67 Problem 11. Fixture guide.

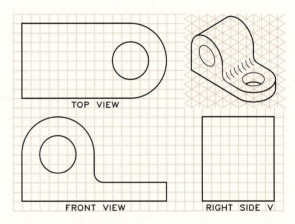

Figure 7.70 Problem 14. Bushing.

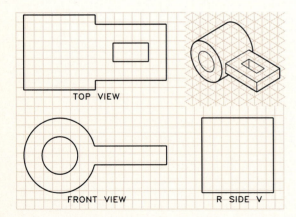

Figure 7.68 Problem 12. Lifting ring.

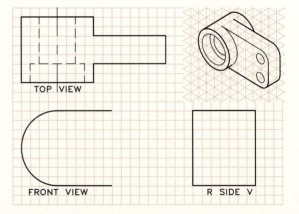

Figure 7.71 Problem 15. Journal.

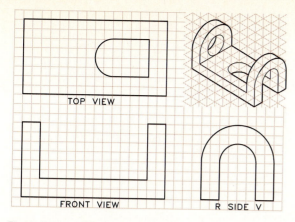

Figure 7.72 Problem 16. End guide.

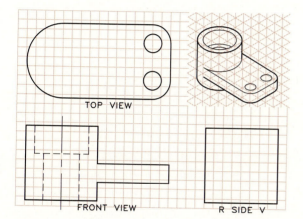

Figure 7.73 Problem 17. Left journal.

Figure 7.74 Problem 18. Tensioner base.

Figure 7.75 Problem 19. Base plate.

18. (Fig. 7.74) Draw three full-size views in millimeters on a size A sheet. The overall dimensions are: height, 120 mm; width, 112 mm; and depth, 56 mm. Estimate the other dimensions.

19. (Fig. 7.75) Draw three full-size views in millimeters on a size A sheet. The overall dimensions are: height, 10 mm; width, 126 mm; and depth, 90 mm. Estimate the other dimensions.

20–45. (Figs. 7.76–7.101) Construct the necessary orthographic views to describe the objects. Label the views and show the overall dimensions of W, D, and H.

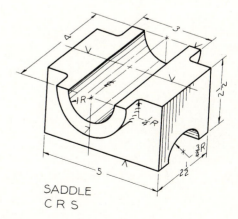

Figure 7.76 Problem 20. Saddle.

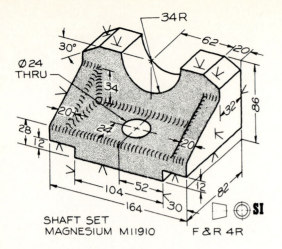

Figure 7.77 Problem 21. Shaft set.

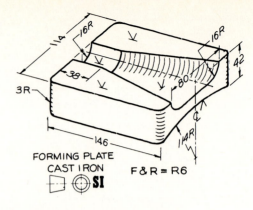

Figure 7.80 Problem 24. Forming plate.

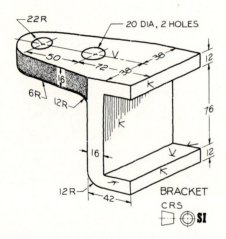

Figure 7.78 Problem 22. Bracket.

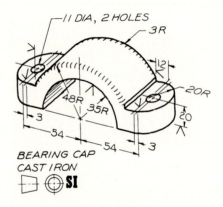

Figure 7.81 Problem 25. Bearing cap.

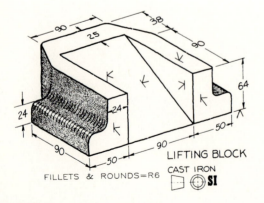

Figure 7.79 Problem 23. Lifting block.

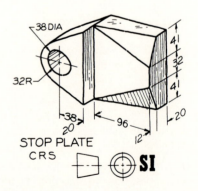

Figure 7.82 Problem 26. Stop plate.

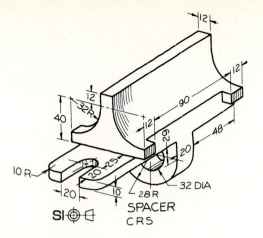

Figure 7.83 Problem 27. Spacer.

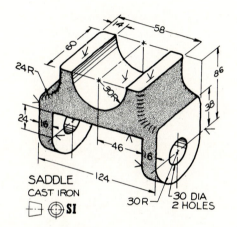

Figure 7.84 Problem 28. Saddle.

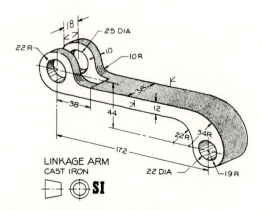

Figure 7.85 Problem 29. Linkage arm.

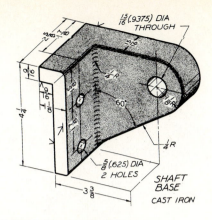

Figure 7.86 Problem 30. Shaft base.

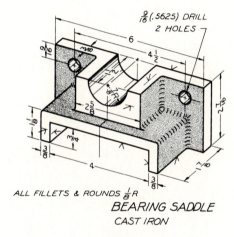

Figure 7.87 Problem 31. Bearing saddle.

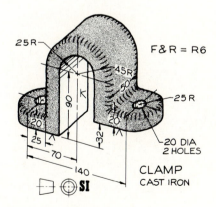

Figure 7.88 Problem 32. Clamp.

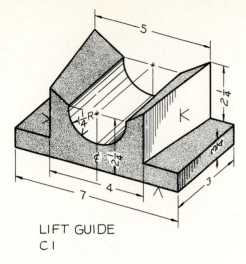

LIFT GUIDE
C I

Figure 7.89 Problem 33. Lift guide.

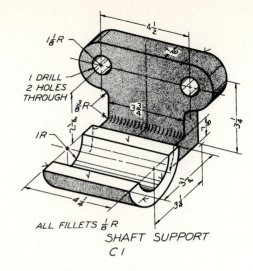

ALL FILLETS $\frac{1}{8}$ R
SHAFT SUPPORT
C I

Figure 7.92 Problem 36. Shaft support.

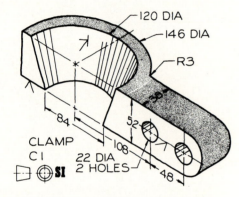

CLAMP
C I
22 DIA
2 HOLES

Figure 7.90 Problem 34. Clamp.

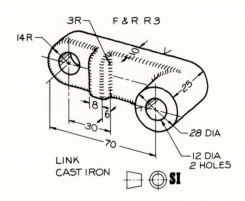

LINK
CAST IRON

Figure 7.93 Problem 37. Link.

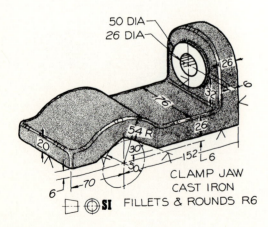

CLAMP JAW
CAST IRON
FILLETS & ROUNDS R6

Figure 7.91 Problem 35. Clamp jaw.

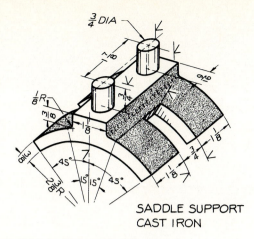

Figure 7.94 Problem 38. Saddle support.

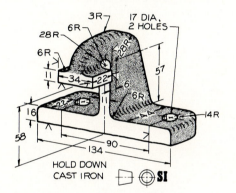

Figure 7.95 Problem 39. Hold down.

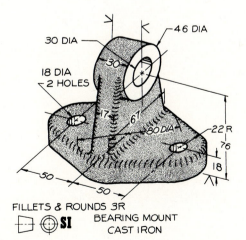

Figure 7.96 Problem 40. Bearing mount.

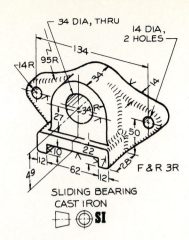

Figure 7.97 Problem 41. Sliding bearing.

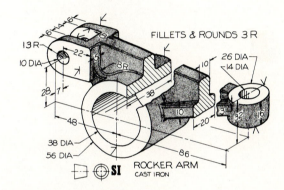

Figure 7.98 Problem 42. Rocker arm.

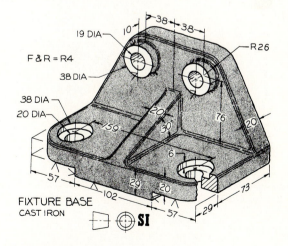

Figure 7.99 Problem 43. Fixture base.

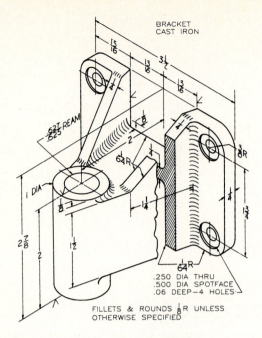

BRACKET
CAST IRON

.637 REAM
.625

64R

64R

1 DIA

2 7/8

2

1 1/2

1 1/4

2

3/8 R

3 1/2

.250 DIA THRU
.500 DIA SPOTFACE
.06 DEEP—4 HOLES

FILLETS & ROUNDS 1/8 R UNLESS
OTHERWISE SPECIFIED

Figure 7.100 Problem 44. Swivel attachment.

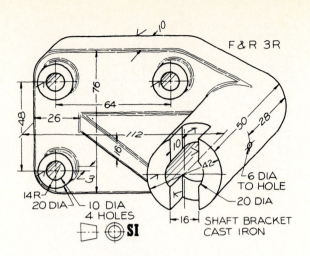

F & R 3R

10

76

64

48

26

112

50

28

16

3

10

42

14R
20 DIA

10 DIA
4 HOLES

SI

6 DIA
TO HOLE

20 DIA

16

SHAFT BRACKET
CAST IRON

Figure 7.101 Problem 45. Shaft bracket.

8

Auxiliary Views

8.1 Introduction

Objects often are designed to have sloping or inclined surfaces that do not appear true size in principal orthographic views. A plane of this type is not parallel to a principal projection plane (horizontal, frontal, or profile) and is therefore a non-principal plane. Its true shape must be projected onto a plane that is parallel to it. This view is called an **auxiliary view**.

An auxiliary view projected from a primary view (principal view) is called a primary auxiliary view. An auxiliary view projected from a primary auxiliary view is a secondary auxiliary view. By the way, get out your dividers; you must use them all the time in drawing auxiliary views.

The inclined surface of the part shown in **Fig. 8.1A** does not appear true size in the top view because it is not parallel to the horizontal projection plane. However, the inclined surface will appear true size in an auxiliary view projected perpendicularly from its edge view in the front view **(Fig. 8.1B)**.

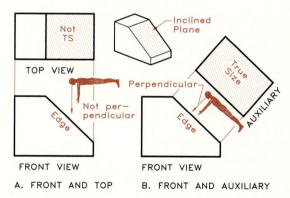

Figure 8.1 A surface that appears as an inclined edge in a principal view can be found true size by an auxiliary view. (A) The top view is foreshortened. (B) The inclined plane is true size in the auxiliary view.

The relationship between an auxiliary view and the view it was projected from is the same as that between any two adjacent orthographic views. **Figure 8.2** shows an auxiliary view pro-

141

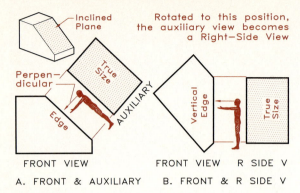

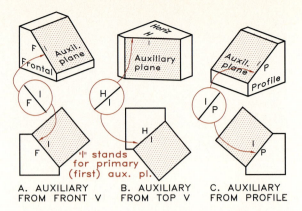

Figure 8.2 An auxiliary view has the same relationship with the view it is projected from as that of any two adjacent principal views.

Figure 8.3 A primary auxiliary plane can be folded from the frontal, horizontal, or profile planes. The fold lines are labeled F–1, H–1, and P–1, with 1 on the auxiliary-plane side and P on the principal-plane side.

jected perpendicularly from the edge view of the sloping surface. By rotating these views (the front and auxiliary views) so that the projectors are horizontal, the views have the same relationship as regular front and right-side views **(Fig. 8.2B)**.

8.2 Folding-Line Theory

The three principal orthographic planes are the **frontal** (F), **horizontal** (H), and **profile** (P) planes. An auxiliary view is projected from a principal orthographic view (a top, front, or side view), and a primary auxiliary plane is perpendicular to one of the principal planes and oblique to the other two.

Think of auxiliary planes as planes that fold into principal planes along a folding line **(Fig. 8.3)**. The plane in **Fig. 8.3A** folds at a 90° angle with the frontal plane and is labeled F–1. F is an abbreviation for frontal, and 1 represents first, or primary, auxiliary plane. **Figures 8.3B** and **8.3C** illustrate the positions for auxiliary planes that fold from the horizontal and profile planes, labeled H–1 and P–1, respectively.

It is important that reference lines be labeled as shown in Fig. 8.3, with the numeral 1 placed on the auxiliary side and the letter H, F, or P on the principal-plane side.

8.3 Auxiliary Views from the Top View

By moving your position about the top view of a part as shown in **Fig. 8.4**, each line of sight is perpendicular to the height dimension. One of the views is a principal view, the front view, while the other positions see nonprincipal views called **auxiliary views**.

Figure 8.5 illustrates how these five views (one of which is a front view) are projected from the top view. The line of sight for each auxiliary view is parallel to the horizontal projection plane; therefore the height dimension is true length in each view projected from a top view.

Folding-Line Method

The inclined plane shown in **Fig. 8.6** is an edge in the top view and is perpendicular to the horizontal plane. If an auxiliary plane is drawn parallel to the inclined surface, the view projected onto it will be a true-size view of the inclined surface. **A surface must appear as an edge in a principal view before it can be found true size in a primary auxiliary view.**

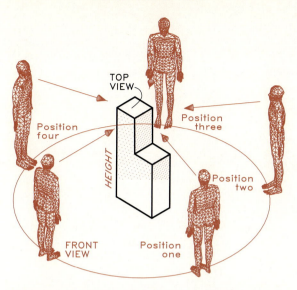

Figure 8.4 By moving your viewpoint around the top view of an object, you will see a series of auxiliary views in which the height dimension (H) is true length.

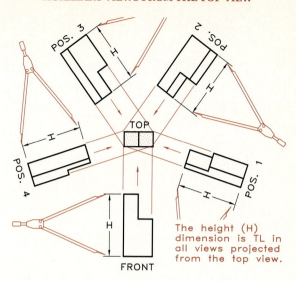

The height (H) dimension is TL in all views projected from the top view.

Figure 8.5 The views shown in Fig. 8.4 would be drawn as shown here with the same height dimensions common to each view.

8.4 Rules of Auxiliary View Construction

The basic rules of drawing auxiliary views are shown in **Fig. 8.7**. **An auxiliary view must be projected perpendicularly from the edge view of the surface to be found true size.** Usually, the inclined surface, or a partial view, is all that is shown in the auxiliary view, but the entire object can be drawn in the auxiliary view if desired, as shown here.

Reference lines (fold lines) should be drawn as thin black lines with a 2H or 3H pencil. Draw the outlines of the auxiliary view as thick visible lines the same as visible lines in principal views, usually with an F or HB pencil. **Construction lines and projectors should be drawn as light gray lines, just dark enough to be seen, with a pencil in the 2H to 4H range.**

Always transfer dimensions from principal views (the front view in this case) perpendicularly from the fold lines to auxiliary views. Use your dividers to transfer these dimensions to the auxil-

iary view. Labeling points with numbers or letters in all views will be helpful. Do your lettering in a professional manner with guidelines.

8.5 Auxiliary Views from the Top View: Application

Figure 8.8 illustrates how the folding-line method is used to find an auxiliary view of a part shown in an imaginary glass box. Because the inclined surface in the top view appears as an edge, it can be found true size in a primary auxiliary view. The height dimension (H) in the frontal plane will be the same as in the auxiliary plane, because both planes are perpendicular to the horizontal plane. In **Fig. 8.9**, the auxiliary plane is rotated about the H–1 fold line into the plane of the top view.

When drawn on a sheet of paper, the views of this object appear as shown in **Fig. 8.10**. The front view is a partial view because the omitted portion would have been hard to draw and would not

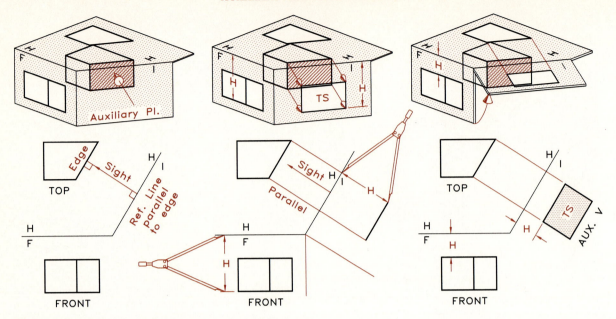

Figure 8.6 Auxiliary view from the top:
Required Find the true-size view of the inclined surface.

Step 1 Draw the line of sight perpendicular to the edge view of the inclined surface. Draw the H–1 line parallel to the edge. Draw the H–F reference line between the top and front views.

Step 2 Project from the edge view of the inclined surface parallel to the line of sight. Transfer the H dimensions from the front view to locate an auxiliary view of a line.

Step 3 Locate the other corners of the inclined surface by projecting to the auxiliary view. Locate the points by transferring the height dimensions (H) from the front view to the auxiliary view.

have been true size. The auxiliary view also is drawn as a partial view because the front view shows the omitted features better.

Reference-Plane Method

A second method of locating an auxiliary view uses **reference planes. Figure 8.11A** shows a horizontal reference plane (HRP) drawn through the center of the front view. Because this view is symmetrical, height dimensions can be conveniently transferred from the front view to the auxiliary view and laid off on both sides of the HRP.

The reference plane can be placed at the base of the front view as shown in **Fig. 8.11B**. In this case, the height dimensions are measured upward

from the HRP in both the front and auxiliary views. You may draw a reference plane (the HRP in this example) in any convenient position in the front view: through the part, above it, or below it.

A similar example of an auxiliary view drawn with a horizontal reference plane is shown in **Fig. 8.12**. In this example, the hole appears as a circle instead of an ellipse.

8.6 Auxiliary Views from the Front View

By moving about the front view of the part as shown in **Fig. 8.13**, you will be looking parallel to the edge view of the frontal plane. Therefore the depth dimension (D) will appear true size in each

RULES FOR DRAWING AUXILIARY VIEWS

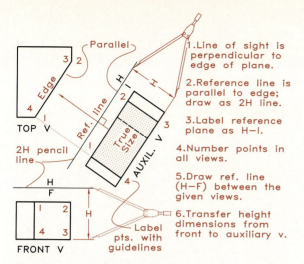

1. Line of sight is perpendicular to edge of plane.

2. Reference line is parallel to edge; draw as 2H line.

3. Label reference plane as H–I.

4. Number points in all views.

5. Draw ref. line (H–F) between the given views.

6. Transfer height dimensions from front to auxiliary v.

Figure 8.7 Apply these rules when drawing auxiliary views. Use thin black lines for reference lines and light gray construction lines (just dark enough to show) for projectors. Use guidelines, label points on the views, and label the fold lines.

VIEW PROJECTED ONTO AUXILIARY PLANE

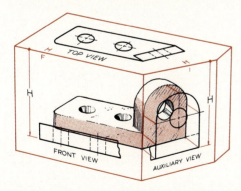

Figure 8.8 By imagining that the object is placed in a glass box, you can see the relationship of the auxiliary projection plane, on which the true-size view is projected, and the horizontal projection plane.

auxiliary view projected from the front view. One of the positions gives a principal view, the right-side view, and position 1 gives a true-size view of

AUXILIARY PLANE ROTATED INTO HORIZONTAL

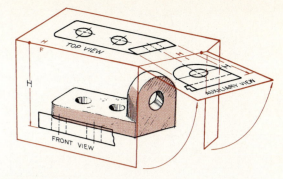

Figure 8.9 Fold the auxiliary plane into the horizontal projection plane by revolving it about the H–1 fold line.

DRAWING THE AUXILIARY VIEW

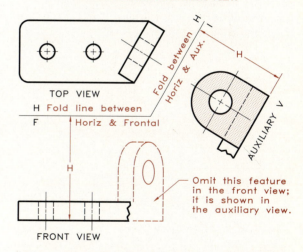

Omit this feature in the front view; it is shown in the auxiliary view.

Figure 8.10 When the views of the object are drawn, they are laid out in this arrangement. The front view is drawn as a partial view because the omitted elliptical features are shown better as a true-size view in the auxiliary view.

the inclined plane. **Figure 8.14** illustrates the relationship between the auxiliary views projected from the front view.

Folding-Line Method

A plane of an object that appears as an edge in the front view (**Fig. 8.15**) is true size in an auxiliary

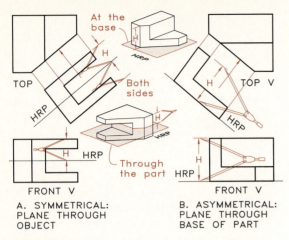

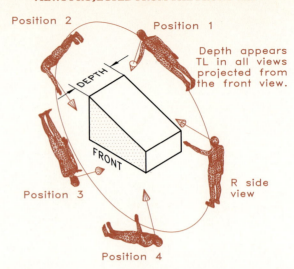

Figure 8.11 A horizontal reference plane (HRP) can be positioned through the part or in contact with it. The dimension of height (H) is measured from the HRP and transferred to the auxiliary view.

Figure 8.13 By moving your viewpoint around the frontal view of an object, you will see a series of auxiliary views in which the depth dimension (D) is true length.

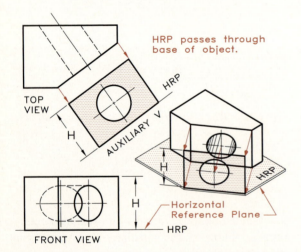

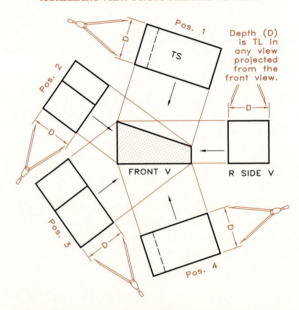

Figure 8.12 An auxiliary view projected from the top view is used to draw a true-size view of the inclined surface using a horizontal reference plane. The HRP is drawn through the bottom of the front view.

Figure 8.14 The auxiliary views shown in Fig. 8.13 would be seen in this arrangement when viewing the front view.

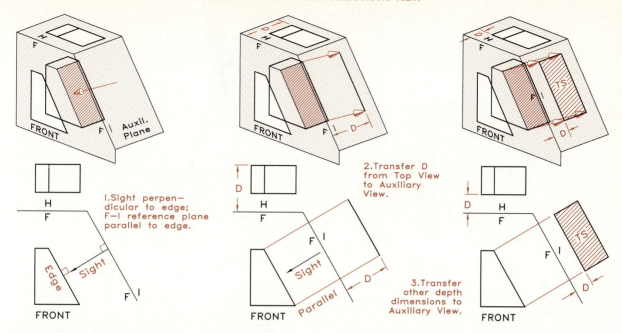

Figure 8.15 Auxiliary from the front—folding-line method:

Step 1 Draw the line of sight perpendicular to the edge of the plane and draw the F–1 reference parallel to the edge. Draw the H–F fold line between the top and front views.

Step 2 Project perpendicularly from the edge view of the inclined surface and parallel to the line of sight. Use the depth dimensions (D) transferred from the top view to locate a line in the auxiliary view.

Step 3 Locate the other corners of the inclined surface by projecting to the auxiliary view. Locate the points by transferring the depth dimensions (D) from the top to the auxiliary view.

view projected perpendicularly from it. Draw fold line F–1 parallel to the edge view of the inclined plane in the front view at a convenient location.

Draw the line of sight perpendicular to the edge view of the inclined plane in the front view. Observed from this direction, the frontal plane appears as an edge; therefore measurements perpendicular to the frontal plane—depth dimensions (D)—will be seen true length. Transfer depth dimensions from the top view to the auxiliary view with your dividers.

The object in **Fig. 8.16** is imagined to be enclosed in a glass box and an auxiliary plane is folded from the frontal plane to be parallel to the

inclined surface. When drawn on a sheet of paper, the views appear as shown in **Fig. 8.17**. The top and side views are drawn as partial views because the auxiliary view eliminates the need for complete views. The auxiliary view, located by transferring the depth dimension measured perpendicularly from the edge view of the frontal plane in the top view and transferred to the auxiliary view, shows the surface's true size.

Reference-Plane Method

The object shown in **Fig. 8.18** has an inclined surface that appears as an edge in the front view;

AUXILIARY VIEW IN 3D

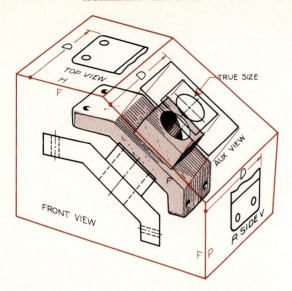

Figure 8.16 This object is shown in an imaginary glass box to illustrate the relationship of the auxiliary plane, on which the true-size view of the inclined surface is projected, with the principal planes.

AUXILIARY VIEW FROM THE FRONT VIEW

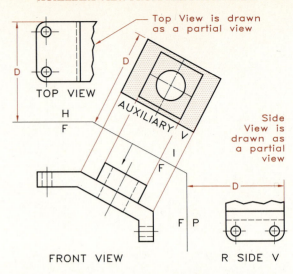

Figure 8.17 The layout and construction of an auxiliary view of the object shown in Fig. 8.16 is shown here.

AUXILIARY VIEW BY FRONTAL REFERENCE-PLANE METHOD

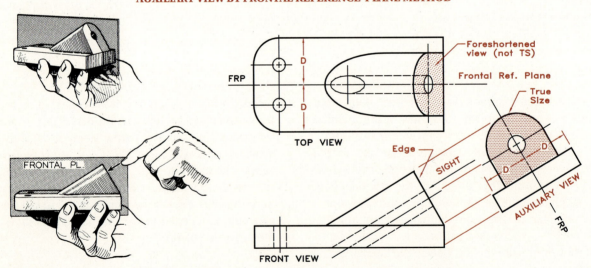

Figure 8.18 Because the inclined surface of this part is symmetrical, it is helpful to use a frontal reference plane (FRP) that passes through the object. Project the auxiliary view perpendicularly from the edge view of the plane in the front view. The FRP appears as an edge in the auxiliary view, and depth dimensions (D) are transferred from each side of it in the top view to locate points on the true-size view of the inclined surface.

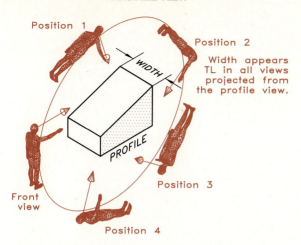

Figure 8.19 By moving your viewpoint around a profile (side) view of an object, you will obtain a series of auxiliary views in which the width dimension (W) is true length.

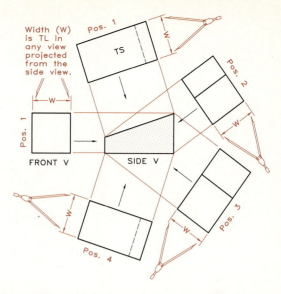

Figure 8.20 The auxiliary views shown in Fig. 8.19 would be seen in this arrangement when projected from the side view.

therefore this plane can be found true size in a primary auxiliary view. It is helpful to draw a reference plane through the center of the symmetrical top view because all depth dimensions can be located on each side of the frontal reference plane. Because the reference plane is a frontal plane, it is labeled FRP in the top and auxiliary views. In the auxiliary view, the FRP is drawn parallel to the edge view of the inclined plane at a convenient distance from it. By transferring depth dimensions from the FRP in the top view to the FRP in the auxiliary view, the symmetrical view of the part is drawn.

8.7 Auxiliary Views from the Profile View

By moving your position about the profile view (side view) of the part as shown in **Fig. 8.19**, you will be looking parallel to the edge view of the profile plane. Therefore, the width dimension will appear true size in each auxiliary view projected

from the side view. One of the positions gives a principal view, the front view, and position 1 gives a true-size view of the inclined plane. **Figure 8.20** illustrates the arrangement of the auxiliary views projected from the side view if they were drawn on a sheet of paper.

Folding-Line Method

Because the inclined surface in **Fig. 8.21** appears as an edge in the profile plane, it can be found true size in a primary auxiliary view projected from the side view. The auxiliary fold line, P–1, is drawn parallel to the edge view of the inclined surface. A line of sight perpendicular to the auxiliary plane shows the profile plane as an edge. Therefore width dimensions (W) transferred from the front view to the auxiliary view appear true length in the auxiliary view.

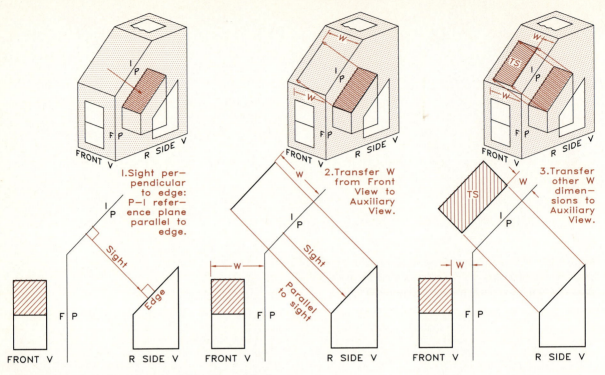

Figure 8.21 Auxiliary from the side—folding-line method:

Step 1 Draw a line of sight perpendicular to the edge view of the inclined surface. Draw the P–1 fold line parallel to the edge view, and draw the F–P fold line between the given views.

Step 2 Project the corners of the edge view parallel to the line of sight. Transfer the W dimensions from the front view to locate a line in the auxiliary view.

Step 3 Find the other corners of the inclined surface by projecting to the auxiliary view. Locate the points by transferring the width dimensions (W) from the front view to the auxiliary view.

Reference-Plane Method

The object shown in **Fig. 8.22** has an inclined surface that appears as an edge in the right-side view, the profile view. This inclined surface may be drawn true size in an auxiliary view by using a profile reference plane (PRP) that is a vertical edge in the front view. Draw the PRP through the center of the front view because the view is symmetrical. Then find the true-size view of the inclined plane by transferring equal width dimensions (W) with your dividers from the edge view

of the PRP in the front view to both sides of the PRP zin the auxiliary view.

8.8 Auxiliary Views of Curved Shapes

The cylinder shown in **Fig. 8.23** has an inclined surface that appears as an edge in the front view. The true-size view of this plane can be seen in an auxiliary view projected from the front view.

Because the cylinder is symmetrical, a frontal reference plane (FRP) is drawn through the center

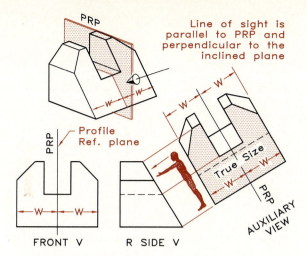

Figure 8.22 An auxiliary view is projected from the right-side view by using a profile reference plane (PRP) to show the true-size view of the inclined surface.

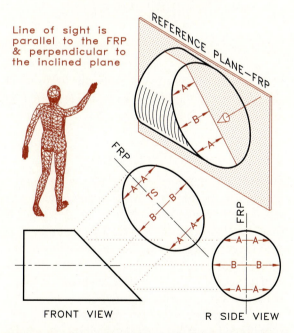

Figure 8.23 The auxiliary view of this elliptical surface was found by locating a series of points about its perimeter. The frontal reference plane (FRP) is drawn through its center in the side view since the object is symmetrical.

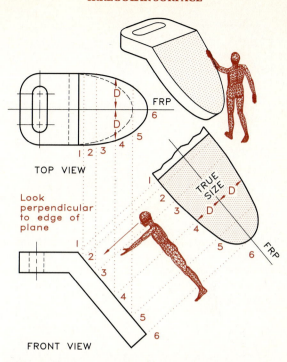

Figure 8.24 The auxiliary view of this curved surface required that a series of points be located in the top view, be projected to the front view, and then projected to the auxiliary view. The FRP was passed through the top view.

of the side view so that equal dimensions can be laid off easily on both sides of it. Points located about the circular right-side view are projected to the edge view of the surface in the front view.

In the auxiliary view, the FRP is drawn parallel to the edge view of the plane in the front view, and the points are projected perpendicularly from the edge view of the plane. Dimensions A and B are shown as examples of depth dimensions used for locating points in the auxiliary view. To construct a smooth elliptical curve, more points than shown are needed.

A true-size auxiliary view of a surface bounded by an irregular curve is shown in **Fig. 8.24**. Project points from the curve in the top view to the front view. Locate these points in the auxiliary view by

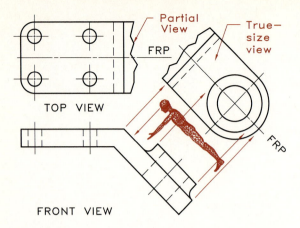

Figure 8.25 Partial views with foreshortened portions omitted can be used to represent objects. The FRP reference line is drawn through the center of the object in the top view because the object is symmetrical to make point location easier.

transferring depth dimensions (D) from the FRP in the top view to the auxiliary view.

8.9 Partial Views

Auxiliary views are used as supplementary views to clarify features that are difficult to depict with principal views alone. Consequently, portions of principal views and auxiliary views may be omitted, provided that the partial views adequately describe the part. The object shown in **Fig. 8.25** is composed of a complete front view, a partial auxiliary view, and a partial top view. These partial views are easier to draw and are more descriptive without sacrificing clarity.

8.10 Auxiliary Sections

In **Fig. 8.26**, a cutting plane labeled A–A is passed through the part to obtain the auxiliary section labeled section A–A. The auxiliary section provides

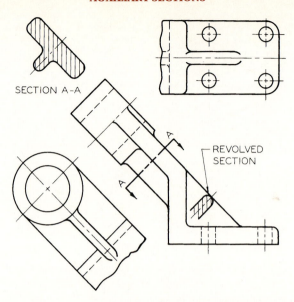

Figure 8.26 A cutting plane labeled A–A is passed through the object and the auxiliary section, section A–A, is drawn as a supplementary view to describe the part. The top and front views are drawn as partial views.

a good and efficient way to describe features of the part that could not be as easily described by additional principal views.

8.11 Secondary Auxiliary Views

Figure 8.27 shows how to project a secondary auxiliary view from a primary auxiliary view. An edge view of the oblique plane is found in the primary auxiliary view by finding the point view of a true-length line (2–3) that lies on the oblique surface. A line of sight perpendicular to the edge view of the plane gives a secondary auxiliary view that shows the oblique plane as true size.

Note that the reference line between the primary auxiliary view and the secondary auxiliary view is labeled 1–2 to represent the fold line between the primary plane (1) and the secondary

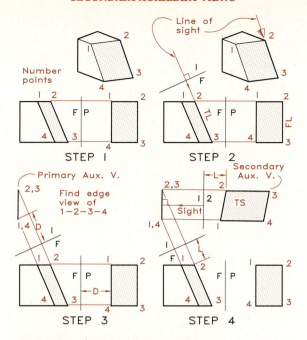

Figure 8.27 Secondary auxiliary views:

Step 1 Draw a fold line F–P between the front and side views. Label the corner points in both views.

Step 2 Line 2–3 is a true-length frontal line in the front view. Draw reference line F–1 perpendicular to line 2–3 at a convenient location with a line of sight parallel to line 2–3.

Step 3 Find the edge view of plane 1–2–3–4 by transferring depth dimensions (D) from the side view.

Step 4 Draw a line of sight perpendicular to the edge view of 1–2–3–4 and draw the 1–2 fold line parallel to the edge view. Find the true-size auxiliary view by transferring the dimensions (L) from the front view to the auxiliary view.

plane (2). The 1 label is placed on the primary side and the 2 label is placed on the secondary side.

Figure 8.28 illustrates the construction of a secondary auxiliary view that gives the true-size view of a surface on a part using these same principles and a combination of partial views. A secondary auxiliary view must be used in this case

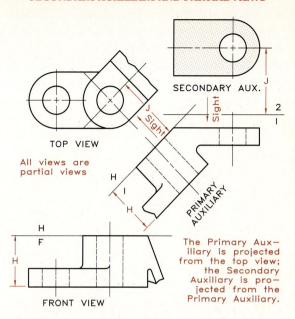

Figure 8.28 A secondary auxiliary view projected from a primary auxiliary view that was projected from the top view is shown here. All views are drawn as partial views.

because the oblique plane does not appear as an edge in a principal view.

Find the point view of a line on the oblique plane to find the edge view of the plane in the primary auxiliary view. The secondary auxiliary view, projected perpendicularly from the edge view of the plane in the primary auxiliary view, gives a true-size view of the plane. In this example all of the views are drawn as partial views.

8.12 Elliptical Features

Occasionally, circular shapes will project as ellipses, which must be drawn with an irregular curve or an ellipse template. The ellipse template (guide) is by far the most convenient method of drawing ellipses. The angle of the ellipse template is the angle the line of sight makes with the edge view of the circular feature. In **Fig. 8.29** the angle is found to be 45° where the curve is an edge in the front view, so the right-side view of the curve is drawn as a 45° ellipse.

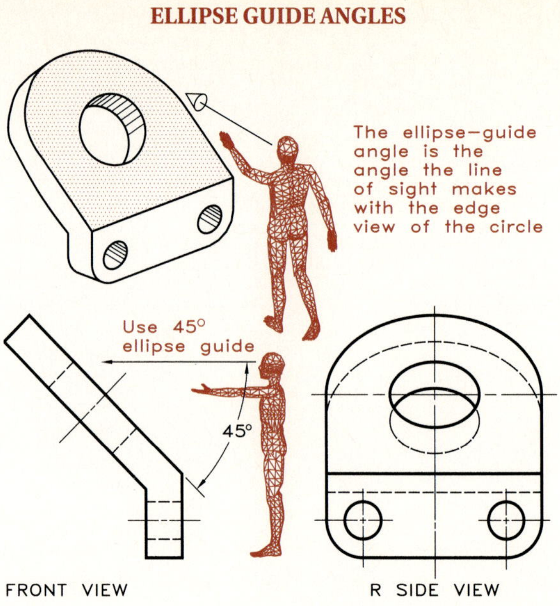

ELLIPSE GUIDE ANGLES

The ellipse–guide angle is the angle the line of sight makes with the edge view of the circle

Use 45° ellipse guide

45°

FRONT VIEW

R SIDE VIEW

Figure 8.29 The ellipse guide angle is the angle that the line of sight makes with the edge view of the circular feature. The ellipse angle for the right-side view is 45°.

Problems

Solve the following problems on size A or size B sheets, as assigned by your instructor.

1–13. (Fig. 8.30) Using the example layout, change the top and front views by substituting the top views given at the right in place of the one given in the example. The angle of inclination in the front view is 45° for all problems, and the height is 38 mm (1.5 inches) in the front view. Construct auxiliary views that show the inclined surface true size. Draw two problems per size A sheet.

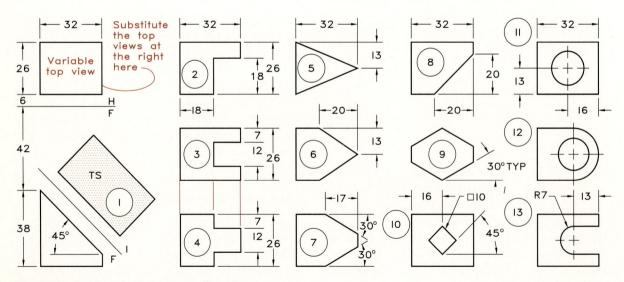

Figure 8.30 Problems 1–13. Primary auxiliary views.

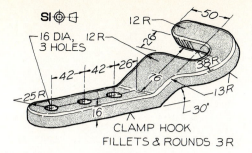

Figure 8.31 Problem 14. Clamp hook.

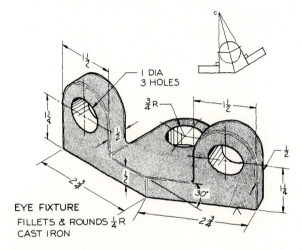

EYE FIXTURE
FILLETS & ROUNDS $\frac{1}{4}$ R
CAST IRON

Figure 8.32 Problem 15. Eye fixture.

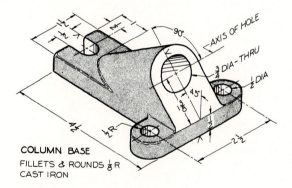

COLUMN BASE
FILLETS & ROUNDS $\frac{1}{8}$ R
CAST IRON

Figure 8.33 Problem 16. Column base.

14–29. (Figs. 8.31–8.46) Draw the necessary primary and auxiliary views to describe the parts shown. Draw one per size A or size B sheet, as assigned. Adjust the scale of each to fit the space on the sheet.

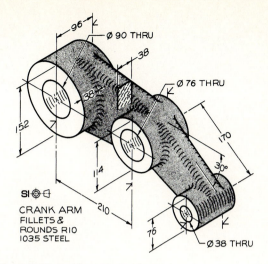

CRANK ARM
FILLETS &
ROUNDS R10
1035 STEEL

Figure 8.34 Problem 17. Crank arm.

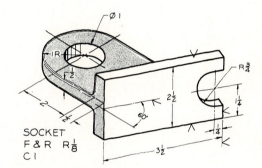

SOCKET
F & R R$\frac{1}{8}$
C I

Figure 8.35 Problem 18. Socket.

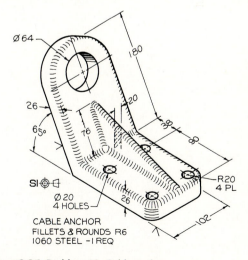

CABLE ANCHOR
FILLETS & ROUNDS R6
1060 STEEL –I REQ

Figure 8.36 Problem 19. Cable anchor.

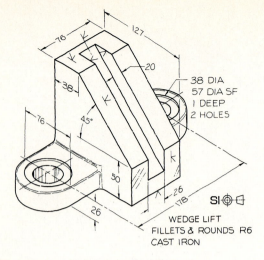

Figure 8.37 Problem 20. Wedge lift.

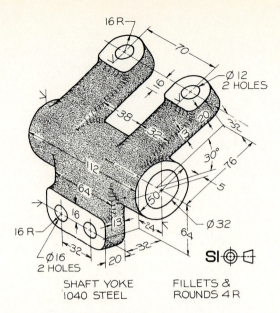

Figure 8.39 Problem 22. Shaft yoke.

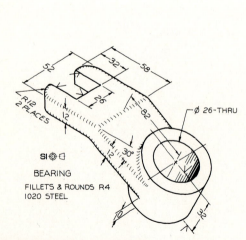

Figure 8.38 Problem 21. Bearing.

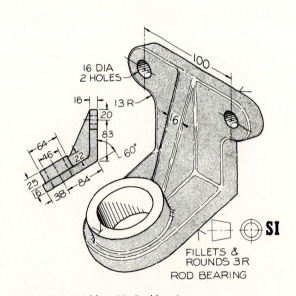

Figure 8.40 Problem 23. Rod bearing.

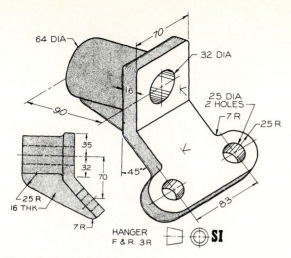

Figure 8.41 Problem 24. Hanger.

64 DIA
70
32 DIA
16
90
25 DIA
2 HOLES
7 R
25 R
45°
83
35
32
70
25 R
16 THK
7 R
HANGER
F & R 3R

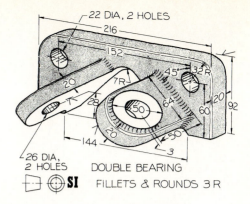

Figure 8.44 Problem 27. Double bearing.

22 DIA, 2 HOLES
216
152
45°
32 R
20
7 R
28
50
64
20
20
60
92
50
26 DIA,
2 HOLES
144
3
DOUBLE BEARING
FILLETS & ROUNDS 3 R
SI

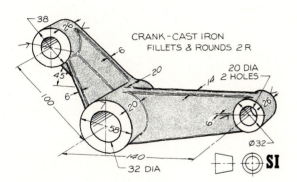

Figure 8.42 Problem 25. Crank.

38
26
6
CRANK - CAST IRON
FILLETS & ROUNDS 2 R
45°
20
14
20 DIA
2 HOLES
6
100
20
26
58
6
Ø32
140
32 DIA
SI

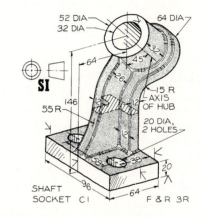

Figure 8.45 Problem 28. Shaft socket.

52 DIA
64 DIA
32 DIA
32
45°
64
26
15 R
AXIS
OF HUB
146
12
55R
12
20 DIA,
2 HOLES
38
20
SHAFT
SOCKET CI
96
64
F & R 3R
SI

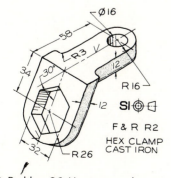

Figure 8.43 Problem 26. Hexagon angle.

Ø16
58
R3
34
30°
12
R 16
12
SI
F & R R2
HEX CLAMP
CAST IRON
32
R 26

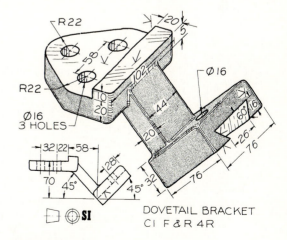

Figure 8.46 Problem 29. Dovetail bracket.

R22
20
5
58
102
Ø16
R22
10
20
44
Ø16
3 HOLES
20
60° 16
32 22 58
28
26
76
70 45°
45°
32
76
DOVETAIL BRACKET
CI F & R 4R
SI

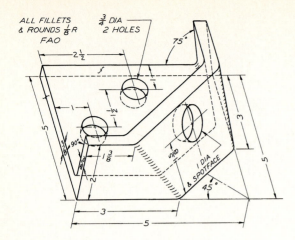

Figure 8.47 Problem 30. Corner bracket.

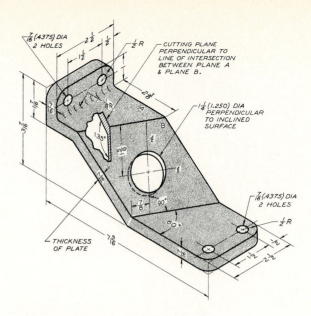

Figure 8.48 Problem 31. Oblique bracket.

30. (Fig. 8.47) Lay out these orthographic views on size B sheets, and complete the auxiliary and primary views.

31. (Fig. 8.48) Construct orthographic views of the given object, and using secondary auxiliary views, draw auxiliary views that give the true-size views of the inclined surfaces. Draw one per size B sheet.

9

Sections

9.1 Introduction

Correctly drawn orthographic views that show all hidden lines may not clearly describe an object's internal details. This shortcoming can be overcome by imagining that part of the object has been cut away and shown in a cross-sectional view, called a **section**.

9.2 Basics of Sectioning

Figure 9.1 shows pictorially a section created by passing an imaginary cutting plane through the object to reveal its internal features. Think of the cutting plane as a knife-edge cutting through the object. **Figure 9.1A** shows the standard top and front views, and **Fig. 9.1B** shows the method of drawing a section. The front view is full section, with the portion cut by the imaginary plane cross-hatched. Hidden lines usually are omitted because they are not needed.

    Figure 9.2 shows two types of cutting planes. Either is acceptable although the one with pairs of

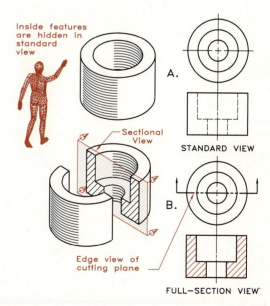

Inside features are hidden in standard view

A.

STANDARD VIEW

Sectional View

B.

Edge view of cutting plane

FULL–SECTION VIEW

Figure 9.1 This drawing compares a standard orthographic view with a full-section view that shows the internal features of the same object.

CUTTING-PLANE LINES

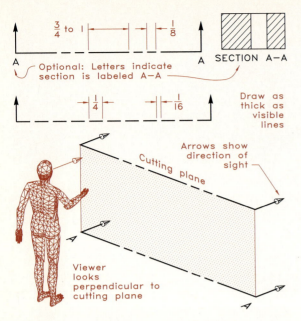

Figure 9.2 Use cutting-plane lines to represent sections (the cutting edge). The cutting plane marked A–A produces a section labeled A–A.

CUTTING-PLANE POSITIONS

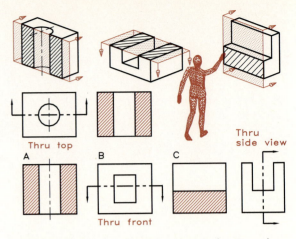

Figure 9.3 The three standard positions of cutting planes through orthographic (A) top, (B) front, and (C) side sectional views as sections. The arrows point in the direction of your line of sight for each section.

short dashes is most often used. The spacing and proportions of the dashes depend on the size of the drawing. The line thickness of the cutting plane is the same as the visible object line. Letters placed at each end of the cutting plane are used to label the sectional view, such as section A–A.

The sight arrows at the ends of the cutting plane are always perpendicular to the cutting plane. In the sectional view, the observer is looking in the direction of the sight arrows, perpendicular to the surface of the cutting plane.

Figure 9.3 shows the three basic positions of sections and their respective cutting planes. In each case perpendicular arrows point in the direction of the line of sight. For example, the cutting plane in **Fig. 9.3A** passes through and removes the front of the top view and the line of sight is perpendicular to the remainder of the top view.

The top view appears as a section when the cutting plane passes through the front view and the line of sight is downward (**Fig. 9.3B**). When the cutting plane passes vertically through the side view (**Fig. 9.3C**), the front view becomes a section.

9.3 Sectioning Symbols

Figure 9.4 shows the hatching symbols used to distinguish between different materials in sections. Although these symbols may be used to indicate the materials in a section, you should provide supplementary notes specifying the materials to ensure clarity.

The cast-iron symbol (evenly spaced section lines) may be used to represent any material and is the symbol used most often. Draw cast-iron symbols with a 2H pencil, slant the lines upward at 30°, 45°, or 60° angles, and space the lines about 1/16 inch apart (close together in small areas and farther apart in larger areas).

STANDARD HATCHING SYMBOLS

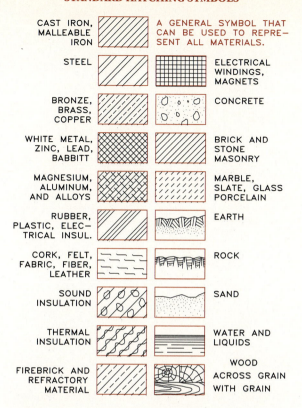

CAST IRON, MALLEABLE IRON		A GENERAL SYMBOL THAT CAN BE USED TO REPRESENT ALL MATERIALS.	
STEEL			ELECTRICAL WINDINGS, MAGNETS
BRONZE, BRASS, COPPER			CONCRETE
WHITE METAL, ZINC, LEAD, BABBITT			BRICK AND STONE MASONRY
MAGNESIUM, ALUMINUM, AND ALLOYS			MARBLE, SLATE, GLASS PORCELAIN
RUBBER, PLASTIC, ELECTRICAL INSUL.			EARTH
CORK, FELT, FABRIC, FIBER, LEATHER			ROCK
SOUND INSULATION			SAND
THERMAL INSULATION			WATER AND LIQUIDS
FIREBRICK AND REFRACTORY MATERIAL			WOOD ACROSS GRAIN WITH GRAIN

Figure 9.4 Use these symbols for hatching parts in section. The cast-iron symbol may be used for any material.

LARGE AND THIN PARTS IN SECTION

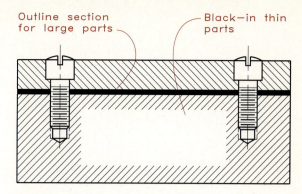

Outline section for large parts

Black—in thin parts

Figure 9.6 Black in thin parts and hatch large areas around their outlines (outline sectioning) to save time and effort.

HATCH-LINE ANGLES

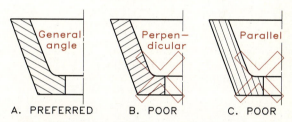

General angle

Perpendicular

Parallel

A. PREFERRED   B. POOR   C. POOR

Figure 9.7 Draw section lines at angles that are neither parallel nor perpendicular to the outline of a part, so that they are not misunderstood as machining features.

SECTION-LINE SPACING

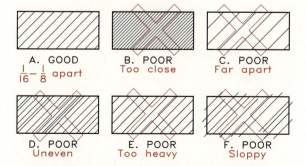

A. GOOD
$\frac{1}{16} - \frac{1}{8}$ apart

B. POOR
Too close

C. POOR
Far apart

D. POOR
Uneven

E. POOR
Too heavy

F. POOR
Sloppy

Figure 9.5 Techniques:
A Section lines are thin lines drawn $\frac{1}{16}$ to $\frac{1}{8}$ in. apart.
B–F Avoid these typical section lining errors.

Figure 9.5A shows properly drawn section lines: thin and evenly spaced. **Figures 9.5B–F** show common errors of section lining.

Section thin parts such as sheet metal, washers, and gaskets by completely blacking in the areas **(Fig. 9.6),** because space does not permit the drawing of section lines. Show large parts with an outline section to save time and effort.

You should hatch sectioned areas with symbols that are neither parallel nor perpendicular to the outlines of the parts lest they be confused with serrations or other machining treatments of the surface **(Fig. 9.7).**

ASSEMBLIES IN SECTION

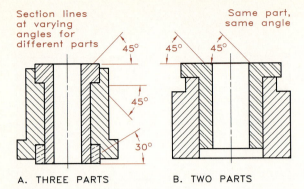

Section lines at varying angles for different parts

Same part, same angle

A. THREE PARTS   B. TWO PARTS

Figure 9.8 Hatching assemblies:
A Draw section lines of different parts in an assembly at varying angles to distinguish the parts.

B Draw section lines on separated portions of the same part (both sides of a hole here) in the same direction.

FULL SECTION

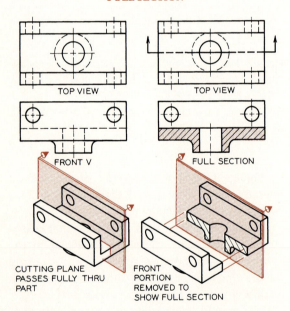

TOP VIEW   TOP VIEW

FRONT V   FULL SECTION

CUTTING PLANE PASSES FULLY THRU PART

FRONT PORTION REMOVED TO SHOW FULL SECTION

Figure 9.9 A full section is found by passing a cutting plane fully through the top view of this part, removing half of it. The arrows at each end of the cutting plane indicate the direction of your sight. The sectional view shows the part's internal features clearly.

FULL SECTION: CYLINDRICAL PART

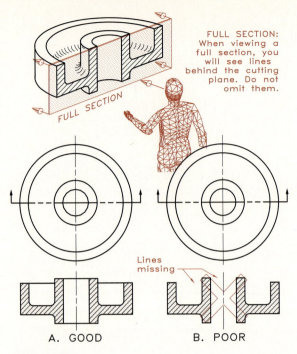

FULL SECTION

FULL SECTION: When viewing a full section, you will see lines behind the cutting plane. Do not omit them.

Lines missing

A. GOOD   B. POOR

Figure 9.10
A When a cutting plane is passed through a cylinder to obtain a full section, you will see lines behind the plane, not just the cut surface.

B Showing only the lines at the cutting plane's surface yields an incomplete view.

9.4 Sectioning Assemblies of Parts

When sectioning an assembly of several parts, draw section lines at varying angles to distinguish the parts from each other (**Fig. 9.8A**). Using different material symbols in an assembly also helps distinguish between the parts and their materials. Cross-hatch the same part at the same angle and with the same symbol even though portions of the part may be separated (**Fig. 9.8B**).

9.5 Full Sections

Passing a cutting plane fully through an object and removing half of it forms a full section view.

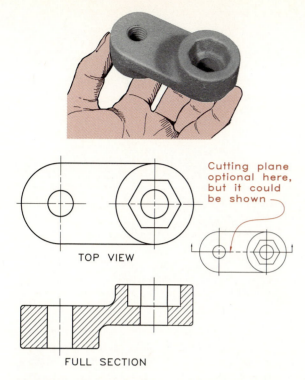

Cutting plane optional here, but it could be shown

TOP VIEW

FULL SECTION

Figure 9.11 The cutting plane of a section can be omitted if its location is obvious.

Figure 9.9 shows two orthographic views of an object with all its hidden lines. We can describe the part better by passing a cutting plane through the top view to remove half of it. The arrows on the cutting plane indicate the direction of sight. The front view becomes a full section, showing the surfaces cut by the cutting plane.

    Figure 9.10 shows a full section through a cylindrical part, with half the object removed. **Figure 9.10A** shows the correctly drawn sectional view. A common mistake in constructing sections is omitting the visible lines behind the cutting plane (**Fig. 9.10B**).

    Omit hidden lines in sectional views unless you consider them necessary for a clear understanding of the view. Also, omit cutting planes if you consid-

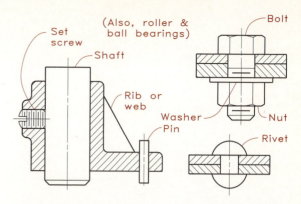

Figure 9.12 By conventional practice these parts are not section lined even though cutting planes pass through them.

er them unnecessary. **Figure 9.11** shows a full section of a part from which the cutting plane was omitted because its path is obvious.

Parts Not Requiring Section Lining

Many standard parts, such as nuts and bolts, rivets, shafts, and set screws, do not require section lining even though the cutting plane passes through them (**Fig. 9.12**). These parts have no internal features, so sections through them would be of no value. Other parts not requiring section lining are roller bearings, ball bearings, gear teeth, dowels, pins, and washers.

Ribs

Ribs are not section lined when the cutting plane passes flatwise through them (**Fig. 9.13A**), because to do so would give a misleading impression of the rib. But ribs do require section lining when the cutting plane passes perpendicularly through them and shows their true thickness (**Fig. 9.13B**).

    Figure 9.14 shows an alternative method of section lining webs and ribs. The outside ribs in **Fig. 9.14A** do not require section lining because the cutting plane passes flatwise through them and they are well identified. As a rule, webs do not

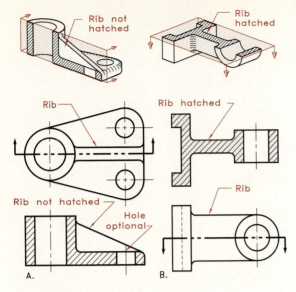

Figure 9.13

A Do not hatch a rib cut in a flatwise direction.

B Hatch ribs when cutting planes pass through them, showing their true thickness.

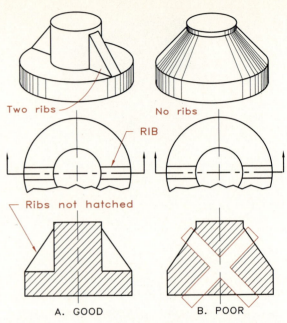

Figure 9.15 In this case (A) the ribs are not hatched to better describe the part than by (B) hatching them. When you use partial views to save space for drawing sections, remove the portion from the side adjacent to the section.

RIBS AND WEBS IN SECTION

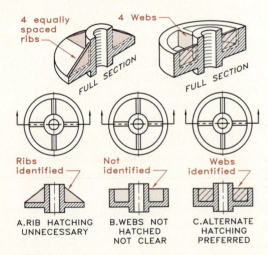

Figure 9.14

A You need not hatch well-defined outside ribs in section.

B Define poorly identified webs by (C) using alternate hatching to call attention to them.

require cross-hatching, but the webs shown in **Fig. 9.14B** are not well identified in the front section and could go unnoticed. Therefore using alternate section lines as shown in **Fig. 9.14C** is better. Here, extending every-other section line through the webs ensures that they can be identified easily.

By not section lining the ribs in **Fig. 9.15A** we provided an effective section view of the part. If we had section lined the ribs, the section would give the impression that the part is solid and conical (**Fig. 9.15B**).

9.6 Half Sections

A half section is a view obtained by passing a cutting plane halfway through an object and removing a quarter of it to show both external and internal features. Half sections are used with

HALF SECTION

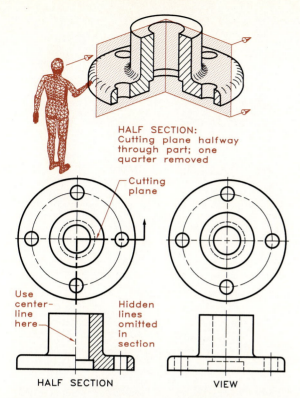

HALF SECTION:
Cutting plane halfway through part; one quarter removed

Cutting plane

Use center-line here

Hidden lines omitted in section

HALF SECTION

VIEW

Figure 9.16 In a half section the cutting plane passes halfway through the object, removing a quarter of it, to show half the outside and half the inside of the object. Omit hidden lines unless you need them to clarify the view.

symmetrical parts and with cylinders, in particular, as shown in **Fig. 9.16**. By comparing the half section with the standard front view, you can see that both internal and external features show more clearly in a half section than in a view. Hidden lines are unnecessary, and we've omitted them to simplify the section. **Figure 9.17** shows a half section of a pulley.

Note omission of the cutting plane from the half section shown in **Fig. 9.18** because the cutting plane's location is obvious. **Because the parting line of the half section is not at a centerline, you may use a solid line or a centerline to separate**

HALF SECTION: PULLEY

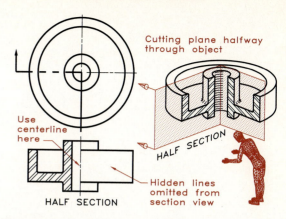

Cutting plane halfway through object

Use centerline here

HALF SECTION

Hidden lines omitted from section view

HALF SECTION

Figure 9.17 This half section describes the part that is shown orthographically and pictorially.

HALF SECTION

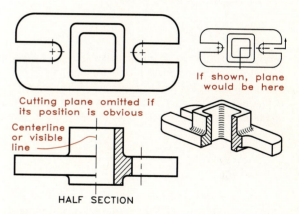

If shown, plane would be here

Cutting plane omitted if its position is obvious

Centerline or visible line

HALF SECTION

Figure 9.18 The cutting plane can be omitted when its location is obvious. The parting line between the section and the view may be a visible line or a centerline if the part is not cylindrical.

the sectional half from the half that appears as an external view.

9.7 Half Views

Figure 9.19 shows **half views**, or conventional methods of representing symmetrical views that

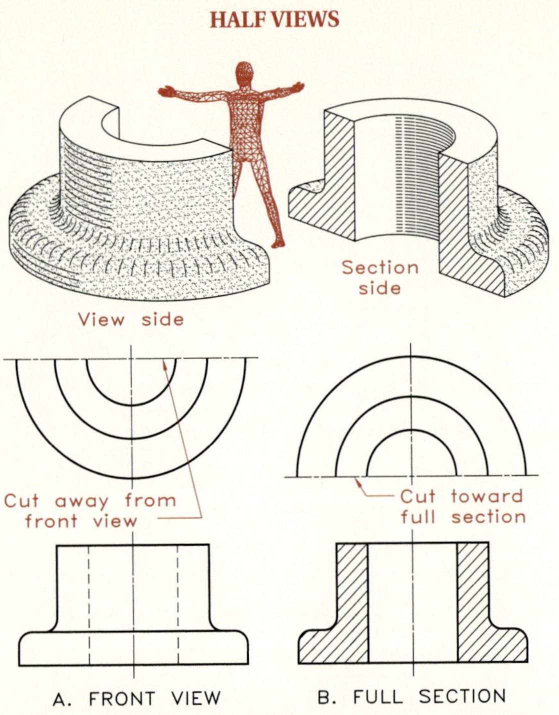

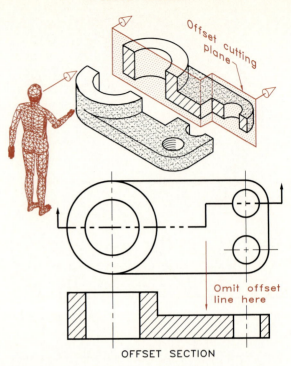

Figure 9.19 Half views of symmetrical objects can be used
to conserve space and drawing time. (A) The omitted portion of the view is away from the front view. (B) The omitted portion of the top view is adjacent to the section. In
half sections, the omitted half view may be either adjacent
to or away from the section.

Figure 9.20 An offset section is formed by a cutting plane
that must be offset to pass through features not in a single
plane. Here, the offset cutting plane is drawn in the top
view and the front view is drawn as an offset section.

require less space and less time to draw than full
views. A half top view is sufficient when drawn
adjacent to the section view or front view. For half
views (not sections), the removed half is the half
away from the adjacent view **(Fig. 9.19A)**. For full
sections, the removed half is the half nearest the
section **(Fig. 9.19B)**. When drawing partial views
with half sections, you may omit either the near or
the far halves of the partial views.

9.8 Offset Sections

An **offset section** is a full section in which the cutting plane is offset to pass through important features that do not lie in a single plane. **Figure 9.20**

shows an offset section in which the plane is offset to
pass through the large hole and one of the small holes.
The cut formed by the offset is not shown in the section
because it is imaginary.

9.9 Broken-Out Sections

A **broken-out section** shows a partial view of a
part's interior features. The broken-out section of
the part shown in **Fig. 9.21** reveals details of the
wall thickness to describe the part better. The
irregular lines representing the break are conventional breaks (discussed later in this chapter).

The broken-out section of the pulley in **Fig.
9.22** clearly depicts the keyway and threaded hole

BROKEN-OUT SECTION

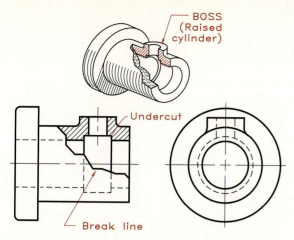

Figure 9.21 To find a broken-out section, imagine that part of the object has been broken away to reveal interior features.

REVOLVED SECTIONS

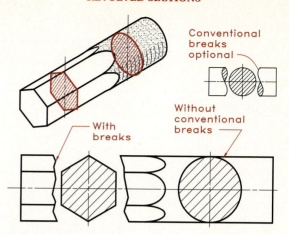

Figure 9.23 Revolved sections show cross-sectional features of a part to eliminate the need for supplementary orthographic views. You may superimpose revolved sections on the given views or use conventional breaks to separate them from the given views.

BROKEN-OUT SECTION: PULLEY

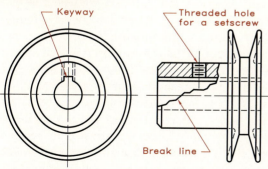

Figure 9.22 This broken-out section effectively shows the keyway and threaded hole for a setscrew in the pulley.

for a setscrew. This method shows the part efficiently, with the minimum of views.

9.10 Revolved Sections

A **revolved section** describes a part when you revolve its cross section about an axis of revolution and place it on the view where the revolution occurred. Note the use of revolved sections to explain two cross sections of the shaft shown in **Fig. 9.23** (with and without conventional breaks). Conventional breaks are optional; you may draw a revolved section on the view without them.

A revolved section helps to describe the part shown in **Fig. 9.24**. Imagine passing a cutting plane through the top view of the part (step 1). Then imagine revolving the cutting plane in the top view to obtain a true-size revolved section in the front view (step 2). Conventional breaks could be used on each side of the revolved section.

Figure 9.25 demonstrates how to use typical revolved sections to show cross sections through

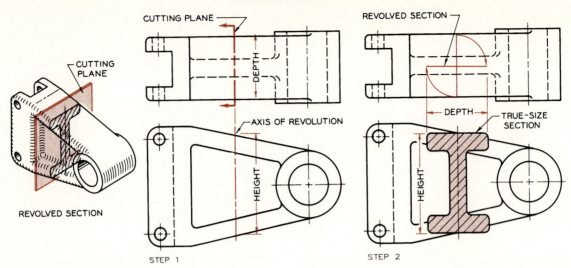

REVOLVED SECTION

Figure 9.24 Drawing revolved sections:
Step 1 Show an axis of revolution in the front view. The cutting plane would appear as an edge in the top view if you were to show it.

Step 2 Revolve the vertical section in the top view to show the section at true size in the front view. Do not draw object lines through the revolved section.

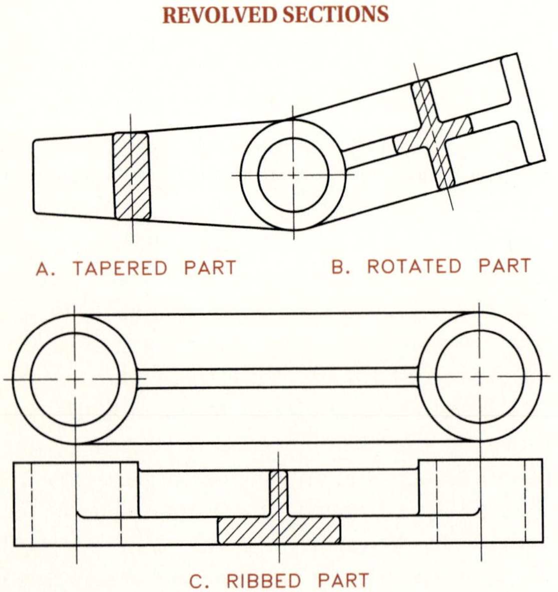

REVOLVED SECTIONS

A. TAPERED PART   B. ROTATED PART

C. RIBBED PART

Figure 9.25 These revolved sections help describe the cross sections of the two parts and make complex orthographic views unnecessary.

parts without having to draw additional orthographic views.

9.11 Conventional Revolutions

In **Fig. 9.26A**, the middle hole is omitted because it does not pass through the center of the circular plate. However, in **Fig. 9.26B**, the hole does pass through the plate's center and is shown in the section. Although the cutting plane does not pass through one of the symmetrically spaced holes in the top view (**Fig. 9.26C**), the hole is revolved to the cutting plane to show the full section.

When ribs are symmetrically spaced about a hub (**Fig. 9.27**), it is conventional practice to revolve them so that they appear true size in both views and sections. **Figure 9.28** illustrates the conventional practice of revolving both holes and ribs (or webs) of symmetrical parts. Revolution gives a better description of the parts in a manner that is easier to draw.

SYMMETRICAL HOLES

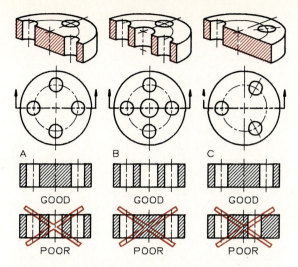

Figure 9.26 Revolve symmetrically spaced holes to show their true radial distances from their centers in sectional views. (A) Do not show the middle hole because it is not at the center of the plate. (B) Show the center hole because it is at the center of the plate. (C) Rotate one of the holes to the cutting plane to make the sectional view symmetrical and more descriptive.

SYMMETRICAL RIBS

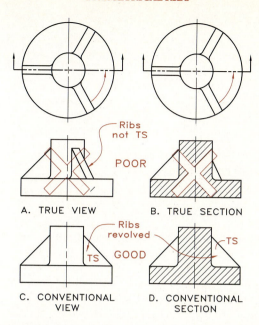

Figure 9.27 Show symmetrically spaced ribs revolved in both orthographic and sectional views to show them true size as a conventional practice.

A cutting plane may be positioned in either of two ways shown in **Fig. 9.29**. Even though the cutting plane does not pass through the ribs and holes in **Fig. 9.29A**, they may appear in section as if the cutting plane passed through them. The path of the cutting plane also may be revolved, as shown in **Fig. 9.29B**. In this case the ribs are revolved to their true-size position in the section view, although the plane does not cut them.

The same principles apply to symmetrically spaced spokes (**Fig. 9.30**). Draw only the revolved, true-size spokes and do not section line them. If the spokes shown in **Fig. 9.31A** were hatched, they could be misunderstood as a solid web, as shown in **Fig. 9.31B**.

Revolving the symmetrically positioned lugs shown in **Fig. 9.32** yields their true size in both the front view and section. The same principles of

RIBS AND HOLES IN SECTION

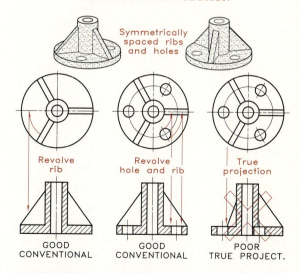

Figure 9.28 Show parts having symmetrically spaced ribs and holes in section with ribs rotated to show their true size and holes rotated to show them at their true radial distance from the center.

9.11 CONVENTIONAL REVOLUTIONS • 169

CUTTING-PLANE POSITIONS

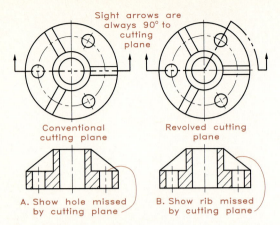

Figure 9.29 Show symmetrically located ribs true size in section whether the cutting plane passes through them or not. You may revolve the path of the cutting plane through certain features if you want, but the sight arrows are always perpendicular to the cutting plane.

SPOKES IN SECTION

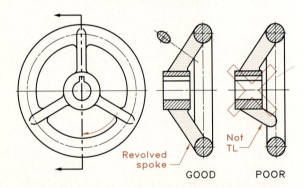

Figure 9.30 Revolve symmetrically spaced spokes to show them at true size in section. Do not section line spokes.

rotation apply to the part shown in **Fig. 9.33**, where the inclined arm appears in the section as if it had been revolved to the centerline in the top view and then projected to the sectional view.

WEBS AND SPOKES IN SECTION

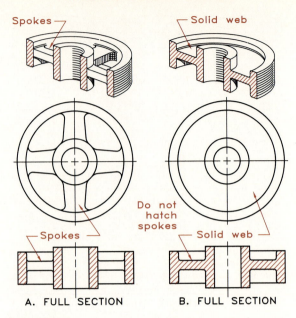

Figure 9.31
A Do not hatch spokes when the cutting plane passes through them.

B Hatch solid webs in sections of this type.

LUGS IN SECTION

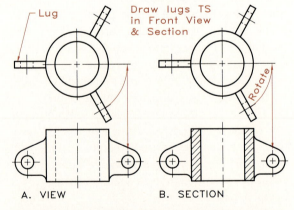

Figure 9.32 Revolve symmetrically spaced lugs (flanges) to show their true size in the (A) front view and (B) in sections.

REVOLVED FEATURES

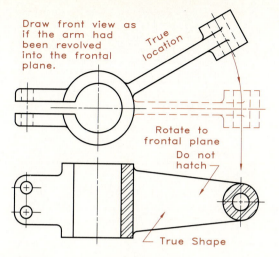

Draw front view as if the arm had been revolved into the frontal plane.

True location

Rotate to frontal plane

Do not hatch

True Shape

Figure 9.33 It is conventional practice to revolve a part with an inclined arm extending from a circular hub as if it were true shape in the sectional view.

REMOVED SECTIONS

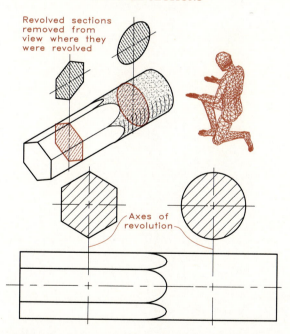

Revolved sections removed from view where they were revolved

Axes of revolution

Figure 9.34 Removed sections are revolved sections that are drawn outside the object along their axes of revolution.

REVOLVED AND REMOVED SECTIONS

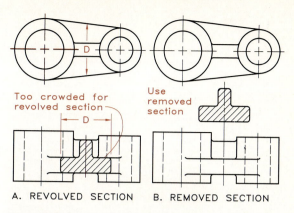

Too crowded for revolved section

Use removed section

A. REVOLVED SECTION   B. REMOVED SECTION

Figure 9.35 Removed sections are necessary when space does not permit the use of revolved sections.

9.12 Removed Sections

A **removed section** is a revolved section that is shown outside the view in which it was revolved (**Fig. 9.34**). Centerlines are used as axes of rotation to show the locations from which the sections are taken. Where space does not permit revolution on the given view (**Fig. 9.35A**), removed sections must be used instead of revolved sections (**Fig. 9.35B**).

Removed sections do not have to position directly along an axis of revolution adjacent to the view from which they were revolved. Instead, removed sections can be located elsewhere on a drawing if they are properly labeled (**Fig. 9.36**). For example, the plane labeled with an A at each end identifies the location of section A–A; the same applies to section B–B.

When a set of drawings consists of multiple sheets, removed sections and the views from which they are taken may appear on different sheets. When this method of layout is necessary, label the cutting plane in the view from which the section was taken and the sheet on which the section appears (**Fig. 9.37**).

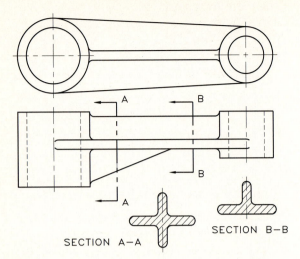

Figure 9.36 Lettering each end of a cutting plane (such as A–A) identifies the removed section labeled Section A–A shown elsewhere on the drawing.

CUTTING PLANE FOR REMOVED SECTIONS

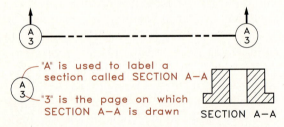

Figure 9.37 If placing a removed section on another page in a set of drawings is necessary, label each end of the cutting plane with a letter and a number. Here, the letters refer to Section A–A, and the numbers mean that Section A–A appears on page 3.

9.13 Conventional Breaks

Figure 9.38 shows types of conventional breaks to use when you remove portions of an object. You may draw the "figure-eight" breaks used for cylindrical and tubular parts freehand **(Fig. 9.39)** or with a compass when they are larger **(Fig. 9.40)**.

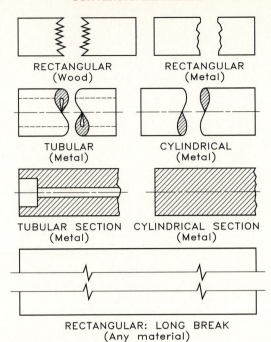

Figure 9.38 These conventional breaks indicate that a portion of an object is not shown.

CYLINDRICAL BREAKS

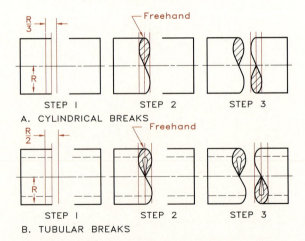

Figure 9.39 Guidelines aid in drawing conventional breaks in (A) cylindrical and (B) tubular sections freehand, as shown here. The radius, R, establishes the width of both "figure-eight" break symbols.

BREAKS WITH INSTRUMENTS

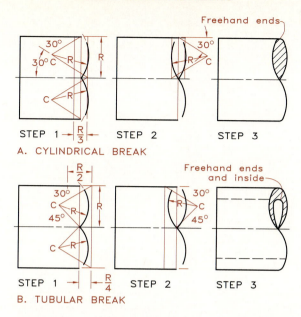

A. CYLINDRICAL BREAK

STEP 1   STEP 2   STEP 3

B. TUBULAR BREAK

STEP 1   STEP 2   STEP 3

Figure 9.40 Instruments help in drawing conventional breaks in larger cylindrical and tubular parts.

APPLICATION OF BREAKS

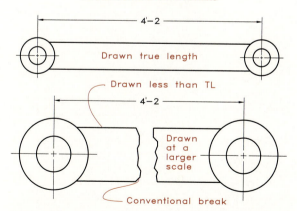

Drawn true length

Drawn less than TL

Drawn at a larger scale

Conventional break

Figure 9.41 The use of conventional breaks allows this part to be drawn effectively at a larger scale. It is permissible to insert a revolved section between the breaks.

One use of conventional breaks is to shorten a long piece by removing the portion between the breaks so that it may be drawn at a larger size (**Fig. 9.41**). The dimension specifies the true length of the part, and the breaks indicate that a portion of the length has been removed.

Problems

Solve the problems shown in **Fig. 9.42** on size A sheets by drawing two solutions per sheet. Each grid space equals 0.20 in., or 5 mm.

1–16. Draw the sections indicated by the cutting planes.

17–20. Draw broken-out sections.

21–24. Draw half sections.

25–29. (Figs. 9.43–9.47) Complete these drawings as full sections. Draw one solution per size AH sheet. Each grid space equals 0.20 in., or 5 mm. Show the cutting planes in each solution.

30, 31. (Figs. 9.48, 9.49) Complete the drawings as half sections with one solution per size AH sheet. Each grid space equals 0.20 in., or 5 mm. Show the cutting planes in each solution.

32, 33. (Figs. 9.50, 9.51) Complete the drawings as offset sections. Draw one solution per size AH sheet. Each grid space equals 0.20 in., or 5 mm. Show the cutting planes in each solution.

34. (Fig. 9.52) Complete the partial view as a full section. Draw the views on a size AH sheet. Each grid space equals 0.20 in., or 5 mm. Show the cutting plane in your solution.

35. (Fig. 9.53) Complete the front view as a full section of the assembly. Draw the views on a size AH sheet. Each grid space equals 0.20 in., or 5 mm. Show the cutting plane in your solution.

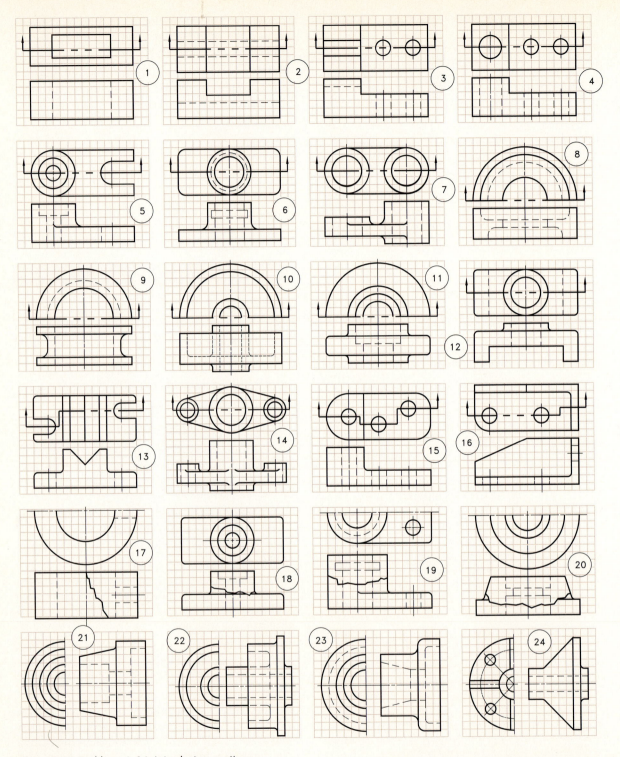

Figure 9.42 Problems 1–24. Introductory sections.

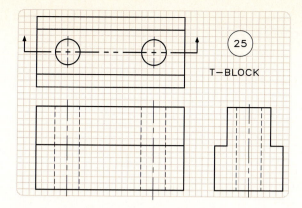

Figure 9.43 Problem 25. Full section.

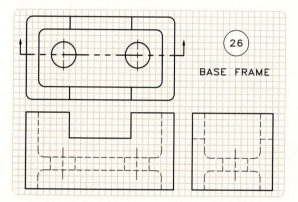

Figure 9.44 Problem 26. Full section.

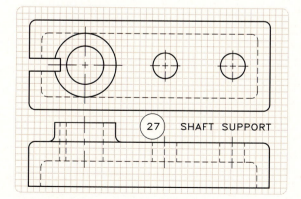

Figure 9.45 Problem 27. Full section.

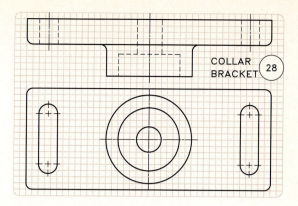

Figure 9.46 Problem 28. Full section.

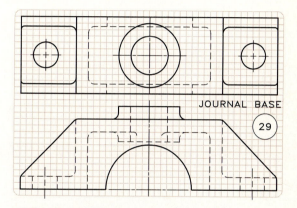

Figure 9.47 Problem 29. Full section.

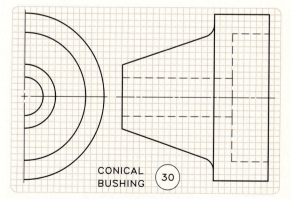

Figure 9.48 Problem 30. Half section.

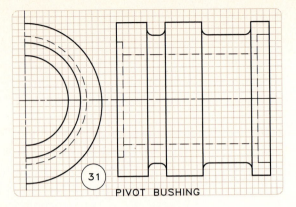

Figure 9.49 Problem 31. Half section.

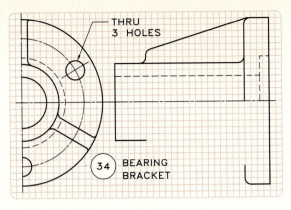

Figure 9.52 Problem 34. Full section.

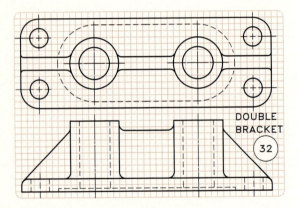

Figure 9.50 Problem 32. Offset section.

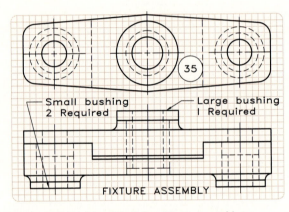

Figure 9.53 Problem 35. Full section in assembly.

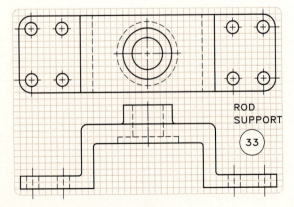

Figure 9.51 Problem 33. Offset section.

10

Screws, Fasteners, and Springs

10.1 Introduction

Screws provide a fast and easy method of fastening parts together, adjusting the position of parts, and transmitting power. **Screws, sometimes called threaded fasteners, should be purchased rather than made as newly designed parts for each product.** Screws are available through commercial catalogs in countless forms and shapes for various specialized and general applications. Such screws are cheap, easy to replace, and interchangeable.

The types of threaded parts most often encountered in industry are covered by current ANSI Standards and include both Unified National (UN) and International Organization for Standardization (ISO) threads. Adoption of the UN thread in 1948 by the United States, Great Britain, and Canada (sometimes called the ABC Standards), a modification of the American Standard and the Whitworth thread, was a major step in standardizing threads. The ISO developed metric standards to unify thread specifications for even broader worldwide applications.

Other types of fasteners include **keys** and **rivets**. **Springs** resist and react to forces and have applications varying from pogo sticks to automobiles. Springs also are available in many forms and styles from specialty manufacturers who supply most of them to industry.

10.2 Threads

Terminology

Understanding threaded parts begins with learning their terminology, which we use throughout this chapter.

External thread: a thread on the outside of a cylinder, such as a bolt **(Fig. 10.1)**.

Internal thread: a thread cut on the inside of a part, such as a nut (Fig. 10.1).

Major diameter: the largest diameter on an internal or external thread **(Fig. 10.2)**.

Minor diameter: the smallest diameter on an internal or external thread (Fig. 10.2).

Figure 10.1 This photo shows examples of external threads (bolts) and internal threads (nuts). (Courtesy of Russell, Burdsall & Ward Bolt and Nut Company.)

THREAD TERMINOLOGY

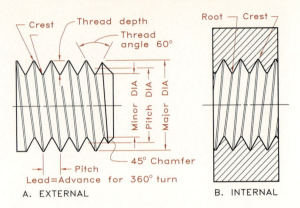

Figure 10.2 This drawing illustrates thread terminology for (A) external and (B) internal threads.

Pitch diameter: the diameter of an imaginary cylinder passing through the threads at the points where the thread width is equal to the space between the threads (Fig. 10.2 and Fig. 10.4).

Lead (pronounced leed): the distance a screw will advance when turned 360°.

Pitch (thread width): the distance between crests of threads, found by dividing 1 inch by the number of threads per inch of a particular thread (Fig. 10.2).

Crest: the peak edge of a screw thread (Fig. 10.2).

Thread angle: the angle between threads cut by the cutting tool, usually 60° (Fig. 10.2).

Root: the bottom of the thread cut into a cylinder to form the minor diameter (Fig. 10.2).

Thread form: the shape of the thread cut into a threaded part (Fig. 10.3).

Thread depth: the depth of the thread from the major diameter to the minor diameter; also measured as the root diameter (Fig. 10.2).

THREAD FORMS

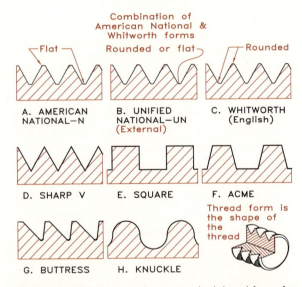

Figure 10.3 This drawing depicts standard thread forms for external threads.

Thread series: the number of threads per inch for a particular diameter, grouped into coarse, fine, extra fine, and eight constant-pitch thread series.

Thread class: the closeness of fit between two mating parts. Class 1 represents a loose fit and Class 3 a tight fit.

Right-hand thread: one that will assemble when turned clockwise. A right-hand external thread slopes downward to the right when its axis is horizontal and in the opposite direction on internal threads.

Left-hand thread: one that will assemble when turned counterclockwise. A left-hand external thread slopes downward to the left when its axis is horizontal and in the opposite direction on internal threads.

Specifications (English System)

Form **Thread form** is the shape of the thread cut into a part (**Fig. 10.3**). The Unified National form is the most widely used form in the United States and is denoted UN in thread notes. The American National form is denoted by N, when it appears occasionally on old drawings.

Transmission of power is achieved with the Acme, square, and buttress threads, which are commonly used in gearing and other machinery applications (Fig. 10.3). The sharp V thread is used for set screws and in applications where friction in assembly is desired.

The Unified National Rolled form, denoted UNR, is specified only for external threads, never for internal threads, because internal threads cannot be formed by rolling. The standard UN form has a flat root (a rounded root is optional) (**Fig. 10.4A**), and the UNR form (**Fig. 10.4B**) has a rounded root that is formed by rolling a cylinder across a die. The UNR form is used instead of the UN form where precision of assembly is less critical.

Series The **thread series** designates the spacing of threads that vary with diameter. The American National and the Unified National (UN/UNR) forms include three graded series: coarse (C), fine (F), and extra fine (EF). Eight constant-pitch series (4, 6, 8, 12, 16, 20, 28, and 32 threads per inch) are also available.

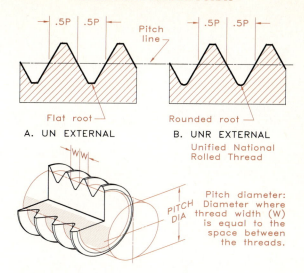

UN AND UNR THREAD FORMS

A. UN EXTERNAL

B. UNR EXTERNAL
Unified National
Rolled Thread

Pitch diameter: Diameter where thread width (W) is equal to the space between the threads.

Figure 10.4

A The UN external thread has a flat root (rounded root is optional) and a flat crest.

B The UNR thread has a rounded root formed by rolling rather than cutting. The UNR form does not apply to internal threads.

A **coarse** Unified National form thread is denoted UNC or UNRC, which is a combination form and series designation. Thus an American National (N) form for a coarse thread is written NC. The coarse thread (UNC/UNRC or NC) has the largest pitch of any series and is suitable for bolts, screws, nuts, and general use with cast iron, soft metals, and plastics when rapid assembly is desired.

Fine threads (NF or UNF/UNRF) are used for bolts, nuts, and screws when a high degree of tightening is required. Fine threads are closer together than coarse threads, and their pitch is graduated to be smaller on smaller diameters.

Extra-fine threads (UNEF/UNREF or NEF) are suitable for sheet-metal screws and bolts, thin nuts, ferrules, and couplings when the length of engagement is limited and high stresses must be withstood.

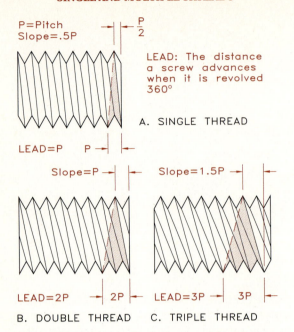

Figure 10.5 This drawing shows (A) single, (B) double, and (C) triple threads.

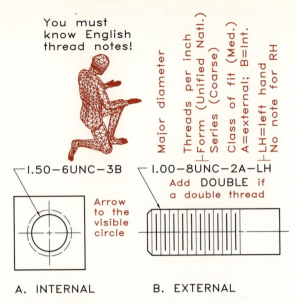

Figure 10.6 These English thread notes apply to (A) internal and (B) external threads.

Constant-pitch threads (4 UN, 6 UN, 8 UN, 12 UN, 16 UN, 20 UN, 28 UN, and 32 UN) are used on larger diameter threads (beginning near the 1/2-inch size) and have the same pitch size regardless of the diameter size. The most commonly used constant-pitch threads are 8 UN, 12 UN, and 16 UN members of the series, which are used on threads of about 1 inch in diameter and larger. Constant-pitch threads may be specified as UNR or N thread forms. The ANSI table in the Appendix shows constant-pitch threads that can be used on larger thread diameters instead of graded pitches of coarse, fine, and extra fine.

Class of Fit The **class of fit** is the tightness of fit between two mating threads, as between a nut and bolt, and is indicated in the thread note by the numbers 1, 2, or 3 followed by the letters A or B. **For UN forms, the letter A represents an external**

thread and the letter B represents an internal thread. The letters A and B do not appear in notes for the now obsolete American National form (N).

Class 1A and 1B threads are used on parts that assemble with a minimum of binding and precision. Class 2A and 2B threads are general-purpose threads for bolts, nuts, and screws used in general and mass-production applications. Class 3A and 3B threads are used in precision assemblies where a close fit is required to withstand stresses and vibration.

Single and Multiple Threads A **single thread (Fig. 10.5A)** advances the distance of its pitch in a revolution of 360°; that is, its pitch is equal to its lead. The crest lines have a slope of 1/2 P, since only 180° of the revolution is visible in the view.

Multiple threads are used wherever quick assembly is required. A **double thread** is composed of two threads that advance a distance of 2P

APPLICATION OF NOTES

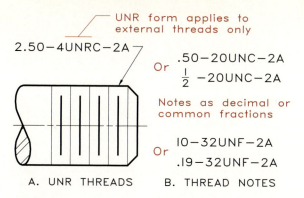

2.50−4UNRC−2A

UNR form applies to external threads only

Or .50−20UNC−2A
$\frac{1}{2}$ −20UNC−2A

Notes as decimal or common fractions

Or 10−32UNF−2A
.19−32UNF−2A

A. UNR THREADS   B. THREAD NOTES

Figure 10.7

A The UNR thread notes apply to external threads only.

B Thread notes may be given as decimal fractions or common fractions.

Nominal Diameter	Basic Diameter	Coarse NC & UNC		Fine NF & UNF		Extra Fine NEF/UNEF	
		Thds per In.	Tap Drill DIA	Thds per In.	Tap Drill DIA	Thds per In.	Tap Drill DIA
1	1.000	8	.875	12	.922	20	.953
1−1/16	1.063	...	...	...	...	18	1.000
1−1/8	1.125	7	.904	12	1.046	18	1.070
1−3/16	1.188	...	...	...	...	18	1.141
1−1/4	1.250	7	1.109	12	1,172	18	1.188
1−5/16	1.313	...	...	...	...	18	1.266
1−3/8	1.375	6	1.219	12	1.297	18	1.313
1−7/16	1.438	...	...	...	...	18	1.375
1−1/2	1.500	6	1.344	12	1.422	18	1.438

Figure 10.8 This portion of the ANSI tables for UN and UNR threads is from Appendix 6.

when turned 360° **(Fig. 10.5B)**; that is, its lead is equal to 2P. The crest lines have a slope of P because only 180° of the revolution is visible in the view. A **triple thread** advances 3P in 360° with a crest line slope of 1-1/2 P in the view where 180° of the revolution is visible **(Fig. 10.5C)**.

Notes

Drawings of threads are only symbolic representations and are inadequate to give the details of a thread unless accompanied by notes (Fig. 10.6). In a thread note, first give the major diameter, then the number of threads per inch, the form and series, the class of fit, and the letter A or B to denote external or internal threads, respectively. For a double or triple thread, include the word **double** or **triple** in the note, and for left-hand threads add the letters LH.

Figure 10.7 shows a UNR thread note for the external thread. (UNR does not apply to internal threads.) When inches are the unit of measurement, write thread notes as decimal fractions, although common fractions may be used. The information for thread notes comes from ANSI tables for English thread specifications.

Using Thread Tables

Figure 10.8 shows a portion of the Appendix, which gives the UN/UNR thread table from which specifications for standardized interchangeable threads can be selected. Note that a 1-1/2-inch-diameter bolt with fine thread (UNF) has 12 threads per inch. Therefore the thread note is written as

1.500-12 UNF-2A or 1-1/2-12 UNF-2A.

If the thread were internal (nut), the thread note would be the same, but you would use the letter B instead of the letter A.

For constant-pitch thread series selected for larger diameters, write the thread note as

1.750-12 UN-2A or 1-3/4-12 UN-2A.

For the UNR thread form (for external threads only) simply substitute UNR for UN in the last three columns, as, for example, UNREF for UNEF (extra fine). **Figure 10.9** shows the preferred placement of thread notes (with leaders) for external and internal threads.

Metric Thread Notes

Metric thread notes usually given as a basic designation are suitable for general applications. However,

PLACEMENT OF THREAD NOTES

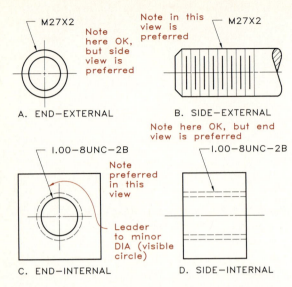

A. END—EXTERNAL

B. SIDE—EXTERNAL

C. END—INTERNAL

D. SIDE—INTERNAL

Figure 10.9 Place notes for external threads on the rectangular view of the threads. Place thread notes for internal threads in the circular view if space permits.

METRIC THREAD TABLE

COARSE		FINE	
MAJ. DIA & THD PITCH	TAP DRILL	MAJ. DIA & THD PITCH	TAP DRILL
M20 X 2.5	17.5	M20 X 1.5	18.5
M22 X 2.5	19.5	M22 X 1.5	20.5
M24 X 3	21.0	M24 X 2	22.0
M27 X 3	24.0	M27 X 2	25.0
M30 X 3.5	26.5	M30 X 2	28.0
M33 X 3.5	29.5	M33 X 2	31.0
M36 X 4	32.0	M36 X 2	33.0
M39 X 4	35.0	M39 X 2	36.0
M42 X 4.5	37.5	M42 X 2	39.0

Figure 10.10 This portion of the ISO tables, which present dimension specifications for metric threads, is from Appendix 8.

METRIC THREAD NOTES

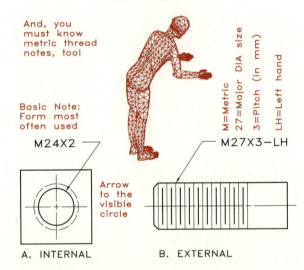

A. INTERNAL

B. EXTERNAL

Figure 10.11 Use this basic type of metric thread note for (A) internal and (B) external threads.

for applications where the assembly of threaded parts is crucial, a complete thread designation should be noted. The ISO thread table in Appendix 8, a portion of which is shown in **Fig. 10.10**, contains specifications for metric thread notes.

Basic Designation **Figure 10.11** shows examples of metric screw thread notes. Each note begins with the letter M, designating the note as metric, followed by the major diameter size in millimeters and the pitch in millimeters separated by the multiplication sign, ×.

Complete Designation The first part of a complete designation note **(Fig. 10.12)** is identical to that for the basic designation, to which is added the tolerance class designation separated by a dash. (A **tolerance** is a specified maximum variation in size that ensures assembly of the threaded parts.) The 5g represents the pitch diameter tolerance, and the 6g represents the crest diameter tolerance.

The numbers 5 and 6 are thread tolerance grades (variations in size from the basic diameter) from **Fig. 10.13**. These grades are for the pitch diameter and the major and minor diameters of medium general-purpose thread similar to class

COMPLETE METRIC DESIGNATION

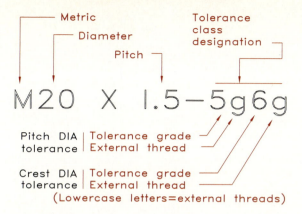

Figure 10.12 A complete designation note for metric threads adds tolerance specifications to the basic note.

TOLERANCE GRADES: METRIC THREADS

External Thread		Internal Thread	
Major Diameter	Pitch Diameter	Minor Diameter	Pitch Diameter
–	3	–	–
4	4	4	4
–	5	5	5
6	6	6	6
–	7	7	7
8	8	8	8
–	9	–	–

(FINE ← MEDIUM → COARSE)

Figure 10.13 Tolerance grades for major and minor diameters and pitch diameters of each range from fine to coarse. Tolerance grades combined with position symbols (such as 6g) become tolerance classes.

2A and 2B threads in the UN system. Grades of less than 6 are best suited to fine-series fits and short lengths of engagement. Grades greater than 6 are best suited to coarse-series fits and long lengths of engagement.

The letters following the grade numbers denote tolerance positions, that is, either external

POSITION, ALLOWANCE, AND ENGAGEMENT

EXTERNAL THREADS (Lowercase letters)
e = Large allowance
g = Small allowance
h = No allowance

INTERNAL THREADS (Uppercase letters)
G = Small allowance
H = No allowance

LENGTH OF ENGAGEMENT
S = Short   N = Normal   L = Long

EXAMPLE: Refer to Fig. 10.15
Position   Lower-case = external threads
           Upper-case = internal threads
Allowance e, g, h, G, H = amount of allowance
Engagement S, N, & L Columns of Fig. 10.15

Figure 10.14 Use symbols to represent position, allowance, and engagement length. Position means either external or internal threads. A lowercase letter indicates an external thread and an uppercase letter signifies an internal thread.

or internal threads. Lowercase letters designate external threads (bolts), as **Fig. 10.14** shows. The letters e, g, and h represent large allowance, small allowance, and no allowance, respectively. (**Allowance** is the permitted variation in size from the basic diameter.) Uppercase letters designate internal threads (nuts). The letters G and H, placed after the tolerance grade number, denote small allowance and no allowance, respectively. For example, 5g designates a medium tolerance with small allowance for the pitch diameter of an external thread, and 6H designates a medium tolerance with no allowance for the minor diameter of an internal thread.

Tolerance classes are fine, medium, and coarse **(Fig. 10.15)**. They represent combinations of tolerance grades, tolerance positions, and lengths of engagement—short (S), normal (N), and long (L). Appendix 22 contains a table of lengths of engagement (the actual length of the assembled thread in mating parts). After deciding whether to use a fine, medium, or coarse class of fit, you should select the thread designation first from those in boxes (commercial threads), second from those in bold print, third from those in medium-size print, and

Quality	External Threads (bolts)									Internal Threads (nuts)					
	Tolerance position e (large allowance)			Tolerance position g (small allowance)			Tolerance position h (no allowance)			Tolerance position G (small allowance)			Tolerance position H (no allowance)		
	Length of engagement			Length of engagement			Length of engagement			Length of engagement			Length of engagement		
	Group S	Group N	Group L	Group S	Group N	Group L	Group S	Group N	Group L	Group S	Group N	Group L	Group S	Group N	Group L
Fine							3h4h	4h	5h4h				4H	5H	6H
Medium	**6e**	7e6e		5g6g	**6g**	7g6g	5h6h	6h	7h6h	5G	6G	7G	**5H**	**6H**	**7H**
Coarse					8g	9g8g					7G	8G		7H	8H

*In selecting tolerance class, select first from the commercial classes in boxes, second from the bold print, third from the medium-size print, and fourth from the small-size print.

Figure 10.15 Tolerance classes for large and medium allowances and for no allowance for internal and external threads are shown here. Select the most commonly used tolerance class, commercial threads (in boxes) first, then the classes in bold print, medium-size print, and small-size print, respectively.

TOLERANCE AND ENGAGEMENT SYMBOLS

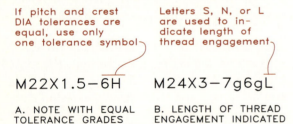

If pitch and crest DIA tolerances are equal, use only one tolerance symbol

Letters S, N, or L are used to indicate length of thread engagement

M22X1.5−6H

A. NOTE WITH EQUAL TOLERANCE GRADES

M24X3−7g6gL

B. LENGTH OF THREAD ENGAGEMENT INDICATED

Figure 10.16 Complete notes:

A When both pitch and crest diameter tolerance grades are the same, show the tolerance class symbol only once.

B The letters S, N, and L indicate the length of the thread engagement.

fourth from those in small print. The 6H class is comparable to the 2B class of fit in the UN system for an interior thread, and the 6g class is similar to the 2A class of fit.

Figure 10.16 shows variations for complete designation thread notes. When the minor and pitch diameters have identical grades, the tolerance class symbol consists of one number and letter, such as 6H **(Fig. 10.16A)**. The uppercase H indicates that the position is internal, with no allowance added to the basic thread note. If necessary, add the length of engagement symbol (S, N, L) to the tolerance class designation **(Fig. 10.16B)**. For unknown lengths of thread engagement, use group N (normal).

Specify the fit between mating threads as shown in **Fig. 10.17**, with a slash separating the tolerance class designations of internal and external threads. Additional information about ISO threads may be obtained from *ISO Metric Screw Threads*, a booklet of standards published by ANSI that was used as the basis for most of this section.

MATING THREADS

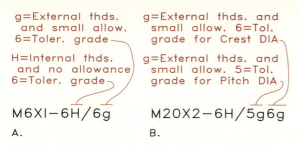

g=External thds. and small allow. 6=Toler. grade

H=Internal thds. and no allowance 6=Toler. grade

g=External thds. and small allow. 6=Tol. grade for Crest DIA

g=External thds. and small allow. 5=Tol. grade for Pitch DIA

M6X1−6H/6g

A.

M20X2−6H/5g6g

B.

Figure 10.17 A slash mark is used to separate the tolerance class designations of mating internal and external threads.

THREAD SYMBOLS

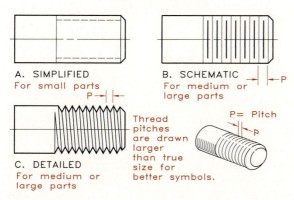

A. SIMPLIFIED
For small parts

P⟶|←

B. SCHEMATIC
For medium or large parts

|←P

C. DETAILED
For medium or large parts

Thread pitches are drawn larger than true size for better symbols.

P= Pitch

|←P

Figure 10.18 The three types of thread symbols used to represent threads are (A) simplified, (B) schematic, and (C) detailed.

10.3 Drawing Threads

Threads may be represented by either detailed, schematic, or simplified symbols (Fig. 10.18). Detailed symbols represent a thread most realistically, simplified symbols represent a thread least realistically, and schematic symbols are a compromise between the two.

Detailed Symbols

UN/UNR Threads **Figure 10.19** illustrates detailed thread symbols for external threads. Instead of helical curves, straight lines depict crest and root lines.

DETAILED SYMBOLS: EXTERNAL

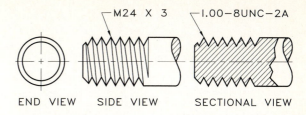

M24 X 3

1.00−8UNC−2A

END VIEW   SIDE VIEW   SECTIONAL VIEW

Figure 10.19 These detailed symbols represent external threads in view and section.

DETAILED SYMBOLS: INTERNAL

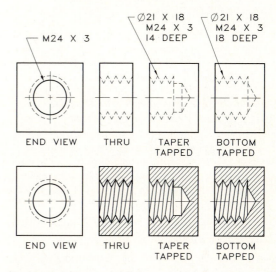

M24 X 3

Ø21 X 18
M24 X 3
14 DEEP

Ø21 X 18
M24 X 3
18 DEEP

END VIEW   THRU   TAPER TAPPED   BOTTOM TAPPED

END VIEW   THRU   TAPER TAPPED   BOTTOM TAPPED

Figure 10.20 These detailed symbols represent internal threads. Approximate the minor diameter as 75% of the major diameter. Tap drill diameters (Ø21) are found in Appendix 8.

Figure 10.20 depicts detailed thread symbols for internal threads in views and sections.

Figure 10.21 shows how to draw a detailed thread representation for both English and metric threads. When using the English tables, calculate the pitch by dividing 1 inch by the number of threads per inch. In the metric system, pitch is given in the tables. **You should draw the spacing between**

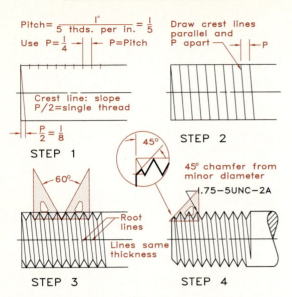

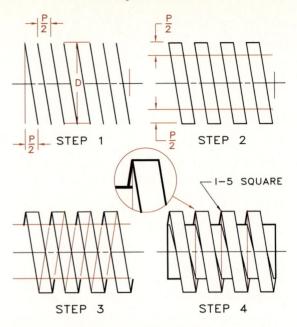

Figure 10.21 Detailed representation of threads:

Step 1 To draw a detailed representation of a 1.75-5 UNC-2A thread, determine the actual pitch by dividing 1 inch by the number of threads per inch, or 5 in this case. In this case, use a pitch of ¼ instead of ⅕ to avoid drawing the threads too close together. Lay off the pitch along the length of the thread and draw a crest line at a slope of P/2, or ⅛ inch in this case.

Step 2 Draw the other crest lines as dark, visible lines parallel to the first crest line.

Step 3 Find the root lines by constructing 60° vees between the crest lines. Draw the root lines from the bottom of the vees. Root lines are parallel to each other but not to crest lines.

Step 4 Construct a 45° chamfer at the end of the thread from the minor diameter. Darken all lines and add a thread note.

Figure 10.22 Drawing the square thread:

Step 1 Lay out the major diameter. Space the crest lines ½P apart and slope them downward to the right for right-hand threads.

Step 2 Connect every other pair of crest lines. Find the minor diameter by measuring ½P inward from the major diameter.

Step 3 Connect the opposite crest lines with light construction lines to establish the profile of the thread form.

Step 4 Connect the inside crest lines with light construction lines to locate the points on the minor diameter where the thread wraps around the minor diameter. Darken the final lines.

crest lines (the pitch) larger than the actual pitch size for a clear, uncrowded representation.

Square Threads **Figure 10.22** shows how to draw and notate a detailed representation of a square thread. Follow the same basic steps to draw views and sections of square internal threads (**Fig.**

10.23). In section, draw both the internal crest and root lines, but in a view draw only the outline of the threads. Place thread notes for internal threads in the circular view, whenever possible, with the leader pointing toward the center and stopping at the visible circle.

When a square thread is long, you may represent it by using phantom lines, without drawing all the threads (**Fig. 10.24**). This conventional

INTERNAL SQUARE THREADS

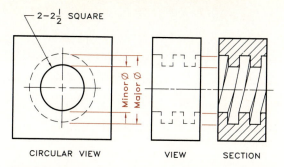

CIRCULAR VIEW   VIEW   SECTION

Figure 10.23 This drawing shows internal square threads in view and section.

SIMPLIFIED SQUARE THREADS

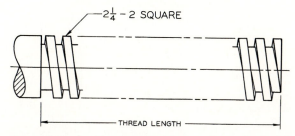

Figure 10.24 The conventional method of showing square threads is to draw sample threads at each end and to connect them with phantom lines.

practice saves time and effort without reducing the drawing's effectiveness.

Acme Threads A modified version of the square thread is the **Acme thread**, which has tapered (15°) sides for easier engagement than square threads. **Figure 10.25** shows the steps involved in drawing detailed Acme threads. Like square threads, Acme threads are used for transmission of force and power, as in screw jacks and lathes. Appendix 9 contains the table for Acme thread specifications and dimensions.

Figure 10.26 shows internal Acme threads in view and section. Slope left-hand internal threads

DRAWING ACME THREADS

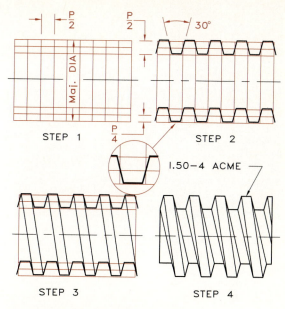

Figure 10.25 Drawing the Acme thread:

Step 1 Lay out the major diameter and thread length and divide the shaft into equal divisions ½P apart. Locate the minor and pitch diameters by using distances ½P and ¼P.

Step 2 Draw construction lines at 15° angles with the vertical along the pitch diameter to make a total angle of 30°.

Step 3 Draw the crest lines across the screw.

Step 4 Darken the lines, draw the root lines, and add the thread note to complete the drawing.

INTERNAL ACME THREADS

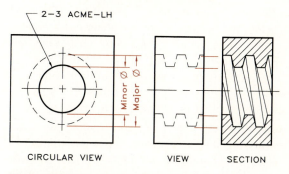

CIRCULAR VIEW   VIEW   SECTION

Figure 10.26 This drawing shows internal Acme threads in view and section.

Figure 10.27 This photo demonstrates cutting an Acme thread on a lathe. (Courtesy of Clausing Corporation.)

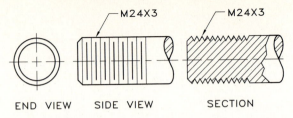

Figure 10.28 These schematic symbols represent external threads in view and section.

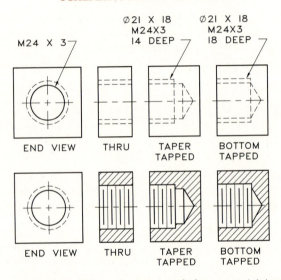

Figure 10.29 These schematic symbols represent internal threads in view and section. Tap drill diameters are found in Appendix 8.

in section to appear the same as right-hand external threads. **Figure 10.27** shows a shaft being threaded with Acme threads on a lathe as the tool travels the length of the shaft.

Schematic Symbols

Figure 10.28 shows schematic representations of external threads, with metric notes. Draw schematic thread symbols by using thin parallel crest lines and thick root lines. Because schematic symbols are easy to draw and adequately represent threads, it is the thread symbol used most often for medium-size threads. Use the same schematic symbols for left-hand and right-hand threads and write LH in the thread note of left-hand threads. Right-hand threads carry no designation in thread notes.

Figure 10.29 shows schematic symbols representing internal threaded holes in view and section. The size of the tap drill diameter is approximately equal to the major diameter minus the pitch. However, the minor diameter usually is drawn a bit smaller to provide better separation between the circles representing the major and minor diameters.

Figure 10.30 shows how to draw threads schematically for English specifications. Draw the minor diameter at approximately three-quarters of the major diameter and the chamfer (bevel) 45° from the minor diameter. Draw crest lines as thin lines and root lines as thick visible lines.

DRAWING SCHEMATIC THREADS

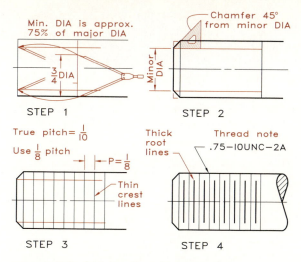

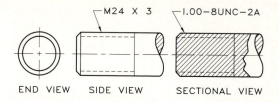

Figure 10.31 These simplified thread symbols represent external threads in view and section.

Figure 10.30 Schematic representation of threads:

Step 1 Lay out the major diameter and locate the minor diameter (about three-quarters of the major diameter). Draw the minor diameter as light construction lines.

Step 2 Chamfer the end of the threads with a 45° angle from the minor diameter.

Step 3 Find the true pitch of a .75-10UNC-2A thread (0.1) by dividing 1 inch by the number of threads per inch (10). Use a larger pitch, ⅛ inch in this case, to draw the thin crest lines ⅛ inch apart.

Step 4 Draw root lines as thick as the visible lines between the crest lines to the construction lines representing the minor diameter. Add a thread note.

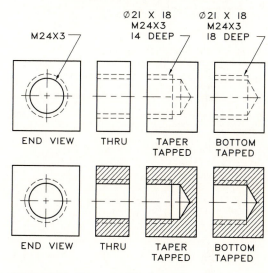

Figure 10.32 These simplified thread symbols represent internal threads in view and section. Draw minor diameters at about ¾ the major diameter.

Simplified Symbols

Figure 10.31 illustrates the use of simplified symbols for external threads and a specifications note. **Figure 10.32** shows the use of simplified symbols for internal threads. **Simplified symbols are the easiest to draw and are the best suited for drawing small threads where schematic and detailed symbols would be crowded.** Draw the minor diameter as hidden lines spaced at about three-quarters the major diameter. **Figure 10.33** shows the steps involved in drawing simplified threads. With experience, you will be able to approximate

the location of the minor diameter of simplified threads by eye.

Drawing Small Threads

Instead of drawing small threads to actual size, draw minor diameters smaller to separate root and crest lines farther for a clear, uncrowded, easy-to-draw representation (Fig. 10.34). Enlarge the thread's pitch to separate thread symbols when drawing all three types of symbols (simplified,

DRAWING SIMPLIFIED THREADS

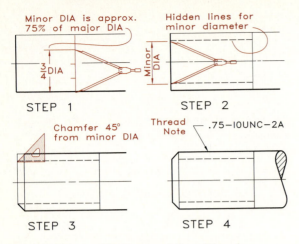

STEP 1   STEP 2

STEP 3   STEP 4

Figure 10.33 Simplified representation of threads:
Step 1 Lay out the major diameter. Locate the minor diameter (about three-quarters of the major diameter).

Step 2 Draw hidden lines to represent the minor diameter.

Step 3 Draw a 45° chamfer from the minor diameter to the major diameter.

Step 4 Darken the lines and add a thread note.

CONVENTIONAL PRACTICES

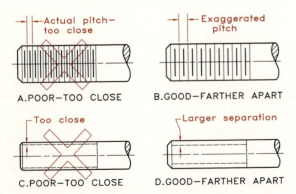

A. POOR—TOO CLOSE   B. GOOD—FARTHER APART

C. POOR—TOO CLOSE   D. GOOD—FARTHER APART

Figure 10.34 Most threads must be drawn using exaggerated dimensions instead of actual measurements to prevent the drawing from having lines drawn too closely together.

Figure 10.35 This photo shows a nut, a bolt, and washers in combination. (Courtesy of Lamson & Sessions.)

TYPES OF BOLTS AND SCREWS

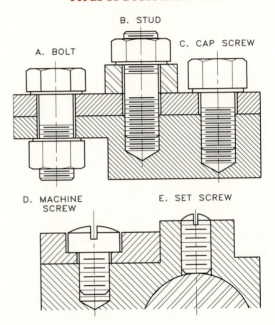

Figure 10.36 This drawing illustrates several types of threaded bolts and screws.

schematic, and detailed). Add a thread note to the symbolic drawing to give the necessary specifications.

10.4 Nuts and Bolts

Nuts and bolts (**Fig. 10.35**) come in many forms and sizes and have many different applications. **Figure 10.36** depicts some common types of

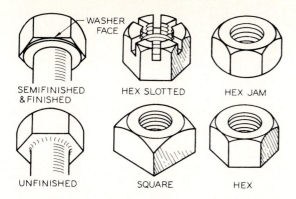

Figure 10.37 The types of finishes for nuts and bolt heads and several types of nuts.

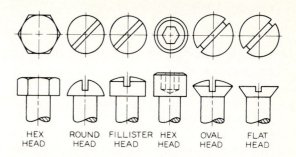

Figure 10.38 These are common types of bolt and screw heads.

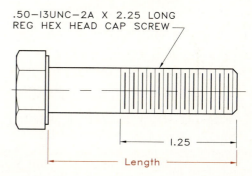

Figure 10.39 A properly dimensioned and noted hexagon-head bolt.

threaded fasteners. A **bolt** is a threaded cylinder with a head and is used with a **nut** to hold parts together. A **stud** is a headless bolt, threaded at both ends, that is screwed into one part with a nut attached to the other end.

A **cap screw** usually does not have a nut, but passes through a hole in one part and screws into another threaded part. A **hexagon-head machine screw** is similar to, but smaller than, a cap screw. Machine screws also come with other types of heads. A **set screw** is used to hold one member fixed in place with another, usually to prevent rotation, as with a pulley on a shaft.

Figure 10.37 shows the types of heads used on regular and heavy bolts and nuts. Heavy bolts have thicker heads than regular bolts for heavier usage. A **finished head** (or nut) has a 1/64-inch-thick washer face (a circular boss) to provide a bearing surface for smooth contact. **Semifinished bolt heads** and nuts are the same as finished bolt heads and nuts. **Unfinished bolt heads** and nuts have no boss and no machined surfaces.

A **hexagon jam nut** does not have a washer face, but it is chamfered (beveled at its corners) on both sides. **Figure 10.38** shows other standard bolt and screw heads for cap screws and machine screws.

Dimensions

Figure 10.39 shows a properly dimensioned bolt. The ANSI tables in Appendixes 11–20 give nut and bolt dimensions, but you may use the following guides for hexagon-head and square-head bolts.

Overall Lengths Hexagon-head bolts are available in 1/4-inch increments up to 8 inches long, in 1/2-inch increments from 8 to 20 inches long, and in 1-inch increments from 20 to 30 inches long. Square-head bolts are available in 1/8-inch increments from 1/2 to 3/4 inch long, in 1/4-inch increments from 3/4 inch to 5 inches long, in 1/2-inch increments from 5 to 12 inches long, and in 1-inch increments from 12 to 30 inches long.

Thread Lengths For both hexagon-head and square-head bolts up to 6 inches long,

$$\text{Thread length} = 2D + \tfrac{1}{4} \text{ in.,}$$

where D is the diameter of the bolt. For bolts more than 6 inches long

$$\text{Thread length} = 2D + \tfrac{1}{2} \text{ inch.}$$

Threads for bolts can be coarse, fine, or 8-pitch threads. The class of fit for bolts and nuts is understood to be 2A and 2B if no class is specified in the note.

Dimension Notes

Designate standard square-head and hexagon-head bolts by notes in one of three forms:

⅜-16 × 1½ SQUARE BOLT—STEEL;

½-13 × 3 HEX CAP SCREW—
SAE GRADE 8—STEEL;

.75 × 5.00 UNC-2A HEX HD LAG SCREW.

The numbers (left to right) represent bolt diameter, threads per inch (omit for lag screws), bolt length, screw name, and material (material designation is optional). When not specified in a note, each bolt is assumed to have a class 2 fit.

Three types of notes for designating nuts are

½-13 SQUARE NUT—STEEL;

¾-16 HEAVY HEX NUT;

1.00-8 UNC-2B HEX THICK SLOTTED
NUT—CORROSION-RESISTANT STEEL.

When nuts are not specified as heavy, they are assumed to be regular. When the class of fit is not specified in a note, it is assumed to be 2B for nuts.

Drawing Square Heads

Appendix 11 gives dimensions for square bolt heads and nuts. However, conventional practice is to draw nuts and bolts by using the general proportions shown in **Fig. 10.40**. The first step in drawing a bolt head or nut is to determine whether the view is to be across corners or across flats—that is, whether the lines at either side of the view rep-

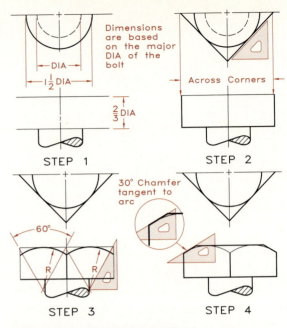

Figure 10.40 Drawing the square head:
Step 1 Draw the major diameter, DIA, of the bolt. Use 1.5 DIA to establish the hexagon-head's diameter and ⅔ DIA to establish its thickness.

Step 2 Draw the top view of the square head at a 45° angle to give an across-corners view.

Step 3 Show the chamfer in the front view by using a 30°–60° triangle to find the centers for the radii.

Step 4 Show a 30° chamfer tangent to the arcs in the front view. Darken the lines.

resent the square's corners or flats. Drawing across corners represents nuts and bolts best, but occasionally you must draw one across flats when the head or nut is truly in this orientation.

Drawing Hexagon Heads

Figure 10.41 shows how to draw the head of a hexagon bolt across corners by using the bolt's major diameter, D, as the basis for all other proportions. Begin by drawing the top view of the head as a circle of a diameter of 1-1/2 D. For a regular head the thickness is 2/3 D and for a heavy head it

DRAWING HEXAGON HEADS

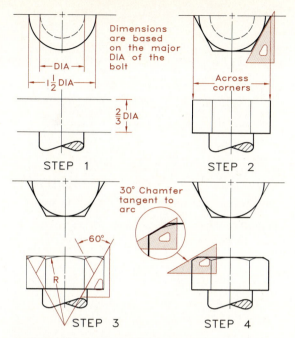

Figure 10.41 Drawing the hexagon head:

Step 1 Draw the major diameter, DIA, of the bolt and use it to establish the head diameter (as 1.5 DIA) and thickness (as ⅔ DIA).

Step 2 Construct a hexagon head with a 30°–60° triangle to give an across-corners view.

Step 3 Find arcs in the front view to show the chamfer of the head.

Step 4 Draw a 30° chamfer tangent to the arcs in the front view. Darken the lines.

is 7/8 D. Circumscribe a hexagon about the circle. Then draw outside arcs in the rectangular view and tangent chamfers (bevels) to complete the drawing.

Drawing Nuts

Use the same techniques to draw a square and a hexagon nut (shown across corners in **Fig. 10.42**) that you did to draw bolt heads. However, nuts are thicker than bolt heads: The thickness of a regular nut is 7/8 D, and the thickness of a heavy nut is 1 D, where D is the bolt diameter. You may insert hidden

DRAWING NUTS ACROSS CORNERS

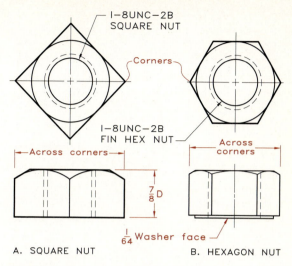

A. SQUARE NUT   B. HEXAGON NUT

Figure 10.42 Drawing square and hexagon nuts across corners involves the same steps used for drawing bolt heads. Add notes to give nut specifications.

lines in the front view to indicate threads, or you may omit them because threading is understood. **Exaggerate the thickness of the 1/64-inch washer face on the finished and semifinished hexagon nuts to about 1/32 inch to make it more noticeable.** Place thread notes on circular views with leaders when space permits. Square nuts that are not labeled heavy are assumed to be regular nuts.

Figure 10.43 shows how to construct square and hexagon nuts across flats. For regular nuts, the distance across flats is 1-1/2 × D (D = major diameter of the thread), and 1-5/8 D for heavy nuts. Draw the top views in the same way you did across-corner top views, but rotate them to give across-flat front views. **Figure 10.44** depicts dimensioned and noted hexagon regular and heavy nuts drawn across corners.

Drawing Nut and Bolt Combinations

Apply the methods of drawing nuts and bolts to drawing nuts and bolts in assembly (**Fig. 10.45**). Use the major diameter, D, of the bolt as the basis

DRAWING NUTS ACROSS FLATS

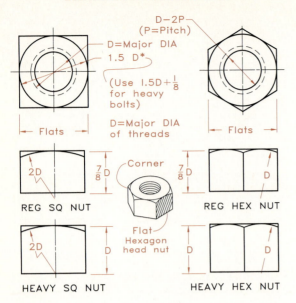

Figure 10.43 These square and hexagon nuts are drawn across flats, with notes added to give nut specifications. Square nuts always are unfinished.

REGULAR AND HEAVY NUTS

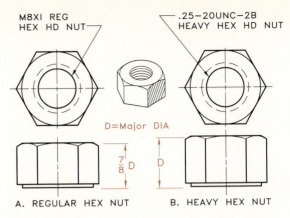

Figure 10.44 These regular and heavy hexagon nuts are drawn across corners, with specification notes added.

for other dimensions. Add a note to give the specifications of the nut and bolt. Here, the views of the bolt heads are across corners, and the views of the nuts are across flats, although both views could have been drawn across corners. Use the half end views to find the front views by projection.

10.5 Screws

Cap Screws

Cap screws are used to hold two parts together without a nut. The cap screw passes through a hole in one part and screws into a threaded hole in the other part. Cap screws are usually larger than machine screws and may also be used with nuts. **Figure 10.46** shows the standard types of cap screw heads drawn on a grid that can be used as a guide for drawing cap screws of other sizes.

BOLT AND NUT PROPORTIONS

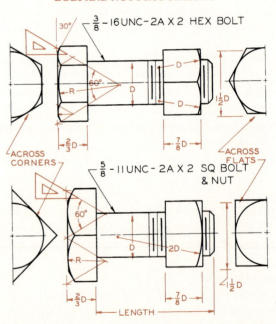

Figure 10.45 This drawing shows hexagon nuts and bolts and square nuts and bolts in assembly and their relative proportions.

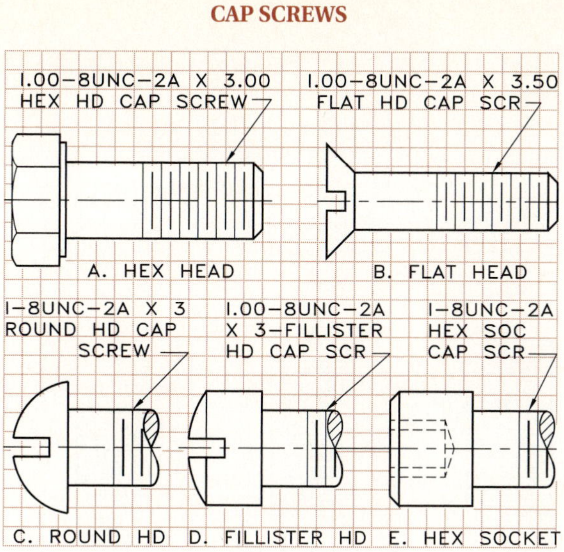

CAP SCREWS

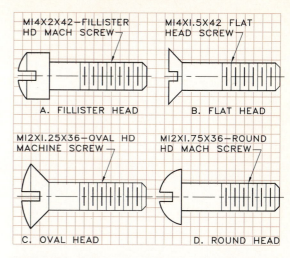

I.00-8UNC-2A X 3.00 HEX HD CAP SCREW

I.00-8UNC-2A X 3.50 FLAT HD CAP SCR

A. HEX HEAD

B. FLAT HEAD

I-8UNC-2A X 3 ROUND HD CAP SCREW

I.00-8UNC-2A X 3-FILLISTER HD CAP SCR

I-8UNC-2A HEX SOC CAP SCR

C. ROUND HD   D. FILLISTER HD   E. HEX SOCKET

Figure 10.46 These cap screws are drawn on a grid to give the proportions for drawing them at different sizes. Notes give thread specifications, length, head type, and bolt name (cap screw).

MACHINE SCREWS

MI4X2X42-FILLISTER HD MACH SCREW

MI4X1.5X42 FLAT HEAD SCREW

A. FILLISTER HEAD

B. FLAT HEAD

MI2X1.25X36-OVAL HD MACHINE SCREW

MI2X1.75X36-ROUND HD MACH SCREW

C. OVAL HEAD

D. ROUND HEAD

Figure 10.47 These are standard types of machine screws. The same proportions may be used to draw machine screws of all sizes.

Appendixes 11–19 give cap screw dimensions, which can aid in drawing them.

Machine Screws

Smaller than most cap screws, **machine screws** usually are less than 1 inch in diameter. They screw into a threaded hole in a part or into a nut. Machine screws are fully threaded when their length is 2 inches or less. Longer screws have thread lengths of 2D + 1/4 inch (D = major diameter of the thread). **Figure 10.47** shows four types of machine screws, along with notes, drawn on a grid that may be used as an aid in drawing them without dimensions from a table. Machine screws range in diameter from No. 0 (0.060 inch) to 3/4 inch, as shown in Appendix 20, which gives the dimensions of round-head machine screws.

Set Screws

Set screws are used to hold parts, such as pulleys and handles on a shaft, together and prevent rotation. **Figure 10.48** shows various types of set screws, with dimensions denoted by letters that correspond to the tables of dimensions in Appendix 21.

Set screws are available in combinations of points and heads. The shaft against which the set screw is tightened may have a machined flat surface to provide a good bearing surface for a **dog** or **flat-point** set screw end to press against. The cup point gives good friction when pressed against round shafts. The **Cone point** works best when inserted into holes drilled in the part being held. The **headless set screw** has no head to protrude above a rotating part. An **exterior square head** is good for applications in which greater force must be applied with a wrench to hold larger set screws in position.

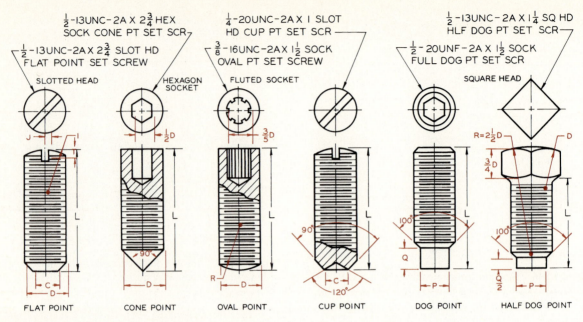

$\frac{1}{2}$-13UNC-2A X 2$\frac{3}{4}$ HEX SOCK CONE PT SET SCR

$\frac{1}{2}$-13UNC-2A X 2$\frac{3}{4}$ SLOT HD FLAT POINT SET SCREW

$\frac{1}{4}$-20UNC-2A X 1 SLOT HD CUP PT SET SCR

$\frac{3}{8}$-16UNC-2A X 1$\frac{1}{2}$ SOCK OVAL PT SET SCREW

$\frac{1}{2}$-13UNC-2A X 1$\frac{1}{4}$ SQ HD HLF DOG PT SET SCR

$\frac{1}{2}$-20UNF-2A X 1$\frac{1}{2}$ SOCK FULL DOG PT SET SCR

SLOTTED HEAD   HEXAGON SOCKET   FLUTED SOCKET   SQUARE HEAD

FLAT POINT   CONE POINT   OVAL POINT   CUP POINT   DOG POINT   HALF DOG POINT

Figure 10.48 Set screws are available with various combinations of heads and points. Notes give their measurements. (See Appendix 21.)

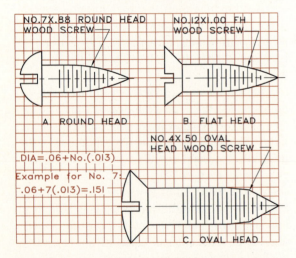

NO.7X.88 ROUND HEAD WOOD SCREW

NO.12X1.00 FH WOOD SCREW

A. ROUND HEAD

B. FLAT HEAD

NO.4X.50 OVAL HEAD WOOD SCREW

DIA=.06+No.(.013)

Example for No. 7:
.06+7(.013)=.151

C. OVAL HEAD

Figure 10.49 Standard types of wood screws are drawn on a grid that gives the proportions for drawing them at other sizes.

Wood Screws

A **wood screw** is a pointed screw having sharp coarse threads that will screw into wood while making its own internal threads. **Figure 10.49** shows the three most common types of wood screws drawn on a grid to show their relative proportions.

Sizes of wood screws are specified by single numbers, such as 0, 6, or 16. From 0 to 10, each digit represents a different size. Beginning at 10, only even-numbered sizes are standard, that is, 10, 12, 14, 16, 18, 20, 22, and 24. Use the following formula to translate these numbers into the actual diameter sizes:

Actual DIA = 0.06 + (screw number × 0.013).

For example, the diameter for the No. 7 wood screw shown in Fig. 10.49 is calculated as follows:

$$DIA = 0.06 + 7(0.013) = 0.151.$$

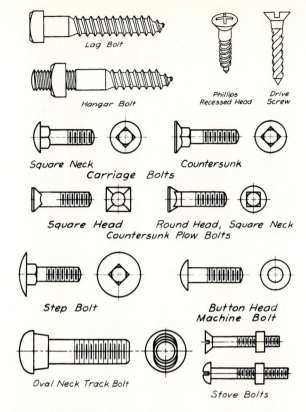

Figure 10.50 This drawing illustrates miscellaneous types of bolts and screws.

10.6 Other Threaded Fasteners

We have space to cover only the more common types of nuts and bolts in this chapter. **Figure 10.50** shows a few of the many other types of threaded fasteners that have their own special applications. Three types of wing screws that are turned by hand are available in incremental lengths of 1/8 inch (**Fig. 10.51**). **Figure 10.52** shows two types of thumb screws, which serve the same purpose as wing screws, and **Fig. 10.53** shows wing nuts that can be screwed together by fingertip without wrenches or screwdrivers.

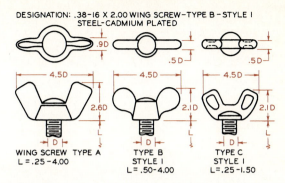

Figure 10.51 These wing screw proportions are for screw diameters of about ⁵⁄₁₆ inch. The same proportions may be used to draw wing screws of any diameter. Type A screws are available in diameters of 4, 6, 8, 10, 12, 0.25", 0.313", 0.375", 0.438", 0.50", and 0.625". Type B screws are available in diameters of 10 to 0.625". Type C screws are available in diameters of 6 to 0.375".

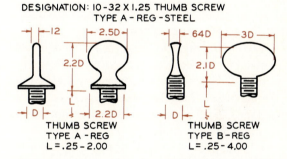

Figure 10.52 These thumb screw proportions are for screw diameters of about ¼ inch. The same proportions may be used to draw thumb screws of any diameter. Type A screws are available in diameters of 6, 8, 10, 12, 0.25", 0.313", and 0.375". Type B thumb screws are available in diameters of 6 to 0.50".

10.7 Tapping a Hole

An internal thread is made by drilling a hole with a tap drill with a 120° point (**Fig. 10.54**). **The depth of the drilled hole is measured to the shoulder of the conical point, not to the point.** The diameter

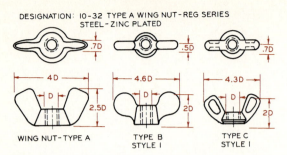

DESIGNATION: 10-32 TYPE A WING NUT-REG SERIES
STEEL - ZINC PLATED

WING NUT-TYPE A

TYPE B
STYLE I

TYPE C
STYLE I

Figure 10.53 These wing nut proportions are for screw diameters of ⅜ inch. The same proportions may be used to draw thumb screws of any size. Type A wing nuts are available in screw diameters of 3, 4, 5, 6, 8, 10, 12, 0.25", 0.313", 0.375", 0.438", 0.50", 0.583", 0.625", and 0.75". Type B nuts are available in sizes from 5 to 0.75". Type C nuts are available in sizes from 4 to 0.50".

of the drilled hole is approximately equal to the root diameter, calculated as the major diameter of the screw thread minus its pitch. (See Appendix 23.) The hole is **tapped**, or threaded, with a tool called a **tap** of one of the types shown.

The taper, plug, and bottoming hand taps have identical measurements, except for the chamfered portion of their ends. The **taper tap** has a long chamfer (8 to 10 threads), the **plug tap** has a shorter chamfer (3 to 5 threads), and the **bottoming tap** has the shortest chamfer (1 to 1-1/2 threads).

When tapping is to be done by hand in open or "through" holes, the taper tap should be used for coarse threads and in harder metals because it ensures straighter alignment and starting. The plug tap may be used in soft metals and for fine-pitch threads. **When a hole is tapped to its bottom, all three taps—taper, plug, and bottoming—are used in that sequence on the same internal threads.**

Notes may be added to specify the depth of a drilled hole and the depth of the threads within it. For example, a note reading 7/8 DIA-3 DEEP × 1–8 UNC-2A × 2 DEEP means that the hole is to be drilled deeper than it is threaded and that the last usable thread will be 2 inches deep in the hole.

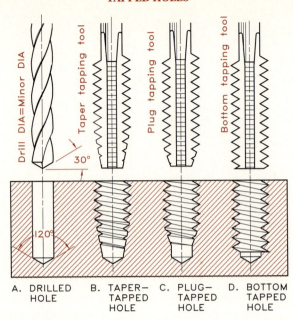

A. DRILLED HOLE

B. TAPER— TAPPED HOLE

C. PLUG— TAPPED HOLE

D. BOTTOM TAPPED HOLE

Figure 10.54 Three types of tapping tools are used to thread internal drilled holes: taper tap, plug tap, and bottom tap.

10.8 Washers, Lock Washers, and Pins

Various types of **washers** are used with nuts and bolts to improve their assembly and increase their fastening strength. Plain washers are noted on a drawing as

.938 × 1.750 × 0.134 TYPE A PLAIN WASHER,

where the numbers (left to right) represent the washer's inside diameter, outside diameter, and thickness. (See Appendixes 29 and 30.)

Lock washers reduce the likelihood that threaded parts will loosen because of vibration and movement. **Figure 10.55** shows several common types of lock washers. Appendix 31 contains a table of dimensions for regular and extra-heavy-duty helical-spring lock washers. Designate them with a note in the form:

HELICAL-SPRING LOCK WASHER
1/4 REGULAR—PHOSPHOR BRONZE,

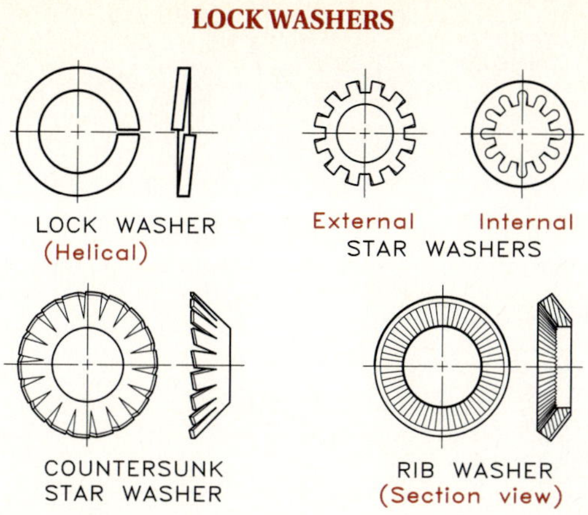

LOCK WASHERS

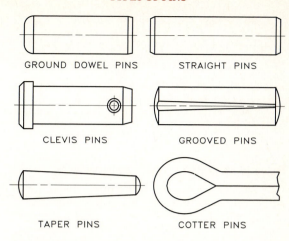

LOCK WASHER
(Helical)

External   Internal
STAR WASHERS

COUNTERSUNK
STAR WASHER

RIB WASHER
(Section view)

Figure 10.55 Lock washers are used to keep threaded parts from vibrating apart.

TYPES OF PINS

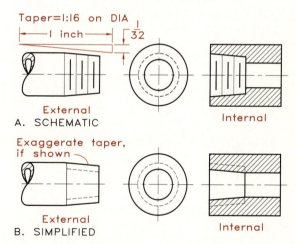

GROUND DOWEL PINS   STRAIGHT PINS

CLEVIS PINS   GROOVED PINS

TAPER PINS   COTTER PINS

Figure 10.56 Pins are used to hold parts together in assembly.

where the 1/4 is the washer's inside diameter. Designate tooth lock washers with a note in one of two forms:

INTERNAL-TOOTH LOCK WASHER
1/4-TYPE A—STEEL;

EXTERNAL-TOOTH LOCK WASHER-562-TYPE B—STEEL.

Pins (Fig. 10.56) are used to hold parts together in a fixed position. Appendix 26 gives dimensions for taper pins. The **cotter pin** is another locking device that everyone who has had a toy wagon is familiar with. Appendix 24 contains a table of dimensions for cotter pins.

10.9 Pipe Threads and Fittings

Pipe threads are used for screwing together connecting pipes and tubing and for lubrication fittings. The most commonly used pipe thread is tapered at a ratio of 1 to 16 on its diameter, but straight pipe threads also are available (**Fig. 10.57**). Tapered pipe threads will engage only for an effective length of

$$L = (0.80D + 6.8)P,$$

PIPE THREAD SYMBOLS

Taper=1:16 on DIA

1 inch $\frac{1}{32}$

External
A. SCHEMATIC

Internal

Exaggerate taper,
if shown

External
B. SIMPLIFIED

Internal

Figure 10.57 These schematic and simplified thread symbols represent pipe threads.

where D is the outside diameter of the threaded pipe and P is the pitch of the thread.

The pipe threads shown in Fig. 10.57 have a taper exaggerated to 1:16 on radius (instead of on diameter) to emphasize it. Drawing them with no taper obviously is easier. You may use either

PIPE THREAD NOTES

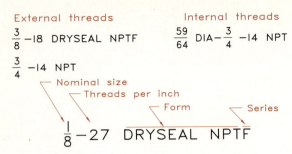

Figure 10.58 These are typical pipe thread notes.

GREASE FITTINGS

Thread size	$\frac{1}{8}$ 3mm		$\frac{1}{4}$ 6mm		$\frac{3}{8}$ 10mm	
Overall length	L=in.	mm	L=in.	mm	L=in.	mm
Straight	.625	16	1.000	25	1.200	30
90° Elbow	.800	20	1.250	32	1.400	36
45° Angle	1.000	25	1.500	38	1.600	41

GREASE FITTINGS
Threads may be NPT
or UN form

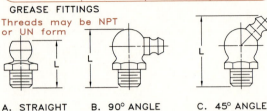

A. STRAIGHT B. 90° ANGLE C. 45° ANGLE

Figure 10.59 These three standard types of grease fittings permit lubrication of moving parts with a grease gun.

schematic or simplified symbols to show the threaded features.

Use the following ANSI abbreviations in pipe thread notes. All begin with NP (for National Pipe thread).

NPT: national pipe taper

NPTF: national pipe thread (dryseal, for pressure-tight joints)

NPS: straight pipe thread

NPSC: straight pipe thread in couplings

NPSI: national pipe straight internal thread

NPSF: straight pipe thread (dryseal)

NPSM: straight pipe thread for mechanical joints

NPSL: straight pipe thread for locknuts and locknut pipe threads

NPSH: straight pipe thread for hose couplings and nipples

NPTR: taper pipe thread for railing fittings

To specify a pipe thread in note form, give the nominal pipe diameter (the common-fraction size of its internal diameter), the number of threads per inch, and the thread-type symbol:

1-1/4-11-1/2 NPT or 3-8 NPTR

Appendix 10 gives a table of dimensions for pipe threads. **Figure 10.58** shows how to present specifications for external and internal threads in note form. Dryseal threads, either straight or tapered, provide a pressure-tight joint without the use of a lubricant or sealer.

Grease Fittings

Grease fittings (Fig. 10.59) allow the application of grease to moving parts that must be lubricated. Threads of grease fittings are available as tapered and straight pipe threads. The ends where grease is inserted with a grease gun are available straight or at 90° and 45° angles. A one-way valve, formed by a ball and spring, permits grease to enter the fitting (forced through by a grease gun) but prevents it from escaping.

10.10 Keys

Keys are used to attach pulleys, gears, or crank handles to shafts, allowing them to remain assembled while moving and transmitting power. The

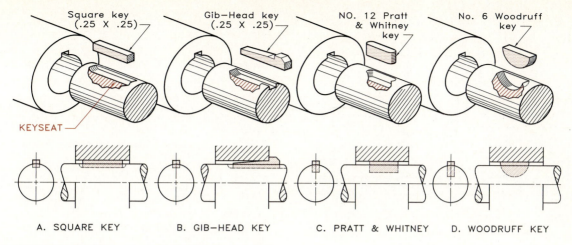

Figure 10.60 Standard keys are used to hold parts on a shaft.

four types of keys shown in **Fig. 10.60** are the most commonly used. Appendixes 27 and 28 contain tables of dimensions for keyways, keys, and keyseats.

10.11 Rivets

Rivets are fasteners that permanently join thin overlapping materials. The rivet is inserted in a hole slightly larger than the diameter of the rivet, and the application of pressure to the projecting end forms the headless end into shape. Forming may be done with either hot or cold rivets, depending on the application.

Figure 10.61 shows typical shapes and proportions of small rivets that vary in diameter from 1/16 to 1-3/4 inches. Rivets are used extensively in pressure-vessel fabrication, heavy construction (such as bridges and buildings), and sheet-metal construction.

Figure 10.62 shows some of the standard ANSI symbols for representing rivets. Rivets that are driven in the shop are called **shop rivets**, and those assembled at the job site are called **field rivets**.

TYPICAL RIVETS

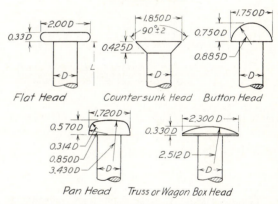

Figure 10.61 This drawing depicts types and proportions of small rivets, which have shank diameters of up to ½ inch.

10.12 Springs

Springs are devices that absorb energy and react with an equal force. Most springs are **helical**, as in a bed, but they can also be **flat** (leaf), as in an automobile chassis. Some of the more common types of springs are **compression, torsion, extension, flat,** and **constant force springs**.

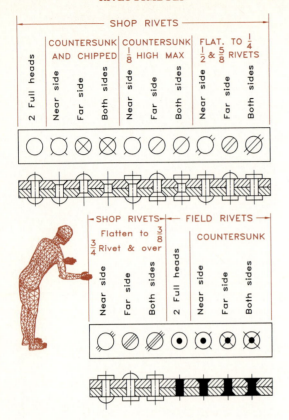

Figure 10.62 These symbols represent rivets in a drawing.

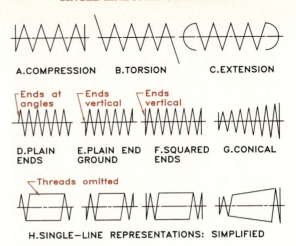

Figure 10.63

A–C These are single-line representations of various types of springs.

D–G These single-line representations of springs show various types of ends.

H These are simplified single-line representations of the springs depicted in D–G.

Figures 10.63A–C show single-line conventional representations of the first three types. **Figures 10.63D–F** represent the types of ends used on compression springs. Plain ends of springs simply end with no special modification of the coil. Ground plain ends are coils that have been machined by grinding to flatten the ends perpendicular to their axes. Squared ends are inactive coils that have been closed to form a circular flat coil at the end of a spring, which may also be ground.

Figure 10.63G represents a conical helical spring. **Figure 10.63H** shows schematic single-line representations of the springs depicted in

Fig. 10.63D–G (conventional method of drawing springs), with phantom outlines instead of all the coils.

Figure 10.64 shows working drawing specifications of a compression spring drawn as a double-line representation. It shows both ends of the spring and the use of phantom lines to omit the central part of the spring's coils in order to save drawing time. Notate the diameter and free length of the spring on the drawing and give the remaining specifications a table near the drawing.

A working drawing of an extension spring (**Fig. 10.65**) is similar to that of a compression spring. An extending spring is designed to resist stretching, whereas a compression spring is designed to resist squeezing. In a drawing of a helical torsion spring, which resists and reacts to a twisting motion (**Fig.**

COMPRESSION SPRING

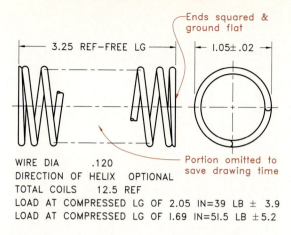

Ends squared & ground flat

3.25 REF—FREE LG

1.05±.02

Portion omitted to save drawing time

WIRE DIA   .120
DIRECTION OF HELIX   OPTIONAL
TOTAL COILS   12.5 REF
LOAD AT COMPRESSED LG OF 2.05 IN=39 LB ± 3.9
LOAD AT COMPRESSED LG OF 1.69 IN=51.5 LB ±5.2

Figure 10.64 This conventional double-line drawing is of a compression spring and includes its specifications.

TORSION SPRING

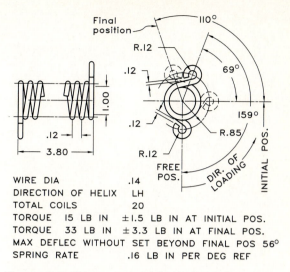

Final position
110°
R.12
.12
69°
159°
.12
R.85
R.12
.12
FREE POS.
DIR. OF LOADING
INITIAL POS.
3.80
1.00

WIRE DIA   .14
DIRECTION OF HELIX   LH
TOTAL COILS   20
TORQUE   15 LB IN   ±1.5 LB IN AT INITIAL POS.
TORQUE   33 LB IN   ±3.3 LB IN AT FINAL POS.
MAX DEFLEC WITHOUT SET BEYOND FINAL POS 56°
SPRING RATE   .16 LB IN PER DEG REF

Figure 10.66 This conventional double-line drawing is of a helical torsion spring and includes its specifications.

EXTENSION SPRING

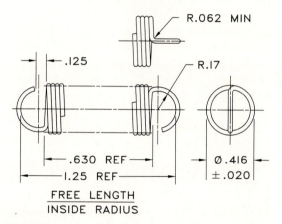

R.062 MIN

.125

R.17

.630 REF

1.25 REF

Ø .416
±.020

FREE LENGTH
INSIDE RADIUS

WIRE DIA   0.42
DIRECTION OF HELIX   OPTIONAL
TOTAL COILS   14 REF
RELATIVE POSITION OF ENDS   180° ±20°
EXTENDED LENGTH INSIDE ENDS
WITHOUT PERMANENT SET   2.45 IN (MAX)
INITIAL TENSION   1.00 LB ±.10 LB
LOAD   4.0 LB ±.4 LB AT 1.56 IN
EXTENDED LG INSIDE ENDS
LOAD   6.30 LB ±.63 LB AT 1.95

Figure 10.65 This conventional double-line drawing is of an extension spring and includes its specifications.

10.66), angular dimensions specify the initial and final positions of the spring as torsion is applied to it. Again, notate the dimensions on the drawing and add specifications to describe their details.

Drawing Springs

Springs may be represented with single-line drawings (see Fig. 10.63) or as more realistic double-line drawings (**Fig. 10.67**). Draw each type shown by first laying out the diameters of the coils and lengths of the springs and then dividing the lengths into the number of active coils (**Fig. 10.67A**). In **Fig. 10.67B**, both end coils are "dead" (inactive) coils, and only six coils are active. **Figure 10.67C** depicts an extension spring with eight active coils.

Figure 10.68 shows the steps involved in drawing a double-line representation of a compression spring. Here, the ends of the spring are to be squared and ground to give flat ends perpendicular to the axis of the spring.

DOUBLE-LINE DRAWINGS OF SPRINGS

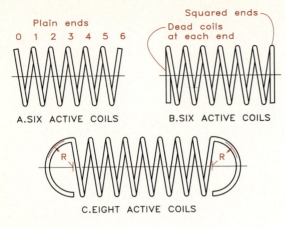

A.SIX ACTIVE COILS

B.SIX ACTIVE COILS

C.EIGHT ACTIVE COILS

Figure 10.67

A This double-line drawing shows a spring with six active coils.

B This double-line drawing shows a spring with six coils and a "dead" coil (inactive coil) at each end.

C This double-line drawing shows an extension spring with eight active coils.

DRAWING A SPRING: DETAILED

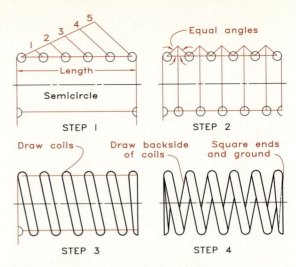

STEP 1

STEP 2

STEP 3

STEP 4

Figure 10.68 Drawing a spring in detail:

Step 1 Lay out the diameter and length of the spring and locate the five coils by the diagonal-line technique.

Step 2 Locate the coils on the lower side along the bisectors of the spaces between the coils on the upper side.

Step 3 Connect the coils on each side. This is a right-hand coil; a left-hand spring would slope in the opposite direction.

Step 4 Construct the back side of the spring and the end coils to complete the drawing. The spring has a square end that is to be ground.

Problems

Solve and draw these problems on size A sheets. Each grid space equals 0.20 inch, or 5 mm.

1. (Fig. 10.69) Draw detailed representations of Acme threads with major diameters of 2 in. Show both external and internal threads as views and sections. Provide a thread note by referring to Appendix 9.

2. Repeat Problem 1, but draw internal and external detailed representations of square threads.

3. Repeat Problem 1, but draw internal and external detailed representations of UN threads. Provide a thread note for a coarse thread with a class 2 fit.

4. Using the notes in **Fig. 10.70**, draw detailed representations of the internal threads and holes in section. Provide thread notes on each as specified.

5. Repeat Problem 4, but use schematic thread symbols.

6. Repeat Problem 4, but use simplified thread symbols.

7. Using the partial views in **Fig. 10.71** and detailed thread symbols, draw external, internal, and end views of the full-size threaded parts. Provide thread notes for UNC threads with a class 2 fit.

8. Repeat Problem 7, but use schematic thread symbols.

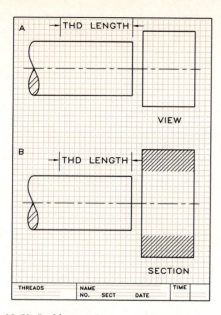

Figure 10.69 Problems 1–3.

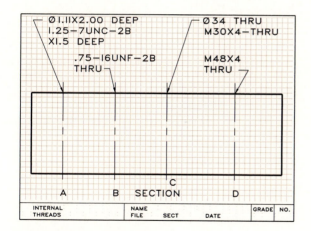

Figure 10.70 Problems 4–6.

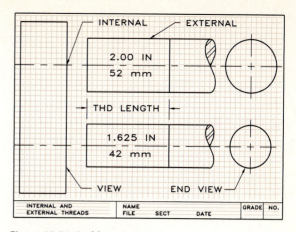

Figure 10.71 Problems 7–9.

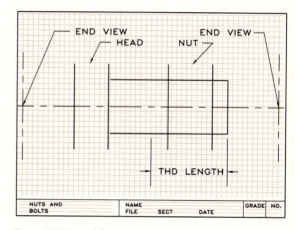

Figure 10.72 Problems 10–12.

9. Repeat Problem 7, but use simplified thread symbols.

10. (Fig. 10.72) Complete the drawing of the finished hexagon-head bolt and a heavy hexagon nut. Draw the bolt head and nut across corners using detailed thread symbols. Provide thread notes in either English or metric forms, as assigned.

11. Repeat Problem 10, but draw the nut and bolt as having unfinished square heads. Use schematic thread symbols.

12. Repeat Problem 10, but draw the bolt with a regular finished hexagon head across flats, using simplified thread symbols. Draw the nut across flats also and provide thread notes for both.

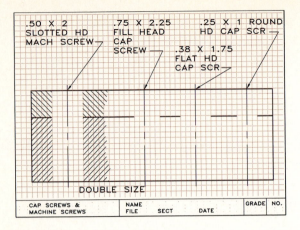

Figure 10.73 Problems 13–15.

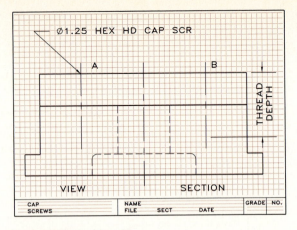

Figure 10.75 Problem 17.

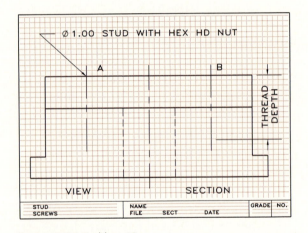

Figure 10.76 Problem 18.

Figure 10.74 Problem 16.

13. Use the notes in **Fig. 10.73** to draw the screws in section and complete the sectional view showing all cross-hatching. Use detailed thread symbols and provide thread notes to the parts.

14. Repeat Problem 13, but use schematic thread symbols.

15. Repeat Problem 13, but use simplified thread symbols.

16. (Fig. 10.74) The pencil pointer has a ¼-in. shaft that fits into a bracket designed to clamp onto a desk top. A set screw holds the shaft in position. Make a drawing of the bracket, estimating its dimensions. Show the details

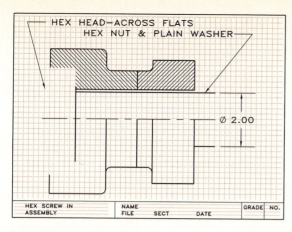

Figure 10.77 Problem 19.

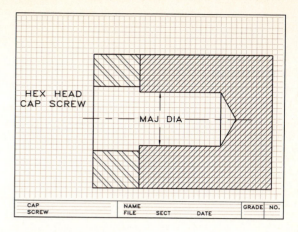

Figure 10.78 Problem 20.

and the method of using the set screw to hold the shaft and provide a thread note.

17. (Fig. 10.75) On axes A and B, construct hexagon-head cap screws (across flats), with UNC threads and a class 2 fit. The cap screws should not reach the bottoms of the threaded holes. Convert the view to a half section.

18. (Fig. 10.76) On axes A and B, draw studs having a hexagon-head nut (across flats) that hold the two parts together. The studs are to be fine series with a class 2 fit, and they should not reach the bottom of the threaded hole. Provide a thread note. Show the view as a half section.

19. (Fig. 10.77) Draw a 2.00-in. (50-mm) diameter hexagon-head bolt, with its head across flats, using schematic symbols. Draw a plain washer and regular nut (across corners) at the right end. Design the size of the opening in the part at the left end to hold the bolt head so that it will not turn. Use a UNC thread with a series 2 fit and provide a thread note.

20. (Fig. 10.78) Draw a 2.00-in. (50-mm) diameter hexa-gon-head cap screw that holds the two parts together. Determine the length of the bolt, show the threads with schematic thread symbols, and provide a thread note.

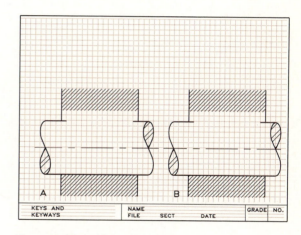

Figure 10.79 Problems 21 and 22.

21. (Fig. 10.79) The part at A is held on the shaft by a square key, and the part at B is held on the shaft by a gib-head key. Using Appendix 28, complete the drawings and provide the necessary notes.

22. Repeat Problem 21, but use Woodruff keys, one with a flat bottom and the other with a round bottom. Using Appendix 27, complete the drawings and provide the necessary notes.

23–26. (Fig. 10.80) Using Table 10.1, make a double-line drawing of the spring assigned.

27–30. Repeat Problem 23, but draw the springs using single-line representations.

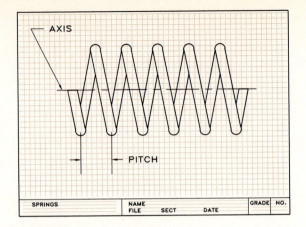

Figure 10.80 Problems 23–30.

Table 10.1
Problems 23–30

Problems	No. of Turns	Pitch	Size Wire	Inside Diameter	Outside Diameter	
23	4	1	No. 4 = 0.2253	3		RH
24	5	$\frac{3}{4}$	No. 6 = 0.1920		2	LH
25	6	$\frac{5}{8}$	No. 10 = 0.1350	2		RH
26	7	$\frac{3}{4}$	No. 7 = 0.1770		$1\frac{3}{4}$	LH

11

Gears and Cams

11.1 Introduction

Gears are toothed wheels whose circumferences mesh to transmit force and motion from one gear to the next. The three most common types are **spur gears, bevel gears**, and **worm gears (Fig. 11.1).**

Cams are irregularly shaped plates and cylinders that control the motion of a follower as they revolve to produce a type of reciprocating action. For example, cams make the needle of a sewing machine move up and down.

Figure 11.1 The three basic types of gears are (A) spur gears, (B) bevel gears, and (C) worm gears. (Courtesy of the Process Gear Company.)

11.2 Spur Gears

Terminology

The **spur gear** is a circular gear with teeth cut around its circumference. Two meshing spur gears transmit power from one shaft to a parallel shaft. When the two meshing gears are unequal in diameter, the smaller gear is called the **pinion** and the larger one the **spur**.

The following terms and corresponding formulas describe the parts of a spur gear, several of which are shown in **Fig. 11.2**:

Pitch circle (PC): the imaginary circle of a gear, as if it were a friction wheel without teeth that contacted another circular friction wheel.

Pitch diameter (PD): the diameter of the pitch circle; $PD = N/DP$, where N is the number of teeth and DP is the diametral pitch.

Diametral pitch (DP): the ratio between the number of teeth on a gear and its pitch diameter; $DP = N/PD$, where N is the number of teeth, and is expressed as teeth per inch of diameter.

GEAR TERMINOLOGY

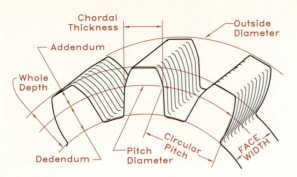

Figure 11.2 These terms apply to spur gears.

Circular pitch (CP): the circular measurement from one point on a tooth to the corresponding point on the next tooth measured along the pitch circle; $CP = 3.14/DP$.

Center distance (CD): the distance from the center of a gear to its mating gear's center; $CD = (N_p + N_S)/(2DP)$, where N_p and N_S are the number of teeth in the pinion and spur, respectively.

Addendum (A): the height of a gear above its pitch circle; $A = 1/DP$.

Dedendum (D): the depth of a gear below the pitch circle; $D = 1.157/DP$.

Whole depth (WD): the total depth of a gear tooth; $WD = A + D$.

Working depth (WKD): the depth to which a tooth fits into a meshing gear; $WKD = 2/DP$, or $WKD = 2A$.

Circular thickness (CRT): the circular distance across a tooth measured along the pitch circle; $CRT = 1.57/DP$.

Chordal thickness (CT): is the straight-line distance across a tooth at the pitch circle; $CT = PD (\sin 90°/N)$, where N is the number of teeth.

Face width (FW): the width across a gear tooth parallel to its axis; a variable dimension, but usually three to four times the circular pitch; $FW = 3CP$ to $4CP$.

Outside diameter (OD): the maximum diameter of a gear across its teeth; $OD = PD + 2A$.

Root diameter (RD): the diameter of a gear measured from the bottom of its gear teeth; $RD = PD - 2D$.

Pressure angle (PA): the angle between the line of action and a line perpendicular to the centerline of two meshing gears; angles of 14.5° and 20° are standard for involute gears.

Base circle (BC): the circle from which an involute tooth curve is generated or developed; $BC = PD \cos PA$.

Tooth Forms

The most common gear tooth is an involute tooth with a 14.5° pressure angle. The 14.5° angle is the angle of contact between two gears when the tangents of both gears are in contact. Gears with pressure angles of 20° and 25° also are used. Gear teeth with larger pressure angles are wider at the base and thus stronger than the standard 14.5° teeth.

Gear Ratios

The diameters of two meshing spur gears establish ratios that are important to their function **(Fig. 11.3)**. If the diameter of a gear is twice that of its pinion (the small gear), the gear has twice as many teeth as the pinion. The pinion then must make twice as many turns as the spur; therefore the revolutions per minute (RPM) of the pinion is twice that of the spur.

The relationship between two meshing gears may be determined by finding the velocity of a point on the pinion that is equal to $\pi PD \times RPM$. The velocity of a point on the large gear equals $\pi PD \times RPM$. The velocity of points on each gear must be equal, so

$$\pi PD_p (RPM_p) = \pi PD_S (RPM_S);$$

GEAR RATIOS

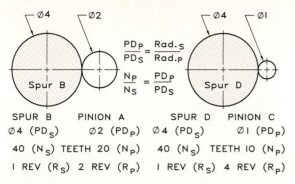

$$\frac{PD_P}{PD_S} = \frac{Rad._S}{Rad._P}$$

$$\frac{N_P}{N_S} = \frac{PD_P}{PD_S}$$

SPUR B	PINION A	SPUR D	PINION C
Ø4 (PD$_S$)	Ø2 (PD$_P$)	Ø4 (PD$_S$)	Ø1 (PD$_P$)
40 (N$_S$) TEETH	20 (N$_P$)	40 (N$_S$) TEETH	10 (N$_P$)
1 REV (R$_S$)	2 REV (R$_P$)	1 REV (R$_S$)	4 REV (R$_P$)

Figure 11.3 These are examples of ratios between meshing spur gears and pinion gears.

therefore

$$\frac{PD_P}{PD_S} = \frac{RPM_S}{RPM_P},$$

If the radius of the pinion is 1 inch, the diameter of the spur is 4 inches, and the RPM of the pinion is 20, the RPM of the spur is

$$\frac{2(1)}{2(4)} = \frac{RPM_S}{20},$$

or

$$RPM_S = \frac{2(20)}{2(4)} = 5\,RPM.$$

Thus the RPM of the spur (5) is one-fourth that of the pinion (20).

The number of teeth on each gear is proportional to the diameters of a pair of meshing gears, or

$$\frac{N_P}{N_S} = \frac{PD_P}{PD_S},$$

where N_P and N_S are the number of teeth on the pinion and spur, respectively, and PD_P and PD_S are their pitch diameters.

Calculations

Before starting a working drawing of a gear, you have to calculate the gear's dimensions.

Problem 1 Calculate the dimensions for a spur that has a pitch diameter of 5 in., a diametral pitch of 4, and a pressure angle of 14.5°.

Solution

Number of teeth: PD(DP) = 5(4) = 20.

Addendum: 1/4 = 0.25".

Dedendum: 1.157/4 = 0.2893".

Circular thickness: 1.5708/4 = 0.3927".

Outside diameter: (20 + 2)/4 = 5.50".

Root diameter: 5 – 2(0.2893) = 4.421".

Chordal thickness:
  5(sin 90°/20) = 5(0.079) = 0.392".

Chordal addendum:
  0.25 + [0.3927^2/(4 × 5)] = 0.2577".

Face width: 3.5(0.79) = 2.75.

Circular pitch: 3.14/4 = 0.785".

Working depth: 0.6366(3.14/4) = 0.4997".

Whole depth: 0.250 + 0.289 = 0.539".

Use these dimensions to draw the spur and to provide specifications necessary for its manufacture.

Problem 2 shows the method of determining design information for two meshing gears when you know their working ratios.

Problem 2 Find the number of teeth and other specifications for a pair of meshing gears with a driving gear that turns at 100 RPM and a driven gear that turns at 60 RPM. The diametral pitch for each is 10, and the center-to-center distance between the gears is 6 in.

Solution

Step 1 Find the sum of the teeth on both gears:

Total teeth = 2(center-to-center distance)(DP)

$$= 2(6)(10) = 120 \text{ teeth.}$$

Step 2 Find the number of teeth for the driving gear:

$$\frac{\text{Driver RPM}}{\text{Driven RPM}} + 1 = \frac{100}{60} + 1 = 2.667,$$

so

$$\frac{\text{Total Teeth}}{\frac{100}{60} + 1} = \frac{120}{2.667} = 45 \text{ teeth.}$$

(The number of teeth must be a whole number since there cannot be fractional teeth on a gear.)

Step 3 Find the number of teeth for the driven gear:

Total teeth – teeth on driver = teeth on driven gear

$$120 - 45 = 75 \text{ teeth.}$$

Step 4 Calculate the other dimensions for the gears as in Problem 1. Adjusting the center distance to yield a whole number of teeth may be necessary.

Drawing Spur Gears

Figure 11.4 shows a conventional drawing of a spur gear. Not having to draw a top view with gear teeth saves a lot of time. Showing only circular and sectional views of the gear and providing a table of dimensions called **cutting data** is acceptable. Circular phantom lines represent the root circle, pitch circle, and outside circle of the gear in the circular view.

A table of dimensions is a necessary part of a gear drawing (**Fig. 11.5**). You may calculate these data or get them from tables of standards in gear handbooks such as *Machinery's Handbook*.

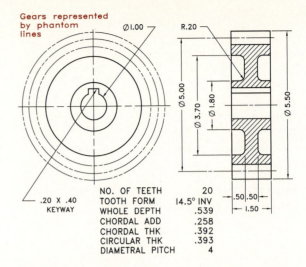

SPUR GEAR

NO. OF TEETH	20
TOOTH FORM	14.5° INV
WHOLE DEPTH	.539
CHORDAL ADD	.258
CHORDAL THK	.392
CIRCULAR THK	.393
DIAMETRAL PITCH	4

Figure 11.4 This detail drawing of a spur gear contains a table of values that supplements the dimensions shown on the view and section.

11.3 Bevel Gears

Terminology

Bevel gears have axes that intersect at angles. The angle of intersection usually is 90°, but other angles also are used. The smaller of the two bevel gears is the pinion, as with spur gears; the larger is the gear.

Figure 11.6 illustrates the terminology of bevel gearing. A further explanation of and the corresponding formula for each feature follow. You may also use gear handbooks to find these dimensions.

Pitch angle of pinion (PA$_p$): tan PA$_p$ = N$_p$/N$_g$, where N$_g$ and N$_p$ are the number of teeth on the gear and pinion, respectively.

Pitch angle of gear (PA$_g$): tan PA$_g$ = N$_g$/N$_p$.

Pitch diameter (PD): the number of teeth, N, divided by the diametral pitch, DP; PD = N/P.

Addendum (A): measured at the large end of the tooth; A = 1/DP.

SPUR GEAR: METRIC

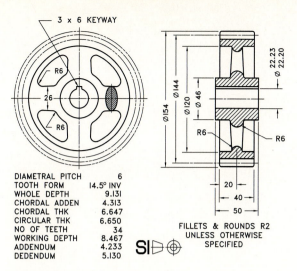

DIAMETRAL PITCH	6
TOOTH FORM	14.5° INV
WHOLE DEPTH	9.131
CHORDAL ADDEN	4.313
CHORDAL THK	6.647
CIRCULAR THK	6.650
NO OF TEETH	34
WORKING DEPTH	8.467
ADDENDUM	4.233
DEDENDUM	5.130

FILLETS & ROUNDS R2
UNLESS OTHERWISE
SPECIFIED

Figure 11.5 This is a detail drawing of a spur gear that was produced on a computer.

BEVEL GEAR TERMINOLOGY

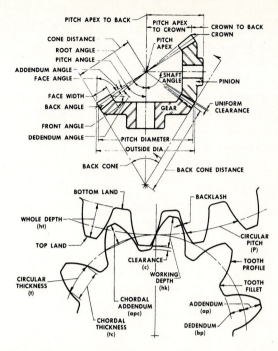

Figure 11.6 These terms apply to bevel gears. (Courtesy of Philadelphia Gear Corporation.)

Dedendum (D): is measured at the large end of the tooth; D = 1.157/DP.

Whole tooth depth (WD): WD = 2.157/DP.

Thickness of tooth (TT): measured at the pitch circle; TT = 1.571/DP.

Diametral pitch: DP = N/PD, where N is the number of teeth.

Addendum angle (AA): the angle formed by the addendum and pitch cone distance; tan AA = A/PCD.

Angular addendum: AK = cos PA × A.

Pitch cone distance:
(PCD): PCD = PD/(2 sin PA).

Dedendum angle (DA): the angle formed by the dedendum and the pitch cone distance; tan DA = D/PCD.

Face angle (FA): the angle between the gear's centerline and the top of its teeth;
FA = 90° − (PCD + AA).

Cutting angle (or root angle) (CA): the angle between the gear's axis and the roots of the teeth; CA = PCD − D.

Outside diameter (OD): the greatest diameter of a gear across its teeth; OD = PD + 2A.

Apex to crown distance (AC): the distance from the crown of the gear to the apex of the cone measured parallel to the axis of the gear; AC = OD/(2 tan FA).

Chordal addendum (CA):
CA = A + [(TT² cos PA)/4PD].

Chordal thickness (CT): measured at the large end of the tooth; CT = PD (sin 90°/N).

Face width (FW): can vary, but should be approximately equal to the pitch cone distance divided by 3; FW = PCD/3.

Calculations

Problem 3 demonstrates use of the preceding formulas. Some of the formulas result in specifications that apply to both gear and pinion.

Problem 3 Two bevel gears intersect at right angles and have a diametral pitch of 3. The gear has 60 teeth, and the pinion has 45 teeth. Find the dimensions of the gear.

Solution

Pitch cone angle of gear:
$$\tan PCA = 60/45 = 1.33; PCA = 53°7'.$$

Pitch cone angle of pinion:
$$\tan PCA = 45/60; PCA = 36°52'.$$

Pitch diameter of gear: $60/3 = 20.00"$.

Pitch diameter of pinion: $45/3 = 15.00"$.

The following calculations yield the same dimensions for both gear and pinion:

Addendum: $1/3 = 0.333"$.

Dedendum: $1.157/3 = 0.3857"$.

Whole depth: $2.157/3 = 0.719"$.

Tooth thickness on pitch circle:
$$1.571/3 = 0.5237".$$

Pitch cone distance:
$$20/(2 \sin 53°7') = 12.5015".$$

Addendum angle:
$$\tan AA = 0.333/12.5015 = 1°32'$$

Dedendum angle:
$$DA = 0.3857/12.5015 = 0.0308 = 1°46'.$$

Face width: $PCD/3 = 4.00"$.

The following dimensions must be calculated separately for gear and pinion:

Chordal addendum of gear:
$$0.333" + [(0.5237^2 \cos 53°7')/(4 \times 20)] = 0.336".$$

Chordal addendum of pinion:
$$0.333" + [(0.5237^2 \cos 36°52')/(4 \times 15)] = 0.338".$$

Chordal thickness of gear:
$$\sin 90°/(60 \times 20") = 0.524".$$

Chordal thickness of pinion:
$$\sin 90°/(45 \times 15") = 0.523".$$

Face angle of gear:
$$90° - (53°7' + 1°32') = 35°21'.$$

Face angle of pinion:
$$90° - (36°52' + 1°32') = 51°36'.$$

Cutting angle of gear: $53°7' - 1°46' = 51°21'$.

Cutting angle of pinion: $36°52' - 1°46' = 35°6'$.

Angular addendum of gear:
$$0.333" \cos 53°7' = 0.1999".$$

Angular addendum of pinion:
$$0.333" \cos 36°52' = 0.2667".$$

Outside diameter of gear:
$$20" + 2(0.1999") = 20.4000".$$

Outside diameter of pinion:
$$15" + 2(0.2667") = 15.533".$$

Apex-to-crown distance of gear:
$$(20.400"/2)(\tan 35°7') = 7.173".$$

Apex-to-crown distance of pinion:
$$(15.533"/2)(\tan 51°36') = 9.800".$$

Drawing Bevel Gears

Use the dimensions calculated to lay out bevel gears in a detail drawing. Because many of these dimensions are difficult to measure with a high degree of accuracy on a drawing, providing a table of cutting data for each gear is important.

Figure 11.7 shows the steps involved in drawing bevel gears. On the finished drawing, the views show certain dimensions, and the table of dimensions contains the rest.

11.4 Worm Gears

A worm gear consists of a threaded shaft called a worm and a circular gear called a spider (Fig. 11.8). When the worm is revolved, it causes the spider to revolve about its axis. Figures 11.8 and

BEVEL GEARS

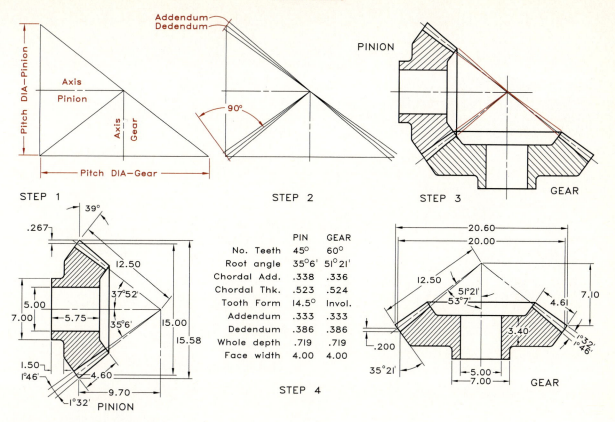

Figure 11.7 Drawing bevel gears:

Step 1 Lay out the pitch diameters and axes of the two bevel gears.

Step 2 Draw construction lines to establish the limits of the teeth by using the addendum and dedendum dimensions.

Step 3 Draw the pinion and gear using the specified or calculated dimensions.

Step 4 Complete the detail drawings of both gears and provide a table of cutting data.

11.9 illustrate the terminology of worm gearing. The following lists further explain these terms and provide the formulas for calculating their dimensions for worm and spider.

Worm Terminology

Linear pitch (P): the distance from one thread to the next, measured parallel to the worm's axis; P = L/N, where N is the number of threads (1 if a single thread, 2 if a double thread, and so on).

Lead (L): the distance a thread advances in a turn of 360°.

Addendum of tooth (AW): AW = 0.3183P.

Pitch diameter (PDW): PDW = OD – 2AW, where OD is the outside diameter.

Whole depth of tooth (WDT): WDT = 0.6866P.

WORM GEARS

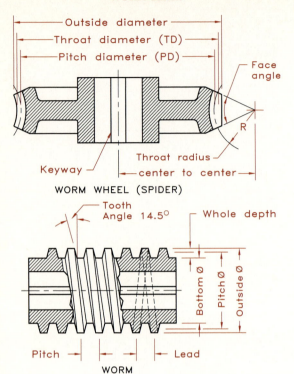

Figure 11.8 These terms apply to worm gears.

WORM GEAR: SPIDER

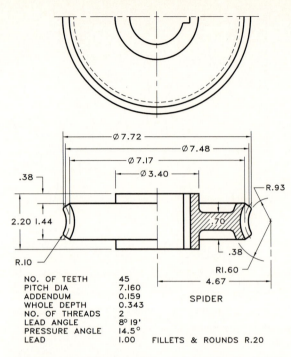

NO. OF TEETH	45
PITCH DIA	7.160
ADDENDUM	0.159
WHOLE DEPTH	0.343
NO. OF THREADS	2
LEAD ANGLE	8° 19'
PRESSURE ANGLE	14.5°
LEAD	1.00

FILLETS & ROUNDS R.20

Figure 11.9 This detail drawing is of a spider for a worm gear with a table of cutting data.

Bottom diameter of worm (BD):
$$BD = OD - 2WDT.$$

Width of thread at root (WT): WT = 0.31P.

Minimum length of worm (MLW):

MLW = $\sqrt{8PDS\,(AW)}$, where PDS is the pitch diameter of the spider.

Helix angle (HA): cot β = 3.14(PDW)/L.

Outside diameter (OD): OD = PD + 2A.

Spider Terminology

Pitch diameter of spider (PDS):

PDS = N(P)/3.14, where N is the number of teeth on the spider.

Throat diameter of spider (TD):
$$TD = PDS + 2A.$$

Radius of spider throat (RST):
$$RST = OD \text{ of worm}/2 - 2A.$$

Face angle (FA): may be selected between 60° and 80° for the average application.

Center-to-center distance (CD):
measured between the worm and spider;
$$CD = PDW + PDS/2.$$

Outside diameter of spider (ODS):
$$ODS = TD + 0.4775P.$$

Face width of gear (FW): FW = 2.38P + 0.25.

WORM GEAR

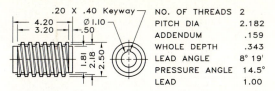

.20 X .40 Keyway	NO. OF THREADS 2
Ø1.10	PITCH DIA 2.182
4.20	ADDENDUM .159
3.20 .50	WHOLE DEPTH .343
1.81 2.18 2.50	LEAD ANGLE 8° 19'
	PRESSURE ANGLE 14.5°
	LEAD 1.00

Figure 11.10 This detail drawing of a worm is based on calculated dimensions.

Figure 11.11 This photo shows three types of machined cams. (Courtesy of Ferguson Machine Company.)

Calculations

Problem 4 demonstrates use of the preceding formulas to find the dimensions for a worm gear.

Problem 4 Calculate the dimensions for a worm gear (worm and spider). The spider has 45 teeth, and the worm has an outside diameter of 2.50 in., a double thread, and a pitch of 0.5 in.

Solution

Lead: $L = 0.5"(2) = 1"$.

Worm addendum: $AW = 0.3183P = 0.1592"$.

Pitch diameter of worm:
$$PDW = 2.50" - 2(0.1592") = 2.1818".$$

Pitch diameter of spider:
$$PDS = (45" \times 0.5)/3.14 = 7.166".$$

Center distance between worm and spider:
$$CD = (2.182" + 7.166")/2 = 4.674".$$

Whole depth of worm tooth:
$$WDT = 0.687(0.5") = 0.3433".$$

Bottom diameter of worm:
$$BD = 2.50" - 2(0.3433") = 1.813".$$

Helix angle of worm:
$$\cot \beta = 3.14(2.1816)/1 = 8°19'.$$

Width of thread at root: $WT = 0.31(1) = 0.155"$.

Minimum length of worm:
$$MLW = \sqrt{8(0.1592) \ (7.1656)} = 3.02"$$

Throat diameter of spider:
$$TD = 7.1656" + 2(0.1592") = 7.484".$$

Radius of spider throat:
$$RST = (2.5/2) - (2 \times 0.1592") = 0.9318".$$

Face width: $FW = 2.38(0.5) + 0.25 = 1.44"$.

Outside diameter of spider:
$$ODS = 7.484 + 0.4775 (0.5) = 7.723".$$

Drawing Worm Gears

Draw and dimension the worm and spider as shown in **Figs. 11.9** and **11.10**. The preceding calculations yield the dimensions needed for scaling and laying out the drawings and providing cutting data.

11.5 Cams

Plate cams are irregularly shaped machine elements that produce motion in a single plane, usually up and down **(Fig. 11.11)**. As the cam revolves about its center, the cam's shape alternately raises and lowers the follower that is in contact with it. Cams utilize the principle of the inclined wedge, with the surface of the cam acting as the wedge, causing a change in the slope of the plane, and thereby producing the desired motion of the follower. **Cams are designed primarily to produce (1) uniform or linear motion, (2) harmonic motion,**

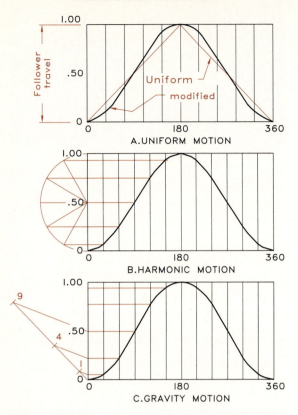

Figure 11.12 These displacement diagrams show three standard motions: uniform, harmonic, and gravity.

(3) gravity motion (uniform acceleration), or (4) combinations of these motions.

Uniform Motion

The uniform motion depicted in **Fig. 11.12A** represents the motion of the cam follower as the cam rotates through 360°. This curve has sharp corners, indicating abrupt changes of velocity that cause the follower to bounce. Therefore uniform motion usually is modified to smooth the changes of velocity. The radius of the modifying arc varies up to a radius of one-half the total displacement, depending on the speed of operation.

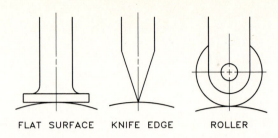

Figure 11.13 Three basic types of cam followers are the flat surface, knife edge, and roller.

Harmonic Motion

The harmonic motion plotted in **Fig. 11.12B** is a smooth, continuous motion based on the change of position of points on a circle. At moderate speeds this displacement gives a smooth operation.

Gravity Motion

The gravity motion (uniform acceleration) illustrated in **Fig. 11.12C** is used for high-speed operation. The variation of displacement is analogous to the force of gravity, with the difference in displacement being 1, 3, 5, 5, 3, 1, based on the square of the number. For instance, $1^2 = 1$, $2^2 = 4$, $3^2 = 9$ give a uniform acceleration. This motion is repeated in reverse order for the remaining half of the follower's motion. Intermediate points are obtained by squaring fractional increments, such as $(2.5)^2$.

Cam Followers

Three basic types of **cam followers** are the **flat surface**, **knife edge**, and **roller (Fig. 11.13)**. Use of flat-surface and knife-edge followers is limited to slow-moving cams, where minor force will be exerted during rotation. The roller follower is able to withstand higher speeds.

Designing Plate Cams

Harmonic Motion   **Figure 11.14** shows the steps involved in designing a plate cam for harmonic motion. Before designing a cam, you must know the motion of the follower, rise of the follower,

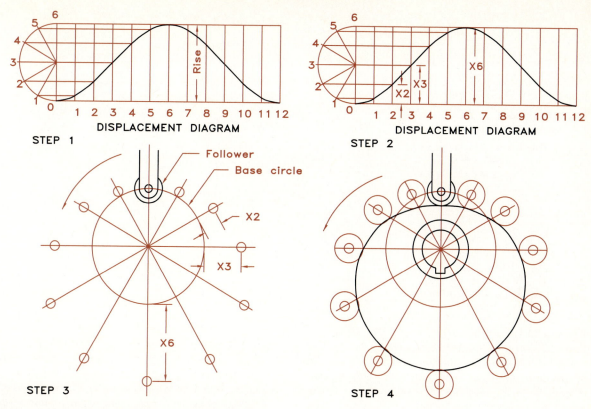

Figure 11.14 Drawing a plate cam for harmonic motion:
Step 1 Construct a semicircle whose diameter equals the rise of the follower. Divide the semicircle into the same number of segments as there are between 0° and 180° on the horizontal axis of the displacement diagram. Plot the displacement curve.

Step 2 Measure distances of rise and fall (X1, X2, X3, . . ., X6) at each interval from the base circle.

Step 3 Construct the base circle and draw the follower. Divide the circle into the same number of sectors as there are divisions on the displacement diagram. Transfer distances from the displacement diagram to the respective radial lines of the circle, measuring outward from it.

Step 4 Draw circles to represent the positions of the roller as the cam revolves counterclockwise. Draw the cam profile tangent to all the rollers to complete the drawing.

diameter of the base circle, and direction of rotation. The displacement diagram shown in step 1 of Fig. 11.14 gives the specifications graphically for the cam.

Gravity Motion **Figure 11.15** shows the steps involved in designing a cam for gravity motion. The same steps used in designing the cam for

harmonic motion apply, but the displacement diagram and knife-edge follower are different.

Cam with an Offset Follower The cam shown in **Fig. 11.16** produces harmonic motion through 360°. In this case, plot the motion directly from the follower rather than from the usual displacement diagram.

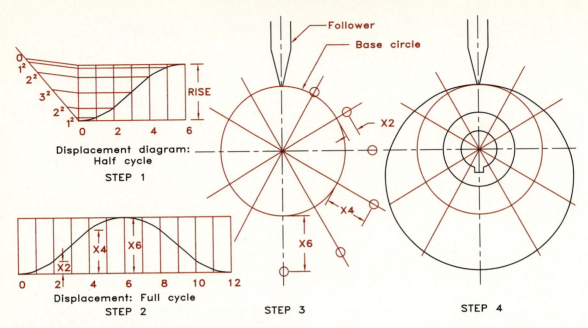

Figure 11.15 Drawing a plate cam for uniform acceleration:
Step 1 Construct a displacement diagram to represent the rise of the follower. Divide the horizontal axis into angular increments of 30°. Draw a construction line through point 0; locate the 1^2, 2^2, and 3^2 divisions and project them to the vertical axis to represent half the rise.

Step 2 Use the same construction to find the right half of the symmetrical curve.

Step 3 Construct the base circle and draw the knife-edge follower. Divide the circle into the same number of sectors as there are divisions in the displacement diagram. Transfer distances from the displacement diagram to their respective radial lines of the base circle, measuring outward from the base circle.

Step 4 Connect the points found in step 3 with a smooth curve to complete the cam profile. Also show the cam hub and keyway.

Draw a semicircle with its diameter equal to the total motion of the follower. Draw the base circle to pass through the center of the roller of the follower. Extend the centerline of the follower downward and draw a circle tangent to the extension with its center at the center of the base circle. Divide the small circle into 30° intervals to establish points through which to draw construction lines tangent to the circle.

Lay out the distances from tangent points to the position points along the path of the follower along the tangent lines drawn at 30° intervals. Locate these points by measuring from the base circle, as shown; for example, point 3 is located distance X from the base circle.

Draw the circular roller in all views, and then draw the profile of the cam tangent to the rollers at all positions.

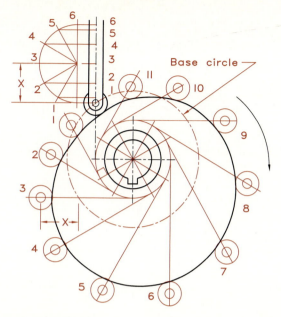

Figure 11.16 Drawing of a plate cam having an offset roller follower.

Problems

Gears

Use size A sheets for the following gear problems. Select appropriate scales so that the drawings will effectively use the available space.

1–5. Calculate the dimensions for the following spur gears, and make a detail drawing of each. Give the dimensions and cutting data for each gear. Provide any other dimensions needed.

Problem	Gear Teeth	Diametral Pitch	14.5° Involute
1	20	5	"
2	30	3	"
3	40	4	"
4	60	6	"
5	80	4	"

6–10. Calculate the gear sizes and number of teeth using the following ratios and data.

Problem	RPM Pinion	RPM Gear	Center to Center	Diametral Pitch
6	100 (driver)	60	6.0"	10
7	100 (driver)	50	8.0"	9
8	100 (driver)	40	10.0"	8
9	100 (driver)	35	12.0"	7
10	100 (driver)	25	14.0"	6

11–20. Make a detail drawing of each gear for which you made calculations in Problems 6–10. Provide a table of cutting data and other dimensions needed to complete the specifications.

21–25. Calculate the specifications for the bevel gears that intersect at 90°, and make detail drawings of each, including the necessary dimensions and cutting data.

Problem	Diametral Pitch	No. of Teeth on Pinion	No. of Teeth on Gear
21	3	60	15
22	4	100	40
23	5	100	60
24	6	100	50
25	7	100	30

26–30. Calculate the specifications for the worm gears and make a detail drawing of each, providing the necessary dimensions and cutting data.

Problem	No. of Teeth in Spider Gear	Outside DIA of Worm	Pitch of Worm	Thread of Worm
26	45	2.50	0.50	double
27	30	2.00	0.80	single
28	60	3.00	0.80	double
29	30	2.00	0.25	double
30	80	4.00	1.00	single

Cams

Use size B sheets for the following cam problems. The standard dimensions are base circle, 3.50 in.; roller follower, 0.60-in. diameter; shaft, 0.75-in. diameter; and hub, 1.25-in. diameter. The direction of rotation is clockwise. The follower is positioned vertically over the center of the base circle. Lay out the problems and displacement diagrams as shown in **Fig. 11.17**.

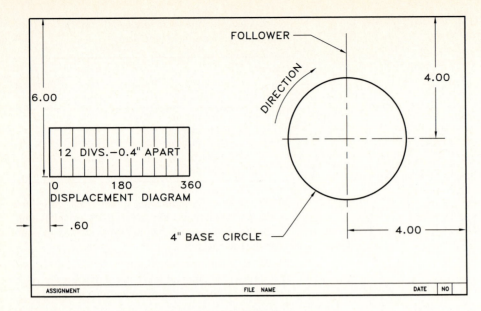

Figure 11.17 Layout for Problems 31–36 on size B sheets.

31. Draw a plate cam with a knife-edge follower for uniform motion and a rise of 1.00 in.

32. Draw a displacement diagram and a cam that will give a modified uniform motion to a knife-edge follower with a rise of 1.7 in. Modify the uniform motion with an arc of one-quarter the rise in the displacement diagram.

33. Draw a displacement diagram and a cam that will give a harmonic motion to a roller follower with a rise of 1.60 in.

34. Draw a displacement diagram and a cam that will give a harmonic motion to a knife-edge follower with a rise of 1.00 in.

35. Draw a displacement diagram and a cam that will give uniform acceleration to a knife-edge follower with a rise of 1.70 in.

36. Draw a displacement diagram and a cam that will give a uniform acceleration to a roller follower with a rise of 1.40 in.

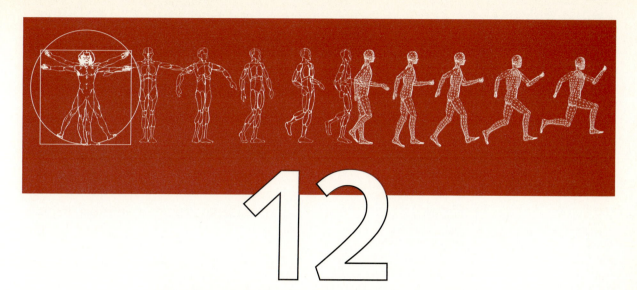

12

Materials and Processes

Figure 12.1 This furnace operator is pouring an aluminum alloy of manganese into ingots (shown at the right) that will be remelted and cast. (Courtesy of the Aluminum Company of America.)

12.1 Introduction

Various materials and manufacturing processes are commonly used to make parts similar to those discussed in this textbook. A large proportion of parts designed by engineers are made of metal, but other materials (such as plastics and ceramics) are available to the designer in increasingly useful applications.

Metallurgy, the study of metals, is a field that is constantly changing as new processes and alloys are developed **(Fig. 12.1)**. These developments affect the designer's specification of metals and their proper application for various purposes. Three associations have standardized and continually update guidelines for designating various types of metals: the American Iron and Steel Institute (AISI), the Society of Automotive Engineers (SAE), and the American Society for Testing Materials (ASTM).

12.2 Commonly Used Metals

Iron*

Metals that contain iron, even in small quantities, are called **ferrous metals**. Three common types of iron are **gray iron, white iron**, and **ductile iron**.

*This section on iron was developed by Dr. Tom Pollock, a metallurgist at Texas A&M University

223

DESIGNATIONS OF GRAY IRON (450 LB / CF)

ASTM Grade (1000 psi)	SAE Grade	Typical Uses
ASTM 25 CI	G 2500 CI	Small engine blocks, pump bodies, clutch plates, transmission cases
ASTM 30 CI	G 3000 CI	Auto engine blocks, heavy castings, flywheels
ASTM 35 CI	G 3500 CI	Diesel engine blocks, tractor transmission cases, heavy & high-strength parts
ASTM 40 CI	G 4000 CI	Diesel cylinders, pistons, camshafts

Figure 12.2 These are the numbering designations of gray iron and its typical uses.

Gray iron contains flakes of graphite, which result in low strength and low ductility and make it easy to machine. Gray iron resists vibration better than other types of iron. **Figure 12.2** shows designations of and typical applications for gray iron.

White iron contains carbide particles that are extremely hard and brittle, enabling it to withstand wear and abrasion. Although the composition of white iron differs from one supplier to another, there are no designated grades of white iron. It is used for parts on grinding and crushing machines, digging teeth on earthmovers and mining equipment, and wear plates on reciprocating machinery used in textile mills.

Ductile iron (also called nodular or spheroidized iron) contains tiny spheres of graphite, making it stronger and tougher than most types of gray iron and more expensive to produce. Three sets of numbers **(Fig. 12.3)** describe the most important features of ductile iron. **Figure 12.4** shows the designations of and typical applications for the commonly used alloys of ductile iron.

Malleable iron is made from white iron by a heat-treatment process that converts carbides into carbon nodules (similar to ductile iron).

DUCTILE IRON NOTE

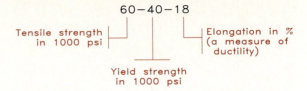

Figure 12.3 This note illustrates the numbering system for ductile iron.

DESIGNATIONS OF DUCTILE IRON (490 LB / CF)

Grade	Typical Uses
60−40−18 CI	Valves, steam fittings, chemical plant equipment, pump bodies
65−45−12 CI	Machine components that are shock loaded, disc brake calipers
80−55−6 CI	Auto crankshafts, gears, rollers
100−70−3 CI	High−strength gears and machine parts
120−90−2 CI	Very high−strength gears, rollers, and slides

Figure 12.4 These are the numbering designations of ductile iron and its typical uses.

Figure 12.5 shows the numbering system for designating grades of malleable iron. **Figure 12.6** shows some of the commonly used grades of malleable iron and their typical applications.

Cast iron is melted and poured into a mold to form it by casting, a commonly used process for producing machine parts. Although cheaper and easier to machine than steel, iron does not have steel's ability to withstand shock and force.

Steel

Steel is an alloy of iron and carbon, which often contains other constituents such as manganese, chromium, or nickel. Carbon (usually between 0.20% and 1.50%) is the ingredient having the greatest effect on the grade of steel. The three major types of steel are **plain carbon steels, free-cutting**

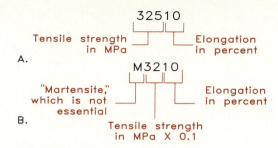

Figure 12.5 These notes illustrate the numbering designations for malleable iron.

DESIGNATIONS OF MALLEABLE IRON (490 LB / CF)

ASTM Grade	Typical Uses
35018 CI	Marine and railroad valves and fittings, "black–iron" pipe fittings (similar to 60–40–18 ductile CI)
45006 CI	Machine parts (similar to 80–55–6 ductile CI)
M3210 CI	Low–stress components, brackets
M4504 CI	Crankshafts, hubs
M7002 CI	High–strength parts, connecting rods, universal joints
M8501 CI	Wear–resistant gears and sliding parts

Figure 12.6 These are the numbering designations of malleable iron and its typical uses.

carbon steels, and **alloy steels. Figure 12.7** gives the types of steels and their designations by four-digit numbers. The first digit indicates the type of steel: 1 is carbon steel, 2 is nickel steel, and so on. The second digit gives content (as a percentage) of the material represented by the first digit. The last two or three digits give the percentage of carbon in the alloy: 100 equals 1%, and 50 equals 0.50%.

Steel weighs about 490 pounds per cubic foot. Some frequently used SAE steels are 1010, 1015, 1020, 1030, 1040, 1070, 1080, 1111, 1118, 1145, 1320, 2330, 2345, 2515, 3130, 3135, 3240, 3310, 4023, 4042, 4063, 4140, and 4320.

DESIGNATIONS OF STEEL (490 LB / CF)

Type of Steel	Number	Applications
Carbon steels		
Plain carbon	10XX	Tubing, wire, nails
Resulphurized	11XX	Nuts, bolts, screws
Manganese steel	13XX	Gears, shafts
Nickel steel	23XX	Keys, levers, bolts
	25XX	Carburized parts
	31XX	Axles, gears, pins
	32XX	Forgings
	33XX	Axles, gears
Molybdenum	40XX	Gears, springs
Chromium–moly.	41XX	Shafts, tubing
Nickel–chromium	43XX	Gears, pinions
Nickel–moly.	46XX	Cams, shafts
	48XX	Roller bearings, pins
Chromium steel	51XX	Springs, gears
	52XX	Ball bearings
Chrom. vanadium	61XX	Springs, forgings
Silicon manganese	92XX	Leaf springs

Figure 12.7 These are the numbering designations of steel and its applications.

Copper

One of the first metals discovered, **copper** is easily formed and bent without breaking. Because it is highly resistant to corrosion and is highly conductive, it is used for pipes, tubing, and electrical wiring. It is an excellent roofing and screening material because it withstands the weather well. Copper weighs about 555 pounds per cubic foot.

Copper has several alloys, including brasses, tin bronzes, nickel silvers, and copper nickels. **Brass** (about 530 pounds per cubic foot) is an alloy of copper and zinc, and **bronze** (about 548 pounds per cubic foot) is an alloy of copper and tin. Copper and copper alloys are easily finished by buffing or plating; joined by soldering, brazing, or welding; and machined.

Wrought copper has properties that permit it to be formed by hammering. A few of the numbered designations of wrought copper are C11000, C11100, C11300, C11400, C11500, C11600, C10200, C12000, and C12200.

ALUMINUM DESIGNATIONS (169 LB / CF)

Composition	Alloy Number	Application
Aluminum (99% pure)	1XXX	Tubing, tank cars
Aluminum alloys		
Copper	2XXX	Aircraft parts, screws, rivets
Manganese	3XXX	Tanks, siding, gutters
Silicon	4XXX	Forging, wire
Magnesium	5XXX	Tubes, welded vessels
Magnesium and silicon	6XXX	Auto body, pipes
Zinc	7XXX	Aircraft structures
Other elements	8XXX	

Figure 12.8 These are the numbering designations of aluminum and aluminum alloys and their applications.

ALUMINUM CASTINGS AND INGOT DESIGNATIONS

Composition	Alloy Number
Aluminum (99% pure)	1XX.X
Aluminum alloys	
Copper	2XX.X
Silicon with copper and/or magnesium	3XX.X
Silicon	4XX.X
Magnesium	5XX.X
Magnesium and silicon	6XX.X
Zinc	7XX.X
Tin	8XX.X
Other elements	9XX.X

Figure 12.9 These are the numbering designations of cast aluminum and aluminum alloys.

Aluminum

Aluminum is a corrosion-resistant, lightweight metal (approximately 169 pounds per cubic foot) that has numerous applications. Most materials called aluminum actually are aluminum alloys, which are stronger than pure aluminum.

The types of wrought aluminum alloys are designated by four digits **(Fig. 12.8)**. The first digit (2 through 9) indicates the alloying element that is combined with aluminum. The second digit indicates modifications of the original alloy or impurity limits. The last two digits identify other alloying materials or indicate the aluminum's purity.

Figure 12.9 shows a four-digit numbering system used to designate types of cast aluminum and alloys. The first digit indicates the alloy group, and the next two digits identify the aluminum alloy or aluminum purity. The number to the right of the decimal point represents the aluminum form: XX.0 indicates castings, XX.1 indicates ingots with a specified chemical composition, and XX.2 indicates ingots with a specified chemical composition other than the XX.1 ingot. **Ingots** are blocks of cast metal to be remelted, and **billets** are castings of aluminum to be formed by forging.

Magnesium

Magnesium is a light metal (109 pounds per cubic foot) available in an inexhaustible supply because it is extracted from seawater and natural brines. Magnesium is an excellent material for aircraft parts, clutch housings, crankcases for air-cooled engines, and applications where lightness is desirable.

Magnesium is used for die and sand castings, extruded tubing, sheet metal, and forging. Magnesium and its alloys may be joined by bolting, riveting, or welding. Some numbered designations of magnesium alloys are M10100, M11630, M11810, M11910, M11912, M12390, M13320, M16410, and M16620.

12.3 Properties of Metals

All materials have properties that designers must utilize to the best advantage. The following terms describe these properties.

Ductility: a softness in some materials, such as copper and aluminum, which permits them to be formed by stretching (drawing) or hammering without breaking.

Brittleness: a characteristic that will not allow metals such as cast irons and hardened steels to stretch without breaking.

Malleability: the ability of a metal to be rolled or hammered without breaking.

Hardness: the ability of a metal to resist being dented when it receives a blow.

Toughness: the property of being resistant to cracking and breaking while remaining malleable.

Elasticity: the ability of a metal to return to its original shape after being bent or stretched.

Modifying Properties by Heat Treatment

The properties of metals can be changed by various types of heat treating. Although heat affects all metals, steels are affected to a greater extent than others.

Hardening: heating steel to a prescribed temperature and quenching it in oil or water.

Quenching: rapidly cooling heated metal by immersing it in liquids, gases, or solids (such as sand, limestone, or asbestos).

Tempering: reheating previously hardened steel and then cooling it, usually by air, to increase its toughness.

Annealing: heating and cooling metals to soften them, release their internal stresses, and make them easier to machine.

Normalizing: heating metals and letting them cool in air to relieve their internal stresses.

Case hardening: hardening a thin outside layer of a metal by placing the metal in contact with carbon or nitrogen compounds that it absorbs as it is heated; afterward, the metal is quenched.

Flame hardening: hardening by heating a metal to within a prescribed temperature range with a flame and then quenching the metal.

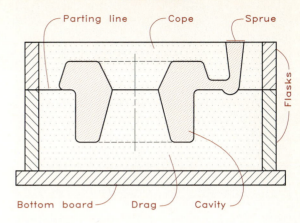

SAND MOLD

Figure 12.10 A two-section sand mold is used for casting a metal part.

12.4 Forming Metal Shapes

Casting

One of the two major methods of forming shapes is **casting**, which involves preparing a mold in the shape of the part desired, pouring molten metal into it, and cooling the metal to form the part. The types of casting, which differ in the way the molds are made, are **sand casting**, **permanent-mold casting**, **die casting**, and **investment casting**.

Sand Casting In the first step of sand casting, a wood or metal form or pattern is made in the shape of the part to be cast. The pattern is placed in a metal box called a **flask** and molding sand is packed around the pattern. When the pattern is withdrawn from the sand, it leaves a void forming the mold. Molten metal is poured into the mold through sprues, or gates. After cooling, the casting is removed and cleaned (**Fig. 12.10**).

Cores formed from sand may be placed in a mold to create holes or hollows within a casting. After the casting has been formed, the cores are broken apart and removed, leaving behind the desired void within the casting.

Because the patterns are placed in and removed from the sand before the metal is

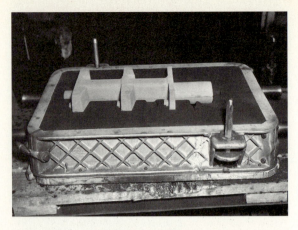

Figure 12.11 This pattern is held in the bottom half (the drag) of a sand mold to form a mold for a casting.

Figure 12.12 The tailstock casting for a lathe has raised bosses that were finished to improve the effectiveness of nuts and bolts. Fillets and rounds were added to the inside and outside corners. (Courtesy L. W. Chuck Company.)

poured, the sides of the patterns must be tapered, called **draft**, for ease of withdrawal from the sand. The angle of draft depends on the depth of the pattern in the sand and varies from 2° to 8° in most applications. **Figure 12.11** shows a pattern held in the sand by a lower flask. Patterns are made oversize to compensate for shrinkage that occurs when the casting cools.

Because sand castings have rough surfaces, features that come into contact with other parts must be machined by drilling, grinding, finishing, or shaping. The tailstock base of a lathe shown in **Fig. 12.12** illustrates raised bosses that have been finished. The casting must be made larger than finished size where metal is to be removed by machining.

Fillets and rounds are used at the inside and outside corners of castings to increase their strength by relieving the stresses in the cast metal (Fig. 12.13). Fillets and rounds also are used because forming square corners by the sand-casting process is difficult and because rounded edges make the finished product more attractive (Fig. 12.12).

Permanent-Mold Casting Permanent molds are made for the mass production of parts. They are generally made of cast iron and coated to prevent

APPLICATION OF FILLETS AND ROUNDS

A. SQUARE CORNERS

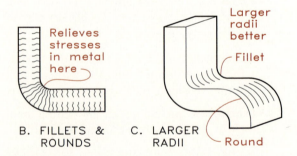

B. FILLETS & ROUNDS   C. LARGER RADII

Figure 12.13

A Square corners cause a failure line to form, causing a weakness at this point.

B Fillets and rounds make the corners of a casting stronger and more attractive.

C The larger the radii of fillets and rounds, the stronger the casting will be.

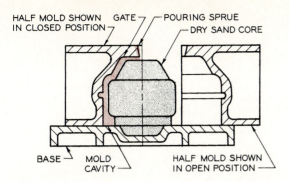

Figure 12.14 Permanent molds are made of metal for repetitive usage. Here, a sand core made from another mold is placed in the permanent mold to create a void within the casting.

Figure 12.16 An investment casting (lost-wax process) is used to produce complex metal objects and art pieces.

DIE CASTING

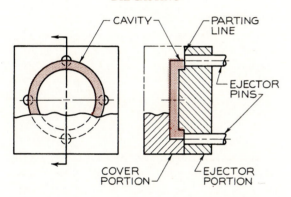

Figure 12.15 This die is used for casting a simple part. The metal is forced into the die to form the casting.

fusing with the molten metal poured into them (**Fig. 12.14**).

Die Casting Die castings are used for the mass production of parts made of aluminum, magnesium, zinc alloys, copper, and other materials. Die castings are made by forcing molten metal into dies (or molds) under pressure. They are inexpensive, meet close tolerances, and have good surface qualities. The same general principles of sand castings—using fillets and rounds, allowing for

shrinkage, and specifying draft angles—apply to die castings (**Fig. 12.15**).

Investment Casting Investment casting is used to produce complicated parts or artistic sculptures that would be difficult to form by other methods (**Fig. 12.16**). A new pattern must be used for each investment casting, so a mold or die is made for casting a wax master pattern. The wax pattern, identical to the casting, is placed inside a container and plaster or sand is poured (invested) around it. Once the investment has cured, the wax pattern is melted, leaving a hollow cavity to serve as the mold for the molten metal. After the casting has set, the plaster or sand is broken away from it.

Forgings

The second major method of forming shapes is **forging**, which is the process of shaping or forming heated metal by hammering or forcing it into a die. Drop forges and press forges are used to hammer metal billets into forging dies. Forgings have the high strength and resistance to loads and impacts required for applications such as aircraft landing gears (**Fig. 12.17**).

Figure 12.18 shows three types of dies. A **single-impression die** gives an impression on one side of the parting line between the mating dies; a **double-**

Figure 12.17 This aircraft landing-gear component was formed by forging. (Courtesy of Cameron Iron Works.)

FORGING DIES

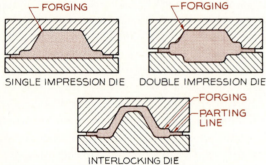

SINGLE IMPRESSION DIE   DOUBLE IMPRESSION DIE

INTERLOCKING DIE

Figure 12.18 This drawing shows three types of forging dies.

impression die gives an impression on both sides of the parting line; and the **interlocking dies** give an impression that may cross the parting line on either side. **Figure 12.19** shows how an object is forged with horizontal dies and a vertical ram to hollow the object.

Figure 12.20 illustrates the sequence of forging a part from a billet by hammering it into different dies. It is then machined to its proper size within specified tolerances.

STEPS OF FORGING

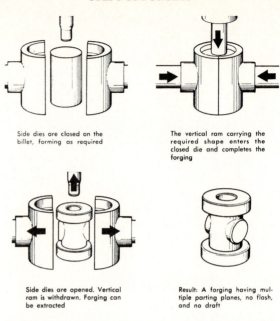

Side dies are closed on the billet, forming as required

The vertical ram carrying the required shape enters the closed die and completes the forging

Side dies are opened. Vertical ram is withdrawn. Forging can be extracted

Result: A forging having multiple parting planes, no flash, and no draft

Figure 12.19 These are the steps involved in forging a part with external dies and an internal ram. (Courtesy of Cameron Iron Works.)

Figure 12.21 shows a working drawing for making a forged part. When preparing forging drawings, you must consider (1) draft angles and parting lines, (2) fillets and rounds, (3) forging tolerances, (4) extra material for machining, and (5) heat treatment of the finished forging.

Draft, the angle of taper, is crucial to the forging process. The minimum radii for inside corners (fillets) are determined by the height of the feature **(Fig. 12.22)**. Similarly, the minimum radii for the outside corners (rounds) are related to a feature's height **(Fig. 12.23)**. **The larger the radius of a fillet or round, the better it is for the forging process.**

Some of the standard steels used for forging are designated by the SAE numbers 1015, 1020, 1025, 1045, 1137, 1151, 1335, 1340, 4620, 5120, and 5140. Iron, copper, and aluminum also can be forged.

FORGING A CONNECTING ROD

Figure 12.20 Steps A through G are required to forge a billet into the finished connecting rod. (Courtesy of the Drop Forging Association.)

FORGING DRAWING

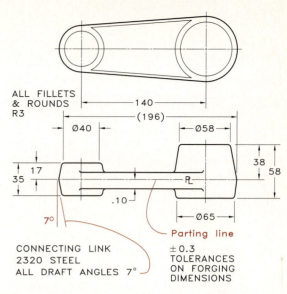

ALL FILLETS & ROUNDS R3

CONNECTING LINK
2320 STEEL
ALL DRAFT ANGLES 7°

± 0.3
TOLERANCES
ON FORGING
DIMENSIONS

Figure 12.21 This working drawing for a forging shows draft angles and the parting line (PL) where the dies come together.

Rolling

Rolling is a type of forging in which the stock is rolled between two or more rollers to shape it. Rolling can be done at right angles or parallel to the axis of the part **(Fig. 12.24)**. If a high degree of shaping is required, the stock usually is heated before rolling. If the forming requires only a slight change in shape, rolling can be done without heating the metal, which is called **cold rolling (CR)**; **CRS** means **cold-rolled steel**. **Figure 12.25** shows a cylindrical rod being rolled.

Stamping

Stamping is a method of forming flat metal stock into three-dimensional shapes. The first step of stamping is to cut out the shapes, called **blanks**,

MINIMUM FILLET RADII FOR FORGINGS: INSIDE CORNERS

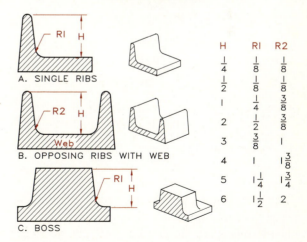

Figure 12.22 These guidelines are for determining the minimum radii for fillets (inside corners) on forged parts.

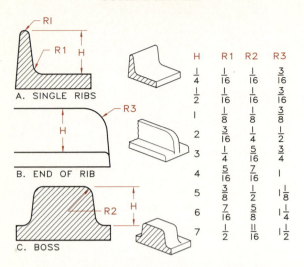

H	R1	R2	R3
$\frac{1}{4}$	$\frac{1}{16}$	$\frac{1}{16}$	$\frac{3}{16}$
$\frac{1}{2}$	$\frac{1}{16}$	$\frac{1}{16}$	$\frac{3}{16}$
1	$\frac{1}{8}$	$\frac{1}{8}$	$\frac{3}{8}$
2	$\frac{3}{16}$	$\frac{1}{4}$	$\frac{1}{2}$
3	$\frac{1}{4}$	$\frac{5}{16}$	$\frac{3}{4}$
4	$\frac{5}{16}$	$\frac{7}{16}$	1
5	$\frac{3}{8}$	$\frac{1}{2}$	$1\frac{1}{8}$
6	$\frac{7}{16}$	$\frac{5}{8}$	$1\frac{1}{4}$
7	$\frac{1}{2}$	$\frac{11}{16}$	$1\frac{1}{2}$

A. SINGLE RIBS

B. END OF RIB

C. BOSS

Figure 12.23 These guidelines are for determining the minimum radii of rounds (outside corners) on forged parts.

Figure 12.25 This cylindrical rod is being rolled to shape.

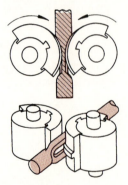

Figure 12.24 Features on parts may be formed by rolling. Here a part is being rolled parallel to its axes. (Courtesy of General Motors Corporation.)

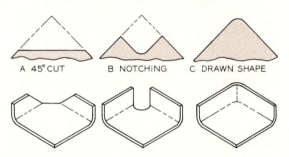

A 45° CUT   B NOTCHING   C DRAWN SHAPE

Figure 12.26 Box-shaped parts formed by stamping:
A A corner cut of 45° permits flanges to be folded with no further trimming.

B Notching has the same effect as the 45° cut and is often more attractive.

C A continuous corner flange requires that the blank be developed so that it can be drawn into shape.

which are formed by bending and pressing them against forms. **Figure 12.26** shows three types of box-shaped parts formed by stamping, and **Fig. 12.27** shows a design for a flange to be formed by stamping. Holes in stampings are made by punching, extruding, or piercing (**Fig. 12.28**).

12.5 Machining Operations

After metal parts have been formed, machining operations must be performed to complete them. The machines used most often are: **lathe, drill**

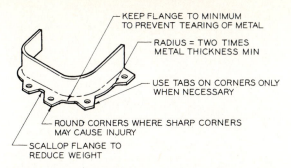

Figure 12.27 This drawing shows a sheet metal flange design with notes that explain design details.

HOLES IN SHEET METAL BY PUNCHING

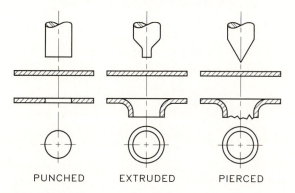

Figure 12.28 These three methods are used to form holes in sheet metal.

press, milling machine, shaper, and planer. Some of these machines require manual operation; others are computer programmed and require minimal operator handling.

Lathe

The lathe shapes cylindrical parts while rotating the workpiece between its centers (Fig. 12.29). The fundamental operations performed on the lathe are turning, facing, drilling, boring, reaming, threading, and undercutting (Fig. 12.30).

Figure 12.29 This typical metal lathe holds and rotates the workpiece between its centers for machining. (Courtesy of the Clausing Corporation.)

LATHE OPERATIONS

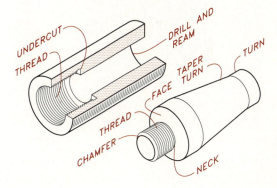

Figure 12.30 These are basic operations performed on a lathe.

Turning forms a cylinder with a tool that advances against and moves parallel to the cylinder being turned between the centers of the lathe (Fig. 12.31). Facing forms flat surfaces perpendic-

TURNING ON A LATHE

Figure 12.31 The most basic operation performed on the lathe is turning, whereby a continuous chip is removed by a cutting tool as the part rotates.

Figure 12.32 Facing on a lathe is the process of machining a surface that is perpendicular to the axis of revolution, as here with a wood cylinder. (Courtesy of Rockwell/Delta Corporation.)

ular to the axis of rotation of the part being rotated (**Fig. 12.32**).

Drilling is performed by mounting a drill in the tail stock of the lathe and rotating the work

STEPS OF DRILLING

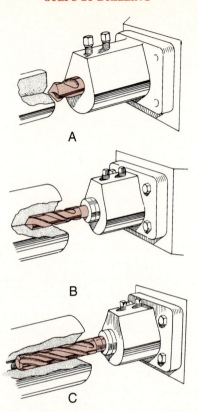

Figure 12.33 Three steps are involved in drilling a hole in the end of a cylinder: (A) start drilling, (B) twist drilling, and (C) core drilling, which enlarges the previously drilled hole to the required size.

BORING A HOLE

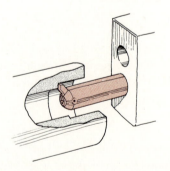

Figure 12.34 Boring is the method of enlarging holes that are larger than available drill bits with a cutting tool attached to a boring bar on the lathe.

REAMING ON A LATHE

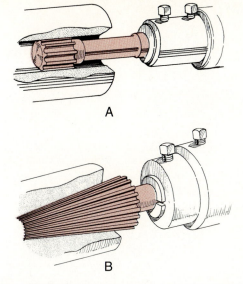

A

B

Figure 12.35 Fluted reamers can be used to finish inside (A) cylindrical and (B) conical holes within a few thousandths of an inch.

Figure 12.36 This hole is being reamed by honing. (Courtesy Barber-Coleman Company.)

while the bit is advanced into the part **(Fig. 12.33)**. **Boring** makes large holes that are too big to be drilled by enlarging smaller drilled holes **(Fig. 12.34)**. **Reaming** removes only thousandths of an

CUTTING THREADS

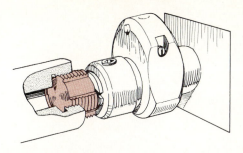

Figure 12.37 Internal threads can be cut on a lathe using a die called a tap. A recess, called a thread relief, was formed at the end of the threaded hole.

Figure 12.38 This die is being used on a lathe to cut internal threads in a part. (Courtesy of the Landis Machine Company.)

inch of material inside cylindrical and conical holes to enlarge them to their required tolerances **(Fig. 12.35)**. **Figure 12.36** shows a close-up view of reaming by honing.

    Threading of external shafts and internal holes can be done on the lathe. The die used for cutting internal holes is called a **tap (Fig. 12.37)**. A tapping die being used to thread a hole held in the chuck of a lathe is illustrated in **Fig. 12.38**.

CUTTING AN UNDERCUT

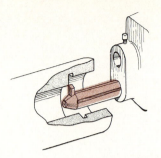

Figure 12.39 A recess (undercut) is formed by using the boring bar that is fed into the rotating stock.

Figure 12.40 A turret lathe performs a sequence of operations.

Undercutting cuts a recess inside a cylindrical hole with a tool mounted on a boring bar. The groove is cut as the tool advances from the center of the axis of revolution into the part (**Fig. 12.39**).

The **turret lathe** is a programmable lathe that can perform sequential operations, such as drilling a series of holes, boring them, and then reaming them. The turret rotates each tool into position for its particular operation (**Fig. 12.40**).

Drill Press

The **drill press** is used to drill small- and medium-sized holes (**Fig. 12.41**). The stock being drilled is held securely by fixtures or clamps (**Fig. 12.42**). **The drill press can be used for counterdrilling, countersinking, counterboring, spotfacing, and threading (Fig. 12.43).** Multiple-head drill presses can be programmed to perform a series of drilling operations for mass production applications (**Fig. 12.44**).

Measuring Cylinders The diameters of cylindrical features of parts made on a drill press (or lathe) are measured. Internal and external micrometer calipers (**Fig. 12.45**) can measure to within one ten-thousandth of an inch.

Broaching Machine

Cylindrical holes can be converted into square, rectangular, or hexagonal holes with a **broach**

Figure 12.41 This small drill press is used to make holes in parts. (Courtesy of Clausing Corporation.)

Figure 12.42 Work stock is held securely in place with fixtures and clamping devices during drilling.

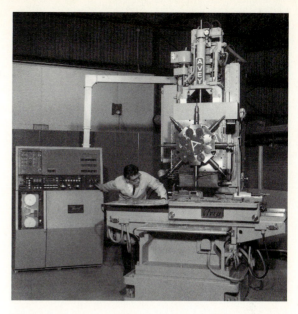

Figure 12.44 This multiple-head drill press can be programmed to perform a series of operations sequentially.

HOLE-MACHINING OPERATIONS

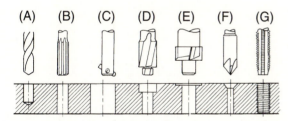

(A) (B) (C) (D) (E) (F) (G)

Figure 12.43 The basic operations performed on the drill press are (A) drilling, (B) reaming, (C) boring, (D) counterboring, (E) spotfacing, (F) countersinking, and (G) tapping (threading).

MEASURING DIAMETERS

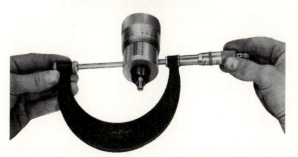

Figure 12.45 Internal and external micrometer calipers are used to measure the diameters of cylinders. (Courtesy of Scherr Tumico Company.)

mounted on a special machine (**Fig. 12.46**). A broach has a series of teeth graduated in size along its axis, beginning with teeth that are nearly the size of the hole to be broached and tapering to the final size of the hole. The broach is forced through the hole by pushing or pulling in a single pass, with each tooth cutting more from the hole as it passes

BROACHING OPERATIONS

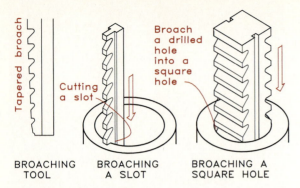

Figure 12.46 A broaching tool can be used to cut slots and holes with square corners on the interior and exterior of parts. Other shapes may be broached also.

Figure 12.47 This milling machine is being used to cut a groove in a workpiece. (Courtesy of the Brown & Sharpe Manufacturing Company.)

through. Broaches can be used to cut external grooves, such as keyways or slots, in a part.

Milling Machine

The **milling machine** uses a variety of cutting tools, rotated about a shaft (**Fig. 12.47**), to form different grooved slots, threads, and gear teeth. The milling machine can cut irregular grooves in cams and finish surfaces on a part within a high degree of tolerance.

Shaper

The **shaper** is a machine that holds a workpiece stationary while the cutter passes back and forth across it to finish the surface or to cut a groove one stroke at a time (**Fig. 12.48**). With each stroke of the cutting tool, the material is shifted slightly to align the part for the next overlapping stroke.

Planer

Unlike the shaper, which holds the workpiece stationary, the **planer** passes the piece under the cutters (**Fig. 12.49**). Like the shaper, the planer can cut grooves or slots and finish surfaces that must meet close tolerances.

SHAPER

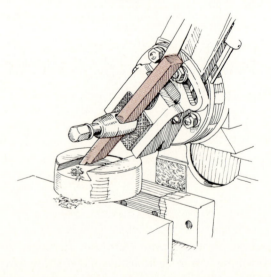

Figure 12.48 The shaper moves back and forth across the part, removing metal as it advances, to finish surfaces, cut slots, and perform other operations.

Figure 12.49 This planer has stationary cutters and a 30-foot bed. Work is fed past the cutters to finish large surfaces. (Courtesy of Gray Corporation.)

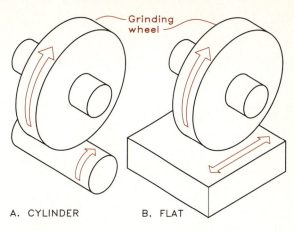

A. CYLINDER   B. FLAT

Figure 12.51 Grinding may be used to finish (A) cylindrical and (B) flat surfaces.

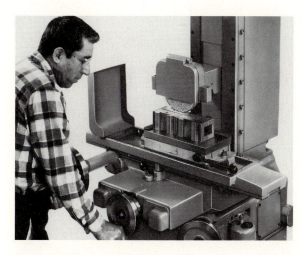

Figure 12.50 The operator is grinding the upper surface of this part to a smooth finish with a grinding wheel. (Courtesy of the Clausing Corporation.)

12.6 Surface Finishing

Surface finishing produces a smooth, uniform surface. It may be accomplished by grinding, polishing, lapping, buffing, and honing.

Grinding involves holding a flat surface against a rotating abrasive wheel (**Fig. 12.50**).

Grinding is used to smooth surfaces, both cylindrical and flat, and to sharpen edges used for cutting, such as drill bits (**Fig. 12.51**). **Polishing** is done in the same way as grinding, except that the polishing wheel is flexible because it is made of felt, leather, canvas, or fabric.

Lapping produces very smooth surfaces. The surface to be finished is held against a lap, which is a large, flat surface coated with a fine abrasive powder that finishes a surface as the lap rotates. Lapping is done only after the surface has been previously finished by a less accurate technique, such as grinding or polishing. Cylindrical parts can be lapped by using a lathe with the lap.

Buffing removes scratches from a surface with a belt or rotating buffer wheel made of wool, cotton, felt, or other fabric. To enhance the buffing, an abrasive mixture is applied to the buffed surface during the process.

Honing finishes the outside or inside of holes within a high degree of tolerance (see Fig. 12.36). The honing tool is rotated as it is passed through the holes to produce the types of finishes found in gun barrels, engine cylinders, and other products requiring a high degree of smoothness.

E=Excellent
G=Good
F=Fair
P=Poor
A=Adhesives

	MACHINABILITY	FORMABILITY	CASTABILITY	WELDABILITY	CORROSION RES.	ABRASION RES.	LB/CU FT	YIELD: 1000 PSI	Typical Applications
THERMOPLASTICS									
ACRYLIC	G	G	E	A	E	F	74	9	Aircraft windows, TV parts, lenses, skylights
ABS	G	G	G	a	E	G	66	66	Luggage, boat hulls, tool handles, pipe fittings
POLYMIDES (NYLON)	E	G	G	–	G	E	73	15	Helmets, gears, drawer slides, hinges, bearings
POLYETHYLENE	G	F	G	A	F	F	58	2	Chemical tubing, containers, ice trays, bottles
POLYPROPYLENE	G	G	G	A	E	G	56	5.3	Card files, cosmetic cases, auto pedals, luggage
POLYSTYRENE	G	E	G	A	P	G	67	7	Jugs, containers, furniture, lighted signs
POLYINYL CHLORIDE	E	E	G	A	G	G	78	4.8	Rigid pipe & tubing, house siding, packaging
THERMOSETS									
EPOXY	F	G	G	–	E	G	69	17	Circuit boards, boat bodies, coatings for tanks
SILICONE	F	G	G	–	G	G	109	28	Flexible hoses, heart valves, gaskets
ELASTOMERS									
POLYURETHANE	G	G	G	A	G	E	74	6	Rigid: Solid tires, bumpers; flexible: foam, sponges
SBR RUBBER	–	–	E	–	F	E	39	3	Belts, handles, hoses, cable coverings
GLASSES									
GLASS	F	G	–	–	F	F	160	10+	Bottles, windows, tumblers, containers
FIBERGLASS	G	–	E	A	G	G	109	20+	Boats, shower stalls, auto bodies, chairs, signs

Figure 12.52 These are the characteristics of and typical applications for commonly used materials.

12.7 Plastics and Other Materials*

Plastics (polymers) are widely used in numerous applications ranging from clothing, containers, and electronics to automobile bodies and components. Plastics are easily formed into irregular shapes, have a high resistance to weather and chemicals, and are available in limitless colors. The three basic types of plastics are **thermoplastics, thermosetting plastics**, and **elastomers**.

Thermoplastics may be softened by heating and formed to the desired shape. If a polymer returns to its original hardness and strength after being heated, it is classified as a thermoplastic. In contrast, **thermosetting plastics** cannot be changed in shape by reheating after they have permanently set. **Elastomers** are rubberlike polymers that are soft, expandable, and elastic, which permits them to be deformed greatly and then return to their original size.

Figure 12.52 shows commonly used plastics and other materials, including glass and fiber-

---

*Parts of this section are based on *Manufacturing Engineering and Technology*, 2nd ed., Serope Kalpakjian, Addison-Wesley, 1992.

Figure 12.53 The use of Dow plastic in this motorized wheelchair (made by Amigo, Inc.) reduced the number of parts by 97% and weight by 10%. It is also safe and easy to clean. (Courtesy of Dow Chemical Corporation.)

glass. The weights and yields of the materials are given, along with examples of their applications.

The motorized wheelchair shown in **Fig. 12.53** is made of plastic. It has fewer parts and weighs less than motorized wheelchairs made of metal. Its rounded corners make it safe, eliminate joints, and make it easy to fabricate and clean.

Ceramics is a material that is being more widely used in products. More innovative materials are expected to come into broad use in the future.

13

Dimensioning

13.1 Introduction

Working drawings must show dimensions and contain notes conveying sizes, specifications, and other information. With the addition of dimensions and notes, drawings will serve as construction documents and legal contracts.

The techniques of dimensioning presented are based primarily on the standards of the American National Standards Institute (ANSI), especially Y14.5M, *Dimensioning and Tolerancing for Engineering Drawings.* Standards of companies such as the General Motors Corporation also are used.

Figure 13.1 This tapered strap is a part of a clamping device.

13.2 Terminology

The strap shown in **Fig. 13.1** is described in **Fig. 13.2** with orthographic views to which dimensions were added. Refer to this drawing as we introduce dimensioning terms.

Dimension lines: thin lines (2H–4H pencil) with arrows at each end and numbers placed near their midpoints to specify size.

Extension lines: thin lines (2H–4H pencil) extending from the part and between which dimension lines are placed.

Centerlines: thin lines (2H–4H pencil) used to locate the centers of cylindrical parts such as holes.

A DIMENSIONED PART

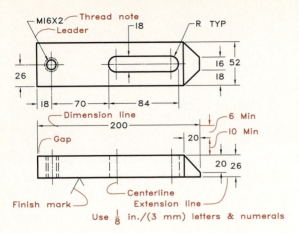

Figure 13.2 This typical dimensioned drawing of the tapered strap shown in Fig. 13.1 introduces the terminology of dimensioning.

Leaders: thin lines (2H–4H pencil) drawn from a note to the feature to which it applies.

Arrowheads: drawn at the ends of dimension lines and leaders and the same length as the height of the letters or numerals, usually 1/8 inch, as shown in **Fig. 13.3**.

Dimension numbers: placed near the middle of the dimension line and usually 1/8-inch high, with no units of measurement (", in., or mm) shown.

13.3 Units of Measurement

The two commonly used units of measurement are the decimal inch in the English (imperial) system, and the millimeter in the metric system (SI) **(Fig. 13.4)**. Giving fractional inches as decimals rather than common fractions simplifies the arithmetic.

Figure 13.5 demonstrates the proper and improper dimensioning techniques with millimeters, decimal inches, and fractional inches. **In general, round off dimensions in millimeters to whole numbers without fractions.** However, when you

ARROWHEADS

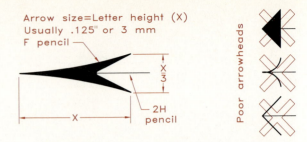

Figure 13.3 Draw arrowheads as long as the height of the letters used on the drawing and one third as wide as they are long.

MILLIMETERS VS. INCHES

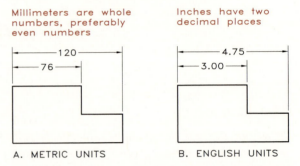

Figure 13.4 For the metric system, round millimeters to the nearest whole number. For the English system, show inches with two decimal places, even for whole numbers such as 3.00.

must show a metric dimension of less than a millimeter, use a zero before the decimal point. Do not use a zero before the decimal point when inches are the unit.

Show decimal inch dimensions with two-place decimal fractions, even if the last numbers are zeros. Omit units of measurement from the dimension because they are understood to be in millimeters or inches. For example, use 112 (not 112 mm) and 67 (not 67" or 5'-7").

Architects use combinations of feet and inches in dimensioning. They show foot marks but omit inch marks, as in 7'-2. Engineers use feet and deci-

DIMENSIONING UNITS

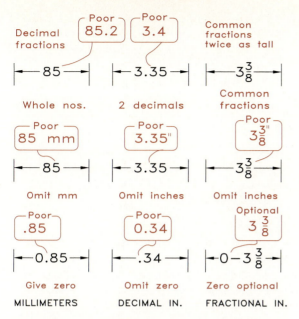

Figure 13.5 This drawing compares the proper and improper ways of notating units in SI and the English system.

DUAL DIMENSIONING

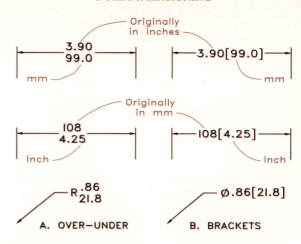

Figure 13.6 In dual dimensioning, place size equivalents in millimeters under or to the right of the inches (in brackets). Place the equivalent measurement in inches under or to the right of millimeters (in brackets). You may need to show millimeters converted from inches as decimal fractions.

mal fractions of feet to dimension large-scale projects such as road designs, as in 252.7'.

13.4 English/Metric Conversions

To convert dimensions in inches to millimeters, multiply by 25.4. Similarly, to convert dimensions in millimeters to inches, divide by 25.4.

When millimeter fractions are required as a result of conversion from inches, one-place fractions usually are sufficient, but two-place fractions are used in some cases. Find the decimal digit by applying the following rules:

- Retain the last digit unchanged if it is followed by a number less than 5; for example, round 34.43 to 34.4.

- Increase by 1 the last digit retained if it is followed by a number greater than 5; for example, round 34.46 to 34.5.

- Retain unchanged the last digit if it is even and is followed by the digit 5; for example, round 34.45 to 34.4.

- Increase by 1 the last digit retained if it is odd and is followed by the digit 5; for example, round 34.75 to 34.8.

13.5 Dual Dimensioning

On some drawings you may have to give both metric and English units, called **dual dimensioning (Fig. 13.6)**. Place the millimeter equivalent either under or over the inch units, or place the converted dimension in brackets to the right of the original dimension. Be consistent in the arrangement you use on any set of drawings.

13.6 Metric Designation

Recall that in the metric system (SI) the first angle of projection positions the front view over the top view and the right-side view to the left of the front

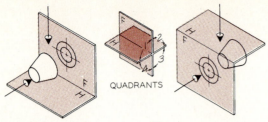

Figure 13.7
A The SI system uses the first angle of orthographic projection, which places the top view under the front view.

B The American system uses the third angle of projection, which places the top view over the front view.

THE SI SYMBOL

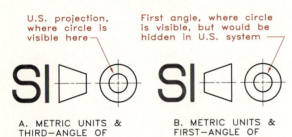

Figure 13.8
A The SI symbol indicates that the millimeter is the unit of measurement, and the truncated cone specifies that third-angle projection was used to position the orthographic views.

B Again, the SI symbol denotes use of the millimeter, but the truncated cone designates that the first-angle projection was used.

view **(Fig. 13.7)**. You should label metric drawings with one of the symbols shown in **Fig. 13.8** to designate the angle of projection. Display either the letters *SI* or the word *metric* prominently in or near the title block to indicate that the measurements are metric.

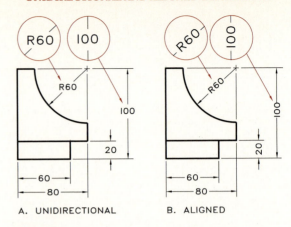

Figure 13.9
A Letter all unidirectional dimensions horizontally on a drawing.

B Aligned dimensions are lettered parallel to angular and vertical dimension lines to read from the right-hand side of the drawing (never from the left).

13.7 Numeric and Symbolic Dimensioning

Vertical Dimensions

Vertical numeric dimensions on a drawing may be aligned or unidirectional. In the **unidirectional-method** all dimensions appear in the standard horizontal position **(Fig. 13.9A)**. **In the aligned method numerals are parallel with vertical and angular dimension lines and read from the right-hand side of the drawing, never from the left-hand side (Fig. 13.9B).** Aligned dimensions are used almost entirely in architectural drawings where dimensions composed of feet, inches, and fractions are too long to fit well unidirectionally (such as 22'-10 1/2).

Placement

Dimensions should be placed on the most descriptive views of the part being dimensioned. The first row of dimensions should be at least three times

PLACEMENT OF DIMENSIONS

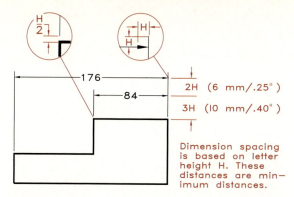

Figure 13.10 Place dimensions on a view as shown here, where all dimensioning geometry is based on the letter height (H) used.

COMMON-FRACTION DIMENSIONS

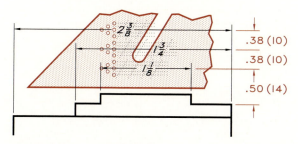

Figure 13.11 Draw guidelines for common-fraction dimensions by aligning the center holes in the Braddock–Rowe triangle with the dimension line.

the letter height (3H) from the object **(Fig. 13.10)**. Successive rows of dimensions should be spaced equally at least two times the letter height apart (0.25 inch, or 6 mm, when 1/8-inch letters are used). Use the Braddock–Rowe lettering guide triangle to space the dimension lines **(Fig. 13.11)**.

Figure 13.12 illustrates how to place dimensions in limited spaces. **Regardless of space limitations, do not make numerals smaller than they appear elsewhere on the drawing.**

DIMENSIONS IN TIGHT SPACES

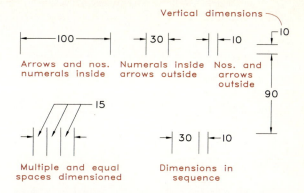

Figure 13.12 When space permits, place numerals and arrows inside extension lines. For smaller spaces use other placements, as shown.

DIMENSIONING SYMBOLS

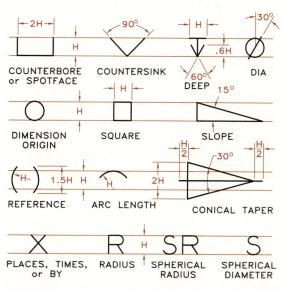

Figure 13.13 These symbols can be used instead of words to dimension parts. Their proportions are based on the letter height, H, which usually is ⅛ inch.

Symbols

Figure 13.13 shows standard dimensioning symbols and their sizes based on the letter height, usually 1/8 inch. Use of these symbols instead of words saves drawing time.

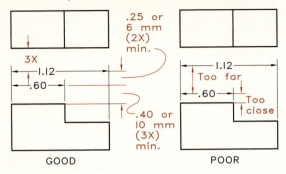

RULE 1: First row 3 times letter height from part, minimum. (X=Letter height)

GOOD   POOR

Figure 13.14 Place the first row of dimensions at least three times the letter height from the object. Successive rows should be at least two times the letter height apart.

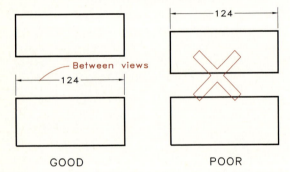

RULE 2: Place dimensions between the views

GOOD   POOR

Figure 13.15 Place dimensions between the views sharing these dimensions.

13.8 Dimensioning Rules

Prisms

There are many rules of dimensioning, and you should become familiar with them in order to place dimensions and notes on drawings most effectively. **From time to time rules of dimensioning must be violated due to the complexity of the part or shortage of space. Figures 13.14–13.26** illustrate the fundamental rules of dimensioning prisms. We simplified these examples to focus on specific rules and to emphasize the logic behind them.

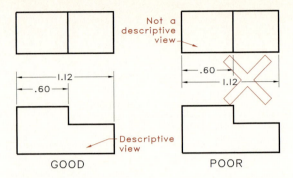

RULE 3: Dimension the most descriptive views

GOOD   POOR

Figure 13.16 Place dimensions on the most descriptive views of an object.

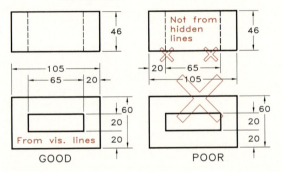

RULE 4: Dimension from visible lines, not hidden lines

GOOD   POOR

Figure 13.17 Dimension visible features, not hidden features.

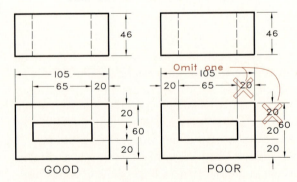

RULE 5: Give an overall dimension and omit one of the chain dimensions

GOOD   POOR

Figure 13.18 Leave the last dimension blank in a chain of dimensions when you also give an overall dimension.

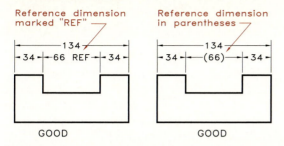

Reference dimension marked "REF"

Reference dimension in parentheses

GOOD   GOOD

Figure 13.19 If you give all dimensions in a chain, mark the reference dimension (the one that would be omitted) with REF or place it in parentheses. Giving a reference dimension is a way of eliminating mathematical calculations in the shop.

RULE 6: Organize and align dimensions for ease of reading

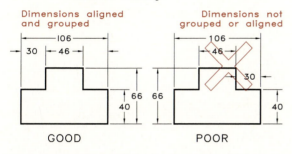

Dimensions aligned and grouped

Dimensions not grouped or aligned

GOOD   POOR

Figure 13.20 Place dimensions in well-organized lines for uncluttered drawings.

RULE 7: Do not repeat dimensions

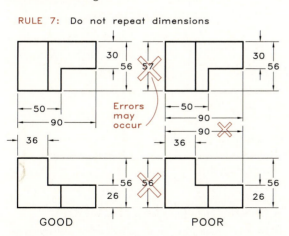

Errors may occur

GOOD   POOR

Figure 13.21 To avoid errors or confusion, do not dupli-cate dimensions on a drawing.

RULE 8: Dimension lines should not cross other lines

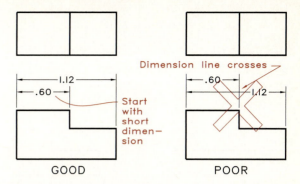

Dimension line crosses

Start with short dimen-sion

GOOD   POOR

Figure 13.22 Dimension lines should not cross any other lines unless absolutely necessary.

RULE 9: Extension lines may cross other lines if they must

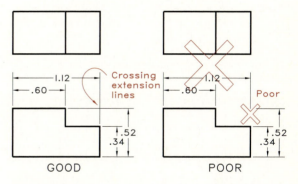

Crossing extension lines

Poor

GOOD   POOR

Figure 13.23 Extension lines may cross other extension lines or object lines if necessary.

Angles

You may dimension angles either by coordinates or angular measurements in degrees (**Fig. 13.27**). Recall that the units for angular measurements are degrees, minutes, and seconds; there are 60 minutes in a degree and 60 seconds in a minute. Seldom will you need to measure angles to the nearest second. **Figures 13.28** and **13.29** illustrate rules for dimensioning angles.

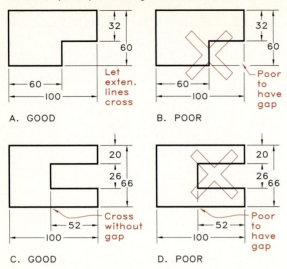

A. GOOD   B. POOR

C. GOOD   D. POOR

Figure 13.24 Leave a small gap from the edges of an object to extension lines that extend from them. Do not leave gaps where extension lines cross object lines or other extension lines.

RULE 10: Do not place dimensions within the views unless necessary

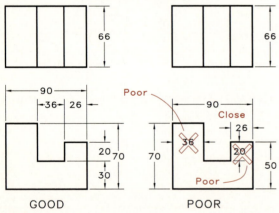

GOOD   POOR

Figure 13.25 Whenever possible, place dimensions outside objects rather than inside their outlines.

Cylindrical Parts and Holes

The diameters of cylinders are measured with a micrometer (**Figs. 13.30** and **13.31**). **Therefore dimension cylinders in their rectangular views**

DIMENSIONING PRISMS

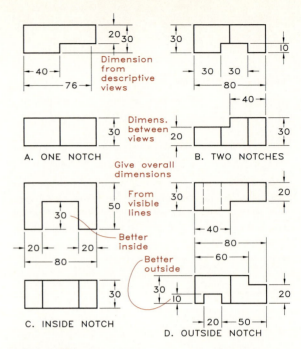

A. ONE NOTCH   B. TWO NOTCHES

C. INSIDE NOTCH   D. OUTSIDE NOTCH

Figure 13.26

A and **B** Dimension prisms from descriptive views and between views.

C You may dimension a notch inside the object if doing so improves clarity.

D Dimension visible lines, not hidden lines.

ANGULAR DIMENSIONS

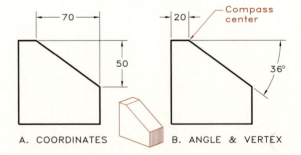

A. COORDINATES   B. ANGLE & VERTEX

Figure 13.27

A Dimension angular planes by using coordinates.

B Measure angles by locating the vertex and measuring the angle in degrees. When accuracy is essential, specify angles in degrees, minutes, and seconds.

RULE 11: Place angular dimensions outside the angle

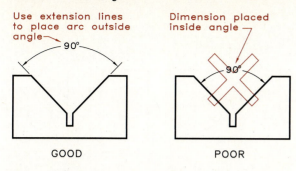

Use extension lines to place arc outside angle

90°

GOOD

Dimension placed inside angle

90°

POOR

Figure 13.28 Place angular dimensions outside angular notches by using extension lines.

RULE 12: Dimension rounded corners to the theoretical intersection

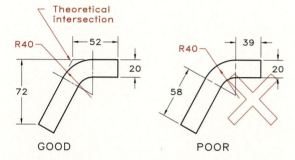

Theoretical intersection

R40   52   20   72

GOOD

R40   39   20   58

POOR

Figure 13.29 Dimension a bent surface rounded corner by locating its theoretical point of intersection with extension lines.

with a diameter (**Figs. 13.32 and 13.33**). Precede all diametral dimensions with the symbol Ø, which indicates that the dimension is a diameter. In the English system you also may use the abbreviation DIA after the diametral dimension.

Stagger dimensions for concentric cylinders to avoid crowding (**Fig. 13.34**). Dimension cylindrical holes in their circular view with leaders (**Fig. 13.35**). Draw leaders specifying hole sizes as shown in **Fig. 13.36**. When you must place diameter notes for holes in the rectangular view instead of the circular view, draw them as shown in **Fig.**

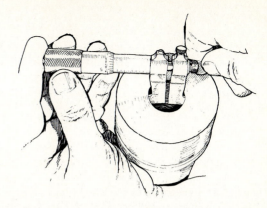

Figure 13.30 This internal micrometer caliper measures internal cylindrical diameters (radii cannot be measured).

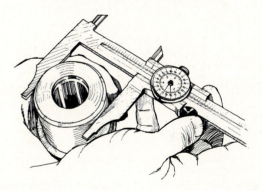

Figure 13.31 This external micrometer caliper measures the diameter of a cylinder.

RULE 13: Dimension cylinders in their rectangular views with diameters

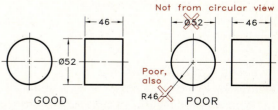

Not from circular view

46   Ø52   46

Ø52

Poor, also   R46

GOOD   POOR

Figure 13.32 Dimension the diameter (not the radius) of a cylinder in the rectangular view.

13.8 DIMENSIONING RULES • 249

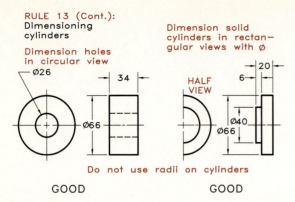

RULE 13 (Cont.):
Dimensioning cylinders

Dimension holes in circular view

Dimension solid cylinders in rectangular views with ø

HALF VIEW

Do not use radii on cylinders

GOOD   GOOD

Figure 13.33 Dimension holes in their circular views with leaders. Dimension concentric cylinders with a series of diameters. Use half views to save drawing time.

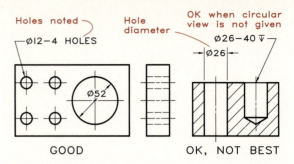

RULE 15: Hole sizes are best given as diameters with leaders in circular views

Holes noted

Hole diameter

OK when circular view is not given

GOOD   OK, NOT BEST

Figure 13.35 Dimension holes in their circular view with leaders whenever possible, but dimension them in their rectangular views if necessary.

RULE 14: Stagger dimension numerals to prevent crowding

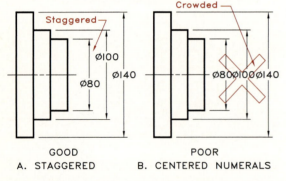

Staggered   Crowded

GOOD   POOR
A. STAGGERED   B. CENTERED NUMERALS

Figure 13.34 Dimensions on concentric cylinders are easier to read if they are staggered within their dimension lines.

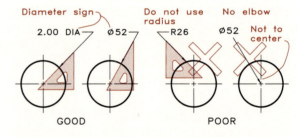

RULE 16: Leaders should have horizontal elbows and point toward the hole centers

Diameter sign   Do not use radius   No elbow

2.00 DIA   Ø52   R26   Ø52 Not to center

GOOD   POOR

Figure 13.36 Draw leaders pointing toward the centers of holes.

13.37. **Figures 13.38** and **13.39** show examples of correctly dimensioned parts having cylindrical features.

Pyramids, Cones, and Spheres

Figures 13.40A–G show three methods of dimensioning pyramids. **Figures 13.40D** and **E** show two acceptable methods of dimensioning cones. Dimension a complete sphere by giving its diameter (**Fig.**

NOTES ON HOLES

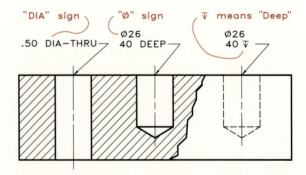

"DIA" sign   "ø" sign   ⊽ means "Deep"

.50 DIA–THRU   Ø26 40 DEEP   Ø26 40 ⊽

Figure 13.37 These are examples of holes noted in their rectangular views.

CYLINDRICAL FEATURES

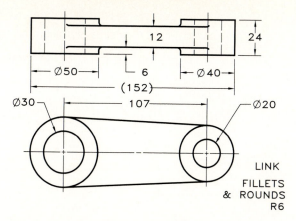

Figure 13.38 This drawing illustrates the application of dimensions to cylindrical features. (F&R R6 means that fillets and rounds have a 6 mm radius.)

DIMENSIONING A CYLINDRICAL PART

A.

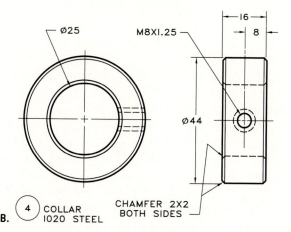

B.

Figure 13.39 (A) This cylindrical part, a collar, is shown drawn and dimensioned in (B).

PYRAMIDS, CONES, AND SPHERES

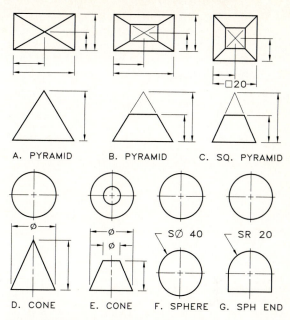

Figure 13.40 This drawing shows the proper way to dimension pyramids, cones, and spheres.

13.40F); give the radius if it is less than a hemisphere (**Fig. 13.40G**). Only one view is needed to describe a sphere.

Leaders

Used to reference notes and dimensions to features, **leaders** most often are drawn at standard angles of triangles (see Fig. 13.36). As **Fig. 13.41** shows, leaders should begin at either the first or last word of a note, with a short horizontal line (elbow) from the note, and extend to the feature being described.

Arcs and Radii

Dimension arcs with radii (**Fig. 13.42**). Current standards specify that radii be dimensioned with an R preceding the dimension (for example, R10). Previously, the standard was for R to follow the

RULE 17: Extend leaders from the first or
the last of a note

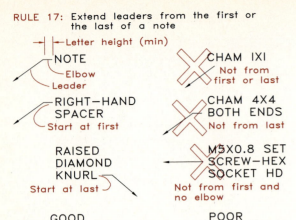

Figure 13.41 Extend leaders from the first or the last word of a note with a horizontal elbow.

RULE 18: Dimensions arcs (less than 180°) with radii

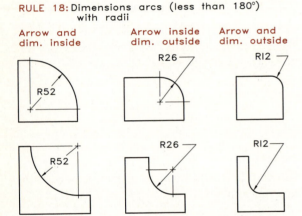

Figure 13.42 When space permits, place dimensions and arrows between the center and the arc. When space is not available for the number, place the arrow between the center and the arc number outside. If there is no space for the arrow inside, place both the dimension and arrow outside the arc with a leader.

dimension (such as 10R). Thus both methods are seen on drawings.

You may dimension large arcs with a false radius (**Fig. 13.43**) by drawing a zigzag to indicate that the line does not represent the true radius.

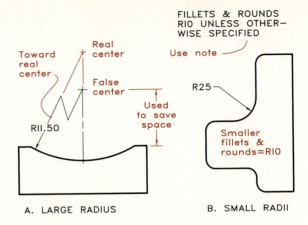

Figure 13.43 Dimensioning radii:
A Show a long radius with a false radius (a line with a zigzag) to indicate that it is not true length. Show its false center on the centerline of the true center.

B Specify fillets and rounds with a note to reduce repetitive dimensions of small arcs.

Where space is not available for radii, dimension small arcs with leaders.

Fillets and Rounds

When all fillets and rounds are equal in size, you may place a note on the drawing stating that condition or use separate notes (**Fig. 13.44**). If most, but not all, of the fillets and rounds have equal radii, the note may read **ALL FILLETS AND ROUNDS R6 UNLESS OTHERWISE SPECIFIED** (or abbreviated as **F&R R6**), with the fillets and rounds of different radii dimensioned separately.

You may note repetitive features as shown in **Fig. 13.45** by using the notes **TYPICAL**, or **TYP**, which means that the dimensioned feature is typical of those not dimensioned. You may use the note **PLACES**, or **PL**, to specify the number of places that identical features appear, although only one is dimensioned.

Figure 13.46A shows a pulley that is drawn and dimensioned in **Fig. 13.46B**. The drawing

FILLETS AND ROUNDS

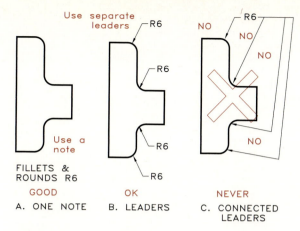

Figure 13.44 Indicate fillets and rounds by (A) notes or (B) separate leaders and dimensions. Never use confusing leaders (C).

NOTES ON PARTS

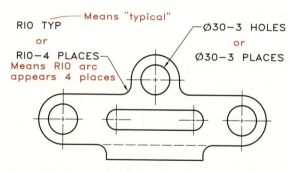

Figure 13.45 Use notes to indicate that identical features and dimensions are repeated on drawings to avoid having to dimension them individually.

demonstrates proper application of many of the rules discussed in this section.

13.9 Dimensioning Other Features

Curved Surfaces
You may dimension an irregular shape comprised of tangent arcs of varying sizes by using a series of

ARCS AND CYLINDERS

A.

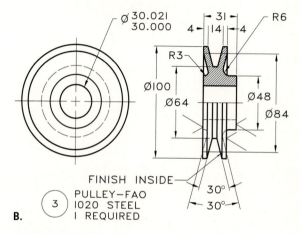

B.

Figure 13.46
A This pulley comprises arcs and circles.

B This drawing illustrates how to dimension the part.

radii **(Fig. 13.47)**. Irregular curves may be dimensioned by using coordinates from two datum lines to locate a series of points along the curve **(Fig. 13.48)**. Placing extension lines at an angle provides additional space for showing dimensions.

Symmetrical Objects
Dimension an irregular symmetrical curve with coordinates **(Fig. 13.49)**. Note the use of dimension lines as extension lines, a permissible violation of dimensioning rules.

PARTS WITH ARCS

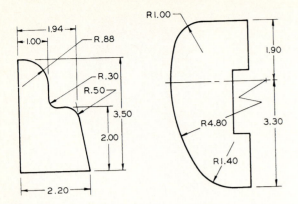

Figure 13.47 These dimension parts comprise a combination of tangent arcs and lines by using radii.

SYMMETRICAL CURVES

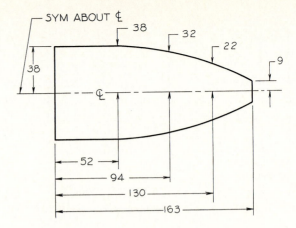

Figure 13.49 Dimensioning symmetrical parts bounded by irregular curves also requires the use of coordinates.

CURVED SURFACES

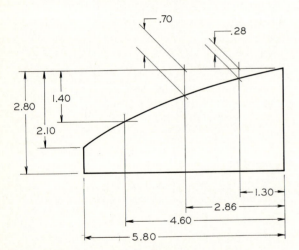

Figure 13.48 Dimensioning points located along an irregular curve requires use of coordinates.

SYMMETRICAL PARTS

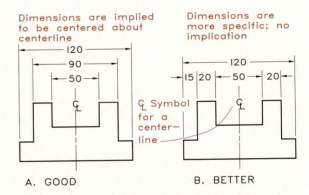

Figure 13.50

A You may dimension symmetrical parts implicitly about their centerlines.

B The better way to dimension symmetrical parts is explicitly about their centerlines.

Dimension other symmetrical objects by using coordinates to imply that the dimensions are symmetrical about the centerline (abbreviated **C**), as shown in **Fig. 13.50A**. **Figure 13.50B** shows a better method of dimensioning this type of object, where symmetry is explicit, not implicit.

13.10 Finished Surfaces

Parts formed in molds, called castings, have rough exterior surfaces. If these parts are to assemble with and move against other parts, they will not

FINISH MARKS

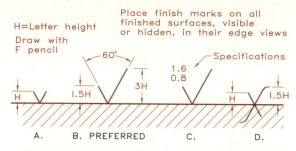

Figure 13.51 Finish marks indicate that a surface is to be machined to a smooth surface.

A The traditional V can be used for general applications.

B The unequal finish mark is the best one for general applications.

C Where surface texture must be specified, this finish mark is used with texture values.

D The f-mark is the least used symbol.

LOCATION DIMENSIONS

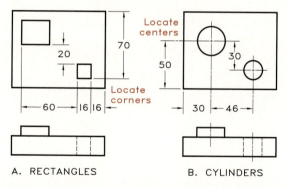

Figure 13.52 Location dimensions give the positions of geometric features with respect to other geometric features, but not their sizes.

function well unless their contact surfaces are machined to a smooth finish by grinding, shaping, lapping, or a similar process.

To indicate that a surface is to be finished, finish marks are drawn on edge views of surfaces to be finished (Fig. 13.51). Finish marks should be

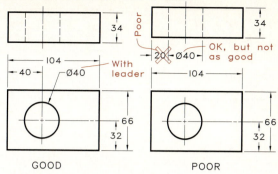

Figure 13.53 Locate cylindrical holes in their circular views by coordinates to their centers.

shown in every view where finished surfaces appear as edges even if they are hidden lines.

The preferred finish mark for the general cases is the uneven mark shown in **Fig. 13.51B**. **When an object is finished on all surfaces, the note FINISHED ALL OVER (abbreviated FAO) is placed on the drawing.**

13.11 Location Dimensions

Location dimensions give the positions, not the sizes, of geometric shapes (**Fig. 13.52**). Locate rectangular shapes by using coordinates of their corners and cylindrical shapes by using coordinates of their centerlines. In each case, dimension the view that shows both measurements. Always extend coordinates from any finished surfaces (even if a finished surface is a hidden line) because smooth machined surfaces allow the most accurate measurements. Locate and dimension single holes as shown in **Fig. 13.53** and multiple holes as shown in **Fig. 13.54**. **Figure 13.55** shows the application of location dimensions to a typical part, with size dimensions omitted.

Baseline dimensions extend from two baselines in a single view (**Fig. 13.56**). The use of baselines

LOCATING CYLINDERS

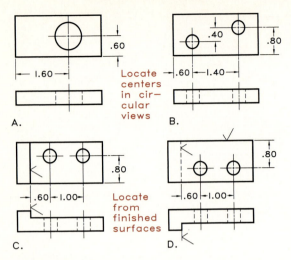

A.

B.

Locate centers in cir-
cular views

C.

Locate from finished surfaces

D.

Figure 13.54

A Locate cylindrical holes in their circular views from two surfaces of the object.

B Locate multiple holes from center to center.

C Locate holes from finished surfaces, even if the finished surfaces are hidden as in (D).

LOCATION DIMENSIONS

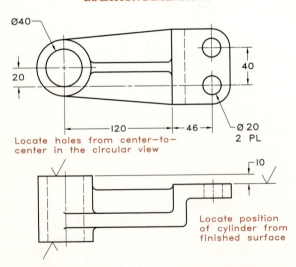

Locate holes from center—to—center in the circular view

Locate position of cylinder from finished surface

Figure 13.55 This example of a dimensioned shaft arm shows the application of location dimensions, with sizes omitted.

BASELINE DIMENSIONING

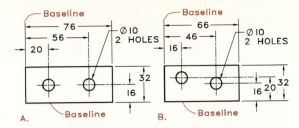

A.

B.

Figure 13.56 Measuring holes from two datum planes is the most accurate way to locate them and reduces the accumulation of errors possible in chain dimensioning.

BOLT CIRCLE

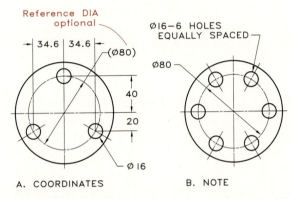

A. COORDINATES

B. NOTE

Figure 13.57 Locate holes on a bolt circle by using (A) coordinates or (B) notes.

eliminates the possible accumulation of errors in size from chain dimensioning.

You may locate holes through circular plates by using coordinates or a note **(Fig. 13.57)**. Dimension the diameter of the imaginary circle passing through the centers of the holes in the circular view as a reference dimension and locate the holes by using coordinates **(Fig. 13.57A)** or a note **(Fig. 13.57B)**. This imaginary circle is called the **bolt circle** or **circle of centers**.

You may also locate holes with radial dimensions and their angular positions in degrees **(Fig. 13.58)**. Holes may be located on their bolt circle even if the shape of the object is not circular.

CIRCLE OF CENTERS

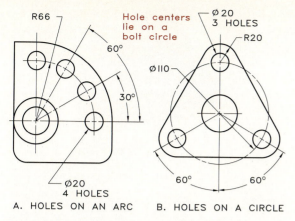

A. HOLES ON AN ARC   B. HOLES ON A CIRCLE

Figure 13.58 Locate centers of holes by using (A) a combination of radii and degrees or (B) a circle of centers.

OBJECTS WITH ROUNDED ENDS

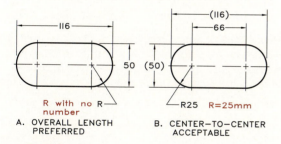

A. OVERALL LENGTH PREFERRED   B. CENTER–TO–CENTER ACCEPTABLE

Figure 13.59

A Dimension objects having rounded ends from end-to-end and give the height.

B A less desirable choice is to dimension the rounded ends from center-to-center and give the radius.

Objects with Rounded Ends

Dimension objects with rounded ends from one rounded end to the other (**Fig. 13.59A**) and show their radii as R without dimensions to specify that the ends are arcs. Obviously, the end radius is half the height of the part.

If you dimension the object from center to center (**Fig. 13.59B**), you must give the radius size. You

ROUNDED FEATURES

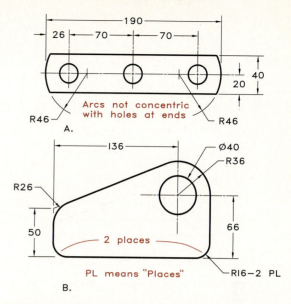

Figure 13.60 These drawings show how to dimension parts having (A) rounded ends that are not concentric with the holes and (B) rounds and cylinders.

may specify the overall width as a reference dimension (116) to eliminate the need for calculations.

Dimension parts with partially rounded ends as shown in **Fig. 13.60A**. Dimension objects with rounded ends that are smaller than a semicircle with a radius and locate the arc's center (**Fig. 13.60B**).

Dimension a single slot with its overall width and height (**Fig. 13.61A**). When there are two or more slots, dimension one slot and use a note to indicate that there are other identical slots (**Fig. 13.61B**).

The tool holder table shown in **Fig. 13.62** illustrates dimensioning of arcs and slots. To prevent dimension lines from crossing, several dimensions are placed on a less descriptive view.

13.12 Outline Dimensioning

Now that you are familiar with most of the rules of dimensioning, you can better understand outline

DIMENSIONING SLOTS

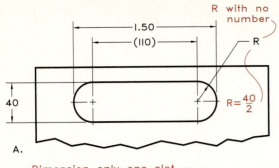

A.

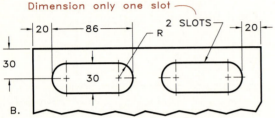

B.

Figure 13.61 These drawings illustrate methods of dimensioning parts that have (A) one slot and (B) more than one slot.

DIMENSIONING ARCS AND SLOTS

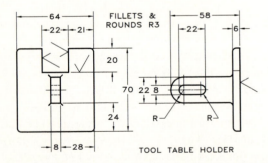

TOOL TABLE HOLDER

Figure 13.62 This dimensioned part has both slots and arcs.

dimensioning, which is a way of applying dimensions to a part's outline (silhouette). By taking this approach, you have little choice but to place dimensions in the most descriptive views of the part. For example, imagine that the T-block shown

OUTLINE DIMENSIONING

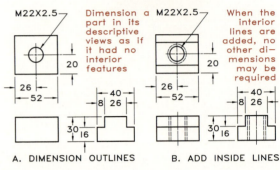

A. DIMENSION OUTLINES   B. ADD INSIDE LINES

Figure 13.63 Outline dimensioning is the placement of dimensions on views as if they had no internal lines. Practice in applying this concept will help you place dimensions on their most descriptive views.

DIMENSIONED PART

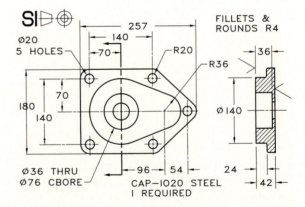

Figure 13.64 This drawing illustrates use of the outline method to dimension the cap in its most descriptive views.

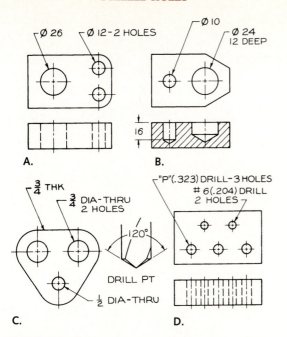

A and **B** You may dimension cylindrical holes by either of these methods.

C and **D** When you use only one view, you have to note the THRU holes or specify their depths.

Figure 13.65

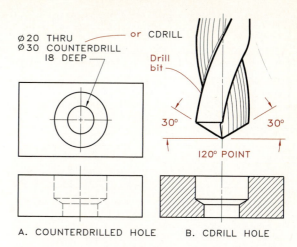

A. COUNTERDRILLED HOLE   B. CDRILL HOLE

Figure 13.66 Counterdrilling notes give the specifications for drilling a larger hole inside a smaller hole. Do not dimension the 120° angle, because it is a byproduct of the drill point. Noting the counterdrill with a leader from the circular view is preferable.

in **Fig. 13.63** has no lines inside its outlines. It is dimensioned beginning with its location dimensions. When the inside lines are added, additional dimensions are seldom needed.

 Figure 13.64 shows an example of outline dimensioning. Note the extension of all dimensions from the outlines of well-defined features.

13.13 Machined Holes

Machined holes are formed by machine operations, such as drilling or boring (**Fig. 13.65**). Give the diameter of the hole with the symbol Ø in front of its dimension (for example, Ø32) with a leader extending from the circular view. You may

also note hole diameters with DIA after their size (for example, 2.00 DIA). Occasionally a machining operation is included in the note, such as 32 DRILL, but the omission of machining operations is preferable.

Drilling Drilling is the basic method of making holes. Dimension the size of a drilled hole with a leader extending from its circular view. You may give its depth in the note or dimension it in the rectangular view (**Fig. 13.65B**). **Dimension the depth of a drilled hole to the usable part of the hole, to the shoulder of the conical point.**

 Counterdrilling involves drilling a large hole inside a smaller hole to enlarge it (**Fig. 13.66**). The drill point leaves a 120° angle as a byproduct of counterdrilling.

 Countersinking is the process of forming conical holes for receiving screw heads (**Fig. 13.67**). Give the diameter of a countersunk hole (the maximum diameter on the surface) and the angle of the

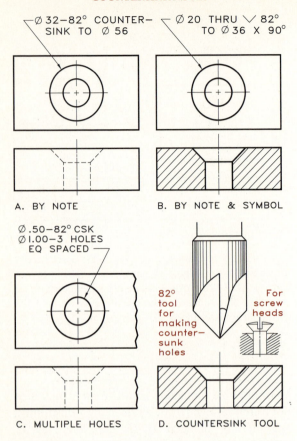

A. BY NOTE   B. BY NOTE & SYMBOL

C. MULTIPLE HOLES   D. COUNTERSINK TOOL

Figure 13.67 These illustrations show methods of noting and specifying countersunk holes for receiving screw heads.

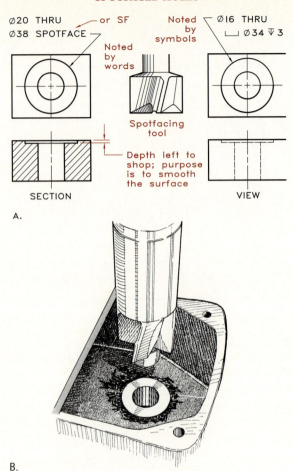

A.

B.

Figure 13.68

A Spotfacing is the smoothing of the surface for contact with a washer or a nut or bolt; dimension for spotfacing as shown.

B This spotfacing tool is used to finish the cylindrical boss to provide a smooth seat for a bolt head.

countersink in a note. Countersunk holes also are used as guides in shafts, spindles, and other cylindrical parts held between the centers of a lathe.

Spotfacing is the process of finishing the surface around holes to provide bearing surfaces for washers or bolt heads (**Fig. 13.68A**). **Figure 13.68B** shows the method of spotfacing a boss (a raised cylindrical element).

Boring Boring is used to make large holes, usually on a lathe with a bore or a boring bar (**Fig.**

13.69). **Counterboring** is the process of enlarging the diameter of a drilled hole (**Fig. 13.70**) to give a flat hole bottom without the tapers as in counterdrilled holes.

Reaming is the operation of finishing or slightly enlarging drilled or bored holes within their prescribed tolerances. A ream is similar to a drill bit.

Figure 13.69 This photo shows the use of a lathe to bore a large hole with a boring bar. (Courtesy of Clausing Corporation.)

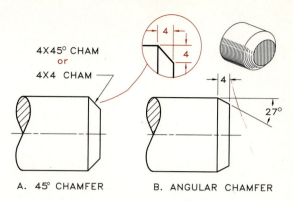

Figure 13.71

A Dimension 45° chamfers by one of the methods shown.

B Dimension chamfers of all other angles as shown.

INSIDE CHAMFERS

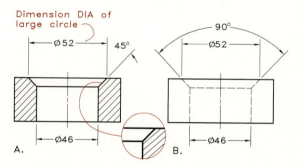

Figure 13.72 Dimension chamfers on the insides of cylinders as shown.

COUNTERBORED HOLES

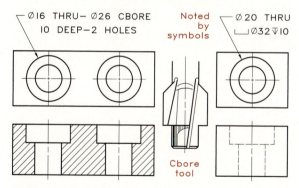

Figure 13.70 Counterbored holes are similar to counterdrilled holes but have flat bottoms instead of tapered sides. Dimension them as shown.

eliminate sharp edges and to make them easier to assemble. When the chamfer angle is 45°, use a note in either of the forms shown in **Fig. 13.71A**. Dimension chamfers of other angles as shown in **Fig. 13.71B**. When inside openings of holes are chamfered, dimension them as shown in **Fig. 13.72**.

13.14 Chamfers

Chamfers are beveled edges cut on cylindrical parts, such as shafts and threaded fasteners, to

13.15 Keyseats

A **keyseat** is a slot cut into a shaft for aligning and holding a pulley or a collar on a shaft. **Figure**

WOODRUFF KEYS

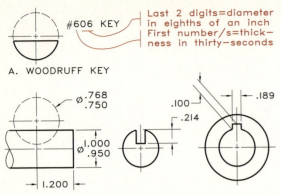

A. WOODRUFF KEY

#606 KEY

Last 2 digits=diameter in eighths of an inch
First number/s=thick-ness in thirty—seconds

B. KEYSEATS: WOODRUFF #606 KEY

Figure 13.73 These drawings show methods of dimensioning (A) Woodruff keys and (B) keyways used to hold a part on a shaft. Appendix 29 gives their tables of sizes.

KNURL NOTES

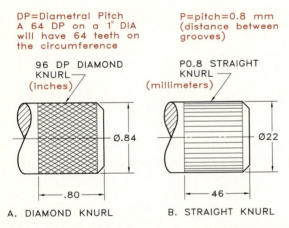

DP=Diametral Pitch
A 64 DP on a 1" DIA will have 64 teeth on the circumference

P=pitch=0.8 mm (distance between grooves)

96 DP DIAMOND KNURL (inches)

P0.8 STRAIGHT KNURL (millimeters)

A. DIAMOND KNURL

B. STRAIGHT KNURL

Figure 13.74 The diamond knurl has a diametral pitch, DP, of 96 and the straight knurl has a linear pitch, P, of 0.8 mm. Pitch is the distance between the grooves on the circumference.

13.73 shows how to dimension keyways and keyseats with dimensions taken from the tables in Appendix 27. The double dimensions on the diameter are tolerances (discussed in Chapter 5).

NECKS

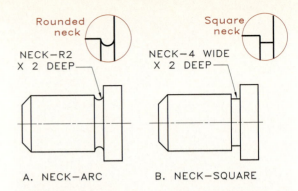

Rounded neck

Square neck

NECK—R2 X 2 DEEP

NECK—4 WIDE X 2 DEEP

A. NECK—ARC

B. NECK—SQUARE

Figure 13.75 Necks are recesses cut in cylinders, with rounded or square bottoms, usually at the intersections of concentric cylinders. Dimension necks as shown.

13.16 Knurling

Knurling is the operation of cutting **diamond-shaped** or **parallel** patterns on cylindrical surfaces for gripping, decoration, or press fits between mating parts that are permanently assembled. Draw and dimension diamond knurls and straight knurls as shown in **Fig. 13.74**, with notes that specify type, pitch, and diameter.

The abbreviation DP means diametral pitch, or the ratio of the number of grooves on the circumference (N) to the diameter (D) expressed as DP = N/D. The preferred diametral pitches for knurling are 64 DP, 96 DP, 128 DP, and 160 DP.

For diameters of 1 inch, knurling of 64 DP, 96 DP, 128 DP, and 160 DP will have 64, 96, 128, and 160 teeth, respectively, on the circumference. The note P0.8 means that the knurling grooves are 0.8 mm apart. Make knurling calculations in inches and then convert them to millimeters. Specify knurls for press fits with the diameter size before knurling and with the minimum diameter size after knurling.

13.17 Necks and Undercuts

A **neck** is a groove cut around the circumference of a cylindrical part. If cut where cylinders of dif-

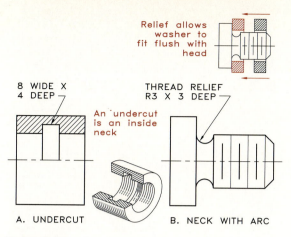

Figure 13.76

A An undercut is a groove cut inside a cylinder.

B A thread relief is a groove cut at the end of a thread to improve the screw's assembly. Dimension both types of necks as shown.

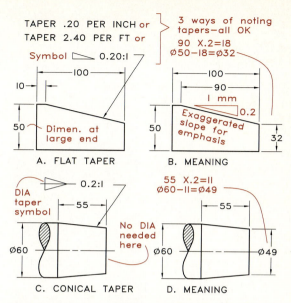

Figure 13.77 Tapers may be specified for either flat or conical surfaces: dimensioning and interpretation for (A and B) a flat taper and (C and D) for a conical taper.

ferent diameters join **(Fig. 13.75)**, a neck ensures that the assembled parts fit flush at the shoulder of the larger cylinder and allows trash that would cause binding to drop out of the way.

An **undercut** is a recessed neck inside a cylindrical hole **(Fig. 13.76A)**. A **thread relief** is a neck that has been cut at the end of a thread to ensure that the head of the threaded part will fit flush against the part it screws into **(Fig. 13.76B)**.

13.18 Tapers

Tapers for both flat planes and conical surfaces may be specified with either notes or symbols. **Flat taper** is the ratio of the difference in the heights at each end of a surface to its length **(Fig. 13.77A and B)**. Tapers on flat surfaces may be expressed as inches per inch (.20 per inch), inches per foot (2.40 per foot), or millimeters per millimeter (0.20:1).

Conical taper is the ratio of the difference in the diameters at each end of a cone to its length **(Fig. 13.77C and D)**. Tapers on conical surfaces may be expressed as inches per inch (.25 per inch), inches per foot (3.00 per foot), or millimeters per millimeter (0.25:1).

13.19 Miscellaneous Notes

Notes on detail drawings provide information and specifications that would be difficult to represent by drawings alone **(Figs. 13.78–13.80)**. Place notes horizontally on the sheet whenever possible, because they are easier to letter and read in that position. Several notes in sequence on the same line should be separated with short dashes between them (for example, 15 DIA-30 DIA SPOTFACE). Use standard abbreviations (see Appendix 1) in notes to save space and time.

MISCELLANEOUS NOTES

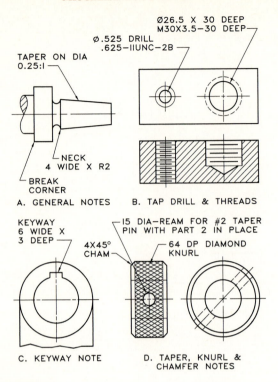

A. GENERAL NOTES

B. TAP DRILL & THREADS

C. KEYWAY NOTE

D. TAPER, KNURL & CHAMFER NOTES

Figure 13.78

A The notes for this part indicate a neck, a taper, and a break corner, which is a slight round to remove sharpness from a corner.

B Threaded holes are sometimes dimensioned by giving the tap drill size in addition to the thread specifications, but selection of the tap drill size usually is left to the shop.

C This note is for dimensioning a keyway.

D The notes for this collar call for knurling, chamfering, and drilling for a #2 taper pin.

Problems

1–24 (a–b). (Figs. 13.81 and **13.82)** Solve these problems on size A paper, one per sheet, if you draw them full size. If you draw them double size, use size B paper. The views are drawn on a 0.20-in. (5-mm) grid.

You will need to vary the spacing between views to provide adequate room for the dimensions. Sketching the

WASHERS AND UNDERCUTS

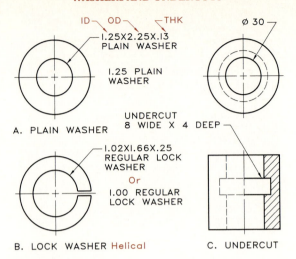

A. PLAIN WASHER

B. LOCK WASHER Helical

C. UNDERCUT

Figure 13.79

A and **B** Dimension washers and lock washers as shown by taking sizes from the tables in the Appendix.

C Dimension an undercut with a note.

KEYWAYS AND SPLINES

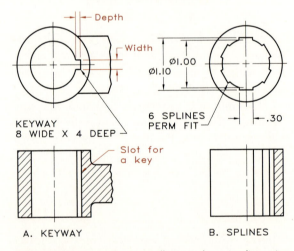

A. KEYWAY

B. SPLINES

Figure 13.80 These drawings illustrate how to dimension (A) keyways and (B) splines.

views and dimensions to determine the required spacing before laying out the solutions with instruments would be helpful. Supply lines that may be missing in all views.

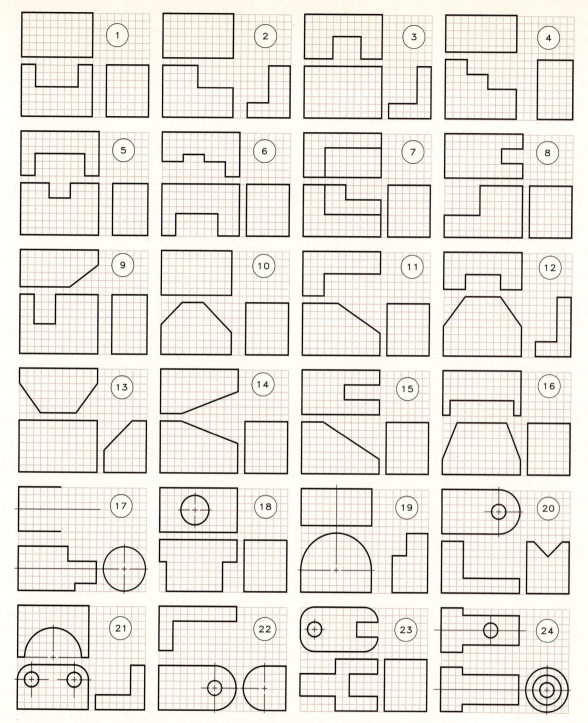

Figure 13.81 Problems 1–24(a). Lay out the views, supply missing lines, and dimension them.

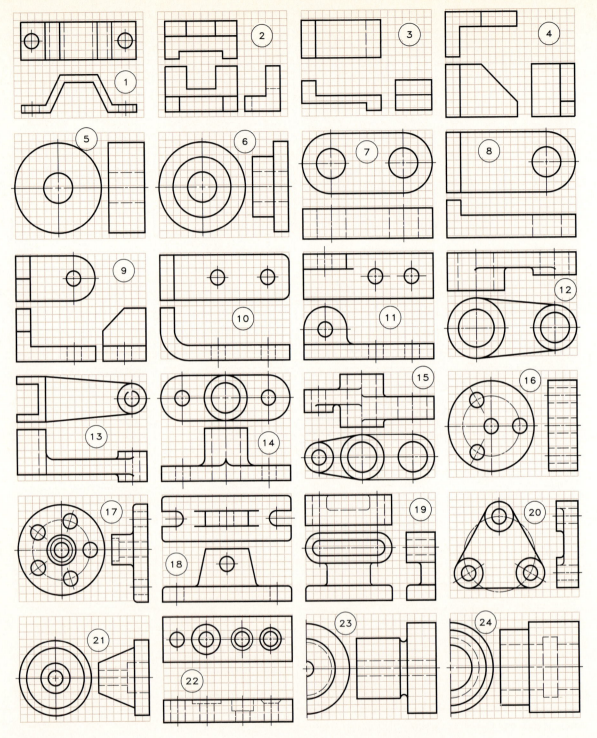

Figure 13.82 Problems 1–24(b). Lay out the views, supply missing lines, and dimension them.

14

Tolerances

14.1 Introduction

Today's technology requires that parts be specified with increasingly exact dimensions. Many parts made by different companies at widely separated locations must be interchangeable, which requires precise size specifications and production.

The technique of dimensioning parts within a required range of variation to ensure interchangeability is called **tolerancing**. Each dimension is allowed a certain degree of variation within a specified zone, or **tolerance**. For example, a part's dimension might be expressed as 20 ± 0.50, which allows a tolerance (variation in size) of 1.00 mm.

A tolerance should be as large as possible without interfering with the function of the part to minimize production costs. Manufacturing costs increase as tolerances become smaller.

The cut-away view of the shaft journal in **Fig. 14.1** illustrates parts that must rotate smoothly on ball bearings. If these parts were not toleranced and manufactured to a high degree of accuracy, they would not function properly.

Figure 14.1 This shaft journal would not rotate smoothly on the ball bearings if adjacent parts had not been manufactured within extremely close tolerances.

14.2 Tolerance Dimensions

Figure 14.2 shows three methods of specifying tolerances on dimensions: unilateral, bilateral, and limit forms. When plus-or-minus tolerancing is used, it is applied to a theoretical dimension

UNILATERAL, BILATERAL, AND LIMIT TOLERANCES

UNILATERAL TOLERANCE
(Variation in one dir.)

2.250 $^{+.000}_{-.005}$

General space

.650
+.003
−.000
Tight Space

Ø.500 $^{+.000}_{-.005}$ DIA Form

Large on top

2.250
2.245

General space

LIMIT FORM

.650
.646

Tight Space

BILATERAL TOLERANCE
(Variation in two dir.)

2.250 ±.003

General space

.650
+.002
−.001
Tight Space

Ø14.000 ±.004 DIA Form

Small to large

Ø14.00−14.20

DIA Form

Figure 14.2 These methods properly position and indicate tolerances in unilateral, bilateral, and limit forms for both general and tight spaces.

ORDER OF NUMBERS

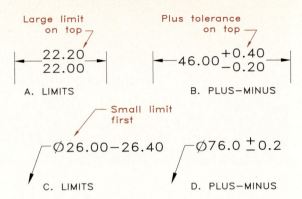

Large limit on top

22.20
22.00

A. LIMITS

Plus tolerance on top

46.00 $^{+0.40}_{-0.20}$

B. PLUS−MINUS

Small limit first

Ø26.00−26.40

C. LIMITS

Ø76.0 ±0.2

D. PLUS−MINUS

Figure 14.3 Place upper limits either above or to the right of lower limits. In plus-and-minus tolerancing, place the plus limits above the minus limits.

POSITIONING OF NUMBERS

$H=\frac{1}{8}$ Same no. of decimal places $\frac{H}{2}=\frac{1}{16}$ H MAX

2.0000 $^{+.0040}_{-.0020}$

A. PLUS−MINUS TOLERANCES

$\frac{H}{2}=\frac{1}{16}$

2.0400
1.9980

B. LIMIT−FORM TOLERANCES

Figure 14.4 This drawing shows the spacing and ratios of numerals used to specify tolerances on dimensions.

called the **basic dimension**. When dimensions can vary in only one direction from the basic dimension (either larger or smaller), tolerancing is **unilateral**. Tolerancing that permits variation in both directions from the basic dimension (larger and smaller) is **bilateral**.

Tolerances may also be given in **limit form**, with dimensions representing the largest and smallest sizes for a feature. When tolerances are shown in limit form, the basic dimension will be unknown.

Figure 14.3 shows the customary methods of applying tolerance values on dimension lines. **Figure 14.4** shows the ratios of tolerance numerals placed in dimension lines.

14.3 Mating Parts

Mating parts must be toleranced to fit within a prescribed degree of accuracy **(Fig. 14.5)**. The upper part is dimensioned with limits indicating its maximum and minimum sizes. The notch in

the lower part is toleranced to be slightly larger, allowing the parts to assemble with a clearance fit.

Mating parts also may be cylindrical forms, such as a pulley, bushing, and shaft **(Fig. 14.6)**. The bushing should force fit inside the pulley to provide a good bearing surface for the rotating shaft. At the same time, the shaft and the bushing should mate so that the pulley and bushing will rotate on the shaft with a free running fit.

MATING PARTS

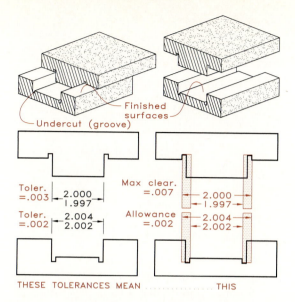

Figure 14.5 These mating parts have tolerances (variations in size) of 0.003" and 0.002", respectively. The allowance (tightest fit) between the assembled parts is 0.002".

TERMINOLOGY OF TOLERANCES

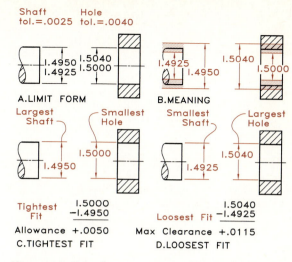

Figure 14.7 The allowance (tightest fit) between these assembled parts is +0.005". The maximum clearance is +0.0115".

CYLINDRICAL FITS

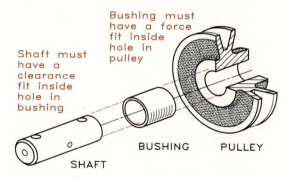

Figure 14.6 These parts must be assembled with cylindrical fits that give a clearance and an interference fit.

ANSI tables (see Appendixes 32–36) prescribe cylindrical-fit tolerances for different applications. Familiarity with the terminology of cylindrical tolerancing is essential to use these tables.

14.4 Tolerancing: English Units

Terminology

Figure 14.7, showing mating of cylindrical parts, illustrates the following tolerancing terminology and definitions.

Tolerance: the difference between the limits prescribed for a single feature, or 0.0025 in. for the shaft and 0.0040 for the hole **(Fig. 14.7A)**.

Limits of tolerance: the extreme measurements permitted by the maximum and minimum sizes of a feature, or 1.4925 and 1.4950 for the shaft and 1.5000 and 1.5040 for the hole **(Fig. 14.7B)**.

Allowance: the tightest fit between the two mating parts, or +0.0050 **(Fig. 14.7C)**, allowance is negative for an interference fit.

Nominal size: an approximate size of shaft and hole, usually expressed with common fractions, or 1.50 in. (1 1/2 in.) **(Fig. 14.7)**.

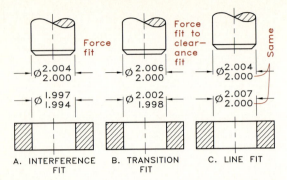

A. INTERFERENCE FIT   B. TRANSITION FIT   C. LINE FIT

Figure 14.8 This drawing shows three types of fits between mating parts in addition to the clearance fit shown in the Fig. 14.7.

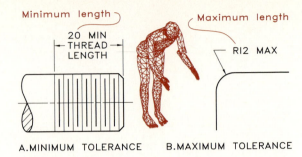

A. MINIMUM TOLERANCE   B. MAXIMUM TOLERANCE

Figure 14.9 Single tolerances can be given in applications of this type in maximum (MAX) or minimum (MIN) form.

Basic size: the exact theoretical size from which limits are derived by the application of plus-and-minus tolerances, or 1.5000 (**Fig. 14.7**). The basic diameter cannot be determined if the tolerances are expressed in limit form.

Actual size: the measured size of the finished part.

Fit: the tightness between two assembled parts. The four types of fit are: clearance, interference, transition, and line.

Clearance fit: the clearance between two assembled mating parts—the fit between the shaft and the hole that permits a minimum clearance of 0.0050 in. and a maximum clearance of 0.0115 in. (**Figs. 14.7C** and **D**).

Interference fit: results in an interference between the two assembled parts—the shaft is larger than the hole, requiring a **force** or **press fit**, an effect similar to welding the two parts (**Fig. 14.8**).

Transition fit: may result in either an interference or a clearance between the assembled parts—the shaft may be either smaller or larger than the hole and still be within the prescribed tolerances (**Fig. 14.8B**).

Line fit: may result in surface contact or clearance when the limits are approached (**Fig. 14.8C**).

Selective assembly: a method of selecting and assembling parts by trial and error and by hand, allowing parts to be made with greater tolerances at less cost as a compromise between a high manufacturing accuracy and ease of assembly.

Single limits: dimensions designated by either minimum (MIN) or maximum (MAX), but not by both (**Fig. 14.9**); depths of holes, lengths, threads, corner radii, chamfers, and so on are sometimes dimensioned in this manner.

14.5 Basic Hole System

The basic hole system utilizes the smallest hole size as the basic diameter for calculating tolerances and allowances. The basic hole system is efficient when standard drills, reamers, and machine tools are available to give precise hole sizes. The smallest hole size is the basic diameter because a hole can be enlarged by machining but not reduced in size.

For example, in Fig. 14.7 the smallest diameter of the hole is 1.500 in. Subtract the allowance, 0.0050, from it to find the diameter of the largest shaft, 1.4950 in. To find the smallest limit for the shaft diameter, subtract the tolerance from 1.4950 in.

14.6 Basic Shaft System

The basic shaft system is applicable when shafts are available in highly precise standard sizes. The largest diameter of the shaft is the basic diameter for applying tolerances and allowances. The largest shaft size is used as the basic diameter because shafts can be machined to smaller size but not enlarged.

For example, if the largest permissible shaft size is 1.500 in., add the allowance to this dimension to obtain the smallest hole diameter into which the shaft fits. If the parts are to have an allowance of 0.0040 in., the smallest hole would have a diameter of 1.5040 in.

14.7 Cylindrical Fits

The ANSI B4.1 standard gives a series of fits between cylindrical features in inches for the basic hole system. The types of fit covered in this standard are:

RC: running or sliding clearance fits

LC: clearance locational fits

LT: transition locational fits

LN: interference locational fits

FN: force and shrink fits

Appendixes 32–36 list these five types of fit, each of which has several classes.

Running or sliding clearance fits (RC) provide a similar running performance, with suitable lubrication allowance, throughout the range of sizes. The clearance for the first two classes (RC 1 and RC 2), used chiefly as slide fits, increases more slowly with diameter size than other classes to maintain an accurate location even at the expense of free relative motion.

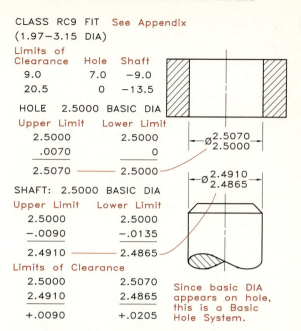

Figure 14.10 This example shows how to calculate limits and allowances for an RC9 fit between a shaft and hole with a basic diameter of 2.5000 inches. Refer to Appendix 32.

Locational fits (LC, LT, LN) determine the location of mating parts and may provide rigid or accurate location (interference fits) or some freedom of location (clearance fits). Locational fits are divided into three groups: **clearance fits (LC), transition fits (LT),** and **interference fits (LN).**

Force fits (FN) are interference fits characterized by the maintenance of constant bore pressures throughout the range of sizes. The interference varies almost directly with diameter, and the difference between its minimum and maximum values is small enough to maintain the resulting pressures within reasonable limits.

Figure 14.10 illustrates how to apply values from the tables in Appendix 32 for an RC 9 fit. The basic diameter of 2.5000 in. falls between 1.97 and 3.15 in. in the size column of the table. Limits are

CALCULATION CHART

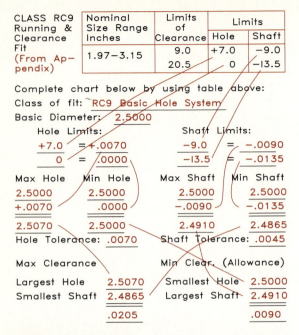

CLASS RC9 Running & Clearance Fit (From Appendix)	Nominal Size Range Inches	Limits of Clearance	Limits	
			Hole	Shaft
	1.97–3.15	9.0	+7.0	–9.0
		20.5	0	–13.5

Complete chart below by using table above:

Class of fit: RC9 Basic Hole System

Basic Diameter: 2.5000

Hole Limits:		Shaft Limits:	
+7.0 = +.0070		–9.0 = –.0090	
0 = .0000		–13.5 = –.0135	

Max Hole	Min Hole	Max Shaft	Min Shaft
2.5000	2.5000	2.5000	2.5000
+.0070	.0000	–.0090	–.0135
2.5070	2.5000	2.4910	2.4865

Hole Tolerance: .0070   Shaft Tolerance: .0045

Max Clearance		Min Clear. (Allowance)	
Largest Hole	2.5070	Smallest Hole	2.5000
Smallest Shaft	2.4865	Largest Shaft	2.4910
	.0205		.0090

Figure 14.11 Cylindrical fit information may be calculated in an organized manner as this chart demonstrates. (Thanks to Steve Horton.)

in thousandths, so convert the values by moving the decimal point three places to the left; for example, +7 is +0.0070 in.

Add the limits (+0.007 and 0.000 in.) to the basic diameter to find the upper and lower limits of the hole (2.5070 and 2.5000 in.). Determine the upper and lower limits of the shaft (2.4910 and 2.4865 in.) by subtracting the two limits (–0.0090 and –0.0135 in.) from the basic diameter (2.5000 in.).

To get the tightest fit between the assembled parts (+0.0090 in.) and the loosest fit (+0.0205 in.), subtract the minimum sizes from the maximum sizes of the holes and shafts. These values appear in the Limit column of the table (Appendix 32).

This same method of using tables of fits applies to other types of fits and their respective tables: force fit, interference fit, transition fit, and

METRIC SYSTEM TERMINOLOGY

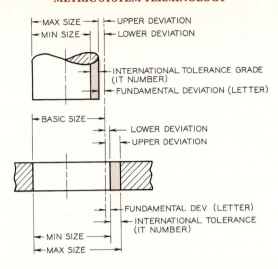

Figure 14.12 The terminology shown here relates to metric fits and limits.

locational fit. Subtract negative limits from the basic diameter and add positive limits to it. **A minus sign preceding a limits of clearance in the tables indicates an interference fit between the assembled features, and a positive limit of clearance indicates a clearance fit.**

Figure 14.11 presents a calculation chart for the tolerances shown in Fig. 14.10. The possibility of errors is reduced if you take the values from the tables and write them down in this manner.

14.8 Tolerancing: Metric System

Terminology

The system recommended by the International Standards Organization (ISO) in ANSI B4.2 for metric measurements relates to fits that usually apply to cylinders—hole and shaft—but you may also use these tables to specify fits between parallel contact surfaces, such as a key in a slot. **Figures 14.12–14.14** illustrate most of the definitions of metric limits and fits.

PREFERRED BASIC SIZES (MILLIMETERS)

First Choice	Second Choice	First Choice	Second Choice	First Choice	Second Choice
1		10		100	
	1.1		11		110
1.2		12		120	
	1.4		14		140
1.6		16		160	
	1.8		18		180
2		20		200	
	2.2		22		220
2.5		25		250	
	2.8		28		280
3		30		300	
	3.5		35		350
4		40		400	
	4.5		45		450
5		50		500	
	5.5		55		550
6		60		600	
	7		70		700
8		80		800	
	9		90		900
				1000	

Figure 14.13 Basic sizes for metric fits should be selected first from the first-choice column and then from the second-choice column.

TOLERANCE SYMBOLS

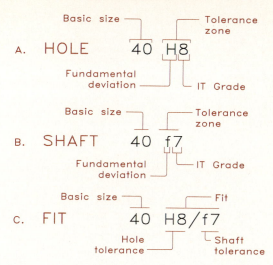

Figure 14.14 These tolerance symbols and their definitions apply to holes and shafts.

Basic size: the theoretical size, usually a diameter from which limits or deviations are calculated (**Fig. 14.12**); select it from the table shown in **Fig. 14.13** under the First Choice column.

Deviation: the difference between the hole or shaft size and the basic size.

Upper deviation: the difference between the maximum permissible size of a part and its basic size (**Fig. 14.12**).

Lower deviation: the difference between the minimum permissible size of a part and its basic size (**Fig. 14.12**).

Fundamental deviation: the deviation closest to the basic size (**Fig. 14.12**); in the note 40 H8 in **Fig. 14.14**, the H represents the fundamental deviation for a hole, and in the note 40 f7, the f represents the fundamental deviation for a shaft.

Tolerance: the difference between the maximum and minimum allowable sizes of a single part.

International tolerance (IT) grade: a series of tolerances that vary with basic size to provide a uniform level of accuracy within a given grade (**Fig. 14.12**); in the note 40 H8 in **Fig. 14.14**, the 8 represents the IT grade; there are 18 IT grades: IT01, IT0, IT1, ..., IT16.

Tolerance zone: a combination of the fundamental deviation and the tolerance grade; the H8 portion of the 40 H8 note in **Fig. 14.14** is the tolerance zone.

Hole basis: a system of fits based on the minimum hole size as the basic diameter, with fundamental deviations; Appendixes 38 and 39 give hole-basis data for tolerances.

Shaft basis: a system of fits based on the maximum shaft size as the basic diameter, with fundamental deviations; Appendixes 40 and 41 give shaft-basis data for tolerances.

Clearance fit: a fit resulting in a clearance between two assembled parts under all tolerance conditions.

ISO SYMBOLS FOR PREFERRED FITS

Hole Basis	Shaft Basis	Description	
H11/c11	C11/h11	Loose Running Fit for wide commercial tolerances on external members	
H9/d9	D9/h9	Free Running Fit for large temperature variations, high running speeds, or high journal pressures	Clearance Fits
H8/f7	F8/h7	Close Running Fit for accurate location and moderate speeds and journal pressures	
H7/g6	G7/h6	Sliding Fit for accurate fit and location and free moving and turning, not free running	
H7/h6	H7/h6	Locational Clearance for snug fits for parts that can be freely assembled	
H7/k6	K7/h6	Locational Transition Fit for accurate locations	Transition Fits
H7/n6	N7/h6	Locational Transition Fit for more accurate locations and greater interference	
H7/p6	P7/h6	Locational Interference Fit for rigidity and alignment without special bore pressures	
H7/s6	S7/h6	Medium Drive Fit for shrink fits on light sections; tightest fit usable for cast iron	Interference Fits
H7/u6	U7/h6	Force Fit for parts that can be highly stressed and for shrink fits.	

Figure 14.15 This list gives the preferred hole-basis and shaft-basis fits for the metric system.

Interference fit: a force fit between two parts, requiring that they be driven together.

Transition fit: may result in either a clearance or an interference fit between assembled parts.

Tolerance symbols: notes giving the specifications of tolerances and fits (**Fig. 14.14**); the basic size is a number, followed by the fundamental deviation letter and the IT number, which combined give the tolerance zone; **uppercase letters indicate the fundamental deviations for holes, and lowercase letters indicate fundamental deviations for shafts.**

TYPES OF FIT

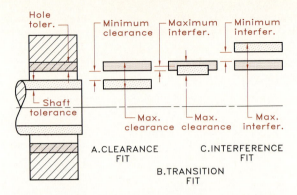

Figure 14.16 Types of fits: (A) clearance fit, (B) transition fit, where there can be either interference or clearance, and (C) interference fit, where the parts must be forced together.

Preferred Sizes and Fits

The table in **Fig. 14.13** shows the preferred basic sizes for computing tolerances. Under the First Choice heading, each number increases by about 25% from the preceding value. Each number in the Second Choice column increases by about 12%. **To minimize cost, select basic diameters from the first column because they correspond to standard stock sizes for round, square, and hexagonal metal products.**

Figure 14.15 shows preferred clearance, transition, and interference fits for the hole-basis and shaft-basis systems. Appendixes 38–41 contain the complete tables.

Preferred Fits: Hole-Basis System Figure 14.16

shows the types of fits for the hole-basis system, in which the **smallest hole is the basic diameter.** Clearance, transition, or interference fits are possible when toleranced with the options of the hole-basis system. **Figure 14.17** compares the preferred fits for a hole-basis system. The lower deviation of the hole is zero, which means that the smallest hole is the basic size. Variations in fit between parts range from a clearance fit of H11/c11 to an interference fit of U7/u6 (see Fig. 14.15).

PREFERRED FITS: HOLE-BASIS SYSTEM

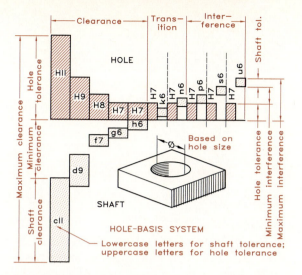

Figure 14.17 This diagram illustrates the preferred fits for the hole-basis system listed in Fig. 14.15. Appendixes 38 and 39 give values for these fits.

PREFERRED FITS: SHAFT-BASIS SYSTEM

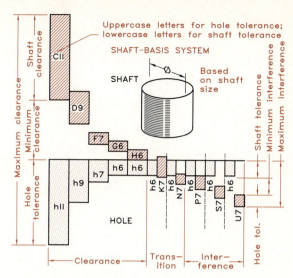

Figure 14.18 This diagram illustrates the preferred fits for a shaft-basis system listed in Fig. 14.15. Appendixes 40 and 41 give values for these fits.

Preferred Fits: Shaft-Basis System **Figure 14.18** compares the preferred fits of the shaft-basis system, in which **the largest shaft is the basic diameter.** Variations in fit between parts range from a clearance fit of C11/h11 to an interference fit of U7/h6 (see Fig. 14.15).

Standard Cylindrical Fits

The following examples demonstrate how to calculate and apply tolerances to cylindrical parts. The solutions involve the use of Appendix 38, Fig. 14.13, and Fig. 14.15.

Example 1 (Fig. 14.19)

Required: Use the hole-basis system, a close running fit, and a basic diameter of 49 mm.

Solution: Use a preferred basic diameter of 50 mm **(Fig. 14.13)** and fit of H8/f7 **(Fig. 14.15).**

Hole: Find the upper and lower limits of the hole in Appendix 38 under H8 and across from 50 mm. These limits are 50.000 and 50.039 mm.

CALCULATION OF METRIC FITS

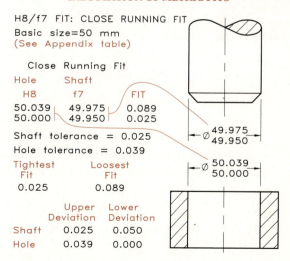

Figure 14.19 This drawing shows how to calculate and apply metric limits and fits to a shaft and hole (Appendix 38).

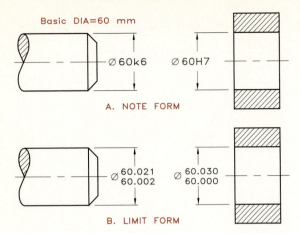

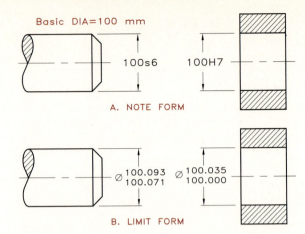

Figure 14.20 These methods are for applying metric tolerances to a hole and shaft with a transition fit (Appendix 39).

Figure 14.21 These methods are for applying metric tolerances to a hole and shaft with an interference fit (Appendix 39).

Shaft: Find the upper and lower limits of the shaft under f7 and across from 50 mm in Appendix 38. These limits are 49.950 and 49.975 mm.

Symbols: **Figure 14.19** shows how to apply toleranced dimensions to the hole and shaft.

Example 2 (Fig. 14.20)

Required: Use the hole-basis system, a location transition fit, and a basic diameter of 57 mm.

Solution: Use a preferred basic diameter of 60 mm (Fig. 14.13) and a fit of H7/k6 (Fig. 14.15).

Hole: Find the upper and lower limits of the hole in Appendix 39 under H7 and across from 60 mm. These limits are 60.000 and 60.030 mm.

Shaft: Find the upper and lower limits of the shaft under k6 and across from 60 mm in Appendix 39. These limits are 60.021 and 60.002 mm.

Symbols: **Figure 14.20** shows two methods of applying the tolerance symbols to a drawing.

Example 3 (Fig. 14.21)

Required: Use the hole-basis system, a medium drive fit, and a basic diameter of 96 mm.

Solution: Use a preferred basic diameter of 100 mm (Fig. 14.13) and a fit of H7/s6 (Fig. 14.15).

Hole: Find the upper and lower limits of the hole in Appendix 39 under H7 and across from 100 mm. These limits are 100.035 and 100.000 mm.

Shaft: Find the upper and lower limits of the shaft under s6 and across from 100 mm in Appendix 39. These limits are 100.093 and 100.071 mm. Appendix 39 gives the tightest fit as an interference of –0.093 mm, and the loosest fit as an interference of –0.036 mm. Minus signs in front of these numbers indicate an interference fit.

Symbols: **Figure 14.21** shows how to apply toleranced dimensions to the hole and shaft.

Nonstandard Fits: Nonpreferred Sizes

You may calculate limits of tolerances for any of the preferred fits shown in Fig. 14.15 for nonstand-

CALCULATION OF NONSTANDARD LIMITS

FIT: H8/f7 Ø45 BASIC DIA

From Appendix

Hole H8	Shaft f7	HOLE LIMITS	45.039 45.000
0.039 0.000	−0.025 −0.050	SHAFT LIMITS	44.975 44.950

Figure 14.22 This calculation is for an H8/f7 fit for a non-standard diameter of 45 mm (Appendixes 42 and 43).

ard sizes that do not appear in Appendixes 38–41. Limits of tolerances for nonstandard hole sizes are in Appendix 42, and limits of tolerances for non-standard shaft sizes are in Appendix 43.

Figure 14.22 shows the hole and shaft limits for an H8/f7 fit and a 45-mm DIA. The tolerance limits of 0.000 and 0.039 mm for an H8 hole are from Appendix 42, across from the size range of 40–50 mm. The tolerance limits of –0.025 and –0.050 mm for the shaft are from Appendix 43. Calculate the hole limits by adding the positive tolerances to the 45-mm basic diameter and the shaft limits by subtracting the negative tolerances from the 45-mm basic diameter.

14.9 Chain Versus Datum-Plane Dimensions

When parts are dimensioned to locate surfaces or geometric features by a chain of dimensions laid end to end **(Fig. 14.23A)**, variations may accumulate in excess of the specified tolerance. For example, the tolerance between surfaces A and B is 0.02, between A and C it is 0.04, and between A and D it is 0.06.

You may eliminate an accumulation of toler-ances by measuring from a single plane called a **datum plane** or **baseline**. A datum plane is usually on the object, but it can also be on the machine used to make the part. Because each plane in **Fig. 14.23B** is located with respect to a datum plane, the tolerances between the intermediate planes do

CHAIN VS. DATUM DIMENSIONS

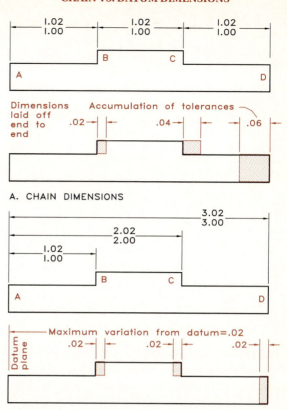

Figure 14.23

A Dimensions given end to end in a chain fashion may result in an accumulation of tolerances of up to 0.06″ at D instead of the specified 0.02″.

B When dimensioned from a single datum, the variations of B, C, and D cannot deviate more than the specified 0.02″ from the datum.

not exceed the maximum tolerance of 0.02. Always base the application of tolerances on the function of a part in relationship to its mating parts.

Origin Selection

When you need to specify a surface as the origin (datum plane) for locating a parallel surface, selection of the shorter one gives more accurate results **(Fig. 14.24)**. However, the angular varia-

ORIGIN SURFACE

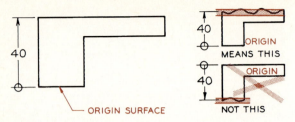

Figure 14.24 Selection of the shorter surface as the origin surface for locating a longer parallel surface gives the greatest accuracy.

TAPER TOLERANCES

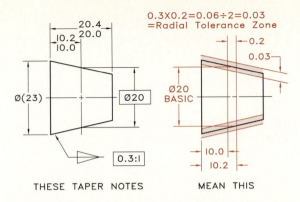

Figure 14.25 Indicate taper with a combination of tolerances and taper symbols. Here, the variation in diameter at any point is 0.06 mm, or 0.03 mm in radius.

tion permitted is less for the longer surface in this case than it would be if the longer surface had been selected as the datum plane.

14.10 Conical Tapers

Recall that taper is a ratio of the difference in the diameters of two circular sections of a cone to the distance between the sections. **Figure 14.25** shows a method of specifying a conical taper by giving a basic diameter and basic taper. The basic diameter of 20 mm is located midway in the length of the cone with a toleranced dimension. **Figure 14.25** shows how to calculate the radial tolerance zone.

14.11 Tolerance Notes

You should tolerance all dimensions on a drawing either by using the rules previously discussed or by placing a note in or near the title block. For example, the note

$$\text{TOLERANCE} \ \pm \frac{1}{64}$$

might be given on a drawing for less critical dimensions.

Some industries give dimensions in inches with two-, three-, and four-decimal-place fractions. A note for dimensions with two and three decimal

places might be given on the drawing as

TOLERANCES XX.XX ±0.10; XX.XXX ±0.005.

Tolerances of four places would be given directly on the dimension lines.

The most common method of noting tolerances is to give as large a tolerance as feasible in a note, such as

TOLERANCES ±0.05

and to give tolerances on the dimension lines for dimensions requiring smaller tolerances. Give angular tolerances in a general note in or near the title block, such as

ANGULAR TOLERANCES ±0.5° or ±30'.

Use one of the techniques shown in **Fig. 14.26** to give specific angular tolerances directly on angular dimensions.

14.12 General Tolerances—Metric Units

All dimensions on a drawing must fall within certain tolerance ranges, even though the tolerances are not shown on dimension lines. Tolerances for dimensions not shown on dimension lines are given by a **general tolerance note** on the drawing.

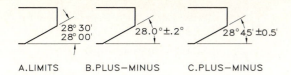

A. LIMITS   B. PLUS—MINUS   C. PLUS—MINUS

Figure 14.26 You may tolerance angles by using any of these techniques.

INTERNATIONAL TOLERANCE GRADES

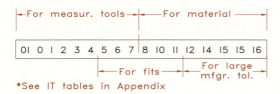

Figure 14.27 This diagram shows the international tolerance (IT) grades and their applications (Appendix 37).

TOLERANCE OF MACHINING

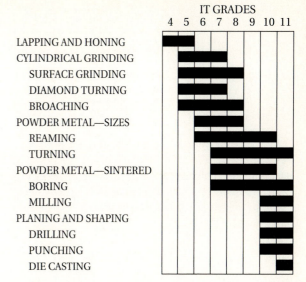

Figure 14.28 Tolerance values may be selected from the international tolerance grades applicable to various machining processes.

Linear Dimensions

Tolerance linear dimensions by indicating plus and minus (±) one half of an international tolerance (IT) grade as given in Appendix 37. You may select the IT grade from the chart in **Fig. 14.27**, where IT grades for mass-produced items range from IT12 through IT16. You may also select IT grades from **Fig. 14.28** for the particular machining process being used.

General tolerances using IT grades may be expressed in a note as follows:

UNLESS OTHERWISE SPECIFIED ALL

UNTOLERANCED DIMENSIONS ARE $\frac{\pm \text{IT}14}{2}$.

This note means that a tolerance of ±0.700 mm is allowed for a dimension between 315 and 400 mm. The value of the tolerance, 1.400 mm, is taken from Appendix 37.

Figure 14.29 shows recommended tolerances for fine, medium, and coarse series for graduated-

GENERAL TOLERANCES: LINEAR DIMENSIONS (MM)

Basic Dimensions	Fine Series	Medium Series	Coarse Series
0.5 to 3	± 0.05	± 0.1	— —
Over 3 to 6	± 0.05	± 0.1	± 0.2
Over 6 to 30	± 0.1	± 0.2	± 0.5
Over 30 to 120	± 0.15	± 0.3	± 0.8
Over 120 to 315	± 0.2	± 0.5	± 1.2
Over 315 to 1000	± 0.3	± 0.8	± 2
Over 1000 to 2000	± 0.5	± 1.2	± 3

Figure 14.29 You may select general tolerance values from this table for fine, medium, and coarse series. Tolerances vary with dimensions.

size dimensions. A medium tolerance, for example, may be specified by the following note:

GENERAL TOLERANCES SPECIFIED IN ANSI B4.3
MEDIUM SERIES APPLY.

TABLE OF GENERAL TOLERANCES

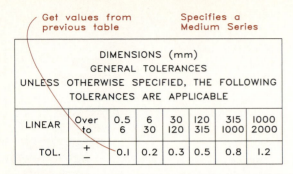

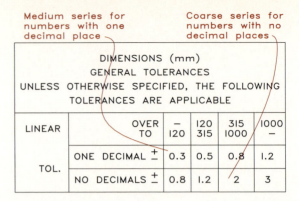

Figure 14.30 This table for a medium series of values was extracted from Fig. 14.29 for insertion on a working drawing to provide the tolerances for a medium series of sizes.

TOLERANCES FOR ONE AND NO DECIMAL PLACES

Figure 14.31 Placed on a drawing, this table of tolerances would indicate the tolerances for dimensions having one or no decimal places, such as 24.0 and 24, denoting medium and coarse series.

Equivalent tolerances may be given in table form (**Fig. 14.30**) on the drawing, the grade—medium in this example—selected from Fig. 14.29. General tolerances may be given in a table for dimensions expressed with one or no decimal places (**Fig. 14.31**).

General tolerances may also be notated in the following form:

UNLESS OTHERWISE SPECIFIED ALL
UNTOLERANCED DIMENSIONS ARE ±0.8 mm.

Use this method only when the dimensions on a drawing are similar in size.

Angular Tolerances

Express angular tolerances as (1) an angle in decimal degrees or in degrees and minutes, (2) a taper expressed in percentage (mm per 100 mm), or (3) milliradians. (To find milliradian, multiply the degrees of an angle by 17.45.) **Figure 14.32** shows the suggested tolerances for each of these units, based on the length of the shorter leg of the angle.

General angular tolerances may be notated on the drawing as follows:

UNLESS OTHERWISE SPECIFIED THE GENERAL
TOLERANCES IN ANSI B4.3 APPLY.

ANGULAR AND TAPER TOLERANCES

Length of shorter leg (mm)	Up to 10	Over 10 to 50	Over 50 to 120	Over 120 to 400
Degrees	±1°	±0° 30'	±0° 20'	±0°10'
mm per 100	±1.8	±0.9	±0.6	±0.3
Millimeters	±18	±9	±6	±3

Figure 14.32 General tolerances for angular and taper dimensions may be taken from this table of values.

A second method involves showing a portion of the table from Fig. 14.32 as a table of tolerances on the drawing (**Fig. 14.33**). A third method is a note with a single tolerance such as:

UNLESS OTHERWISE SPECIFIED ANGULAR
TOLERANCES ARE ±0°30' (or ±0.5°).

14.13 Geometric Tolerances

Geometric tolerancing specifies tolerances that control location form, profile, orientation, and

280 • CHAPTER 14 TOLERANCES

ANGULAR TOLERANCES				
LENGTH OF SHORTER LEG (mm)	UP TO 10	OVER 10 TO 50	OVER 50 TO 120	OVER 120 TO 400
TOLERANCE	±1°	±0°30'	±0°20'	±0°10'

Values in degrees and minutes taken from previous table

Figure 14.33 Extracted from Fig. 14.32, this table of values inserted on a drawing would indicate general tolerances for angles in degrees and minutes

GEOMETRIC SYMBOLS

	TOLERANCE	CHARACTERISTIC	SYMBOL
INDIVIDUAL FEATURES	FORM	STRAIGHTNESS	—
		FLATNESS	▱
		CIRCULARITY	○
		CYLINDRICITY	⌭
INDIVIDUAL OR RELATED FEATURES	PROFILE	PROFILE OF A LINE	⌒
		PROFILE OF A SURFACE	⌓
RELATED FEATURES	ORIENTATION	ANGULARITY	∠
		PERPENDICULARITY	⊥
		PARALLELISM	//
	LOCATION	POSITION	⌖
		CONCENTRICITY	◎
	RUNOUT	CIRCULAR RUNOUT	↗
		TOTAL RUNOUT	↗↗

Figure 14.34 These symbols specify the geometric characteristics of a part's features.

runout on a dimensioned part as covered by the ANSI *Y14.5M-1982 Standards* and the *Military Standards (Mil-Std)* of the U.S. Department of Defense. Before discussing those types of tolerancing, however, we need to introduce you to symbols, size limits, rules, three-datum-plane concepts, and applications.

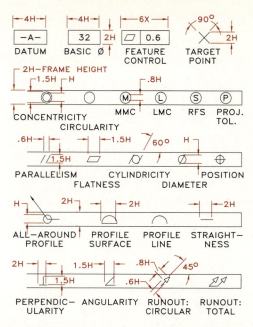

Figure 14.35 Use these general proportions (based on the letter height used) for drawing feature control symbols and frames.

Symbols

Figure 14.34 shows various symbols used to represent geometric characteristics of dimensioned drawings. **Figure 14.35** shows additional symbols, feature control frames, and their proportions, which are based on the letter height, H. On most drawings, a 1/8-in. or 3-mm letter height is recommended. **Figure 14.36** depicts some feature control frames and their proportions.

Size Limits

Three conditions of size are used when geometric tolerances are applied: **maximum material condition, least material condition,** and **regardless of feature size.**

In the **maximum material condition (MMC),** a feature contains the maximum amount of material.

SIZES OF FRAMES

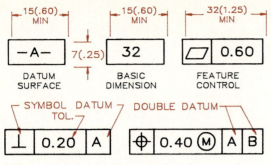

DATUM
SURFACE

BASIC
DIMENSION

FEATURE
CONTROL

SYMBOL DATUM
TOL.

DOUBLE DATUM

FEATURE CONTROL SYMBOLS

Figure 14.36 These are examples of geometric tolerancing frames used to indicate datum planes, basic dimensions, and feature control symbols.

MAXIMUM MATERIAL CONDITION (MMC)

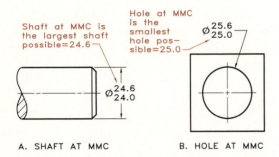

Shaft at MMC is the largest shaft possible=24.6

Hole at MMC is the smallest hole possible=25.0

A. SHAFT AT MMC

B. HOLE AT MMC

Figure 14.37 A shaft is at maximum material condition (MMC) when it is at the largest size permitted by its tolerance. A hole is at MMC when it is at its smallest size.

For example, the shaft shown in **Fig. 14.37** is at MMC when it has the largest permitted diameter of 24.6 mm. The hole is at MMC when it has the most material, or the smallest diameter of 25.0 mm.

The **least material condition (LMC)** indicates that a feature contains the least amount of material. The shaft in Fig. 14.37 is at LMC when it has the smallest diameter of 24.0 mm. The hole is at LMC when it has the least material, or the largest diameter of 25.6 mm.

SIZE PRESCRIBES FORM

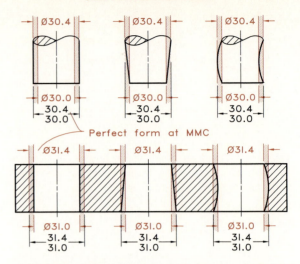

Perfect form at MMC

Figure 14.38 When only a tolerance of size is specified on a feature, the limits prescribe the form of the features, as shown for these shafts and holes having identical limits.

TOLERANCES OF POSITION

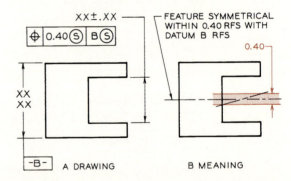

XX±.XX

FEATURE SYMMETRICAL
WITHIN 0.40 RFS WITH
DATUM B RFS

A DRAWING

B MEANING

Figure 14.39 Tolerances of position should include the note of M, S, or L to indicate maximum material condition, regardless of feature size, or least material condition.

The **regardless of feature size (RFS)** condition indicates that tolerances apply to a geometric feature regardless of its size. These sizes range from MMC to LMC.

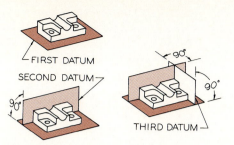

Figure 14.40 When an object is referenced to a primary datum plane, it comes into contact with the datum plane at at least three points. The vertical surface contacts the secondary datum plane at at least two points. The third datum plane comes into contact with at least one point on the object. The datum planes are listed order of priority in the feature control frame.

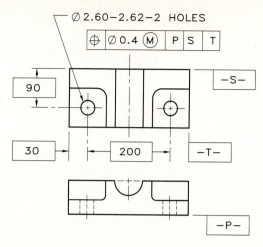

Figure 14.41 Label the three planes of the reference system where they appear as edges. The primary datum plane (P) is given first in the feature control frame; the secondary plane (S), second; and the tertiary plane (T), third. Numbers in frames are exact basic dimensions.

14.14 Rules for Tolerancing

Three general rules of tolerancing geometric features should be followed.

Rule 1 (Individual Feature Size)   When only a tolerance of size is specified on a feature, the limits of size control the variation in its geometric form. The forms of the shaft and hole shown in **Fig. 14.38** are permitted to vary within the tolerance ranges of the dimensions.

Rule 2 (Tolerances of Position)   When a tolerance of position is specified on a drawing, MMC, LMC, or RFS must be specified with respect to the tolerance, datum, or both. The specification of symmetry of the part in **Fig. 14.39** is based on a tolerance at RFS from a datum at RFS.

Rule 3 (All Other Geometric Tolerances)   The RFS condition applies to all other geometric tolerances for individual tolerances and datum references if no modifying symbol is given in the feature control frame. If a feature is to be at MMC, it must be specified.

Three-Datum-Plane Concept

A datum plane is used as the origin of a part's features that have been toleranced. Datum planes usually relate to manufacturing equipment, such as machine tables or locating pins.

Three mutually perpendicular datum planes are required to dimension a part accurately. For example, the part shown in **Fig. 14.40** sits on the primary datum plane, with at least three points of its base in contact with the datum. The part is related to the secondary plane by at least two contact points. The third (tertiary) datum is in contact with at least one point on the object.

The priority of datum planes is presented in sequence in feature control frames. For example, in **Fig. 14.41**, the primary datum is surface P, the secondary datum is surface S, and the tertiary datum is surface T. **Figure 14.42** lists the order of priority of datum planes A–C sequentially in the feature control frames.

SPECIFICATION OF THREE DATUM PLANES

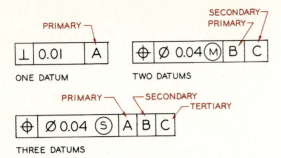

Figure 14.42 Use feature control frames to indicate from one to three datum planes in order of priority.

HOLES AT TRUE POSITION

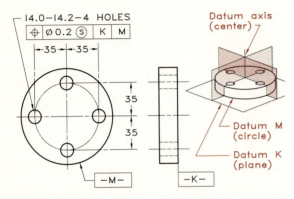

Figure 14.43 These true-position holes are located with respect to primary datum K and secondary datum M. Because datum M is a circle, the implication is that the holes are located about two intersecting datum planes formed by the crossing centerlines in the circular view, satisfying the three-plane concept.

14.15 Cylindrical Datum Features

Figure 14.43 illustrates a part with a cylindrical datum feature that is the axis of a true cylinder. Datum K is the primary datum. Datum M is associated with two theoretical planes—the second and third in a three-plane relationship.

The two theoretical planes are represented in the circular view by perpendicular centerlines that intersect at the point view of the datum axis. All

EFFECTS OF DATUM PLANES

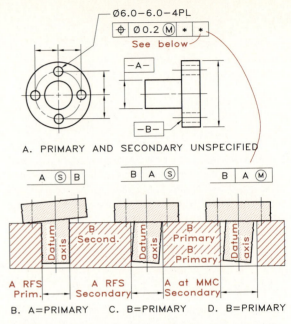

Figure 14.44 For the unspecified datum planes in (A), examples (B)–(D) illustrate the effects of selecting the datum planes in order of priority and of RFS and MMC.

dimensions originate from the datum axis perpendicular to datum K; the other two intersecting datum planes are used for measurements in the x and y directions.

The priority of the datum planes in the feature control frame is significant in the manufacturing and inspection processes. The part shown in **Fig. 14.44** is dimensioned in three ways to show the effects of datum-plane selection and material condition on the location of the hole pattern.

Figure 14.44B illustrates the effect of specifying diameter A at RFS as the primary datum plane and surface B as the secondary datum plane. During production the part is centered on cylinder A. The part is mounted in a chuck, mandrel, or centering device on the processing equipment, which centers the part at RFS. Any variation from perpendicular in surfaces A and B will affect the degree of contact of surface B with its datum plane.

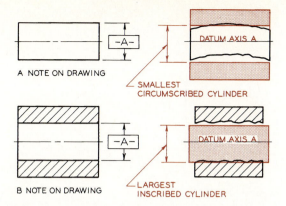

Figure 14.45 The datum axis of a shaft is the smallest circumscribed cylinder in contact with the shaft. The datum axis of a hole is the centerline of the largest inscribed cylinder in contact with the hole.

If surface B were specified as the primary datum feature, it would contact datum plane B at no fewer than three points (**Fig. 14.44C**). The axis of datum cylinder A will be gauged by the smallest cylinder that is perpendicular to the first datum that will contact cylinder A at RFS. This cylinder identifies variation from perpendicular between planes A and B and size variations.

In **Fig. 14.44D**, plane B is specified as the primary datum feature and cylinder A as the secondary datum feature at MMC. The part is mounted on the processing equipment so that at least three points on feature B come into contact with datum B. The datum axis is the axis of a circumscribed cylinder of a fixed size that is perpendicular to datum B. Using the modifier to specify MMC gives a more liberal tolerance zone than when RFS is specified.

Datum Features at RFS

When size dimensions are applied to a feature at RFS, the processing equipment that comes into contact with surfaces of the part establishes the datum. Variable machine elements, such as chucks or center devices, are adjusted to fit the external or internal features and establish datums.

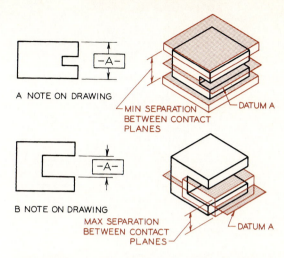

Figure 14.46 The datum plane for external parallel surfaces is the center plane between two contact parallel planes at their minimum separation. The datum plane for internal parallel surfaces is the center plane between two contact parallel surfaces at their maximum separation.

Primary Diameter Datums For an external cylinder (shaft) at RFS, the datum axis is the axis of the smallest circumscribed cylinder that contacts the cylindrical feature (**Fig. 14.45A**). That is, the largest diameter of the part making contact with the smallest cylinder of the machine element holding the part is the datum axis.

For an internal cylinder (hole) at RFS, the datum axis is the axis of the largest inscribed cylinder making contact with the hole. That is, the smallest diameter of the hole making contact with the largest cylinder of the machine element inserted in the hole is the datum axis (**Fig. 14.45B**).

Primary External Parallel Datums The datum for external features at RFS is the center plane between two parallel planes—at minimum separation—that contact the planes of the object (**Fig. 14.46A**). These are planes of a viselike device at minimum separation that holds the part.

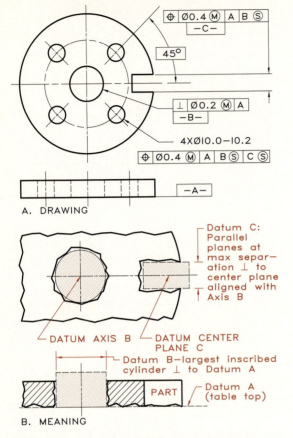

Figure 14.47 A part located with respect to primary, secondary, and tertiary datum planes.

Primary Internal Parallel Datums The datum for internal features is the center plane between two parallel planes—at their maximum separation—that contact the inside planes of the object (**Fig. 14.46B**).

Secondary Datums The secondary datum (axis or center plane) for both external and internal diameters (or distances between parallel planes) has the additional requirement that the cylinder in contact with the parallel elements of the hole be perpendicular to the primary datum (**Fig. 14.47**). Datum axis B is the axis of cylinder B.

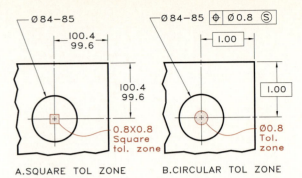

Figure 14.48

A These dimensions give a square tolerance zone for the axis of the hole.

B Basic dimensions (in frames) locate the true center about which a circular tolerance zone of 0.8 mm is specified.

Tertiary Datums The third datum (axis or center plane) for both external and internal features has the further requirement that either the cylinder or parallel planes be oriented angularly to the secondary datum. Datum C in Fig. 14.47 is the tertiary datum plane.

14.16 Location Tolerancing

Tolerances of location deal with position, concentricity, and symmetry.

Position

Toleranced location dimensions yield a square (or rectangular) coordinate tolerance zone for the center of a hole (**Fig. 14.48A**). **In contrast, true-position dimensions, called basic dimensions, locate the exact position of a hole's center, about which a circular tolerance zone is specified (Fig. 14.48B).**

In both the coordinate and true-position methods, the hole diameter is toleranced by identical notes. In the true-position method, a feature control frame specifies the diameter of the circular tolerance zone inside which the hole's center must

THE SQUARE TOLERANCE ZONE

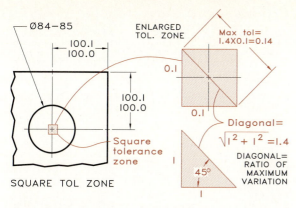

Figure 14.49 The coordinate method of tolerancing gives a square tolerance zone with a diagonal that exceeds the specified tolerance by a factor of 1.4.

lie. **A circular position zone gives a more precise tolerance of the hole's true position than a square.**

Figure 14.49 shows an enlargement of the square tolerance zone resulting from the use of coordinates to locate a hole's center. The diagonal across the square zone is greater than the specified tolerance by a factor of 1.4. Therefore the true-position method, shown enlarged in **Fig. 14.50**, can have a larger circular tolerance zone by a factor of 1.4 and still have the same degree of accuracy specified by the 0.1 square zone. If a variation of 0.14 across the diagonal of the square tolerance zone is acceptable in the coordinate method, a circular tolerance zone of 0.14, which is greater than the 0.1 tolerance permitted by the square zone, should be acceptable in the true-position tolerance method.

The circular tolerance zone specified in the circular view of a hole extends the full depth of the hole. **Therefore the tolerance zone for the centerline of the hole is a cylindrical zone inside which the axis must lie.** Because both the size of the hole and its position are toleranced, these two tolerances establish the diameter of a gauge cylinder for checking conformance of hole sizes and their locations against specifications (**Fig. 14.51**).

THE CIRCULAR TOLERANCE ZONE (TRUE-POSITION TOLERANCING)

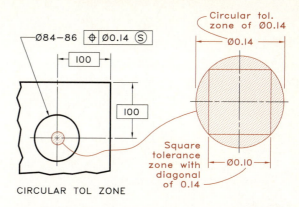

Figure 14.50 The true-position method of tolerancing gives a circular tolerance zone with its center at the true position of the hole. The circular tolerance zone can be 1.4 times greater than the square tolerance zone and still be as accurate.

CYLINDRICAL TOLERANCE ZONE

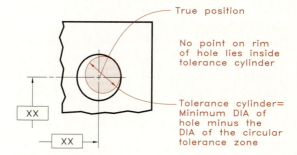

Figure 14.51 When a hole at MMC is located at true position, no element of the hole will be inside the imaginary cylinder obtained by subtracting the circular tolerance zone from the minimum diameter of the hole.

Subtracting the true-position tolerance from the hole at MMC (the smallest permissible hole) yields the circle that represents the least favorable condition when the part is gauged or assembled with a mating part. When the hole is not at MMC, it is larger and permits greater tolerance and easier assembly.

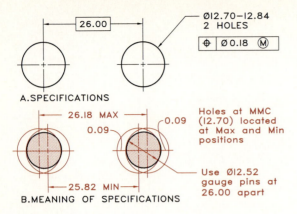

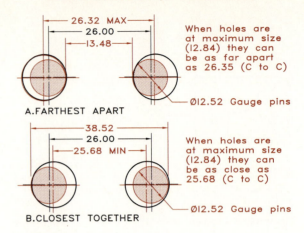

Figure 14.52

A These two holes at MMC are to be located at true position, as specified.

B The two holes may be gauged with pins 12.52 mm in diameter located 26.00 mm apart.

Figure 14.53

A These two holes at MMC may have their centers spaced as far as 26.32 mm apart and still be acceptable.

B The holes may be placed as close as 25.68 mm apart when they are at maximum size.

Gauging a Two-Hole Pattern

Gauging is a technique of checking dimensions to determine whether they meet specified tolerances (**Fig. 14.52**). The two holes, with diametral size limits of 12.70–12.84, are located at true position 26.00 mm apart within a diameter of 0.18 at MMC. The gauge pin diameter is calculated to be 12.52 mm (the smallest hole's size, 12.70, minus the true-position tolerance, 0.18), as **Fig. 14.52B** shows. Thus two pins with diameters of 12.52 mm spaced exactly 26.00 mm apart could be used to check the diameters and positions of the holes at MMC, the most critical size. If the pins can be inserted into the holes, the holes are properly sized and located.

When the holes are not at MMC, or larger than the minimum size, these gauge pins permit a greater range of variation (**Fig. 14.53**). When the holes are at their maximum size of 12.84 mm, they can be located as close as 25.68 mm from center to center or as far apart as 26.32 mm from center to center.

Concentricity

Concentricity is a feature of location because it specifies the relationship of two cylinders that share the same axis. In **Fig. 14.54**, the large cylinder is labeled as datum A, which means the large diameter is used as the datum for locating the small cylinder's axis.

We use feature control frames of the type shown in **Fig. 14.55** to specify concentricity and other geometric characteristics throughout the remainder of this chapter.

Symmetry

Symmetry also is a feature of location in which a feature is symmetrical with the same contour and size on opposite sides of a central plane. **Figure 14.56A** shows how to apply a symmetry feature symbol to the notch that is symmetrical about the part's central datum plane B for a zone of 0.6 mm (**Fig. 14.56B**).

CONCENTRICITY

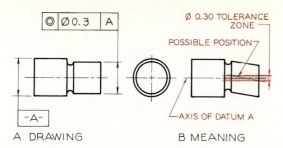

Figure 14.54 Concentricity is a tolerance of location. Here, the feature control frame specifies that the axis of the small cylinder be concentric to datum cylinder A, within a tolerance of 0.3 mm diameter.

FEATURE CONTROL FRAME

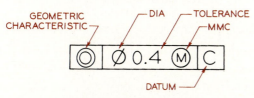

FEATURE CONTROL FRAME

Figure 14.55 This typical feature control frame indicates that a surface is concentric to datum C within a cylindrical diameter of 0.4 mm at MMC.

SYMMETRY

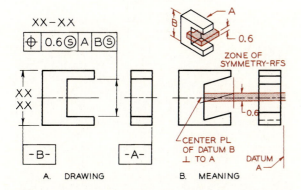

Figure 14.56 Symmetry is a tolerance of location. It specifies that a part's features be symmetrical about the center plane between parallel surfaces of the part.

FLATNESS

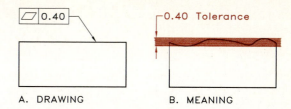

Figure 14.57 Flatness is a tolerance of form. It specifies a tolerance zone within which an object's surface must lie.

STRAIGHTNESS

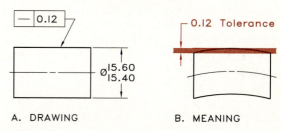

Figure 14.58 Straightness is a tolerance of form, indicating that elements of a surface are straight lines. The tolerance frame is applied to the views in which elements appear as straight lines.

14.17 Form Tolerancing

Flatness A surface is flat when all its elements are in one plane. A feature control frame specifies flatness within a 0.4 mm tolerance zone in **Fig. 14.57** where no point on the surface may vary more than 0.40 from the highest to the lowest point.

Straightness A surface is straight if all its elements are straight lines within a specified tolerance zone. The feature control frame shown in **Fig. 14.58** specifies that the elements of a cylinder must be straight within 0.12 mm. On flat surfaces, straightness is measured in a plane passing through control-line elements, and it may be specified in two directions (usually perpendicular) if desired.

ROUNDNESS: CYLINDER

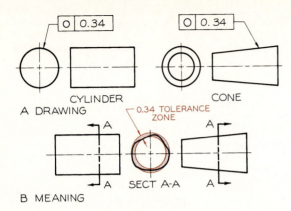

Figure 14.59 Roundness is a tolerance of form. It indicates that a cross section through a surface of revolution is round and lies within two concentric circles.

ROUNDNESS: SPHERE

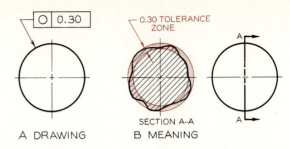

Figure 14.60 Roundness of a sphere means that any cross section through it is round within the specified tolerance.

CYLINDRICITY

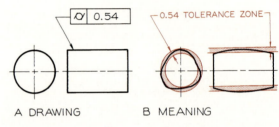

Figure 14.61 Cylindricity is a tolerance of form that is a combination of roundness and straightness. It indicates that the surface of a cylinder lies within a tolerance zone formed by two concentric cylinders.

Roundness A surface of revolution (a cylinder, cone, or sphere) is round when all points on the surface intersected by a plane perpendicular to its axis are equidistant from the axis. In **Fig. 14.59** the feature control frame specifies roundness of a cone and cylinder, permitting a tolerance of 0.34 mm on the radius. **Figure 14.60** specifies a 0.30 mm tolerance zone for the roundness of a sphere.

Cylindricity A surface of revolution is cylindrical when all its elements lie within a cylindrical tolerance zone, which is a combination of tolerances of roundness and straightness (**Fig. 14.61**). Here, a cylindricity tolerance zone of 0.54 mm on the radius of the cylinder is specified.

14.18 Profile Tolerancing

Profile tolerancing involves specifying tolerances for a contoured shape formed by arcs or irregular curves and can apply to a surface or a single line. The surface with the unilateral profile tolerance shown in **Fig. 14.62A** is defined by coordinates. **Figure 14.62B** shows how to specify bilateral and unilateral tolerance zones.

PROFILE: PLANE

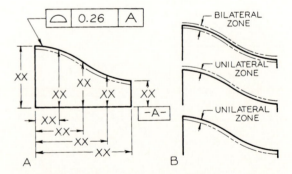

Figure 14.62 Profile is a tolerance of form for irregular curves of planes. (A) The curving plane is located by coordinates and is toleranced unidirectionally. (B) The tolerance may be applied by any of these methods.

PROFILE: LINE

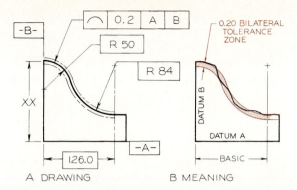

Figure 14.63 The profile of a line is a tolerance of form that specifies the variation allowed from the path of a line. Here, the line is formed by tangent arcs. The tolerance zone may be either bilateral or unilateral, as shown in Fig. 14.62.

PARALLELISM: CYLINDER

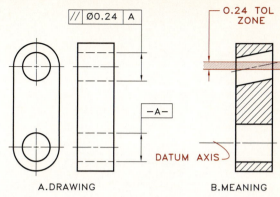

Figure 14.65 You may specify parallelism of one centerline to another by using the diameter of one of the holes as the datum.

PARALLELISM: PLANE

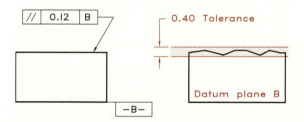

Figure 14.64 Parallelism is a tolerance of form. It indicates that a plane is parallel to a datum plane within specified limits. Here, plane B is the datum plane.

A profile tolerance for a single line is specified as shown in **Fig. 14.63**. The curve is formed by tangent arcs whose radii are given as basic dimensions. The radii are permitted to vary ±0.10 mm from the basic radii.

14.19 Orientation Tolerancing

Tolerances of orientation include **parallelism, perpendicularity**, and **angularity.**

Parallelism A surface or line is parallel when all its points are equidistant from a datum plane or axis. Two types of parallelism tolerance zones follow:

1. A **planar tolerance** zone parallel to a datum plane within which the axis or surface of the feature must lie **(Fig. 14.64)**. This tolerance also controls flatness.

2. A **cylindrical tolerance** zone parallel to a datum feature within which the axis of a feature must lie **(Fig. 14.65)**.

Figure 14.66 shows the effect of specifying parallelism at MMC, where the modifier M is given in the feature control frame. Tolerances of form apply at RFS when not specified. Specifying parallelism at MMC means that the axis of the cylindrical hole must vary no more than 0.20 mm when the holes are at their smallest permissible size.

As the hole approaches its upper limit of 30.30, the tolerance zone increases to a maximum of 0.50 DIA. Therefore a greater variation is given at MMC than at RFS.

Perpendicularity Figure 14.67 specifies perpendicularity of a plane to a datum plane. The feature

PARALLELISM AT MMC

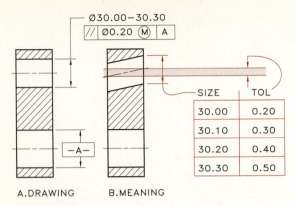

SIZE	TOL
30.00	0.20
30.10	0.30
30.20	0.40
30.30	0.50

A. DRAWING   B. MEANING

Figure 14.66 The critical tolerance exists when features are at MMC. (A) The upper hole must be parallel to the hole used as datum A within a 0.20 DIA. (B) As the hole approaches its maximum size of 30.30 mm, the tolerance zone approaches 0.50 mm.

PERPENDICULARITY: PLANE

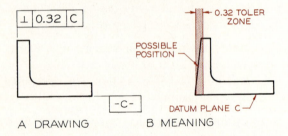

A DRAWING   B MEANING

Figure 14.67 Perpendicularity is a tolerance form that gives a tolerance zone for a plane perpendicular to a specified datum plane.

control frame shows that the surface perpendicular to datum plane C has a tolerance of 0.32 in. In **Fig. 14.68** a hole is specified as perpendicular to datum plane A.

Angularity A surface or line is angular when it is at an angle (other than 90°) from a datum or an axis. The angularity of the surface shown in **Fig. 14.69** is dimensioned with a basic angle (exact angle) of 30° and an angularity tolerance zone of 0.25 mm inside of which the plane must lie.

PERPENDICULARITY: CYLINDER

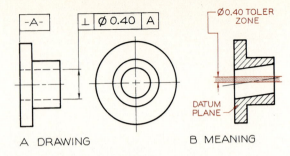

A DRAWING   B MEANING

Figure 14.68 Perpendicularity can apply to the axis of a feature, such as the centerline of a cylinder.

ANGULARITY

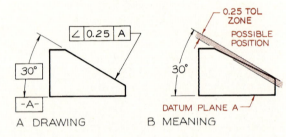

A DRAWING   B MEANING

Figure 14.69 Angularity is a tolerance of form specifying the tolerance zone for an angular surface with respect to a datum plane. Here, the 30° angle is a true, or basic, angle to which a tolerance of 0.25 mm is applied.

14.20 Runout Tolerancing

Runout tolerancing is a way of controlling multiple features by relating them to a common datum axis. Features so controlled are surfaces of revolution about an axis and surfaces perpendicular to the axis.

The datum axis, such as diameter B in **Fig. 14.70**, is established by a circular feature that rotates about the axis. When the part is rotated about this axis, the features of rotation must fall within the prescribed tolerance at **full indicator movement (FIM).**

The two types of runout are **circular runout** and **total runout.** One arrow in the feature control

RUNOUT: CIRCULAR

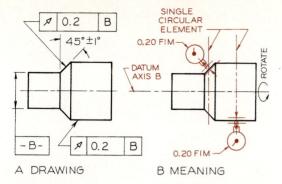

A DRAWING   B MEANING

Figure 14.70 Runout tolerance, a composite of several tolerance of form characteristics, is used to specify concentric cylindrical parts. The part is mounted on the datum axis and is gauged as it is rotated.

RUNOUT: TOTAL

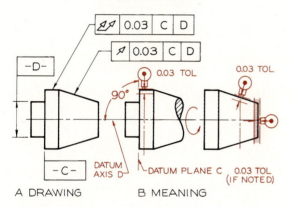

A DRAWING   B MEANING

Figure 14.71 Here, runout tolerance is measured by mounting the object on the primary datum plane C and the secondary datum cylinder D. The cylinder and conical surface are gauged to check their conformity to a tolerance zone of 0.03 mm. The runout at the end of the cone could have been noted.

frame indicates circular runout; two arrows indicate total runout.

Circular Runout Rotating an object about its axis 360° determines whether a circular cross section

APPLICATION OF GEOMETRIC TOLERANCES

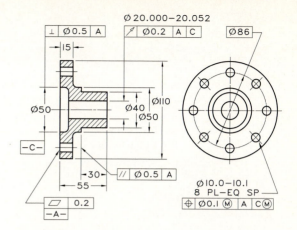

Figure 14.72 A combination of notes and symbols describe this part's geometric features.

exceeds the permissible runout tolerance at any point (**Fig. 14.71**). This same technique is used to measure the amount of wobble in surfaces perpendicular to the axis of rotation.

Total Runout Used to specify cumulative variations of circularity, straightness, coaxiality, angularity, taper, and profile of a surface (Fig. 14.71), total runout tolerances are measured for all circular and profile positions as the part is rotated 360°. When applied to surfaces perpendicular to the axis, total runout tolerances control variations in perpendicularity and flatness.

Conclusion

The dimensioned part shown in **Fig. 14.72** illustrates several of the techniques of geometric tolerancing described in this and previous sections.

14.21 Surface Texture

Because the surface texture of a part affects its function, it must be precisely specified instead of giving an unspecified finished mark such as a ✔.

SURFACE TEXTURE

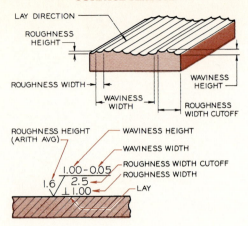

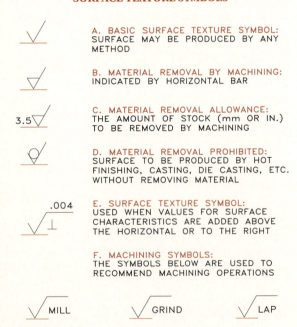

Figure 14.73 These are the definitions of surface texture for a finished surface.

SURFACE TEXTURE SYMBOLS

A. BASIC SURFACE TEXTURE SYMBOL: SURFACE MAY BE PRODUCED BY ANY METHOD

B. MATERIAL REMOVAL BY MACHINING: INDICATED BY HORIZONTAL BAR

C. MATERIAL REMOVAL ALLOWANCE: THE AMOUNT OF STOCK (mm OR IN.) TO BE REMOVED BY MACHINING

D. MATERIAL REMOVAL PROHIBITED: SURFACE TO BE PRODUCED BY HOT FINISHING, CASTING, DIE CASTING, ETC. WITHOUT REMOVING MATERIAL

E. SURFACE TEXTURE SYMBOL: USED WHEN VALUES FOR SURFACE CHARACTERISTICS ARE ADDED ABOVE THE HORIZONTAL OR TO THE RIGHT

F. MACHINING SYMBOLS: THE SYMBOLS BELOW ARE USED TO RECOMMEND MACHINING OPERATIONS

MILL   GRIND   LAP

Figure 14.74 Use surface texture symbols to specify surface finish on the edge views of finished surfaces.

SURFACE TEXTURE

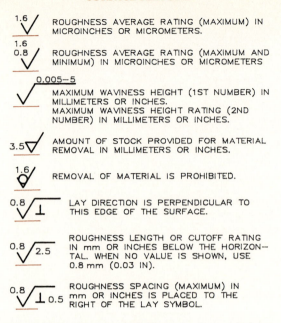

Figure 14.75 Values may be added to surface control symbols for more precise specifications.

Figure 14.73 illustrates most of the terms that apply to surface texture (surface control):

Surface texture: the variation in a surface, including roughness, waviness, lay, and flaws.

Roughness: the finest of the irregularities in the surface caused by the manufacturing process used to smooth the surface.

Roughness height: the average deviation from the mean plane of the surface measured in microinches (μin.) or micrometers (μm), or millionths of an inch and a meter, respectively.

Roughness width: the width between successive peaks and valleys forming the roughness measured in microinches or micrometers.

ROUGHNESS HEIGHT RATING

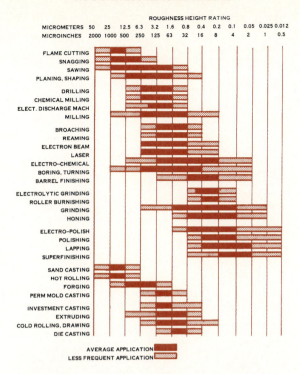

Figure 14.76 Various types of production methods result in the surface roughness heights shown in micrometers and microinches (millionths of a meter or an inch).

PREFERRED ROUGHNESS AVERAGE VALUES

Micrometers	Microinches		Micrometers	Microinches
μ m	μ in.		μ m	μ in.
0.025	1		1.6	63
0.050	2		3.2	125
0.10	4		6.3	250
0.20	8		12.5	500
0.40	16		25	1000
0.80	32		Micrometers=0.001 mm	

Figure 14.77 This range of roughness heights is recommended in ANSI Y14.36 standards.

Roughness width cutoff: the largest spacing of repetitive irregularities that includes average roughness height (measured in inches or millimeters); when not specified, a value of 0.8 mm (0.030 in.) is assumed.

Waviness: a widely spaced variation that exceeds the roughness width cutoff measured in inches or millimeters; roughness may be regarded as a surface variation superimposed on a wavy surface.

Waviness height: the peak-to-valley distance between waves measured in inches or millimeters.

Waviness width: the spacing between wave peaks or wave valleys measured in inches or millimeters.

Lay: the direction of the surface pattern caused by the production method used.

Flaws: irregularities or defects occurring infrequently or at widely varying intervals on a surface, including cracks, blow holes, checks, ridges, scratches, and the like; the effect of flaws is usually omitted in roughness height measurements.

Contact area: the surface that will make contact with a mating surface.

Figure 14.74 shows symbols for specifying surface texture. The point of the ✔ must touch the edge view of the surface, an extension line from the surface, or a leader pointing to the surface. **Figure 14.75** shows how to specify values as a part of surface texture symbols.

Roughness height values are related to the processes used to finish surfaces and may be taken from the table in **Fig. 14.76**. The preferred values of roughness height are listed in **Fig. 14.77**.

The preferred roughness width cutoff values in **Fig. 14.78** are for specifying the sampling width

ROUGHNESS WIDTH CUTOFF VALUES

MILLIMETERS	0.08	0.25	0.80	2.5	8.0	25
INCHES	.003	.010	.030	.1	.3	1

Figure 14.78 This range of roughness width cutoff values is recommended in ANSI Y14.36 standards.

MAXIMUM WAVINESS HEIGHT VALUES

mm	in.	mm	in.
0.0005	.00002	0.025	.001
0.0008	.00003	0.05	.002
0.0012	.00005	0.08	.003
0.0020	.00008	0.12	.005
0.0025	.0001	0.20	.008
0.005	.0002	0.25	.010
0.008	.0003	0.38	.015
0.012	.0005	0.50	.020
0.020	.0008	0.80	.030

Figure 14.79 This range of maximum waviness height values is recommended in ANSI Y14.36 standards.

used to measure roughness height. A value of 0.80 mm is assumed if no value is given. When required, maximum waviness height values may be selected from the recommended values shown in **Fig. 14.79**.

Lay symbols indicating the direction of texture (markings made by the machining operation) on a surface (Fig. 14.80) may be added to surface texture symbols as shown in Fig. 14.81. The perpendicular sign indicates that lay is perpendicular to the edge view of the surface in this view (where the surface control symbol appears). **Figure 14.82** illustrates how to apply a variety of surface texture symbols to a part.

LAY SYMBOLS

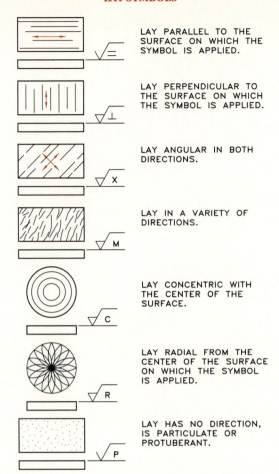

Figure 14.80 These symbols are used to indicate the direction of lay with respect to the surface where the control symbol is placed.

SURFACE TEXTURE SYMBOLS

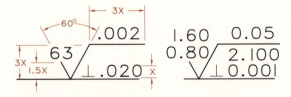

Figure 14.81 These are examples and sizes of typical fully specified surface texture symbols.

THE APPLICATION OF SURFACE TEXTURE SYMBOLS

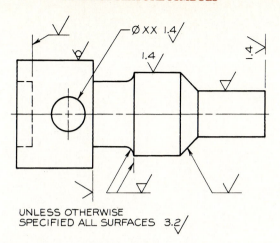

Figure 14.82 Techniques of applying surface texture symbols to a part are illustrated here.

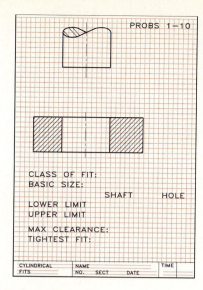

Figure 14.83 Problems 1–10.

Problems

Solve the following problems on size A sheets laid out on a grid of 0.20 in. or 5 mm.

Cylindrical Fits

1. (Fig. 14.83) Draw the shaft and hole shown (it need not be to scale), give the limits for each diameter, and complete the table of values. Use a basic diameter of 1.00 in. (25 mm) and a class RC 1 fit or a metric fit of H8/f7.

2. Repeat Problem 1, but use a basic diameter of 1.75 in. (45 mm) and a class RC 9 fit or a metric fit of H11/c11.

3. Repeat Problem 1, but use a basic diameter of 2.00 in. (51 mm) and a class RC 5 fit or a metric fit of H9/d9.

4. Repeat Problem 1, but use a basic diameter of 12.00 in. (305 mm) and a class LC 11 fit or a metric fit of H7/h6.

5. Repeat Problem 1, but use a basic diameter of 3.00 in. (76 mm) and a class LC 1 fit or a metric fit of H7/h6.

6. Repeat Problem 1, but use a basic diameter of 8.00 in. (203 mm) and a class LC 1 fit or a metric fit of H7/k6.

7. Repeat Problem 1, but use a basic diameter of 102 in. (2591 mm) and a class LN 3 fit or a metric fit of H7/n6.

8. Repeat Problem 1, but use a basic diameter of 11.00 in. (279 mm) and a class LN 2 fit or a metric fit of H7/p6.

9. Repeat Problem 1, but use a basic diameter of 6.00 in. (152 mm) and a class FN 5 fit or a metric fit of H7/s6.

10. Repeat Problem 1, but use a basic diameter of 2.60 in. (66 mm) and a class FN 1 fit or a metric fit of H7/u6.

Position Tolerancing

11. (Fig. 14.84) Make an instrument drawing of the part shown. Locate the two holes with a size tolerance of 1.00 mm and a position tolerance of 0.50 DIA. Insert the proper symbols and dimensions.

12. Repeat Problem 11, but locate three holes using the same tolerances for size and position.

13. Give the specifications for a two-pin gauge that can be used to measure the correctness of the two holes

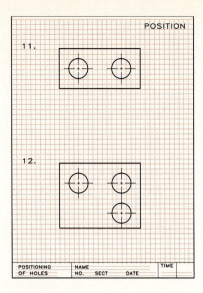

Figure 14.84 Problems 11–13.

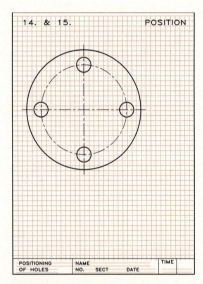

Figure 14.85 Problems 14 and 15.

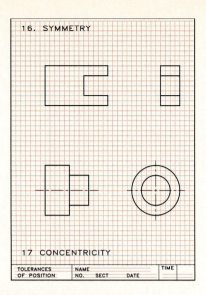

Figure 14.86 Problems 16 and 17.

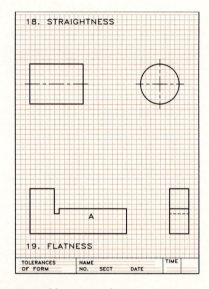

Figure 14.87 Problems 18 and 19.

specified in Problem 11. Make a sketch of the gauge and show the proper dimensions on it.

14. (Fig. 14.85) Using positioning tolerances, locate the holes and properly note them to provide a size tolerance of 1.50 mm and a locational tolerance of 0.60 DIA.

15. Repeat Problem 14, but locate six equally spaced, equally sized holes using the same tolerances of position.

16. (Fig. 14.86) Using a feature control symbol and the necessary dimensions, indicate that the notch is

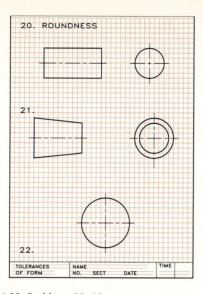

Figure 14.88 Problems 20–22.

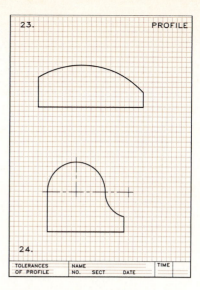

Figure 14.89 Problems 23 and 24.

symmetrical to the left-hand end of the part within 0.60 mm.

17. (Fig. 14.86) Using a feature control symbol and the necessary dimensions, indicate that the small cylinder is concentric with the large one (the datum cylinder) within a tolerance of 0.80.

18. (Fig. 14.87) Using a feature control symbol and the necessary dimensions, indicate that the elements of the cylinder are straight within a tolerance of 0.20 mm.

19. (Fig. 14.87) Using a feature control symbol and the necessary dimensions, indicate that surface A of the object is flat within a tolerance of 0.08 mm.

20–22. (Fig. 14.88) Using feature control symbols and the necessary dimensions, indicate that the cross sections of the cylinder, cone, and sphere are round within a tolerance of 0.40 mm.

23. (Fig. 14.89) Using a feature control symbol and the necessary dimensions, indicate that the profile of the irregular surface of the object lies within a bilateral or unilateral tolerance zone of 0.40 mm.

24. (Fig. 14.89) Using a feature control symbol and the necessary dimensions, indicate that the profile of the line formed by tangent arcs lies within a bilateral or unilateral tolerance zone of 0.40 mm.

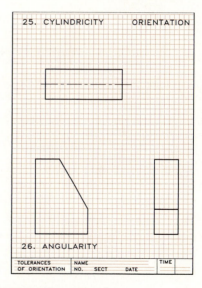

Figure 14.90 Problems 25 and 26.

25. (Fig. 14.90) Using a feature control symbol and the necessary dimensions, indicate that the cylindricity of the cylinder is 0.90 mm.

26. (Fig. 14.90) Using a feature control symbol and the necessary dimensions, indicate that the angularity toler-

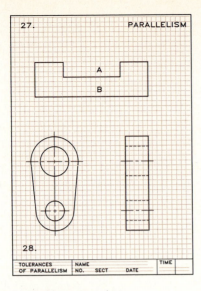

Figure 14.91 Problems 27 and 28.

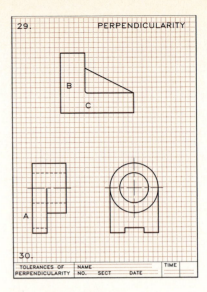

Figure 14.92 Problems 29 and 30.

ance of the inclined plane is 0.7 mm from the bottom of the object, the datum plane.

27. (Fig. 14.91) Using a feature control symbol and the necessary dimensions, indicate that surface A of the object is parallel to datum B within 0.30 mm.

28. (Fig. 14.91) Using a feature control symbol and the necessary dimensions, indicate that the small hole is parallel to the large hole, the datum, within a tolerance of 0.80 mm.

29. (Fig. 14.92) Using a feature control symbol and the necessary dimensions, indicate that the vertical surface B is perpendicular to the bottom of the object, the datum C, within a tolerance of 0.20 mm.

30. (Fig. 14.92) Using a feature control symbol and the necessary dimensions, indicate that the hole is perpendicular to datum A within a tolerance of 0.08 mm.

31. (Fig. 14.93) Using a feature control symbol and cylinder A as the datum, indicate that the conical feature has a runout of 0.80 mm.

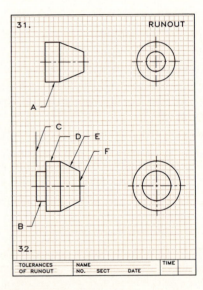

Figure 14.93 Problems 31 and 32.

32. (Fig. 14.93) Using a feature control symbol with cylinder B as the primary datum and surface C as the secondary datum, indicate that surfaces D, E, and F have a runout of 0.60 mm.

15

Welding

15.1 Introduction

Welding is the process of permanently joining metal by heating a joint to a suitable temperature with or without applying pressure and with or without using filler material. The welding practices described in this chapter comply with the standards developed by the American Welding Society and the American National Standards Institute (ANSI).

Welding is done in shops, on assembly lines, or in the field, as shown in **Fig. 15.1**, where a welder is joining pipes. Welding is a widely used method of fabrication that you must become familiar with in order to make and read drawings containing welding notes and specifications.

Advantages of welding over other methods of fastening include (1) simplified fabrication, (2) economy, (3) increased strength and rigidity, (4) ease of repair, (5) creation of gas- and liquid-tight joints, and (6) reduction in weight and size.

Figure 15.1 This welder is joining two pipes in accordance with specifications on a set of drawings. (Courtesy of Texas Eastern; *TE Today*; photo by Bob Thigpen.)

15.2 Welding Processes

Figure 15.2 shows various types of welding processes. The three main types are **gas welding**, **arc welding**, and **resistance welding**.

TYPES OF WELDING PROCESSES

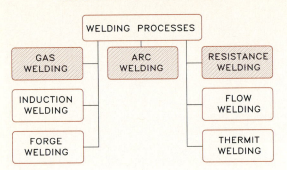

Figure 15.2 The three main types of welding processes are gas welding, arc welding, and resistance welding.

GAS WELDING PROCESS

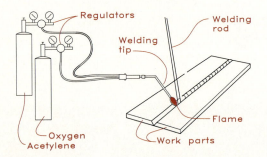

Figure 15.3 The gas welding process burns gases such as oxygen and acetylene in a torch to apply heat to a joint. The welding rod supplies the filler material. (Courtesy of General Motors Corporation.)

Gas welding involves the use of gas flames to melt and fuse metal joints. Gases such as acetylene or hydrogen are mixed in a welding torch and burned with air or oxygen (**Fig. 15.3**). The oxyacetylene method is widely used for repair work and field construction.

Most oxyacetylene welding is done manually with a minimum of equipment. Filler material in the form of welding rods is used to deposit metal at the joint as it is heated. Most metals, except for low- and medium-carbon steels, require fluxes to aid the process of melting and fusing the metals.

ARC WELDING

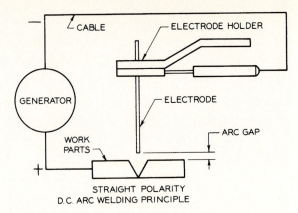

Figure 15.4 In arc welding, either AC or DC current is passed through an electrode to heat the joint

Arc welding involves the use of an electric arc to heat and fuse joints, with pressure sometimes required in addition to heat (**Fig. 15.4**). The filler material is supplied by a consumable or nonconsumable electrode through which the electric arc is transmitted. Metals well-suited to arc welding are wrought iron, low- and medium-carbon steels, stainless steel, copper, brass, bronze, aluminum, and some nickel alloys. In electric-arc welding, **the flux is a material coated on the electrodes that forms a coating on the metal being welded.** This coating protects the metal from oxidation so that the joint will not be weakened by overheating.

Flash welding is a form of arc welding, but it is similar to resistance welding because both pressure and electric current (**Fig. 15.5**) are applied. The pieces to be welded are brought together, and an electric current is passed through them, causing heat to build up between them. As the metal burns the current is turned off, and the pressure between the pieces is increased to fuse them.

Resistance welding comprises several processes by which metals are fused both by the heat produced from the resistance of the parts to an electric current and by pressure. Fluxes and filler materials

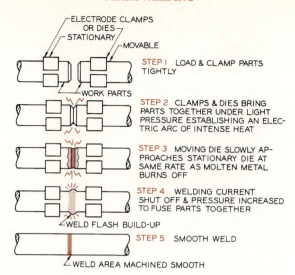

STEP 1 LOAD & CLAMP PARTS TIGHTLY

STEP 2 CLAMPS & DIES BRING PARTS TOGETHER UNDER LIGHT PRESSURE ESTABLISHING AN ELECTRIC ARC OF INTENSE HEAT

STEP 3 MOVING DIE SLOWLY APPROACHES STATIONARY DIE AT SAME RATE AS MOLTEN METAL BURNS OFF

STEP 4 WELDING CURRENT SHUT OFF & PRESSURE INCREASED TO FUSE PARTS TOGETHER

STEP 5 SMOOTH WELD

Figure 15.5 Flash welding, a type of arc welding, uses a combination of electric current and pressure to fuse two parts.

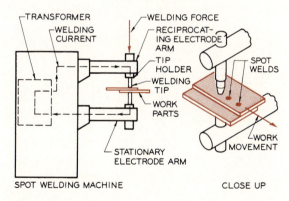

SPOT WELDING MACHINE   CLOSE UP

Figure 15.6 Resistance spot welding may be used to join lap and butt joints.

Material	Spot Welding	Flash Welding
Low—carbon mild steel		
SAE 1010	Rec.	Rec.
SAE 1020	Rec.	Rec.
Medium—carbon steel		
SAE 1030	Rec.	Rec.
SAE 1050	Rec.	Rec.
Wrought alloy steel		
SAE 4130	Rec.	Rec.
SAE 4340	Rec.	Rec.
High—alloy austenitic stainless steel		
SAE 30301—30302	Rec.	Rec.
SAE 30309—30316	Rec.	Rec.
Ferritic and martensistic stainless steel		
SAE 51410—51430	Satis.	Satis.
Wrought heat—resisting alloys		
19—9—DL	Satis.	Satis.
16—25—6	Satis.	Satis.
Cast iron	NA	Not Rec.
Gray iron	NA	Not Rec.
Aluminum & alum. alloys	Rec.	Satis.
Nickel & nickel alloys	Rec.	Satis.

Rec.—Recommended   Satis.—Satisfactory
Not Rec.— Not   NA—Not applicable
    recommended

Figure 15.7 Resistance welding processes for various materials are shown here.

Fig. 15.6. A series of small welds spaced at intervals, called **spot welds**, secure the parts. **Figure 15.7** lists welding processes that may be used for different materials.

15.3 Weld Joints and Welds

Figure 15.8 shows the five standard weld joints. The **butt joint** can be joined with the square groove, V-groove, bevel groove, U-groove, and J-groove welds. The **corner joint** can be joined with these welds and with the fillet weld. The **lap joint** can be joined with the bevel groove, J-groove,

normally are not used. All resistance welds are either lap- or butt-type welds.

Resistance spot welding is performed by pressing the parts together, and an electric current fuses them as illustrated in the lap joint weld in

STANDARD WELD JOINTS

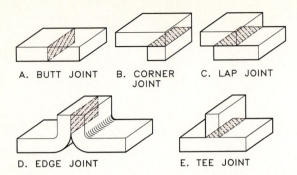

Figure 15.8 These diagrams depict the five standard weld joints.

STANDARD WELDS AND IDEOGRAPHS

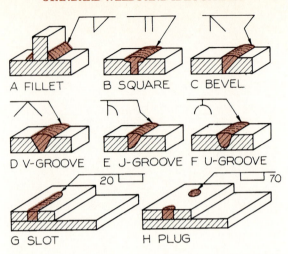

Figure 15.9 These views illustrate standard welds and their corresponding ideographs.

fillet, slot, plug, spot, projection, and seam welds. The **edge joint** uses the same welds as the lap joint along with the square groove, V-groove, U-groove, and seam welds. The **tee joint** can be joined by the bevel groove, J-groove, and fillet welds.

Figure 15.9 depicts commonly used welds and their corresponding ideographs (symbols). The **fillet weld** is a built-up weld at the intersection (usually 90°) of two surfaces. The **square, bevel, V-groove, J-groove,** and **U-groove welds** all have grooves, and the weld is made in these grooves. **Slot** and **plug welds** have intermittent holes or openings where the parts are welded. Holes are unnecessary when resistance welding is used.

15.4 Welding Symbols

If a drawing has a general welding note such as **ALL JOINTS ARE WELDED THROUGHOUT**, the designer has transferred responsibility to the welder. Welding is too important to be left to chance and should be specified more precisely.

Symbols convey welding specifications on a drawing. **Figure 15.10** shows the symbol in its complete form, but it usually appears on a drawing in modified form (less detail). The scale of the welding symbol is based on the letter height used on the drawing, or the size of the grid on which

WELDING SYMBOL

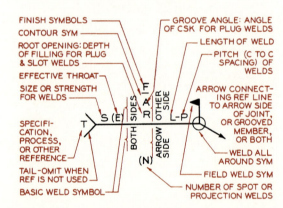

Figure 15.10 The welding symbol. Usually it is modified to a simpler form for use on drawings.

the symbol is drawn, as shown in **Fig. 15.11**. The standard height of lettering on a drawing is usually 1/8 in. or 3 mm.

The **ideograph** is the symbol that denotes the type of weld desired, and it generally depicts the cross-sectional representation of the weld. **Figure 15.12** shows the ideographs used most often. They

WELDING SYMBOL PROPORTIONS

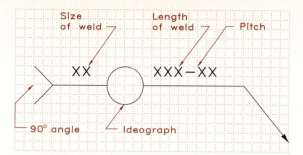

Figure 15.11 Welding symbol proportions are based on the letter height used on a drawing, usually ⅛ in. or 3 mm. This grid is equal to the letter height.

WELDING IDEOGRAPHS

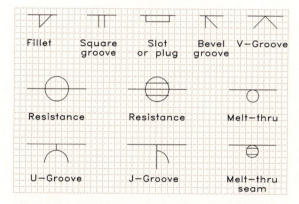

Figure 15.12 The sizes of the ideographs shown on the ⅛-in. (3 mm) grid (the letter height) are proportional to the size of the welding symbol (Fig. 15.11).

are drawn to scale on the 1/8-in. (3-mm) grid (equal to the letter height), which represents their full size when added to the welding symbol.

15.5 Application of Symbols

Fillet Welds

In **Fig. 15.13A**, placement of the fillet weld ideograph below the horizontal line of the symbol indicates that the weld is at the joint on the arrow

FILLET WELDS

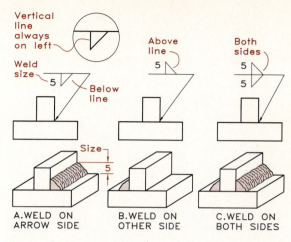

Figure 15.13 Fillet welds may be noted with abbreviated symbols. (A) When the ideograph appears below the horizontal line, it specifies a weld on the arrow side. (B) When it is above the line, it specifies a weld on the opposite side. (C) When it is on both sides of the line, it specifies a weld on each side.

side—the right side in this case. The vertical leg of the ideograph is always on the left side.

A numeral (either a common fraction or a decimal value) to the right of the ideograph indicates the size of the weld. You may omit this number from the symbol if you insert a general note elsewhere on the drawing to specify the fillet size, such as:

ALL FILLET WELDS 1/4 IN. UNLESS
OTHERWISE NOTED.

Placing the ideograph above the horizontal line **Fig. 15.13B** indicates that the weld is to be on the other side, that is, the joint on the other side of the part away from the arrow. When the part is to be welded on both sides, use the ideograph shown in **Fig. 15.13C**. You may omit the tail and other specifications from the symbol when you provide detailed specifications elsewhere.

A single arrow often is used to specify a weld that is to be made all around two joining parts

FILLET WELDS: ALL AROUND

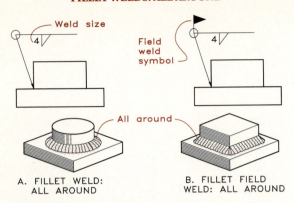

Figure 15.14 These symbols indicate fillet welds all around two types of parts.

FILLET WELD SYMBOLS

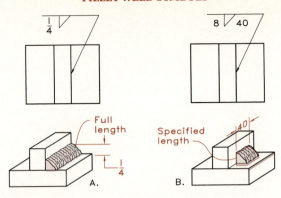

Figure 15.15
A This symbol indicates full-length fillet welds.

B This symbol indicates fillet welds of specified, but less than, full length.

(**Fig. 15.14A**); a circle, 6 mm (twice the letter height) in diameter, drawn at the bend in the leader of the symbol denotes this type of weld. If the welding is to be done in the field rather than in the shop, a solid black triangular "flag" is used (**Fig. 15.14B**).

You may specify a fillet weld that is to run the full length of the two parts as in **Fig. 15.15A**. The ideograph is on the lower side of the horizontal line, so the weld is on the arrow side. You may specify a fillet weld that is to run shorter than full length as in **Fig. 15.15B**, where 40 represents the weld's length in millimeters.

You may specify fillet welds to run different lengths and be positioned on both sides of a part as in **Fig. 15.16A**. The dimension on the lower side of the horizontal gives the length of the weld on the arrow side, and the dimension on the upper side of the horizontal gives the length on the opposite side.

Intermittent welds have a specified length and are spaced uniformly, center to center, at an interval called the **pitch**. In **Fig. 15.16B**, the welds are equally spaced on both sides, are 60 mm long, and have pitches of 120 mm, as indicated by the symbol shown. The symbol shown in **Fig. 15.16C** speci-

INTERMITTENT WELDING

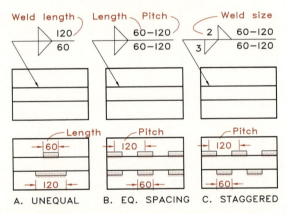

Figure 15.16 These symbols specify intermittent welds of varying lengths and alignments.

fies intermittent welds that are staggered in alternate positions on opposite sides.

Groove Welds

Figure 15.17 shows standard types of groove welds. When you do not give the depth of the grooves, angle of the chamfer, and root openings on a sym-

GROOVE WELDS

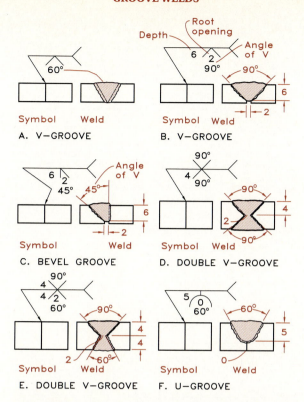

Figure 15.17 This drawing shows the various types of groove welds and their general specifications.

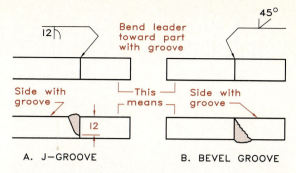

Figure 15.18 J-groove welds and bevel welds are specified by bent arrows pointing to the side of the joint to be grooved or beveled.

WELDING PROCESS SYMBOLS

CAW	Carbon–arc w.	IB	Induction brazing
CW	Cold welding	IRB	Infrared brazing
DB	Dip brazing	OAW	Oxyacetylene w.
DFW	Diffusion welding	OHW	Oxyhydrogen w.
EBW	Electric beam w.	PGW	Pressure gas w.
ESW	Electroslag welding	RB	Resist. brazing
EXW	Explosion welding	RPW	Projection weld.
FB	Furnace brazing	RSEW	Resist. seam w.
FOW	Forge welding	RSW	Resist. spot w.
FRW	Friction welding	RW	Resist. welding
FW	Flash welding	TB	Torch brazing
GMAW	Gas metal arc w.	UW	Upset welding
GTAW	Gas tungsten w.		w.=welding

Figure 15.19 These abbreviations represent the various types of welding processes and are used in welding symbols.

bol, you must specify them elsewhere on the drawing or in supporting documents. In **Figs. 15.17A** and **B**, the angles of the **V-joints** are labeled 60° and 90° under the ideographs. In **Fig. 15.17B**, the depths of the weld (6) and the root opening (2)—the gap between the two parts—are given.

In a **bevel groove** weld, only one of the parts is beveled. The symbol's leader is bent and pointed toward the beveled part to call attention to it (**Figs. 15.17C** and **15.18B**). This practice also applies to J-groove welds, where one side is grooved and the other is not (**Fig. 15.18A**).

Notate double V-groove welds by weld size, bevel angle, and root opening (**Fig. 15.17D** and **E**). Omit root opening sizes or show a zero on the

symbol when parts fit flush. Give the angle and depth of the groove in the symbol for a **U-groove** weld (**Fig. 15.17F**).

Seam Welds

A seam weld joins two lapping parts with either a continuous weld or a series of closely spaced spot welds. The seam weld process to be used is identified by abbreviations in the tail of the weld symbol (**Fig. 15.19**). The circular ideograph for a resistance weld is about 12 mm (four times the letter height)

SEAM WELDS

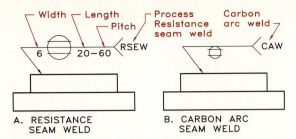

A. RESISTANCE SEAM WELD
B. CARBON ARC SEAM WELD

Figure 15.20 The process used for (A) resistance seam welds and (B) arc-seam welds is indicated in the tail of the symbol. For the arc weld the symbol must specify the arrow side or the other side of the piece.

SPOT WELDS

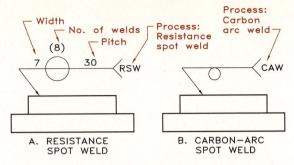

A. RESISTANCE SPOT WELD
B. CARBON–ARC SPOT WELD

Figure 15.21 The process to be used for (A) resistance spot welds and (B) arc spot welds is indicated in the tail of the symbol. For the arc weld the symbol must specify the arrow side or the other side of the piece.

in diameter and is centered over the horizontal line of the symbol (**Fig. 15.20A**). The weld's width, length, and pitch are given.

When the seam weld is to be made by arc welding (CAW), the diameter of the ideograph is about 6 mm (twice the letter height) and goes on the upper or lower side of the symbol's horizontal line to indicate whether the seam is to be applied to the arrow side or opposite side (**Fig. 15.20B**). When the length of the weld is not shown, the seam weld is understood to extend between abrupt changes in the direction of the seam.

Spot welds are similarly specified with ideographs and specifications by diameter, number of welds, and pitch between the welds. The process of resistance spot welding (RSW) is noted in the tail of the symbol (**Fig. 15.21A**). For arc welding, the arrow side or other side must be indicated by a symbol (**Fig. 15.21B**).

Built-Up Welds

When the surface of a part is to be enlarged, or built-up, by welding, indicate this process with a symbol, as shown in **Fig. 15.22**. Dimension the width of the built-up weld in the view. Specify the height of the weld above the surface in the symbol to the left of the ideograph. The radius of the circular segment is 6 mm (twice the letter height).

SURFACE BUILT-UP WELD

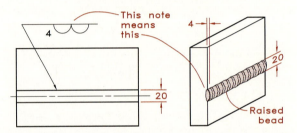

Figure 15.22 Use this method to apply a symbol to a built-up weld on a surface.

15.6 Surface Contouring

Contour symbols are used to indicate which of the three types of contours—flush, concave, or convex—is desired on the surface of the weld. **Flush** contours are smooth with the surface or flat across the hypotenuse of a fillet weld. **Concave** contours bulge inward with a curve, and **convex** contours bulge outward with a curve (**Fig. 15.23**).

Finishing the weld by an additional process to obtain the desired contour often is necessary. These processes, which may be indicated by their abbreviations, are **chipping** (C), **grinding** (G),

CONTOUR SYMBOLS

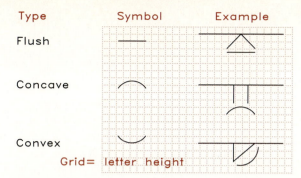

Figure 15.23 These contour symbols specify the desired surface finish of a weld.

USING CONTOUR SYMBOLS

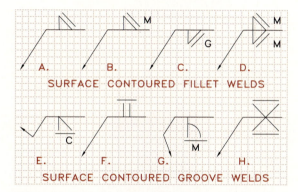

Figure 15.24 These examples of contoured weld symbols with letters added indicate the type of finishing to be applied to the weld (M, machining; G, grinding; C, chipping).

hammering (H), **machining** (M), **rolling** (R), and **peening** (P), as shown in **Fig. 15.24**.

15.7 Brazing

Brazing is a method much like welding for joining pieces of metal. Brazing entails heating joints to more than 800°F and distributing by capillary action a nonferrous filler material, with a melting

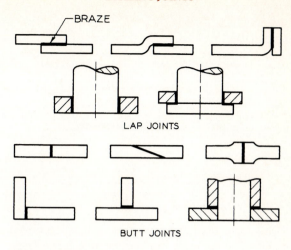

Figure 15.25 The two basic types of brazing joints are lap joints and butt joints.

point below that of the base materials, between the closely fitting parts.

Before brazing the parts must be cleaned and the joints fluxed. The brazing filler is added before or just as the joints are heated beyond the filler's melting point. After the filler material has melted, it is allowed to flow between the parts to form the joint. As **Fig. 15.25** shows, there are two basic brazing joints: **lap joints** and **butt joints**.

Brazing is used to join parts, to provide gas- and liquid-tight joints, to ensure electrical conductivity, and to aid in repair and salvage. Brazed joints withstand more stress, higher temperature, and more vibration than soft-soldered joints.

15.8 Soft Soldering

Soldering is the process of joining two metal parts with a third metal that melts below the temperature of the metals being joined. Solders are alloys of nonferrous metals that melt below 800°F. Widely used in the automotive and electrical industries, soldering is one of the basic techniques of welding and often is done by hand with a soldering iron

SOLDERING IRON

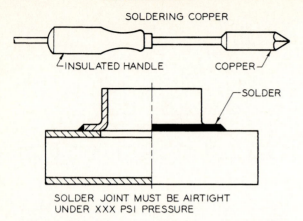

Figure 15.26 This typical hand-held soldering iron is used to soft-solder two parts together. The method of notating a drawing for soldering also is shown.

like the one depicted in **Fig. 15.26**. The iron is placed on the joint to heat it and to melt the solder. Figure 15.26 also shows how to notate a soldered joint.

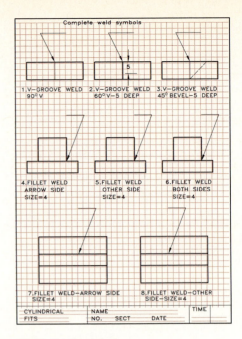

Figure 15.27 Problems 1–8.

Problems

Solve these problems on size A sheets laid out on a grid of 0.20 inch (5 mm).

1–8. **(Fig. 15.27)** Give welding notes to include the information specified for each problem. You may omit instructional information from the solution.

9. **(Fig. 15.28)** Draw the shaft socket and give fillet weld symbols.

Figure 15.28 Problem 9.

16
Working Drawings

16.1 Introduction

Working drawings are the drawings from which a design is implemented. All principles of orthographic projection and techniques of graphics can be used to communicate the details of a project in working drawings. A **detail drawing** is a working drawing of a single part (or detail) within the set of working drawings.

Specifications are the written instructions that accompany working drawings. When the design can be represented on a few sheets, the specifications are usually written on the drawings to consolidate the information into a single format.

All parts must interact with other parts to some degree to yield the desired function from a design. Before detail drawings of individual parts are made the designer must thoroughly analyze the working drawing to ensure that the parts fit properly with mating parts, that the correct tolerances are applied, that the contact surfaces are properly finished, and that the proper motion is possible between the parts.

Much of the work in preparing working drawings is done by the drafter, but the designer, who is usually an engineer, is responsible for their correctness. It is working drawings that bring products and systems into being.

16.2 Working Drawings as Legal Documents

Working drawings are legal contracts that document the design details and specifications as directed by the engineer. Therefore drawings must be as clear, precise, and thorough as possible. Revisions and modifications of a project at the time of production or construction are much more expensive than when done in the preliminary design stages.

Poorly executed working drawings result in wasted time and resources and increase implementation costs. To be economically competitive, drawings must be as error-free as possible.

Working drawings specify all aspects of the design, reflecting the soundness of engineering and function of the finished product and economy of fabrication. The working drawing is the instrument that is most likely to establish the responsibility for any failure to meet specifications during implementation.

16.3 Dimensions and Units

English System

The inch is the basic unit of the English system, and virtually all shop drawings are dimensioned in inches. This practice is followed even when dimensions are several feet in length.

The clamp illustrated in **Fig. 16.1** is detailed in working drawings (**Figs. 16.2–16.4**), which are dimensioned in inches. Decimal fractions are

Figure 16.1 This revolving clamp assembly holds parts while they are being machined. (Courtesy of Jergens, Incorporated.)

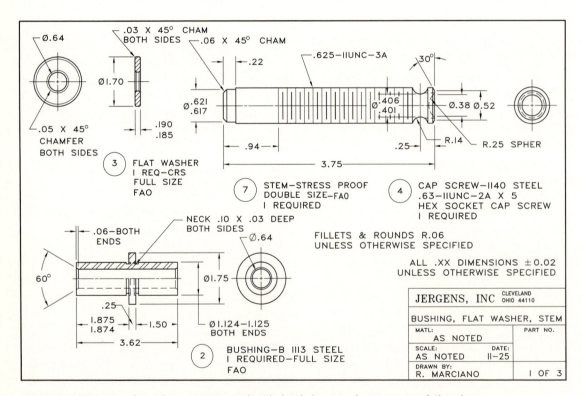

Figure 16.2 Sheet 1 of 3: This computer-produced detail drawing depicts parts of the clamp assembly shown in Fig. 16.1. (Figures 16.2–16.4 courtesy of Jergens, Incorporated.)

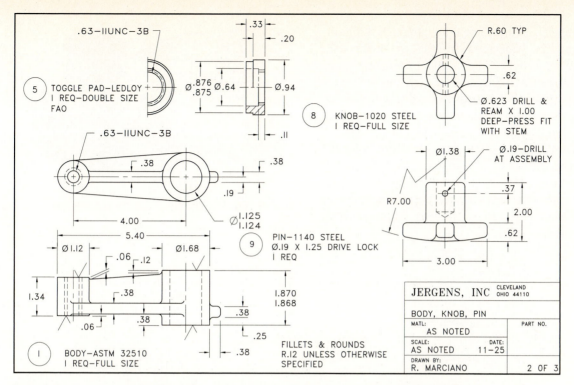

Figure 16.3 Sheet 2 of 3: This continuation of Fig. 16.2 shows additional parts of the clamp assembly.

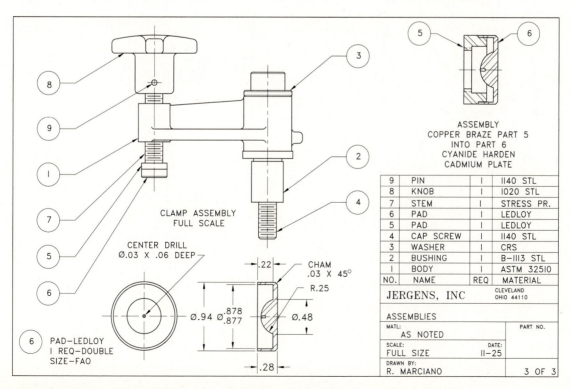

Figure 16.4 Sheet 3 of 3: This continuation of Fig. 16.2 shows the clamp assembly at full scale, an orthographic assembly drawing of the clamp assembly, and a parts list.

preferable to common fractions, although common fractions are still used (mostly by architects). Arithmetic can be done with greater ease with decimal fractions than with common fractions.

Inch marks (") are omitted from dimensions on working drawings because the units are understood to be in inches, and their omission saves drafting time. Usually, several dimensioned orthographic views of parts may be shown on each sheet. However, some companies have policies that views of only one part be drawn on a sheet, even if the part is extremely simple, such as a threaded fastener.

Figure 16.5 This photo is of a pulley and setscrew.

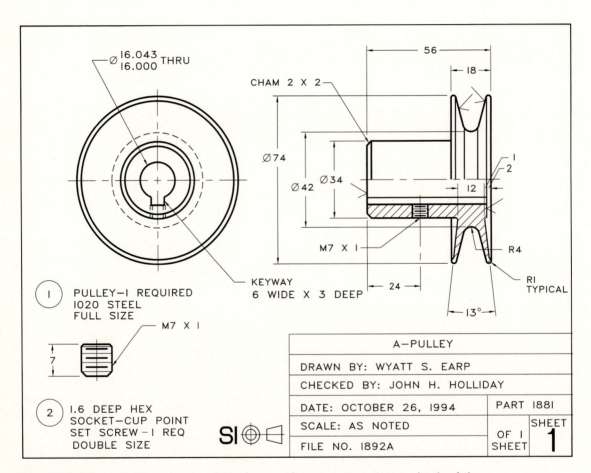

Figure 16.6 This computer-produced working drawing (dimensions in mm) gives details of the pulley and setscrew shown in Fig. 16.5.

The arrangement of views of parts on the sheet has no relationship to how the parts fit together; the views are simply positioned to best fit the available space on the sheet. **The views of each part are labeled with a part number, a name for identification, the material it is made of, and any other notes necessary to explain manufacturing procedures.**

The purpose of the orthographic **assembly drawing** shown on sheet 3 (**Fig. 16.4**) is to illustrate how the parts are to fit together. Each part is numbered and cross-referenced with the numbers in the **parts list**, which serves as a bill of materials.

Metric System

The millimeter is the basic unit of the metric system, and dimensions usually are given to the nearest whole millimeter without decimal fractions (except to specify tolerances). Metric abbreviations (mm) after the numerals are omitted from dimensions because the SI symbol near the title block indicates that all units are metric. If you have trouble relating to the length of a millimeter, recall that the fingernail of your index finger is about 10 mm wide.

The pulley (**Fig. 16.5**) is depicted and dimensioned in millimeters in the working drawings shown in **Fig. 16.6**. Dimensions and notes along with the descriptive views give the information needed to construct the pieces.

The left-end handcrank (**Fig. 16.7**) is detailed on two size B sheets in **Figs. 16.8** and **16.9**. The orthographic, sectioned assembly drawing of the left-end handcrank shown in Fig. 16.9 demonstrates how the parts are to be put together. The numbers in the balloons provide a cross-reference in the parts list, which goes just above the title block.

Figure 16.10 is a photograph of a lifting device used to level equipment such as lathes and milling machines; **Figs. 16.11** and **16.12** show working drawings that give details of its parts. The SI symbol indicates that the dimensions are in millime-

Figure 16.7 This photo is of a left-end handcrank.

ters, and the truncated cone indicates third-angle projection views. The assembly drawing in Fig. 16.12 illustrates how the parts are to be assembled after they have been made.

Dual Dimensions

Some working drawings carry both inch and millimeter dimensions as shown in **Fig. 16.13** where the dimensions in parentheses or brackets are millimeters. The units may also appear as millimeters first and then be converted and shown in brackets as inches. Converting from one unit to the other results in fractional round-off errors. An explanation of the primary unit system for each drawing should be noted in the title block.

16.4 Laying Out a Detail Drawing

When making a drawing by hand with instruments on paper or film, first lay out the views and dimensions on a different sheet of paper. Then overlay the drawing with vellum or film and trace it to obtain the final drawing. You must use guidelines for lettering for each dimension and note. Lightly draw them or underlay the drawing with a sheet containing guidelines.

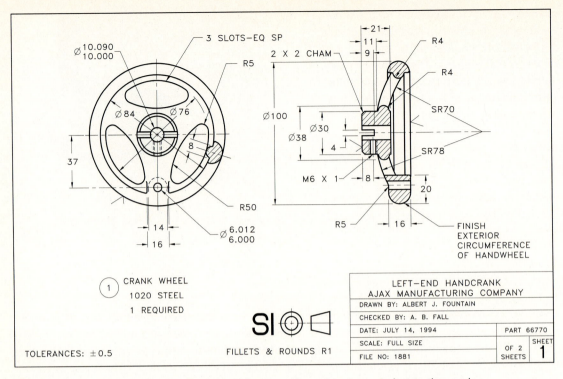

Figure 16.8 Sheet 1 of 2: This set of working drawings (dimensions in mm) depicts the crank wheel of the left-end handcrank shown in Fig. 16.7.

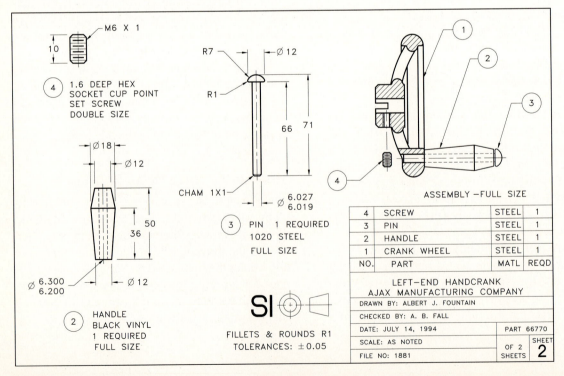

Figure 16.9 Sheet 2 of 2: This continuation of Fig. 16.8 includes an assembly drawing and parts list.

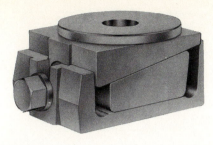

Figure 16.10 This Lev-L-Line lifting device is used to level heavy machinery. (Courtesy of Unisorb Machinery Installation Systems.)

Figure 16.14 shows the standard sheet sizes for working drawings. Paper, film, cloth, and reproduction materials are available in these modular sizes, so good practice requires that you make drawings in one of these standard sizes.

16.5 Notes and Other Information

Title Blocks and Parts Lists

Figure 16.15 shows a **title block** and **parts list** suitable for student assignments. Title blocks usually are placed in the lower right-hand corner of the drawing sheet against the borders. The parts list (Fig. 16.15) should be placed directly over the title block (see also Figs. 16.9 and 16.12).

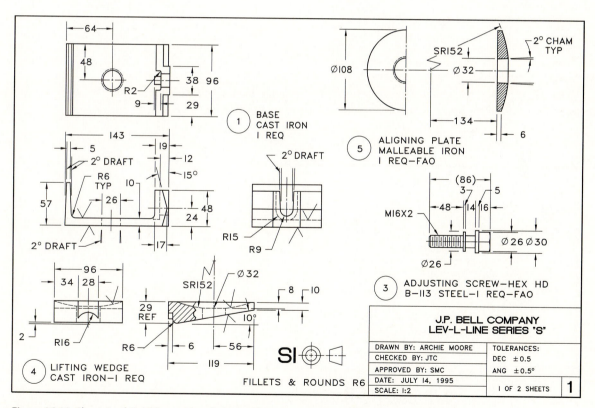

Figure 16.11 Sheet 1 of 2: This working drawing (dimensioned in SI units) is of the lifting device shown in Fig. 16.10. (Courtesy of Unisorb Machinery Installation Systems.)

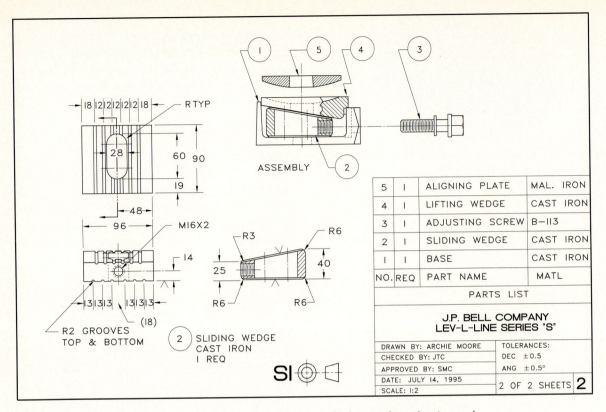

Figure 16.12 Sheet 2 of 2: This continuation of Fig. 16.11 is a further working drawing and assembly drawing of the lifting device. (Courtesy of Unisorb Machinery Installation Systems.)

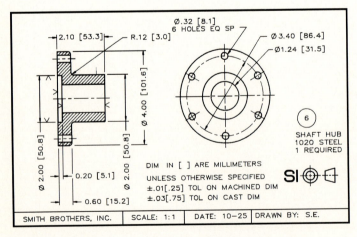

Figure 16.13 In this dual-dimensioned drawing, dimensions are shown in millimeters with their equivalents in inches given in brackets.

DRAWING SHEET SIZES

ENGLISH SIZES			METRIC SIZES		
A	11 x 8.5		A4	297 X 210	
B	17 X 11		A3	420 X 297	
C	22 X 17		A2	594 X 420	
D	34 X 22		A1	841 X 594	
E	44 X 34		A0	1189 X 841	

Figure 16.14 These are the standard sheet sizes for working drawings dimensioned in inches and millimeters.

PARTS LIST AND TITLE BLOCK

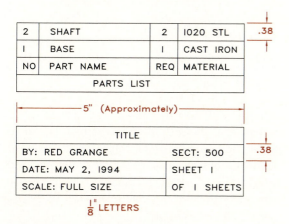

Figure 16.15 This typical title block and parts list is suitable for most student assignments.

Title Blocks In practice, title blocks usually contain the title or part name, drafter, date, scale, company, and sheet number. Other information, such as tolerances, checkers, and materials, also may be given. **Figure 16.16** shows another example of a title block, which is typical of those used by various industries. Any modifications or changes added after the first version to improve the design are shown in the revision blocks.

Depending on the complexity of the project, a set of working drawings may contain from one to more than a hundred sheets. Therefore, giving the

A TYPICAL TITLE BLOCK

REVISIONS	COMPANY NAME COMPANY ADDRESS		
CHG. HEIGHT	TITLE: LEFT—END BEARING		
FAO	DRAWN BY: JOHNNY RINGO		
	CHECKED BY: FRED DODGE		
	DATE: JULY 14, 1995		
	SCALE HALF SIZE	OF 3 SHEETS	SHEET 1

Figure 16.16 This title block, which includes a revision block, is typical of those used in industry.

number of each sheet and the total number of sheets in the set on each sheet is important (for example, sheet 2 of 6, sheet 3 of 6, and so on).

Parts List The part numbers and part names in the parts list correspond to those given to each part depicted on the working drawings. In addition, the number of identical parts required is given along with the material used to make each part. Because the exact material (for example, 1020 STEEL) is designated for each part on the drawing, the material in the parts list may be shortened to STEEL, which requires less space.

Patent Rights Note
Figure 16.17 shows the use of a note near the title block that names Jack Omohundro as the inventor of the part or process. An associate, J. B. Hickok, signs and dates the drawing as a witness to the designer's work. This type of note establishes ownership of the ideas and dates of their development to help the inventor obtain a patent. An even better case for design ownership is made if a second witness signs and dates the drawing.

Scale Specification
If all working drawings in a set are the same scale, you need to indicate it only once in the title block

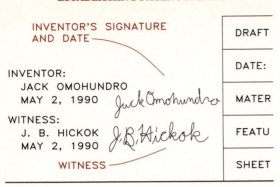

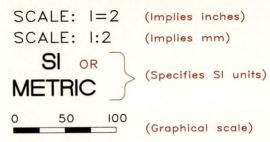

Figure 16.18 Specify scales in English and SI units on working drawings with these methods.

Figure 16.17 This note next to the title block names the inventor and is witnessed by an associate to establish ownership of a design for patent purposes.

on each sheet. If several detail drawings on a working drawing are different scales, indicate them on the drawing under each set of views. In this case, indicate "as shown" in the title block opposite *scale*. When a drawing is not to scale, place the abbreviation NTS (not to scale) in the title block.

Figure 16.18 shows several methods of indicating scales. Use of the colon (for example, 1:2) implies the metric system; use of the equal sign (for example, 1=2) implies the English system—but these are not absolute rules. The SI symbol or *metric* designation on a drawing specifies that millimeters are the units of measurement.

In some cases, you may want to show a graphical scale with calibrations on a drawing to permit the interpretation of linear measurements by transferring them with dividers from the drawing to the scale.

Tolerances

Recall from Chapter 14 that you may use general notes on working drawings to specify the dimension tolerances. **Figure 16.19** shows a table of values with boxes in which you can make a check mark to

indicate whether the units are in inches or millimeters. Position plus-and-minus tolerances under each common or decimal fraction. For example, this table specifies that each dimension with two-place decimals will have a tolerance of ±0.10 in. You may also give angular tolerances in general notes (±0.5°, for example).

Part Names and Numbers

Give each part a name and number, using letters and numbers 1/8-in. (3 mm) high **(Fig. 16.20)**. **Place part numbers inside circles, called *balloons*, having diameters approximately four times the height of the numbers.**

Place part numbers near the views to which they apply, so their association will be clear. On assembly drawings, balloons are especially important because the same part numbers are used in the parts list.

16.6 Checking a Drawing

People who check drawings must have special qualifications that enable them to identify errors and to suggest revisions and modifications that

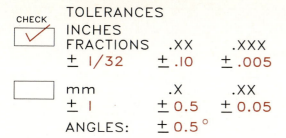

Figure 16.19 General tolerance notes on working drawings specify the dimension tolerances permitted.

Figure 16.20 Name and number each part on a working drawing for use in the parts list.

will result in a better product at a lower cost. A checker may be a chief drafter experienced in drafting and manufacturing processes or the engineer or designer who originated the project. In large companies, personnel in the various shops involved in production review the drawings to ensure that the most efficient production methods are specified for each part.

Checkers never check the original drawing; instead, they mark corrections with a colored pencil on a diazo (blue-line) print. They return the marked-up print to the drafter who revises the original and makes another print for final approval.

In **Fig. 16.21**, the various modifications made by checkers are labeled with letters that are circled and placed near the revisions. The drafter lists and dates changes in the revision record, which lists the revisions made.

Checkers inspect a working or detail drawing for correctness and soundness of design. In addition, they are responsible for the drawing's completeness, quality, readability, and clarity, which reflect the lettering and drafting techniques used. **Lettering and text quality is especially important** because the shop person is guided by lettered notes and dimensions.

Checking Students' Work

The best way for you to check your drawings for adequate dimensions is to rapidly make a scale drawing of the part using the dimensions from the working drawings. You can identify missing dimensions more easily in this way than by reading a drawing by eye. **Figure 16.22** shows a grading scale for checking working drawings prepared by students, with hypothetical grading shown. Use this list as an outline for reviewing working drawings to ensure that you have met the main requirements.

16.7 Drafter's Log

In addition to the individual revision records, drafters should keep a log of all changes made during a project. As the project progresses, the drafter should record the changes, dates, and people involved. Such a log allows anyone reviewing the project in the future to understand easily and clearly the process used to arrive at the final design.

Calculations often are made during a drawing's preparation. If they are lost or poorly done, they may have to be redone; therefore they should be a permanent part of the log.

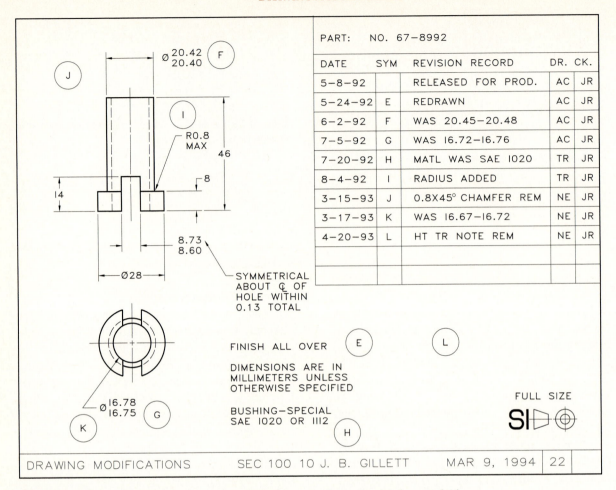

| PART: | | NO. 67–8992 | | |
DATE	SYM	REVISION RECORD	DR.	CK.
5–8–92		RELEASED FOR PROD.	AC	JR
5–24–92	E	REDRAWN	AC	JR
6–2–92	F	WAS 20.45–20.48	AC	JR
7–5–92	G	WAS 16.72–16.76	AC	JR
7–20–92	H	MATL WAS SAE 1020	TR	JR
8–4–92	I	RADIUS ADDED	TR	JR
3–15–93	J	0.8X45° CHAMFER REM	NE	JR
3–17–93	K	WAS 16.67–16.72	NE	JR
4–20–93	L	HT TR NOTE REM	NE	JR

SYMMETRICAL ABOUT ℄ OF HOLE WITHIN 0.13 TOTAL

FINISH ALL OVER

DIMENSIONS ARE IN MILLIMETERS UNLESS OTHERWISE SPECIFIED

BUSHING–SPECIAL SAE 1020 OR 1112

FULL SIZE

DRAWING MODIFICATIONS   SEC 100 10 J. B. GILLETT   MAR 9, 1994   22

Figure 16.21 The modifications to this working drawing are noted near the details revised. The letters in balloons correspond to those in the revision table.

16.8 Assembly Drawings

After parts have been made according to the specifications of the working drawings, they will be assembled (**Fig. 16.23**) in accordance with the directions of an **assembly drawing**. Two general types of assembly drawings are **orthographic assemblies** and **pictorial assemblies**. Dimensions usually are omitted from assembly drawings.

The lifting device shown in Fig. 16.10 is depicted in an isometric assembly in **Fig. 16.24**. Each part is numbered with a balloon and leader to cross reference them to the parts list, where more information about each part is given.

Figure 16.25 shows an orthographic exploded assembly drawing. In many applications, the arrangement of parts may be easier to understand

EVALUATION BY INSTRUCTOR

TITLE BLOCK (5 points)

Student's name	1	1
Checker's name	1	1
Date	1	1
Scale	1	1
Sheet number	1	1

DRAWING DETAILS (19 pts)

Properly drawn views	10	9
Spacing of views	5	4.5
Part names and numbers	2	1.5
Sections & conventions	2	1.5

DESIGN INFORMATION (12 pts)

Proper tolerances	5	4
Surface texture symbols	2	2
Thread notes & symbols	5	4.5

DIMEN. PRACTICES (20 pts)

Proper arrowheads	3	2.5
Positions of dimensions	3	2.5
Completeness of dimens	4	3
Fillet & round notes	2	2
Machined-hole notes	2	1.5
Inch/mm marks omitted	2	2
Dimensions from best views	4	3.5

DRAFTSMANSHIP (19 points)

Thicknesses of lines	6	5.5
Lettering	6	5
Neatness	3	1.5
Reproduction quality	4	3

GENERAL NOTES (5 points)

SI symbol	2	2
Third angle symbol	2	2
General tolerance note	1	1

ASSEMBLY DRAWING (15 points)

Descriptive views	6	5.5
Clarity of assembly	3	2.8
Parts list completeness	4	3.6
Part numbers in balloons	2	2

PRESENTATION (5 points)

Properly stapled	2	2
Properly trimmed	1	1
Properly folded	1	1
Grade sheet attached	1	1
Total 100		88

Figure 16.22 This checklist may be used to evaluate a student's working drawing assignment.

Figure 16.23 An assembly drawing explains how the parts of a product, such as this Ford tractor, are to be assembled. (Courtesy of Ford Motor Company.)

PICTORIAL ASSEMBLY: ASSEMBLED

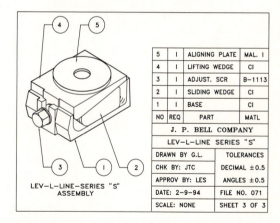

Figure 16.24 This isometric assembly drawing depicts the parts of the lifting device shown in Fig. 16.10 fully assembled. Dimensions usually are omitted from assembly drawings and a parts list is given.

ORTHOGRAPHIC ASSEMBLY: EXPLODED

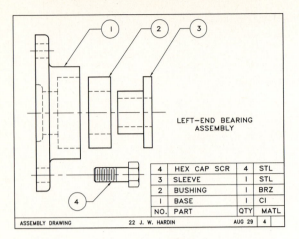

Figure 16.25 This exploded orthographic assembly illustrates how the parts shown are to be put together.

EXPLODED ASSEMBLY

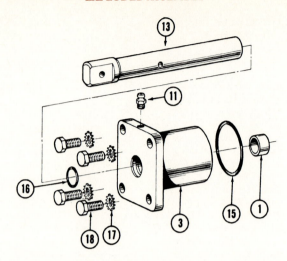

Figure 16.27 This exploded pictorial assembly drawing is of a shaft bearing assembly. (Courtesy of Cameron Iron Works, Incorporated.)

ORTHOGRAPHIC ASSEMBLY:
SECTIONED AND ASSEMBLED

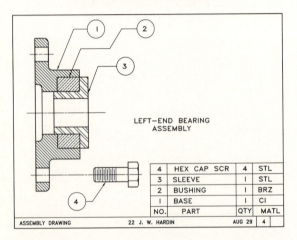

Figure 16.26 This sectioned orthographic assembly shows the parts from Fig. 16.25 in their assembled positions, except for the exploded bolt.

A FREEHAND WORKING DRAWING

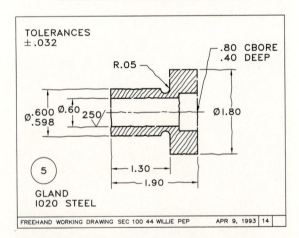

Figure 16.28 A freehand working drawing with the essential dimensions can be as adequate as an instrument-drawn detail drawing for simple parts.

when the parts are shown *exploded* along their centerlines. These views are shown as regular orthographic views, with some lines shown as hidden lines and others omitted.

Assembly of the same part is shown in **Fig. 16.26** in an orthographic assembly drawing, in which the parts are depicted in their assembled positions. The views are sectioned to make them easier to understand.

Figure 16.27 shows a brake pedal assembly in an exploded pictorial assembly drawing, illustrating how the parts fit together. Special balloons refer to a variety of information given in notes on the complete drawing.

16.9 Freehand Working Drawings

A freehand sketch can serve the same purpose as an instrument drawing, provided that the part is sufficiently simple and that the essential dimensions are shown **(Fig. 16.28)**. Use the same principles of making working drawings with instruments when making working drawings freehand.

16.10 Working Drawings for Forged Parts and Castings

The two parts shown in **Fig. 16.29** illustrate the difference between a forged part and a machined part. Recall from Chapter 12 that a forging is a rough form made by hammering (forging) the metal into shape or pressing it between two forms (called dies). The forging is then machined to its finished dimensions and tolerances.

A casting, like a forging, must be machined so that it will fit and function with other parts when assembled; therefore additional material is added to the areas where metal will be removed by machining. Recall (Chapter 12) that a casting is formed by pouring molten metal into a mold formed by a pattern that is slightly larger than the finished part to compensate for metal shrinkage **(Fig. 16.30)**. For the pattern to be removable from

Figure 16.29 The left part is a blank that has been forged. It will look like the part on the right after it has been machined.

TWO-PART SAND MOLD

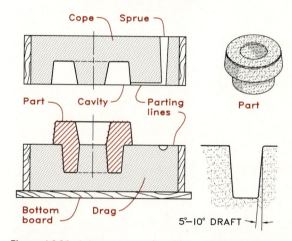

Figure 16.30 A two-part sand mold is used to produce a casting. A draft of from 5° to 10° is needed to permit withdrawal of the pattern from the sand. Some machining is usually required to finish various features of the casting within specified tolerances.

the sand that forms the mold, its sides must be tapered. This taper of from 5° to 10° is called **draft**.

In some industries, working drawings for forged and cast parts are prepared separately **(Fig. 16.31A)**. More often, however, they are shown on the regular working drawing, with the understanding that the features to be machined by operations such as grinding or shaping are made oversize.

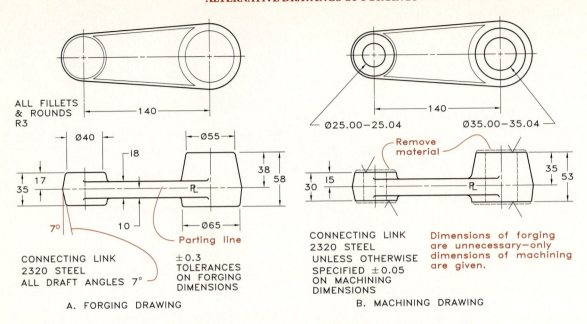

Figure 16.31 These separate working drawings, (A) a forging drawing and (B) a machining drawing, give the details of the same part. Often, this information is combined into a single drawing.

Problems

General

The dimensions given in the problems do not always represent good dimensioning practices because of space limitations and the nature of three-dimensional pictorial drawings, but they are adequate to provide dimensions for making the working drawings. In cases where dimensions may be missing, use your own judgment to approximate them. Provide all the necessary information, notes, and dimensions to describe the views completely. Use any of the previously covered principles, conventions, and techniques to present the views with the maximum clarity and simplicity.

Working Drawing Practice

Reproduce the drawings shown in **Figs. 16.32–16.39**, as directed. Some have only one sheet and others have more. You may use the dimensions given or convert them to the other system (from millimeters to inches, for example). The purpose of these assignments is to give you experience in laying out a working drawing and improve your draftsmanship on the board or at the computer.

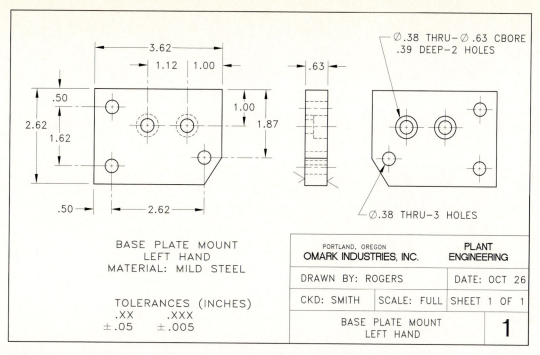

Figure 16.32 Duplicate the working drawing of the base plate mount by computer or drafting instruments on a size B sheet. (Courtesy of Omark Industries, Incorporated.)

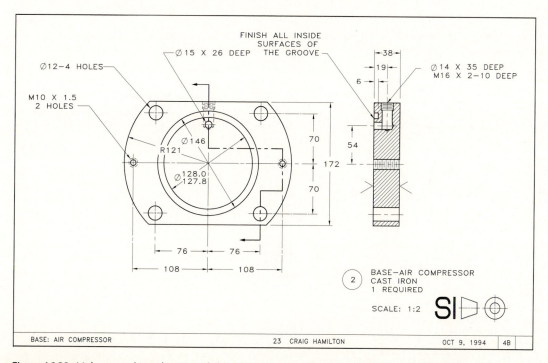

Figure 16.33 Make a working drawing of the air compressor base by computer or drafting instruments on a size B sheet.

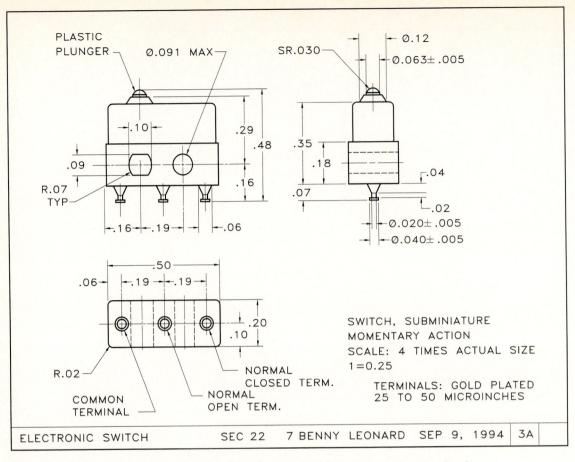

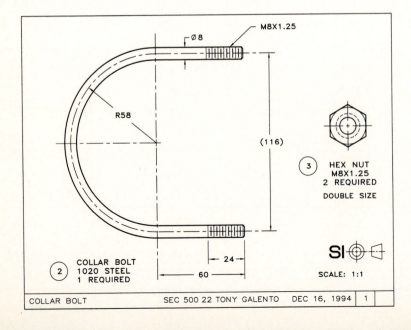

Figure 16.34 Make a drawing of the switch by computer or drafting instruments on a size A sheet. Note that the views are enlarged by a factor of 4.

Figure 16.35 Sheet 1 of 3: Make full-size working drawings, with an assembly drawing (in mm), of a pipe hanger on size A sheets.

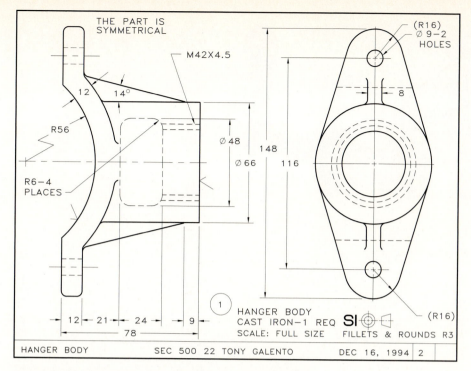

Figure 16.36 Sheet 2 of 3: The pipe hanger working drawings.

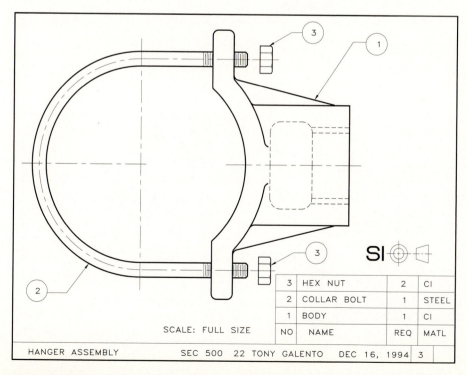

Figure 16.37 Sheet 3 of 3: The assembly of the pipe hanger.

Figure 16.38 This photo is of a ball crank assembly.

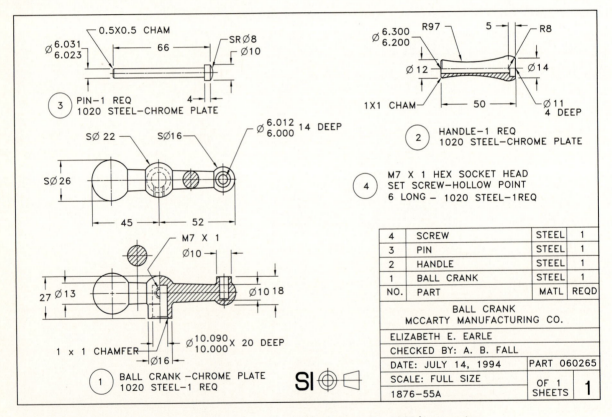

Figure 16.39 Make a working drawing of the ball crank assembly shown in Fig. 16.38 by computer or drafting instruments on a size B sheet. On a second size B sheet make an assembly drawing of the parts of the ball crank.

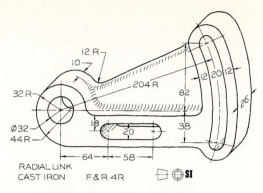

Working Drawings of Single Parts
Make working drawings by hand or by computer, as assigned, of the single parts shown in **Figs. 16.40–16.53** on the sheet sizes specified for each. Include a title block and the dimensions and notes necessary for constructing the part.

Figure 16.40 Make a half-size detail drawing of this radial link on a size B sheet.

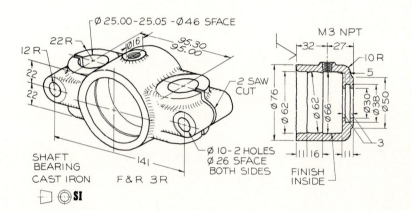

Figure 16.41 Make a full-size detail drawing of this shaft bearing on a size B sheet.

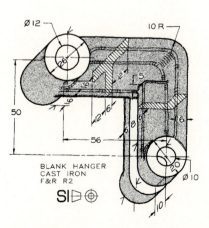

Figure 16.42 Make a full-size detail drawing of this blank hanger on a size B sheet.

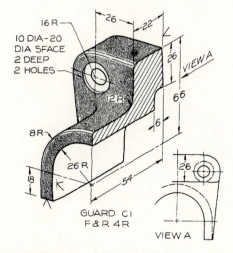

Figure 16.43 Make a full-size detail drawing of this guard on a size B sheet.

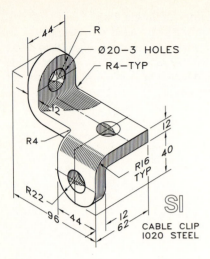

R
∅20-3 HOLES
R4-TYP
44
12
R4
R16
TYP
12
40
R22
96
44
12
62
SI

CABLE CLIP
1020 STEEL

Figure 16.44 Make a half-size detail drawing of this spindle head on a size B sheet.

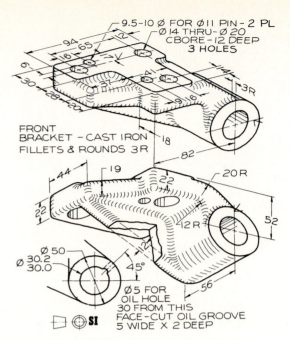

9.5-10 ∅ FOR ∅11 PIN - 2 PL
∅ 14 THRU-∅ 20
CBORE - 12 DEEP
3 HOLES
94
65
6
30
28
20
18
3R
82

FRONT
BRACKET - CAST IRON
FILLETS & ROUNDS 3R
18

44
19
22
20R
22
12R
52
∅ 30.2
∅ 30.0
∅ 50
45°
12
56
∅5 FOR
OIL HOLE
30 FROM THIS
FACE-CUT OIL GROOVE
5 WIDE X 2 DEEP
SI

Figure 16.46 Make a half-size detail drawing of this front bracket drawing on a size B sheet.

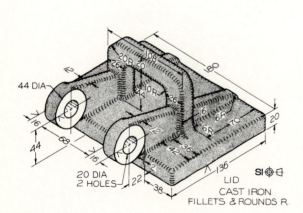

44 DIA
12
20R 20
26
108
180
10R
44
26
16
6R
70
20
6R
68
16
36
42
16
2
136
20 DIA
2 HOLES
22
38
SI

LID
CAST IRON
FILLETS & ROUNDS R

Figure 16.45 Make a half-size detail drawing of this lid on a size B sheet.

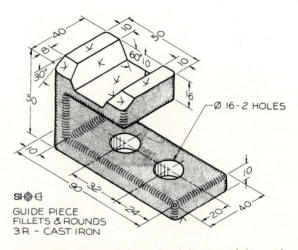

40
10
50
8
K
60° 10
30°
10
16
50
∅ 16-2 HOLES
10
90
32
24
20
40
10
SI

GUIDE PIECE
FILLETS & ROUNDS
3R - CAST IRON

Figure 16.47 Make a full-size detail drawing of this guide piece on a size B sheet.

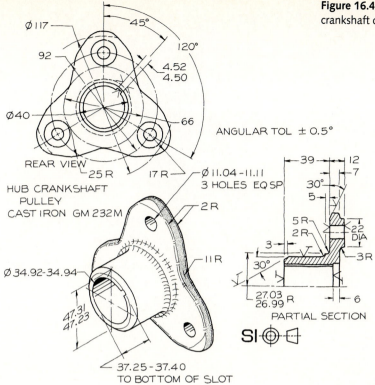

Ø 117
45°
92
120°
4.52
4.50
Ø40
66
REAR VIEW
25 R
17 R
HUB CRANKSHAFT
PULLEY
CAST IRON GM 232M
2 R
11 R
Ø 34.92-34.94
47.31
47.23
37.25 - 37.40
TO BOTTOM OF SLOT

ANGULAR TOL ± 0.5°

Ø 11.04-11.11
3 HOLES EQ SP

39   12
7
30°
5
5 R
2 R   22
DIA
3   3 R
30°
27.03 R   6
26.99
PARTIAL SECTION
SI

Figure 16.48 Make a full-size detail drawing of this hub crankshaft on a size B sheet.

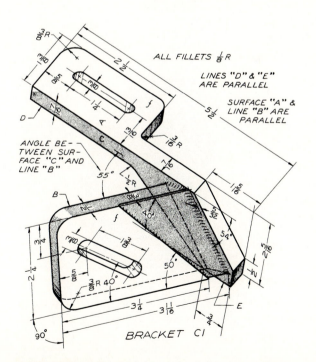

3/8 R
ALL FILLETS 1/8 R
2 1/2
LINES "D" & "E"
ARE PARALLEL
1/4
5 1/2
SURFACE "A" &
LINE "B" ARE
f   PARALLEL
D
7/16
A
3/16 R
C
ANGLE BE-
TWEEN SUR-
FACE "C" AND
LINE "B"   7/16
55°   1 5/16
1/2 R
B   40°
f   5 3/32
54°   2 5/16
3/4   1/4
2 1/4   50°
3/8 R 40°
3 1/4   3 11/16
90°   3/4
E
BRACKET C1

Figure 16.49 Make a full-size detail drawing of this bracket brace on a size B sheet.

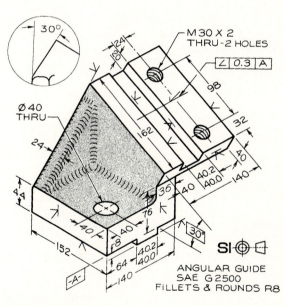

30°

M 30 X 2
THRU-2 HOLES
∠ 0.3 A
24
20
98
Ø 40
THRU
162   32
24   40
40.2
40.0   140
36
40
76
30°
40
8
152   8   SI
64   40.2
140   40.0   ANGULAR GUIDE
SAE G 2500
FILLETS & ROUNDS R8
-A-
44

Figure 16.50 Make a half-size detail drawing of this angular guide on a size B sheet.

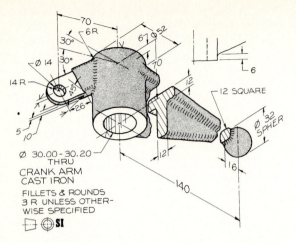

Figure 16.51 Make a full-size detail drawing of this crank arm on a size B sheet.

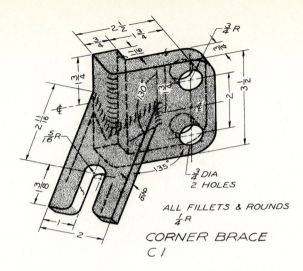

Figure 16.53 Make a full-size detail drawing of this corner brace on a size B sheet.

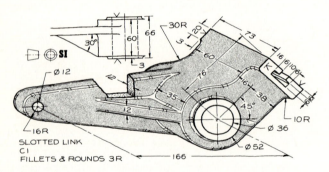

Figure 16.52 Make a half-size detail drawing of this slotted link on a size B sheet.

Figure 16.54 Make detail drawings of this 7-in. diameter pulley on a size A sheet.

Working Drawings of Single Parts Involving Design Features

Make working drawings of the single parts shown in **Figs. 16.54–16.59** on size A sheets. These problems require that you use your judgment and creativity to depict design features. Include a title block and the dimensions and notes necessary for making the part.

Figure 16.55 Make detail drawings of this 3-in.-ID shaft socket on a size A sheet.

Figure 16.57 Make detail drawings of this 4-in.-high angle on a size A sheet.

Figure 16.58 Make detail drawings of this shaft arm that fits shafts of 1.00 and 2.00 in. in diameter, with 6.00 in. between centers, on a size A sheet.

Figure 16.56 Make detail drawings of this hanger bracket that extends 8 in. from the wall and supports a 0.50-in.-diameter bolt on a size A sheet.

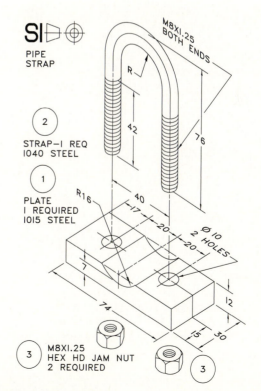

Figure 16.59 Make full-size working drawings of this U-bolt pipe strap on size A sheets.

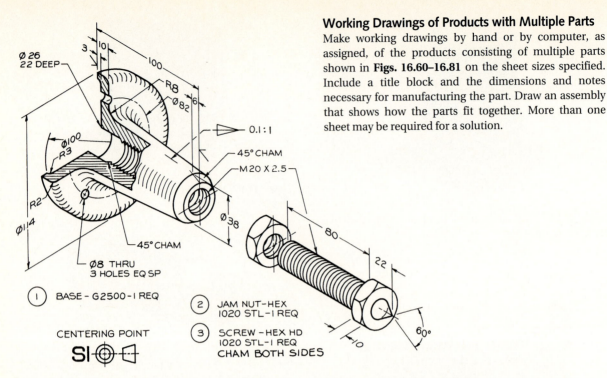

Working Drawings of Products with Multiple Parts

Make working drawings by hand or by computer, as assigned, of the products consisting of multiple parts shown in **Figs. 16.60–16.81** on the sheet sizes specified. Include a title block and the dimensions and notes necessary for manufacturing the part. Draw an assembly that shows how the parts fit together. More than one sheet may be required for a solution.

Figure 16.60 Make half-size working drawings, with an assembly drawing, of this centering point on size A sheets.

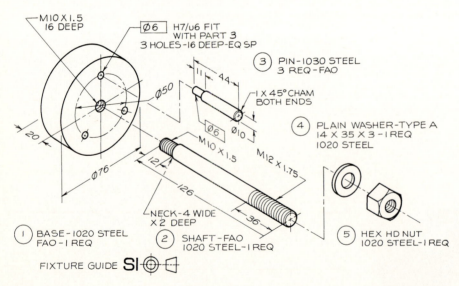

Figure 16.61 Make full-size working drawings, with an assembly drawing, of this fixture guide on size A sheets.

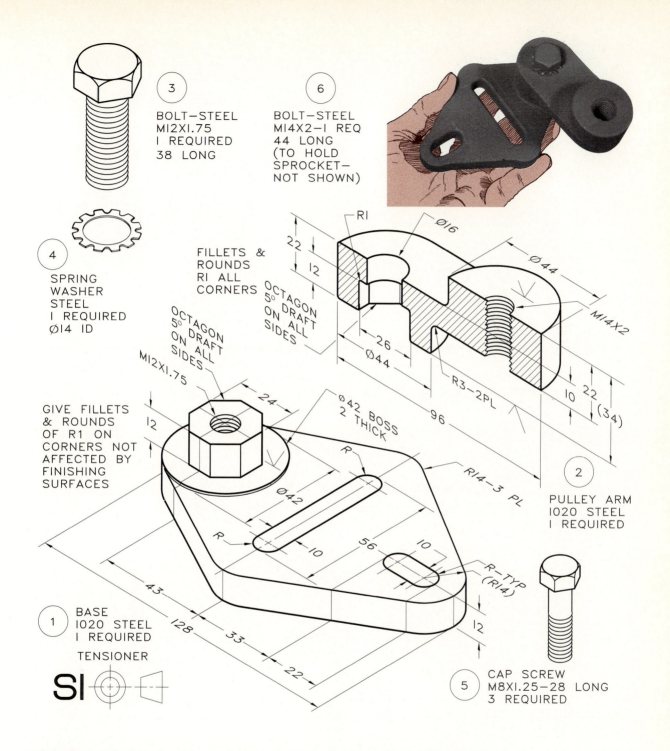

3 BOLT—STEEL
MI2X1.75
1 REQUIRED
38 LONG

6 BOLT—STEEL
MI4X2—1 REQ
44 LONG
(TO HOLD
SPROCKET—
NOT SHOWN)

4 SPRING
WASHER
STEEL
1 REQUIRED
Ø14 ID

FILLETS &
ROUNDS
R1 ALL
CORNERS

R1

Ø16

Ø44

OCTAGON
5° DRAFT
ON ALL
SIDES

OCTAGON
5° DRAFT
ON ALL
SIDES

MI4X2

22

12

26

Ø44

96

R3—2PL

10

22
(34)

2 PULLEY ARM
1020 STEEL
1 REQUIRED

OCTAGON
5° DRAFT
ON ALL
SIDES

MI2X1.75

GIVE FILLETS
& ROUNDS
OF R1 ON
CORNERS NOT
AFFECTED BY
FINISHING
SURFACES

24

12

Ø42 BOSS
2 THICK

Ø42

R

R14—3 PL

R

10

56

10

R—TYP
(R14)

12

43

128

33

22

1 BASE
1020 STEEL
1 REQUIRED

TENSIONER

SI

5 CAP SCREW
M8X1.25—28 LONG
3 REQUIRED

Figure 16.62 Make full-size working drawings, with an assembly drawing, of this tensioner on size B sheets.

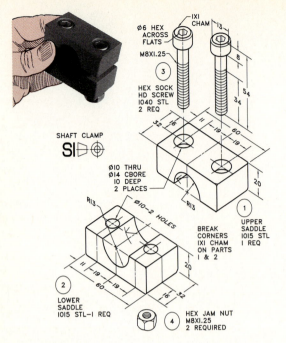

Figure 16.63 Make full-size working drawings, with an assembly drawing, of this shaft clamp on size A sheets.

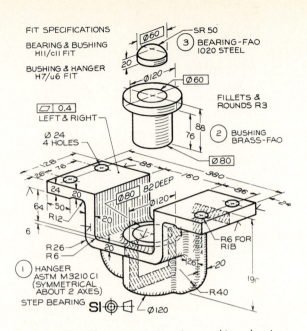

Figure 16.64 Make one-quarter size working drawings, with an assembly drawing, of this step bearing on size B sheets.

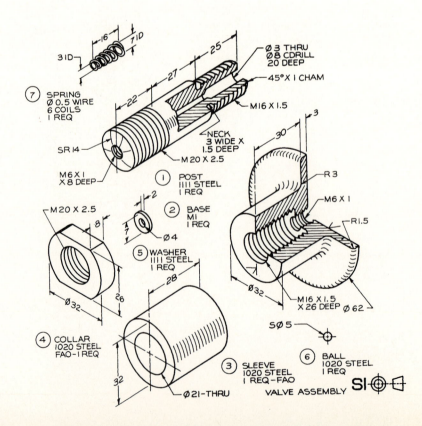

Figure 16.65 Make full-size working drawings, with an assembly drawing, of this valve assembly on size B sheets.

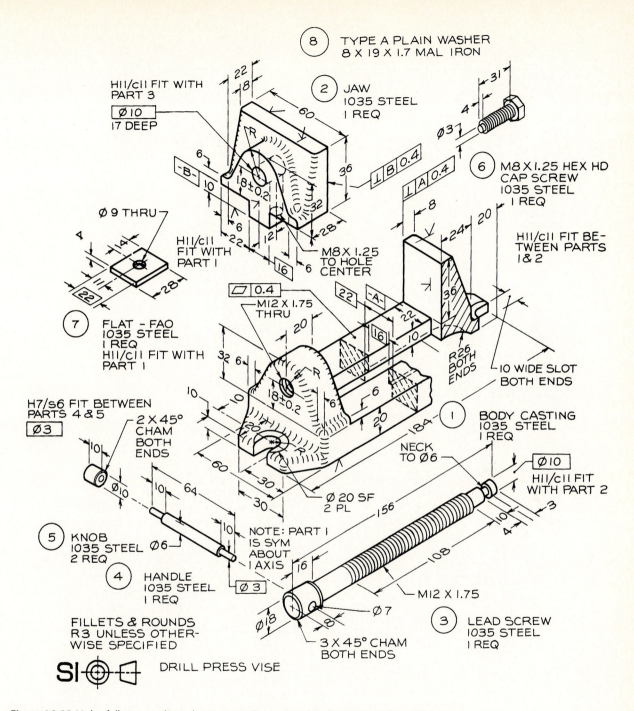

Figure 16.66 Make full-size working drawings, with an assembly drawing, of this drill press vise on size B sheets.

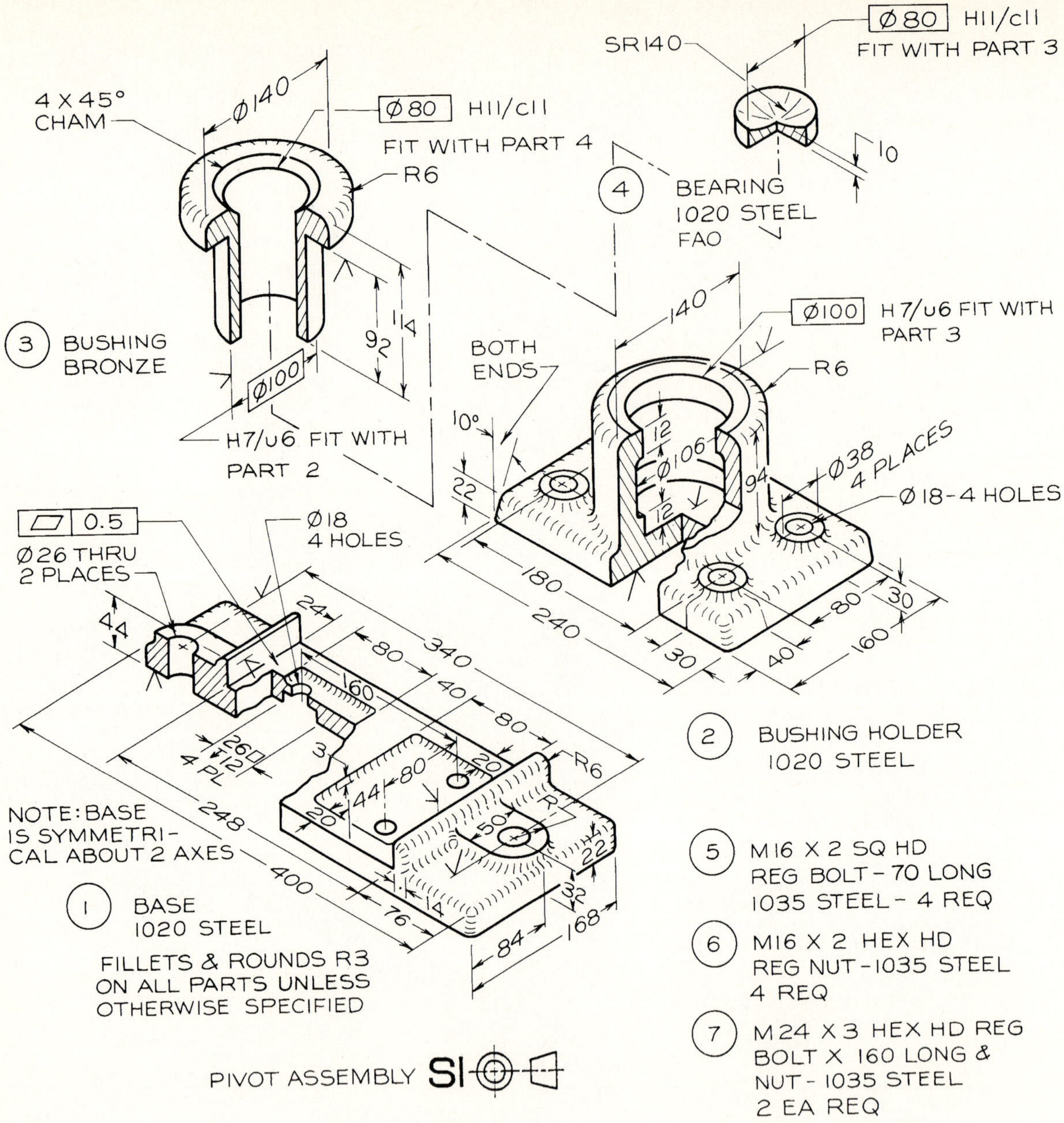

SR140
Ø80 H11/c11
FIT WITH PART 3
4 X 45°
CHAM
Ø140
Ø80 H11/c11
FIT WITH PART 4
R6
4
BEARING
1020 STEEL
FAO
10
3 BUSHING
BRONZE
114
92
Ø100
H7/u6 FIT WITH
PART 2
140
Ø100 H7/u6 FIT WITH
PART 3
BOTH
ENDS
R6
10°
22
12
Ø106
12
94
Ø38
4 PLACES
Ø18-4 HOLES
180
240
30
80
30
40
160
0.5
Ø26 THRU
2 PLACES
Ø18
4 HOLES
44
24
340
80
160
40
80
26
12
4 PL
3
20
44
80
R6
R
20
50
22
NOTE: BASE
IS SYMMETRI-
CAL ABOUT 2 AXES
248
400
76
14
32
84
168
1 BASE
1020 STEEL
FILLETS & ROUNDS R3
ON ALL PARTS UNLESS
OTHERWISE SPECIFIED
2 BUSHING HOLDER
1020 STEEL
5 M16 X 2 SQ HD
REG BOLT - 70 LONG
1035 STEEL - 4 REQ
6 M16 X 2 HEX HD
REG NUT - 1035 STEEL
4 REQ
7 M24 X 3 HEX HD REG
BOLT X 160 LONG &
NUT - 1035 STEEL
2 EA REQ
PIVOT ASSEMBLY SI

Figure 16.67 Make a working drawing, with an assembly drawing, of this pivot assembly on size B sheets.

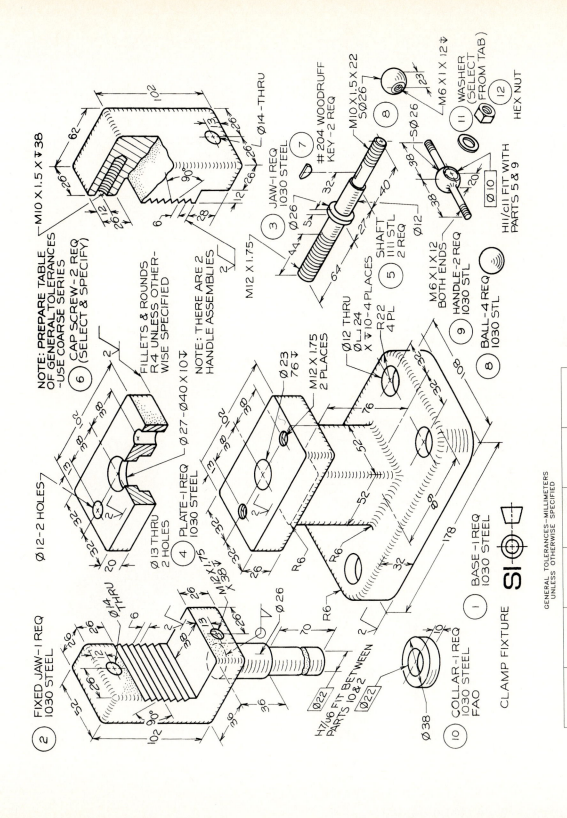

Figure 16.68 Make half-size working drawings, with an assembly drawing, of this clamp fixture on size B sheets.

341

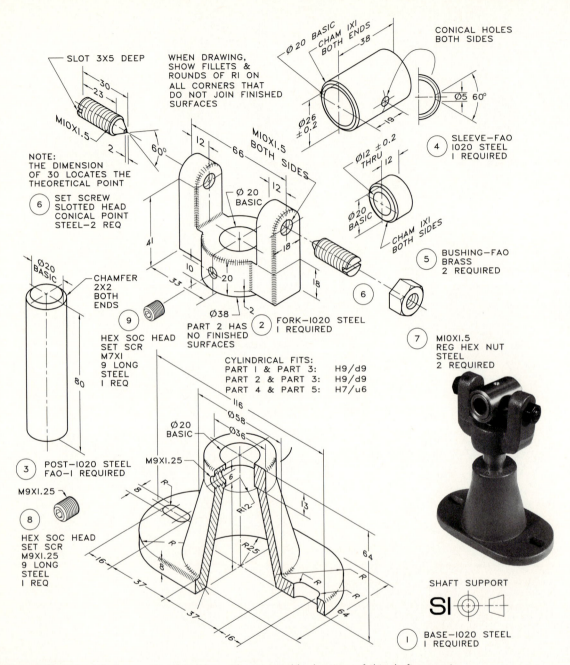

SLOT 3X5 DEEP

30
23

M10X1.5

2

60°

NOTE:
THE DIMENSION
OF 30 LOCATES THE
THEORETICAL POINT

⑥ SET SCREW
SLOTTED HEAD
CONICAL POINT
STEEL—2 REQ

WHEN DRAWING,
SHOW FILLETS &
ROUNDS OF R1 ON
ALL CORNERS THAT
DO NOT JOIN FINISHED
SURFACES

Ø 20 BASIC   CHAM 1X1
BOTH ENDS   38

CONICAL HOLES
BOTH SIDES

Ø26
±0.2

19

Ø5 60°

④ SLEEVE—FAO
1020 STEEL
1 REQUIRED

M10X1.5
BOTH SIDES

12
66
12

Ø 20
BASIC

18

Ø12 ±0.2
THRU   12

Ø 20
BASIC

CHAM 1X1
BOTH SIDES

⑤ BUSHING—FAO
BRASS
2 REQUIRED

Ø20
BASIC

CHAMFER
2X2
BOTH
ENDS

⑨

HEX SOC HEAD
SET SCR
M7X1
9 LONG
STEEL
1 REQ

41

10
33

20

Ø38

⑥

② FORK—1020 STEEL
1 REQUIRED

PART 2 HAS
NO FINISHED
SURFACES

⑥

⑦ M10X1.5
REG HEX NUT
STEEL
2 REQUIRED

80

CYLINDRICAL FITS:
PART 1 & PART 3:   H9/d9
PART 2 & PART 3:   H9/d9
PART 4 & PART 5:   H7/u6

③ POST—1020 STEEL
FAO—1 REQUIRED

M9X1.25

⑧

HEX SOC HEAD
SET SCR
M9X1.25
9 LONG
STEEL
1 REQ

116
Ø58
Ø36
Ø20
BASIC

M9X1.25

6

8

R

R12

R25

13

R

R

R

64

16

8

37

37

16

64

SHAFT SUPPORT

S1

① BASE—1020 STEEL
1 REQUIRED

Figure 16.69 Make full-size working drawings, with an assembly drawing, of this shaft support on size B sheets.

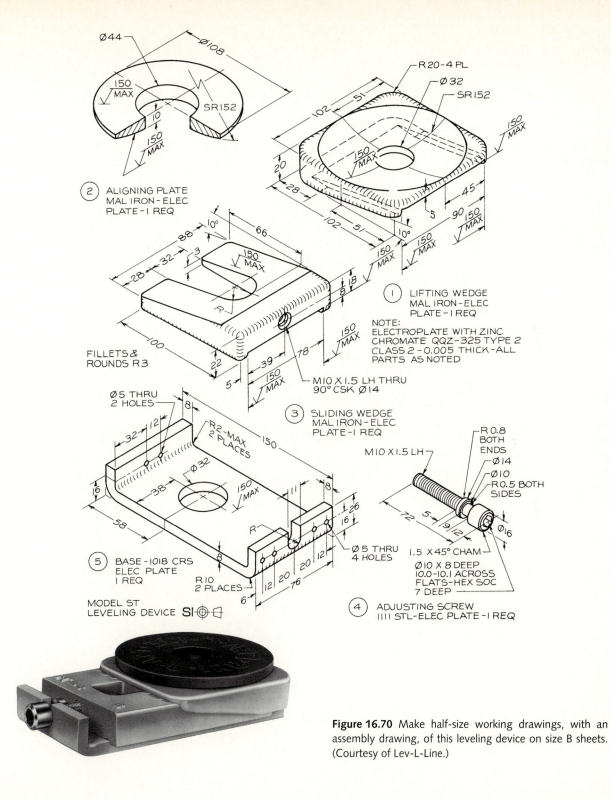

Ø44
Ø108

150 MAX

SR152

10

150 MAX

150 MAX

② ALIGNING PLATE
MAL IRON – ELEC
PLATE – I REQ

R20-4 PL
Ø32
SR152

102
51

20

28

150 MAX

102
51

150 MAX

150 MAX

10°

45

5

90

150 MAX

150 MAX

① LIFTING WEDGE
MAL IRON – ELEC
PLATE – I REQ

NOTE:
ELECTROPLATE WITH ZINC
CHROMATE QQZ–325 TYPE 2
CLASS 2 – 0.005 THICK – ALL
PARTS AS NOTED

10°
88
66

150 MAX

28 32 3

150 MAX

R

18

8

100

22

FILLETS &
ROUNDS R3

5

39 78

150 MAX

M10 X 1.5 LH THRU
90° CSK Ø14

③ SLIDING WEDGE
MAL IRON – ELEC
PLATE – I REQ

Ø5 THRU
2 HOLES

8

32 12

R2 – MAX
2 PLACES

150

Ø32

38

150 MAX

16

11

8

R

26

16

58

150 MAX

M10 X 1.5 LH

R 0.8
BOTH
ENDS

Ø14

Ø10

R0.5 BOTH
SIDES

72

5

9 12

Ø16

1.5 X 45° CHAM

Ø10 X 8 DEEP
10.0-10.1 ACROSS
FLATS-HEX SOC
7 DEEP

Ø 5 THRU
4 HOLES

⑤ BASE – 1018 CRS
ELEC PLATE
I REQ

R10
2 PLACES

8

12 20 20 12

76

6

④ ADJUSTING SCREW
IIII STL–ELEC PLATE – I REQ

MODEL ST
LEVELING DEVICE SI ⊕ ⊲

Figure 16.70 Make half-size working drawings, with an assembly drawing, of this leveling device on size B sheets. (Courtesy of Lev-L-Line.)

Figure 16.71 Make half-size working drawings, with an assembly drawing, of this C-clamp on size B sheets.

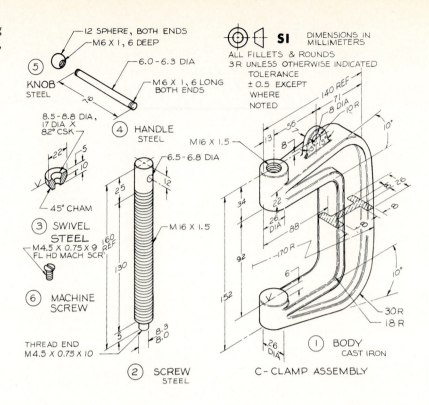

Figure 16.72 Make half-size working drawings, with an assembly drawing, of this indicating lever on size B sheets.

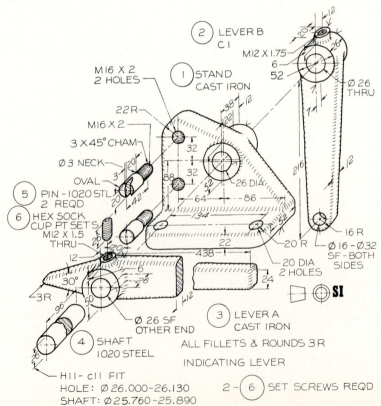

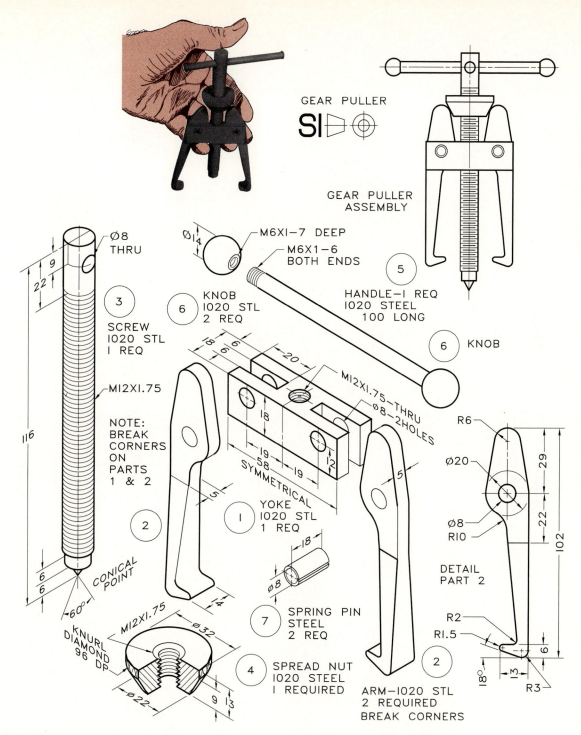

GEAR PULLER

SI ⊳ ⊕

GEAR PULLER
ASSEMBLY

Ø8
THRU

Ø14

M6X1—7 DEEP

M6X1—6
BOTH ENDS

⑤

③

SCREW
1020 STL
1 REQ

M12X1.75

NOTE:
BREAK
CORNERS
ON
PARTS
1 & 2

⑥ KNOB
1020 STL
2 REQ

HANDLE—1 REQ
1020 STEEL
100 LONG

⑥ KNOB

116

M12X1.75—THRU
Ø8—2HOLES

18 6
6

20

18

19
58   19   12

SYMMETRICAL

① YOKE
1020 STL
1 REQ

R6

Ø20

Ø8
R10

29

22

102

DETAIL
PART 2

②

6

22

②

5

5

R2

R1.5

18°   13   R3

6

6

6

60°

CONICAL
POINT

KNURL
DIAMOND
96 DP

M12X1.75

Ø32

②

18

Ø8

⑦ SPRING PIN
STEEL
2 REQ

④ SPREAD NUT
1020 STEEL
1 REQUIRED

Ø22   9 13

② ARM—1020 STL
2 REQUIRED
BREAK CORNERS

Figure 16.73 Make double-size working drawings, with an assembly drawing, of this gear puller on size B sheets.

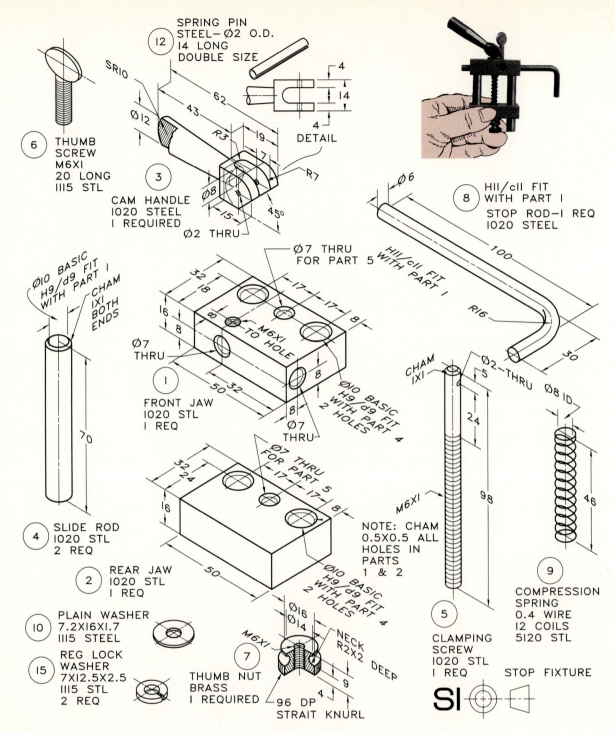

SPRING PIN
STEEL—Ø2 O.D.
14 LONG
DOUBLE SIZE

⑫

4

14

4

DETAIL

⑥ THUMB SCREW
M6X1
20 LONG
1115 STL

SR10

Ø12

62

43

R3

19

7

R7

⑧ H11/c11 FIT
WITH PART 1
STOP ROD—1 REQ
1020 STEEL

Ø6

100

③ CAM HANDLE
1020 STEEL
1 REQUIRED

Ø8

15

45°

Ø2 THRU

R16

H11/c11 FIT
WITH PART 1

30

Ø10 BASIC
H9/d9 FIT
WITH PART 1

CHAM
1X1
BOTH
ENDS

Ø7 THRU
FOR PART 5

32

18

16

8

8

Ø7
THRU

M6X1
TO HOLE

① FRONT JAW
1020 STL
1 REQ

50

32

17 17   8

8

Ø10
H9/d9 FIT
WITH PART 4
2 HOLES

8

Ø7
THRU

70

CHAM
1X1

Ø2 THRU

5

6

24

Ø8 ID

M6X1

98

④ SLIDE ROD
1020 STL
2 REQ

② REAR JAW
1020 STL
1 REQ

Ø7 THRU
FOR PART 5

32

24

16

17 17   8

50

Ø10 BASIC
H9/d9 FIT
WITH PART 4
2 HOLES

NOTE: CHAM
0.5X0.5 ALL
HOLES IN
PARTS
1 & 2

46

⑨ COMPRESSION
SPRING
0.4 WIRE
12 COILS
5120 STL

⑩ PLAIN WASHER
7.2X16X1.7
1115 STEEL

⑮ REG LOCK
WASHER
7X12.5X2.5
1115 STL
2 REQ

Ø16
Ø14

M6X1

⑦ THUMB NUT
BRASS
1 REQUIRED

NECK
R2X2 DEEP

4

9

96 DP
STRAIT KNURL

⑤ CLAMPING
SCREW
1020 STL
1 REQ

SI

STOP FIXTURE

Figure 16.74 Make full-size working drawings, with an assembly drawing, of this stop fixture on size B sheets.

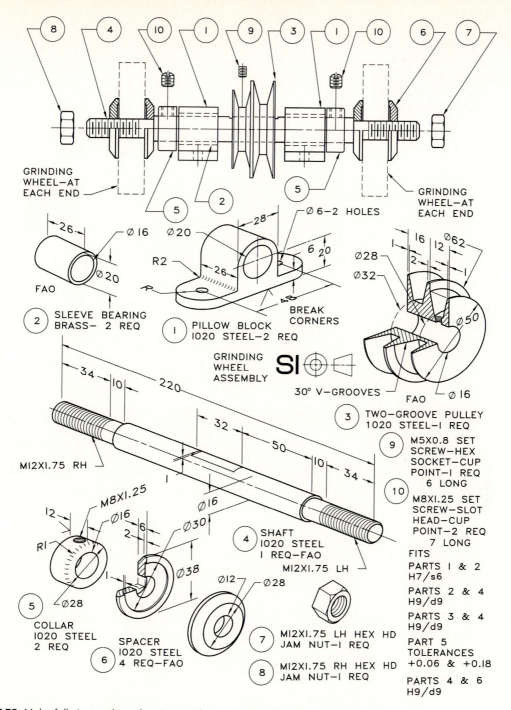

8 • GRINDING WHEEL—AT EACH END

4

10

1

9

3

1

10

6

7 • GRINDING WHEEL—AT EACH END

5

2

— 26 —
Ø16
Ø20

FAO

2 SLEEVE BEARING BRASS— 2 REQ

— 28 —
R2
Ø20
— 26 —
6 20
Ø 6—2 HOLES
BREAK CORNERS
48

1 PILLOW BLOCK 1020 STEEL—2 REQ

GRINDING WHEEL ASSEMBLY

SI

30° V-GROOVES

1 16 12 Ø62
Ø28
2 1
Ø32
Ø50
Ø 16
FAO

3 TWO-GROOVE PULLEY 1020 STEEL—1 REQ

— 34 — 10 — 220 —
32
50
10 — 34 —

M12X1.75 RH

9 M5X0.8 SET SCREW—HEX SOCKET—CUP POINT—1 REQ 6 LONG

10 M8X1.25 SET SCREW—SLOT HEAD—CUP POINT—2 REQ 7 LONG

M8X1.25
12
Ø16
R1
Ø28
2 6
Ø16
Ø30

5 COLLAR 1020 STEEL 2 REQ

Ø38

6 SPACER 1020 STEEL 4 REQ—FAO

Ø12 Ø28

4 SHAFT 1020 STEEL 1 REQ—FAO
M12X1.75 LH

7 M12X1.75 LH HEX HD JAM NUT—1 REQ

8 M12X1.75 RH HEX HD JAM NUT—1 REQ

FITS

PARTS 1 & 2 H7/s6

PARTS 2 & 4 H9/d9

PARTS 3 & 4 H9/d9

PART 5 TOLERANCES +0.06 & +0.18

PARTS 4 & 6 H9/d9

Figure 16.75 Make full-size working drawings, with an assembly drawing, of this grinding wheel assembly on size B sheets.

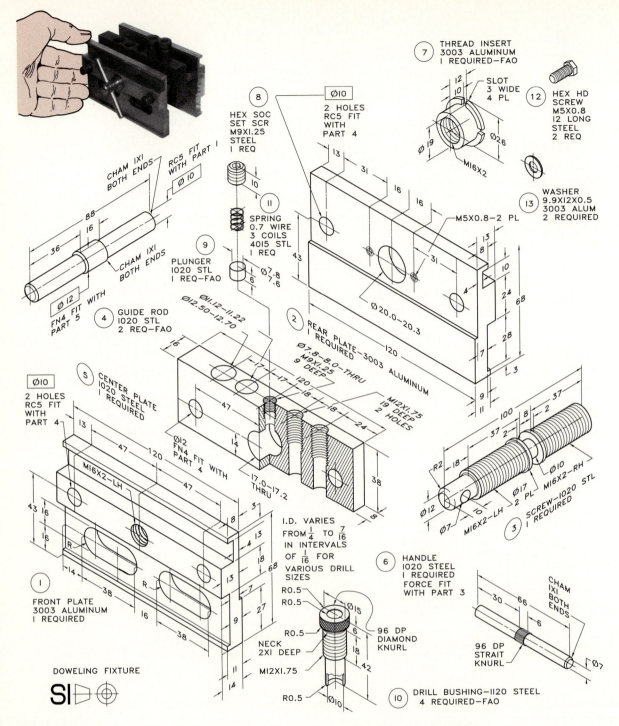

Figure 16.76 Make full-size working drawings, with an assembly drawing, of this dowelling fixture on size B sheets.

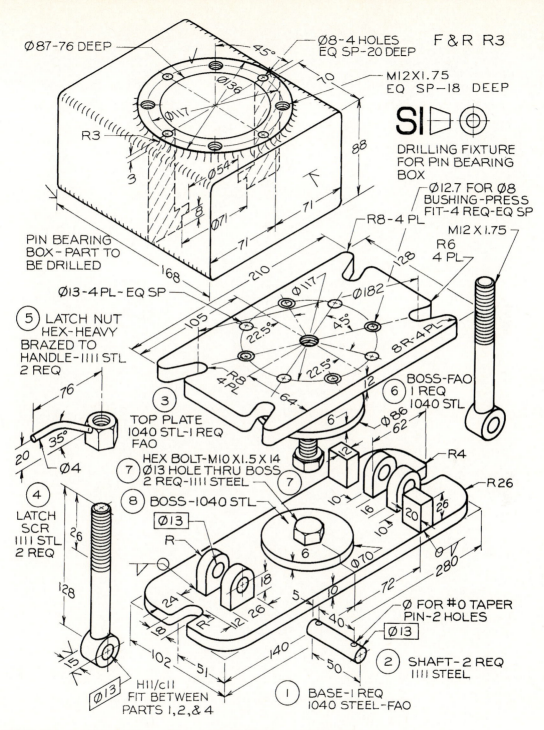

Ø87-76 DEEP

Ø8-4 HOLES
EQ SP-20 DEEP

45°

F & R R3

70

M12X1.75
EQ SP-18 DEEP

Ø136

Ø117

88

R3

3

Ø54

DRILLING FIXTURE
FOR PIN BEARING
BOX

Ø12.7 FOR Ø8
BUSHING-PRESS
FIT-4 REQ-EQ SP

8

Ø71

M12 X 1.75

R8-4 PL

R6
4 PL

PIN BEARING
BOX - PART TO
BE DRILLED

168

71

71

210

128

Ø13-4 PL-EQ SP

105

Ø117

Ø182

22.5°

45°

8R-4 PL

⑤ LATCH NUT
HEX-HEAVY
BRAZED TO
HANDLE-1111 STL
2 REQ

76

R8
4 PL

22.5°

12

BOSS-FAO
⑥ 1 REQ
1040 STL

64

6

Ø86

62

35°

Ø4

③ TOP PLATE
1040 STL-1 REQ
FAO

12

R4

20

R26

④ LATCH
SCR
1111 STL
2 REQ

HEX BOLT-M10 X1.5 X 14
⑦ Ø13 HOLE THRU BOSS
2 REQ-1111 STEEL

⑦

10

16

26

26

⑧ BOSS-1040 STL

Ø13

R

6

10

Ø70

V

128

18

Ø13

5

10

72

280

24

26

12

Ø FOR #0 TAPER
PIN-2 HOLES

15

18

R

40

Ø13

Ø13

102

51

140

50

② SHAFT-2 REQ
1111 STEEL

H11/c11
FIT BETWEEN
PARTS 1,2,& 4

① BASE-1 REQ
1040 STEEL-FAO

Figure 16.77 Make working drawings, with an assembly drawing, of this drilling fixture on size B sheets.

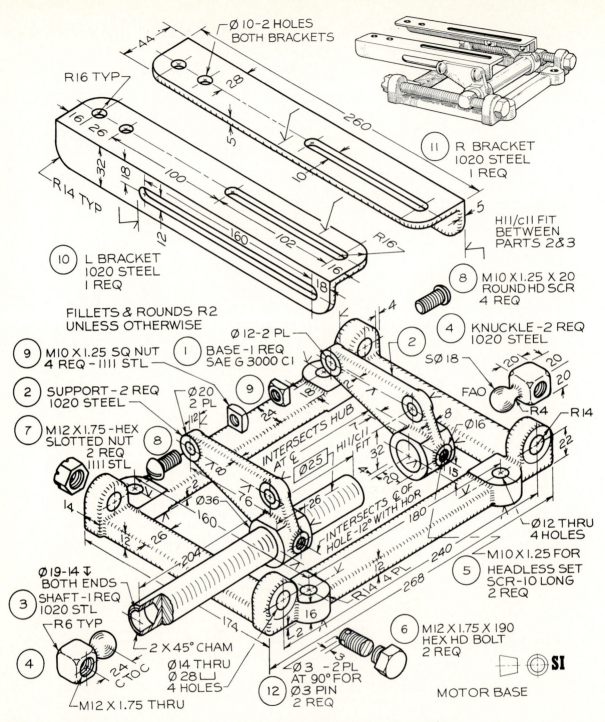

Ø10-2 HOLES
BOTH BRACKETS

44

R16 TYP

28

260

16 26

⑪ R BRACKET
1020 STEEL
I REQ

32

18

R14 TYP

100

5

10

R16

H11/C11 FIT
BETWEEN
PARTS 2&3

5

⑩ L BRACKET
1020 STEEL
I REQ

160   102

16

18

⑧ M10 X1.25 X 20
ROUND HD SCR
4 REQ

12

FILLETS & ROUNDS R2
UNLESS OTHERWISE

Ø12-2 PL

②

④ KNUCKLE -2 REQ
1020 STEEL

SØ18

20   20

⑨ M10 X1.25 SQ NUT
4 REQ -1111 STL

① BASE-I REQ
SAE G 3000 C1

⑨

18

FAO

20

② SUPPORT-2 REQ
1020 STEEL

Ø20
2 PL

INTERSECTS HUB
AT ₵

H11/C11
FIT

R4   R14

12

Ø25

⑦ M12 X1.75 -HEX
SLOTTED NUT
2 REQ
1111 STL

⑧

24

32

Ø16

22

40

8

15

14

76

4

29

Ø36

2

26

INTERSECTS ₵ OF
HOLE-12° WITH HOR

180

Ø12 THRU
4 HOLES

160

12

Ø19-14
BOTH ENDS

204

26

240

268

M10 X1.25 FOR
⑤ HEADLESS SET
SCR-10 LONG
2 REQ

③ SHAFT-I REQ
1020 STL

R6 TYP

16

R14 4 PL

174

2

⑥ M12 X1.75 X 190
HEX HD BOLT
2 REQ

④

2 X 45° CHAM

24
C TO C

Ø14 THRU
Ø28
4 HOLES

Ø3 -2PL
AT 90° FOR
Ø3 PIN
2 REQ

⑫

SI

M12 X1.75 THRU

MOTOR BASE

Figure 16.78 Make working drawings, with an assembly drawing, of this motor base on size B sheets.

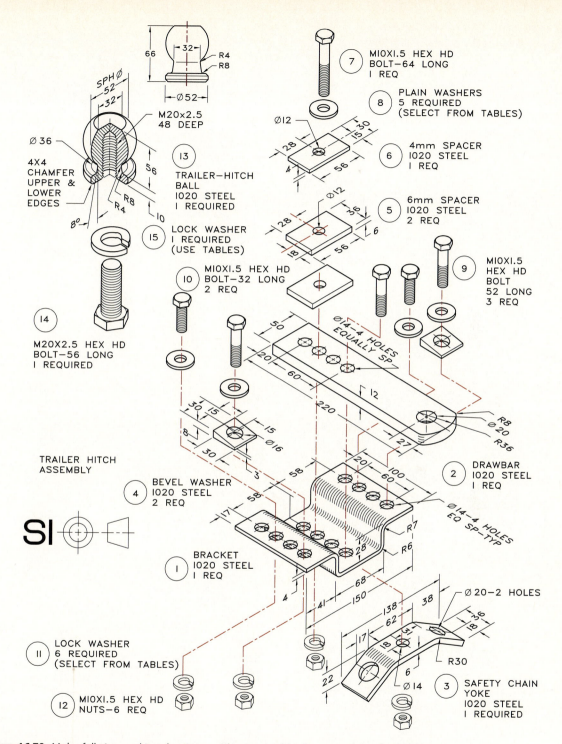

66

32
R4
R8

SPHØ
52
32
Ø52

Ø36

M20x2.5
48 DEEP

4X4
CHAMFER
UPPER &
LOWER
EDGES

56

R8
R4

10

8°

(13) TRAILER–HITCH
BALL
1020 STEEL
1 REQUIRED

(14)

M20X2.5 HEX HD
BOLT–56 LONG
1 REQUIRED

(15) LOCK WASHER
1 REQUIRED
(USE TABLES)

(7) M10X1.5 HEX HD
BOLT–64 LONG
1 REQ

(8) PLAIN WASHERS
5 REQUIRED
(SELECT FROM TABLES)

Ø12

30
15
28
56
4

(6) 4mm SPACER
1020 STEEL
1 REQ

Ø12

30
28
6
18
56

(5) 6mm SPACER
1020 STEEL
2 REQ

(10) M10X1.5 HEX HD
BOLT–32 LONG
2 REQ

(9) M10X1.5
HEX HD
BOLT
52 LONG
3 REQ

50
Ø14–4 HOLES
EQUALLY SP
20
60
12
220
27

R8
Ø 20
R36

(2) DRAWBAR
1020 STEEL
1 REQ

Ø14–4 HOLES
EQ SP–TYP

20
100
60

30
15
15
8
30
Ø16
3
58
58
17

(4) BEVEL WASHER
1020 STEEL
2 REQ

R7
R6
28

(1) BRACKET
1020 STEEL
1 REQ

TRAILER HITCH
ASSEMBLY

SI

4
41
68
150
138
62
17
18
6
22
Ø14

Ø 20–2 HOLES
6
18

R30

(3) SAFETY CHAIN
YOKE
1020 STEEL
1 REQUIRED

(11) LOCK WASHER
6 REQUIRED
(SELECT FROM TABLES)

(12) M10X1.5 HEX HD
NUTS–6 REQ

Figure 16.79 Make full-size working drawings, with an assembly drawing, of this trailer hitch on size B sheets.

Figure 16.80 Make full-size working drawings, with an assembly drawing, of this chisel and blade honer on size B sheets.

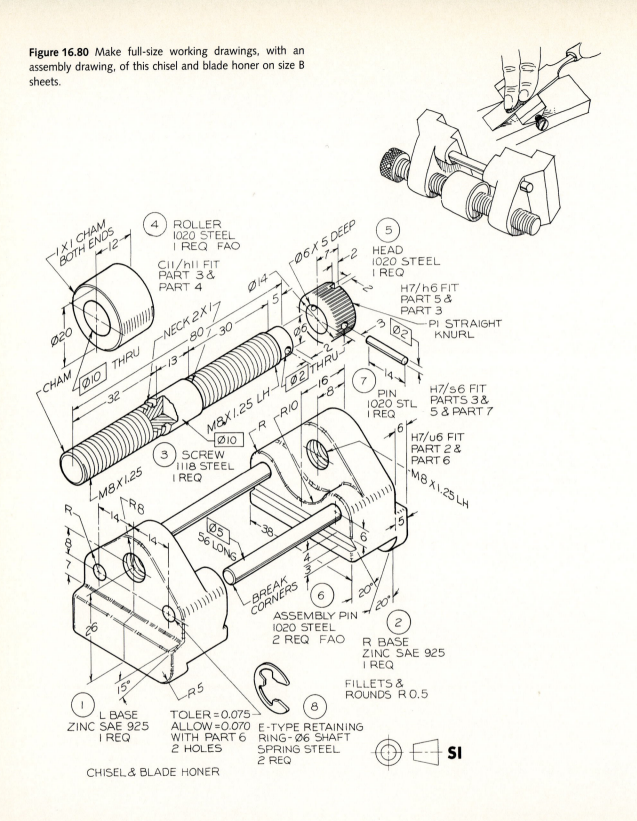

1 X 1 CHAM BOTH ENDS

4 ROLLER
1020 STEEL
I REQ FAO

C11/h11 FIT
PART 3 &
PART 4

Ø6 X 5 DEEP

5 HEAD
1020 STEEL
I REQ

H7/h6 FIT
PART 5 &
PART 3

PI STRAIGHT KNURL

Ø20

Ø10 THRU

CHAM

32

NECK 2 X 1

Ø14

80   30

13

5

Ø6

Ø2

H7/s6 FIT
PARTS 3 &
5 & PART 7

7 PIN
1020 STL
I REQ

Ø2 THRU

M8 X 1.25 LH

Ø10

R   R10

16

8

6

H7/u6 FIT
PART 2 &
PART 6

3 SCREW
1118 STEEL
I REQ

M8 X 1.25

M8 X 1.25 LH

5

R   R8

14

14

Ø5
56 LONG

38

6

4

3

BREAK CORNERS

20°   20°

26

15°

R5

6 ASSEMBLY PIN
1020 STEEL
2 REQ FAO

2 R BASE
ZINC SAE 925
I REQ

FILLETS & ROUNDS R 0.5

1 L BASE
ZINC SAE 925
I REQ

TOLER = 0.075
ALLOW = 0.070
WITH PART 6
2 HOLES

8 E-TYPE RETAINING
RING - Ø6 SHAFT
SPRING STEEL
2 REQ

SI

CHISEL & BLADE HONER

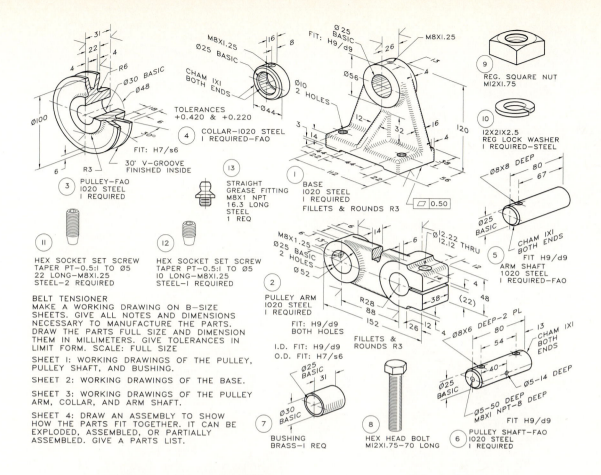

Figure 16.81 Make full-size working drawings, with an assembly drawing, of this belt tensioner on size B sheets.

Working Drawings of Multiple Parts Involving Design Features

Make dimensioned working drawings of the multiple parts shown in **Figs. 16.82–16.93** on a sheet size of your choice with the necessary dimensions and notes to fabricate the parts. Each part is given in a general format, which requires some design on your part. You must consider the addition of fillets and rounds, the application of finish marks, and the modification of features of the parts to make them functional and practical. Apply the tolerance to the parts in limit form by using the tables of cylindrical fits in the Appendix. Make an assembly drawing and parts list to show how the parts are to be put together.

Figure 16.82 Design: Make working drawings, with an assembly drawing, of this turn buckle on size B sheets.

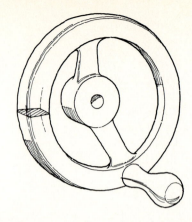

Figure 16.85 Design: Make working drawings, with an assembly drawing, of this hand wheel having a 10-in.-OD on size B sheets.

Figure 16.83 Design: Make working drawings, with an assembly drawing, of this I-beam clamp with a $^3/_4$-in.-diameter screw on size B sheets. (Courtesy of Grinnel Corporation.)

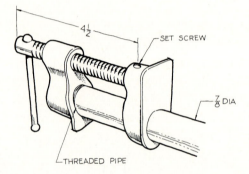

Figure 16.86 Design: Make working drawings, with an assembly drawing, of this clamping assembly on size B sheets.

Figure 16.84 Design: Make working drawings, with an assembly drawing, of this lathe dog with a $^3/_4$-in.-diameter screw on size B sheets.

Figure 16.87 Design: Make working drawings, with an assembly drawing, of this roller chain puller (for stretching a chain for assembly) on size B sheets. The prongs should join when closed.

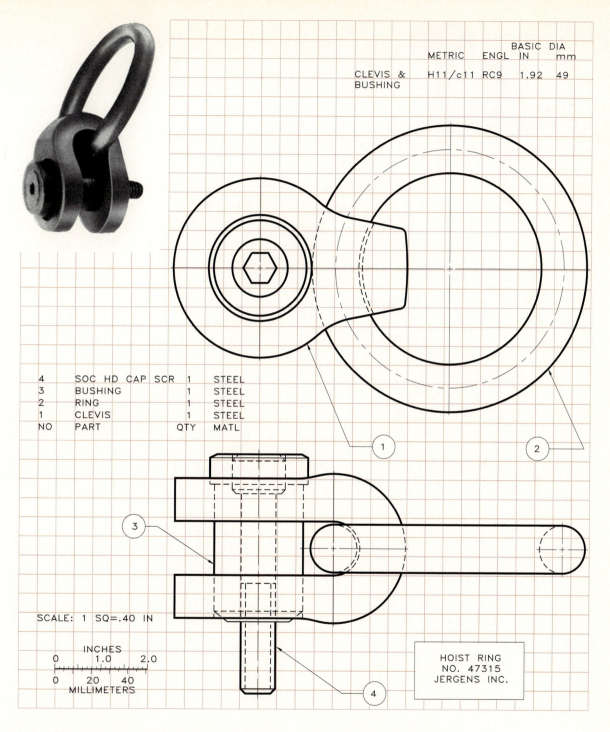

Metric / English / Basic Dia table:

	METRIC	ENGL	BASIC DIA IN	mm
CLEVIS & BUSHING	H11/c11	RC9	1.92	49

Parts list:

NO	PART	QTY	MATL
4	SOC HD CAP SCR	1	STEEL
3	BUSHING	1	STEEL
2	RING	1	STEEL
1	CLEVIS	1	STEEL

SCALE: 1 SQ=.40 IN

INCHES
0   1.0   2.0
0   20   40
MILLIMETERS

HOIST RING
NO. 47315
JERGENS INC.

Figure 16.88 Design: Make full-size working drawings, with an assembly drawing, of this clevis and bushing on size B sheets. (Courtesy of Jergens, Incorporated.)

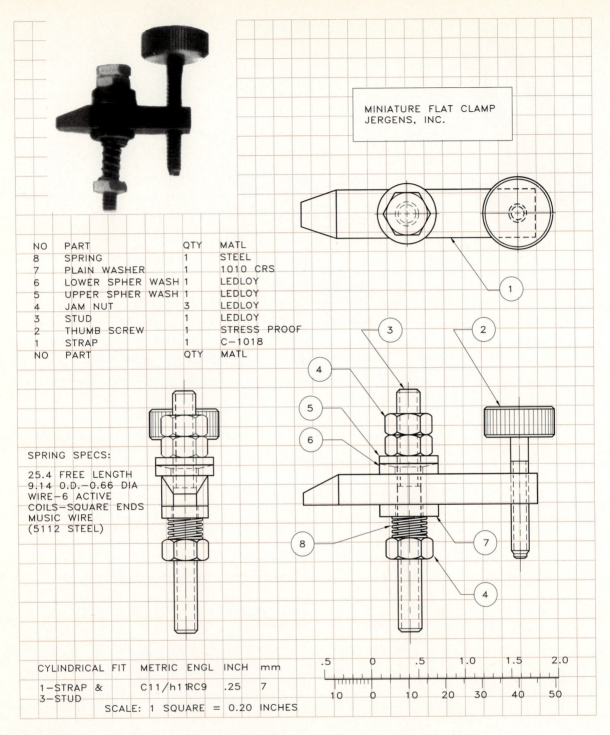

MINIATURE FLAT CLAMP
JERGENS, INC.

NO	PART	QTY	MATL
8	SPRING	1	STEEL
7	PLAIN WASHER	1	1010 CRS
6	LOWER SPHER WASH	1	LEDLOY
5	UPPER SPHER WASH	1	LEDLOY
4	JAM NUT	3	LEDLOY
3	STUD	1	LEDLOY
2	THUMB SCREW	1	STRESS PROOF
1	STRAP	1	C−1018
NO	PART	QTY	MATL

SPRING SPECS:

25.4 FREE LENGTH
9.14 O.D.−0.66 DIA
WIRE−6 ACTIVE
COILS−SQUARE ENDS
MUSIC WIRE
(5112 STEEL)

CYLINDRICAL FIT	METRIC	ENGL	INCH	mm
1−STRAP & 3−STUD	C11/h11 RC9	.25	7

SCALE: 1 SQUARE = 0.20 INCHES

Figure 16.89 Design: Make double-size working drawings, with an assembly drawing, of this miniature flat clamp on size B sheets. (Courtesy of Jergens, Incorporated.)

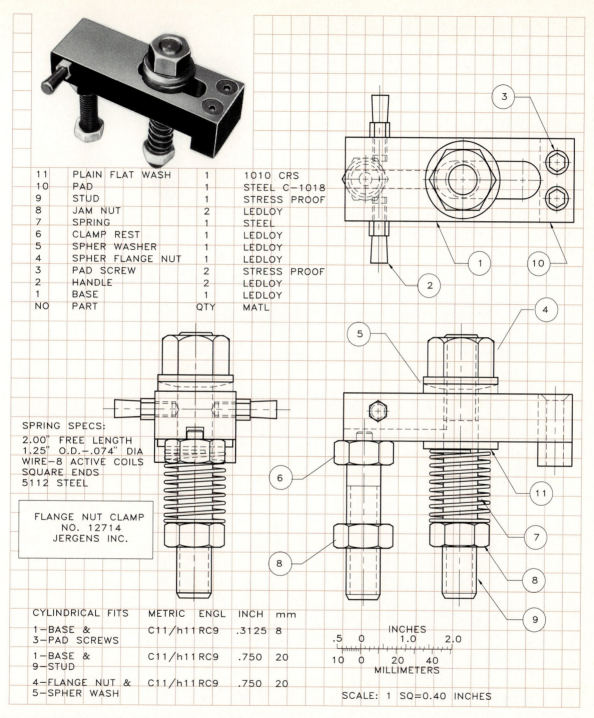

NO	PART	QTY	MATL
11	PLAIN FLAT WASH	1	1010 CRS
10	PAD	1	STEEL C-1018
9	STUD	1	STRESS PROOF
8	JAM NUT	2	LEDLOY
7	SPRING	1	STEEL
6	CLAMP REST	1	LEDLOY
5	SPHER WASHER	1	LEDLOY
4	SPHER FLANGE NUT	1	LEDLOY
3	PAD SCREW	2	STRESS PROOF
2	HANDLE	2	LEDLOY
1	BASE	1	LEDLOY

SPRING SPECS:
2.00" FREE LENGTH
1.25" O.D.−.074" DIA
WIRE−8 ACTIVE COILS
SQUARE ENDS
5112 STEEL

FLANGE NUT CLAMP
NO. 12714
JERGENS INC.

CYLINDRICAL FITS	METRIC	ENGL	INCH	mm
1−BASE & 3−PAD SCREWS	C11/h11	RC9	.3125	8
1−BASE & 9−STUD	C11/h11	RC9	.750	20
4−FLANGE NUT & 5−SPHER WASH	C11/h11	RC9	.750	20

INCHES
.5 0   1.0   2.0
10 0   20   40
MILLIMETERS

SCALE: 1 SQ=0.40 INCHES

Figure 16.90 Design: Make full-size working drawings, with an assembly drawing, of this flange nut clamp on size B sheets. (Courtesy of Jergens, Incorporated.)

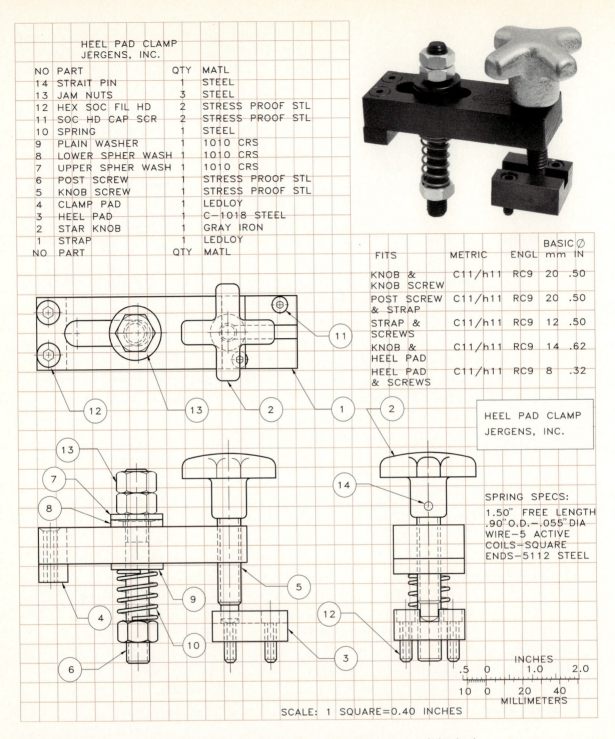

HEEL PAD CLAMP
JERGENS, INC.

NO	PART	QTY	MATL
14	STRAIT PIN	1	STEEL
13	JAM NUTS	3	STEEL
12	HEX SOC FIL HD	2	STRESS PROOF STL
11	SOC HD CAP SCR	2	STRESS PROOF STL
10	SPRING	1	STEEL
9	PLAIN WASHER	1	1010 CRS
8	LOWER SPHER WASH	1	1010 CRS
7	UPPER SPHER WASH	1	1010 CRS
6	POST SCREW	1	STRESS PROOF STL
5	KNOB SCREW	1	STRESS PROOF STL
4	CLAMP PAD	1	LEDLOY
3	HEEL PAD	1	C—1018 STEEL
2	STAR KNOB	1	GRAY IRON
1	STRAP	1	LEDLOY
NO	PART	QTY	MATL

FITS	METRIC	ENGL	BASIC ⌀ mm	IN
KNOB & KNOB SCREW	C11/h11	RC9	20	.50
POST SCREW & STRAP	C11/h11	RC9	20	.50
STRAP & SCREWS	C11/h11	RC9	12	.50
KNOB & HEEL PAD	C11/h11	RC9	14	.62
HEEL PAD & SCREWS	C11/h11	RC9	8	.32

HEEL PAD CLAMP
JERGENS, INC.

SPRING SPECS:
1.50" FREE LENGTH
.90" O.D.—.055" DIA
WIRE—5 ACTIVE
COILS—SQUARE
ENDS—5112 STEEL

INCHES
.5 0   1.0   2.0
10 0   20   40
MILLIMETERS

SCALE: 1 SQUARE=0.40 INCHES

Figure 16.91 Design: Make full-size working drawings, with an assembly drawing, of this heel pad clamp on size B sheets. (Courtesy of Jergens, Incorporated.)

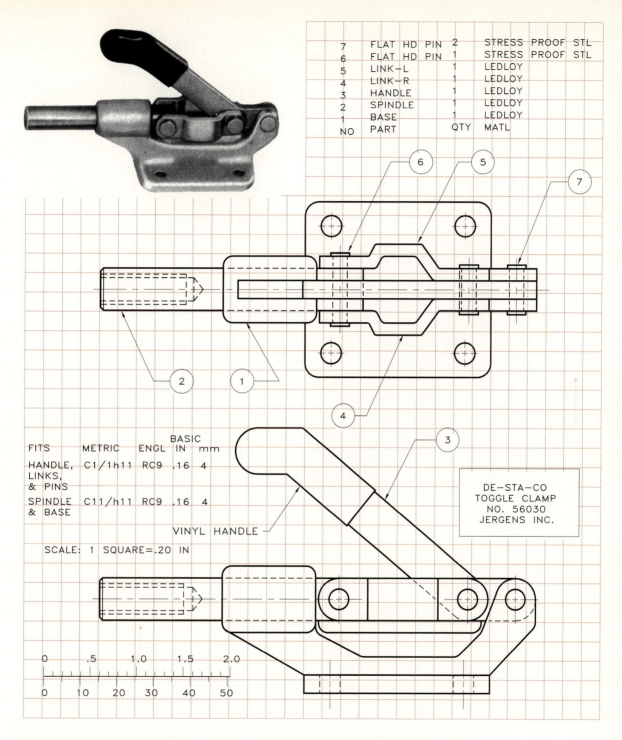

7	FLAT HD PIN	2	STRESS PROOF STL
6	FLAT HD PIN	1	STRESS PROOF STL
5	LINK—L	1	LEDLOY
4	LINK—R	1	LEDLOY
3	HANDLE	1	LEDLOY
2	SPINDLE	1	LEDLOY
1	BASE	1	LEDLOY
NO	PART	QTY	MATL

			BASIC		
FITS	METRIC	ENGL	IN	mm
HANDLE,	C1/1h11	RC9	.16	4
LINKS,				
& PINS				
SPINDLE	C11/h11	RC9	.16	4
& BASE				

VINYL HANDLE

SCALE: 1 SQUARE=.20 IN

DE—STA—CO
TOGGLE CLAMP
NO. 56030
JERGENS INC.

0   .5   1.0   1.5   2.0

0   10   20   30   40   50

Figure 16.92 Design: Make double-size working drawings, with an assembly drawing, of this toggle clamp on size B sheets. (Courtesy of Jergens, Incorporated.)

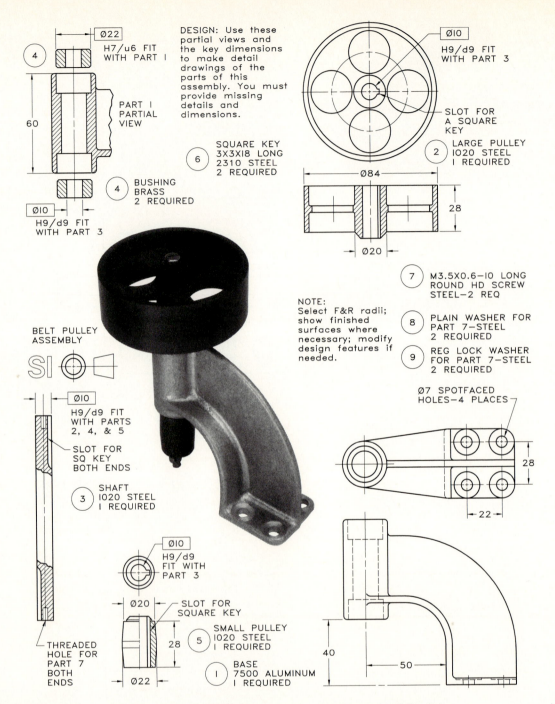

4   Ø22
H7/u6 FIT WITH PART I

PART I PARTIAL VIEW

60

4   BUSHING BRASS 2 REQUIRED

Ø10
H9/d9 FIT WITH PART 3

DESIGN: Use these partial views and the key dimensions to make detail drawings of the parts of this assembly. You must provide missing details and dimensions.

6   SQUARE KEY 3X3XI8 LONG 2310 STEEL 2 REQUIRED

Ø10
H9/d9 FIT WITH PART 3

SLOT FOR A SQUARE KEY

2   LARGE PULLEY 1020 STEEL I REQUIRED

Ø84

28

Ø20

7   M3.5X0.6—I0 LONG ROUND HD SCREW STEEL—2 REQ

NOTE:
Select F&R radii; show finished surfaces where necessary; modify design features if needed.

8   PLAIN WASHER FOR PART 7—STEEL 2 REQUIRED

9   REG LOCK WASHER FOR PART 7—STEEL 2 REQUIRED

BELT PULLEY ASSEMBLY

SI

Ø10
H9/d9 FIT WITH PARTS 2, 4, & 5

SLOT FOR SQ KEY BOTH ENDS

3   SHAFT 1020 STEEL I REQUIRED

Ø7 SPOTFACED HOLES—4 PLACES

28

22

THREADED HOLE FOR PART 7 BOTH ENDS

Ø10
H9/d9 FIT WITH PART 3

Ø20   SLOT FOR SQUARE KEY

28

5   SMALL PULLEY 1020 STEEL I REQUIRED

Ø22

I   BASE 7500 ALUMINUM I REQUIRED

40

50

Figure 16.93 Design: Make full-size working drawings, with an assembly drawing, of this belt pulley assembly on size B sheets. Use your design ability to supply missing details, specifications, and notes.

Reproduction of Drawings

17.1 Introduction

So far we have discussed the preparation of drawings and specifications through the working-drawing stage where detailed drawings are completed on tracing film or paper. Now the drawings must be reproduced, folded, and prepared for transmittal to those who will use them to prepare bids or to fabricate the parts. Several methods of reproduction are available to engineers and technologists for making copies of their drawings. However, most reproduction methods require strong, well-executed line work on the originals in order to produce good copies.

17.2 Types of Reproduction

Drawings made by a drafter are of little use in their original form. If original drawings were handled by checkers and by workers in the field or shop, they would quickly be soiled and damaged, and no copy would be available as a permanent record of the job. Therefore the reproduction of

drawings is necessary for making inexpensive, expendable copies for use by the people who need to use them.

The most often used processes of reproducing engineering drawings are (1) diazo printing, (2) microfilming, (3) xerography, and (4) photostating.

Diazo Printing

The **diazo print** more correctly is called a **whiteprint** or **blue-line print** than a blueprint, because it has a white background and blue lines. Other colors of lines are available, depending on the type of diazo paper used. (Blueprinting, which creates a print with white lines and a blue background, is a wet process that is almost obsolete at the present.) **Figure 17.1** shows a typical diazo printer.

Diazo printing requires that original drawings be made on semitransparent tracing paper, cloth, or film that allows light to pass through the drawing. The diazo paper on which the blue-line print is made is chemically treated, giving it a yellow

Figure 17.1 This typical whiteprinter operates on the diazo process. (Courtesy of Blu-Ray, Incorporated, Essex, CT.)

tint on one side. Diazo paper must be stored away from heat and light to prevent spoilage.

Making a diazo print first requires that the tracing-paper or film drawing be placed face up on the yellow side of the diazo paper (**Fig. 17.2 A**) and then run through the diazo-process machine, exposing the drawing to a built-in light (**Fig. 17.2B**). Light rays pass through the tracing paper and burn away the yellow tint on the diazo paper except where the drawing lines have shielded the paper from the light, similar to how a photographic negative works. The exposed diazo paper becomes a duplicate of the original drawing except that the lines are light yellow and not permanent. When the diazo paper is passed through the developing unit of the diazo machine (**Figs. 17.2C** and **D**), ammonia fumes develop the yellow lines on it into permanent blue lines (**Fig. 17.2E**).

The speed at which the drawing passes under the light determines the darkness of the copy; **the faster the speed, the darker the print is**. A slow speed burns out more of the yellow and produces a clear white background, but some of the lighter lines of the drawing may be lost. Most diazo copies are made at a speed fast enough to give a light tint of blue in the background and dark lines on the copy. Ink drawings give the best reproductions.

Microfilming
Microfilming is a photographic process that converts large drawings into film copies—either aper-

ture cards or roll film. Drawings are photographed on either 16-mm or 35-mm film (**Fig. 17.3**).

The roll film or aperture cards are placed in a microfilm enlarger–printer, where the individual drawings can be viewed on a built-in screen (**Fig. 17.4**). The selected drawings can be printed from the film in standard sizes. Microfilm copies are usually made smaller than the original drawings to save paper and make the drawings easier to use.

Microfilming eliminates the need for large, bulky files of drawings, because hundreds of drawings can be stored in miniature on a small amount of film. The aperture cards shown in **Fig. 17.4** are data processing cards that can be cataloged and recalled by a computer to make them accessible with a minimum of effort.

Xerography
Xerography is an electrostatic process of duplicating drawings on ordinary, unsensitized paper. Originally developed for business and clerical uses, xerography more recently has been used for the reproduction of engineering drawings. The xerographic process is used to reduce the sizes of the drawings being copied (**Fig. 17.5**). The Xerox 2080 can reduce a 24-×-36-inch drawing to 8 × 10 inches.

Photostating
Photostating is a method of enlarging or reducing drawings photographically. **Figure 17.6** shows a combination camera and processor used for photographing drawings and producing high-contrast copies.

The drawing is placed under the glass of the exposure table, which is lit by built-in lamps. The image appears on a glass plate inside the darkroom where it is exposed on photographically sensitive paper. The exposed negative paper is placed in contact with receiver paper, and the two are fed through the developing solution to obtain a photostatic copy. Photostating also can be used to make reproductions on transparent films and for reproducing halftones (photographs with tones of gray).

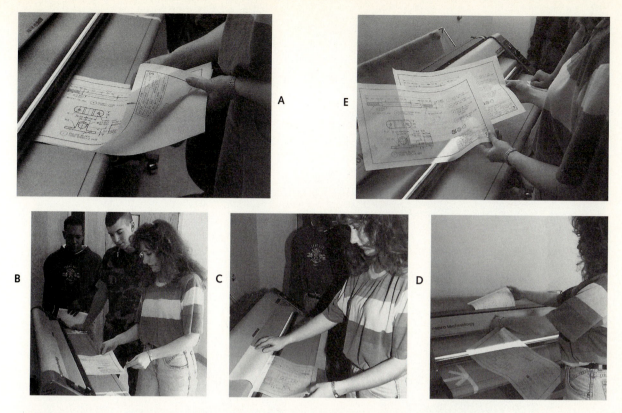

Figure 17.2 Blue-line prints are made by (A) placing the original readable side up and on top of the yellow side of the diazo paper, (B) feeding them under the light of the diazo machine, and (C) feeding the exposed diazo sheet through the ammonia chamber for developing the yellow lines into permanent blue lines. When the final print emerges (D), it is a full-size copy of the original (E).

Figure 17.3 The Micro-Master 35-mm camera and copy table are used for microfilming engineering drawings. (Courtesy of Keuffel & Esser Company, Morristown, NJ.)

Figure 17.4 The Bruning 1200 microfilm enlarger–printer makes drawings up to 18″ × 24″ from aperture cards and roll film. (Courtesy of Bruning Company.)

Figure 17.5 This Xerox Flat Sorter-36 and the Xerox 5080 copier offer plain-paper copying and sorting of drawings larger than 11" × 17". (Courtesy of Xerox Corporation.)

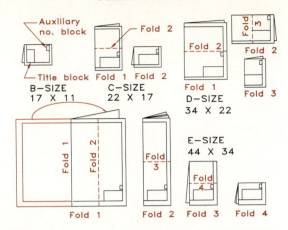

Figure 17.7 All standard drawing sheets can be folded to 8½" × 11" size for filing and storage.

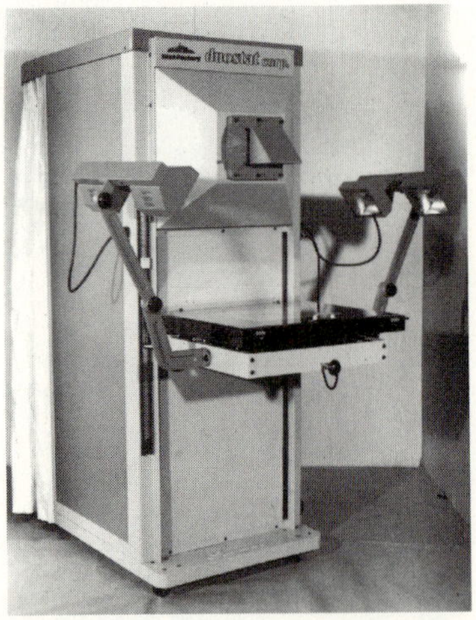

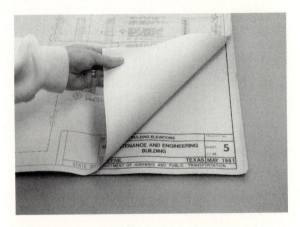

Figure 17.6 This camera–processor enlarges and reduces drawings to be reproduced as photostats. (Courtesy of the Duostat Corporation.)

Figure 17.8 The title block should appear at the right, usually in the lower right-hand corner of the sheet.

17.3 Assembling Drawing Sets

After the original drawings have been copied, they should be stored flat without folding in a file for future use and updating. Prints made from the originals, however, usually are folded or rolled for ease of transmittal from office to office. **Figure 17.7** shows how to fold size B, C, D, and E sheets so that the image will appear on the outside of the fold. Drawings should be folded so that the title

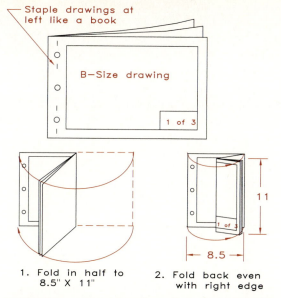

Staple drawings at left like a book

B−Size drawing

1 of 3

11

8.5

1. Fold in half to 8.5" X 11"

2. Fold back even with right edge

Figure 17.9 A set of size B drawings can be assembled by stapling, punching, and folding, as shown here, for safe-keeping in a three-ring notebook with the title block visible on top.

WORKING DRAWING CHECKLIST

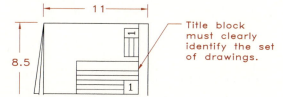

1. Staple along left edge, like a book. Use several staples, never just one.

2. Fold with drawing on outside.

3. Fold drawings as a set, not separately, one at a time.

4. Fold to an 8.5" X 11" modular size.

5. The title block must be visible after folding.

6. Sheets of a set should be uniform in size.

11

8.5

1

1

Title block must clearly identify the set of drawings.

Figure 17.10 Follow these basic rules for assembling sets of working drawing prints.

Figure 17.11 Fax machines, such as this Xerox 7124, can transmit large drawings throughout the country within three minutes over Kinko's Copy Center network. (Courtesy of Xerox Corporation.)

block always shows on the outside at the right, usually in the lower right-hand corner of the page **(Fig. 17.8)**. The final size after folding is 8 1/2 × 11 inches (or 9 × 12 inches).

An alternative method of folding and stapling size B sheets often is used for student assignments so that they can be kept in a three-ring notebook **(Fig. 17.9)**. The basic rules of assembling drawings are listed in **Fig. 17.10**.

17.4 Transmittal of Drawings

Prints of drawings must be delivered to contractors, manufacturers, fabricators, and others who must use the drawings for implementing the project.

Prints usually are placed in standard 9-×-12-inch envelopes and are delivered by hand or mail. Sets of large drawings, which may be 30 × 40 inches in size and contain four or more sheets, usually are rolled and mailed in a mailing tube when folding becomes impractical.

An advanced method of transmitting drawings is by use of the Xerox 7124 engineering fax machines at Kinko's Copy Centers (Fig. 17.11). Within three minutes, large documents can be scanned and transmitted to more than 150 sites throughout the country.

Computer drawings can be transmitted on disk by mailing them to their destination, where hard copies can be plotted and reproduced. This procedure offers substantial savings in shipping charges.

In the future, more drawings will be sent electronically as data and as scanned images over telephone wires, making them available instantaneously at the desired location. What was once a fantasy is now a reality.

18

Three-Dimensional Pictorials

18.1 Introduction

A **three-dimensional pictorial** is a drawing that shows an object's three principal planes, much as they would be captured by a camera. This type of pictorial is an effective means of illustrating a part that is difficult to visualize when only orthographic views are given. Pictorials are especially helpful when a design is complex and when the reader of the drawings is unfamiliar with orthographic drawings.

Sometimes called **technical illustrations**, pictorials are widely used to describe products in catalogs, parts manuals, and maintenance publications. The ability to sketch pictorials rapidly to explain a detail to an associate in the field is an important communication skill.

The four commonly used types of pictorials are obliques, isometrics, axonometrics, and perspectives **(Fig. 18.1)**.

Oblique pictorials: three-dimensional drawings made by projecting from the object with

TYPES OF PICTORIAL SYSTEMS

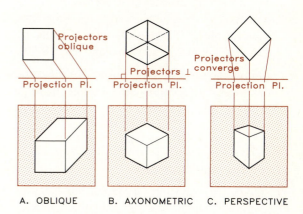

Figure 18.1 There are three pictorial projection systems: (A) oblique pictorials, with parallel projectors oblique to the projection plane; (B) axonometric (including isometric) pictorials, with parallel projectors perpendicular to the projection plane; and (C) perspectives, with converging projectors that make varying angles with the projection plane.

367

OBLIQUES VS. ORTHOGRAPHIC VIEWS

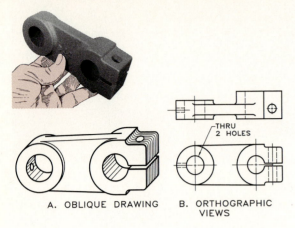

Figure 18.2 The oblique drawing of this part makes it easier to visualize than its representation by orthographic views.

OBLIQUES ARE EASY!

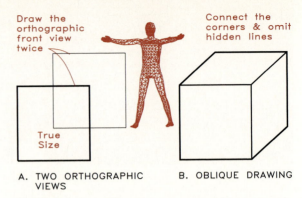

Figure 18.3 Draw two true-size surfaces of a box, connect them at the corners, and you have an oblique.

parallel projectors that are oblique to the picture plane (**Fig. 18.1A**).

Isometric and axonometric pictorials: three-dimensional drawings made by projecting from the object with parallel projectors that are perpendicular to the picture plane (**Fig. 18.1B**).

Perspective pictorials: three-dimensional drawings made with projectors that converge at the viewer's eye and make varying angles with the picture plane (**Fig. 18.1C**).

18.2 Oblique Drawings

The pulley arm shown in **Fig. 18.2** is illustrated by orthographic views and an oblique pictorial. Because most parts are drawn before they actually exist, photographs cannot be taken; therefore the next best option is to draw a three-dimensional pictorial of the part. Details can usually be drawn with more clarity than can be shown in a photograph.

Oblique pictorials are easy to draw. If you can drawn an orthographic view of a part, you are but one step away from drawing an oblique. For example, **Fig. 18.3** shows that drawing a front

view of a box twice and connecting its corners yields an oblique drawing.

Thus an oblique is an orthographic view with a receding axis, drawn at an angle to show the depth of the object. An oblique is a pictorial that does not exist in reality (a camera cannot give an oblique). This type of pictorial is called an **oblique** because its parallel projectors from the object are oblique to the picture plane. These projection principles are covered in Section 18.3.

Types of Obliques

The three basic types of oblique drawings are: cavalier, cabinet, and general (**Fig. 18.4**). For each type, the angle of the receding axis with the horizontal can be at any angle between 0° and 90°. **Measurements along the receding axes of the cavalier oblique are laid off true length, and measurements along the receding axes of the cabinet oblique are laid off half size. The general oblique has measurements along the receding axes that are greater than half size and less than full size.**

Figure 18.5 shows three examples of cavalier obliques of a cube. The receding axis for each is drawn at a different angle, but all are drawn true length. **Figure 18.6** compares cavalier with cabinet obliques.

TYPES OF OBLIQUES

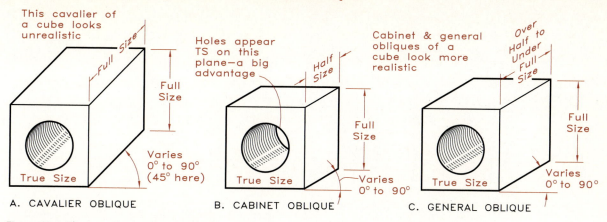

This cavalier of a cube looks unrealistic

Full Size

Full Size

True Size

Varies 0° to 90° (45° here)

A. CAVALIER OBLIQUE

Holes appear TS on this plane—a big advantage

Half Size

Full Size

True Size

Varies 0° to 90°

B. CABINET OBLIQUE

Cabinet & general obliques of a cube look more realistic

Over Half to Under Full Size

Full Size

True Size

Varies 0° to 90°

C. GENERAL OBLIQUE

Figure 18.4 There are three types of obliques:

A The cavalier oblique has a receding axis at any angle and true-length measurements along the receding axis.

B The cabinet oblique has a receding axis at any angle and half-size measurements along the receding axis.

C The general oblique has a receding axis at any angle and measurements along the receding axis larger than half size and less than full size.

CAVALIER OBLIQUES

Drawn with standard angles

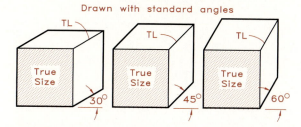

TL

True Size

30°

TL

True Size

45°

TL

True Size

60°

Figure 18.5 A cavalier oblique usually has its receding axis as one of the standard angles of drafting triangles. Each gives a different view of a cube.

CAVALIER VS. CABINET OBLIQUES

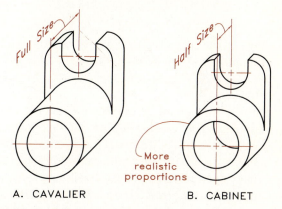

Full Size

Half Size

More realistic proportions

A. CAVALIER

B. CABINET

Figure 18.6 Measurements along the receding axis of a cavalier oblique are full size, and those in a cabinet oblique are half size.

Constructing Obliques

You can easily begin a cavalier oblique by drawing a box using the overall dimensions of height, width, and depth with light construction lines. As demonstrated in **Fig. 18.7**, first draw the front view as a true-size orthographic view. True mea-

surements must be made parallel to the three axes and transferred from the orthographic views with your dividers. Then remove the notches from the

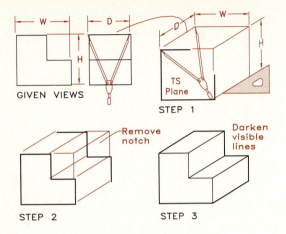

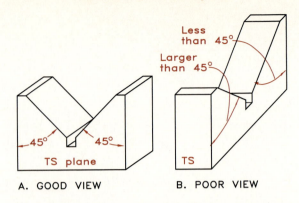

Figure 18.7 Constructing a cavalier oblique:
Step 1 Draw the front surface of the object as a true-size plane. Draw the receding axis at a convenient angle and measure its depth as the true distance D transferred from the side view with dividers.

Step 2 Draw the notch in the front plane and project it to the rear plane.

Step 3 Darken the lines to complete the drawing.

Figure 18.8 Objects with angular features should be drawn in oblique so that the angles appear true size, the good view is as descriptive as possible, and its construction is simple.

LOCATING ANGLES WITH COORDINATES

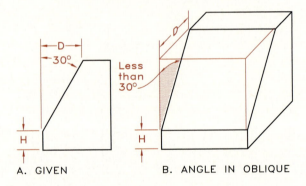

blocked-in construction box to complete the oblique.

Angles

Angular measurements can be made on the true-size plane of an oblique, but not on the other two planes. Note in **Fig. 18.8** that a true angle can be measured on a true-size surface, but in **Fig. 18.9** angles along receding planes are either smaller or larger than their true sizes. **A better, easier-to-draw oblique is obtained when angles are drawn to appear true size.**

To construct an angle in an oblique on one of the receding planes, you must use coordinates, as shown in Fig. 18.9. To find the surface that slopes 30° from the front surface, locate the vertex of the angle, H distance from the bottom. To find the upper end of the sloping plane, measure the distance D along the receding axis. Transfer H and D

Figure 18.9 Angles that do not lie in a true-size plane of an oblique must be located with coordinates.

to the oblique with your dividers. The angle in the oblique is not equal to the 30° angle in the orthographic view.

Cylinders

The major advantage of an oblique is that circular features can be drawn as true circles on its frontal plane (Fig. 18.10). Draw the centerlines of the circular end at A and construct the receding axis at

CAVALIER OBLIQUE CYLINDER

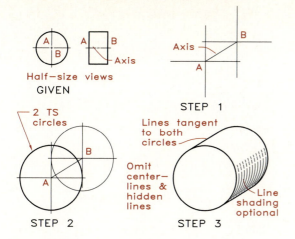

Figure 18.10 Drawing an oblique of a cylinder:
Step 1 Draw axis AB and locate the centers of the circular ends of the cylinder at A and B. Because the axis is true length, this is a cavalier oblique.

Step 2 Draw a true-size circle with its center at A by using a compass or computer-graphics techniques.

Step 3 Draw the other circular end with its center at B and connect the circles with tangent lines parallel to axis AB.

SEMICIRCULAR FEATURES

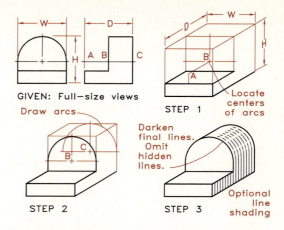

Figure 18.11 Drawing semicircular features in oblique:
Step 1 Block in the overall dimensions of the cavalier oblique with light construction lines, ignoring the semicircular features.

Step 2 Locate centers B and C and draw arcs with a compass or by computer tangent to the sides of the construction boxes.

Step 3 Connect the arcs with lines tangent to each arc and parallel to axis BC and darken the lines.

the desired angle. Locate the end at B by measuring along the axis, draw circles at each end at centers A and B, and draw tangents to both circles.

These same principles apply to construction of the object having semicircular features shown in **Fig. 18.11**. Position the oblique so that the semicircular features are true size. Locate centers A, B, and C and the two semicircles. Then complete the cavalier oblique.

Circles

Circular features drawn as true circles on a true-size plane of an oblique pictorial appear on the receding planes as ellipses.

The four-center ellipse method is a technique of constructing an approximate ellipse with a compass and four centers (**Fig. 18.12**). The ellipse

is tangent to the inside of a rhombus drawn with sides equal to the circle's diameter. Drawing the four arcs produces the ellipse.

The four-center ellipse method will not work for the cabinet or general oblique, but coordinates must be used. **Figure 18.13** illustrates the method of locating coordinates on the planes of cavalier and cabinet obliques. For the cabinet oblique, the coordinates along the receding axis are half size, and the coordinates along the horizontal axis (true-size axis) are full size. Draw the ellipse with an irregular curve or an ellipse template that approximates the plotted points.

Whenever possible, oblique drawings of objects with circular features should be positioned so circles can be drawn as true circles instead of ellipses. The left view in **Fig. 18.14** is

FOUR-CENTER ELLIPSE

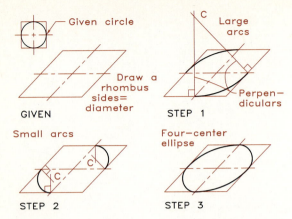

Figure 18.12 Constructing a four-center ellipse in oblique:

Given Block in the circle to be drawn in oblique with a square tangent to the circle. This square becomes a rhombus on the oblique plane.

Step 1 Draw construction lines perpendicular to the points of tangency to locate the centers for drawing two segments of the ellipse.

Step 2 Locate the centers for the two remaining arcs with perpendiculars drawn from adjacent tangent points.

Step 3 Draw the four arcs, which yield an approximate ellipse.

CIRCLES ON FACES OF CUBES

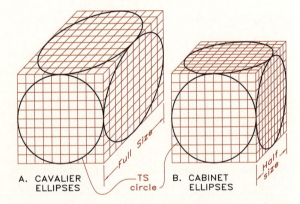

Figure 18.13 Circular features on the faces of cavalier and cabinet obliques are compared here. Ellipses on the receding planes of cabinet obliques must be plotted by coordinates. The spacing of the coordinates along the receding axis of cabinet obliques is half size.

VIEWPOINTS FOR OBLIQUES

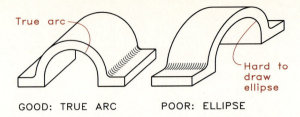

Figure 18.14 An oblique should be positioned so that circular and curving features may be drawn most easily.

CURVES BY COORDINATES

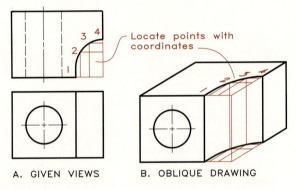

Figure 18.15 Coordinates are used to find points along irregular curves in oblique. Projecting the points downward a distance equal to the height of the object yields the lower curve.

better than the one on the right because it gives a more descriptive view of the part and is easier to draw.

Curves

Irregular curves in oblique pictorials must be plotted point by point with coordinates **(Fig. 18.15)**. Transfer the coordinates from the orthographic to the oblique view and draw the curve through the plotted points with an irregular curve. If the object has a uniform thickness, plot the points for the lower curve by projecting vertically downward from the upper points a distance equal to the object's height.

PLOTTING ELLIPTICAL FEATURES

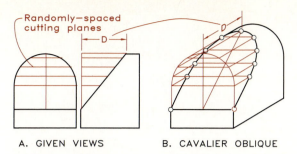

A. GIVEN VIEWS   B. CAVALIER OBLIQUE

Figure 18.16 Construction of an elliptical feature on an inclined surface in oblique requires the use of three-dimensional coordinates to locate points on the curve.

SKETCHING OBLIQUES

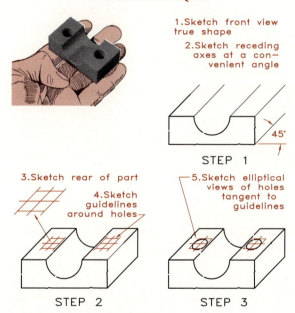

1. Sketch front view true shape
2. Sketch receding axes at a convenient angle

STEP 1

3. Sketch rear of part
4. Sketch guidelines around holes
5. Sketch elliptical views of holes tangent to guidelines

STEP 2   STEP 3

Figure 18.17 Sketching obliques:

Step 1 Sketch the front of the object as true-size surface and draw a receding axis from each corner.

Step 2 Lay off the depth, D, along the receding axes to locate the rear of the part. Lightly sketch pictorial boxes as guidelines for drawing the holes.

Step 3 Sketch the holes inside the boxes and darken all lines.

DIMENSIONING AN OBLIQUE

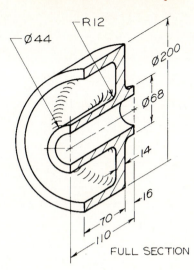

FULL SECTION

Figure 18.18 Oblique pictorials can be drawn as sections and dimensioned to serve as working drawings.

To obtain the elliptical feature on the inclined surface shown in **Fig 18.16**, use a series of coordinates to locate points along its curve. Connect the plotted points by using an irregular curve or ellipse template.

Sketching

Understanding the principles of oblique construction is essential for sketching obliques freehand. The sketch of the part shown in **Fig. 18.17** is based on the principles discussed, but its proportions were determined by eye instead of with scales and dividers.

Lightly drawn guidelines need not be erased when you darken the final lines. When sketching on tracing vellum, you can place a printed grid under the sheet to provide guidelines. Refer to Chapter 6 to review sketching techniques if needed.

Dimensioned Obliques

Dimensioned sectional views of obliques provide excellent, easily understood descriptions of objects (**Fig. 18.18**). Apply numerals and lettering

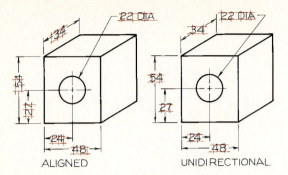

Figure 18.19 Either of these methods—aligned or unidirectional—is acceptable for dimensioning obliques.

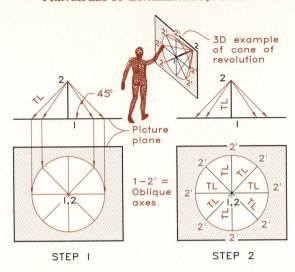

Figure 18.20 This drawing demonstrates the underlying principle of the cavalier oblique by using a series of projectors to form a cone:

Step 1 Each element from point 2 makes a 45° angle with the picture plane.

Step 2 The projected lengths of 1–2' are equal in length to line 1–2, which is perpendicular to the picture plane. Thus the receding axis of a cavalier oblique is true length and at any angle.

in oblique pictorials by using either the aligned method (with numerals aligned with the dimension lines) or the unidirectional method (with numerals positioned horizontally regardless of the direction of the dimension lines), as shown in **Fig. 18.19**. Notes connected with leaders are positioned horizontally in both methods.

18.3 Oblique Projection Theory

Now that you have a general understanding of oblique pictorials, you should know the theory on which this system is based. **Oblique projection (Fig. 18.20)** is the basis of oblique drawings. Receding axis 1–2 is perpendicular to the frontal projection plane. Projectors drawn from point 2 at 45° to the projection plane yield lengths on the front surface that are the same length as 1–2 (true length, in other words). Infinitely many 45° projectors form a cone of projectors with its apex at 2.

The true-length projections of lines 1–2' represent receding axes that can be used for cavalier obliques, which by definition, have true-length dimensions along their receding axes. Do not use a vertical or a horizontal receding axis, but one between those limits.

To distinguish oblique projection from oblique drawing, as described in this chapter so far,

observe the top and side views of a part and the picture planes shown in **Fig. 18.21**. In an oblique projection, projectors from the top and side views are oblique to the edge views of the projection planes, hence the name *oblique*.

Your line of sight can yield obliques with receding axes longer than true length (which should be avoided). Because of this shortcoming and the complexity of construction, **oblique pictorials usually are oblique drawings rather than oblique projections.**

18.4 Isometric Pictorials

In **Fig. 18.22** the pulley arm is drawn in orthographic views and in a three-dimensional pictorial

PRINCIPLES OF OBLIQUE PROJECTION

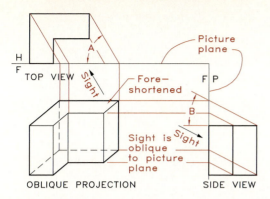

Figure 18.21 An oblique projection may be drawn at varying angles of sight. However, a line of sight making an angle of less than 45° with the picture plane would result in a receding axis longer than its true length, thereby distorting the pictorial.

ISOMETRICS VS. ORTHOGRAPHIC VIEWS

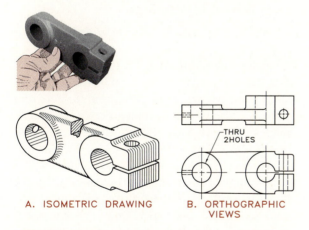

Figure 18.22 An isometric drawing gives a more realistic view than an oblique, and it is easier to visualize than are orthographic views.

drawing. The pictorial is an isometric drawing in which the three planes of the object are equally foreshortened, representing the object more realistically than an oblique drawing can.

PROJECTION VS. DRAWING

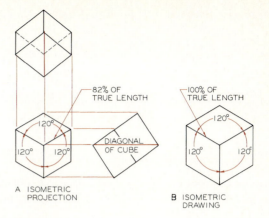

Figure 18.23

A A true isometric projection is found by constructing a view in which the diagonal of a cube appears as a point and the axes are foreshortened.

B An isometric drawing is not a true projection because the dimensions are true size rather than foreshortened.

With more realism comes more difficulty of construction. In particular, circles and curves do not appear true shape on any of the three isometric planes.

Isometric Projection Versus Drawing

In isometric projection, parallel projectors are perpendicular to the imaginary projection (picture) plane in which the diagonal of a cube appears as a point (Fig. 18.23). An isometric pictorial constructed by projection is called an **isometric projection**, with the three axes foreshortened to 82% of their true lengths and 120° apart. The name *isometric*, which means equal measurement, aptly describes this type of projection because the planes are equally foreshortened.

An **isometric drawing** is a convenient approximate isometric pictorial in which the measurements are shown full size along the three axes rather than at 82% as in isometric projection **(Fig. 18.24).** Thus the isometric drawing method allows you to measure true dimensions with standard

PROJECTION VS. DRAWING

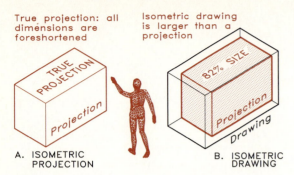

Figure 18.24 The true isometric projection is foreshortened to 82% of full size. The isometric drawing is drawn full size for convenience.

POSITIONING OF AXES

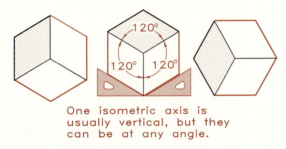

One isometric axis is usually vertical, but they can be at any angle.

Figure 18.25 Isometric axes are spaced 120° apart, but they can be revolved into any position. Usually, one axis is vertical, but it can be at any angle with axis spacing remaining the same.

scales and lay them off with dividers along the three axes. The only difference between the two is the larger size of the drawing. Consequently, **isometric drawings are used much more often than isometric projections.**

The axes of isometric drawings are separated by 120° (**Fig. 18.25**), but more often than not, one of the axes selected is vertical, since most objects have vertical lines. Isometrics without a vertical axis are still isometrics.

ISOMETRIC LINES AND PLANES

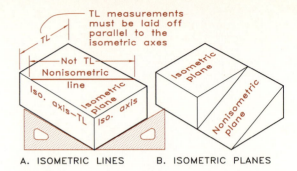

Figure 18.26
A Isometric lines (parallel to the three axes) give true measurements, but nonisometric lines do not.

B Here, the three isometric planes are equally foreshortened, and the nonisometric plane is inclined at an angle to one of the isometric planes.

18.5 Isometric Drawings

An isometric drawing is begun by drawing three axes 120° apart. Lines parallel to these axes are called **isometric lines** (**Fig. 18.26A**). You can make true measurements along isometric lines but not along nonisometric lines. The three surfaces of a cube in an isometric drawing are called **isometric planes** (**Fig. 18.26B**). Planes parallel to those planes also are isometric planes.

To draw an isometric pictorial, you need a scale, dividers, and a 30°–60° triangle (**Fig. 18.27**). Begin selecting the three axes and then constructing a plane of the isometric from the dimensions of height, H, and depth, D. Add the third dimension of width, W, and complete the isometric drawing.

Use light construction lines to block in all isometric drawings (**Fig. 18.28**) and the overall dimensions W, D, and H. Take other dimensions from the given views with dividers and measure along their isometric lines to locate notches in the blocked-in drawing.

Figure 18.29 shows an isometric drawing of a slightly more complex object, with two notches.

ISOMETRIC OF A BOX

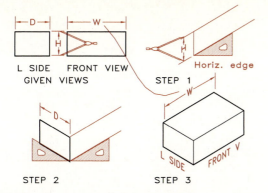

Figure 18.27 Drawing an isometric of a box:
Step 1 Use a 30°–60° triangle and a horizontal straight-edge to construct a vertical line equal to the height, H, and draw two isometric lines through each end.

Step 2 Draw two 30° lines and locate the depth, D, by transferring this dimension from the given views with dividers.

Step 3 Locate the width, W, of the object, complete the surfaces of the isometric box, and darken the lines.

ISOMETRIC OF A SIMPLE OBJECT

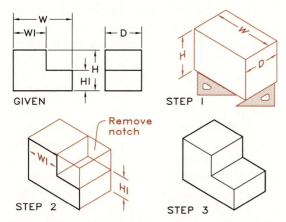

Figure 18.28 Constructing an isometric of a simple part:
Step 1 Construct an isometric drawing of a box by using the overall dimensions W, D, and H from the given views.

Step 2 Locate the notch in the box by transferring dimensions W1 and H1 from the given views with dividers.

Step 3 Darken the lines to complete the drawing.

ISOMETRIC DRAWING

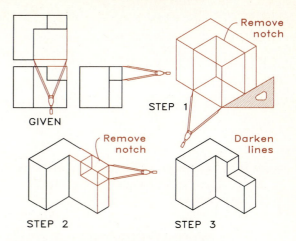

Figure 18.29 Laying out an isometric drawing:
Step 1 Use the overall dimensions given to block in the object with light lines and remove the large notch.

Step 2 Remove the small notch.

Step 3 Darken the lines to complete the drawing.

The object was blocked in by using the H, W, and D dimensions. The notches in the block are removed to complete the drawing.

Angles

You cannot measure an angle's true size in an isometric drawing because the surfaces of an isometric are not true size. Instead, you must locate angles with isometric coordinates measured parallel to the axes (**Fig. 18.30**). Lines AD and BC are equal in length in the orthographic view, but they are shorter and longer than true length in the isometric drawing. **Figure 18.31** shows a similar situation, where two angles drawn in isometric are less than and greater than their true dimensions in the orthographic view.

Figure 18.32 shows how to construct an isometric drawing of an object with inclined surfaces. Blocking in the object with its overall dimensions with light construction lines is followed by removal of the inclined portions.

ISOMETRIC: INCLINED SURFACES

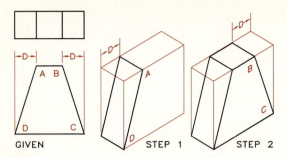

Figure 18.30 Use coordinates measured along the isometric axes to obtain inclined surfaces. Angular lines are not true length in isometric.

ANGLES IN ISOMETRIC

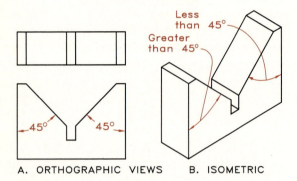

Figure 18.31 Angles in isometric may appear larger or smaller than they actually are.

Circles

Three methods of constructing circles in isometric drawings are **point plotting**, **four-center ellipse construction**, and **ellipse template usage**.

Point plotting is a method of using a series of x and y coordinates to locate points on a circle in the given orthographic views. The coordinates are then transferred with dividers to the isometric drawing to locate the points on the ellipse one at a time (**Fig. 18.33**).

Block in the cylinder with light construction lines and show the centerlines. Draw coordinates on the

ISOMETRIC: INCLINED PLANES

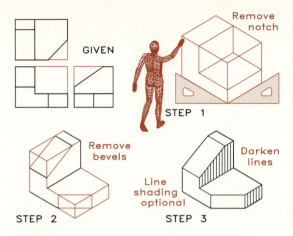

Figure 18.32 Drawing inclined planes in isometric:
Step 1 Block the object with light lines, using the overall dimensions, and remove the notch.

Step 2 Locate the ends of the inclined planes by using measurements parallel to the isometric axes.

Step 3 Darken the lines to complete the drawing.

upper plane and use the height dimension to locate the points on the lower plane. Draw the ellipses with an irregular curve or an ellipse template.

A plotted ellipse is a true ellipse and is equivalent to a 35° ellipse drawn on an isometric plane. An example of a design composed of circular features drawn in isometric is the handwheel shown in **Fig. 18.34**.

Four-center ellipse construction is the method of producing an approximate ellipse by using four arcs drawn with a compass (**Fig. 18.35**). Draw an isometric rhombus with its sides equal to the diameter of the circle to be represented. Find the four centers by constructing perpendiculars to the sides of the rhombus at the midpoints of each side, and draw the four arcs to complete the ellipse. You may draw four-center ellipses on all three isometric planes because each plane is equally foreshortened (**Fig. 18.36**). Although it is only an approximate ellipse, the four-center ellipse technique is accept-

POINT-BY-POINT PLOTTED CYLINDERS

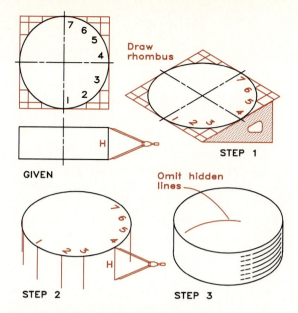

Figure 18.33 Plotting circles in isometric:

Step 1 Block in the circle by using its overall dimensions. Transfer the coordinates used to locate points on the circle to the isometric plane and connect them with a smooth curve.

Step 2 Drop each point a distance equal to the height of the cylinder to obtain the lower ellipse.

Step 3 Connect the two ellipses with tangent lines and darken the lines.

INDUSTRIAL EXAMPLE

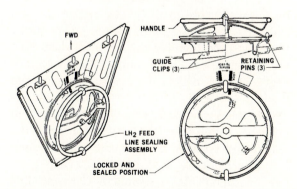

Figure 18.34 This handwheel assembly proposed for use in an orbital workshop is an example of parts with circular features drawn as ellipses in isometric. (Courtesy of NASA.)

FOUR-CENTER ELLIPSE

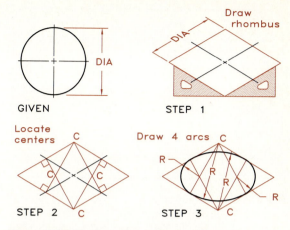

Figure 18.35 The four-center ellipse method:

Step 1 Use the diameter of the given circle to draw an isometric rhombus and the centerlines.

Step 2 Draw light construction lines perpendicularly from the midpoints of each side to locate four centers.

Step 3 Draw four arcs from the centers to represent an ellipse tangent to the rhombus.

APPLICATION OF FOUR-CENTER ELLIPSES

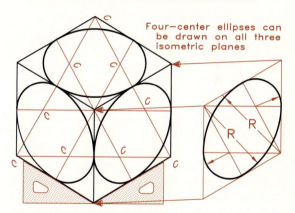

Figure 18.36 Four-center ellipses may be drawn on all three surfaces of an isometric drawing.

able for drawing large ellipses and as a way to draw ellipses when an ellipse template is unavailable.

Isometric ellipse templates are specially designed for drawing ellipses in isometric (**Fig.**

THE ISOMETRIC ELLIPSE TEMPLATE

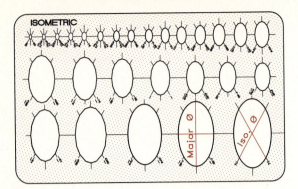

Figure 18.37 The isometric template (a 35° ellipse) is designed for drawing elliptical features in isometric. The isometric diameters of the ellipses are not their major diameters but are diameters that are parallel to the isometric axes.

CYLINDER: FOUR-CENTER METHOD

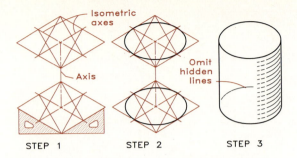

Figure 18.39 A cylinder using the four-center method:
Step 1 Draw an isometric rhombus at each end of the cylinder's axis.

Step 2 Draw a four-center ellipse within each rhombus.

Step 3 Draw lines tangent to each rhombus to complete the drawing.

ELLIPSE TERMINOLOGY

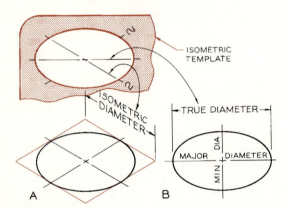

Figure 18.38
A Measure the diameter of a circle along the isometric axes. The major diameter of an isometric ellipse thus is larger than the measured diameter.

B The minor diameter is perpendicular to the major diameter.

18.37). The numerals on the templates represent the isometric diameters of the ellipses because diameters are measured parallel to the isometric axes of an isometric drawing (**Fig. 18.38**). Recall that the **maximum diameter across the ellipse is**

its major diameter, which is a true diameter. Thus the size of the diameter marked on the template is less than the ellipse's major diameter. You may use the isometric ellipse template to draw an ellipse by constructing centerlines of the ellipse in isometric and aligning the ellipse template with those isometric lines (Fig. 18.38).

Cylinders

A cylinder may be drawn in isometric by using the four-center ellipse method (**Fig. 18.39**). Use the isometric axes and centerline axis to construct a rhombus at each end of the cylinder. Then draw the ellipses at each end, connect them with tangent lines, and darken the lines to complete the drawing.

An easier way to draw a cylinder is to use an isometric ellipse template (**Fig. 18.40**). **Draw the axis of the cylinder and construct perpendiculars at each end. Because the axis of a right cylinder is perpendicular to the major diameter of its elliptical ends, position the ellipse template with its major diameter perpendicular to the axis.** Draw the ellipses at each end, connect them with

CYLINDER: ELLIPSE TEMPLATE

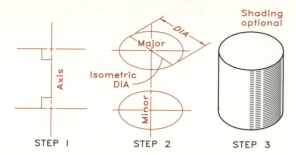

Figure 18.40 A cylinder using ellipse template method:
Step 1 Establish the length of the axis of the cylinder and draw perpendiculars at each end.

Step 2 Draw the elliptical ends by aligning the major diameter of the ellipse template with the perpendiculars at the ends of the axis. The isometric diameters of the isometric ellipse template will align with two isometric axes.

Step 3 Connect the ellipses with tangent lines to complete the drawing and omit hidden lines.

USING THE ELLIPSE TEMPLATE

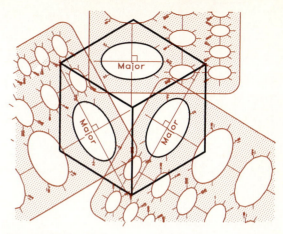

Figure 18.42 Position the isometric ellipse template as shown for drawing ellipses of various sizes on the three isometric planes.

CYLINDRICAL HOLES IN ISOMETRIC

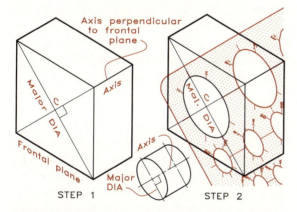

Figure 18.41 Constructing cylindrical holes through a block:
Step 1 Locate the center of the hole on a face of the isometric drawing. Draw the axis of the cylinder from the center parallel to the isometric axis perpendicular to the plane of the circle. The major diameter is perpendicular to this axis.

Step 2 Use the 2-in. ellipse template to draw the ellipse by aligning guidelines on the template with the major and minor diameters drawn on the front surface.

tangent lines, and darken the visible lines to complete the drawing.

To construct a cylindrical hole in a block (**Fig. 18.41**), begin by locating the center of the hole on the isometric plane. Draw the axis of the cylinder parallel to the isometric axis that is perpendicular to the plane of the ellipse through its center. Align the ellipse template with the major diameter, which makes a 90° angle with the cylindrical axis and complete the elliptical view of the cylindrical hole.

The isometric ellipse template can be used to draw ellipses on all three planes of an isometric drawing. On each plane, the major diameter is perpendicular to the isometric axis of the adjacent perpendicular plane. The isometric diameters marked on the template align with the isometric axes. All ellipses drawn on isometric planes must align in the directions shown in **Fig. 18.42**.

Rounded Corners

The rounded corners of an object may be drawn with an ellipse template (**Fig. 18.43**). Block in each corner with light construction lines, draw centerlines, draw the major diameter, and construct

ROUNDED CORNERS

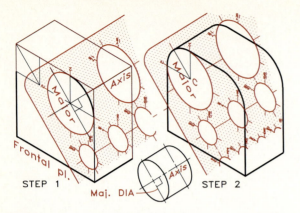

Figure 18.43 Drawing rounded corners:
Step 1 Draw the centerlines and isometric axes at the corners. Align the ellipse template with these guidelines and draw one quarter of the ellipse.

Step 2 Draw the other elliptical corner in the same manner with the same size ellipse.

ISOMETRIC: CONE

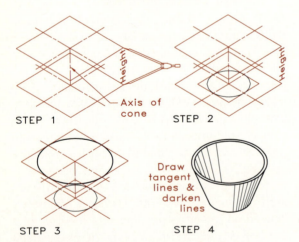

Figure 18.44 Constructing a cone in isometric:
Step 1 Draw the axis of the cone and block in the larger end at both ends.

Step 2 Block in the smaller end of the cone.

Step 3 Block in the larger end of the cone.

Step 4 Connect the ellipses with tangents, draw the cone's wall thickness, and darken the lines to complete the drawing.

INCLINED SURFACE

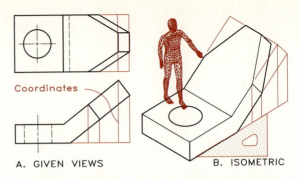

A. GIVEN VIEWS   **B. ISOMETRIC**

Figure 18.45 Inclined surfaces in isometric must be located with three-dimensional coordinates parallel to the isometric axes. True angles cannot be measured in isometric drawings.

ellipses at each corner by positioning the template as shown. The rounded corners may also be constructed by using the four-center ellipse method (see Fig. 18.39) or by plotting points with coordinates (see Fig. 18.33).

A similar drawing involving the construction of ellipses is the conical shape shown in **Fig. 18.44**. Block in the ellipses on the upper and lower surfaces. Then draw the circular features by using a template or the four-center method, and draw lines tangent to each ellipse.

Inclined Planes
Inclined planes in isometric may be located by coordinates, but they cannot be measured with a protractor because they do not appear true size. **Figure 18.45** illustrates the coordinate method. Use horizontal and vertical coordinates (in the x and y directions) to locate key points on the orthographic views. Transfer these coordinates to the isometric drawing with dividers to show the features of the inclined surface.

Curves
Irregular curves in isometric must be plotted point by point, with coordinates locating each point. Locate points A through F in the ortho-

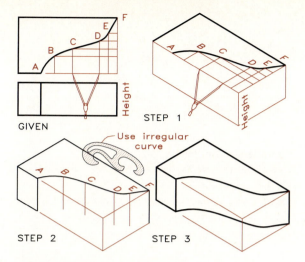

GIVEN

STEP 1

Use irregular curve

STEP 2

STEP 3

Figure 18.46 Plotting irregular curves:

Given Locate a series of points on the irregular curve with coordinates parallel to the W, D, and H dimensions.

Step 1 Block in the shape by using the overall dimensions. Locate points on the irregular curve with coordinates transferred from the orthographic views.

Step 2 Project these points downward the distance H from the upper points to obtain the lower curve.

Step 3 Connect the points and darken the lines.

graphic view with coordinates of width and depth (**Fig. 18.46**). Then transfer them to the isometric view of the blocked-in part and connect them with an irregular curve.

Project points on the upper curve downward a distance of H, the height of the part, to locate points on the lower ellipse. Connect these points with an irregular curve and darken the lines to complete the isometric.

Ellipses on Nonisometric Planes

Ellipses on nonisometric planes in an isometric drawing, such as the one shown in **Fig. 18.47**, must be found by locating a series of points on the curve. Locate three-dimensional coordinates in the orthographic views and then transfer them to

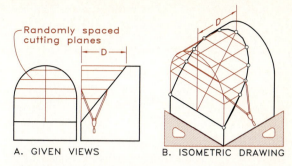

A. GIVEN VIEWS   B. ISOMETRIC DRAWING

Figure 18.47 To construct ellipses on inclined planes, draw coordinates to locate points in the orthographic views. Then transfer the three-dimensional coordinates to the isometric drawing and connect them with a smooth curve.

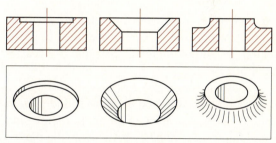

A. SPOTFACE   B. COUNTERSUNK   C. BOSS

Figure 18.48 These examples of circular features in isometric may be drawn by using ellipse templates.

the isometric with dividers. Connect the plotted points with an irregular curve or an ellipse template selected to approximate the plotted points. It will not be an isometric ellipse template, but one that fits the plotted points.

18.6 Technical Illustration

Machine Parts

Figure 18.48 shows orthographic and isometric views of a **spotface**, **countersink**, and **boss**. These

THREADS IN ISOMETRIC

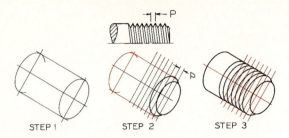

STEP I STEP 2 STEP 3

Figure 18.49 Threads in isometric:
Step 1 Using an ellipse template, draw the cylinder to be threaded.

Step 2 Lay off perpendiculars, spacing them apart at a distance equal to the pitch of the thread, P.

Step 3 Draw a series of ellipses to represent the threads. Draw the chamfered end by using an ellipse whose major diameter is equal to the root diameter of the threads.

NUT IN ISOMETRIC

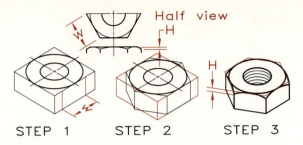

STEP 1 STEP 2 STEP 3

Figure 18.50 Constructing a nut:
Step 1 Use the overall dimensions of the nut to block in the nut.

Step 2 Construct the hexagonal sides at the top and bottom.

Step 3 Draw the chamfer with an irregular curve. Draw the threads to complete the drawing.

---

features may be drawn in isometric by point-by-point plotting of the circular features, the four-center or ellipse template method (the easiest method).

A threaded shaft may be drawn in isometric as shown in **Fig. 18.49**. First draw the cylinder in isometric. Draw the major diameters of the crest lines equally separated by distance P, the pitch of the thread. Then draw ellipses by aligning the major diameter of the ellipse template with the perpendiculars to the cylinder's axis. Use a smaller ellipse at the end for the 45° chamfered end.

Figure 18.50 shows how to draw a hexagon-head nut with an ellipse template. Block in the nut and draw an ellipse tangent to the rhombus. Construct the hexagon by locating distance W across a flat parallel to the isometric axes. To find the other sides of the hexagon, draw lines tangent to the ellipse. Lay off distance H at each corner to establish the chamfers.

Figure 18.51 depicts a hexagon-head bolt in two positions. The washer face is on the lower side of the head, and the chamfer is on the upper side.

Figure 18.52 shows how to use a portion of a sphere to draw a round-head screw. Construct a hemisphere and locate the centerline of the slot

BOLT IN ISOMETRIC

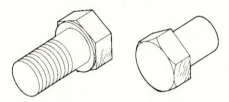

Figure 18.51 Isometric drawings of the lower and upper sides of a hexagon-head bolt.

BOLT HEAD IN ISOMETRIC

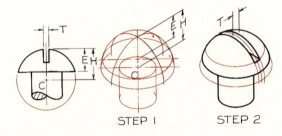

STEP I STEP 2

Figure 18.52 Drawing spherical features:
Step 1 Use an isometric ellipse template to draw the elliptical features of a round-head screw.

Step 2 Draw the slot in the head and darken the lines to complete the drawing.

SECTION IN ISOMETRIC

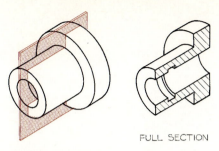

FULL SECTION

Figure 18.53 Isometric sections can be used to clarify the internal features of a part.

ALIGNED VS. UNIDIRECTIONAL DIMENSIONS

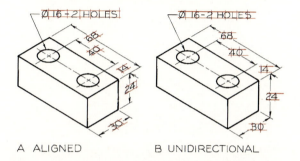

A ALIGNED   B UNIDIRECTIONAL

Figure 18.54 Either of the techniques shown—aligned or unidirectional—is acceptable for placing dimensions on isometric drawings. Guidelines should always be used for lettering.

along one of the isometric planes. Measure the head's thickness, E, from the highest point on the sphere.

Sections

A full section drawn in isometric can clarify internal details that might otherwise be overlooked (**Fig. 18.53**). Half sections also may be used advantageously.

Dimensioned Isometrics

When you dimension isometric drawings, place numerals on the dimension lines, using either

FILLETS & ROUNDS IN ISOMETRIC

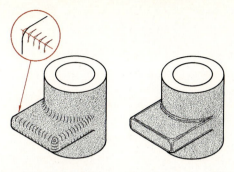

Figure 18.55 These are two methods of representing fillets and rounds on a part.

aligned or unidirectional numerals (**Fig. 18.54**). In both cases, notes connected with leaders usually are positioned horizontally, but drawing them to lie in an isometric plane is permissible. Always use guidelines for your lettering and numerals.

Fillets and Rounds

Fillets and rounds in isometric may be represented by either of the techniques shown in **Fig. 18.55** for added realism. The enlarged detail in the balloon shows how to draw intersecting guidelines equal in length to the radii of the fillets and rounds with arcs drawn tangent to them. These arcs may be drawn either freehand or with an ellipse template. The stipple shading was applied by using an adhesive overlay film.

When fillets and rounds of a dimensional part are shown, it is much easier to understand its features than it is when the part is represented by orthographic views (**Fig. 18.56**).

Assemblies

Assembly drawings illustrate how to put parts together. **Figure 18.57A** shows common mistakes in applying leaders and balloons to an assembly, and **Fig. 18.57B** shows the correct method of applying them. The numbers in the balloons correspond to the part numbers in the parts list. **Figure 18.58** shows an exploded assembly that

DIMENSIONED 3-D PICTORIAL

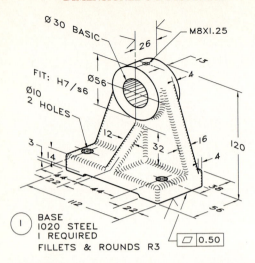

Figure 18.56 This three-dimensional drawing has been drawn to show fillets and rounds, and dimensions and notes are given so it can be used as a working drawing.

LEADERS IN ISOMETRIC

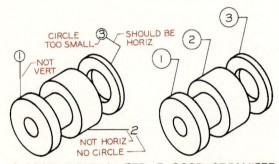

Figure 18.57 This drawing shows (A) common mistakes in applying leaders and part numbers in balloons of an assembly, and (B) acceptable techniques of applying leaders and part numbers to an assembly.

illustrates the relationship of four mating parts. Illustrations of this type are excellent for inclusion in parts catalogs and maintenance manuals.

EXPLODED ASSEMBLY

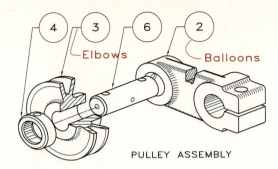

Figure 18.58 This exploded isometric assembly shows how parts are to be put together.

TYPES OF AXONOMETRICS

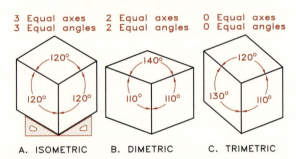

Figure 18.59 This drawing illustrates the three types of axonometric projection.

18.7 Axonometric Projection

An axonometric projection is a type of orthographic projection in which the **pictorial view is projected perpendicularly onto the picture plane with parallel projectors**. The object is positioned at an angle to the picture plane so that its pictorial projection will be a three-dimensional view. The three types of axonometric projections are: **isometric, dimetric,** and **trimetric (Fig. 18.59)**.

Recall that the isometric projection is the type of pictorial in which the diagonal of a cube is seen as a point, the three axes and planes of the cube are equally foreshortened, and the axes are equally spaced 120° apart. Measurements along the three axes will be equal but less than true length because the isometric projection is true projection.

A **dimetric projection** is a pictorial in which two planes are equally foreshortened and two of the planes are equally foreshortened and two of the axes are separated by equal angles. Measurements along two axes of the cube are equal.

A **trimetric projection** is a pictorial in which all three planes are unequally foreshortened. The lengths of the axes are unequal, and the angles between them are different.

Draw your solutions to the following problems (**Fig. 18.60**) on size A or B sheets, as assigned. Select an appropriate scale to take advantage of the space available on each sheet. By letting each square represent 0.20 in. (5 mm), you can draw two solutions on each size A sheet. By setting each square to 0.40 inch (10 mm), you can draw one solution on each size B sheet.

Oblique Pictorials
1–24. Construct cavalier, cabinet, or general obliques of the parts assigned.

Isometric Pictorials
1–24. Construct isometrics of the parts assigned.

Perspective Pictorials
1–24. On size B sheets lay out perspective views of the parts assigned.

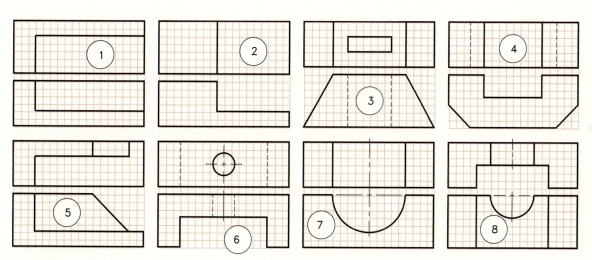

Figure 18.60 Problems 1–24.

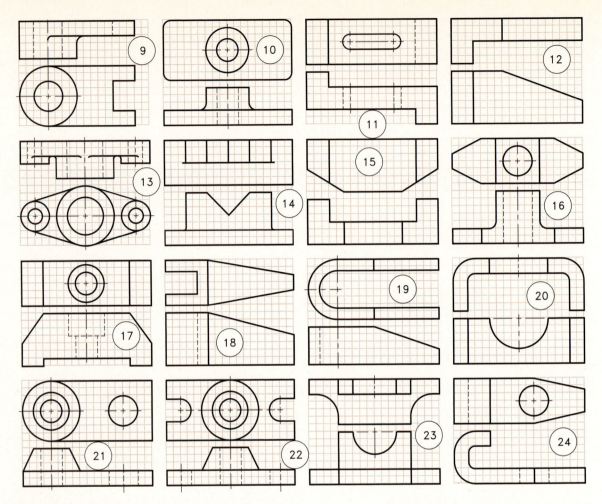

Figure 18.60 (continued)

19

Points, Lines, and Planes

19.1 Introduction

Points, lines, and planes are the basic geometric elements used in three-dimensional (3D) spatial geometry, called descriptive geometry. You need to understand how to locate and manipulate these elements in their simplest form because they will be applied to 3D spatial problems in Chapters 19 through 24.

The unmanned spacecraft designed to explore Mars comprises many points, lines, and planes. Its geometry had to be established with great precision in order for it to function properly (**Fig. 19.1**).

The labeling of points, lines, and planes is an essential part of 3D projection because it is your means of analyzing their spatial relationships. **Figure 19.2** illustrates the fundamental requirements for properly labeling these elements in a drawing:

> **Lettering:** use 1/8-inch letters with guidelines for labels; label lines at each end and planes at each corner with either letters or numbers.

Figure 19.1 The geometry of points, lines, and planes must be established with great precision in the design of this unmanned Mars orbiter spacecraft. (Courtesy of The Boeing Company.)

> **Points:** mark with two short perpendicular dashes forming a cross, not a dot; each dash should be approximately 1/8 inch long.

389

LABELING A DRAWING

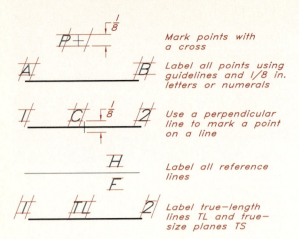

Mark points with a cross

Label all points using guidelines and 1/8 in. letters or numerals

Use a perpendicular line to mark a point on a line

Label all reference lines

Label true-length lines TL and true-size planes TS

Figure 19.2 These are standard practices for labeling points, lines, and planes.

Points on lines: mark with a short perpendicular dash crossing the line, not a dot.

Reference lines: label these thin dark lines as described in Chapter 7.

Object lines: draw these lines used to represent points, lines, and planes heavier than reference lines with an H or F pencil; draw hidden lines thinner than visible lines.

True-length lines: label TRUE LENGTH or TL.

True-size planes: label TRUE SIZE or TS.

Projection lines: draw precisely with a 2H or 4H pencil as thin lines, just dark enough to be visible so they need not be erased.

19.2 Projection of Points

A **point** is a theoretical location in space having no dimensions other than its location. However, a series of points establishes lengths, areas, and volumes of complex shapes.

A point must be located in at least two adjacent orthographic views to establish its position in

THREE VIEWS OF A POINT

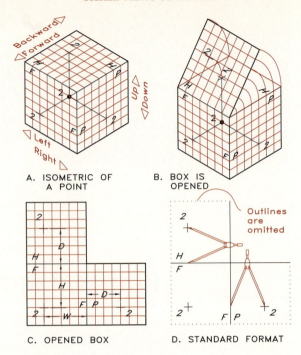

A. ISOMETRIC OF A POINT

B. BOX IS OPENED

C. OPENED BOX

D. STANDARD FORMAT

Figure 19.3

A This drawing shows three projections of point 2 pictorially.

B The projection planes are opened into a single plane.

C In the opened box, point 2 is 5 units to the left of the profile, 5 units below the horizontal, and 4 units behind the frontal view.

D The outlines of the projection are omitted in orthographic projection.

3D space (**Fig. 19.3**). When the planes of the projection box (**Fig. 19.3A**) are opened onto the plane of the drawing surface (**Fig. 19.3C**), the projectors from each view of point 2 are perpendicular to the reference lines between the views. Letters H, F, and P represent the horizontal, frontal, and profile planes, the three principal projection planes.

A point may be located from verbal descriptions with respect to the principal planes. For example, point 2 in Fig. 19.3 may be described as being 5 units left of the profile plane, 5 units

THREE PROJECTIONS OF A LINE

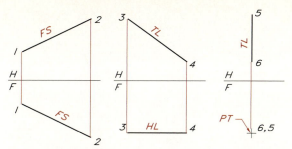

A. FORESHORTENED   B. TRUE LENGTH   C. POINT

Figure 19.4 A line in orthographic projection can appear as foreshortened (FS), true length (TL), or a point (PT).

A 3D LINE

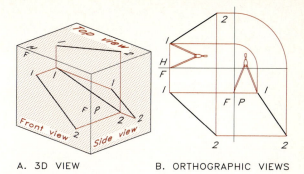

A. 3D VIEW   B. ORTHOGRAPHIC VIEWS

Figure 19.5

A This pictorial shows three views of a line in 3D space.

B These are the standard three orthographic views of a line.

below the horizontal plane, and 4 units behind the frontal plane.

When you look at the front view of the box, the horizontal and profile planes appear as edges. In the top view, the frontal and profile planes appear as edges. In the side view, the frontal and horizontal planes appear as edges.

19.3 Lines

A **line** is the straight path between two points in 3D space. A line may appear as foreshortened, true-length, or a point **(Fig. 19.4).**

Oblique lines are neither parallel nor perpendicular to a principal projection plane **(Fig. 19.5)**. When line 1–2 is projected onto the horizontal, frontal, and profile planes, it appears foreshortened in each view.

Principal lines are parallel to at least one of the principal projection planes. A principal line is true length in the view where the principal plane to which it is parallel appears true size. The three types of principal lines are **horizontal, frontal,** and **profile** lines.

Figure 19.6A shows a **horizontal line** (HL) that appears true length in the horizontal (top) view. Any line shown in the top view will appear

true length as long as it is parallel to the horizontal plane.

When looking at the top view, you cannot tell whether the line is horizontal. You must look at the front or side views to do so. In those views, an HL will be parallel to the edge view of the horizontal, the HF fold line **(Fig 19.7)**. A line that projects as a point in the front view is a combination horizontal and profile line.

A **frontal line** (FL) is parallel to the frontal projection plane. It appears true length in the front view because your line of sight is perpendicular to it in this view. In **Fig. 19.6B** line 3–4 is an FL because it is parallel to the edge of the frontal plane in the top and side views.

A **profile line** (PL) is parallel to the profile projection planes and appears true length in the side (profile) views. To tell whether a line is a PL, you must look at a view adjacent to the profile view, or the top or front view. In **Fig. 19.6C**, line 5–6 is parallel to the edge view of the profile plane in both the top and side views.

Locating a Point on a Line

Figure 19.8 shows the top and front views of a line 1–2 with point O located at its midpoint. To find

PRINCIPAL LINES

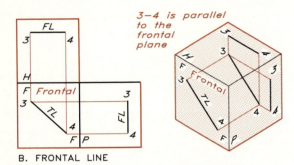

A. HORIZONTAL LINE

1–2 is parallel to the horizontal plane

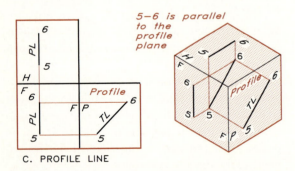

B. FRONTAL LINE

3–4 is parallel to the frontal plane

C. PROFILE LINE

5–6 is parallel to the profile plane

Figure 19.6 Principal lines:

A The horizontal line is true length in the horizontal (top) view. It is parallel to the edge view of the horizontal plane in the front and side views.

B The frontal line is true length in the front view. It is parallel to the edge view of the frontal plane in the top and side views.

C The profile line is true length in the profile (side) view. It is parallel to the edge view of the profile plane in the top and front views.

DETERMINATION OF PARALLELISM

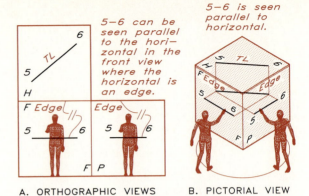

5–6 can be seen parallel to the horizontal in the front view where the horizontal is an edge.

5–6 is seen parallel to horizontal.

A. ORTHOGRAPHIC VIEWS   **B. PICTORIAL VIEW**

Figure 19.7 To determine that a line is horizontal, you must use the front or side views in which the horizontal projection plane is an edge. Line 5–6 is seen parallel to the horizontal and is therefore a horizontal line, too.

LOCATE A POINT ON A LINE

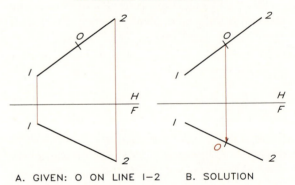

A. GIVEN: O ON LINE 1–2   **B. SOLUTION**

Figure 19.8 Point O on the top view of line 1–2 may be found in the front view by projection. The projector is perpendicular to the HF reference line between the views.

the front view of the point, recall that, in orthographic projection, the projector between the views is perpendicular to the HF fold line. Use that projector to project point O to line 1–2 in the front view. A point located at a line's midpoint will be at the line's midpoint in all orthographic views of the line.

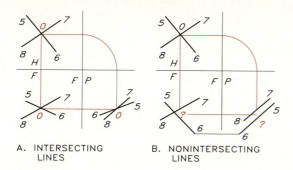

A. INTERSECTING LINES

B. NONINTERSECTING LINES

Figure 19.9
A These lines intersect because O, the point of intersection, projects as a common point of intersection in all views.

B The lines cross in the top and front views, but they do not intersect because there is no common point of intersection in all views.

Intersecting and Nonintersecting Lines

Lines that intersect have a common point of intersection lying on both lines. Point O in **Fig. 19.9A** is a point of intersection because it projects to a common crossing point in all three views.

However, the crossing point of the lines in **Fig. 19.9B** in the top and front views is not a point of intersection. Point O does not project to a common crossing point in the top and front views, so the lines do not intersect; they simply cross, as shown in the profile view.

19.4 Visibility

Crossing Lines

In **Fig. 19.10** nonintersecting lines AB and CD cross in certain views. Therefore portions of the lines are visible or hidden at the crossing points (here, line thickness is exaggerated for purposes of illustration). Determining which line is above or in front of the other is referred to as finding a line's **visibility**, a requirement of many 3D problems.

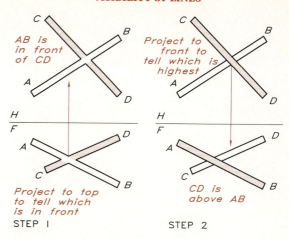

STEP 1   STEP 2

Figure 19.10 Determining visibility of lines:
Required Find the visibility of the lines in both views.

Step 1 Project the crossing point from the front to the top view. This projector strikes line AB before it strikes line CD, indicating that line AB is in front and thus is visible in the front view.

Step 2 Project the crossing point from the top view to the front view. This projector strikes line CD before it strikes line AB, indicating that line CD is above line AB and thus is visible in the top view.

You have to determine line visibility by analysis. For example, select a crossing point in the front view and project it to the top view to determine which line is in front of the other. Because the projector contacts line AB first, you know that line AB is in front of CD and is visible in the front view.

Repeat this process by projecting downward from the intersection in the top view to find that line CD is above line AB and is visible in the top view. If only one view were available, visibility would be impossible to determine.

A Line and a Plane

The principles of visibility analysis also apply to determining visibility for a line and a plane (**Fig.**

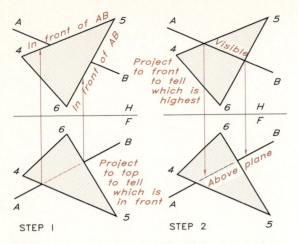

STEP 1   STEP 2

Figure 19.11 Determining visibility of a line and a plane: **Required** Find the visibility of the plane and the line in both views.

Step 1 Project the points where line AB crosses the plane from the front view to the top view. These projectors intersect lines 4–6 and 5–6 of the plane first, indicating that the plane is in front of the line and making line AB hidden in the front view.

Step 2 Project the points where line AB crosses the plane in the top view to the front view. These projectors encounter line AB first, indicating that line AB is higher than the plane and making the line visible in the top view.

19.11). First, project the intersections of line AB with lines 4–5 and 5–6 to the top view to determine that the lines of the plane (4–5 and 5–6) lie in front of line AB in the front view. Therefore line AB is a hidden line in the front view.

Similarly, project the two intersections of line AB in the top view to the front view, where line AB is found to lie above lines 4–5 and 5–6 of the plane. Because line AB is above the plane, it is a visible line in the top view.

19.5 Planes

A **plane** may be represented in orthographic projection by any of the four combinations shown in

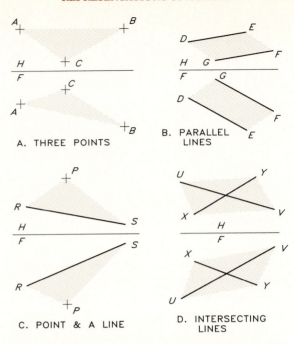

A. THREE POINTS

B. PARALLEL LINES

C. POINT & A LINE

D. INTERSECTING LINES

Figure 19.12 A plane may be represented as (A) three points not on a straight line, (B) two parallel lines, (C) a line and a point not on the line or its extension, and (D) two intersecting lines.

Fig. 19.12. In orthographic projection, a plane may appear as **an edge, a true-size plane,** or **a foreshortened plane (Fig. 19.13).**

Oblique planes (the general case) are not parallel to principal projection planes in any view **(Fig. 19.14). Principal planes** are parallel to principal projection planes **(Fig. 19.15).** The three types of principal planes are **horizontal, frontal,** and **profile.**

A **horizontal plane** is parallel to the horizontal projection plane and is true size in the top view **(Fig. 19.15A).** To determine that the plane is horizontal, you must observe the front or profile views, where you can see its parallelism to the edge view of the horizontal plane.

A **frontal plane** is parallel to the frontal projection plane and appears true size in the front view

THREE PROJECTIONS OF A PLANE

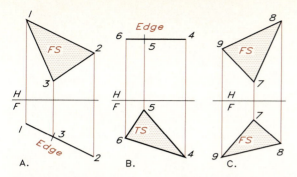

Figure 19.13 A plane in orthographic projection can appear as (A) an edge, (B) true size (TS), or (C) foreshortened (FS). A plane that is foreshortened in all principal views is an oblique plane.

OBLIQUE PLANE—GENERAL CASE

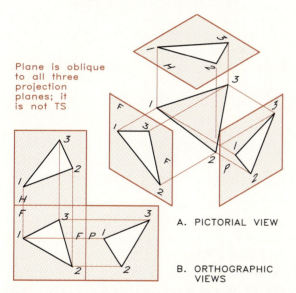

Plane is oblique to all three projection planes; it is not TS

A. PICTORIAL VIEW

B. ORTHOGRAPHIC VIEWS

Figure 19.14 An oblique plane is neither parallel nor perpendicular to a projection plane. It is the general-case plane.

(Fig. 19.15B). To determine that the plane is frontal, you must look at the top or profile views, where you can see its parallelism to the edge view of the frontal plane.

PRINCIPAL PLANES

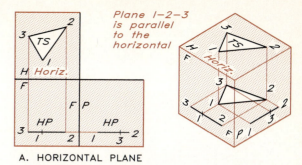

Plane 1–2–3 is parallel to the horizontal

A. HORIZONTAL PLANE

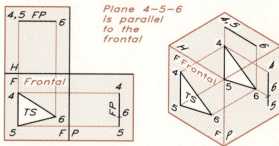

Plane 4–5–6 is parallel to the frontal

B. FRONTAL PLANE

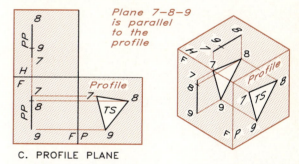

Plane 7–8–9 is parallel to the profile

C. PROFILE PLANE

Figure 19.15 Principal planes:

A The horizontal plane is true size in the horizontal (top) view. It is parallel to the edge view of the horizontal plane in the front and profile views.

B The frontal plane is true size in the front view. It is parallel to the edge view of the frontal plane in the top and profile views.

C The profile plane is true size in the profile view. It is parallel to the edge view of the profile plane in the top and front views.

A **profile plane** is parallel to the profile projection plane and is true size in the side view **(Fig. 19.15C)**. To determine that the plane is profile,

LINE ON A PLANE

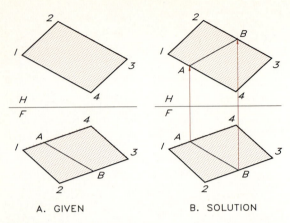

A. GIVEN   B. SOLUTION

Figure 19.16 If line AB lying on the plane is given, the line's top view can be found. Project points A and B to lines 1–4 and 2–3 and connect them to get the top view of line AB.

LOCATION OF A POINT ON A PLANE

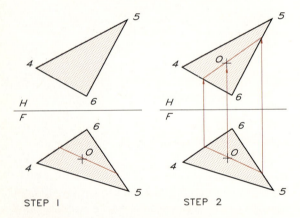

STEP 1   STEP 2

Figure 19.17 Locating a point on a plane:
Required Find the top view of point O on the plane.

Step 1 In the front view, draw a line through point O in any convenient direction except vertical.

Step 2 Project the ends of the line to the top view and draw the line. Project point O to this line.

you must observe the top or front views, where you can see its parallelism to the edge view of the profile plane.

LINES ON A PLANE

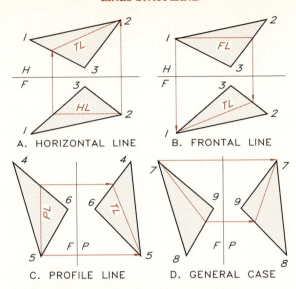

A. HORIZONTAL LINE   B. FRONTAL LINE

C. PROFILE LINE   D. GENERAL CASE

Figure 19.18 Finding principal lines on a plane:
A First, draw a horizontal line in the front view parallel to the edge view of the horizontal plane. Then, project it to the top view, where it is true length.

B First, draw a frontal line in the top view parallel to the edge view of the frontal plane. Then, project it to the front view, where it is true length.

C First, draw a profile line in the front view parallel to the edge view of the profile plane. Then project it to the profile view, where it is true length.

D A general-case line is not parallel to the frontal, horizontal, or profile planes and is not true length in any principal view.

A Line on a Plane

Line AB on the plane in the front view is given in **Fig. 19.16**, and it is to be found in the top view. Project points A and B, lying on lines 1–4 and 2–3, to the top view of lines 1–4 and 2–3. Connecting points A and B gives the top view of line AB.

A Point on a Plane

Point O on the front view of plane 4–5–6 in **Fig. 19.17** is to be located on the plane in the top view. First, draw a line in any direction (except vertical) through the point to establish a line on the plane.

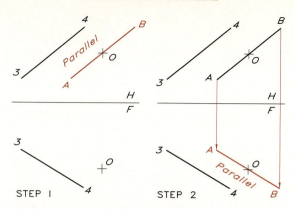

Figure 19.19 Constructing a line parallel to a line:

Required Draw a line through point O parallel to line 3–4.

Step 1 Draw line AB parallel to the top view of line 3–4, with its midpoint at O.

Step 2 Draw the front view of line AB parallel to the front view of 3–4 through point O.

Then project this line to the top view and project point O from the front view to the top view of the line.

Principal Lines on a Plane

Principal lines may be found in any view of a plane when at least two orthographic views of the plane are given. Any number of principal lines can be drawn on any plane.

Figure 19.18A shows a **horizontal line** parallel to the edge view of the horizontal projection plane in the front view. When projected to the top view, this line is true length.

Figure 19.18B shows a **frontal line** parallel to the edge view of the frontal projection plane in the top view. When projected to the front view, this line is true length.

Figure 19.18C shows a **profile line** parallel to the edge view of the profile projection plane in the front. When projected to the profile view, this line is true length.

In the **general case (oblique)**, a line is not parallel to the edge view of any principal projection

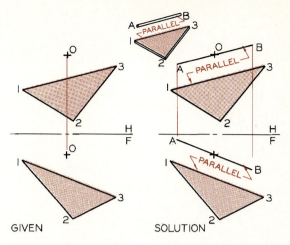

Figure 19.20 A line may be drawn through point O parallel to plane 1–2–3 if the line is parallel to any line in the plane. Draw line AB parallel to line 1–3 of the plane in the front and top views, making it parallel to the plane.

plane (**Fig. 19.18D**). Therefore it is not true length in any principal view.

19.6 Parallelism

Lines

Two parallel lines appear parallel in all views, except in views where both appear as points. Parallelism of lines in 3D space cannot be determined without at least two adjacent orthographic views. In **Fig. 19.19**, line AB was drawn parallel to the horizontal view of line 3–4 and through point O, which is the midpoint. Projecting points A and B to the front view with projectors perpendicular to the HF reference plane yields the length of line AB, which is parallel to line 3–4 through point O.

A Line and a Plane

A line is parallel to a plane when it is parallel to any line in the plane. In **Fig. 19.20**, a line with its midpoint at point O is to be drawn parallel to plane 1–2–3. In this case line AB was drawn parallel to a line in the plane, or line 1–3, in the top

LINE PARALLEL TO A PLANE

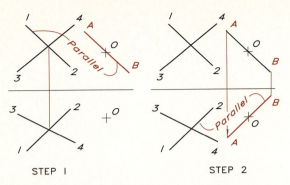

Figure 19.21 Constructing a line parallel to plane:
Required Draw a line through point O that is parallel to plane 1–2–3–4 represented by intersecting lines.

Step 1 Draw line AB parallel to line 1–2 through point O.

Step 2 Draw line AB parallel to the same line, line 1–2, in the front view, which makes line AB parallel to the plane.

PARALLELISM: TWO PLANES

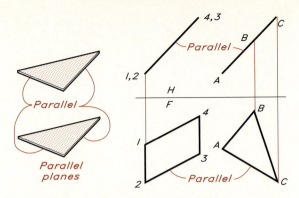

Figure 19.22 Two planes are parallel when intersecting lines in one are parallel to intersecting lines in the other. When parallel planes appear as edges, their edges are parallel.

PLANE PARALLEL TO A PLANE

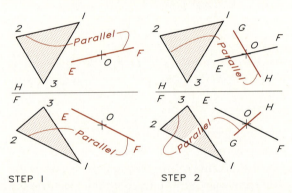

Figure 19.23 Constructing a plane through a point parallel to a plane:
Required Draw a plane through point O parallel to the given plane.

Step 1 Draw line EF parallel to any line in the plane (line 1–2 in this case). Show the line in both views.

Step 2 Draw a second line parallel to line 2–3 in the top and front views. These intersecting lines passing through O represent a plane parallel to 1–2–3.

and front views. The line could have been drawn parallel to any line in the plane, making infinite solutions possible.

Figure 19.21 shows a similar example. Here, a line parallel to the plane, with its midpoint at O, was drawn. In this case, the plane is represented by two intersecting lines instead of an outlined area.

Planes

Two planes are parallel when intersecting lines in one plane are parallel to intersecting lines in the other (Fig. 19.22). Determining whether planes are parallel is easy when both appear as edges in a view.

In **Fig. 19.23**, a plane is to be drawn through point O parallel to plane 1–2–3. First, draw line EF through point O parallel to line 1–2 in the top and front views. Then draw a second line through point O parallel to line 2–3 of the plane in the front and top views. These two intersecting lines form a plane parallel to plane 1–2–3, as intersecting lines on one plane are parallel to intersecting lines on the other.

19.7 Perpendicularity

Lines

When two lines are perpendicular, draw them with a true 90° angle of intersection in views

PERPENDICULARITY: TWO LINES

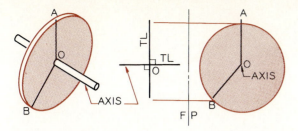

Figure 19.24 Perpendicular lines have a true angle of 90° between them in a view where one or both of them appear true length.

LINE PERPENDICULAR TO A LINE

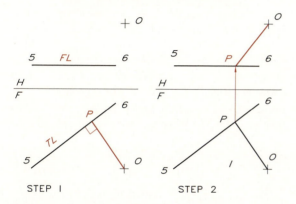

Figure 19.25 Constructing a line perpendicular to a principal line:

Required Draw a line from point O perpendicular to line 5–6.

Step 1 Line 5–6 is a frontal line and is true length in the front view, so a perpendicular from point O makes a true 90° angle with it in the front view.

Step 2 Project point P to the top view and connect it to point O. As neither line is true length in the top view, they do not intersect at 90° in this view.

LINE PERPENDICULAR TO AN OBLIQUE LINE

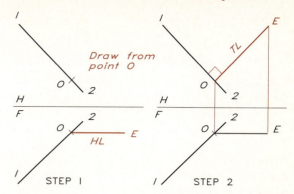

Figure 19.26 Constructing a line perpendicular to an oblique line:

Required Draw a line from point O on line 1–2 perpendicular to the line.

Step 1 Draw a horizontal line (OE) from point O in the front view.

Step 2 Horizontal line OE is true length in the top view, so draw it perpendicular to line 1–2 in this view.

---

perpendicular to the axis in the front view. Spokes OA and OB are examples of true length foreshortened axes, respectively, in the front view.

A Line Perpendicular to a Principal Line In **Fig. 19.25**, a line is to be constructed through point O perpendicular to frontal line 5–6, which is true length in the front view. First, draw OP perpendicular to line 5–6 because it is true length. Then, project point P to the top view of line 5–6. In the top view, line OP is not perpendicular to line 5–6 because neither of the lines is true length in this view.

A Line Perpendicular to an Oblique Line In **Fig. 19.26**, a line is to be constructed from point O perpendicular to oblique line 1–2. First, draw a horizontal line from O to some convenient length in the front view, say, to E.

Locate point O in the top view by projection and draw line OE to make a 90° angle with the top view of 1–2. Line OE is true length in the top view, so it makes a true 90° angle with line 1–2.

---

where one or both of them appear true length **(Fig. 19.24)**. In a view where neither of two perpendicular lines is true length, the angle between is not a true 90° angle.

In Fig. 19.24, the axis is true length in the front view; therefore any spoke of the circular wheel is

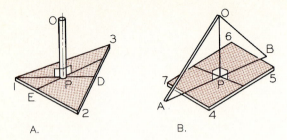

Figure 19.27
A A line is perpendicular to a plane when it is perpendicular to two intersecting lines on the plane.

B A plane is perpendicular to another plane if it contains a line that is perpendicular to the other plane.

Planes

A line is perpendicular to a plane when it is perpendicular to any two intersecting lines in the plane (Fig. 19.27A). A plane is perpendicular to another plane when a line in one plane is perpendicular to the other plane (Fig. 19.27B).

A Line Perpendicular to a Plane

In **Fig. 19.28**, a line is to be drawn perpendicular to the plane from point O on the plane. First, draw a frontal line on the plane in the top view through O. Project the line to the front view, where it is true length. Draw line P at a convenient length perpendicular to the true-length line.

Then, draw a horizontal line through point O

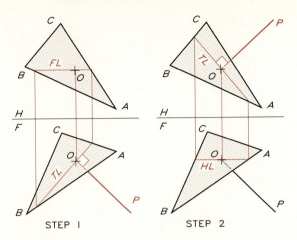

Figure 19.28 Constructing a line perpendicular to a plane:
Required From point O on the plane, draw a line perpendicular to the plane.

Step 1 Construct a frontal line on the plane through O in the top view. This line is true length in the front view, so draw line OP perpendicular to this true-length line.

Step 2 Construct a horizontal line through point O in the front view. This line is true length in the top view, so draw line OP perpendicular to it.

in the front view and project it to the top view of the plane, perpendicular to the true-length line. This construction results in a line perpendicular to the plane because the line is perpendicular to two intersecting lines, a horizontal and a frontal line, in the plane.

Problems

Use size A sheets for the following problems and lay out your solutions with instruments. Each square on the grid is equal to 0.20 in. or 5 mm. You can use either grid paper or plain paper. Label all reference planes and points in each problem with $1/8$-in. letters and numbers, using guidelines.

1. (Fig. 19.29)

(A–D) Draw three views (top, front, and right-side views) of the given point.

(E, F) Draw the three views of the points and connect them to form lines.

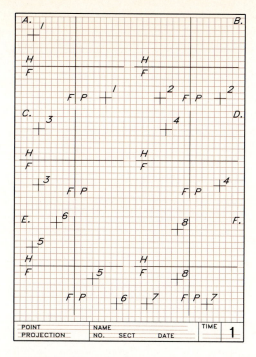

Figure 19.29 Problem 1 (A–F).

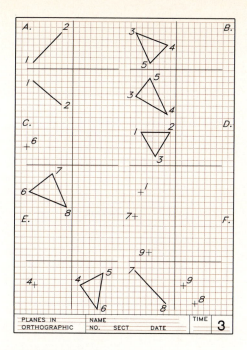

Figure 19.31 Problem 3 (A–F).

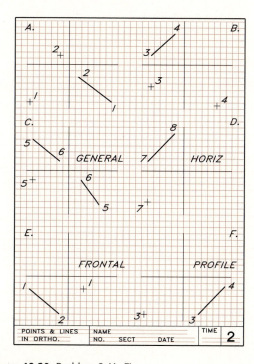

Figure 19.30 Problem 2 (A–F).

2. (Fig. 19.30)

(A–C) Draw three views (top, front, and right-side views) of the partially drawn lines.

(D–F) Draw the missing views of the lines so that 7–8 is a horizontal line, 1–2 is a frontal line, and 3–4 is a profile line.

3. (Fig. 19.31)

(A, B) Draw the right-side view of line 1–2 and plane 3–4–5.

(C–E) Draw the missing views of the planes so that 6–7–8 is a frontal plane, 1–2–3 is a horizontal plane, and 4–5–6 is a profile plane.

(F) Complete the top and side views of the plane that appears as an edge in the front view.

4. (Fig. 19.32)

(A) Draw the side view of the plane and locate point A on the plane in all views.

(B) Draw the side view and two horizontal lines on each view.

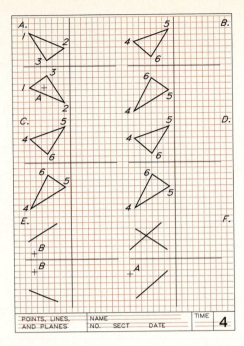

Figure 19.32 Problem 4 (A–F).

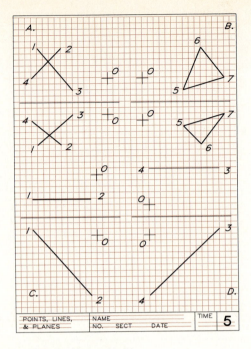

Figure 19.33 Problem 5 (A–D).

(C) Draw the side view and two frontal lines on each view.

(D) Draw the side view and two profile lines on each view.

(E) Draw a line through B that is parallel to and equal in length to the given line.

(F) Complete the three views of the intersecting lines.

5. (Fig. 19.33)

(A, B) Draw 1.50-in. lines that pass through point O and are parallel to their respective planes.

(C, D) Through point O draw the top and front views of lines that are perpendicular to their respective lines.

20

Primary Auxiliary Views in Descriptive Geometry

20.1 Introduction

Descriptive geometry is the projection of three-dimensional (3D) orthographic views onto a two-dimensional (2D) plane of paper to allow graphical determination of lengths, angles, shapes, and other geometric information. Orthographic projection is the basis for laying out and solving problems by descriptive geometry.

The **primary auxiliary view**, which permits analysis of 3D geometry, is essential to descriptive geometry. For example, the design of the space-craft shown in **Fig. 20.1** contains many complex geometric elements (lines, angles, and surfaces) that were analyzed by descriptive geometry prior to its fabrication.

20.2 True-Length Lines

Primary Auxiliary View
Figure 20.2 shows the top and front views of line 1–2 pictorially and orthographically. Line 1–2 is

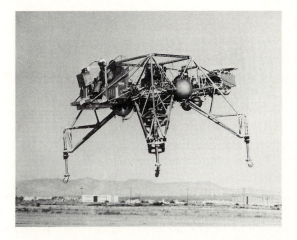

Figure 20.1 This lunar vehicle could not have been designed without the use of descriptive geometry to determine lengths, angles, and areas of its component parts. (Courtesy of Ryan Aircraft Corporation.)

not a principal line, so it is not true length in a principal view. Therefore a primary auxiliary view is required to find its true-length view.

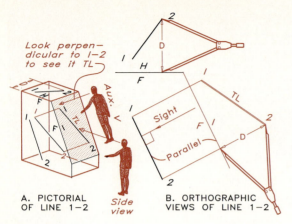

Figure 20.2

A A pictorial of line 1–2 is shown inside a projection box where an auxiliary plane is parallel to the line and perpendicular to the frontal plane.

B The auxiliary view is projected from the front orthographic view to find 1–2 true length.

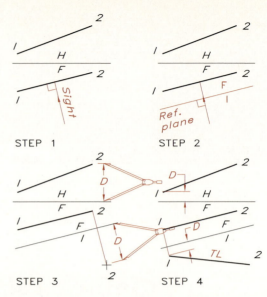

Figure 20.3 The true length of a line:

Step 1 To find the true length of line 1–2, the line of sight must be perpendicular to one of its views, the front view here.

Step 2 Draw the F1 reference line parallel to the line and perpendicular to the line of sight.

Step 3 Project point 2 perpendicularly from the front view. Transfer distance D from the top view to locate point 2 in the auxiliary view.

Step 4 Locate point 1 in the same manner to find line 1–2 true length in the auxiliary view.

In **Fig. 20.2A**, the line of sight is perpendicular to the front view of the line and reference line F1 is parallel to the line's frontal view. The auxiliary plane is parallel to the line and perpendicular to the frontal plane, accounting for its label, F1, where F and 1 are abbreviations for frontal and primary planes, respectively.

Projecting parallel to the line of sight and perpendicular to the F1 reference line yields the auxiliary view. Transferring distance D with dividers to the auxiliary view locates point 2 because the frontal plane appears as an edge in both the top and auxiliary views. Point 1 is located in the same manner, and the points are connected to find the true-length view of the line.

Figure 20.3 summarizes the steps of finding the true-length view of an oblique line. Letter all reference planes using the notation suggested in Chapter 19 and as shown in the examples throughout this chapter, with the exception of

noted dimensions such as D. Use your dividers to transfer dimensions.

A primary auxiliary view projected parallel from a true-length view of a line in a principal view shows the point view of the line (**Fig. 20.4**). The auxiliary view projected from the line's front view gives a foreshortened view, not a point view, because the line is not true length in the front view.

True Length by Analytical Geometry

Figure 20.5 shows how to find the true length of a frontal line (line 3–4) mathematically. The

POINT VIEW OF A LINE

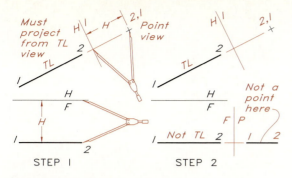

Figure 20.4 The point view of a line:
Step 1 The point view of a line is found in a primary auxiliary view projected from the true-length view of the line.

Step 2 An auxiliary view projected from a foreshortened view of a line gives a foreshortened view of the line, not its point view.

Pythagorean theorem states that the hypotenuse of a right triangle is equal to the square root of the sum of the squares of the other two sides. Because the line is true length in the front view, measuring that length provides a check on the mathematical solution.

The true length of a line shown pictorially in **Fig. 20.6A** (line 1–2) is determined by analytical geometry from its length in the front view where the X and Y distances form a right triangle. **Figure 20.6B** shows a second right triangle, 1–0–2, whose hypotenuse is the true length of line 1–2. Thus the true length of an oblique line is the square root of the sum of the squares of the X, Y, and Z distances that correspond to the width, height, and depth of the triangles shown orthographically in **Fig. 20.6C**.

True-Length Diagram

A true-length diagram utilizes two perpendicular lines to find a line of true length (**Fig. 20.7**). This method does not give the line's direction, only its true length.

The two measurements laid out on the true-length diagram may be transferred from any two

TRUE LENGTH OF A FRONTAL LINE

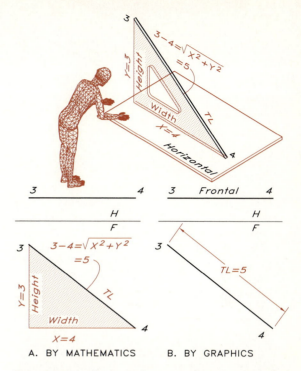

Figure 20.5 Apply the Pythagorean theorem to calculate the length of a line that appears true length in a view, the front view here. Because line 3–4 is true length in the front view, it can be measured to find its length graphically.

adjacent orthographic views. One measurement is the distance between the endpoints in one of the views. The other measurement, from the adjacent view, is the distance between the endpoints perpendicular to the reference line between the two views. Here, these dimensions are vertical, V, and horizontal, H, between points 1 and 2.

20.3 Angles Between Lines and Principal Planes

To measure the angle between a line and a plane, the line must appear true length and the plane as an edge in the same view (Fig. 20.8). A principal plane appears as an edge in a primary auxil-

TRUE-LENGTH LINES
BY THE PYTHAGOREAN THEOREM

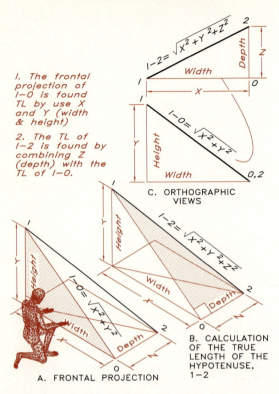

I. The frontal projection of 1–0 is found TL by use X and Y (width & height)

2. The TL of 1–2 is found by combining Z (depth) with the TL of 1–0.

$$1-2 = \sqrt{X^2 + Y^2 + Z^2}$$

$$1-0 = \sqrt{X^2 + Y^2}$$

C. ORTHOGRAPHIC VIEWS

$$1-2 = \sqrt{X^2 + Y^2 + Z^2}$$

$$1-0 = \sqrt{X^2 + Y^2}$$

B. CALCULATION OF THE TRUE LENGTH OF THE HYPOTENUSE, 1–2

A. FRONTAL PROJECTION

Figure 20.6 To calculate the true length of a 3D line that is not true length in principal view, find (A) the frontal projection, line 1–O, by using the X and Y distances, and (B) the hypotenuse of the right triangle 1–O–2 by using the length of line 1–O and the Z distance. Then apply the Pythagorean theorem to find its length of 5. Orthographic views are shown in (C).

iary view projected from it, so the angle a line makes with this principal plane can be measured if the line is true length in this auxiliary view.

20.4 Sloping Lines

Slope is the angle that a line makes with the horizontal plane when the line is true length and the plane is an edge. Figure 20.9 shows the three methods for specifying slope: slope angle, percent grade, and slope ratio.

TRUE-LENGTH DIAGRAM

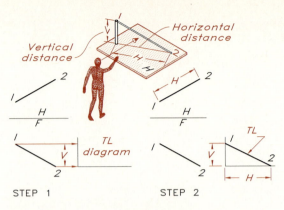

STEP 1   STEP 2

Figure 20.7 Using a true-length diagram:
Step 1 Transfer the vertical distance between the ends of line 1–2 to the vertical leg of the TL diagram.

Step 2 Transfer the horizontal length of the line in the top view to the horizontal leg of the TL diagram. The diagonal is the true length of line 1–2.

ANGLES WITH PRINCIPAL PLANES

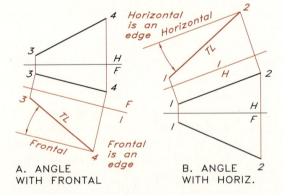

A. ANGLE WITH FRONTAL

B. ANGLE WITH HORIZ.

Figure 20.8 Angles between lines and principal planes:
A An auxiliary view projected from the front view that shows the line true length will show the frontal plane as an edge, where its angle with the frontal plane can be measured.

B An auxiliary view projected from the top that shows the line true length will show the horizontal plane as an edge, where its angle with the horizontal plane can be measured.

MEASURING SLOPES OF LINES

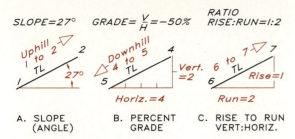

A. SLOPE (ANGLE) B. PERCENT GRADE C. RISE TO RUN VERT:HORIZ.

Figure 20.9 The inclination of a line with the horizontal may be measured and expressed as: (A) slope angle, (B) percent grade, and (C) slope ratio.

PERCENT GRADE OF A LINE

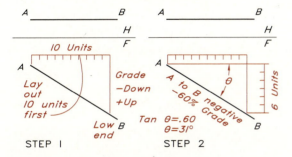

STEP 1 STEP 2

Figure 20.10 The percent grade of a line:
Step 1 The percent grade of a line may be measured in the view where the horizontal appears as an edge and the line is true length (here, the front view). Lay off ten units parallel to the horizontal from the end of the line.

Step 2 A vertical distance from the end of the 10 units to the line measures 6 units. The percent grade is 6 divided by 10, or 60%. This is a negative grade from A to B because the line slopes downward from A. The tangent of this slope angle is 6/10, or 0.60, which can be used to find the slope of 31° from trigonometric function tables.

The **slope angle** of line AB in **Fig. 20.10** is 31°. It can be measured in the front view where the line is true length.

The **percent grade** is the ratio of the vertical (rise) divided by the horizontal (run) between the ends of a line, expressed as a percentage. The

SLOPE RATIO OF A LINE

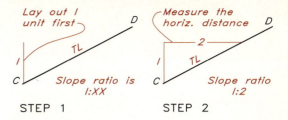

STEP 1 STEP 2

Figure 20.11 Slope ratio:
Step 1 Slope ratio always begins with 1, so lay out a vertical distance of 1 from end C.

Step 2 Lay off a horizontal distance from the end of the vertical line and measure it. It is 2, so the slope ratio (always expressed as 1:XX) of this line is 1:2.

percent grade of line AB is determined in the front view of Fig. 20.10 where the line is true length and the horizontal plane is an edge. Line AB has a –60% grade from A to B because the line slopes downward; it would be positive (upward) from B to A. Trigonometric tables reveal a slope angle of 31° for the angle's tangent of 0.60 (6/10).

The **slope ratio** is the ratio of a rise of 1 to the run. The rise is always written as 1, followed by a colon and the run (for example, 1:10, 1:200). **Figure 20.11** illustrates the graphical method of finding the slope ratio. The rise of 1 unit is laid off on the true-length view of CD. The corresponding run measures 2 units, for a slope ratio of 1:2.

The slopes of oblique lines are found true length in an auxiliary view projected from the top view so that the horizontal reference plane will appear as an edge **(Fig. 20.12A)**. The slope is expressed as an angle, or 26°.

To find the percent grade of an oblique line **(Fig. 20.12B)**, lay off 10 units horizontally, parallel to the H1 reference line. The corresponding vertical distance measures 4.5 units, for a –45% grade from point 3 to point 4.

The principles of true-line length and angles between lines and planes are useful in applications such as the design of aggregate conveyors

SLOPE OF OBLIQUE LINE

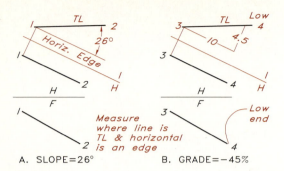

A. SLOPE=26° B. GRADE=−45%

Figure 20.12
A Find the slope angle of an oblique line (26° in this case) in a view where the horizontal appears as an edge and the line is true length;

B Find the percent grade in an auxiliary view projected from the top view where line 3–4 is true length (−45% from 3 to 4, the low end, in this case).

Figure 20.13 The design of these aggregate conveyors required the application of sloping-line principles in order to obtain their optimal slopes. (Courtesy of Smith Engineering Works.)

(Fig. 20.13) where slope is crucial to optimal operation of the equipment.

20.5 Bearings and Azimuths of Lines

Two types of bearings of a line's direction are compass bearings and azimuths. **Compass bearings** are angular measurements from north or south. The line in **Fig. 20.14A** that makes a 30° angle with north has a bearing of N 30° W. The line making a 60° angle with south toward the east has a bearing of south 60° east, or S 60° E. Because a compass can be read only when held level, bearings of a line must be found in the top, or horizontal, view.

Azimuths are measured clockwise from north through 360° **(Fig. 20.14B)**. Azimuth bearings are written N 120°, N 210°, and so on, indicating that they are measured from north.

The bearing of a line is toward the low end of the line unless otherwise specified. For example, line 2–3 in **Fig. 20.15** has a bearing of N 45° E because the line's low end is point 3 in the front view.

COMPASS DIRECTIONS

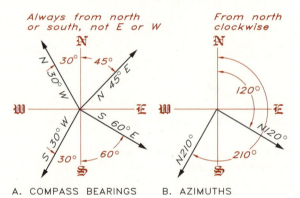

A. COMPASS BEARINGS B. AZIMUTHS

Figure 20.14
A Compass bearings are measured with respect to north and south.

B Azimuths are measured clockwise from north up to 360°.

Figure 20.16 shows how to find the bearing and slope of a line. This information may be used verbally to describe the line as having a bearing of S 60° E and a slope of 26° from point 5 to point 6. This information and the location of one point in

COMPASS BEARING OF A SLOPING LINE

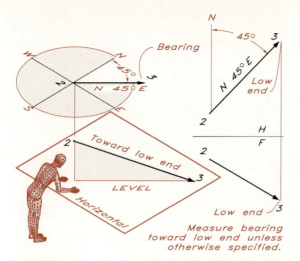

Figure 20.15 Measure the compass bearing of a line in the top view toward its low end (unless otherwise specified). Line 2–3 has a bearing of N 45° E toward the low end at 3.

the top and front views is sufficient to complete a 3D drawing of a line **(Fig. 20.17)**.

20.6 Contour Maps and Profiles

A **contour map** depicts variations in elevation of the earth in two dimensions **(Fig. 20.18)**. Three-dimensional representations involve (1) conventional orthographic views of the contour map combined with profiles and (2) contoured surface views (often in the form of models).

    Contour lines are horizontal (level) lines that represent constant elevations from a horizontal datum such as sea level. The vertical interval of spacing between the contours shown in **Fig. 20.18** is 10 feet. Contour lines may be thought of as the intersection of horizontal planes with the surface of the earth as shown in the model in **Fig. 20.19**.

    Contour maps contain contour lines that connect points of equal elevation on the earth's surface and therefore are continuous **(Fig. 20.18)**. The closer the contour lines are to each other, the steeper the terrain is.

SLOPE AND BEARING OF A LINE

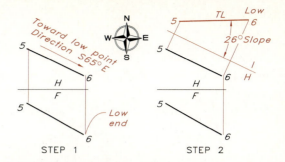

Figure 20.16 The slope and bearing of a line:
Step 1 Measure the bearing in the top view toward its low end, or S 65° E in this case.

Step 2 Measure the slope angle of 26° from the H1 reference line in an auxiliary view projected from the top view where the line is true length.

LINE FROM SPECIFICATIONS

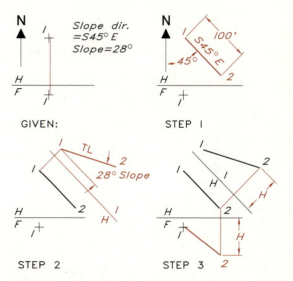

Figure 20.17 A line from slope specifications:
Required Draw a line through point 1 that bears S 45° E for 100 ft horizontally and slopes 28°.

Step 1 Draw the bearing and the horizontal distance in the top view from point 1.

Step 2 Project an auxiliary view from the top view and draw the line at a slope of 28°.

Step 3 Find the front view of line 1–2 by locating point 2 in the front view.

CONTOUR MAP

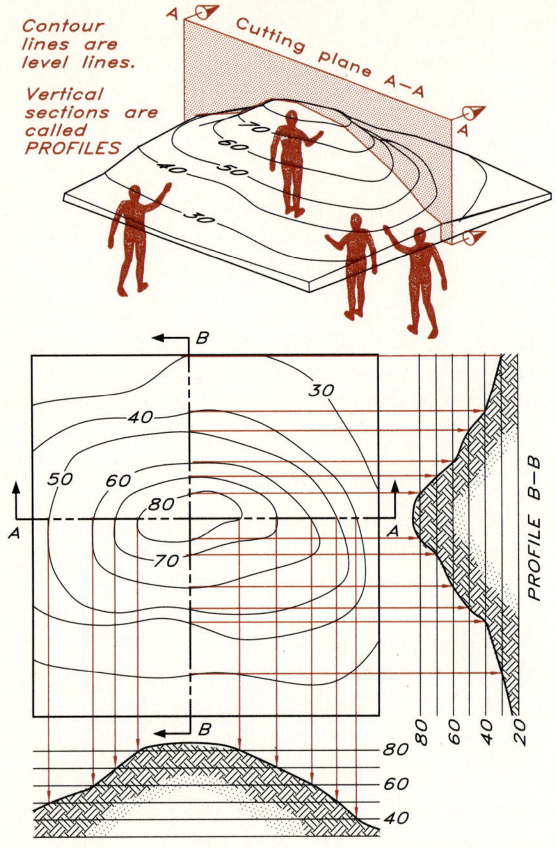

Contour lines are level lines.

Vertical sections are called PROFILES

Cutting plane A–A

PROFILE B–B

PROFILE A–A

Figure 20.18 A contour map shows variations in elevation on a surface. A profile is a vertical section through the contour map. To construct a profile, draw elevation lines parallel to the cutting planes, spacing them equally to show the difference in elevations of the contours (10 ft in this case). Then project crossing points of contours and the cutting plane to their respective elevations in the profile and connect them.

Profiles are vertical sections through a contour map that show the earth's surface at any desired location **(Fig. 20.18)**. Contour lines represent edge views of equally spaced horizontal planes in profiles. True representation of a profile involves use of a vertical scale equal to the scale

Figure 20.19 This model illustrates the use of contour lines in 3D space. (Courtesy of Burlington Industries.)

of the contour map; however, **the vertical scale usually is drawn larger to emphasize changes in elevation that often are slight compared to horizontal dimensions.**

Contoured surfaces also are depicted in drawings with contour lines **(Fig. 20.18)** or on models. When applied to objects other than the earth's surface—such as airfoils, automobile bodies, ship hulls, and household appliances—this technique of showing contours is called **lofting**.

Station numbers identify distances on a contour map. Surveyors use a chain (metal tape) 100 feet long, so primary stations are located 100 feet apart **(Fig. 20.20)**. For example, station 7 is 700 feet from the beginning point, station 0; a point 32 feet beyond station 7 is station 7 + 32.

A **plan–profile** combines a section of a contour map (a plan view) and a vertical section (a profile view). Engineers use plan–profile drawings extensively for construction projects such as pipelines, roadways, and waterways.

Application: Vertical Sections
In **Fig. 20.21**, a vertical section passed through the top view of an underground pipe gives a profile

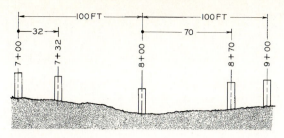

Figure 20.20 Primary station points are located 100 ft apart; for example, station 7 is 700 ft from station 0 (not shown). A point 32 ft beyond station 7 is labeled station 7 + 32. A point 870 ft from the origin is labeled station 8 + 70.

VERTICAL SECTIONS

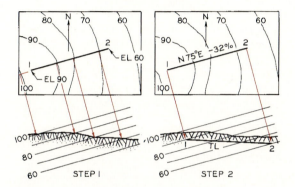

Figure 20.21 Drawing profiles (vertical sections):

Step 1 An underground pipe has elevations of 90 ft and 60 ft at its ends. Project an auxiliary view perpendicularly from the top view and draw contours at 10-ft intervals corresponding to their elevations in the plan view. Locate the ground surface by projecting from the contour lines in the plan view.

Step 2 Locate points 1 and 2 at elevations of 90 ft and 60 ft in the profile. Line 1–2 is TL in the section, so measure its slope (percent grade) here and label its bearing and slope in the top view.

Figure 20.22 Pipeline construction relies on the principles of descriptive geometry, true-length lines, and slopes of 3D lines. (Courtesy of Consumers Power Company.)

pipe in profile. To measure the true lengths and angles of slope in the profile, use the same scale for both the contour map and the profile.

Pipeline installation (**Fig. 20.22**) requires major outlays for engineering design and construction. The use of profiles, found graphically, is the best way to make cost estimations for constructing ditches for laying underground pipe.

20.7 Plan–Profiles

A plan–profile drawing shows an underground drainage system from manhole 1 to manhole 3 in **Figs. 20.23** and **20.24**. The profile has a larger vertical scale to emphasize variations in the earth's surface and the grade of the pipe, although the vertical scale may be drawn at the same scale as the plan if desired.

The location of manhole 1 is projected to the profile orthographically, **but the remaining points are not (Fig. 20.23)**. Instead, transfer the distances where the contour lines cross the top view of the pipe to their respective elevations in the profile with your dividers to show the surface of the ground over the pipe.

view. The pipe is known to have elevations of 90 feet at point 1 and 60 feet at point 2. Project an auxiliary view perpendicularly from the top view, locate contour lines, and draw the top of the earth over the

PLAN–PROFILE: VERTICAL SECTION

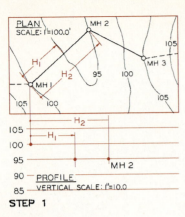

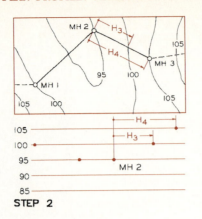

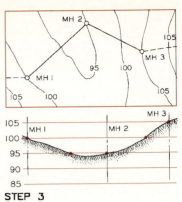

STEP 1   STEP 2   STEP 3

Figure 20.23 Plan–profile:

Required Find the profile of the earth's surface over the pipeline.

Step 1 Transfer distances H_1 and H_2 from manhole 1 in the plan view to their respective elevations in the profile view. This is not a true orthographic projection from the top view.

Step 2 Measure distances H_3 and H_4 from manhole 2 in plan and transfer them to their respective elevations in profile. These points represent elevations of points on the earth above the pipe.

Step 3 Connect these points with a freehand line and crosshatch the drawing to represent the earth's surface. Draw centerlines to show the locations of the three manholes.

PLAN–PROFILE: MANHOLE LOCATION

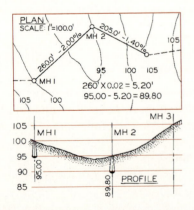

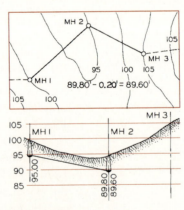

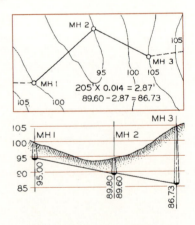

Figure 20.24 Determining manhole location in plan–profile:

Step 1 Multiply the horizontal distance from manhole 1(MH1) to manhole 2 (MH2) by the percent grade. Calculate the elevation of the bottom of MH2 by subtracting the amount of fall from the elevation of MH1.

Step 2 The lower side of MH2 is 0.20 ft lower than the inlet side to compensate for loss of head (pressure) because of the turn in the pipeline. Find the elevation on the lower side (89.60') and label it.

Step 3 Calculate the elevation of MH3 (86.73 ft) from the 1.40% grade from MH2 to MH3. Draw the flow line of the pipeline from manhole to manhole and label the elevations.

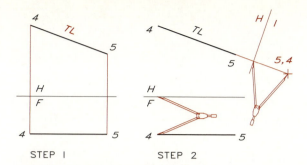

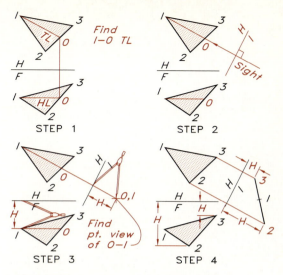

Figure 20.25 The point view of a line:

Step 1 Line 4–5 is horizontal in the front view and therefore is true length in the top view.

Step 2 Find the point view of line 4–5 by projecting parallel to its true length to the auxiliary view.

Figure 20.26 The edge view of a plane:

Step 1 To find the edge view of plane 1–2–3, draw horizontal line 1–O on its front view of the plane and project it to the top view, where it is true length.

Step 2 Draw a line of sight parallel to the true-length line 1–O. Draw reference line H1 perpendicular to the line of sight.

Step 3 Find the point view of 1–O in the auxiliary view by transferring height (H) from the front view.

Step 4 Locate points 2 and 3 in the same manner to find the edge view of the plane.

Figure. 20.24 shows the manholes, their elevations, and the bottom line of the pipe. Find the drop from manhole 1 to manhole 2 (5.20 ft) by multiplying the horizontal distance of 260.00 ft by a –2.00% grade. The pipes intersect at manhole 2 at an angle, so the flow of the drainage is disrupted at the turn. A drop of 0.20 ft across the bottom of the manhole compensates for the loss of pressure (head) through the manhole.

You cannot measure the true lengths of the pipes in the profile view when the vertical scale is different from the horizontal scale; you have to use trigonometry to calculate them.

20.8 Edge Views of Planes

Edge View

The edge view of a plane appears in a view where any line on the plane appears as a point. Recall that you can find a line as a point by projecting from its true-length view (**Fig. 20.25**). You may obtain a true-length line on any plane by drawing a line parallel to one of the principal planes and projecting it to the adjacent view (**Fig. 20.26**). You then get the edge view of the plane in an auxiliary view by finding the point view of line 3–4 on its surface.

Dihedral Angle

The angle between two planes, a dihedral angle, is found in a view where the line of intersection between two planes appears as a point. In this view, both planes appear as edges and the angle between them is true size. The line of intersection, line 1–2, between the two planes shown in **Fig. 20.27** is true length in the top view. Project an auxiliary view from the top view to find the point view of line 1–2 and the edge views of both planes.

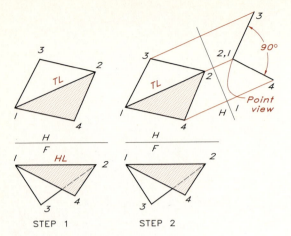

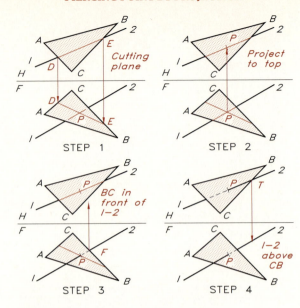

Figure 20.27 A dihedral angle:
Step 1 The line of intersection between the planes, line 1–2, is true length in the top view.

Step 2 The angle between the planes (the dihedral angle) is found in the auxiliary view where the line of intersection appears as a point and both planes are edges.

Figure 20.28 A piercing point by projection:
Step 1 Pass a vertical cutting plane through the top view of line 1–2, which cuts the plane along line DE. Project line DE to the front view to locate piercing point P.

Step 2 Project point P to the top view of line 1–2.

Step 3 Determine visibility in the front view by projecting the crossing point of lines CB and 1–2 to the top view. Because CB is encountered first, it is visible in front of line 1–2, making segment PF hidden in the front view.

Step 4 Determine visibility in the top view by projecting the crossing point of lines CB and 1–2 to the front view. Because line 1–2 is encountered first, it is above line CB, making TP visible in the top view.

20.9 Planes and Lines

Piercing Points

By Projection   **Figure 20.28** shows how to use projection to find the piercing point where line 1–2 passes through the plane. Pass cutting planes through the line and plane in the top view. Then project the trace of this cutting plane, line DE, to the front view to find piercing point P. Locate the top view of P and determine the visibility of the line.

By Auxiliary View   You may also find the piercing point of a line and a plane by auxiliary view in which the plane is an edge **(Fig. 20.29)**. The location of piercing point P in step 2 is where line AB crosses the edge view of the plane. Project point P to AB in the top view from the auxiliary view, and then to the front view. To verify the location of point P in the front view, transfer dimension H from the auxiliary view with dividers.

You can easily determine visibility for the top view because you see in the auxiliary view that line AP is higher than the plane and therefore is visible in the top view. Similarly, the top view shows that endpoint A is the forward-most point and line AP therefore is visible in the front view.

Perpendicular to a Plane
A perpendicular line appears true length and perpendicular to a plane where the plane appears as

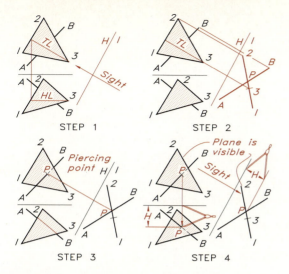

STEP 1   STEP 2

STEP 3   STEP 4

Figure 20.29 A piercing point by auxiliary view:

Step 1 Draw a horizontal line on the plane in the front view and project it to the top view where it is true length on the plane.

Step 2 Find the edge view of the plane in an auxiliary view and project line AB to this view. Point P is the piercing point.

Step 3 Project point P to line AB in the top view. Line AP is nearest the H1 reference line, so it is the highest end of the line and is visible in the top view.

Step 4 Project point P to line AB in the front view. Line AP is visible in the front view because line AP is in front of 1–2.

an edge. In **Fig. 20.30**, a line is to be drawn from point O perpendicular to the plane. Obtain an edge view of the plane and draw the true-length perpendicular to locate piercing point P. Locate point P in the top view by drawing line OP parallel to the H1 reference line. (This principle is reviewed in **Fig. 20.31**.) Line OP also is perpendicular to a true-length line in the top view of the plane. Obtain the front view of point P, along with its visibility, by projection.

Intersection

Auxiliary View Method To find the intersection between planes, find the edge view of one of the

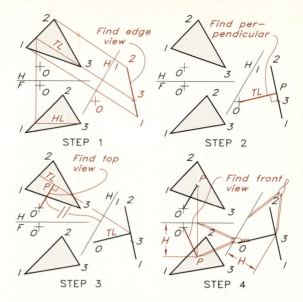

STEP 1   STEP 2

STEP 3   STEP 4

Figure 20.30 A line perpendicular to a plane:

Step 1 Find the edge view of the plane by finding the point view of a line on it in an auxiliary view. Project point O to this view, also.

Step 2 Draw line OP perpendicular to the edge view of the plane, which is true length in this view.

Step 3 Because line OP is true length in the auxiliary view, it must be parallel to the H1 reference line in the preceding view. Line OP is visible in the top view because it appears above the plane in the auxiliary view.

Step 4 Project point P to the front view and locate it by transferring height H from the auxiliary view with dividers.

planes (**Fig. 20.32**). Then project piercing points L and M from the auxiliary view to their respective lines, lines 5–6 and 4–6, in the top view. Plane 4–5–L–M is visible in the top view because sight line 1 has an unobstructed view of the 4–5–L–M portion of the plane in the auxiliary view. Plane 4–5–L–M is visible in the front view because sight line 2 has an unobstructed view of the top view of this portion of the plane.

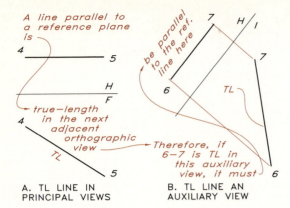

A. TL LINE IN
PRINCIPAL VIEWS

B. TL LINE AN
AUXILIARY VIEW

Figure 20.31 In the top view of Fig. 20.30, line OP is parallel to the H1 reference line because it is true length in the auxiliary view. Here, lines 4–5 and 6–7 are examples of this principle: Both are true length in one view and parallel to the reference line in the preceding view.

INTERSECTION BETWEEN PLANES

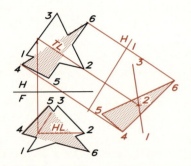
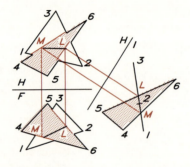
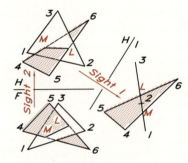

Figure 20.32 The intersection of planes by auxiliary view:

Step 1 Locate the edge view of one of the planes in an auxiliary view and project the other plane to this view.

Step 2 Piercing points L and M appear on the edge view of the plane. Project line LM to the top and front views.

Step 3 The line of sight from the top view strikes line L–5 first in the auxiliary view, indicating that line L–5 is visible in the top view. Line 4–5 is farthest forward in the top view and is visible in the front view.

20.10 Sloping Planes

Slope and Direction of Slope

The slope of a plane is described as follows:

Angle of Slope: the angle that the plane's edge view makes with the edge of the horizontal plane.

Direction of Slope: the compass bearing of a line perpendicular to a true-length line in the top view of a plane toward its low side (the direction in which a ball would roll on the plane).

As **Fig. 20.33** shows, a ball would roll perpendicular to all horizontal lines on the roof toward the low side. **Figure 20.34** shows how to find a plane's direction of slope and slope angle.

You can establish a plane in three dimensions by working from slope and direction specifica-

SLOPE OF PLANE: DEFINITION

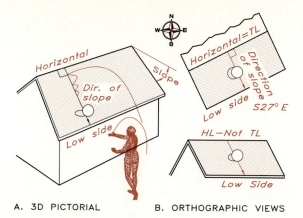

A. 3D PICTORIAL   B. ORTHOGRAPHIC VIEWS

Figure 20.33 Slope definition:

A The direction of slope of a plane is the compass bearing of the direction in which a ball on the plane will roll.

B Slope direction is measured in the top view toward the low side of the plane and perpendicular to a horizontal line on the plane.

SLOPE AND BEARING OF A PLANE

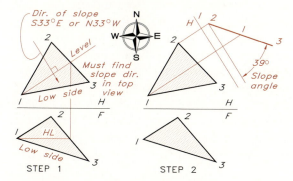

STEP 1   STEP 2

Figure 20.34 The slope and bearing of a plane:

Step 1 Slope direction is perpendicular to a true-length, level line in the top view toward the low side of the plane, or S 33° E in this case.

Step 2 Find the slope in an auxiliary view where the horizontal is an edge and the plane is an edge, or 39° in this case.

FINDING A PLANE FROM SLOPE SPECIFICATIONS

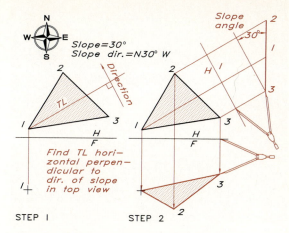

STEP 1   STEP 2

Figure 20.35 A plane from slope specifications:

Step 1 If the top view of a plane, the front view of point 1, and slope specifications are given, you can complete the front view. Draw the direction of slope in the top view and a true-length horizontal line on the plane perpendicular to the slope direction.

Step 2 Find a point view of the TL line in the auxiliary view to locate point 1. Draw the edge view of the plane through point 1 at a slope of 30°, according to the specifications. Find the front view by transferring height dimensions from the auxiliary view to the front view.

tions (**Fig. 20.35**). Draw the direction of slope in the top view to locate a perpendicular true-length line on the plane. Find the edge view of the plane by locating point 1 and constructing a slope of 30° through it in an auxiliary view. Transfer points 3 and 2 to the front view from the auxiliary view.

Application: Cut and Fill

A level roadway through irregular terrain and the embankment for an earthen dam (**Fig. 20.36**) involve the principles of cut and fill. **Cut and fill** is the process of cutting away high ground and filling low areas, generally of equal volumes.

In **Fig. 20.37**, a level roadway at an elevation of 60 feet is to be constructed along a specified centerline with specified angles of cut and fill. First,

Figure 20.36 This dam was built by applying the principles of cut and fill. (Courtesy of the Bureau of Reclamation, U.S. Department of the Interior.)

draw the roadway in the top view. Use contour intervals in the profile view of 10 feet to match those in the top view.

Next, measure and draw the cut angles on both sides of the roadway. Project the points where the cut angles cross each elevation line to the respective contour lines in the plan view to find the limits of cut.

Then, measure and draw the fill angles in the profile view. Project the points where the fill angles cross each elevation line to the respective contour lines in the plan view to find the limits of fill. Finally, draw new contour lines inside the areas of cut parallel the centerline.

Application: Design of a Dam

Some of the terms used in designing a dam are (1) *crest,* or the top of the dam; (2) *water level;* and (3) *freeboard,* or the height of the crest above the water level (**Fig. 20.38**). The earthen dam shown in **Fig. 20.39** is an arc in plan view, with its center at C. The finished plan–profile drawing depicts both

the dam and the level of the water held by the dam.

Figure 20.40 is a photo of the 726-foot-high Hoover Dam, built in the 1930s. Because it was constructed of reinforced concrete instead of earth, the dam was designed in the shape of an arch bowed toward the water, taking advantage of the compressive strength of concrete.

Strike and Dip

Strike and dip are terms used in geology and mining engineering to describe the location of strata of ore under the surface of the earth:

> **Strike:** the compass bearings (two are possible) of a level line in the top view of a plane.

> **Dip:** the angle that the edge view of a plane makes with the horizontal and its general compass direction, such as NW or SW.

The dip angle lies in the primary auxiliary view projected from the top view. The dip direction is perpendicular to the strike and toward its low side.

Figure 20.41 demonstrates how to find the strike and dip of a plane. Here, the true-length line in the top view of the plane has a strike of N 66° W or S 66° E. The dip angle appears in an auxiliary view projected from the top view that shows the horizontal (H1) and the plane as edges.

You may construct a plane from strike and dip specifications (**Fig. 20.42**). First, draw the strike as a true-length horizontal line on the plane and the dip direction perpendicular to the strike. Then find the edge view of the plane in the auxiliary view through point 1 at a dip of 30°. Locate points 2 and 3 in the front view by transferring them from the auxiliary view.

20.11 Ore-Vein Applications

The principles of descriptive geometry can be applied to find the distance from a point to a plane. Techniques of finding such distances often are used to solve mining and geological problems.

CUT AND FILL OF A LEVEL ROADWAY

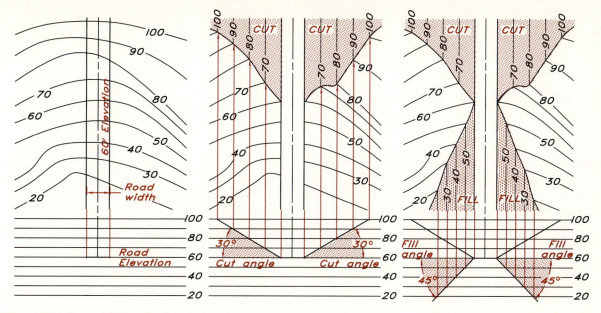

Figure 20.37 Cut and fill for a level roadway:

Step 1 Draw and label a series of elevation planes in the front view at the same scale as the contour map. Draw the width and elevation (60′ in this case) of the roadway in the top and front views.

Step 2 Draw the cut angles on the higher sides of the road in the front view. Project the points of intersection between the cut angles and the contour planes in the front view to their respective contour lines in the top view to determine the limits of cut.

Step 3 Draw the fill angles on the lower sides of the road in the front view. Project the points in the front view where the fill angles cross the contour lines to their respective contour lines in the top view to give the limits of fill. Draw contour lines parallel to the centerline in the cut-and-fill areas to indicate the new contours.

TERMINOLOGY OF DAMS

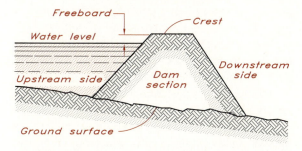

Figure 20.38 These terms and symbols are used in the design of a dam.

Application: Underground Ore Veins

Geologists and mining engineers usually assume that strata of ore veins have upper and lower planes that are parallel. In **Fig. 20.43**, point O is on the upper surface of the earth and plane 1–2–3 is an underground ore vein. Point 4 is on the lower plane of the vein.

Find the edge view of plane 1-2-3 by projecting from the top view and then draw the lower plane through point 4 parallel to the upper plane. Draw the horizontal distance from point O to the plane parallel to the H1 reference line and the vertical

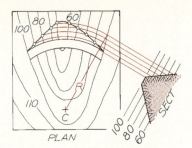

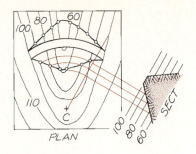

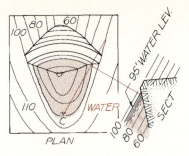

Figure 20.39 An arc-shaped dam:
Step 1 An arc-shaped dam with its center at C has a crest elevation of 100'. Draw radius R from C, project perpendicularly from this line, and draw a section (profile) through the dam from the specifications. Project the downstream side of the dam to radial line R. Use the radii from C to locate points on their respective contours.

Step 2 Project the elevations of the dam on the upstream side of the section to the radial line R. Use center C and your compass to locate points on their respective contour lines in the plan view as you project them from the profile.

Step 3 Draw the water level (95') in the profile. Project the points where the water intersects the dam to the radial line in the plan view as an arc from center C. Draw the upper limit of the water level between the 90' and 100' contour lines in the top view.

Figure 20.40 The Hoover Dam and Lake Mead, built from 1931 to 1935, is a classic dam design and a major civil engineering achievement. (Courtesy of the Bureau of Reclamation, U.S. Department of the Interior.)

distance perpendicular to line H1. The shortest distance is perpendicular to the ore vein. These three lines from point O are true length in the auxiliary view where the ore vein appears as an edge.

Application: Ore-Vein Outcrop

The same assumption regarding parallel planes is made in analyzing the orientation of underground ore veins that are inclined to the earth's surface and outcrop on its surface. When ore veins outcrop, open-pit mining can be used to reduce costs.

Figure 20.44 shows how to find the outcrop of an ore vein from the locations of sample drillings given on a contour map. Points A, B, and C are located on the upper plane of the ore vein, and point D is located on the lower plane of the vein. Draw them in the front view at their determined elevations.

STRIKE AND DIP OF A PLANE

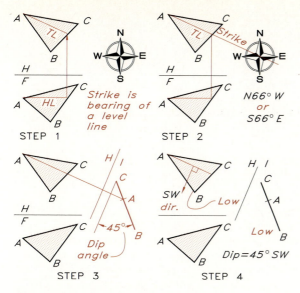

Figure 20.41 The strike and dip of a plane:

Step 1 Draw a horizontal line on the plane in the front view and project it to the top view, where it is true length.

Step 2 Strike is the compass direction of a level line on the plane in the top view—here, either N 66° W or S 66° E.

Step 3 Find the edge view of the plane in the auxiliary view. The dip angle of 45° is the angle between the H1 reference line and the edge view of the plane.

Step 4 The general compass direction of dip is toward the low side, and perpendicular to a strike in the top view or SW in this case. Dip direction in this example is 45 SW.

Find the edge view of the ore vein in an auxiliary view projected from the top view. Then project points on the upper surface where the vein crosses elevation lines back to their respective contour lines in the top view. Also project points on the lower surface of the vein (through point D) to the top. If the ore vein extends uniformly at its angle of inclination to the earth's surface, the area between these two lines will be the outcrop of the vein.

FINDING A PLANE FROM STRIKE AND DIP SPECS

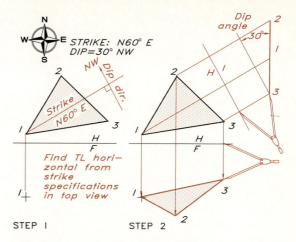

Figure 20.42 Strike and dip specifications:
Step 1 Draw the strike in the top view of the plane as a true-length horizontal line. Draw the direction of dip perpendicular to the strike toward the NW as specified.

Step 2 Find the point view of strike in the auxiliary view to locate point 1 where the edge view of the plane passes through it at a 30° dip, as specified. Complete the front view by transferring height (H) dimensions from the auxiliary to the front view.

DISTANCES FROM A POINT TO A PLANE

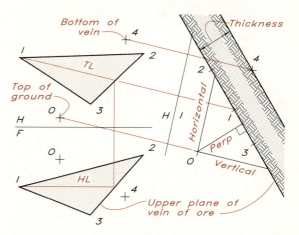

Figure 20.43 To find the vertical, horizontal, and perpendicular distances from a point to an ore vein, project an auxiliary view from the top view, where the vein appears as an edge. The thickness of an ore vein is perpendicular to the upper and lower planes of the vein.

ORE-VEIN OUTCROP

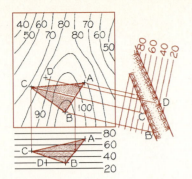
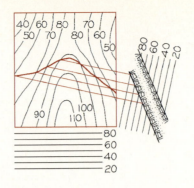
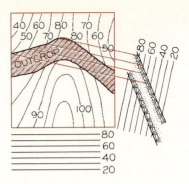

Figure 20.44 Locating an ore-vein outcrop:

Step 1 Use points A, B, and C on the upper surface of the ore vein to find its edge view by projecting an auxiliary from the top view. Draw the lower surface of the vein parallel to the upper plane through point D.

Step 2 Project points of intersection between the upper plane of the vein and the contour lines in the auxiliary view to their respective contours in the top view to find a line of the outcrop.

Step 3 Project points from the lower plane in the auxiliary view to their respective contours in the top view to find the second line of outcrop. Crosshatch the area between the lines to depict the outcrop of the vein.

INTERSECTION BETWEEN PLANES: STRIKE AND DIP METHOD

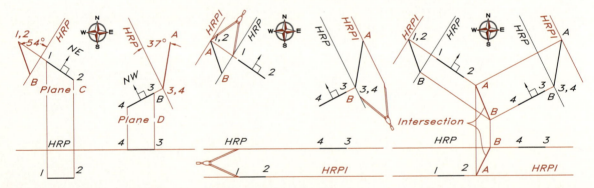

Figure 20.45 The intersection of planes by the strike and dip method:

Step 1 Lines 1–2 and 3–4 are strike lines and are true length in the top view. Use a common reference plane, HRP, to find the point view of each strike line by auxiliary views. Find the edge views by drawing the dip angles with the HRP line through the point views. The low side is the side of the dip arrow.

Step 2 Draw a supplementary horizontal plane, HRP1, at a convenient location in the front view. This plane, shown in both auxiliary views, is located H distance from HRP. The HRP1 cuts through each edge in both auxiliary views, locating A and B on each plane.

Step 3 Project points A from both auxiliary views of HRP1 in the top view to their intersection at A. Project points B and HRP1 to their intersection in the top view. Project points A and B to their respective planes in the front view. Line AB is the line of intersection between the two planes.

20.12 Intersections Between Planes

Strike and Dip Method

Figure 20.45 shows how to locate the intersection of two planes located with strike and dip specifications. The given strike lines are true-length level lines in the top view, so the edge view of the planes appear in the auxiliary views where the strikes appear as points. Draw the edge views using the given dip angles and directions.

Use the additional horizontal datum plane HRP1 to find lines on each plane at equal elevations that intersect when projected to the top view from their auxiliary views. Connect points A and B as the line of intersection between the two planes in the top view and project it to the front view to establish line AB in three dimensions.

Cutting Plane Method

In **Fig. 20.46**, top and front views of two planes are given and the line of intersection between them, if they were extended, is to be determined. Draw cutting planes through both planes in either view at any angle and project them to the top view. Find points L and M in the top view to establish the line of intersection. Find the front view of line LM, the line of intersection, by projecting its endpoints from the top view to their respective planes in the front view.

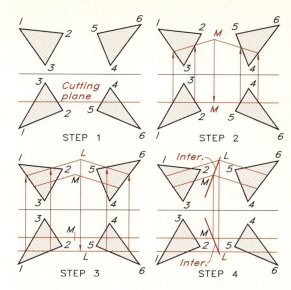

Figure 20.46 The intersection of planes by the cutting plane method:

Step 1 Draw a cutting plane that passes through both planes in the front view in any convenient direction.

Step 2 Project the intersections of the cutting plane to the top views of the planes. Find intersection point M in the top view and project it to the front view.

Step 3 Draw a second cutting plane through the front view of the planes and project it to the top view. Find intersection point L in the top view and project it to the front view.

Step 4 Connect points L and M in the top and front views to represent the 3D line of intersection of the extended planes.

Problems

Use size A sheets for your solutions to the following problems and lay out the solutions using instruments. Each square on the grid is equal to 0.20 inch (5 mm). You may use either grid or plain paper. Label all reference planes and points with $1/8$-in. (3 mm) letters or numbers, using guidelines.

1. (Fig. 20.47)

(A–D) Find the true-length views of the lines by auxiliary view as indicated by the given lines of sight. Alternative method: Find the true length of the lines by the Pythagorean theorem.

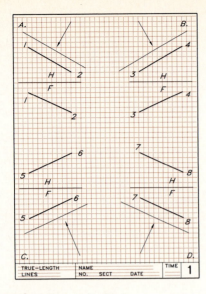

Figure 20.47 Problem 1 (A–D).

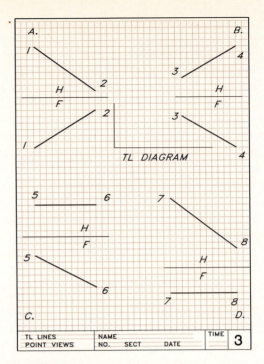

Figure 20.49 Problem 3 (A–D).

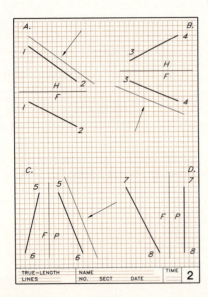

Figure 20.48 Problem 2 (A–D).

2. (Fig. 20.48)

(A–D) Find the true-length views of the lines by auxiliary view as indicated by the lines of sight. Alternative method: Find the true length of the lines by the Pythagorean theorem.

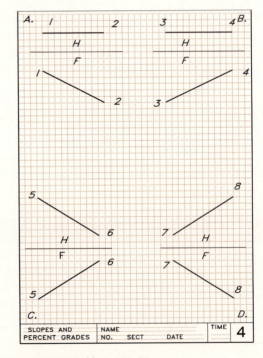

Figure 20.50 Problem 4 (A–D).

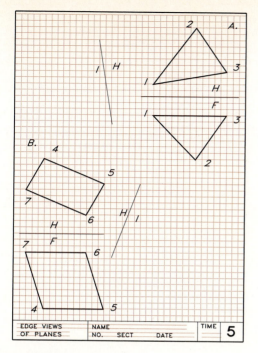

Figure 20.51 Problem 5 (A, B).

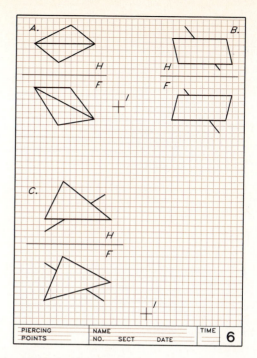

Figure 20.52 Problem 6 (A–C).

3. (Fig. 20.49)

(A, B) Find the true length of the lines with a true-length diagram.

(C, D) Find the point views of the lines.

4. (Fig. 20.50)

(A–D) Find the slope angle, tangent of the slope angle, and the percent grade of the four lines.

5. (Fig. 20.51)

(A, B) Find the edge views of the planes.

6. (Fig. 20.52)

(A) Find the angle between the planes.

(B) By projection, find the projection point between the line and plane and show visibility.

(C) By the auxiliary view method, find the point of intersection between the line and plane and show visibility.

7. (Fig. 20.53)

(A) Construct a 1-in. line perpendicular from point O on the plane and show it in all views.

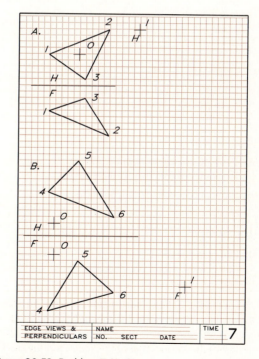

Figure 20.53 Problem 7 (A, B).

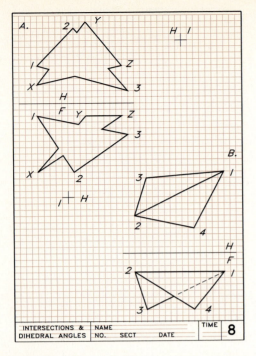

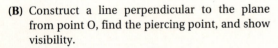

| INTERSECTIONS & | NAME | | TIME | 8 |
| DIHEDRAL ANGLES | NO. SECT DATE | | | |

Figure 20.54 Problem 8 (A, B).

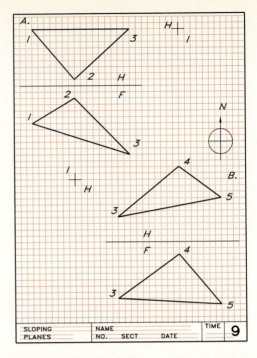

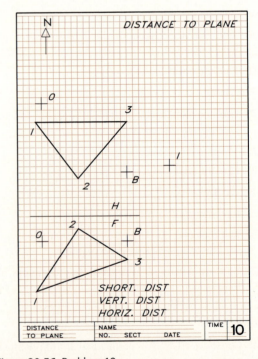

| SLOPING | NAME | | TIME | 9 |
| PLANES | NO. SECT DATE | | | |

Figure 20.55 Problem 9 (A, B).

(B) Construct a line perpendicular to the plane from point O, find the piercing point, and show visibility.

8. (Fig. 20.54)

   (A) Find the line of intersection between the intersecting planes by using an auxiliary view.

   (B) Find the angle between the planes by using an auxiliary view.

9. (Fig. 20.55)

(A, B) Find the direction of slope and the slope angle of the planes. Alternative method: Find the strike and dip of the planes.

10. (Fig. 20.56) Find the shortest distance, the horizontal distance, and the vertical distance from point O to the underground ore vein represented by plane 1–2–3. Point B is on the lower plane of the vein. Find the thickness of the vein.

DISTANCE TO PLANE

SHORT. DIST
VERT. DIST
HORIZ. DIST

| DISTANCE | NAME | | TIME | 10 |
| TO PLANE | NO. SECT DATE | | | |

Figure 20.56 Problem 10.

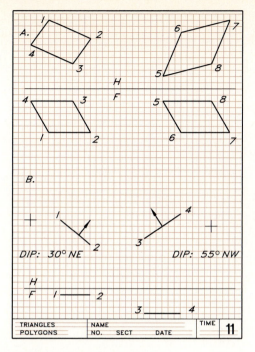

Figure 20.57 Problem 11 (A, B).

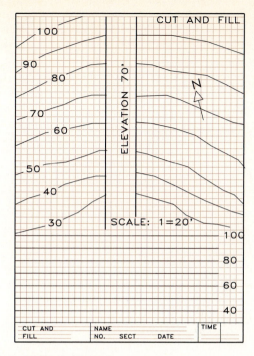

Figure 20.58 Problem 12.

11. (Fig. 20.57)

(A) Find the line of intersection between the two planes by the cutting plane method.

(B) Find the line of intersection between the two planes indicated by strike lines 1–2 and 3–4. The plane with strike line 1–2 has a dip of 30°, and the plane with strike line 3–4 has a dip of 55°.

12. (Fig. 20.58) Find the limits of cut and fill in the plan view of the roadway. Use a cut angle of 35° and fill angle of 40°.

13. (Fig. 20.59) Find the outcrop of the ore vein represented by plane 1–2–3 on its upper surface. Point B is on the lower surface.

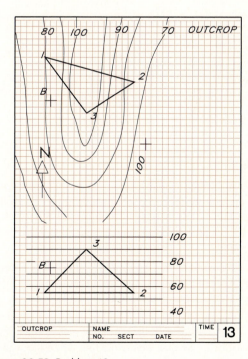

Figure 20.59 Problem 13.

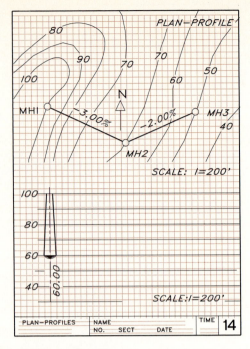

Figure 20.60 Problem 14.

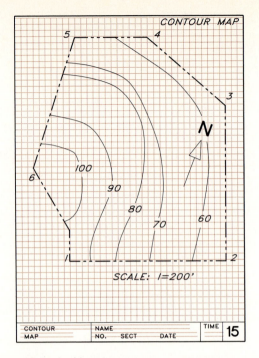

Figure 20.61 Problem 15.

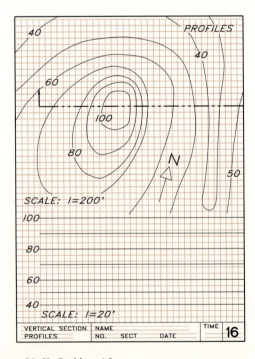

14. (Fig. 20.60) Complete the plan–profile drawing of the drainage system from manhole 1 through manhole 2 to manhole 3, using the grades indicated. Allow a drop of 0.20 ft across each manhole to compensate for loss of pressure.

15. (Fig. 20.61) Draw the contour map with its contour lines. Give the lengths of the sides, their compass directions, interior angles, scale, and north arrow.

16. (Fig. 20.62) Draw the contour map and construct the profile (vertical section) as indicated by the cutting plane line in the plan view. Note that the profile scale is different from the plan scale.

Figure 20.62 Problem 16.

21

Successive Auxiliary Views

21.1 Introduction

A detailed drawing and specifications for a design cannot be completed without determining its geometry, which usually requires the application of descriptive geometry. The structural supports for the shopping mall shown in **Fig. 21.1** are examples of complex descriptive geometry problems in which lengths must be determined, angles between lines and planes calculated, and 3D connectors designed.

The process of determining the 3D geometry of a design requires the use of secondary and successive auxiliary views. **Secondary auxiliary views are views projected from primary auxiliary views, and successive auxiliary views are views projected from secondary auxiliary views.**

21.2 Point View of a Line

Recall that, when a line appears true length, you can find its point view in a primary auxiliary view projected parallel from it. In **Fig. 21.2**, line 1–2 is true length in the top view because it is horizontal

Figure 21.1 This structural support of the roof system of a shopping mall was designed and fabricated through the application of descriptive geometry. (Courtesy of Lorna Stuckgold, Kaiser Engineers.)

POINT VIEW OF A LINE

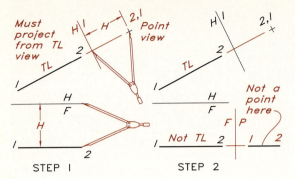

Figure 21.2 To find the point of view of a line, project an auxiliary view from the true-length view of the line.

POINT VIEW OF AN OBLIQUE LINE

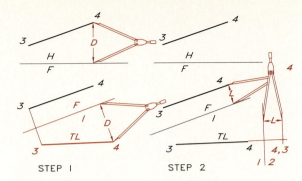

Figure 21.3 A point view of an oblique line:

Step 1 Draw a line of sight perpendicular to one of the views, the front view in this case. Line 3–4 is found true length in an auxiliary view projected perpendicularly from the front view.

Step 2 Draw a secondary reference line, 1–2, perpendicular to the true-length view of line 3–4. Find the point view by transferring dimension L from the front view to the secondary auxiliary view.

in the front view. To find its point view in the primary auxiliary view, first construct reference line H1 perpendicular to the true-length line. Transfer the height dimension, H, to the auxiliary view to locate the point view of 1–2.

Line 3–4 in **Fig. 21.3** is not true length in either view. Finding the line's true length by a primary auxiliary view allows you to find its point view. To obtain a true-length view of line 3–4, project an auxiliary view from the front view (or from the top view). Projecting parallel from the true-length view to a secondary auxiliary view yields the point view of line 3–4. Label the line 4–3 because you see point 4 first in the secondary auxiliary view. Label the reference line between the primary and secondary planes 1–2 to represent the primary (1) and secondary (2) planes.

21.3 Dihedral Angles

Recall that the angle between two planes is called **a dihedral angle and can be found in a view where the line of intersection appears as a point.** The line of intersection lies on both planes, so both appear as edges when the intersection is a point view.

The planes shown in **Fig. 21.4** represent a special case because their line of intersection, line 1–2, is true length in the top view. This condition

DIHEDRAL ANGLE

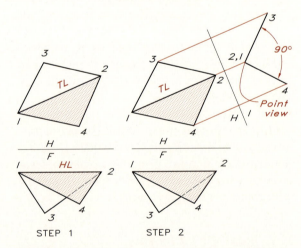

Figure 21.4 The angle between planes (the dihedral angle) appears in the view where their line of intersection projects as a point. The line of intersection, 1–2, is true length in the top view, so it can be found as a point in a view projected from the top view.

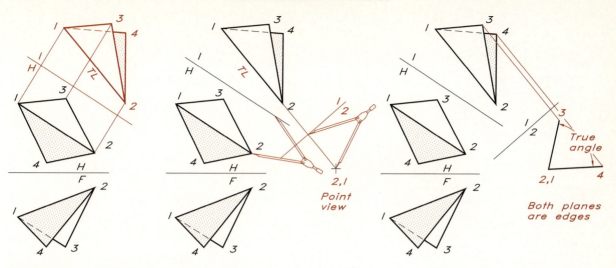

Figure 21.5 The angle between two planes:

Step 1 The angle between two planes is found in a view where the line of intersection (1–2) appears as a point. Find the true-length view of the intersection in a primary auxiliary view projected perpendicularly from it in the top view.

Step 2 Obtain the point view of the line of intersection in the secondary auxiliary view by projecting parallel to the true-length view of line 1–2.

Step 3 Complete the edge views of the planes in the secondary auxiliary view by locating points 3 and 4. Measure the angle between the planes (the dihedral angle) in this view.

permits you to find the line's point view in a primary auxiliary view and measure the true angle between the planes.

Figure 21.5 presents a more typical case. Here, the line of intersection between the two planes is not true length in either view. The line of intersection, line 1–2, is true length in a primary auxiliary view, and the point view of the line appears in the secondary auxiliary view, where you measure the dihedral angle.

This principle was applied to determine the angles between wall panels of the control tower shown in **Fig. 21.6**. That allowed the corner braces to be designed and the structure to be assembled correctly.

21.4 True Size of a Plane

A plane can be found true size in a view projected perpendicularly from an edge view of a plane. The front view of plane 1–2–3 in **Fig. 21.7** appears as an edge in the front view as a special case. The plane's true size is in a primary auxiliary view projected perpendicularly from the edge view.

Figure 21.8 depicts a general case in which you can find the true-size view of plane 1–2–3 by finding the edge view of the plane and constructing a secondary auxiliary view projected perpendicularly from the edge view to find the plane true size.

This principle can be applied to find the angle between lines such as bends in an automobile

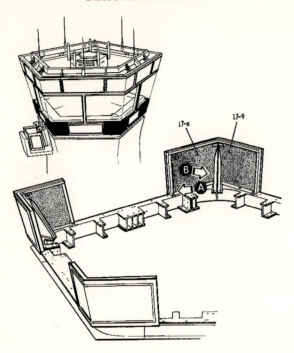

Figure 21.6 These control tower wall panels that intersect at compound angles illustrate the application of methods used to measure dihedral angles. The designer had to determine the angles between the wall panels in order to design corner connectors for securing the panels at their joints.

exhaust pipe **(Fig. 21.9)**. **Figure 21.10** shows how to solve this type of problem. The top and front views of intersecting centerlines are given, the angles of bend and the radii of curvature must be found. Angle 1–2–3 is an edge in the primary auxiliary view and true size in the secondary view, where it can be measured and the radius of curvature drawn.

21.5 Shortest Distance from a Point to a Line: Line Method

The shortest distance from a point to a line can be measured in the view where the line appears

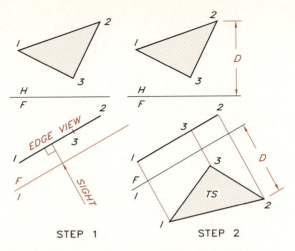

STEP 1   STEP 2

Figure 21.7 The true size of a plane (special case):
Step 1 Because plane 1–2–3 appears as an edge in the front view, it is a special case. Draw the line of sight perpendicular to its edge and the F1 reference line parallel to the edge.

Step 2 Find the true size of plane 1–2–3 in the primary auxiliary view by locating the vertex points with the depth D dimension.

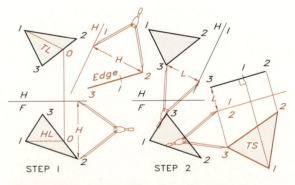

STEP 1   STEP 2

Figure 21.8 The true size of a plane (general case):
Step 1 Find the edge view of plane 1–2–3 by obtaining the point view of true-length line 1–O in a primary auxiliary view.

Step 2 Find a true-size view by projecting a secondary auxiliary view perpendicularly from the edge view of the plane.

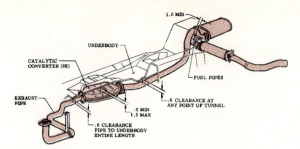

Figure 21.9 The designer determined the angles of bend in this automobile exhaust pipe by applying the principles of the angle between two lines. (Courtesy of General Motors Corporation.)

ANGLE BETWEEN LINES

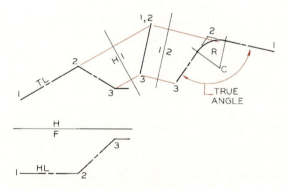

Figure 21.10 The angle between two lines is obtained by finding the plane of the two lines true size.

as a point. The shortest distance from point 3 to line 1–2 that appears in a primary auxiliary view in **Fig. 21.11** (Step 1) is a special case. The distance from point 3 to the line is true length in the auxiliary view where the line is a point, so it is parallel to reference line F1 in the front view.

Figure 21.12 shows how to solve a general-case problem of this type, where neither line appears true length in the given views. Line 1–2 is true length in the primary auxiliary projected perpendicularly from the front view. The point view

SHORTEST DISTANCE TO A LINE

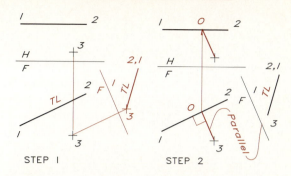

Figure 21.11 The shortest distance from a point to a line:
Step 1 The shortest distance from a point to a line is the true length where the line (1–2) appears as a point. The true-length view of the connecting line appears in the primary auxiliary view.

Step 2 When the connecting line is projected back to the front view, it must be parallel to the F1 reference line in the front view. Project line 3–O back to the top view.

of line 1–2 lies in the secondary auxiliary view, where the distance from point 3 is true length. Because line O–3 is true length in this view, it will be parallel to reference line 1–2 in the preceding view, the primary auxiliary view. It is also perpendicular to the true-length view of line 1–2 in the primary auxiliary view.

21.6 Shortest Distance Between Skewed Lines: Line Method

Randomly positioned (nonparallel) lines are called **skewed lines**. **The shortest distance between two skewed lines is found in the view where one of the lines appears as a point.**

The shortest distance between two lines is a line perpendicular to both lines. The location of the shortest distance between lines is both functional and economical. **Figure 21.13** shows standard 90° pipe connectors (tees and elbows) that are used to make the shortest connections between skewed pipes.

SHORTEST DISTANCE FROM A POINT TO A LINE

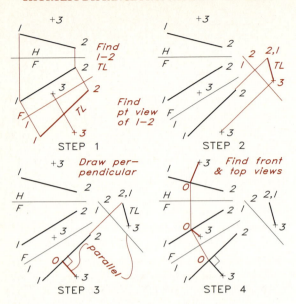

Figure 21.12 The shortest distance from a point to a line:
Step 1 The shortest distance from a point to a line is found in the view where the line appears as a point. Find the true length of line 1–2 by projecting from the front view.

Step 2 Line 1–2 is a point in a secondary auxiliary view projected from the true-length view of line 1–2. The shortest distance to it is true length in this view.

Step 3 Since 3–O is true length in the secondary auxiliary view, it is parallel to the 1–2 reference line in the primary auxiliary view and perpendicular to the line.

Step 4 Find the front and top views of 3–O by projecting from the primary auxiliary view in sequence.

Figure 21.14 illustrates how to find the shortest distance between skewed lines with the line method. Find the true length of line 3–4 and then its point view in the secondary auxiliary view, where the shortest distance is perpendicular to line 1–2. Because the distance between the lines is true length in the secondary auxiliary view, it is parallel to reference line 1–2 in the primary auxiliary view. Find point O by projection and draw OP perpendicular to line 3–4. Project the line back to the given principal views.

PIPE CONNECTORS

Tee

90° Elbow

Figure 21.13 The shortest distance between two lines or two planes is a line perpendicular to both. Thus the most economical and functional connection of pipes is by 90° tees and elbows, which are standard connectors.

21.7 Shortest Distance Between Skewed Lines: Plane Method

You may also determine the shortest distance between skewed lines by the plane method, which requires construction of a plane through one of the lines parallel to the other **(Fig. 21.15)**. The top and front views of line O–2 are parallel to their respective views of line 3–4. Therefore plane 1–2–O is parallel to line 3–4. Both lines will appear parallel in an auxiliary view, where plane 1–2–0 appears as an edge.

Figure 21.16 demonstrates this principle. First construct plane 3–4–O. When its edge view is found in a primary auxiliary view, the lines appear parallel. To find the secondary auxiliary view where both lines are true length and cross, project a secondary auxiliary view perpendicularly from these parallel lines. The crossing point is the point view of the shortest distance between the lines. That distance is true length and perpendicular to both lines when projected to the primary auxiliary view as line LM. Project LM back to the given views to complete the solution.

The principle of the shortest distance between two skewed lines is used to determine the separation of power lines, where clearance is critical **(Fig. 21.17)**.

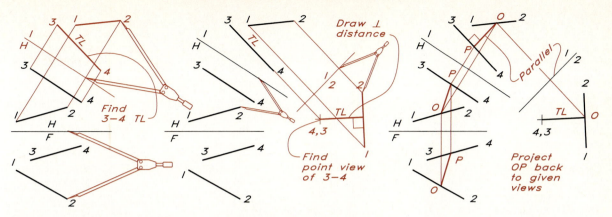

Figure 21.14 The shortest distance between skewed lines (line method):

Step 1 The shortest distance between two skewed lines appears in the view where one of the lines is a point. Find the true length of line 3–4, by projecting it from the top view along with line 1–2.

Step 2 Find the point view of line 3–4 in a secondary auxiliary view projected from the true-length view of line 3–4. The shortest distance between the lines is perpendicular to line 1–2.

Step 3 The shortest distance is true length in the secondary auxiliary view, so it must be parallel to the 1–2 reference line in the preceding view. Project line OP back to the given views.

PLANE PARALLEL TO A LINE

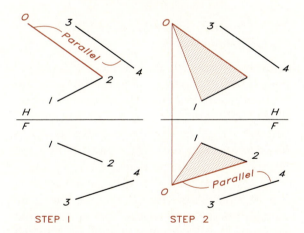

STEP 1 STEP 2

Figure 21.15 A plane through a line and parallel to another line:

Step 1 Draw line O–2 parallel to line 3–4 to a convenient length.

Step 2 Draw the front view of line O–2 parallel to the front view of line 3–4. Find the length of line O–2 in the front view by projecting from the top view of O. Plane 1–2–O is parallel to line 3–4.

21.8 Shortest Level Distance Between Skewed Lines

The shortest level (horizontal) distance between two skewed lines can be found by the plane method but not by the line method. In **Fig. 21.18**, plane 3–4–O is constructed parallel to line 1–2, and its edge view is found in the primary auxiliary view. Lines 1–2 and 3–4 appear parallel in this view, and the horizontal reference plane H1 appears as an edge.

A line of sight parallel to H1 is used, and the secondary reference line, 1–2, is drawn perpendicular to H1. The crossing point of the lines in the secondary auxiliary view locates the point view of the shortest horizontal distance between the lines. This line, LM, is true length in the primary auxiliary view and parallel to the H1 plane. Line LM is projected back to the given views. As a check on construction, LM must be parallel to the HF line in the front view, verifying that it is a level or horizontal line.

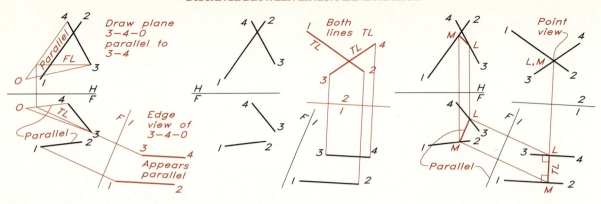

Figure 21.16 The shortest distance between skewed lines (plane method):

Step 1 Construct a plane through line 3–4 parallel to line 1–2. Find plane 3–4–O as an edge by projecting it from the front view, and the two lines will appear parallel.

Step 2 The shortest distance is true length in the primary auxiliary view and perpendicular to both lines. Project the secondary auxiliary view perpendicularly from the lines in the primary auxiliary to find both lines true length.

Step 3 The crossing point of the two lines is the point view of the perpendicular distance (LM) between them. Project LM to the primary auxiliary view, where it is true length, and back to the given views.

Figure 21.17 The determination of clearance between power lines is an electrical engineering problem that involves the application of methods of finding the distance between skewed lines. (Courtesy of the Tennessee Valley Authority.)

21.9 Shortest Grade Distance Between Skewed Lines

Features of many applications (such as highways, power lines, or conveyors) are connected to other features at specified grades other than horizontal or perpendicular. For example, the design of conveyors, such as the one shown in **Fig. 21.19,** for transporting aggregate or grain involves the specification of slopes for optimum operation.

If you need to find a 40% grade connector between two lines (Fig. 21.20), use the plane method. To obtain an edge view of the horizontal plane from which the 40% grade is constructed, you must project the primary auxiliary view from the top view. Construct a view in which the lines appear parallel and draw a 40% grade line from the edge view of the horizontal (H1) by laying off rise and run units of 4 and 10, respectively. The grade line may be constructed in two directions

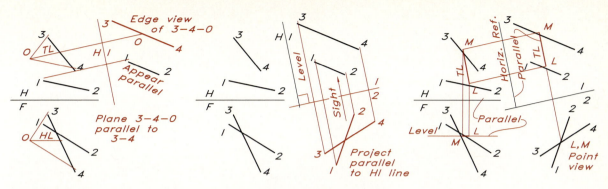

Figure 21.18 The shortest level distance between skewed lines (plane method):

Step 1 Construct plane O–3–4 parallel to line 1–2 by drawing line O–4 parallel to line 1–2. Find the edge view of plane O–3–4 by projecting off the top view, where the lines appear parallel. Project the auxiliary view from the top view to find the horizontal plane as an edge.

Step 2 Infinitely many horizontal (level) lines may be drawn parallel to reference line H1 between the lines in the auxiliary view, but the shortest one appears true length. Construct the secondary auxiliary view by projecting parallel to H1 to find the point view of the shortest level line.

Step 3 The crossing point of the two lines in the secondary auxiliary view is the point view of the level connector, LM. Project line LM back to the given views. Line LM is parallel to the horizontal reference plane in the front view, verifying that it is a level line.

Figure 21.19 The design of these conveyors involved the principles of skewed lines on a grade. (Courtesy of the American Aggregate Corporation.)

from the H1 reference line, but the shortest distance is the direction most nearly perpendicular to both lines.

Project the secondary auxiliary view parallel to this 40% grade line to find the crossing point of the lines to locate the shortest connector, LM. Project line LM back to all views; it is true length in the primary auxiliary view, where the given lines appear parallel.

The shortest distances between skewed lines—perpendicular, horizontal, and perpendicular—are true length in the view where the lines appear parallel. The plane method is the general-case method that can be used to find any shortest connector between two lines.

21.10 Angular Distance to a Line

Standard connectors used to connect pipes and structural members are available in two standard angles: 90° (see Fig. 21.13) and 45°. Specifying these standard connectors in a design is far more economical than calling for fabrication of specially made connectors.

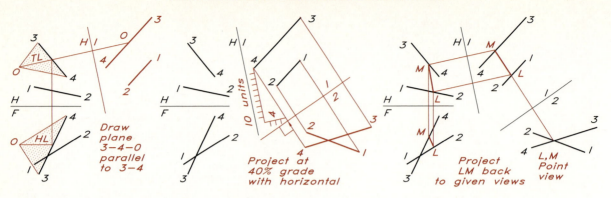

Figure 21.20 The grade distance between skewed lines:

Step 1 To find a level line or a line on a grade between two skewed lines, the primary auxiliary must be projected from the top view. Construct plane 3–4–O parallel to line 1–2. Find the edge view of the plane, and the lines appear parallel.

Step 2 Construct a 40% grade line from the edge view of the H1 reference line in the primary auxiliary view that is most nearly perpendicular to the lines. Project the secondary auxiliary view parallel to the grade line. The shortest grade distance appears true length in the primary auxiliary.

Step 3 The point of crossing of the two lines in the secondary auxiliary view establishes the point view of the 40% grade line, LM. Project LM back to the previous views in sequence.

In **Fig. 21.21**, a line from point O that makes an angle of 45° with line 1–2 is to be found. Connect point O with the line's endpoints, 1 and 2, to find plane 1–2–O in the top and front views, and find its edge view in a primary auxiliary view. Find the true-size view of plane 1–2–O by projecting perpendicularly from its edge view. Measure the angle of the line from point O in this view, **where the plane of the line and point is true size**.

Draw the 45° connector from point O toward point 2 (the low point) if it slopes downward or toward point 1 if it slopes upward. Determine the upper and lower ends of line 1–2 by referring to the front view, where the height is easily seen. Project the 45° line, OP, back to the given views.

21.11 Angle Between a Line and a Plane: Plane Method

The angle between a line and a plane can be measured in the view **where the plane appears as**

an edge and the line appears true length. In **Fig. 21.22**, the edge view of plane 1–2–3 lies in a primary auxiliary view projected from the top view and is true size (step 2) where the line appears foreshortened. Line AB is true length in a third successive auxiliary view projected perpendicularly from the secondary auxiliary view of line AB. The line appears true length and the plane appears as an edge in the third successive auxiliary view.

21.12 Angle Between a Line and a Plane: Line Method

An alternative method (not illustrated here) of finding the angle between a line and a plane is the line method. In that method, the line, rather than the plane, is the primary geometric element that is projected. The line is found as true length in a primary auxiliary view, it is found as a point in the secondary auxiliary view, and the plane is found as

ANGULAR DISTANCE TO A LINE

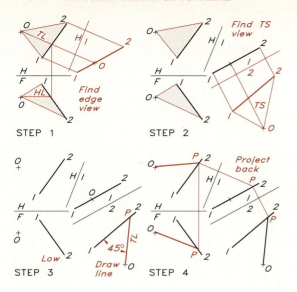

STEP 1

STEP 2

Find TS view

STEP 3

Low *Draw line*

STEP 4

Project back

Figure 21.21 A line through a point with a given angle to a line:

Step 1 Connect O to each end of the line to form plane 1–2–O in both views. Draw a horizontal line in the front view of the plane and project it to the top view, where it is true length. Find the point view of AO and the edge view of the plane.

Step 2 Find the true size of plane 1–2–O in the primary auxiliary view by projecting perpendicularly from its edge view. Omit the outline of the plane in this view and only show line 1–2 and point O.

Step 3 Construct Line OP at an angle of 45° with line 1–2. If you draw the angle toward point 2 (the low end), the line slopes downward; if toward point 1, it slopes upward.

Step 4 Project line OP back to the other views in sequence.

ANGLE BETWEEN A LINE AND A PLANE

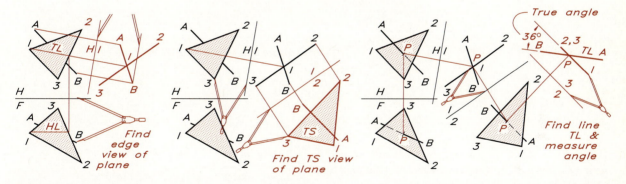

Find edge view of plane

Find TS view of plane

Find line TL & measure angle

Figure 21.22 The angle between a line and plane (plane method):

Step 1 The angle between a line and a plane in the view where the plane is an edge and the line is true length. Find the plane as an edge by projecting it from the top view along with the line AB.

Step 2 To find the plane's true size, project perpendicularly from the edge view of the plane. A view projected in any direction from a true-size plane will show the plane as an edge.

Step 3 Project a third successive auxiliary view perpendicularly from line AB. The line appears true length and the plane as an edge in this view, where the angle is true size. Project line AB back in sequence to the given views and determine the piercing points and visibility in each view.

an edge in the third successive auxiliary view. Because this last view is projected from the true-length view of the line, the line appears true length where the plane is an edge. When you project the piercing point back to the views in sequence, you can determine visibility for each view.

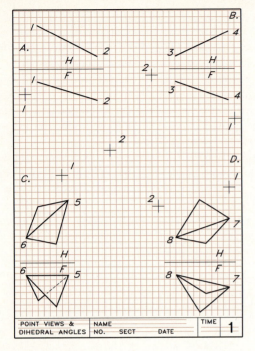

Figure 21.23 Problem 1 (A–D).

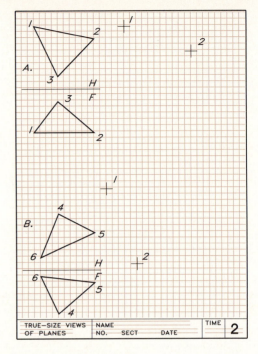

Figure 21.24 Problem 2 (A, B).

Use size A sheets for the following problems and lay out your solutions with instruments on grid or plain paper. Each square on the grid is equal to 0.20 in. (5 mm). Label all reference planes and points in each problem with $1/8$-in. letters or numbers, using guidelines.

Use the crosses marked "1" and "2" for positioning the primary and secondary reference lines. Primary reference lines should pass through "1" and secondary reference lines through "2."

1. (Fig. 21.23)

(A, B) Find the point views of the lines.

(C, D) Find the angles between the planes.

2. (Fig. 21.24)

(A, B) Find the true-size views of the planes.

3. (Fig. 21.25)

(A, B) Find the angles between the lines.

4. (Fig. 21.26)

(A, B) Find the shortest distances from the points to the lines. Show this distance in all views.

5. (Fig. 21.27)

(A, B) Find the shortest distances between the lines by the line method. Show this distance in all views.

6. (Fig. 21.28) Find the shortest distance between the lines by the plane method. Show the line in all views. Alternative problem: Find the shortest horizontal distance between the two lines and show the distance in all views.

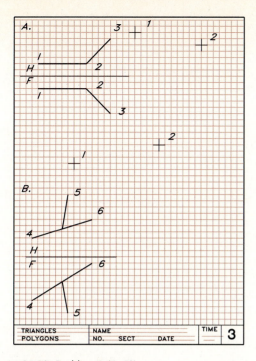

Figure 21.25 Problem 3 (A, B).

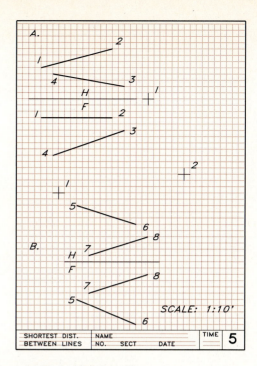

Figure 21.27 Problem 5 (A, B).

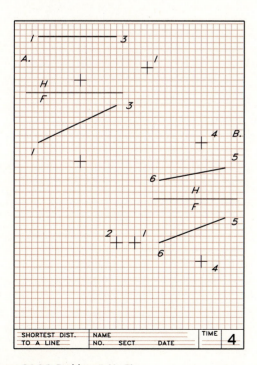

Figure 21.26 Problem 4 (A, B).

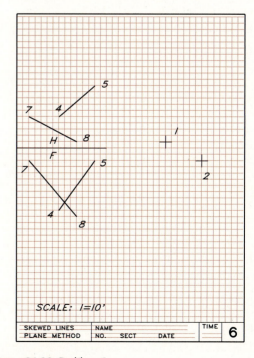

Figure 21.28 Problem 6.

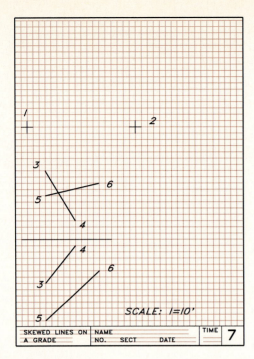

Figure 21.29 Problem 7.

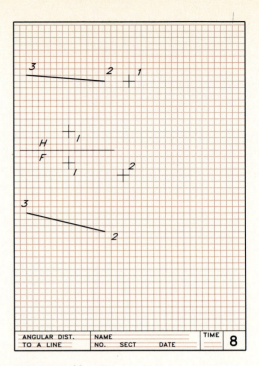

Figure 21.30 Problem 8.

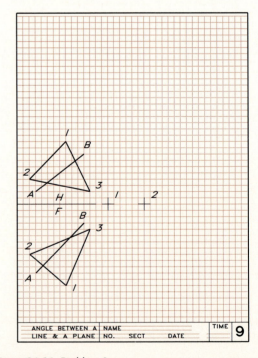

7. (Fig. 21.29) Find the shortest 20% grade distance between the two lines. Show this distance in all views.

8. (Fig. 21.30) Find the connector from point O that intersects intersect line 1–2 at 60°. Show this line in all views. Project from the top view. Scale: full size.

9. (Fig. 21.31) Find the angle between the line and the plane by the plane method. Show visibility in all views.

Figure 21.31 Problem 9.

22

Revolution

22.1 Introduction

An automobile's front suspension was designed to revolve about several axes at each wheel. This design is just one of many based on the principles of revolution. **Revolution** is a technique of revolving an orthographic view into a new position to yield a true-size view of a surface or a line. Revolution was used to solve descriptive geometry problems before the introduction of the auxiliary-view method.

22.2 True-Length Lines

In the Front View

Figure 22.1 compares the auxiliary view and revolution methods of obtaining the true size of inclined surfaces. In the auxiliary view method, the observer changes position to an auxiliary vantage point and looks perpendicularly at the object's inclined surface. In the revolution method, the top view of the object is revolved about the axis until the edge view of the inclined

AUXILIARY VIEWS VS. REVOLVED VIEWS

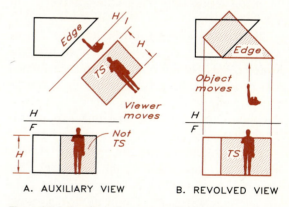

A. AUXILIARY VIEW   B. REVOLVED VIEW

Figure 22.1 Auxiliary views vs. revolved views:
A The surface is found true size in an auxiliary view.
B The surface is revolved to be seen true size in the front view.

plane is parallel to the frontal plane and perpendicular to the standard line of sight from the front view. In other words, the observer's line of sight

TRUE LENGTH IN FRONT VIEW

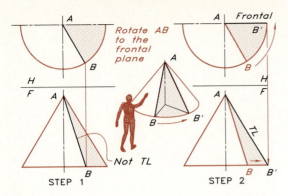

Figure 22.2 Determining true length in the front view:
Step 1 Use the top view of line AB as a radius to draw the base of a cone with point A as the apex. Draw the front view of the cone with a horizontal base through point B.

Step 2 Revolve the top view of line AB to be parallel to the frontal plane. When projected to the front view, frontal line AB' is the outside element of the cone and is true length.

does not change, but the object is revolved until the plane appears true size in the observer's normal line of sight.

To find a true-length line in the front view by revolution (Fig. 22.2), revolve line AB into the frontal plane. The top view represents the circular base of a right cone, and the front view is the triangular view of a cone. Line AB' is the outside element of the cone's frontal line and is true length in the front view.

Figure 22.3 illustrates the technique of finding line 1–2 true length in the front view. The observer's line of sight is not perpendicular to the triangle containing line 1–2 in its first position, and line 1–2 is not seen true length. When the triangle is revolved into the frontal plane, the observer's line of sight is perpendicular to the plane, and line 1–2 is seen true length.

In the Top View

A surface that appears as an edge in the front view may be found true size in the top view by a primary auxiliary view or by a single revolution (**Fig. 22.4**).

LINE TRUE LENGTH BY REVOLUTION

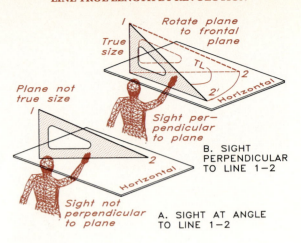

Figure 22.3
A Line 1–2 of the triangle does not appear true length in the front view because the observer's line of sight is not perpendicular to it.

B When the triangle is revolved into the frontal plane, the observer's line of sight is perpendicular to it and line 1–2' is seen true length.

AUXILIARY VIEWS VS. REVOLVED VIEWS

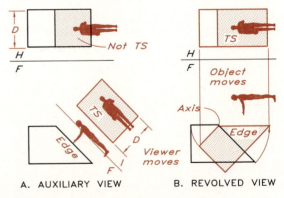

Figure 22.4 Auxiliary views vs. revolved views:
A The inclined plane is true size in an auxiliary view with a line of sight perpendicular to its edge in the front view.

B The surface is true size in the top view after the front view is revolved parallel to the horizontal plane.

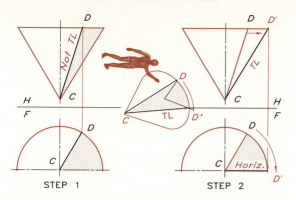

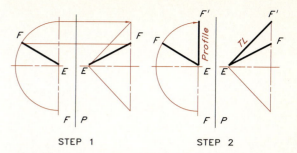

Figure 22.5 Obtaining true length of a line in the top view:

Step 1 Use the front view of line CD as a radius to draw the base of a cone with point C as the apex. Draw the top view of the cone with the base shown as a frontal plane.

Step 2 Revolve the front view of line CD into a horizontal position, CD'. When projected to the top view, CD' is the outside element of the cone and is true length.

Figure 22.6 Finding true length of a line in the side view:

Step 1 Use the front view of line EF as a radius to draw the circular view of the base of a cone. Draw the side view of the cone with its base through point F, which gives a frontal edge.

Step 2 Revolve line EF in the frontal view to position EF' where it is a profile line. Line EF' in the profile view is true length because it is a profile line and the outside element of the cone.

The axis of revolution is a point in the front view and true length in the top view. Revolving the edge view of the plane into the horizontal in the front view and projecting it to the top view yields the surface's true size. As in the auxiliary view method, the depth dimension, D, does not change.

In Fig. 22.5, revolving line CD into the horizontal gives its true length in the top view. The arc of revolution in the front view represents the base of the cone of revolution. Line CD' is true length in the top view because it is an outside element of the cone. Note that the depth in the top view does not change.

In the Profile View

In Fig. 22.6, revolving the front view of line EF into the profile plane gives its true length. Projecting the circular view of the cone to the side view yields a triangular view of the cone. Because line EF' is a profile line, it is true length in the side view, where it is the outside element of the cone.

22.3 Angles with a Line and Principal Planes

The angle between a line and plane appears true size in the view where the plane is an edge and the line is true length. In orthographic projection, two principal planes appear as edges in any principal view. Therefore, when a line appears true length in a principal view, the angle between the line and the two principal planes can be measured. The angle between the horizontal and the profile planes can be measured in **Fig. 22.7A** in the front view. The angle between horizontal and profile planes can be measured in the top view in **Fig. 22.7B**.

22.4 True Size of a Plane

When a plane appears as an edge in a principal view (the top view in **Fig. 22.8**), it can be revolved parallel to the frontal reference plane. The new front view is true size when projected horizontally across from its original front view.

ANGLES WITH PRINCIPAL PLANES

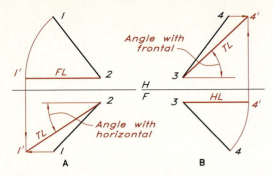

Figure 22.7 Angles with principal planes:

A The angle with the horizontal plane may be measured in the front view if the line appears true length.

B The angle with the frontal plane may be measured in the top view if the line appears true length.

TRUE SIZE OF A PLANE

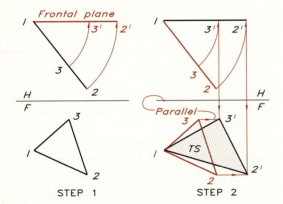

Figure 22.8 Determining true size of a plane:

Step 1 Revolve the edge view of the plane until it is parallel to the frontal plane.

Step 2 Project points 2' and 3' to the horizontal projectors from points 2 and 3 in the front view.

The combination of an auxiliary view and a single revolution finds the plane in **Fig. 22.9** true size. After finding the plane as an edge by finding the point of view of a true-length line in the plane,

TRUE SIZE OF A PLANE

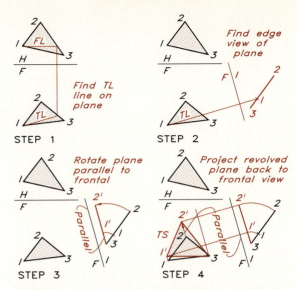

Figure 22.9 Obtaining true size of a plane by revolution:

Step 1 To find the edge view of the plane by revolution, draw a frontal line on the plane that is true length in the front view.

Step 2 Find the edge view of the plane by finding the point view of the frontal line.

Step 3 Revolve the edge view of the plane until it is parallel to the F1 reference line.

Step 4 Project the revolved points 1' and 2' to the front view to the projectors from points 1 and 2 that are parallel to the F1 reference line.

revolve the edge view to be parallel to the F1 reference line. To find the true size of the plane, project the original points (1, 2, and 3) in the front view parallel to the F1 line to intersect the projectors from 1' and 2'. The true size of the plane also may be found by projecting from the top view to find the edge view.

By Double Revolution

You may find the edge view of a plane by revolution without using auxiliary views (**Fig. 22.10**). Draw a frontal line on plane 1–2–3, and project it to the front view where it is true length. Revolve

EDGE VIEW OF A PLANE

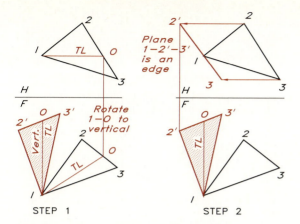

STEP 1

STEP 2

Figure 22.10 Finding the edge view of a plane:
Step 1 Draw a true-length frontal line on the front view of the plane. Revolve the front view until the true-length line is vertical.

Step 2 The true-length line, 1–O is vertical, so it appears as a point in the top view, and the plane appears as edge 1–2'-3'.

TRUE-SIZE VIEW OF A PLANE

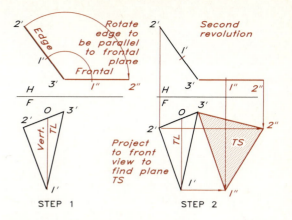

STEP 1

STEP 2

Figure 22.11 Finding true size of a plane:
Step 1 When a plane appears as an edge in the principal view (as in Fig. 22.10), you may revolve it to a position parallel to a reference line, or the frontal line in this case (3'–1"–2").

Step 2 Project points 1" and 2" to the front view to intersect with the horizontal projectors from the original points 1' and 2'. The plane 1"–2"–3' is true size in this view.

the plane until the true-length line is vertical in the front view. The true-length line projects as a point in the top view; therefore the plane appears as an edge in this view. Projectors from points 2 and 3 from the top view are parallel to the HF reference line.

A second revolution, called a **double revolution**, positions this edge view of the plane parallel to the frontal plane, as shown in step 1 of **Fig. 22.11**. Projecting the top views of points 1" and 2" to the front view gives a true-size plane 1"–2"–3" (step 2). We could have shown this second revolution in Fig. 22.10, but it would have resulted in overlapping views, making observation of the separate steps difficult.

Figure 22.12 shows how to use double revolution to find the true size of the oblique plane (1–2–3) of the object. Revolve the true-length line 1–2 on the plane in the top view until it is perpendicular to the frontal plane. Line 1–2 appears as a

point in the front view, and the plane appears as an edge. This revolution changes the width and depth but not the height. Then revolve the edge view of the plane into a vertical position parallel to the profile plane. To find the plane in true size, project to the profile view, where the depth remains unchanged but the height is greater.

22.5 Angle Between Planes

The angle between the planes of the nuclear detection satellite shown in **Fig. 22.13** may be found by revolution instead of by auxiliary views. This application of geometry was essential to the design of the satellite.

In **Fig. 22.14**, finding the **dihedral** angle involves drawing its edge view perpendicular to the line of intersection and projecting the plane of the angle to the front view. Revolving the edge view of the angle until it is a frontal plane in the

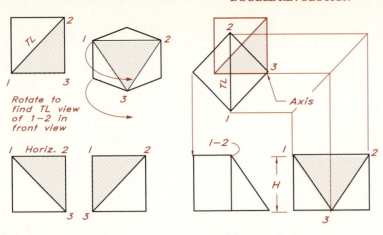
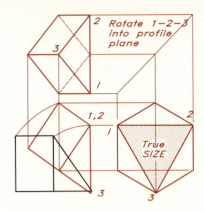

Figure 22.12 Obtaining true size of a plane by double revolution:

Given Three views of a block with an oblique plane across one corner.

Required Find the true size of the plane by revolution.

Step 1 Line 1–2 is horizontal in the frontal view and true length in the top view. Revolve the top view so that line 1–2 appears as a point in the front view.

Step 2 Plane 1–2–3 is an edge in step 1, so you can revolve this plane into a vertical position in the front view to obtain its true size in the side view. The depth dimension does not change.

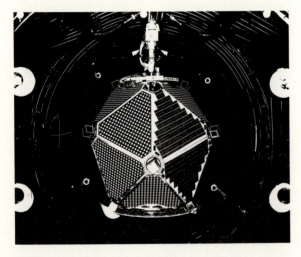

Figure 22.13 The use of revolution principles allows determination of the angles between the planes of this nuclear detection satellite. (Courtesy of TRW Space Technology Laboratories.)

top view and projecting it to the front view yields its true-size view.

Figure 22.15 shows how to solve a similar problem. Here, the line of intersection does not appear true length in the given views; therefore an auxiliary view is needed to find its true length. Draw the plane of the dihedral angle as an edge perpendicular to the true-length line of intersection. Project the foreshortened view of plane 1–2–3 to the top view. Then revolve the edge view of plane 1–2–3 in the primary auxiliary view until it is parallel to the H1 reference line. Project the revolved edge view of the angle back to the top view, where it is true size.

22.6 Determining Direction

To solve more advanced problems of revolution, you must be able to locate the basic directions of up, down, forward, and backward in any given view. In **Fig. 22.16A**, directional arrows in the top

ANGLE BETWEEN PLANES

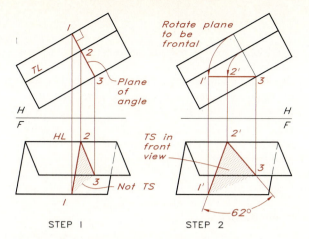

STEP I   STEP 2

Figure 22.14 Finding the angle between planes:
Step 1 Draw a plane of the angle perpendicular to the true-length line of intersection between the planes in the top view and project it to the front view. The angle is not true size in the front view.

Step 2 Revolve the edge view of the plane of the angle to position angle 1'–2'–3 in the top view parallel to the frontal plane. Project this angle to the frontal view, where it is true size.

ANGLE BETWEEN OBLIQUE PLANES

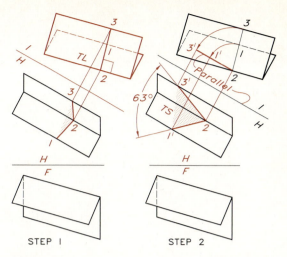

STEP I   STEP 2

Figure 22.15 Determining the angle between oblique planes:
Step 1 To find a true-length view of the line of intersection, project it to an auxiliary view from the top view. Draw the plane of the angle perpendicular to the true length of the line of intersection and project it to the top view.

Step 2 Revolve the edge view of the plane of the angle until it is parallel to the H1 reference line so that the plane appears true size in the top view. The angle between the planes is 2–1'–3'.

and front views identify the directions of backward and up. Pointing backward in the top view, line 4–5 appears as a point in the front view. Projecting arrow 4–5 to the auxiliary view as you would any other line determines the direction of backward. By drawing the arrow on the other end of the line, you would find the direction of forward.

Locate the direction of up in **Fig. 22.16B** by drawing line 4–6 in the direction of up in the front view and as a point in the top view. Then find the arrow in the primary auxiliary by the usual projection method. The direction of down is in the opposite direction.

You find the location of directions in secondary auxiliary views in the same way. To determine the direction of up in **Fig. 22.17**, begin with an arrow that points up in the front view and

DIRECTIONS OF FORWARD, BACK, UP, AND DOWN

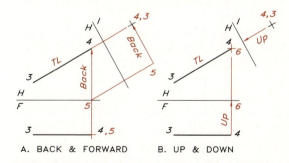

A. BACK & FORWARD   B. UP & DOWN

Figure 22.16 The directions of backward, forward, up, and down may be identified in the given views with arrows pointing in these directions. These directional arrows may be projected to successive auxiliary views. This drawing shows the directions of (A) backward and (B) up.

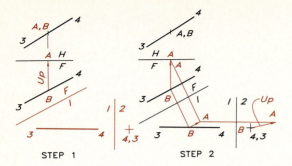

STEP 1   STEP 2

Figure 22.17 Finding direction in a secondary auxiliary view:

Step 1 To find the direction of up in the secondary auxiliary view, draw arrow AB pointing up in the front view. It appears as a point in the top view.

Step 2 Project arrow AB to the primary and secondary auxiliary views like any other line. Locate the direction of up in the secondary auxiliary view.

REVOLUTION OF A POINT ABOUT AN AXIS

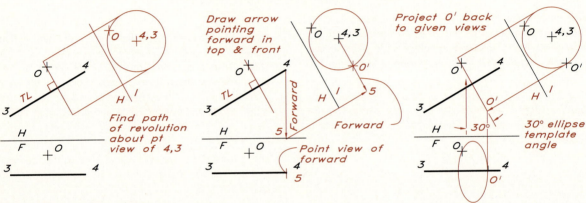

Figure 22.18 Revolving a point about an axis:

Step 1 To rotate point O about axis 3–4 to its most forward position, find the point view of the axis in a primary auxiliary view. The circular path of revolution appears as a circle in the auxiliary views and as an edge perpendicular to the axis in the top view.

Step 2 Locate the most forward position of point O by drawing an arrow pointing forward in the top view. It appears as a point in the front view. Find the arrow, 4–5, in the auxiliary view to locate point O'.

Step 3 Project point O' back to the given views. The path of revolution appears as an ellipse in the front view because the axis is not true length in this view. Draw a 30° ellipse because this is the angle of your line of sight with the circular path in the front view.

appears as a point in the top view. Project the arrow AB from the front view to the primary auxiliary view and then to a secondary auxiliary view to show the direction of up. Identify the other directions in the same way by beginning with the two principal views of a known direction.

22.7 Revolution About an Axis

A Point

In **Fig. 22.18**, point O is to be revolved about axis 3–4 to its most forward position. **Draw the circular path of revolution in the primary auxiliary**

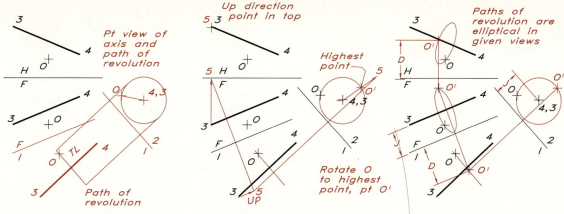

Figure 22.19 Revolving a point about an oblique axis:

Step 1 To rotate O about axis 3–4 to its highest position, find the axis as a point in a secondary auxiliary and draw the circular path. The path of revolution appears as an edge in the primary auxiliary view perpendicular to the true-length view of the axis.

Step 2 To locate the highest position on the path of revolution, draw arrow 3–5 pointing up in the top view and project it to the secondary auxiliary view to find O'.

Step 3 Project point O' back to the given views by transferring the dimensions J and D with your dividers. The highest point lies over the line in the top view, verifying its position. The path of revolution is elliptical wherever the axis is not true length.

view, where the axis is a point. Draw the direction of forward and find the new location of point O at O'. Project back through the successive views to find point O' in each view. Note that point O' lies on the line in the front view, verifying that point O' is in its most forward position.

In **Fig. 22.19** an additional auxiliary view is needed in order to rotate a point about an axis because axis 3–4 is not true length in the given views. You must find the true length of the axis before you can find it as a point in the secondary auxiliary view, where the path of revolution appears as a circle. Revolve point O into its highest position, O', and locate the up arrow, 3–5, in the secondary auxiliary view.

Project back to the given views to locate O in each view. Its position in the top view is over the axis, which verifies that the point is at its highest position.

The paths of revolution appear as edges when their axes are true length and as ellipses when their axes are not true length. The angle of the ellipse template for drawing the ellipse in the front view is the angle the projectors from the front view make with the edge view of the revolution in the primary auxiliary view. To find the ellipse in the top view, project an auxiliary view from the top view to obtain the path of revolution as an edge perpendicular to the true-length axis.

The handcrank of a casement window (**Fig. 22.20)** is an example of the application of revolution techniques. The designer must determine the clearances between the sill and the window frame when designing the crank.

A Right Prism
The coal chute shown in **Fig. 22.21** conveys coal continuously between two buildings. The sides of

HANDCRANK REVOLUTION

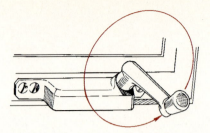

Figure 22.20 The handcrank on a casement window is an example of a problem solved by applying revolution principles. The handle must be properly positioned so as not to interfere with the windowsill or wall.

CONVEYOR-CHUTE DESIGN

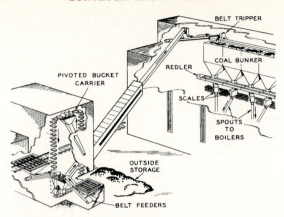

Figure 22.21 A conveyor chute must be installed so that two edges of its right section are vertical for the conveyors to function properly. (Courtesy of Stephens-Adamson Manufacturing Company.)

REVOLVING A PRISM ABOUT ITS AXIS

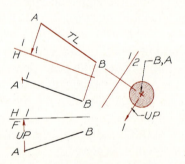

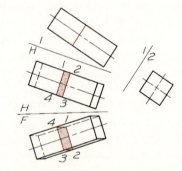

Figure 22.22 Revolving a prism about its axis:

Step 1 To draw a chute with two of its square sides vertical, locate the point view of centerline AB in the secondary auxiliary view and draw a circle about the axis with a diameter equal to the square section. Draw a vertical arrow in the front and top views and project it to the secondary auxiliary view to indicate the direction of vertical.

Step 2 Draw the right section, 1–2–3–4, in the secondary auxiliary view with two sides parallel to the vertical directional arrow. Project this section back to the successive views by transferring measurements with dividers. The edge view of the section may be anywhere along centerline AB in the primary auxiliary view.

Step 3 Draw the lateral edges of the prism through the corners of the right section parallel to the centerline in all views. Terminate the ends of the prism in the primary auxiliary view where they appear as edges perpendicular to the centerline. Project the corner points of the ends to the top and front views to establish the ends in these views.

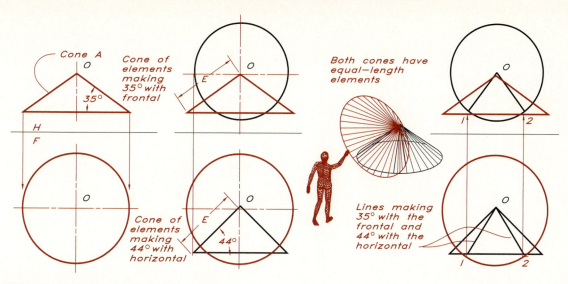

Figure 22.23 Constructing a line at specified angles:

Step 1 To draw lines making angles of 35° and 44° with the frontal and horizontal planes, respectively, begin by drawing a cone in the top view with outside elements making a 35° angle with the frontal plane. Construct the circular view of the cone in the front view with point O as the apex. All elements of this cone make an angle of 35° with the frontal plane.

Step 2 Draw a second cone in the front view with outside elements that make an angle of 44° with the horizontal plane. Draw the elements of this cone equal in length to element E of cone A. All elements of cone B make an angle of 44° with the horizontal plane.

Step 3 Because elements A and B are equal in length, two elements lie on the surface of each cone: lines O–1 and O–2. Locate points 1 and 2 at the point where the bases of the cones intersect in both views. These lines slope forward and down from this point at the specified angles.

the enclosed chute must be vertical and the bottom of the chute's right section must be horizontal. Design of the chute required application of the technique of revolving a prism about its axis.

In **Fig. 22.22**, the right section is to be positioned about centerline AB so that two of its sides will be vertical. To do so, find the point view of the axis and project the direction of up to this view. Draw the right section about the axis so that two of its sides are parallel to the up arrow. Find the right section in the other views. Then construct the sides of the chute parallel to the axis. The bottom of the chute's right section will be horizontal and properly positioned for conveying coal.

22.8 A Line at a Specified Angle with Two Principal Planes

In **Fig. 22.23**, a line is to be drawn through point O that makes angles of 35° with the frontal plane and 44° with the horizontal plane and slopes forward and down.

First, draw the cone containing elements making 35° with the frontal plane and then the cone with elements making 44° with the horizontal plane. The length of the elements of both cones must be equal so that the cones will intersect with equal elements. Finally, find lines O–1 and O–2, which are elements that lie on each cone and make the specified angles with the principal planes.

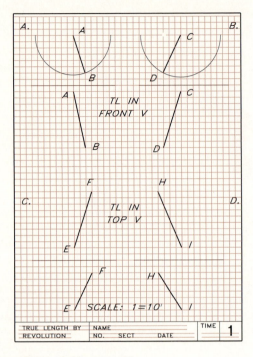

Figure 22.24 Problem 1 (A–D).

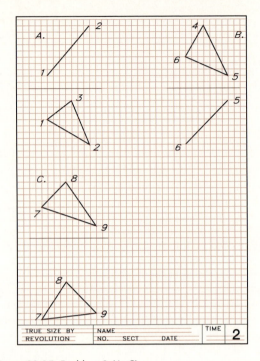

Figure 22.25 Problem 2 (A–C).

Use size A sheets for the following problems and lay out your solutions using instruments on grid or plain paper. Each square on the grid is equal to 0.20 in. (5mm). Label all reference planes and points in each problem with $1/8$-in. letters or numbers, using guidelines.

Use the crosses marked "1" and "2" for positioning primary and secondary reference lines. The primary reference line should pass through "1" and the secondary reference line through "2."

1. (Fig. 22.24)

(A, B) Find the true-length views of the lines in their front views by revolution.

(C, D) Find the true-length views of the lines in their top views by revolution.

2. (Fig. 22.25)

(A, B) By revolution, find the true-size views of plane 1–2–3 in the front view and plane 4–5–6 in the top view.

(C) By using an auxiliary view projected from the top view and one revolution, find the true-size view of plane 7–8–9.

3. (Fig. 22.26)

(A, B) Find the angles between the planes by revolution. Show construction.

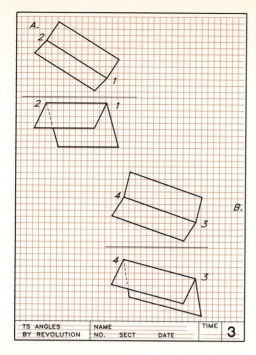

Figure 22.26 Problem 3 (A, B).

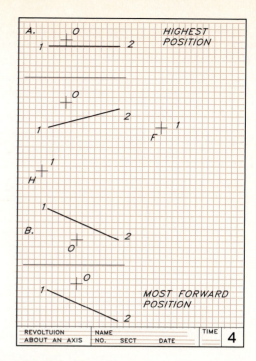

Figure 22.27 Problem 4 (A, B).

4. (Fig. 22.27)

(A) Perform the construction necessary to show point O revolved into its highest position.

(B) Repeat part (A) but show point O in its most forward position.

5. (Fig. 22.28) Construct a chute from A to B that has the cross section shown. The longer sides are to be vertical sides.

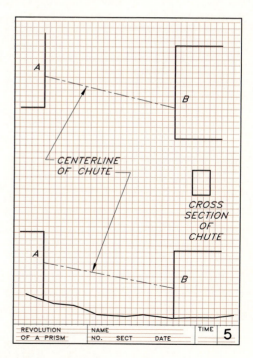

Figure 22.28 Problem 5.

6. (Fig. 22.29) Draw the views of the line that is 3.2 in. long that makes a 30° angle with the frontal plane and a 52° angle with the horizontal plane.

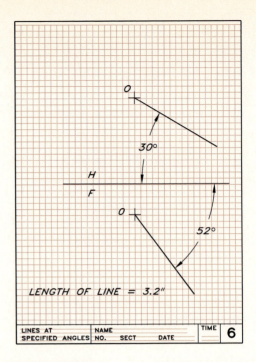

Figure 22.29 Problem 6.

23

Vector Graphics

23.1 Introduction

Design of a structural system requires analysis of each member to determine the loads they must support and whether those loads are in tension or compression. Forces may be represented graphically by **vectors** and their magnitudes and directions determined in 3D space. Graphical methods are useful in the solution of vector problems as alternatives to conventional trigonometric and algebraic methods. Quantities such as distance, velocity, and electrical properties also may be represented as vectors for graphical solution.

23.2 Definitions

To help you understand more easily the discussion of vectors in this chapter, we define the following terms.

Force: a push or pull tending to produce motion. All forces have (1) magnitude, (2) direction, and (3) a point of application. The

REPRESENTATION OF A FORCE BY A VECTOR

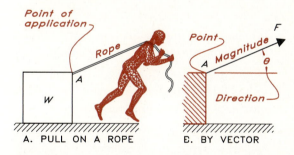

Figure 23.1 A force applied to an object (A) may be represented by vectors depicting the magnitude and direction of the force (B).

person shown pulling the rope in **Fig. 23.1A** is applying a force to the weight W.

Vector: a graphical representation of a force drawn to scale and depicting magnitude, direction, and point of application. The vector

RESULTANT: PARALLELOGRAM METHOD

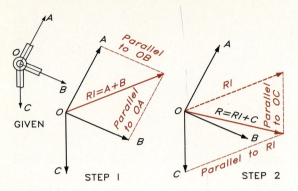

Figure 23.2 Determining the resultant by the parallelogram method:
Step 1 Draw a parallelogram with its sides parallel to vectors A and B. The diagonal R1 is the resultant of forces A and B.
Step 2 Draw a parallelogram using vectors R1 and C to find diagonal R, or the overall resultant that can replace forces A, B, and C.

in **Fig. 23.1B** represents the force applied through the rope to pull the weight W.

Magnitude: the amount of push or pull represented by the length of the vector line, usually measured in pounds or kilograms.

Direction: the inclination of a force (with respect to a reference coordinate system) indicated by a line with an arrow at one end.

Point of application: the point through which the force is applied on the object or member (point A in **Fig. 23.1A**).

Compression: the state created in a member by pushing forces that tend to shorten it. Compression is represented by the letter C or a plus sign (+).

Tension: the state created in a member by pulling forces that tend to stretch it. Tension is represented by the letter T or a minus sign (–).

System of forces: the combination of all forces acting on an object as shown (forces A, B, and C in **Fig. 23.2**).

Resultant: a single force that can replace all the forces of a force system and have the same effect as the combined forces (force R1 in **Fig. 23.2**).

Equilibrant: the opposite of a resultant; the single force that can be used to counterbalance all forces of a force system.

Components: separate forces that, if combined, would result in a single force; forces A and B are components of resultant R1 in **Fig. 23.2**.

Space diagram: a diagram depicting the physical relationship between structural members, as given in **Fig. 23.2**.

Vector diagram: a diagram of vectors representing the forces in a system and used to solve for unknown vectors in the system.

Metric units: standard units of weights and measures; the kilogram (kg) is the unit of mass (load), and one kilogram is approximately 2.2 pounds.

23.3 Coplanar, Concurrent Force Systems

When several forces, represented by vectors, act through a common point of application, the system is **concurrent**. In **Fig. 23.2** vectors A, B, and C act through a single point; therefore this system is concurrent. When all vectors lie in the same plane, the system is **coplanar** and only one view is necessary to show them true length.

The **resultant** is the single vector that can replace all forces acting on the point of application. Resultants may be found graphically by (1) the parallelogram method and (2) the polygon method.

An **equilibrant** has the same magnitude, orientation, and point of application as the resultant in a system of forces, but in the opposite direc-

RESULTANT VS. EQUILIBRANT

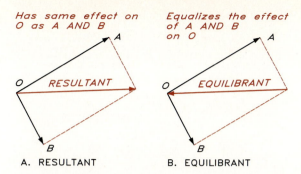

Has same effect on O as A AND B

Equalizes the effect of A AND B on O

A. RESULTANT

B. EQUILIBRANT

Figure 23.3 The (A) resultant and (B) equilibrant are equal in all respects except in direction (shown by arrowhead).

RESULTANT: POLYGON METHOD

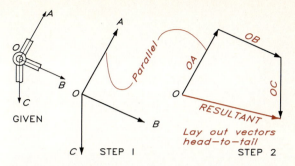

GIVEN

STEP 1

Lay out vectors head−to−tail

STEP 2

Figure 23.4 The resultant of a coplanar, concurrent system may be determined by the polygon method, in which the vectors are drawn head-to-tail. The vector that closes the polygon is the resultant.

tion. The resultant of the system of forces shown in **Fig. 23.3** is balanced by the equilibrant applied at point O, thereby causing the system to be in equilibrium.

Resultant: Parallelogram Method

In **Fig. 23.2**, the vectors lie in the same plane, act through a common point, and are scaled to their known magnitudes. Use of the parallelogram method to determine resultants requires that the vectors be drawn to scale. Vectors A and B form two sides of a parallelogram. Constructing parallels to these vectors completes the parallelogram. Its diagonal, R1, is the resultant of forces A and B; that is, resultant R1 is the *vector sum* of vectors A and B.

Replaced by R1, vectors A and B now may be disregarded. Resultant R1 and vector C are two sides of a second parallelogram. Its diagonal, R, is the vector sum of R1 and C and the resultant of the entire system. Resultant R may be thought of as the only force acting on the point, thereby simplifying further analysis.

Resultant: Polygon Method

Figure 23.4 shows the same system of forces, but here the resultant is determined by the **polygon**

method. Again, the vectors are drawn to scale but in this case head-to-tail, in their true directions to form the polygon. The vectors are laid out in a clockwise sequence beginning with vector A. The polygon does not close, so the system is not in equilibrium but tends to be in motion. The resultant R (from the tail of vector A to the head of vector C) closes the polygon.

23.4 Noncoplanar, Concurrent Force Systems

When vectors lie in more than one plane of projection, they are **noncoplanar**, requiring 3D views for analysis of their spatial relationships. The resultant of a system of noncoplanar forces may be obtained by the parallelogram method if their projections are given in two adjacent orthographic views. Otherwise, it must be determined by the polygon method.

Resultant: Parallelogram Method

In **Fig. 23.5** vectors 1 and 2 were used to construct the top and front views of a parallelogram and its diagonal R1 in both views. The front view of R1

RESULTANT BY PARALLELOGRAM

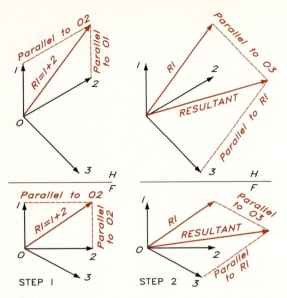

RESULTANT BY POLYGON

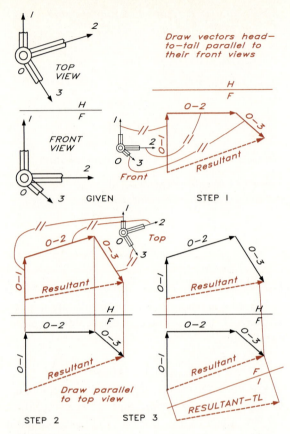

Figure 23.5 Finding the resultant by the parallelogram method:

Step 1 Use vectors 1 and 2 to construct a parallelogram in the top and front views. Diagonal R1 is the resultant of vectors 1 and 2.

Step 2 Use vectors 3 and R1 to construct a second parallelogram to find the overall resultant, R.

Figure 23.6 Obtaining the resultant by the polygon method:

Required Find the resultant of this system of forces by the polygon method.

Step 1 Lay off each vector head-to-tail in the front view parallel to the given view and find the front view of the resultant.

Step 2 Draw the same vectors head-to-tail in the top view, a 3D polygon projected above the front view.

Step 3 The resultant is found true length in an auxiliary view projected from the front view.

must be an orthographic projection of its top view.

Then resultant R1 and vector 3 are resolved to form the overall resultant in both views. The top and front views of the resultant must project orthographically. The overall resultant replaces vectors 1, 2, and 3. However, it is an oblique line, so an auxiliary view (**Fig. 23.6**) or revolution must be used to obtain its true length.

Resultant: Polygon Method

Figure 23.6 shows the solution of the same system of forces for the resultant by the polygon method. **Each vector is laid head-to-tail clockwise, beginning with vector 1 in the front view.**

Then the vectors are projected orthographically from the front view to the top view of the vector polygon. The vector polygon does not close, so the system is not in equilibrium. In both views, the

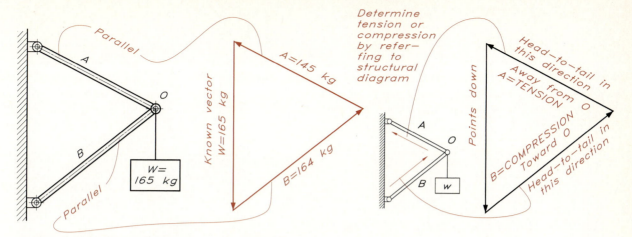

Figure 23.7 Determining coplanar forces in equilibrium:

Required Find the forces in the structural members supporting the 165-kg load.

Step 1 Draw the load of 165-kg as a vector. Draw vectors A and B parallel to their directions from the ends of the load and head-to-tail.

Step 2 Vector A points away from point O when transferred to the structural diagram and thus is in tension. Vector B points toward point O and thus is in compression.

resultant (from the tail of vector 1 to the head of vector 3) closes the polygon. However, the resultant is an oblique line, requiring an auxiliary view to obtain its true length.

23.5 Forces in Equilibrium

A structure in equilibrium is one that is static with no motion taking place; the members balance each other.

The coplanar, concurrent structure depicted in **Fig. 23.7** is designed to support a load of W = 165 kg. The maximum loading of each structural member determines the material and size of the members to be used in the design.

A single view of a vector polygon in equilibrium allows you to find only two unknown values. (Later, we show how to solve for three unknowns by using descriptive geometry.) Lay off the only known force, W = 165 kg, parallel to its given direc-

tion (here pointing vertically downward). Then draw the unknown forces A and B parallel to the supports to form the force polygon and scale (or calculate) the magnitude of these forces.

Analyze vectors A and B to determine whether they are in tension or compression and thus find their direction. Vector B points upward to the left, which is toward point O when transferred to the structural diagram shown in the small drawing. Vectors that act toward their point of application are in compression. Vector A points away from point O when transferred to the structural diagram and therefore is in tension.

Figure 23.8 is a similar example involving determination of the loads in the structural members caused by the weight of 110 pounds acting through a pulley. The only difference between this solution and the previous one is the construction of two equal vectors at the outset to represent the cable loads on both sides of the pulley.

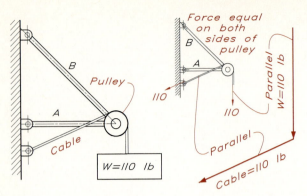
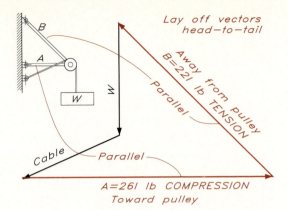

Figure 23.8 Obtaining forces in equilibrium (pulley application):

Required Find the forces in the members supporting the load of 110 lb on the pulley.

Step 1 The force in the cable is equal to 110 lb on both sides of the pulley. Draw these two forces as vectors head-to-tail and parallel to their directions in the space diagram.

Step 2 Draw A and B head-to-tail to close the polygon. Vector A points toward the point of application and thus is in compression. Vector B points away from the point and is in tension

23.6 Coplanar Truss Analysis

Designers use vector polygons to determine the loads in each member of a truss by two graphical methods: (1) joint-by-joint analysis and (2) Maxwell diagrams.

Joint-by-Joint Analysis

In the Fink truss shown in **Fig. 23.9**, 3000-lb loads are applied at its joints. This method of designating forces is called **Bow's notation**. The exterior forces on the truss are labeled with letters placed between them, and numerals are placed between the interior members. Each vector is referred to by the number on each of its sides clockwise about its joint. For example, the vertical load at the left is denoted AB, with A at the tail and B at the head of the vector.

First analyze the joint at the left end with a reaction of 4500 lb. When you read clockwise about the joint, the force is EA, where E is the tail and A is the head of the vector. Continuing clock-

wise, the next forces are A–1 and 1–E, which close the polygon at E, the beginning letter. Place arrowheads in a head-to-tail sequence beginning with the known vector EA.

Determine tension and compression by relating the directions of each vector to the original joint. For example, A–1 points toward the joint and is in compression, whereas 1–E points away and is in tension. The truss is symmetrical and equally loaded, so the loads in the members on the right will be equal to those on the left.

Analyze the other joints in the same way. The directions of the vectors are opposite at each end. For example, vector A–1 is toward the left in step 1 and toward the right in step 2.

Maxwell Diagrams

The Maxwell diagram is virtually the same as the joint-by-joint analysis, with the exception that the polygons overlap, with some vectors common to more than one polygon. In **Fig. 23.10** (step 1) the

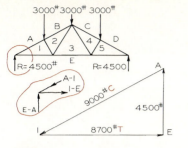

STEP 1

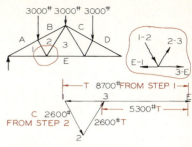

STEP 2   STEP 3

Figure 23.9 Analyzing a truss (joint-by-joint method):

Step 1 Use Bow's notation to label the truss, with letters between the exterior loads and numbers between interior members. Because it has only two unknowns, A–1 and 1–E, you may analyze the left joint. Find vectors A–1 and 1–E, by drawing them parallel to their directions from both ends of EA in a head-to-tail sequence.

Step 2 Using vector 1–A from step 1 and load AB, find the two unknowns, B–2 and 2–1. Draw the known vectors beginning with vector 1–A and then draw vectors B–2 and 2–1 to close the polygon, moving clockwise about the joint. A vector pointing toward the point of application is in compression. A vector pointing away from the point of application is in tension.

Step 3 Analyze the third joint by laying out vectors E–1 and 1–2 from the preceding steps. Vectors 2–3 and 3–E close the polygon and are parallel to their directions in the space diagram. Vectors 2–3 and 3–E point away from the point of application and thus are in tension.

exterior loads are laid out head-to-tail in clockwise sequence—AB, BC, CD, DE, and EA—with a letter placed at each end of each vector. The forces are parallel so this force diagram is a vertical line.

Vector analysis begins at the left end where the force EA of 4500 lb is known. A free-body diagram is sketched to isolate this joint. The two unknowns, A–1 and 1–E, are drawn parallel to their directions in the truss, with A–1 beginning at point A, 1–E beginning at point E, and both extended to point 1.

Because resultant EA points upward, A–1 must have its tail at A and its direction toward point 1. The free-body diagram shows that the direction is toward the point of application, which means that A–1 is in compression. Vector 1–E points away from the joint, which means that it is in tension. The vectors are coplanar and may be scaled to determine their magnitudes.

In step 2, where vectors 1–A and AB are known, the unknown vectors, B–2 and 2–1 may be determined. Vector B–2 is drawn parallel to its structural member through point B in the Maxwell diagram, and the line of vector 2–1 is extended from point 1 to intersect with B–2 at point 2. The arrows of each vector are drawn head-to-tail. Vectors B–2 and 2–1 point toward the joint in the free-body diagram and therefore are in compression.

In step 3, the next joint is analyzed to find the forces in 2–3 and 3–E. The truss and its loading are symmetrical, so the Maxwell diagram will be symmetrical when completed.

If the last force polygon in the series does not close perfectly, an error in construction has occurred. A slight error may be disregarded, as a rounding error may be disregarded in mathematics. Arrowheads are unnecessary and usually are omitted on Maxwell diagrams because each vec-

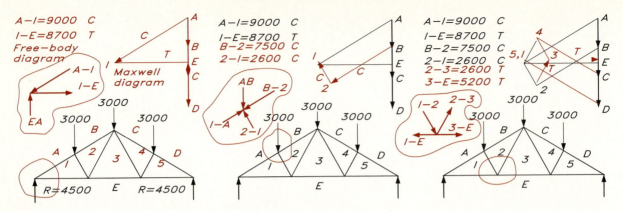

Figure 23.10 Analyzing a truss (Maxwell diagram method):

Step 1 Label the spaces between the outer loads on the truss with letters and the internal spaces with numbers using Bow's notation. Add the vertical loads end-to-end in a Maxwell diagram, and sketch a free-body diagram of the first joint. Use vectors EA, A–1, and 1–E (head-to-tail) to draw a vector diagram to find their magnitudes. Vector A–1 is in compression because it points toward the joint, and 1-E is in tension because it points away from the joint.

Step 2 Sketch the next joint to be analyzed. Because AB and A–1 are known, only 2–1 and B–2 are unknown. Draw them parallel to their direction (head-to-tail) in the Maxwell diagram using the previously found vector. Vectors B–2 and 2–1 are in compression, as each points toward the joint. Vector A–1 becomes vector 1–A when read in a clockwise direction.

Step 3 Sketch a free-body diagram of the next joint to be analyzed, where the unknowns are 2–3 and 3–E. Draw their vectors in the Maxwell diagram parallel to their given members to find point 3. Vectors 2–3 and 3–E are in tension because they point away from the joint. Repeat this process to find the vectors on the opposite side.

tor will have the opposite direction when applied to a different joint.

23.7 Noncoplanar Vector Analysis

Special Case

The solution of 3D vector systems requires the use of descriptive geometry because the system must be analyzed in 3D space. An example is the manned flying system (MFS) shown in **Fig. 23.11**, which was analyzed to determine the loads on its support members. Weight on the moon is 0.165 of earth weight. Thus a tripod that must support 182 lb on earth needs to support only 30 lb on the moon.

Figure 23.11 The structural members of this tripod support for a moon vehicle may be analyzed graphically to determine design load requirement. (Courtesy of NASA.)

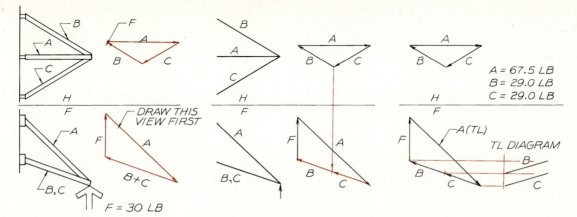

Figure 23.12 Noncoplanar structural analysis (special case):

Step 1 Forces B and C coincide in the front view, where there are only two unknowns. Draw vector F (30 lb) and the two unknown forces parallel to their front view in the front view of the vector polygon. To find the top view of A, project from the front and draw vectors B and C parallel to their top views.

Step 2 Project the point of intersection of vectors B and C in the top view to the front view to separate the head-to-tail vectors. Vectors B and C are in tension because they act away from the point in the space diagram, whereas vector A is in compression.

Step 3 The lengths of vectors B and C are not true length in their top and front views. Construct a true-length diagram and scale the lengths of these lines to obtain their magnitudes.

In general, only two unknown vectors can be determined in a single view of a vector polygon that is in equilibrium. However, the system shown in **Fig. 23.12 is a special case because members B and C lie in the same edge view of the plane in the front view**. Therefore solving for three unknowns is possible in this case.

Construct a vector polygon in the front view by drawing force F as a vector and using the other vectors as the sides of the polygon. Draw the top view using vectors B and C to form the polygon that closes at each end of vector A. Then find the front view of vectors B and C.

A true-length diagram gives the lengths of the vectors; measure them to determine their magni-tudes. Vector A is in compression because it points toward the point of application. Vectors B and C are in tension because they point away from the point.

General Case

The structural frame shown in **Fig. 23.13** is attached to a vertical wall to support a load of W = 1200 lb. There are three unknowns in each of the views, so begin by projecting an auxiliary view from the top view to obtain the edge view of a plane containing vectors A and B, thereby reducing the number of unknowns to two. You no longer need refer to the front view.

Draw a vector polygon with vectors parallel to their members in the auxiliary view. Then draw

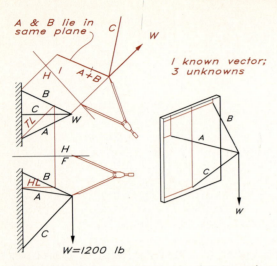

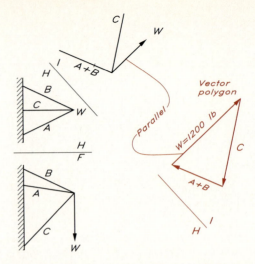

Figure 23.13 Noncoplanar structural analysis (general case): **Given** The top and front views of a structural frame that supports a load of 1200 lb.

Required Find the loads in the structural members.

Step 1 To limit the unknowns to two, draw an auxiliary view where vectors A and B lie in the edge view of a plane. Draw a vector polygon parallel to the members in the auxiliary view in which W = 1200 lb is the only known vector.

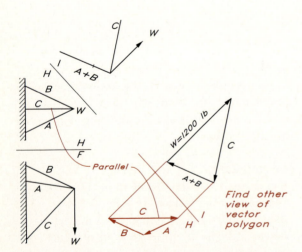

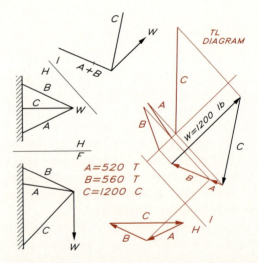

Step 2 Construct an orthographic projection of the vector polygon from step 1, with its vectors parallel to the members in the top view. The reference plane between the two views is parallel to the H1 plane. (This portion of the solution is closely related to that in Fig. 23.12.)

Step 3 Project the intersection of A and B in the top view of the vector polygon to the auxiliary view polygon. Find the magnitudes of vectors A, B, and C in a true-length diagram and analyze them for tension or compression by referring to the top and auxiliary views.

Figure 23.14 Tractor sidebooms represent noncoplanar, concurrent systems of forces that can be solved graphically. (Courtesy of Trunkline Gas Company.)

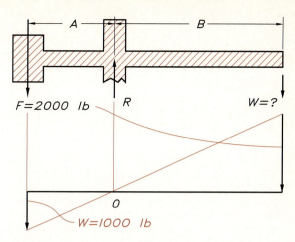

Figure 23.15 The load W required to balance the beam can be found by this diagram for a system of parallel, nonconcurrent forces.

an adjacent orthographic view of the vector polygon with vectors parallel to their members in the top view. Use a true-length diagram to find the true length of the vectors and measure their magnitudes.

An application of a 3D vector system is the side-boom tractors used to lower pipe into ditches during pipeline construction (**Fig. 23.14**).

23.8 Resultant of Parallel, Nonconcurrent Forces

The beam depicted in **Fig. 23.15** is part of a rotational crane used to move building materials. The counterbalance weight is 2000 lb and the magnitude of the weight W is to be found, assuming that the support cables have been omitted.

To obtain the graphical solution, construct a line to represent the distance between forces F and W. Project point O, the pivot point of balance, from the space diagram. Draw vectors F and W by transposing them to the opposite ends of the

beam. Draw a line from the end of vector F through point O and extend it to intersect the extension of vector W to locate the end of vector W. When you scale it, you find that its magnitude is 1000 lb.

The beam depicted in **Fig. 23.16** must carry the three loads shown. The requirement is to determine the magnitude of supports R_1 and R_2, the resultant of the loads, and the resultant's location. Begin by labeling the spaces between all vectors clockwise with Bow's notation and draw a vector diagram.

Extend the lines of force in the space diagram and draw the strings from the vector diagram in their respective spaces, parallel to their original directions. For example, string oa is parallel to string oA in space A between forces EA and AB, and string ob is in space B, beginning at the intersection of oa with vector AB. The last string, oe, closes the diagram, called a **funicular diagram**.

Transfer the direction of string oe to the force diagram, and lay it off through point O to intersect

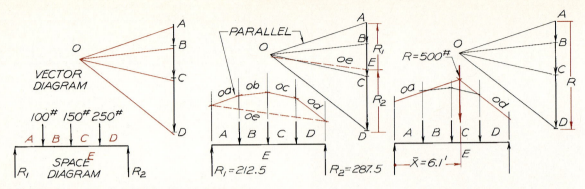

Figure 23.16 Analyzing parallel, nonconcurrent loads:

Step 1 Letter the spaces between the loads using Bow's notation. Find the sum of the vertical loads by drawing them head-to-tail in a vector diagram. Locate pole point O at a convenient location and draw strings from O to each end of the vectors.

Step 2 Extend the lines of vertical loads and draw a funicular diagram with string oa in the A space, ob in the B space, oc in the C space, and so on. The last string drawn, oe, closes the diagram. Transfer oe to the vector polygon to locate point E, thus establishing R_1 and R_2, which are EA and DE, respectively.

Step 3 The resultant of the three downward forces equals their graphical summation, line AD. Locate the resultant by extending strings oa and od in the funicular diagram to a point of intersection. The resultant, R = 500 lb, acts through this point in a downward direction at distance $\bar{X}$ from the left end.

the load line at E. Vector DE represents R_2 (refer to Bow's notation as it was applied in step 1), and vector EA represents R_1.

The magnitude of the resultant of the loads is the sum of the downward forces, or the distance from A to D. To find the location of the resultant, extend the outside strings of the funicular diagram, oa and od, to intersect. The resultant has a magnitude of 500 lb, a vertical downward direction, and a point of application at $\bar{X}$.

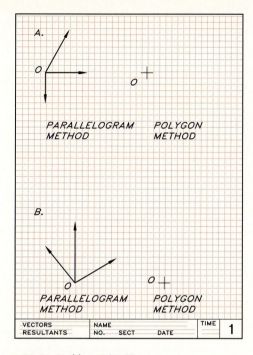

Figure 23.17 Problem 1 (A, B).

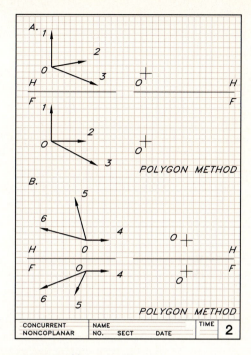

Figure 23.18 Problem 2 (A, B).

Draw your solutions to these problems with instruments on size A grid or plain sheets. Each grid square represents 0.20 in. (5mm). Make all notes, sketches, drawings, and graphical work neatly and use good design practices. Letter written matter legibly, using $^1/_8$-in. guidelines.

1. (Fig. 23.17)

(A, B) Find the resultants of the force systems by the parallelogram and polygon methods. Scale: 1" = 100 lb.

2. (Fig. 23.18)

(A, B) Find the resultants of the force systems by the parallelogram and polygon methods. Scale: 1" = 100 lb.

3. (Fig. 23.19)

(A, B) Find the forces in the coplanar force systems. Label the members, assign the forces in each of them, and indicate whether the forces are compression or tension.

4. (Fig. 23.20) Find the forces in each member of the truss by using a Maxwell diagram. Make a table of forces and indicate compression and tension.

5. (Fig. 23.21) Find the forces in the members of the concurrent noncoplanar force system. Make a table of forces and indicate compression and tension.

6. (Fig. 23.22) Find the forces in the members of the concurrent noncoplanar force system. Make a table of forces and indicate compression and tension.

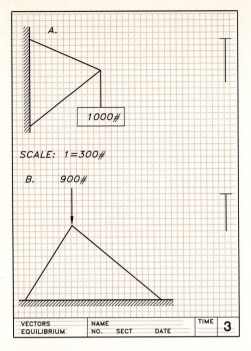

Figure 23.19 Problem 3 (A, B).

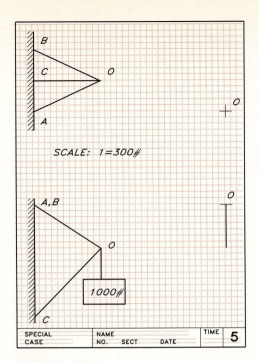

Figure 23.21 Problem 5.

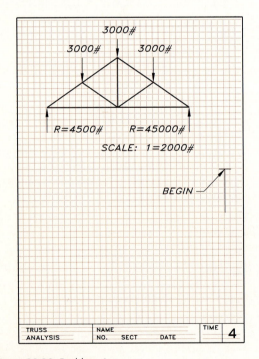

Figure 23.20 Problem 4.

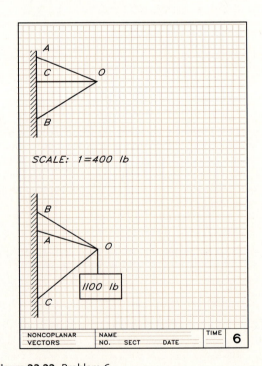

Figure 23.22 Problem 6.

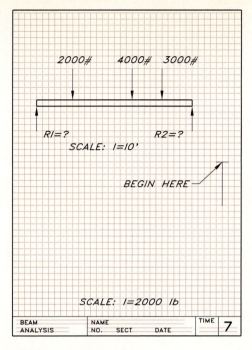

Figure 23.23 Problem 7 (A, B).

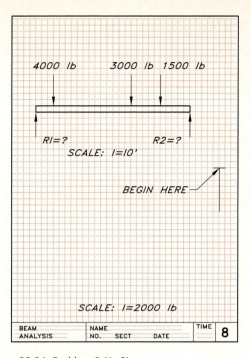

Figure 23.24 Problem 8 (A, B).

7. (Fig. 23.23)

(A) Find the forces in reactions R1 and R2 necessary to equalize the loads applied to the beam.

(B) Find the value and location of the single support that could replace both R1 and R2.

8. (Fig. 23.24) Repeat Problem 7 for this configuration.

9. (Fig. 23.25) Find the forces in the support members. Make a table of forces and indicate compression and tension.

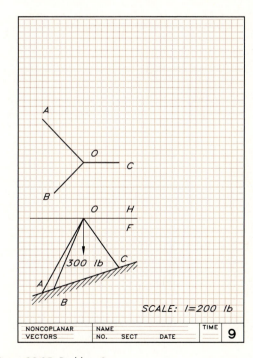

Figure 23.25 Problem 9.

10. (Fig. 23.26) Find the forces in the coplanar force system. Label the members, make a table of forces, and indicate compression and tension.

11. Repeat Problem 4, but use the joint-by-joint analysis instead of the Maxwell diagram method.

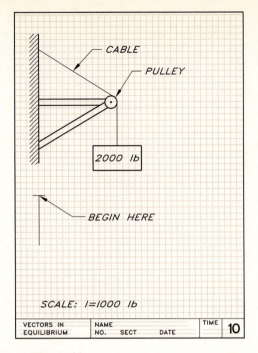

Figure 23.26 Problem 10.

24
Intersections and Developments

24.1 Introduction

Several methods may be used to find lines of intersection between parts that join. Usually such parts are made of sheet metal, or of plywood if used as forms for concrete. After **intersections** are found, **developments**, or flat patterns, can be laid out on sheet metal and cut to the desired shape. The refinery shown in **Fig. 24.1** illustrates many examples of intersections and developments.

24.2 Intersections of Lines and Planes

Figure 24.2 illustrates how to find the intersection between a line and a plane. This example is a special case in which the point of intersection clearly shows in the view where the plane appears as an edge. Projecting the piercing point, P, to the front view completes the visibility of the line.

This same principle is applied to finding the line of intersection between two planes **(Fig. 24.3)**. By locating the piercing points of lines AB

and DC and connecting these points, the line of intersection is found.

The angular intersection of two planes at a corner gives a line of intersection that bends around the corner **(Fig. 24.4)**. First, find piercing points 2' and 1'. Then project corner point 3 from the side view where the vertical corner pierces the plane to the front view of the corner. Point 2' is hidden in the front view because it is on the back side.

Figure 24.5 shows how to find the intersection between a plane and prism where the plane appears as an edge. Obtain the piercing points for each corner line and connect them to form the line of intersection. Show visibility to complete the intersection.

Figure 24.6 depicts a more general case of an intersection between a plane and prism. Passing vertical cutting planes through the planes of the prism in the top view yields traces (cut lines) on the front view of the oblique plane on which the piercing points of the vertical corner lines lie.

Figure 24.1 The design of this refinery in Borger, Texas, involved the application of many principles of intersections and developments. (Courtesy of Phillips Petroleum Company.)

LINE AND A PLANE

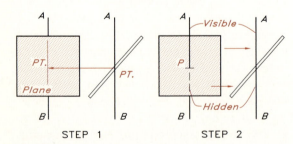

STEP 1   STEP 2

Figure 24.2 Intersection of a line and a plane:

Step 1 Find the point of intersection in the view where the plane appears as an edge, the side view in this case, and project it to the front view.

Step 2 Determine visibility in the front view by looking from the front view to the right-side view.

BETWEEN PLANES

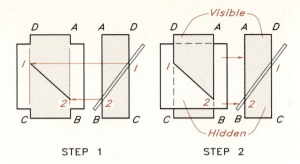

STEP 1   STEP 2

Figure 24.3 Intersection of planes:

Step 1 Find the piercing points of lines AB and DC with the plane where the plane appears as an edge and project them to the front view.

Step 2 Line 1–2 is the line of intersection. Determine visibility by looking from the front view to the right-side view.

PLANE AT A CORNER

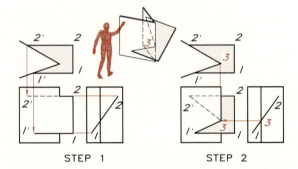

STEP 1   STEP 2

Figure 24.4 The intersection of a plane at a corner:

Step 1 The intersecting plane appears as an edge in the side view. Project intersection points 1' and 2' from the top and side views to the front view.

Step 2 The line of intersection from 1' to 2' must bend around the vertical corner at 3' in the top and side views. Project point 3' to the front view to locate line 1'–3'–2'.

Connect the points and determine visibility to complete the solution.

In **Fig. 24.7**, finding the intersection between a foreshortened plane and an oblique prism involves finding an auxiliary view to obtain the

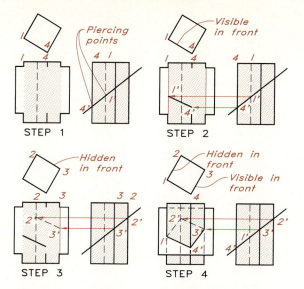

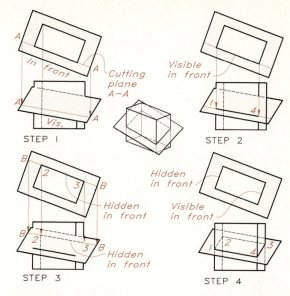

Figure 24.5 The intersection of a plane and a prism:

Step 1 Vertical corners 1 and 4 intersect the edge view of the plane in the side view at points 1' and 4'.

Step 2 Project points 1' and 4' from the side view to lines 1 and 4 in the front view. Connect them to form a visible line of intersection.

Step 3 Vertical corners 2 and 3 intersect the edge view of the plane at points 2' and 3' in the side view. Project points 2' and 3' to the front view to form a hidden line of intersection.

Step 4 Connect points 1', 2', 3', and 4' and determine visibility by analyzing the top and side views.

Figure 24.6 The intersection of an oblique plane and a prism:

Step 1 Pass vertical cutting plane A–A through corners 1 and 4 in the top view and project endpoints to the front view.

Step 2 Locate piercing points 1' and 4' in the front view where line A–A crosses lines 1 and 4.

Step 3 Pass vertical cutting plane B–B through corners 2 and 3 in the top view and project them to the front view to locate piercing points 2' and 3'.

Step 4 Connect the four piercing points and determine visibility by analysis of the top view.

edge view of the plane and simplify the problem. The piercing points of the corner lines of the prism lie in the auxiliary view and project back to the given views. Points 1, 2, and 3, projected from the auxiliary view to the given views, are shown as examples. Analysis of crossing lines determines visibility to complete the line of intersection in the top and front views.

24.3 Intersections Between Prisms

The techniques used to find the intersection between planes and lines also apply to finding the

intersection between two prisms **(Fig. 24.8)**. Project piercing points 1, 2, and 3 from the side and top views to the front view. Point X lies in the side view where line of intersection 1–2 bends around the vertical corner of the vertical prism. Connect points 1, X, and 2 and determine visibility.

Figure 24.9 illustrates how to find the line of intersection between an inclined prism and a vertical prism. An auxiliary view reveals the end view of the inclined prism where its planes appear as edges. In the auxiliary view, plane 1–2 bends around corner AB at point P. Project points of

OBLIQUE PLANE AND PRISM

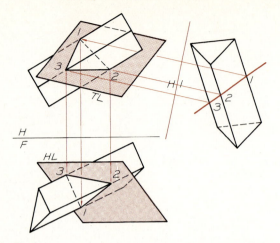

Figure 24.7 To find the intersection between a plane and a prism, construct a view in which the plane appears as an edge. Project piercing points 1, 2, and 3 back to the top and front views.

PERPENDICULAR PRISMS

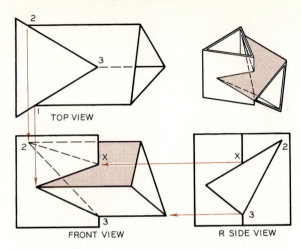

Figure 24.8 These are three views of intersecting prisms. The points of intersection are best found where intersecting planes appear as edges.

INTERSECTION BETWEEN PRISMS

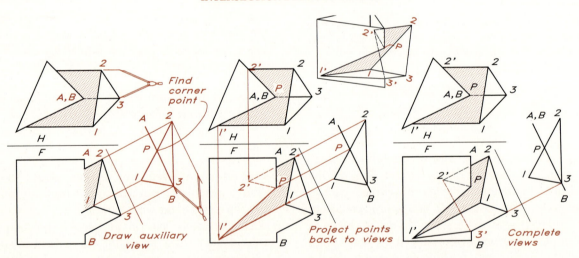

Figure 24.9 The intersection of prisms by auxiliary view:
Step 1 Construct the end view of the inclined prism by projecting an auxiliary view from the front view. Show line AB of the vertical prism in the auxiliary view.

Step 2 Locate piercing points 1' and 2' in the top and front views. Intersection line 1'–2' bends around corner AB at point P (projected from the auxiliary view).

Step 3 Intersection lines from 2' and 1' to 3' do not bend around the corner and are straight lines. Line 1'–3' is visible, and line 2'–3' is invisible.

INCLINED PRISM

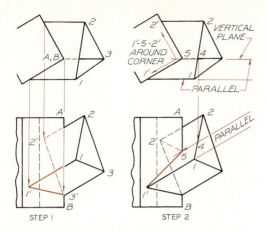

Figure 24.10 The intersection of prisms by projection:
Step 1 Project the piercing points of lines 1, 2, and 3 from the top view to the front view to locate piercing points 1', 2', and 3'.

Step 2 Pass a cutting plane through corner AB in the top view to locate point 5, where intersection line 1'–2' bends around the vertical prism. Find point 5 in the front view and draw line 1'–5–2'.

DESIGN APPLICATION: CONDUIT CONNECTOR

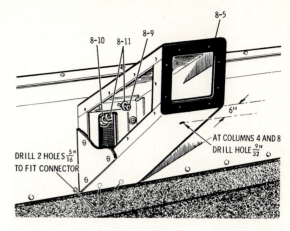

Figure 24.11 The design of this conduit connector involved the use of the principles of the intersection of a plane and prism. (Courtesy of the Federal Aviation Administration.)

intersection 1' and 2' from the top and auxiliary to their intersections in the front view. Then draw the line of intersection 1'–P–2' for this portion of the line of intersection. Connect the remaining lines, 1'–3' and 2'–3' to complete the solution.

Figure 24.10 shows an alternative method of solving this type of problem. Piercing points 1' and 2' appear in the front view as projections from the top view. Point 5 is the point where line 1'–5–2' bends around vertical corner AB. To find point 5 in the front view, pass a cutting plane through corner AB in the top view and project its trace to the front view. Draw the lines of intersection, 1'–5–2'.

The conduit connector shown in **Fig. 24.11** is an application of the principles of intersecting plane and prism.

24.4 Intersections Between Planes and Cylinders

Figure 24.12 shows how to find the intersection between a plane and a cylinder. Cutting planes passed vertically through the top view of the cylinder establish pairs of elements on the cylinder and their piercing points. Space the cutting planes conveniently apart by eye. Then project the piercing points to each view and draw the elliptical line of intersection.

Figure 24.13 shows the solution of a more general problem. Here, the cylinder is vertical and the plane is oblique and does not appear as an edge. Passing vertical cutting planes through the cylinder and the plane in the top view gives elements on the cylinder and their piercing points on the plane. Projecting these points to the front view completes the elliptical line of intersection. The

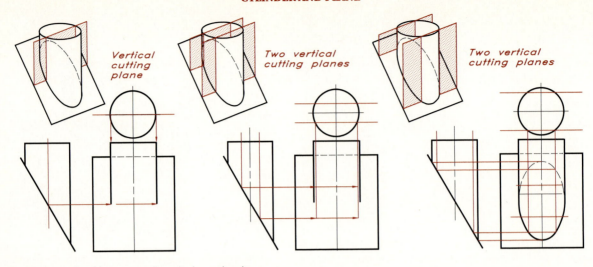

Figure 24.12 The intersection of a cylinder and a plane:

Step 1 Pass a vertical cutting plane through the cylinder parallel to its axis to find two points of intersection.

Step 2 Use two more cutting planes to find four additional points in the top and left side views. Project these points to the front view.

Step 3 Use additional cutting planes to find more points. Connect these points to give an elliptical line of intersection.

more cutting planes used, the more accurate the line of intersection will be.

Figure 24.14 demonstrates the general case of the intersection between a plane and cylinder, where both are oblique in the given views. An auxiliary view is used to show the edge view of the plane. Cutting planes passed through the cylinder parallel to its axis in the auxiliary view determine elements on the cylinder and their piercing points. An elliptical line of intersection is found when the points are connected and projected back to the given views.

24.5 Intersections Between Cylinders and Prisms

An inclined prism intersects a vertical cylinder in **Fig. 24.15**. A primary auxiliary view is drawn to show the end view of the inclined prism where its planes appear as edges. A series of vertical cutting planes in the top view establish lines lying on the surfaces of the cylinder and prism. The cutting planes, also shown in the auxiliary view, are the same distance apart as in the top view.

Projecting the line of intersection from 1 to 3 from the auxiliary view to the front view yields an elliptical line of intersection. The visibility of this line changes from visible to hidden at point X, which appears in the auxiliary view and is projected to the front view. Continuing this process gives the lines of intersection of the other two planes of the prism.

24.6 Intersections Between Two Cylinders

To find the line of intersection between two perpendicular cylinders, pass cutting planes through them parallel to their centerlines (**Fig. 24.16**). Each cutting plane locates a pair of elements on both cylinders that intersect at a piercing point.

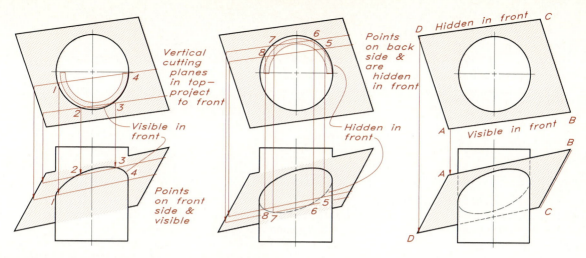

Figure 24.13 Intersection of a cylinder and an oblique plane:

Step 1 Pass vertical cutting planes through the cylinder in the top view to establish elements on its surface and lines on the oblique plane. Project piercing points 1, 2, 3, and 4 to the front view of their respective lines and connect them with a visible line.

Step 1 Pass vertical cutting planes through the cylinder in the top view to establish elements on its surface and lines on the oblique plane. Project piercing points 1, 2, 3, and 4 to the front view of their respective lines and connect them with a visible line.

Step 3 Determine visibility of the plane and cylinder in the front view. Line AB is visible by inspection of the top view, and line CD is hidden.

OBLIQUE CYLINDER AND OBLIQUE PLANE

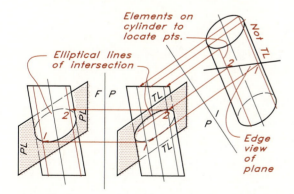

Figure 24.14 To find the intersection between an oblique cylinder and an oblique plane, construct a view that shows the plane as an edge. Cutting planes passed through the cylinder locate points on the line of intersection.

Connecting the points and determining visibility completes the solution. The design and fabrication of the vessels and pipes shown in **Fig. 24.17** required application of these principles.

Figure 24.18 illustrates how to find the intersection between nonperpendicular cylinders. This method involves passing a series of vertical cutting planes through the cylinders parallel to their centerlines. Points 1 and 2, labeled on cutting plane D, are typical of points on the line of intersection. Other points may be found in the same manner. Although the auxiliary view is not essential to the solution, it is an aid in visualizing the problem. Projecting points 1 and 2 on cutting plane D in the auxiliary view to the front view provides a check on the projections from the top view.

CYLINDER AND A PRISM

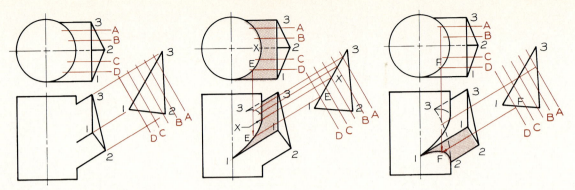

Figure 24.15 The intersection of a cylinder and a prism:

Step 1 Project an auxiliary view of the triangular prism from the front view to show the edge views of its planes. Draw frontal cutting planes through the top view of the cylinder and locate them in the auxiliary view with your dividers.

Step 2 Locate points along intersection line 1–3 in the top view and project them to the front view. For example, find point E on cutting plane D in the top and auxiliary views and project it to the front view where the projectors intersect. Visibility changes in the front view at point X.

Step 3 Determine all the remaining points of intersection by using the other cutting planes. Project point F, shown in the top and auxiliary views, to the front view of line 1–2. Connect the points and determine visibility.

INTERSECTION BETWEEN CYLINDERS

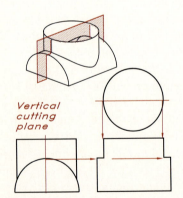

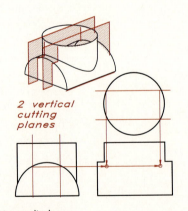

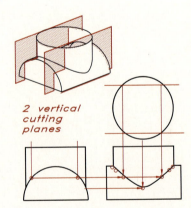

Figure 24.16 Obtaining the intersection of two cylinders:

Step 1 Pass a cutting plane through the cylinders parallel to their axes, locating two points of intersection.

Step 2 Use two more cutting planes in order to find four additional points of intersection.

Step 3 Use two more cutting planes to locate four more points. Connect the points to find the line of intersection.

Figure 24.17 These vessels and pipes are examples of intersections between cylinders. (Courtesy of Lone Star Gas Company.)

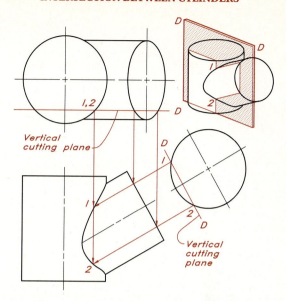

Figure 24.18 To find intersection of these cylinders, locate the end view of the inclined cylinder in an auxiliary view. Then use vertical cutting planes to find the piercing points of the cylindrical elements and the line of intersection.

24.7 Intersections Between Planes and Cones

To find points of intersection on a cone, use cutting planes that are **(1) perpendicular to the cone's axis** or **(2) parallel to the cone's axis**. The vertical planes in the top view of **Fig. 24.19A** cut radial lines on the cone and establish elements on its surface. The horizontal planes in **Fig. 24.19B** cut circular sections that appear true size in the top view of a right cone.

A series of **radial cutting planes** define elements on a cone (**Fig. 24.20**). These elements cross the edge view of the plane in the front view

to locate piercing points of each element that, when projected to the top view of the same elements, lie on the line of intersection.

A series of **horizontal cutting planes** may be used to determine the line of intersection between a cone and an oblique plane (**Fig. 24.21**). The sections cut by these imaginary planes are circles in the top view. The cutting planes also locate lines on the oblique plane that intersect the circular sections cut by each respective cutting plane. The points of intersection found in the top view project to the front view. We could have used the horizontal cutting-plane method in Fig. 24.20 to obtain the same results.

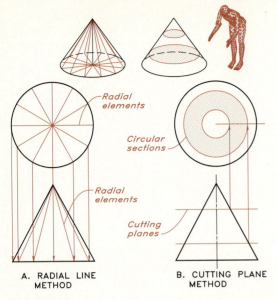

Figure 24.19 To find intersections on conical surfaces, you may use (A) radial cutting planes that pass through the cone's centerline and are perpendicular to its base, or (B) cutting planes that are parallel to the cone's base.

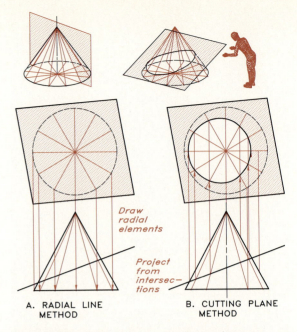

Figure 24.20 The intersection of a plane and a cone:
Step 1 Divide the base evenly in the top view and connect these points with the apex to establish elements on the cone. Project these elements to the front view.

Step 2 Project the piercing point of each element on the edge view of the plane to the top view of the same elements, and connect them to form the line of intersection.

24.8 Intersections Between Cones and Prisms

A primary auxiliary view gives the end view of the inclined prism that intersects the cone in **Fig. 24.22**. Cutting planes that radiate from the apex of the cone in the top view locate elements on the cone's surface that intersect the prism in the auxiliary view. These elements project to the front view.

Wherever the edge view of plane 1–3 intersects an element in the auxiliary view, the piercing points project to the same element in the front and top views. Passing an extra cutting plane through point 3 in the auxiliary view locates an element that projects to the front and top views. Piercing point 3 projects to this element in sequence from the auxiliary view to the top view.

This same procedure yields the piercing points of the other two planes of the prism. All projections of points of intersection originate in the auxiliary view, where the planes of the prism appear as edges.

In **Fig. 24.23**, horizontal cutting planes passed through the front view of the cone and cylinder give a series of circular sections in the top view. Points 1 and 2, shown on cutting plane C in the top view, are typical and project to the front view. The same method produces other points.

OBLIQUE PLANE AND A CONE

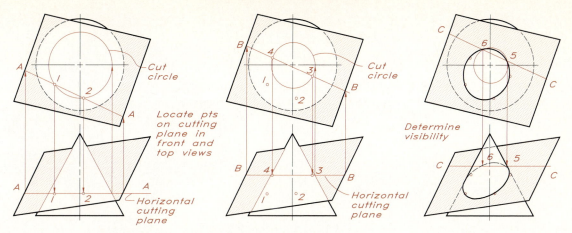

Figure 24.21 Determining the intersection of an oblique plane and a cone:

Step 1 Pass a horizontal cutting plane through the front view to establish a circular section on the cone and a line on the plane in the top view. The piercing points of this line are on the circular section. Project piercing points 1 and 2 to the front view.

Step 2 Pass horizontal cutting plane B–B through the front view in the same manner to locate piercing points 3 and 4 in the top view. Project these points to the horizontal plane in the front view from the top view.

Step 3 Use additional horizontal planes to find a sufficient number of points to complete the line of intersection and then determine visibility.

CONE AND PRISM

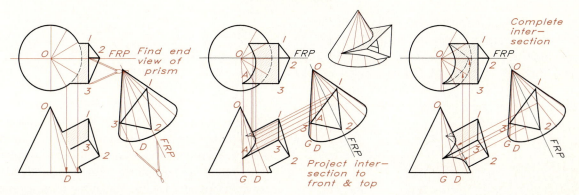

Figure 24.22 The intersection of a cone and a prism:

Step 1 Construct an auxiliary view to obtain the edge views of the lateral surfaces of the prism. In the auxiliary view, pass cutting planes through the cone that radiate from the apex to find elements on the cone. Project the elements to the front and auxiliary views.

Step 2 Locate the piercing points of the cone's elements with the edge view of plane 1–3 in the primary view and project them to the front and top views. For example, point A lies on element OD in the primary auxiliary view, so project it to the front and top views of OD.

Step 3 Locate the piercing points where the conical elements intersect the edge views of the planes of the prism in the auxiliary view. For example, find point B on O in the primary auxiliary view and project it to the front and top views of OE.

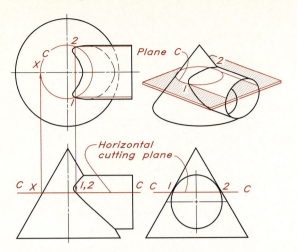

Figure 24.23 Horizontal cutting planes are used to find the intersection between the cone and the cylinder. The cutting planes cut circles in the top view. Only one cutting plane is shown here as an example.

Figure 24.24 This electrically operated distributor is an application of intersections between a cone and a series of cylinders. (Courtesy of GATX.)

This method is feasible only when the center-line of the cylinder is perpendicular to the axis of the cone, producing circular sections in the top view (rather than elliptical sections, which would be difficult to draw). The distributor housing in **Fig. 24.24** is an example of an intersection between cylinders and a cone.

24.9 Intersections Between Prisms and Pyramids

Figure 24.25 shows how to find the intersection of an inclined prism with a pyramid. An auxiliary view shows the end view of the inclined prism and the pyramid. The radial lines OB and OA drawn through corners 1 and 3 in the auxiliary view project back to the front and top views. Projection locates intersecting points 1 and 3 on lines OB and OA in each view. Point P is the point where line

1–3 bends around corner OC. Finding lines of intersection 1–4 and 4–3 and determining visibility completes the solution.

Figure 24.26 shows a horizontal prism that intersects a pyramid. An auxiliary view depicts the end view of the horizontal prism with its planes as edges. Passing a series of horizontal cutting planes through the corner points of the horizontal prism and the pyramid in the auxiliary view gives the lines of intersection, which form triangular sections in the top view.

The cutting plane through corner point P in the auxiliary view is an example of a typical cutting plane. At point P the line of intersection of this plane bends around the corner of the pyramid. Other cutting planes are passed through the corner lines of the prism in the auxiliary and front

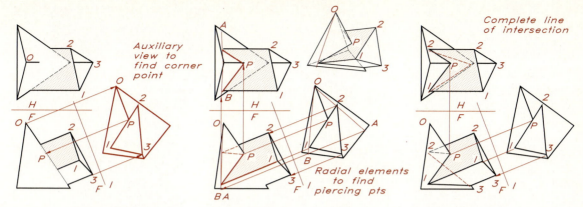

Figure 24.25 The intersection of a prism and a pyramid:

Step 1 Find the edge view of the surfaces of the prism by projecting an auxiliary view from the front view. Project the pyramid into this view also, showing only the visible surfaces.

Step 2 Pass planes A and B through apex O and points 1 and 3 in the auxiliary view. Project lines OA and OB to the front and top views and project points 1 and 3 to them. Point 2 lies on line OC. Connect points 1, 2, and 3 to give the intersection of the upper plane.

Step 3 Point 3 lies on line OC in the auxiliary view. Project this point to the principal views. Connect point 3 to points 1 and 2 to complete the intersections and show visibility. Assume that these geometric shapes are constructed of sheet metal.

views. Each corner line extends in the top view to intersect the triangular section formed by the cutting plane, as shown at P.

24.10 Principles of Developments

The sheet metal mixing unit shown in **Fig. 24.27** was designed for fabrication from flat, sheet-metal stock. The part's flat pattern was developed and laid out in the plane of the stock and then folded and joined to form the 3D shape.

Figure 24.28 illustrates some of the standard edges and joints for sheet metal. The application determines the type of seam that is used.

Figure 24.29 shows the development of patterns for three typical shapes. The sides of a box are unfolded into a common plane. The cylinder is rolled out along a stretch-out line equal in length to its circumference. The pattern of a right

cone is developed with the length of an element serving as a radius for drawing the base arc.

The construction of patterns for geometric shapes with parallel elements, such as the prisms and cylinders shown in **Figs. 24.30A** and **B**, begins with drawing **stretch-out lines parallel to the edge views of the shapes' right sections**. The distance around the right section becomes the length of the stretch-out line. The prism and cylinder in **Figs. 24.30C** and **D** are inclined, so their right sections are perpendicular to their sides, not parallel to their bases.

In development, **an inside pattern is preferable to an outside pattern** for two reasons: (1) most bending machines are designed to fold metal inward, and (2) markings and scribings will be hidden. The designer labels patterns with a series of lettered or numbered points on the layouts. **All lines on developments must be true**

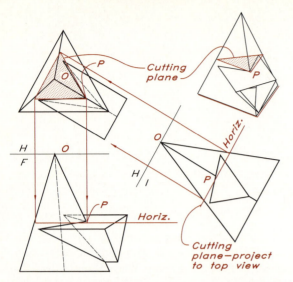

Figure 24.26 To locate the intersection of this pyramid and prism, obtain the end view of the prism in an auxiliary view. Pass horizontal cutting planes through the fold lines of the prism to find the piercing points and the line of intersection. A typical cutting plane is shown to find a corner point where a plane bends around a corner of the pyramid.

Figure 24.27 The design of this mixing unit required the application of the principles of intersections and developments. Its flat pattern was developed on flat sheet-metal stock that was bent into shape. These flat patterns are called developments.

length. **Patterns should be laid out so that the seam line (a line where the pattern is joined) is the shortest line in order to reduce the expense of riveting or welding the seams**.

24.11 Development of Rectangular Prisms

Figure 24.31 illustrates the development of a flat pattern for a rectangular prism. The edges of the prism are vertical and true length in the front view. The right section is perpendicular to these sides and the right section is true size in the top view. The stretch-out line begins with point 1 and is drawn parallel to the edge view of the right section.

If an inside pattern is to be laid out to the right, you must determine which point is to the right of

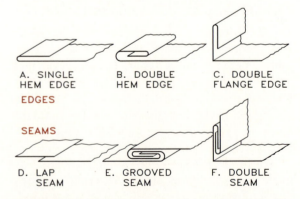

Figure 24.28 These are examples of several types of edges and seams used to join sheet-metal developments. Other seams are joined by riveting and welding.

TYPES OF DEVELOPMENTS

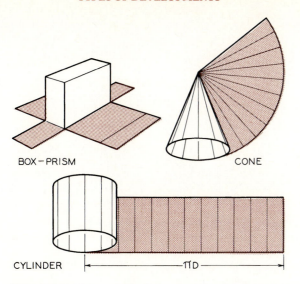

BOX – PRISM

CONE

CYLINDER

πD

Figure 24.29 Three standard types of developments are the box, cylinder, and cone.

RECTANGULAR PRISM

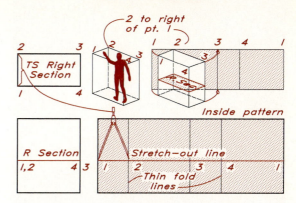

Figure 24.31 To develop a rectangular prism for an inside pattern, draw the stretch-out line parallel to the edge view of the right section. Transfer the distances between the fold lines from the true-size right section to the stretch-out line.

STRETCH-OUT LINES

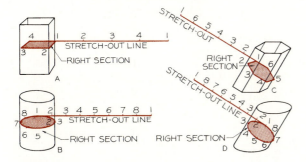

Figure 24.30

A and **B** To obtain the developments of right prisms and right cylinders, roll out the right sections along a stretch-out line.

C and **D** Draw stretch-out lines parallel to the edge views of the right section of cylinders and prisms, or perpendicular to their true-length elements.

the beginning point, point 1. Let's assume that you are standing inside the top view and are looking at point 1: You will see point 2 to the right of point 1.

To locate the fold lines of the pattern, transfer lines 2–3, 3–4, and 4–1 with your dividers from the right section in the top view to the stretch-out line. The length of each fold line is its projected true length from the front view. Connect the ends of the fold lines to form the boundary of the developed surface. Draw the fold lines as thin, dark lines and the outside lines as thicker, visible object lines.

The can-crushing machine shown in **Fig. 24.32** comprises prisms and pyramids and was designed using the principles of development.

Development of the prism depicted in **Fig. 24.33** is similar to that shown in Fig. 24.31. Here, though, one of its ends is beveled (truncated) rather than square. The stretch-out line is parallel to the edge view of the right section in the front view. Lay off the true-length distances around the

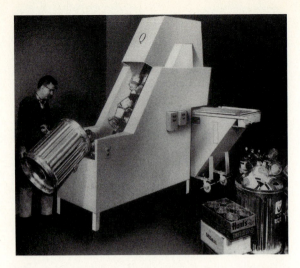

Figure 24.32 The principles of intersections and developments were applied to the design and construction of this can-crushing machine hopper.

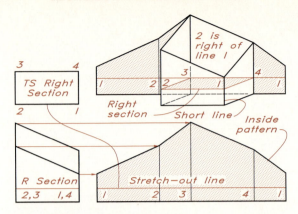

Figure 24.33 To develop an inside pattern of a rectangular prism with a beveled end, draw the stretch-out line parallel to the right section. Then find the fold lines by transferring distances between the fold lines from the true-size right section to the stretch-out line.

OBLIQUE PRISM

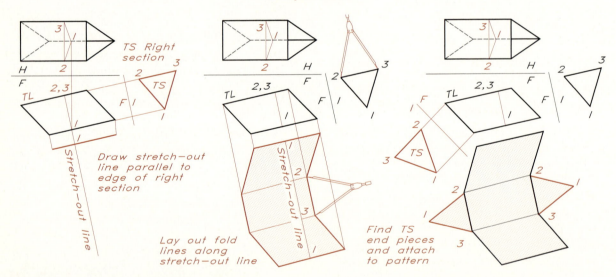

Figure 24.34 Development of an oblique prism:

Step 1 The edge view of the right section is perpendicular to the true-length axis of the prism in the front view. Find the true-size view of the right section by an auxiliary view. Draw the stretch-out line parallel to the edge view of the right section. The line through point 1 is the first line of the development.

Step 2 Because the pattern is to be laid out to the right from line 1, the next point is line 2 (from the auxiliary view). Transfer true-length lines 1–2, 2–3, and 3–1 from the right section to the stretch-out line to locate fold lines. Determine the lengths of bend lines by projection.

Step 3 Find true-size views of the end pieces by projecting auxiliary views from the front view. Connect these ends to the development to form the completed pattern. Draw fold lines as thin, dark lines and outside lines as thicker, visible object lines.

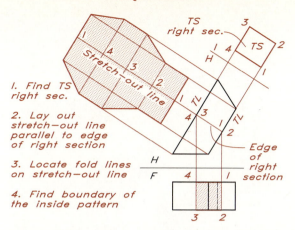

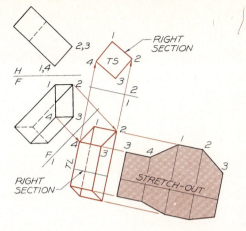

Figure 24.35 To develop this oblique chute, locate the right section true size in the auxiliary view. Draw the stretch-out line parallel to its right section. Find fold lines by transferring their spacing from the true-size right section to the stretch-out line.

Figure 24.36 To develop an oblique prism, draw a primary auxiliary view in which the fold lines are true length and a secondary auxiliary view in which the right section appears true size. Use these views to develop the pattern the same way as in Fig. 24.35.

right section along the stretch-out line (beginning with the shortest one) and locate the fold lines. Find the lengths of the fold lines by projecting from the front view of these lines.

24.12 Development of Oblique Prisms

The prism shown in **Fig. 24.34** is inclined to the horizontal plane, but its fold lines are true length in the front view. The right section is an edge perpendicular to these fold lines, and the stretch-out line is parallel to the edge of the right section. A true-size view of the right section is found in the auxiliary view.

Transfer the distances between the fold lines from the true-size right section to the stretch-out line. Find the lengths of the fold lines by projecting from the front view. Determine the ends of the prism and attach them to the pattern so that they can be folded into position.

In **Fig. 24.35**, the fold lines of the prism are true length in the top view, and the edge view of the right section is perpendicular to them. The stretch-out line is parallel to the edge view of the right section, and the true size of the right section appears in an auxiliary view projected from the top view. Transfer the distances about the right section to the stretch-out line to locate the fold lines, beginning with the shortest line. Find the lengths of the fold lines by projecting from the top view. Attach the end portions to the pattern to complete the construction.

A prism that does not project true length in either view may be developed as shown in **Fig. 24.36**. The fold lines are true length in an auxiliary view projected from the front view. The right section appears as an edge perpendicular to the fold lines in the auxiliary view and true size in a secondary auxiliary view.

Draw the stretch-out line parallel to the edge view on the right section. Locate the fold lines on

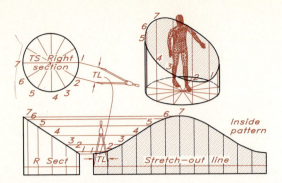

Figure 24.37 To develop an inside pattern for a truncated right cylinder, draw the stretch-out line parallel to the right section. Transfer points 1–7 from the top view to the stretch-out line that is parallel to the right section. Point 2 is to the right of point 1 for an inside pattern.

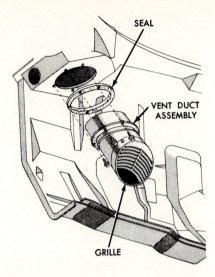

Figure 24.38 The design of this automobile ventilator air duct involved the use of development principles. (Courtesy of Ford Motor Company.)

the stretch-out line by measuring around the right section in the secondary auxiliary view, beginning with the shortest one. Then project the lengths of the fold lines to the development from the primary auxiliary view.

24.13 Development of Cylinders

Figure 24.37 illustrates how to develop a flat pattern of a right cylinder. The elements of the cylinder are true length in the front view, so the right section appears as an edge in this view and true size in the top view. **The stretch-out line is parallel to the edge view of the right section,** and point 1 is the beginning point because it lies on the shortest element.

Let's assume that you are standing inside the cylinder in the top view and are looking at point 1: You will see that point 2 is to the right of point 1. Therefore lay off point 2 to the right of point 1 for developing an inside pattern.

By drawing radial lines at 15° or 30° intervals, you can equally space the elements in the top view and conveniently lay them out along the stretch-out line as equal measurements. To complete the pattern, find the lengths of the elements by projecting from the front view. An application of a developed cylinder with a beveled end is the automobile air-conditioning duct shown in **Fig. 24.38**.

24.14 Development of Oblique Cylinders

The pattern for an oblique cylinder **(Fig. 24.39)** involves the same determinations as the preceding cases, but with the additional step of finding a true-size view of the right section in an auxiliary view. First, locate a series of equally spaced elements around the right section in the auxiliary view and project them back to the true-length

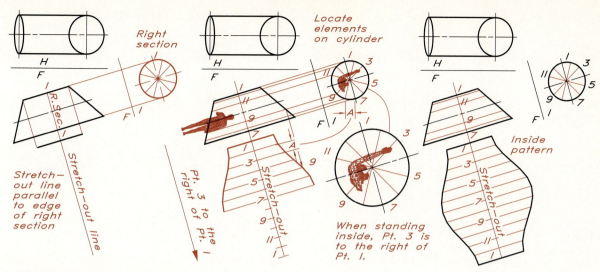

Figure 24.39 Development of an oblique cylinder:

Step 1 The right section is an edge perpendicular to the true-length axis in the front view. Draw an auxiliary view to find the right section true size. Divide the right section into equal chords. Draw a stretch-out line parallel to the edge view of the right section. Locate the shortest element at 1.

Step 2 Project elements from the right section to the front view. Transfer the chordal measurements in the auxiliary view to the stretch-out line to locate cylindrical elements and determine their lengths by projection.

Step 3 Locate the remaining elements to complete the inside pattern.

view. Draw the stretch-out line parallel to the edge view of the right section in the front view.

Lay out the spacing between the elements along the stretch-out line, and draw the elements through these points perpendicular to the stretch-out line. Find the lengths of the elements by projecting from the front view and complete the pattern.

A more general case is the oblique cylinder shown in **Fig. 24.40**, where the elements are not true length in the given views. A primary auxiliary view gives the elements true length, and a secondary auxiliary view yields a true-size view of the right section. Draw the stretch-out line parallel to

the edge view of the right section in the primary auxiliary view. Transfer the elements to the stretch-out line from the true-size right section.

Draw the elements perpendicular to the stretch-out line and find their lengths by projecting from the primary auxiliary view. Connect the endpoints with a smooth curve to complete the pattern.

24.15 Development of Pyramids

All lines used to draw patterns must be true length, but pyramids have few lines that are true length in the given views. For this reason you

GENERAL-CASE CYLINDER

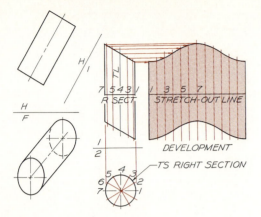

Figure 24.40 To develop an oblique cylinder, construct a primary auxiliary view in which the elements appear true length. The right section is found true size in a secondary auxiliary view. Complete the drawing as in Fig. 24.39.

TRUE LENGTH BY REVOLUTION (PYRAMID)

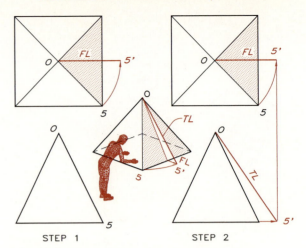

STEP 1   STEP 2

Figure 24.41 True length of a pyramid by revolution:
Step 1 To find the true length of corner line O–5 of a pyramid, revolve it into the frontal plane in the top view, to O–5'.

Step 2 Project point 5' to the front view, where frontal line O–5' is true length.

must find the sloping corner lines true length before drawing a development.

Figure 24.41 shows the method of finding the corner lines of a pyramid true length by revolution. Revolve line O–5 into the frontal plane to line O–5' in the top view so that it will be true length in the front view. An application of the development of a pyramid is the sheet-metal hopper shown in **Fig. 24.42**.

Figure 24.43 shows the development of a right pyramid. Line O–1 is revolved into the frontal plane in the top view to find its true length in the front view. Because it is a right pyramid, all corner lines are equal in length. Line O–1' is the radius for the base circle of the development. When you transfer distance 1–2 from the base in the top view to the development, it forms a chord on the base circle. Find lines 2–3, 3–4, and 4–1 in the same manner and in sequence. Draw the fold lines as thin lines from the base to the apex, point O.

DESIGN APPLICATION: HOPPER

Figure 24.42 This sheet-metal hopper is an application of a design involving development of a pyramid. (Courtesy of Gar–Bro.)

DEVELOPMENT OF A RIGHT PYRAMID

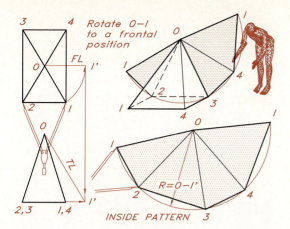

Figure 24.43 To develop this right pyramid, lay out an arc by using the true length of corner line O–1' as the radius. Transfer true-length distances around the base in the top view to the arc and darken the lines.

DEVELOPMENT OF A RIGHT PYRAMID

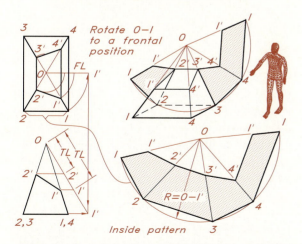

Figure 24.44 To develop an inside pattern of a truncated right pyramid, use the method shown in Fig. 24.41. Find the true lengths of elements O–1', O–2', O–3', and O–4' in the front view by revolution. Lay them off along their respective elements to find the upper boundary of the pattern.

TRUE LENGTH BY REVOLUTION (CONE)

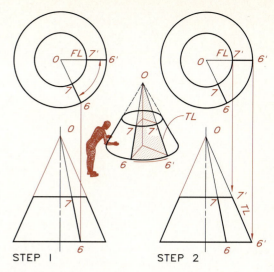

Figure 24.45 True length by revolution (cone):

Step 1 Revolve an element of a cone, O–6, into a frontal plane in the top view.

Step 2 Project point 6' to the front view, where it is a true-length outside element of the cone. Find the true length of line O–7' by projecting point 7' to the outside element in the front view.

A variation of this case is the truncated pyramid (**Fig. 24.44**). Development of the inside pattern proceeds as in the preceding case, but establishing the upper lines of the development requires an additional step. Revolution yields the true-length lines from the apex to points 1', 2', 3', and 4'. Lay off these distances along their respective lines on the pattern to find the upper boundary of the pattern.

24.16 Development of Cones

All elements of a right cone are equal in length (**Fig. 24.45**). Revolving element O–6 into its

DEVELOPMENT OF A RIGHT CONE

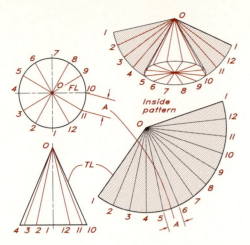

Figure 24.46 To develop an inside pattern of a right cone, use a true-length element (O–4 or O–10 in the front view) as the radius. Transfer chordal distances from the true-size base in the top view and mark them off along the arc.

Figure 24.47 This conical shape was formed from metal panels by applying principles of developments.

frontal position at O–6' gives its true length. When projected to the front view, line O–6' is true length and is the outside element of the cone. Projecting point 7 horizontally to element O–6' locates point 7'.

To develop the right cone depicted in **Fig. 24.46**, divide the base into equally spaced elements in the top view and project them to the front view, where they radiate to the apex at O. The outside elements in the front view, O–10 and O–4, are true length.

Using element O–10 as a radius, draw the base arc of the development. The spacing of the elements along the base circle is equal to the chordal distances between them on the base in the top

view. Inspection of the top view from the inside, where point 2 is to the right of point 1, indicates that this is an inside pattern. The sheet-metal chambers in **Fig. 24.47** are applications of conical development.

Figure 24.48 shows the development of a truncated cone. To find its pattern, lay out the entire cone by using the true-length element O–1 as the radius, ignoring the portion removed from it. Locate the hyperbolic section formed by the inclined plane through the front view of the cone in the top view by projecting points on each element of the cone to the top view of these elements. For example, determine the true length of line O–3' by projecting point 3' horizontally to the true-

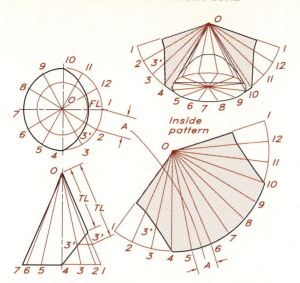

Figure 24.48 To develop a conical surface with a side opening, begin by laying it out as in Fig. 24.46. Find true-length elements by revolution in the front view and transfer them to their respective elements in the pattern.

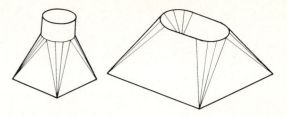

Figure 24.49 These are examples of transition pieces that connect parts having different cross sections.

Figure 24.50 Transition pieces were used to join a circular shape with a rectangular section in this application. (Courtesy of Western Precipitation Group, Joy Manufacturing Company.)

length element O–1 in the front view. Lay off these distances, and others, along their respective elements to establish a smooth curve.

24.17 Development of Transition Pieces

A transition piece changes the shape of a section at one end to a different shape at the other end (Fig. 24.49). In industrial applications, transition pieces may be huge **(Fig. 24.50)** or relatively small (Fig. 24.47).

Figure 24.51 shows development of a transition piece. Radial elements extend from each corner to the equally spaced points on the circular end of the piece. Revolution gives the true length

of each line. True-length lines 2–D, 3–D, and 2–3 yield the inside pattern of 2–3–D.

The true-length radial lines, used in combination with the true-length chordal distance in the top view, give a series of adjacent triangles to form the pattern beginning with element D2. Adding the triangles A–1–2 and G–3–4 at each end of the pattern completes the development of a half-pattern.

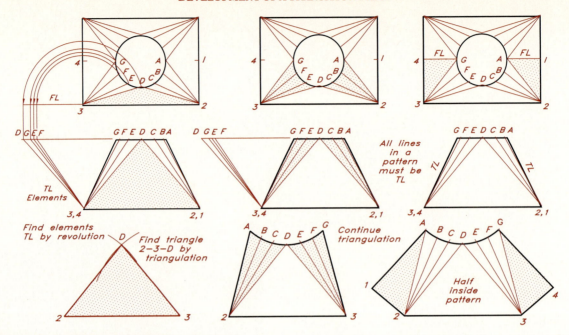

Figure 24.51 Development of a transition piece:

Step 1 Divide the circular end into equal parts in the top view and connect these points with lines to corner points 2 and 3. Find the true length of these lines by revolving and projecting them to the front view. Using true-length lines, draw triangle 2–3–D.

Step 2 Using other true-length lines and the chord distances on the circular end in the top view, draw a series of triangles joined at common sides. For example, draw arcs 2–C from point 2. To find point C, draw arc DC from point D. Chord DC is true length in the top view.

Step 3 Construct the two remaining planes, A–1–2 and G–3–4, by triangulation to complete the inside half-pattern of the transition piece. Draw the fold lines, where the surface is to be bent, as thin lines. The seam line for the pattern is line A–1, the shortest line.

Problems

The scale of these problems allows you to fit two solutions on a size A sheet for a grid size of 0.20 in. (5 mm). For a grid size of 0.40 in. (10 mm), you can fit only one solution on a size A sheet.

Intersections

1–24. (Fig. 24.52) Lay out the problems and find the intersections that are necessary to complete the views.

Developments

25–48. (Fig. 24.53) Lay out the problems and draw the developments. Orient the long side of the sheet horizontally to allow space at the right of the given views for the development.

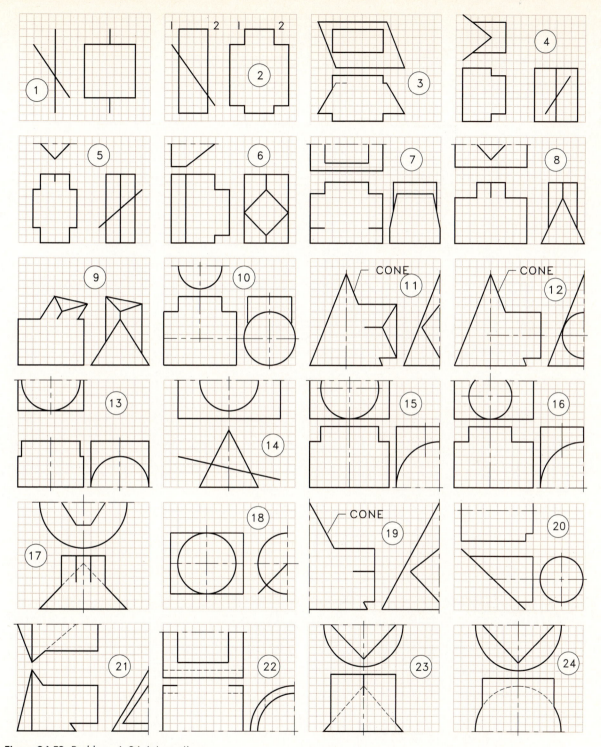

Figure 24.52 Problems 1–24. Intersections.

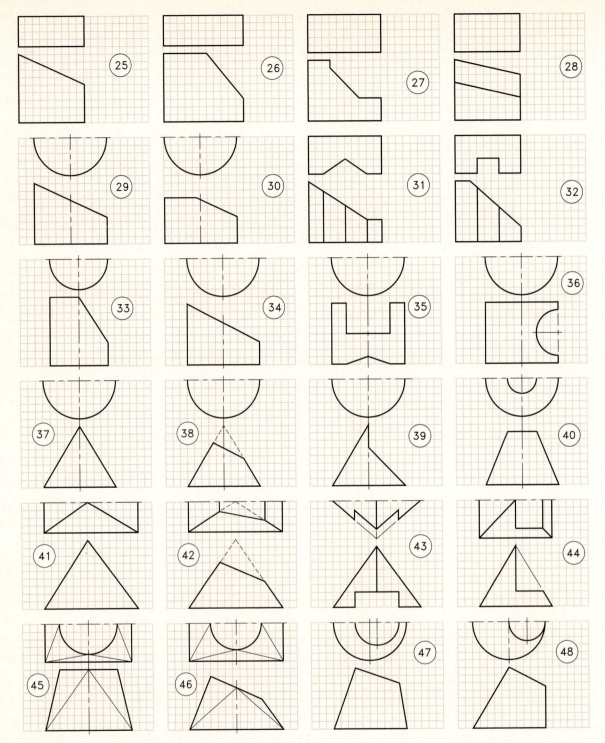

Figure 24.53 Problems 25–48. Developments.

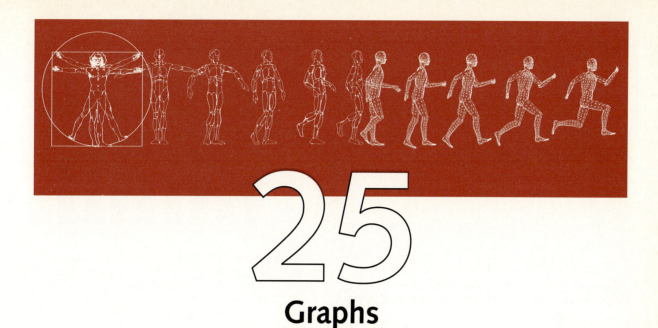

25

Graphs

25.1 Introduction

Data and information expressed as numbers and words are usually difficult to analyze or evaluate unless transcribed into graphical form, or as a **graph**. The term **chart** is an acceptable substitute for graph, but it is more appropriate when applied to maps, a specialized form of graphs.

Graphs are especially useful in presenting data at briefings, when the data must be interpreted and communicated quickly to those in attendance. Graphs are a convenient way to condense and present data visually, allowing the data to be grasped much more easily than when presented as tables of numbers or verbally.

Several different types of graphs are widely used, depending on the nature of the presentation required. The most common types of graphs are:

- Pie graphs
- Bar graphs
- Linear coordinate graphs
- Logarithmic coordinate graphs
- Semilogarithmic coordinate graphs
- Polar graphs
- Schematics and diagrams.

Proportions

Graphs are used on large display boards, and in technical reports, as slides for a projector, or as transparencies for an overhead projector. Consequently, the proportion of the graph must be determined before it is constructed to match the page, slide, or transparency.

A graph that is to be photographed with a 35-mm camera must be drawn to the proportions of the film, or approximately 3×2 **(Fig. 25.1)**. This area may be enlarged or reduced proportionally by using the diagonal-line method.

The proportions of an overhead projector transparency are approximately 10×8. The image size should not exceed 9.5 inches $\times$ 7.5 inches to allow adequate margin for mounting the transparency on a frame (usually of cardboard).

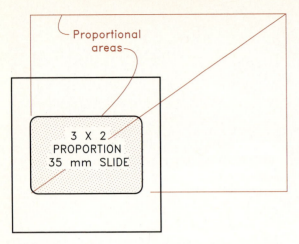

Figure 25.1 This diagonal-line method may be used to lay out drawings that are proportional to the area of a 35-mm slide.

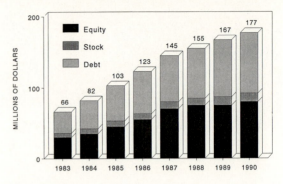

Figure 25.2 This computer-produced bar graph was generated by a program that converts numerical data into various types of graphs. (Courtesy of SlideWrite.)

Graphing by Computer

Many computer programs are available for converting numerical data into various types of graphs to improve comprehension and interpretation. These programs vary from data representation as bar graphs, coordinate graphs, and pie graphs to 3D mathematical models.

Computer-produced graphs are especially useful for preparing visual aids for projection on a screen for a presentation. They are equally valuable as graphs for technical reports. **Figure 25.2** is an example of a 3D bar graph printed by a laser printer from data that were input in tabular form. It could have also been plotted with a pen plotter or an impact printer.

25.2 Pie Graphs

Pie graphs compare the relationship of parts to a whole. For example, **Fig. 25.3** shows a pie graph that compares industry's use of various types of computer graphics software as percentages of the total, or their market share.

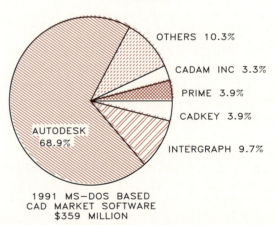

Figure 25.3 A pie graph shows the relationship of parts to a whole. It is most effective when there are only a few parts. (Courtesy of Autodesk.)

Figure 25.4 illustrates the steps involved in drawing a pie graph. The data in this example, as simple as it is, are not as easily compared in numerical form as when drawn as a pie graph. Position thin sectors of a pie graph as nearly

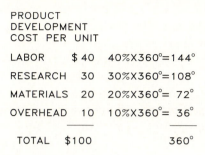

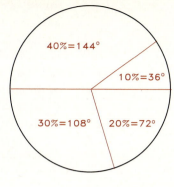

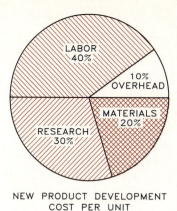

PRODUCT
DEVELOPMENT
COST PER UNIT

LABOR	$ 40	40%×360°=144°
RESEARCH	30	30%×360°=108°
MATERIALS	20	20%×360°= 72°
OVERHEAD	10	10%×360°= 36°
TOTAL	$100	360°

NEW PRODUCT DEVELOPMENT
COST PER UNIT

Figure 25.4 Pie graphs:

Step 1 Find the sum of the parts and the percentage that each is of the total. Multiply each percentage by 360° to obtain the angle of each sector of the graph.

Step 2 Draw the circle and construct each sector using the degrees of each from step 1. Place small sectors as nearly horizontal as possible.

Step 3 Label sectors with their proper names and percentages. Exact numbers also may be included in each sector.

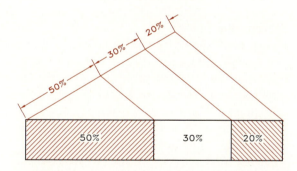

Figure 25.5 The diagonal-line method may be used to find the percentages of the parts to the whole, where the total bar represents 100%.

horizontal as possible to provide more space for labeling. When space is not available within the sectors, place labels outside the pie graph and, if necessary, use leaders (see Fig. 25.3). Showing the percentage represented by each sector is impor-

tant, and giving the actual numbers or values as part of the label is also desirable.

25.3 Bar Graphs

Bar graphs are widely used for comparing values because the general public understands them. A bar graph may be a single bar **(Fig. 25.5)** where the length of the bar representing 100% is divided into lengths proportional to the percentages of its three parts. In **Fig. 25.6** the bars show not only the overall production of timber (the total heights of the bars), but also the percentages of the total devoted to three uses of the timber.

Figure 25.7 shows how to convert data into a bar graph that can be used in a report or briefing. The axes of the graph carry labels, and its title appears inside the graph where space is available.

The bars of a bar graph should be sorted in ascending or descending order unless there is an overriding reason not to, such as a chronological sequence. An arbitrary arrangement of the bars, such as in alphabetical or numerical order, makes

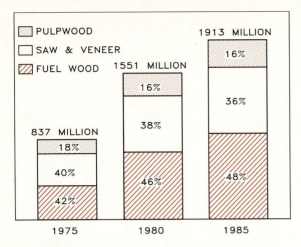

WORLDWIDE TIMBER PRODUCTION

Figure 25.6 In this bar graph, each bar represents 100% of the total amount and shows the percentages of the parts to the total.

a graph difficult to evaluate **(Fig. 25.8A)**. However, ranking the categories by bar length allows easier comparisons from smallest to largest **(Fig. 25.8B)**. If the data are sequential and involve time, such as sales per month, a better arrangement of the bars is chronologically, to show the effect of time.

Bars in a bar graph may be horizontal **(Fig. 25.9)** or vertical. Data cannot be compared accurately unless each bar is full length and originates at zero. Also, bars should not extend beyond the limits of the graph (giving the impression that the data were "too hot" to hold). Another form of bar graph shows plus and minus changes from a base value **(Fig. 25.10)**.

25.4 Linear Coordinate Graphs

Figure 25.11 shows a typical **linear coordinate graph**, with notes explaining its important features. Divided into equal divisions, the axes are referred to as **linear scales**. Data points are plotted

on the grid by using measurements, called **coordinates**, along each axis from zero. The plotted points are marked with symbols such as circles or squares that may be easily drawn with a template.

The horizontal scale of the graph is called the **abscissa or x axis**. The vertical scale is called the **ordinate or y axis**.

When the points have been plotted, a curve is drawn through them to represent the data. The line drawn to represent data points is called a **curve** regardless of whether it is a smooth straight line, curve, or broken line. The curve should not extend through the plotted points; rather, the points should be **left as open circles or other symbols**.

The curve is the most important part of the graph, so it should be drawn as the most prominent (thickest) line. If there are two curves in a graph, they should be drawn as different line types and labeled. The title of the graph is placed in a box inside the graph and units are given along the x and y axes with labels identifying the scales of the graph.

Broken-Line Graphs

Figure 25.12 shows the steps required to draw a linear coordinate graph. Because the data points represent sales, which have no predictable pattern, the data do not give a smooth progression from point to point. Therefore the points are connected with a **broken-line curve** drawn as an angular line from point to point.

Again, leave the symbols used to mark the data points open rather than extending grid lines or the data curve through them **(Fig. 25.13)**. Each circle or symbol used to plot points should be about 1/8 in. (3 mm) in diameter. **Figure 25.14** shows typical data-point symbols and lines.

Titles   The title of a graph may be located in any of the positions shown in **Fig. 25.15**. A graph's title should never be as meaningless as "graph" or "coordinate graph." Instead, it should identify concisely what the graph shows.

BAR GRAPH CONSTRUCTION

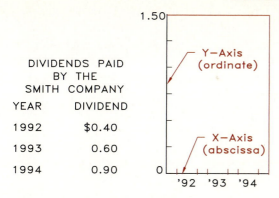

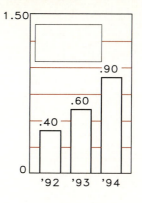

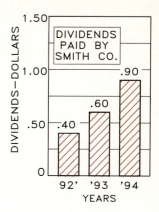

Figure 25.7 Constructing a bar graph:

Given These data are to be plotted as a bar graph.

Step 1 Scale the vertical and horizontal axes so that the data will fit on the grid. Bars should begin at zero on the ordinate.

Step 2 Draw and label the bars. The width of the bars should be greater than the space between them. Grid lines should not cross the bars.

Step 3 Strengthen lines, title the graph, label the axes, and cross-hatch the bars.

ARRANGING BARS BY LENGTH

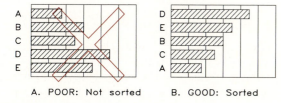

Figure 25.8
A When the bars are arbitrarily arranged, such as alphabetically, the bar graph is difficult to interpret.
B When the bars are sorted by length, the graph is much easier to interpret.

HORIZONTAL BAR GRAPH

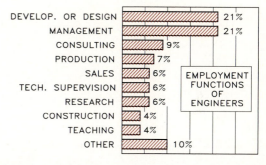

Figure 25.9 The horizontal bars of this graph (showing employment of engineers) are arranged in descending order. Note that the final category, "Other", is made up of variations that represent less than 4% each of the total.

Scale and Labeling The calibration and labeling of the axes affects the appearance and readability of a graph. **Figure 25.16A** shows a properly calibrated and labeled axis. **Figures 25.16B** and **25.16C** illustrate common mistakes: placing the grid lines too close together and labeling too many divisions along the axis. In **Fig. 25.16C**, the choice of the interval between the labeled values (9 units) makes interpolation between them diffi-

BAR GRAPH: PLUS AND MINUS BARS

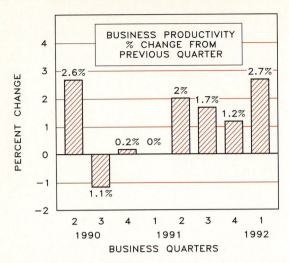

Figure 25.10 Bar graphs may be drawn with bars in both negative and positive directions.

MAJOR FEATURES OF A GRAPH

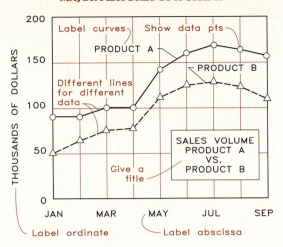

Figure 25.11 This basic linear coordinate graph illustrates the important features on a graph.

BROKEN-LINE GRAPH CONSTRUCTION

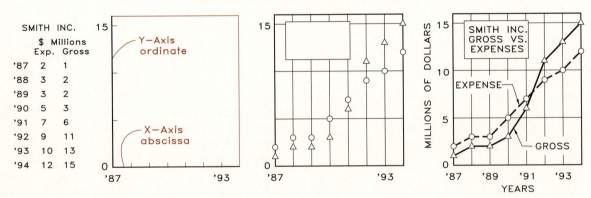

Figure 25.12 A broken-line graph:

Given A record of the Smith Company's gross income and expenses.

Step 1 Lay off the vertical (ordinate) and horizontal (abscissa) axes to provide space for the largest values.

Step 2 Draw division lines and plot data points for their respective years, using different symbols for each curve.

Step 3 Connect data points with straight lines, label the axes, title the graph, darken the lines, and label the curves.

DATA POINTS

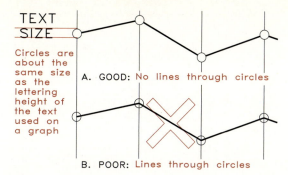

Figure 25.13 The curve of a graph drawn from point to point should not extend through the symbols used to represent data points.

SYMBOLS FOR DATA POINTS

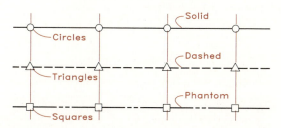

Figure 25.14 Symbols and lines such as these may be used to represent different curves on a graph. The data-point symbols should be drawn about the same size as the letter height being used, usually a little less than $1/8$ in. (3 mm) in diameter.

cult. For example, locating the value 22 by eye is more difficult on this scale than on the one shown in Fig. 25.16A.

Smooth-Line Graphs

The strength of concrete related to its curing time is plotted in **Fig. 25.17**. The strength of concrete changes gradually and continuously in relation to curing time. Therefore the data points are connected with a **smooth-line curve** rather than a

PLACEMENT OF TITLES ON GRAPHS

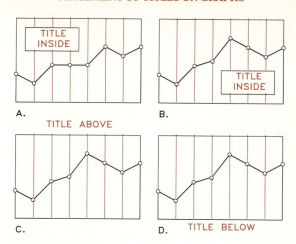

Figure 25.15

A and **B** The title of a graph may be placed inside a box within the graph. Box perimeter lines should not coincide with grid lines.

C Titles may be placed over the graph.

D Titles may be placed below the graph.

CALIBRATION OF GRAPH SCALES

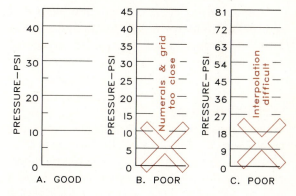

Figure 25.16

A The scale is properly labeled and calibrated. It has about the right number of grid lines and divisions, and the numbers are well spaced and easy to interpolate.

B The numbers are too close together, and there are too many grid lines.

C The increments selected make interpolation difficult.

SMOOTH-LINE GRAPH

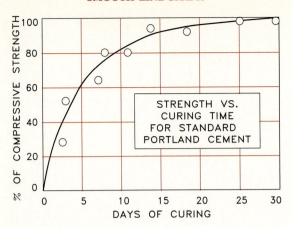

Figure 25.17 When the data being graphed involve gradual, continuous changes in relationships, the curve is drawn as a smooth line.

STRAIGHT-LINE GRAPH

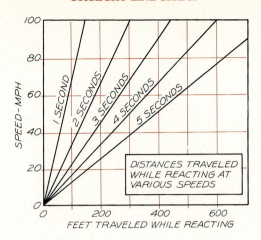

Figure 25.18 This graph may be used to determine a third value from the other two variables. For example, select a speed of 70 mph and a time of 5 seconds to find a distance traveled of 550 ft.

TWO-SCALE GRAPH

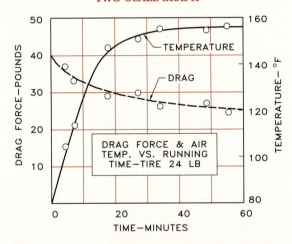

Figure 25.19 A two-scale graph has different scales along each *y* axis, and labels identify which scale applies to which curve.

broken-line curve. These relationships are represented by the **best-fit curve**, a smooth curve that is an average representation of the points.

A smooth-line curve on a graph implies that interpolations between data points can be made to estimate other values. Data points connected by a broken-line curve imply that interpolations between the plotted points cannot be made.

Straight-Line Graphs

Some graphs have neither broken-line curves nor smooth-line curves, but **straight-line curves (Fig. 25.18)**. On this graph, a third value can be determined from the two given values. For example, if you are driving 70 miles per hour and you take 5 seconds to react and apply your brakes, you will have traveled 550 feet in that time.

Two-Scale Coordinate Graphs

Graphs may contain different scales in combination, as shown in **Fig. 25.19**, where the vertical scale at the left is in units of pounds and the one at the right is in degrees of temperature. Both curves are drawn with respect to their *y* axes and each curve is labeled. Two-scale graphs of this

OPTIMIZATION GRAPH

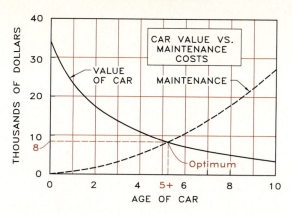

Figure 25.20 This graph shows the optimum time to sell a car based on the intersection of curves representing the depreciating value of the car and its increasing maintenance costs.

OPTIMIZATION GRAPH CONSTRUCTION

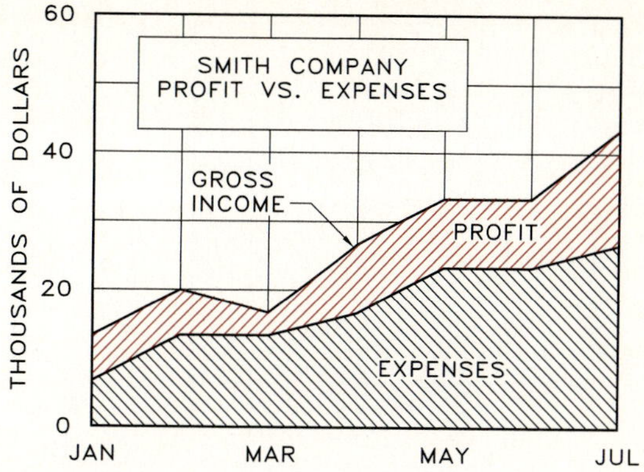

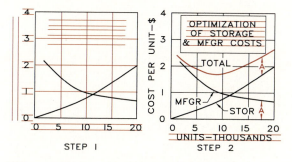

Figure 25.21 Constructing an optimization graph:
Step 1 Lay out the graph and plot the curves from the data given.

Step 2 Graphically add the two curves to find a third curve. For example, transfer distance A to locate a point on the third curve. The lowest point of the "total" curve is the optimum point, or 8000 units.

type may be confusing unless they are clearly labeled. Two-scale graphs are effective for comparing related variables, as shown here.

COMPOSITE GRAPH

Figure 25.22 This composite graph is a combination of a coordinate graph and an area graph. The upper area represents the difference between the two plotted curves.

Optimization Graphs

Figure 25.20 depicts the optimization of an automobile's depreciation in terms of maintenance cost increases. These two sets of data cross at an *x*-axis value of slightly more than five years, or the optimum point. At that time the cost of maintenance is equal to the value of the car, indicating that it might be a desirable time to buy a new car.

Figure 25.21 illustrates the steps involved in drawing an optimization graph. Here, the manufacturing cost per unit reduces as more units are made, causing warehousing costs to increase. Adding the two curves to get a third (total) curve indicates that the optimum number to manufacture at a time is about 8000 units (the low point on the total curve). When more or fewer units are manufactured, the total cost per unit is greater.

Composite Graphs

The graph shown in **Fig. 25.22** is a composite (or combination) of an area graph and a coordinate graph. The upper curve is a plot of the company's gross income. The lower curve is a plot of the company's expenses. The difference between the two is the company's profit. Cross-hatching the areas

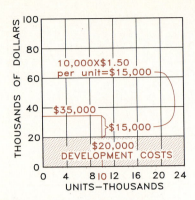

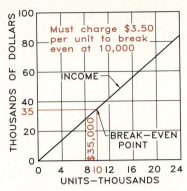

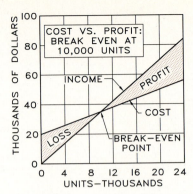

Figure 25.23 A break-even graph:
Step 1 Draw the graph and plot the development cost ($20,000 in this case). If each unit costs $1.50 to manufacture, the total investment would be $35,000 for 10,000 units, the break-even point.

Step 2 To break even at 10,000, the manufacturer must sell each unit for $3.50. Draw a line from zero through the break-even point of $35,000.

Step 3 The manufacturer incurs a loss of $20,000 at zero units, but it becomes progressively less until the break-even point is reached. Profit is the difference between cost and income to the right of the break-even point.

emphasizes the relative sizes of expenses and profits.

Break-Even Graphs

Break-even graphs help in evaluating marketing and manufacturing costs to determine the selling price of a product. As **Fig. 25.23** shows, if the desired break-even point for a product is 10,000 units, it must sell for $3.50 each to cover the costs of manufacturing and development.

25.5 Semilogarithmic Coordinate Graphs

Semilogarithmic graphs are called **ratio graphs** because they **graphically represent ratios**. One scale, usually the vertical scale, is logarithmic, and the other is linear (divided into equal divisions).

Figure 25.24 shows the same data plotted on a linear grid and on a semilogarithmic grid. The semilogarithmic graph reveals that the percentage change from 0 to 5 is greater for curve B than for curve A because here curve B is steeper. The plot

PERCENT INCREASE

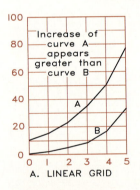

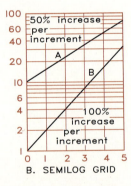

Figure 25.24 When plotted on a linear grid, curve A appears to be increasing at a greater rate than curve B. However, plotting the data on a semilogarithmic grid reveals the true rate of change.

on the linear grid appears to show the opposite result.

Figure 25.25 shows the relationship between the linear scale and the logarithmic scale. Equal

LINEAR VS. LOGARITHMIC SCALES

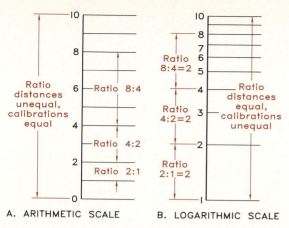

Figure 25.25 The divisions on an arithmetic scale are equal and represent unequal ratios between points. The divisions on logarithmic scales are unequal and represent equal ratios.

SEMILOGARITHMIC GRAPH

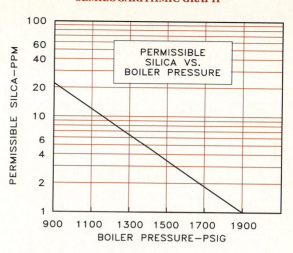

Figure 25.27 This semilogarithmic graph relates permissible silica (parts per million) to boiler pressure

LAYING OUT LOG SCALES

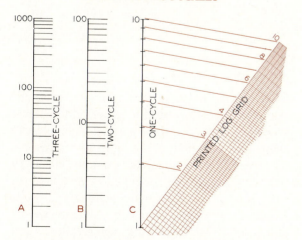

Figure 25.26 Logarithmic paper (either bought or drawn) may have several cycles: (A) three-cycle scales; (B) two-cycle scales, and (C) one-cycle scales. Calibrations may be projected to a scale of any length from a printed scale, as shown in (C).

divisions along the linear scale have unequal ratios, but equal divisions along the log scale have equal ratios.

Log scales may have one or many cycles. Each cycle increases by a factor of 10. For example, the scale shown in **Fig. 25.26A** is a three-cycle scale, and the one shown in **Fig. 25.26B** is a two-cycle scale. When scales must be drawn to a certain length, commercially printed log scales may be used to transfer graphically the calibrations to the scale being used (**Fig. 25.26C**).

Figure 25.27 illustrates an application of a semilogarithmic graph for presenting industrial data. People who do not realize that semilog graphs are different from linear coordinate graphs may misunderstand them. Also, zero values cannot be shown on log scales.

Percentage Graphs

The percentage that one number is of another, or the percentage increase of one number to a greater number, can be determined on a semilogarithmic graph (Fig. 25.28). Data plotted in

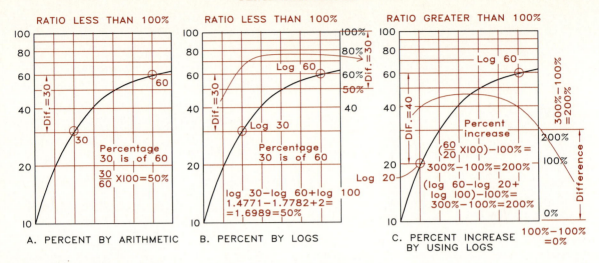

Figure 25.28 Percentage graphs:

A To find the percentage that one data point is of another point (the percentage that 30 is of 60, for example) you may calculate it mathematically: (30/60)(100) = 50%.

B You may also find the percentage that 30 is of 60 mathematically by using the logarithms of the numbers. Or you may find it graphically by transferring the distance between 30 and 60 to the scale at the right, which shows that 30 is 50%.

C To find a percentage increase greater than 100%, divide the smaller number into the larger number. Find the difference between the logs of 60 and 20 with dividers and measure upward from 100% to find the percentage increase of 200%.

Fig. 25.28A are used to find the percentage that 30 is of 60 (two points on the curve) by arithmetic. The vertical distance between them is the difference between their logarithms, so the percentage can be found graphically in **Fig 25.28B**. The distance from 30 to 60 is transferred to the log scale at the right of the graph and subtracted from the log of 100 to find the value of 50% as a direct reading of percentage.

In **Fig. 25.28C**, the percentage increase between two points is transferred from the grid to the lower end of the log scale and measured upward because the increase is greater than zero. These methods may be used to find percentage increases or decreases for any set of points on the grid.

25.6 Polar Graphs

Polar graphs comprise a series of concentric circles with the origin at the center. Lines drawn from the center toward the perimeter of the graph allow data to be plotted through 360° by measuring values from the origin. For example, **Fig. 25.29** shows the maximum illumination of a lamp of 5500 lumens at 35° from the vertical and lesser amounts elsewhere. Printed graph paper may be purchased for use in drawing polar graphs.

25.7 Schematics

The organization of a group of people can be represented in an organizational graph (usually

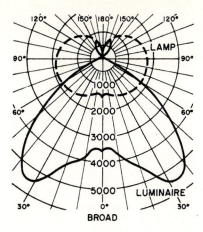

Figure 25.29 A polar graph is used to show the illumination characteristics of luminaires.

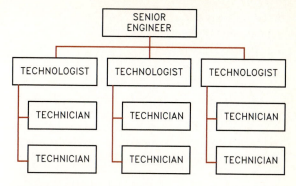

Figure 25.30 This block diagram shows the organization of a design team.

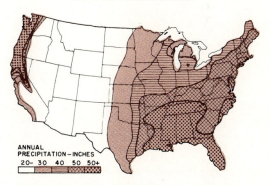

Figure 25.31 This map chart shows annual precipitation for various parts of the United States. (Courtesy of the Structural Clay Products Institute.)

called an organization chart), as shown in **Fig. 25.30**. The positions represented by the blocks in the lower part of the graph are responsible to those represented by the blocks above them. Lines of authority connecting the blocks give the routes for communication from one position to another, both upward and downward.

Geographical charts are used to combine maps and other relationships, such as weather (**Fig. 25.31**). Here, different hatching symbols represent the annual rainfall in various parts of the nation.

Problems

Draw your solutions to these problems on size A sheets in pencil or ink, as specified. Utilize the techniques presented and the examples given in this chapter.

Pie Graphs

1. Draw a pie graph that shows the comparative sources of retirees' income: investments, 34%; employment, 24%; social security, 21%; pensions, 19%; other, 2%.

2. Draw a pie graph that shows the number of members of the technological team: engineers, 985,000; technicians, 932,000; scientists, 410,000.

3. Construct a pie graph of the employment status of graduates of two-year technician programs a year after graduation: employed, 63%; continuing full-time study, 23%; considering job offers, 6%; military, 6%; other, 2%.

Table 25.1

Angle with vertical	0°	10°	20°	30°	40°	50°	60°	70°	80°	90°
Candlepower (thous.) 2–400W	37	34	25	12	5.5	2.5	2	0.5	0.5	0.5
Candlepower (thous.) 1–1000W	22	21	19	16	12.3	7	3	2	0.5	0.5

4. Construct a pie graph that shows the types of degrees held by engineers in aeronautical engineering: bachelor's, 65%; master's, 29%; Ph.D., 6%.

Bar Graphs

5. Draw a bar graph that shows expected job growth in Texas in 1995: Austin, 1.3%; San Antonio, 0.8%; Houston, 1.6%; Fort Worth, 0%; Dallas, 0.4%; all of Texas, 0.8%.

6. Draw a single-bar bar graph that represents 100% of a die casting alloy. The proportional parts of the alloy are: tin, 16%; lead, 24%; zinc, 38.8%; aluminum, 16.4%; copper, 4.8%.

7. Draw a bar graph that compares the number of skilled workers employed in various occupations. Use the following data and arrange the graph for ease of comparing occupations: carpenters, 82,000; all-round machinists, 310,000; plumbers, 350,000; bricklayers, 200,000; appliance servicers, 185,000; automotive mechanics, 760,000; electricians, 380,000; painters, 400,000.

8. Draw a bar graph that shows the characteristics of a typical U.S. family's spending: housing, 29.6%; food, 15.1%; transportation, 16.7%; clothing, 5.9%; retirement, 8.6%; entertainment, 4.9%; insurance, 5.2%; health care, 3.0%; charity, 3.1%; other, 7.9%.

9. Draw a bar graph that compares the corrosion resistance of the materials listed in the following table.

	Loss in Weight (%)	
	In Atmosphere	*In Seawater*
Common steel	100	100
10% nickel steel	70	80
25% nickel steel	20	55

10. Draw a bar graph using the data from Problem 1.

11. Draw a bar graph using the data from Problem 2.

12. Draw a bar graph using the data from Problem 3.

13. Construct a bar graph comparing sales and earnings of Apple Computer from 1980 through 1989. Data are by year for sales and earnings (profit) in billions of dollars: 1980, 0 and 0; 1981, 0.33 and 0.05; 1982, 0.60 and 0.07; 1983, 1.00 and 0.09; 1984, 1.51 and 0.08; 1985, 1.90 and 0.07; 1986, 1.85 and 0.12; 1987, 2.70 and 0.25; 1988, 4.15 and 0.40; 1989, 5.50 and 0.45.

Linear Coordinate Graphs

14. Draw a linear coordinate graph to show the estimated population growth in the United States from 1992 through 2050 in millions of people: 1992, 255; 2000, 270; 2010, 295; 2020, 325; 2030, 348; 2040, 360; 2050, 383.

15. Plot the data shown in Table 25.1 as a linear coordinate graph to assist in deciding which lamps should be selected to provide economical lighting for an industrial plant. The table gives the candlepower directly under the lamps (0°) and at various angles from the vertical for lamps mounted at a height of 25 ft.

16. Construct a linear coordinate graph that shows the relationship of energy costs (mills per kilowatt-hour) on the y axis to the percent capacity of a nuclear power plant and a gas- or oil-fired power plant on the x axis. Gas- or oil-fired plant data: 17 mills, 10%; 12 mills, 20%; 8 mills, 40%; 7 mills, 60%; 6 mills, 80%; 5.8 mills, 100%. Nuclear plant data: 24 mills, 10%; 14 mills, 20%; 7 mills, 40%; 5 mills, 60%; 4.2 mills, 80%; 3.7 mills, 100%.

17. Plot the data from Problem 13 as a linear coordinate graph.

18. Construct a linear coordinate graph to show the relationship between the transverse resilience in inch-pounds (ip) on the y axis and the single-blow impact in foot-pounds (fp) on the x axis of gray iron. Data: 21 fp, 375 ip; 22 fp, 350 ip; 23 fp, 380 ip; 30 fp, 400 ip; 32 fp, 420 ip; 33 fp, 410 ip; 38 fp, 510 ip; 45 fp, 615 ip; 50 fp, 585 ip; 60 fp, 785 ip; 70 fp, 900 ip; 75 fp, 920 ip.

19. Draw a linear coordinate graph to illustrate the trends in the export of U.S. services and products from 1980 through 1993: 1980, +8.5%; 1981, +2.5%; 1982, −7.5%; 1983, −4.5%; 1984, +7%; 1985, −2%; 1986, +7%; 1987, +12.5%; 1988, +17.5%; 1989, +10%; 1990, +6%; 1991, +3%; 1992, +5%; 1993, +7%.

20. Draw a linear coordinate graph that shows the voltage characteristics for a generator as given in the following table of values: abscissa, armature current in amperes, (I_a); ordinate, terminal voltage in volts, (E_t).

I_a	E_t	I_a	E_t	I_a	E_t
0	288	31.1	181.8	41.5	68
5.4	275	35.4	156	40.5	42.5
11.8	257	39.7	108	39.5	26.5
15.6	247	40.5	97	37.8	16
22.2	224.5	40.7	90	13.0	0
26.2	217	41.4	77.5		

21. Draw a linear coordinate graph for the centrifugal pump test data in the following table. The units along the x axis are to be gallons per minute. Use four curves to represent the variables given.

Gallons per Minute	Discharge Pressure	Water HP	Electric HP	Efficiency (%)
0	19.0	0.00	1.36	0.0
75	17.5	0.72	2.25	32.0
115	15.0	1.00	2.54	39.4
154	10.0	1.00	2.74	36.5
185	5.0	0.74	2.80	26.5
200	3.0	0.63	2.83	22.2

Table 25.2

F°	Ultimate Strength	Elastic Limit
400	257,500	208,000
500	247,000	224,500
600	232,500	214,000
700	207,500	193,500
800	180,500	169,000
900	159,500	146,500
1000	142,500	128,500
1100	126,500	114,000
1200	114,500	96,500
1300	108,000	85,500

22. Draw a linear coordinate graph that compares two of the values shown in Table 25.2—ultimate strength and elastic limit—with degrees of temperature (x axis).

Break-Even Graphs

23. Construct a break-even graph that shows the earnings for a new product that has a development cost of $12,000. The break-even point is at 8000 units, and each costs $0.50 to manufacture. What would be the profit at volumes of 20,000 and 25,000?

24. Repeat Problem 23 except that the development costs are $80,000, the manufacturing cost of the first 10,000 units is $2.30 each, and the desired break-even point is 10,000 units. What would be the profit at volumes of 20,000 and 30,000?

Logarithmic Graphs

25. Use the data given in Table 25.3 to construct a logarithmic graph. Plot the vibration amplitude (A) as the ordinate and the vibration frequency (F) as the abscissa. The data for curve 1 represent the maximum limits of machinery in good condition with no danger from

Table 25.3

F	100	200	500	1000	2000	5000	10,000
A(1)	0.0028	0.002	0.0015	0.001	0.0006	0.0003	0.00013
A(2)	0.06	0.05	0.04	0.03	0.018	0.005	0.001

vibration. The data for curve 2 are the lower limits of machinery that is being vibrated excessively to the danger point. The vertical scale should be three cycles, and the horizontal scale should be two cycles.

26. Plot the following data on a two-cycle log graph to show the current in amperes (y axis) versus the voltage in volts (x axis) of precision temperature-sensing resistors. Data: 1 volt, 1.9 amps; 2 volts, 4 amps; 4 volts, 8 amps; 8 volts, 17 amps; 10 volts, 20 amps; 20 volts, 30 amps; 40 volts, 36 amps; 80 volts, 31 amps; 100 volts, 30 amps.

27. Plot the data from Problem 14 as a logarithmic graph.

28. Plot the data from Problem 20 as a logarithmic graph.

Semilogarithmic Graphs

29. Construct a semilogarithmic graph with the y axis a two-cycle log scale from 1 to 100 and the x axis a linear scale from 1 to 7. The objective of the graph is to show the survivability of a shelter at varying distances from the atmospheric detonation of a one-megaton thermonuclear bomb. Plot overpressure in psi along the y axis, and distance from ground zero in miles along the x axis. The data points represent an 80% chance of survival of the shelter. Data: 1 mile, 55 psi; 2 miles, 11 psi; 3 miles, 4.5 psi; 4 miles, 2.5 psi; 5 miles, 2.0 psi; 6 miles, 1.3 psi.

30. The growth of two divisions of a company, Division A and Division B, is represented by the following data. Plot the data on a rectilinear graph and on a semilog graph with a one-cycle log scale on the y axis for sales in thousands of dollars and a linear scale on the x axis for years. Data: first year, A = $11,700 and B = $44,000; second year, A = $19,500 and B = $50,000; third year, A = $25,000 and B = $55,000; fourth year, A = $32,000 and B = $64,000; fifth year, A = $42,000 and B = $66,000; sixth year, A = $48,000 and B = $75,000. Which division has the better growth rate?

31. Draw a semilog chart showing probable engineering progress based on the following indices: 40,000 B.C., 21; 30,000 B.C., 21.5; 20,000 B.C., 22; 16,000 B.C., 23; 10,000 B.C., 27; 6000 B.C., 34; 4000 B.C., 39; 2000 B.C., 49; 500 B.C., = 60; A.D. 1900, 100. Use a horizontal scale of 1 in. = 10,000 years, a height of about 5 in., and two-cycle printed paper, if available.

32. Plot the data from Problem 20 as a semilogarithmic graph.

33. Plot the data from Problem 22 as a semilogarithmic graph.

Percentage Graphs

34. Plot the data below as a semilog graph to determine percentages and ratios for the data. What is the percentage increase in the demand for water from 1890 to 1920? What percentage of demand is the supply for 1900, 1930, and 1970?

	Supply*	Demand*		Supply*	Demand*
1890	80	35	1940	240	125
1900	90	35	1950	270	200
1910	110	60	1960	315	320
1920	135	80	1970	380	410
1930	155	110	1980	450	550

*Billions of gallons per day

35. Using the graph plotted in Problem 30, determine the percentage of increase of Division A and Division B growth from year 1 to year 4. What percentage of sales of Division A are the sales of Division B at the end of year 2? At the end of year 6?

36. Plot the values for water horsepower and electric horsepower from Problem 21 on semilog paper against gallons per minute along the x axis. What percentage of electric horsepower is water horsepower when 75 gallons per minute are being pumped? What percentage increase in electric horsepower corresponds to an increase in pumping volume from 0 to 185 gallons per minute?

Polar Graphs

37. Construct a polar graph from the data in Problem 15.

38. Construct a polar graph of the following illumination, in lumens at various angles, emitted from a luminaire. The 0° position is vertically under the overhead lamp. Data: 0°, 12,000; 10°, 15,000; 20°, 10,000; 30°, 8000; 40°, 4200; 50°, 2500; 60°, 1000; 70°, 0. The illumination is symmetrical about the vertical.

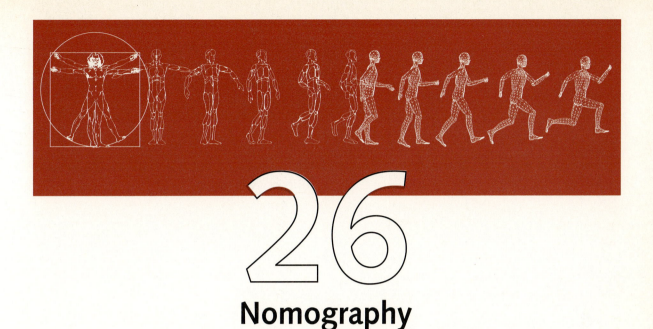

26

Nomography

26.1 Introduction

An additional aid in analyzing data is a graphical computer called a **nomogram**, **nomograph**, or "number chart." Basically, it is any graphical arrangement of calibrated scales and lines that may be used for calculations, usually those of a repetitive nature.

The term *nomogram* frequently denotes a specific type of scale arrangement called an **alignment chart** (which we call an *alignment graph*). **Figure 26.1** shows two examples of alignment graphs. Other types have curved scales or different scale arrangements for use with more complex problems.

An alignment graph usually is constructed to solve for one or more unknowns in a formula or empirical relationship between two or more quantities. For example, such a graph can be used to convert degrees Celsius to degrees Fahrenheit or to find the size of a structural member to sustain a certain load. To read an alignment graph, **place a straightedge or draw a line, called an isopleth**, across the scales of the graph and read corre-

EXAMPLES OF NOMOGRAPHS

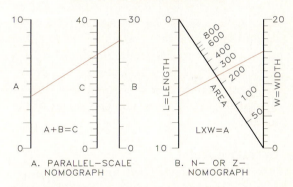

Figure 26.1 These two types of alignment graphs are typical nomographs.

sponding values from the scale on this line. **Figure 26.2** shows readings for the formula $W = U + V$.

26.2 Alignment Graph Scales

To construct any alignment graph, you must first determine the graduations of the scales that give

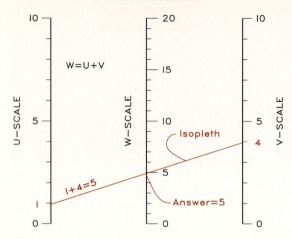

Figure 26.2 This graph illustrates the use of an isopleth to solve graphically for unknowns in an equation, $W = U + V$.

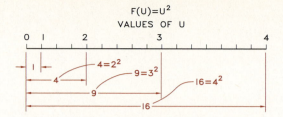

Figure 26.3 This functional scale contains units of measurement proportional to $F(U) = U2$.

the desired relationships. Alignment graph scales, called **functional scales**, are graduated according to values of some function of a variable. **Figure 26.3** illustrates a functional scale for $F(U) = U^2$. Substituting a value of $U = 2$ into the equation gives the position of U on the functional scale 4 units from zero, or $2^2 = 4$. Repeating this procedure for as many values of U as required yields a scale for finding all corresponding values of the function.

The Scale Modulus

Because the graduations on a functional scale are spaced in proportion to values of the function, a proportionality, or **scaling factor**, is needed. This constant of proportionality is called the **scale modulus**, m:

$$m = \frac{L}{F(U2) - F(U1)} \qquad (1)$$

where

> m = scale modulus, in inches per functional unit,
>
> L = desired length of the scale, in inches,

$F(U2)$ = functional value at the end of the scale, and

$F(U1)$ = functional value at the start of the scale.

For example, suppose that you are to construct a functional scale for $F(U) = \sin U$ with $0° \le U \le 45°$ and a scale 6 in. in length. Thus $L = 6$ in., $F(U2) = \sin 45° = 0.707$, $F(U1) = \sin 0° = 0$. Substituting these values into Eq. (1) gives

$$m = \frac{6}{0.707 - 0} = 8.49 \text{ in.}$$

per (sine) unit.

The Scale Equation

A **scale equation** makes possible graduation and calibration of functional scales. The general form of this equation is a variation of Eq. (1):

$$X = m[F(U) - F(U1)], \qquad (2)$$

where

> X = distance from the measuring point of the scale to any graduation point,
>
> m = scale modulus,
>
> $F(U)$ = functional value at the graduation point,
>
> $F(U1)$ = functional value at the measuring point of the scale.

CONSTRUCTION OF A FUNCTIONAL SCALE

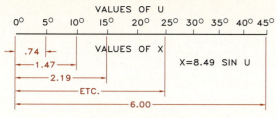

TABLE OF VALUES

U	0°	5°	10°	15°	20°	25°	30°	35°	40°	45°
X	0	1.47	2.90	4.24	5.45					
	.74	2.19	3.58	4.86	6.00					

Figure 26.4 This drawing depicts a functional scale calibrated with values from the table, which were derived from the scale equation, X = 8.49 sin U.

FUNCTIONAL SCALE CALIBRATION

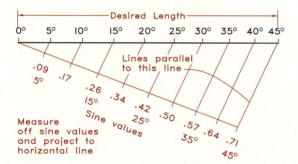

Figure 26.5 This functional scale shows the sine of the angles from 0° to 45° drawn graphically by the proportional line method. Draw the scale to a desired length and lay off the sine values of angles at 5° intervals along a construction line passing through the 0° end of the scale

For example, let's construct a functional scale for the equation, $F(U) = \sin U$ $(0° \leq U \leq 45°)$. We have already determined that $m = 8.49$, $F(U) = \sin U$, and $F(U1) = \sin 0° = 0$. Thus, by substitution, Eq. (2) becomes

$$X = 8.49(\sin U - 0) = 8.49 \sin U.$$

Using this equation, we can substitute values of U and construct a table of positions. In this case, we calibrated the scale at 5° intervals, as shown in **Fig. 26.4**. The values of X give the positions, in inches, for the corresponding graduations measured from the start of the scale ($U = 0°$). The initial measuring point does not have to be at one end of the scale, but an end is usually the most convenient point, especially if the functional value is zero at that point.

Figure 26.5 shows graphically how to locate functional values along a scale with the proportional line method. Measure the sine functions along a line at 5° intervals, with the end of the line passing through the 0° end of the scale. Transfer these functions from the inclined line with parallel lines back to the scale and label the functions.

26.3 Concurrent Scales

Concurrent scales aid in the rapid conversion of terms in one system of measurement into terms of a second system of measurement. Formulas of the type $F1 = F2$, which relate two variables, may be adapted to the concurrent scale format. A typical example is the Fahrenheit–Celsius temperature relation:

$$°F = \frac{9}{5}°C + 32.$$

Another is the area of a circle:

$$A = \pi r^2.$$

Construction of a concurrent scale chart involves determining a functional scale for each side of the mathematical formula so that the position and lengths of each scale coincide. For example, to construct a conversion chart 5 inches long that gives the areas of circles whose radii range from 1 to 10, we first write $F1(A) = A$, $F2(r) = \pi r^2$, $r1 = 1$, and $r2 = 10$. The scale modulus for r is

$$m_r = \frac{L}{F2\,(r2) - F2\,(r1)}$$

$$= \frac{5}{\pi(10)^2 - \pi(1)^2} = 0.0161.$$

CALIBRATION OF RADIUS SCALE

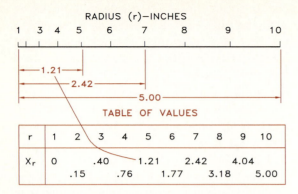

Figure 26.6 Calibrate one scale of a concurrent scale chart by using values from the table that have been calculated.

COMPLETED CONCURRENT SCALE GRAPH

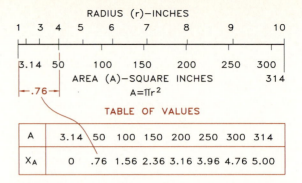

Figure 26.7 This completed concurrent scale chart is for the formula $A = \pi r^2$. Values for the A scale are from table.

Thus the scale equation for *r* becomes

$$X_r = m_r[F2(r) - F2(r1)]$$

$$= 0.0161[\pi r^2 - \pi(1)^2]$$

$$= 0.0161\pi(r^2 - 1)$$

$$= 0.0505(r^2 - 1).$$

Figure 26.6 shows a table of values for X_r and *r*. The *r*-scale values come from this table. From the original formula, $A = \pi r^2$, the limits of *A* are found to be $A1 = \pi = 3.14$ and $A2 = 100\pi = 314$. The scale modulus for concurrent scales is always the same for equal-length scales; therefore $m_A = m_r = 0.0161$, and the scale equation for *A* becomes

$$X_A = m_A[F1(A) - F1(A1)]$$

$$= 0.0161(A - 3.14).$$

We then compute the corresponding table of values for selected values of *A*, as shown in **Fig. 26.7**. We superimposed the *A* scale on the *r* scale and placed its calibrations on the other side of the line to facilitate reading.

To expand or contract one of the scales, simply use the alternative arrangement shown in **Fig. 26.8**. Draw the two scales parallel at any conve-

CONCURRENT GRAPH—UNEQUAL SCALES

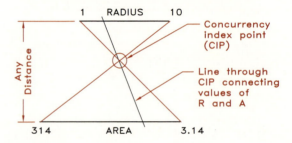

Figure 26.8 This construction is used to draw a concurrent graph with unequal scales.

nient distance and calibrate them in opposite directions. You must calculate a different scale modulus and corresponding scale equation for each scale if they are not the same length.

To construct concurrent scales graphically, use the proportional line method, as shown in **Fig. 26.9**. There are 101.6 mm in 4 in. Project millimeter units to the upper side of the inch scale with a series of parallel projectors.

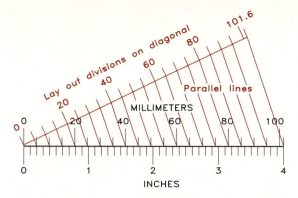

Figure 26.9 The proportional line method may be used to construct an alignment graph that converts inches to millimeters. The units at each end of the scales must be known. For example, there are 101.6 mm in 4 in.

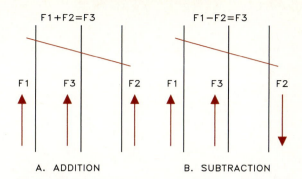

Figure 26.10 These two common forms of parallel scale alignment nomographs show the directions in which the scales increase for addition and subtraction.

26.4 Alignment Graphs with Three Variables

For a formula containing three functions (of one variable each), draw a nomograph by selecting the lengths and positions of two scales according to the range of variables and size of the chart desired. Calibrate these scales by using the scale equations presented in Section 26.4. Although mathematical relationships may be used to locate the third scale, graphical constructions are simpler and usually less subject to error. Examples of the various forms of these nomographs are presented in the following sections.

26.5 Parallel Scale Graphs

Linear Scales

Any formula of the type $F1 + F2 = F3$ may be represented as a parallel scale alignment graph (**Fig. 26.10**). For addition, the three scales increase (functionally) in the same direction, and the function of the middle scale represents the sum of the other two. Reversing the direction of any scale changes the sign of its function in the formula, as for $F1 - F2 = F3$.

We can use the formula $Z = X + Y$ to illustrate this type of alignment graph (**Fig. 26.11**). First, draw and calibrate the outer scales for X and Y. Then use two sets of data that yield a Z of 8 to locate the parallel Z scale. Divide the Z scale into 16 equal units. Add various values of X and Y to the finished nomograph to find their sums along the Z scale.

Figure 26.12 illustrates how the outer scales of a parallel-scale nomograph are calibrated for solving the equation $U + 2V = 3W$. The scales are placed any distance apart and are divided into linear divisions from 0 to 14 and 0 to 8 for U and V, respectively. These scales are used to complete the nomograph explained in **Fig. 26.13**.

Obtain the limits of calibration for the middle scale by connecting the endpoints of the outer scales and substituting these values into the formula. Here, W is 0 and 10 at the extreme ends. Select two pairs of corresponding values of U and

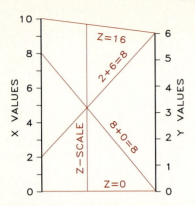 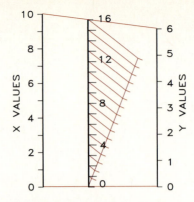 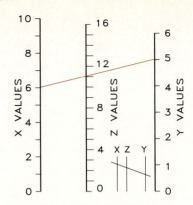

Figure 26.11 Constructing a parallel scale nomograph (linear scales):

Step 1 Draw two parallel scales at any length and calibrate them. Locate the parallel Z scale by selecting two sets of values that give the same value of Z (8 in this case). The ends of the Z scale have values of 0 and 16, or the sum of the end values of X and Y.

Step 2 Draw the Z scale through the point located in step 1 parallel to the other scales. Calibrate the scale from 0 to 16 by using the proportional line method.

Step 3 Calibrate and label the Z scale. Draw a key to show how to use the nomograph. If the Y scale were calibrated with 0 at the upper end instead of at the bottom, a different Z scale could be computed and the nomograph could be used for Z = X − Y.

CALIBRATION OF SCALES

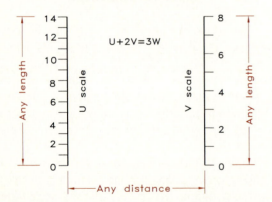

Figure 26.12 This calibration is of the outer scales for the formula U + 2V = 3W, where $0 \leq U \leq 14$ and $0 \leq V \leq 8$.

V that give the same value of W. For example, U = 0 and V = 7.5 give W = 5. Also W = 5 when U = 14 and V = 0.5.

Because the W scale is linear (3W is a linear function), you may subdivide it into uniform

intervals by equal parts. For a nonlinear scale, determine the scale modulus (and the scale equation) by substituting length and its two end values into Eq. (1). You may use the scales to obtain infinitely many problem solutions.

Logarithmic Scales

You may solve problems involving formulas of the type (F1)(F2) = F3 in a manner similar to that described in Fig. 26.11 by using logarithmic scales instead of linear scales (as shown in Fig. 26.15).

The first step in drawing a nomograph with logarithmic scales is to transfer the logarithmic functions to the scales. **Figure 26.14** shows the graphical method, which involves projecting units from a printed logarithmic scale to the nomographic scale.

Figure 26.15 illustrates the conversion of the formula Z = XY into a nomograph. The desired limits for the X and Y scales are 1 and 10. Sets of values of X and Y that yield the same value of Z, 10 in this case, are used to locate the Z axis. The limits of the Z axis are 1 and 100.

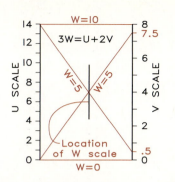

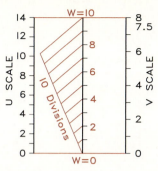

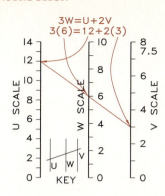

Figure 26.13 Constructing parallel scale nomograph (linear scales):

Step 1 Substitute the end values of the U and V scales into the formula to find the end values of the W scale: $W = 10$ and $W = 0$. Select two sets of U and V that will give the same value of W. For example, when $U = 0$ and $V = 7.5$, $W = 5$, and when $U = 14$ and $V = 0.5$, $W = 5$. Connect these sets of values to locate the W scale.

Step 2 Draw the W scale parallel to the outer scales to the limit lines of W = 10 and W = 0. This scale is 10 linear divisions long, so divide it graphically into 10 units. The W scale is a linear scale; construct it as shown in Fig. 26.11.

Step 3 Use the nomograph as illustrated by selecting any two known variables and connecting them with an isopleth to determine the third unknown. The key shows how to use the nomograph. The values of $U = 12$ and $V = 3$ verify the graph's accuracy.

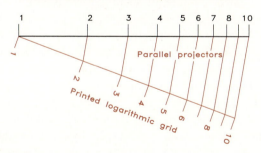

Figure 26.14 Here, a scale is calibrated graphically by projection from a printed logarithmic scale.

The Z axis is drawn and calibrated as a two-cycle log scale. A key explains how to use an isopleth to add the logarithms of X and Y to give the log of Z. Recall that the addition of logarithms

performs the operation of multiplication. Had the Y axis been calibrated in the opposite direction, with 1 at the upper end and 10 at the lower end, a new Z axis could have been calibrated. The nomograph then could be used for the formula $Z = Y/X$, involving the subtraction of logarithms.

26.6 N or Z Nomographs

Whenever $F2$ and $F3$ are linear functions, we can avoid using logarithmic scales for formulas of the type

$$F1 = \frac{F2}{F3}.$$

To do so, we use an **N graph (Fig. 26.16)**. The outer scales, or "legs," of the N are functional scales and therefore are linear if $F2$ and $F3$ are linear. If a parallel-scale graph were used for the same formula, all its scales would be logarithmic.

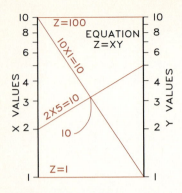 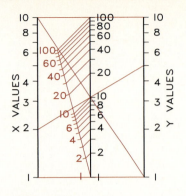 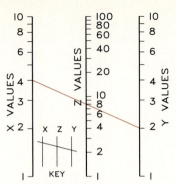

Figure 26.15 Parallel scale nomograph (logarithmic scales):

Step 1 For the equation $Z = XY$, draw parallel log scales. Construct sets of X and Y points that yield the same value of Z (10 in this case). Their intersection locates the Z scale with end values of 1 and 100.

Step 2 Graphically calibrate the Z axis as a two-cycle logarithmic scale from 1 to 100. This scale is parallel to the X and Y scales.

Step 3 Draw a key. An isopleth confirms that $4 \times 2 = 8$. By reversing the Y value scale from 1 downward to 10 and computing a different Z scale, the nomograph could be redrawn for the equation $Z = Y/X$.

N NOMOGRAPH FOR DIVISION

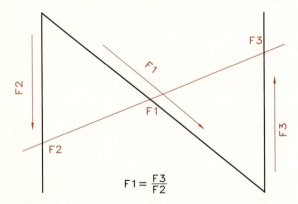

Figure 26.16 This N graph solves an equation of the form $F1 = F2/F3$.

Some main features of the N graph are:

1. The outer scales are parallel functional scales of $F2$ and $F3$.

2. The outer scales increase (functionally) in opposite directions.

3. The diagonal scale connects the (functional) zeros of the outer scales.

4. In general, the diagonal scale is not a functional scale for the function $F1$ and is nonlinear.

Construction of an N nomograph is simplified because locating the middle (diagonal) scale is usually less of a problem than it is for a parallel scale graph. Calibration of the diagonal scale is most easily accomplished by graphical methods.

Figure 26.17 shows how to construct a basic N graph of the equation $Z = Y/X$. Draw the diagonal to connect the zero ends of the scales. Then locate whole values along the diagonal by using combinations of X and Y values. Be sure to locate whole-value units along the diagonal that are easy to interpolate between. Label the diagonal and give a key explaining how to use the nomograph. Note that a sample **isopleth** verifies the correctness of the graphical relationship between the scales.

We can construct a more advanced N graph for the equation

$$A = \frac{B + 2}{C + 5},$$

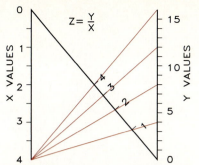

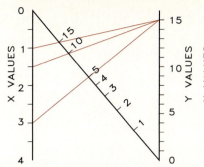

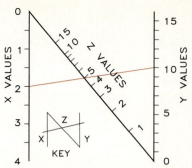

Figure 26.17 Constructing an N graph:
Step 1 Draw an N graph for the equation of $Z = Y/X$ with two parallel scales. Connect the zero ends of each scale with a diagonal scale. Use isopleths to locate units along the diagonal.

Step 2 Draw additional isopleths to locate other units along the diagonal. The units on the diagonal should be whole units to make interpolation easy.

Step 3 Label the diagonal scale and draw a key. An isopleth confirms that $10/2 = 5$. The accuracy of the N graph is greatest at the 0 end of the diagonal. The diagonal approaches infinity at the other end.

where $0 \le B \le 8$ and $0 \le C \le 15$. This equation takes the form:

$$F1 = \frac{F2}{F3},$$

where

$$F1(A) = A,$$

$$F2(B) = B + 2, \quad \text{and}$$

$$F3(C) = C + 5.$$

Thus the outer scales will be for $B + 2$ and $C + 5$, and the diagonal scale will be for A.

Begin the construction in the same manner as for a parallel scale graph by selecting the layout of the outer scales (**Fig. 26.18**). Determine the limits of the diagonal scale by connecting the endpoints on the outer scales, giving $A = 0.1$ for $B = 0$, $C = 15$ and $A = 2.0$ for $B = 8$, and $C = 0$. **Figure 26.18** shows these relationships and also gives the remainder of the construction.

Locate the diagonal scale by finding the **function zeros** of the outer scales (that is, the points where $B + 2 = 0$ or $B = -2$ and $C + 5 = 0$ or $C = -5$). Then draw the diagonal scale by connecting these points.

Calibrating the diagonal scale is most easily accomplished by substituting into the formula. Selecting the upper limit of an outer scale, say, $B = 8$, gives the formula:

$$A = \frac{10}{C + 5}.$$

Then solve this equation for the other outer scale variable:

$$C = \frac{10}{A - 5}.$$

Using it as a "scale equation," make a table of values for the desired values of A and corresponding values of C (up to the limit of C in the graph), as shown in Table 26.1. Connect isopleths from $B = 8$ to the tabulated values of C. Their intersections with the diagonal scale give the required calibrations for approximately half the diagonal scale.

Table 26.1

A	2.0	1.5	1.0	0.9	0.8	0.7	0.6	0.5
C	0	1.67	5.0	6.11	7.50	9.28	11.7	15.0

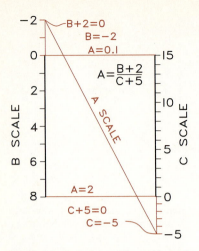

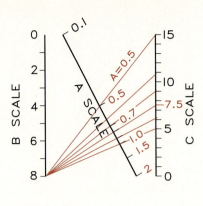

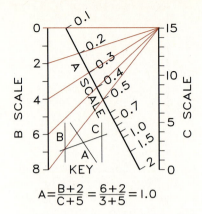

$$A = \frac{B+2}{C+5} = \frac{6+2}{3+5} = 1.0$$

Figure 26.18 Constructing an N graph: **Step 1** Locate the diagonal scale by finding the functional zeros of the outer scales. Do so by setting $B + 2 = 0$ and $C + 5 = 0$, which gives a zero value for A.

Step 2 Select the upper limit of one of the outer scales ($B = 8$ in this case) and substitute it into the equation to obtain a series of values of C for the desired values of A (see Table 26.1). Draw isopleths from $B = 8$ to the values of C to calibrate the A scale.

Step 3 Calibrate the remainder of the A scale in the same manner by substituting $C = 15$ into the equation to determine a series of values on the B scale for desired values on the A scale (see Table 26.2). Draw isopleths from $C = 15$ to calibrate the A scale, as shown.

Calibrate the remainder of the diagonal scale by substituting the end value of the other outer scale ($C = 15$) into the formula, giving

$$A = \frac{B + 2}{20}.$$

Solving for B yields

$$B = 20A - 2.$$

Construct a table for the desired values of A as shown in Table 26.2. Isopleths connecting $C = 15$ with the tabulated values of B locate the remaining calibrations on the A scale.

Table 26.2

A	0.5	0.4	0.3	0.2	0.1
B	8.0	6.0	4.0	2.0	0

Problems

Use the principles covered in this chapter to solve the following problems; use size A sheets. For problems involving geometric construction and mathematical calculations, show both the construction and calculations in the solutions. If the calculations are extensive, use a separate sheet for them.

Concurrent Scales

Construct concurrent scales for converting one type of unit to the other. The range of units for the scales is given for each relationship.

1. Kilometers and miles:

   1.609 km = 1 mile; from 10 to 100 miles.

2. Liters and U.S. gallons:

   1 L = 0.2692 U.S. gal; from 1 to 10 L.

3. Knots and miles per hour:

   1 knot = 1.15 mph; from 0 to 45 knots.

4. Horsepower and British thermal units:

   1 hp = 42.4 Btu; from 0 to 1200 hp.

5. Centigrade and Fahrenheit:

   $°F = \dfrac{9}{5}°C + 32$; from 32°F to 212°F.

6. Radius and area of a circle:

   $A = \pi r^2$; from $r = 0$ to 10.

7. Inches and millimeters:

   1 in. = 25.4 mm; from 0 to 5 in.

8. Numbers and their logarithms:

   Use logarithm tables; numbers from 1 to 10.

Addition and Subtraction Nomographs

Construct parallel scale nomographs to solve the following addition and subtraction problems.

9. $A = B + C$, where $B = 0$ to 10 and $C = 0$ to 5.

10. $Z = X + Y$, where $X = 0$ to 8 and $Y = 0$ to 12.

11. $Z = Y - X$, where $X = 0$ to 6 and $Y = 0$ to 24.

12. $A = C - B$, where $C = 0$ to 30 and $B = 0$ to 6.

13. $W = 2V + U$, where $U = 0$ to 12 and $V = 0$ to 9.

14. $W = 3U + V$, where $U = 0$ to 10, and $V = 0$ to 10.

15. Electrical current at a circuit junction:

$$I = I1 + I2,$$

where

I = current entering the junction in amperes (amps),

$I1$ = current leaving the junction, varying from 2 to 15 amps, and

$I2$ = current leaving junction, varying from 7 to 36 amps.

16. Pressure change in fluid flowing in a pipe:

$$\Delta P = P2 - P1,$$

where

ΔP = pressure change between two points in pounds per square inch (psi),

$P1$ = pressure upstream, varying from 3 psi to 12 psi, and

$P2$ = pressure downstream, varying from 10 psi to 15 psi.

Multiplication and Division: Parallel Scales

Construct parallel scale nomographs having logarithmic scales for performing the following multiplication and division operations.

17. Area of a rectangle: $A = H \times W$, where $H = 1$ to 10 and $W = 1$ to 12.

18. Area of a triangle: $A = {}^1/_2 B \times H$, where $B = 1$ to 10, and $H = 1$ to 5.

19. Electrical potential between terminals of a conductor:

$$E = IR,$$

where

E = electrical potential in volts,

I = current, varying from 1 to 10 amps, and

R = resistance, varying from 5 to 30 ohms.

20. Pythagorean theorem:

$$C^2 = A^2 + B^2,$$

where

C = hypotenuse of a right triangle in centimeters (cm),

A = one leg of the right triangle, varying from 5 to 50 cm, and

B = second leg of the right triangle, varying from 20 to 80 cm.

21. Allowable pressure on a shaft bearing:

$$P = \frac{ZN}{100},$$

where

P = pressure in psi,

Z = viscosity of lubricant, varying from 15 to 50 (cp), and centipoise, and

N = angular velocity of shaft, varying from 10 to 1000 rpm.

22. Miles per gallon (mpg) an automobile gets: Miles vary from 1 to 500; gallons vary from 1 to 24.

23. Cost per mile (cpm) of an automobile: Miles vary from 1 to 500; cost varies from $1 to $28.

24. Angular velocity of a rotating body:

$$W = \frac{V}{R},$$

where

W = angular velocity, in radians per second,

V = peripheral velocity, varying from 1 to 100 m^{-1}, and

R = radius, varying from 0.1 to 1 m.

N Nomographs

Construct N graphs that will solve the following equations.

25. Stress = P/A, where P varies from 0 to 1000 psi and A varies from 0 to 15 in^2.

26. Volume of a cylinder:

$$V = \pi r^2 h,$$

where

V = volume in in^3,

r = radius, varying from 5 to 10 ft, and

h = height, varying from 2 to 20 in.

27. Repeat Problem 17.

28. Repeat Problem 18.

29. Repeat Problem 19.

30. Repeat Problem 20.

31. Repeat Problem 21.

32. Repeat Problem 22.

33. Repeat Problem 23.

34. Repeat Problem 24.

27 Empirical Equations and Calculus

27.1 Introduction

Graphical methods are useful supplements to mathematical techniques of solving problems dealing with experimental data, especially when the data do not fit a mathematical equation. Data from laboratory experiments or from field tests are called **empirical data**. Empirical data often are expressed as one of three types of equations: linear, power, or exponential.

Analysis of empirical data begins with plots of the data on linear, logarithmic, or semilogarithmic grids. Fitting curves to the data determines which of the grids gives a straight-line relationship (**Fig. 27.1**). Data that yield a straight-line plot on one of these grids may be written as a mathematical equation.

27.2 Curve Equations

Two methods of finding the equation of a curve are (1) the selected-points method and (2) the slope-intercept method (**Fig. 27.2**).

LINEAR, LOGARITHMIC, AND SEMILOG GRIDS

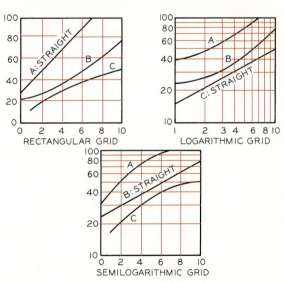

Figure 27.1 Plotting empirical data on each type of grid determines which yields a straight-line plot. A straight-line plot on one of these grids means that a mathematical equation can be written to describe the data.

EQUATION OF A LINE

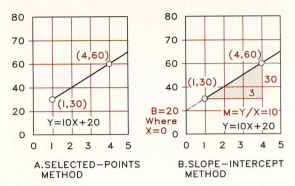

A. SELECTED−POINTS METHOD

B. SLOPE−INTERCEPT METHOD

Figure 27.2

A One way to determine the equation of a straight line on a grid is by selecting any two points on the line.

B A second way is to use the slope-intercept equation. It requires finding the Y intercept (where $X = 0$), involving the extension of the curve to the Y axis.

THE LINEAR EQUATION: $Y = MX + B$

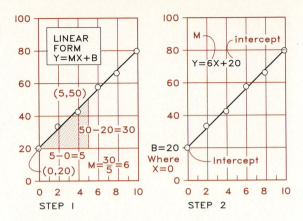

STEP 1

STEP 2

Figure 27.3 The linear equation, $Y = MX + B$:

Step 1 A straight line on an arithmetic grid has an equation that takes the form $Y = MX + B$. Here, the slope, M, is 6.

Step 2 The intercept, $B = 20$, is substituted in the equation to obtain $Y = 6X + 20$.

Selected-Points Method

Two widely separated points on the line in **Fig. 27.2A**, (1, 30) and (4, 60), are selected and substituted into the equation

$$\frac{Y - 30}{X - 1} = \frac{60 - 30}{4 - 1}.$$

The resulting equation is

$$Y = 10X + 20.$$

Slope-Intercept Method

The slope-intercept method may be used when the Y intercept of the curve (where $X = 0$) is known. If the X axis is logarithmic, the log of $X = 1$ is 0, and the intercept is at $X = 1$.

In **Fig. 27.2B**, the curve does not intercept the Y axis, so it must be extended to find the intercept at $X = 0$, or $B = 20$ in this case. The slope of the curve, $M = 10$, is determined ($\Delta Y / \Delta X$ or 30/3), and it is substituted into the linear equation form to obtain $Y = 10X + 20$.

APPLICATION: LINEAR FORM

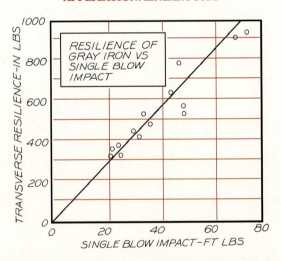

Figure 27.4 The relationship between the transverse strength of gray iron and impact resistance plots as a straight line yielding an equation of the form $Y = MX + B$ or $Y = 13.3X$.

528 • **CHAPTER 27 EMPIRICAL EQUATIONS AND CALCULUS**

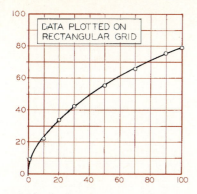

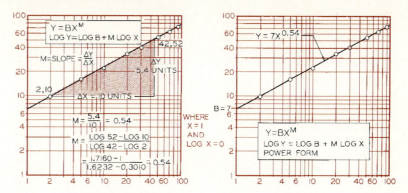

Figure 27.5 The power equation, $Y = BX^M$:

Given Plotting these data on a rectangular grid gives a parabolic curve. Because the curve is not a straight line on the rectangular grid, its equation is not linear.

Step 1 The data plot as a straight line on a logarithmic grid. Find the slope, M, graphically with an engineer's scale by setting ΔX at 10 units and measuring ΔY with the same scale to get 5.4 units. Thus $M = 5.4/10$, or 0.54.

Step 2 The intercept $B = 7$ lies at $X = 1$. Substitute the slope and intercept into the equation, which becomes $Y = 7X^{0.54}$.

27.3 The Linear Equation: $Y = MX + B$

The curve shown in **Fig. 27.3** representing experimental data is a straight line on a linear graph, which identifies the data as **linear**, meaning that each measurement along the Y axis is directly proportional to the measurement along the X axis. We may use either the slope-intercept method or the selected-points method to find the equation for the data.

By using the slope-intercept method first, we select two known points along the curve. The vertical and horizontal differences between the coordinates of each point establish the adjacent sides of a right triangle. In the slope-intercept equation, $Y = MX + B$, the slope, M, is the tangent of the angle between the curve and the horizontal, B is the Y intercept of the curve (where $X = 0$), and X and Y are variables. Here, $M = 30/5 = 6$, and the intercept is at 20.

Substituting these values into the slope-intercept equation, we obtain $Y = 6X + 20$, from which we may determine values of Y by substituting any value of X into the equation. If the curve had sloped downward to the right, the slope would have been negative.

Let's now use the selected-points method, assuming that we do not know the Y intercept. Select two widely separated points, say (2, 32) and (10, 80), and write the equation in the form

$$\frac{Y - 32}{X - 2} = \frac{80 - 32}{10 - 2}$$

or

$$Y = 6X + 20.$$

Thus both methods give the same equation for the curve, or $Y = MX + B$.

Figure 27.4 shows the relationship between the transverse strength and impact resistance of gray iron obtained from empirical data. Plotted on a linear grid, the data are best represented by a straight line, so its equation takes the linear form.

27.4 The Power Equation: $Y = BX^M$

Data plotted on a logarithmic grid that yields a straight line **(Fig. 27.5)** may be expressed in the

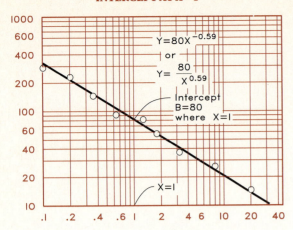

Figure 27.6 Use of the slope-intercept method with a logarithmic grid means that the intercept lies at $X = 1$. Here, the intercept lies at 80 (near the middle of the graph).

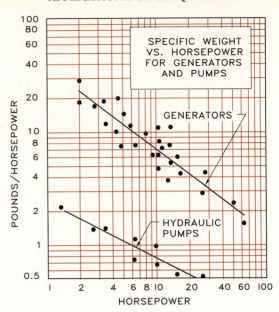

Figure 27.7 Empirical data plotted on a logarithmic grid showing the specific weight versus horsepower of electric generators and hydraulic pumps are straight lines. Their equations take the power form, $Y = BX^M$.

power equation form in which Y is a function of X raised to a power, or $Y = BX^M$. We obtain the equation of the data by using the Y intercept as B and the slope of the curve as M.

Select two points on the curve to form the slope triangle and use an engineer's scale to measure its slope. If you draw the horizontal side of the right triangle as 1 or a multiple of 10, you may read the vertical distance directly. Here, the slope M (tangent of the angle) is 0.54 and the Y intercept, B, is 7; thus the equation is $Y = 7X^{0.54}$, which in logarithmic form is

$$\log Y = \log B + M \log X,$$

$$= \log 7 + 0.54 \log X.$$

We used base-10 logarithms in these examples, but natural logs may be used with e (2.718) as the base.

In **Fig. 27.6** the intercept, B, lies on the Y axis where $X = 1$ because the curve is plotted on a logarithmic grid. The Y intercept ($B = 80$) is found where $X = 1$. Recall that the intercept at this point is analogous to the linear form of the equation because the log of 1 is 0. The curve slopes downward to the right making the slope, M, negative.

Figure 27.7 shows plots of empirical data that relate the specific weight (pounds per horsepower) of generators and hydraulic pumps to horsepower. The plots of the data are represented by straight lines on a logarithmic grid, which means that their equations take the power form.

27.5 The Exponential Equation: $Y = BM^X$

When data plotted on a semilogarithmic grid (**Fig. 27.8**) yield a straight line, the equation takes the form $Y = BM^X$, where B is the Y intercept, and M is the slope of the curve. Select two points along the curve, draw a right triangle, and find its slope, M. The slope of the curve is

$$\log M = \frac{\log 40 - \log 6}{8 - 3} = 0.1648,$$

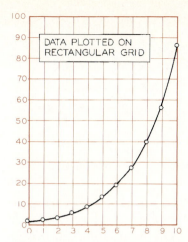

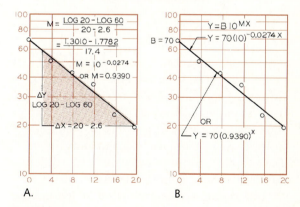

Figure 27.8 The exponential equation, $Y = BM^X$:

Given These data give a straight line on a semilogarithmic grid. Therefore the data take the equation form $Y = BM^X$.

Step 1 You must find the slope mathematically, not graphically, because the X and Y scales are unequal. Write the slope equation in either of the forms shown.

Step 2 Find the intercept, $B = 2$, where $X = 0$. Substitute the values for M and B into the equation to get $Y = 2(10)^{0.1648X}$ or $Y = 2(1.46)^X$.

or

$$M = (10)^{0.1648} = 1.46.$$

Substitute this value of M into the exponential equation:

$$Y = BM^X \quad \text{or} \quad Y = 2(1.46)^X,$$

$$Y = B(10)^{MX} \quad \text{or} \quad Y = 2(10)^{0.1648X},$$

where X is a variable that can be substituted into the equation to give infinitely many values for Y. In logarithmic form, the equation is

$$\log Y = \log B + X \log M,$$

or

$$\log Y = \log 2 + X \log 1.46.$$

The same methods give the negative slope of a curve. The curve shown in **Fig. 27.9** slopes downward to the right and therefore has a negative slope. The slope, M, is the antilog of -0.0274. The intercept of 70 and the slope yield the equation for the curve.

NEGATIVE SLOPE (M)

Figure 27.9

A When a curve slopes downward to the right, its slope is negative.

B Substitution gives these two forms of the equation for the curve.

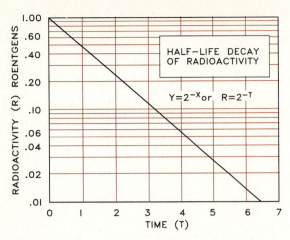

Figure 27.10 The decay of radioactivity is represented by a straight line on a semilog grid, indicating that its equation takes the exponential form, $Y = BM^X$ or $R = 2^{-T}$.

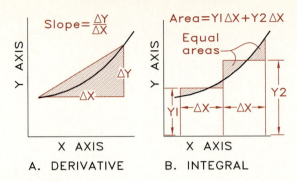

Figure 27.11
A The derivative of a curve is the rate of change at any point on the curve, or its slope, $\Delta Y / \Delta X$.

B The integral of a curve is the cumulative area enclosed by the curve, or the summation of the incremental areas comprising the whole.

The half-life decay of radioactivity plotted in **Fig. 27.10** compares decay to time. The half-life of different isotopes varies, so different values would be assigned along the X axis for them. However, the curves for all isotopes would be straight lines and take the exponential equation form.

27.6 Graphical Calculus

If the equation of a curve is known, calculus may be used to perform certain types of calculations. However, experimental data often do not fit standard mathematical equations, making impossible the application of calculus mathematically. In these cases, graphical calculus must be used. The two basic forms of calculus are (1) differential calculus and (2) integral calculus.

Differential calculus is used to determine the rate of change of one variable with respect to another **(Fig. 27.11A)**. The rate of change at any instant along the curve is the slope of a line tangent to the curve at that point. Constructing a chord at any interval allows approximation of this slope. The tangent, $\Delta Y / \Delta X$, may represent miles per hour, weight versus length, or various other rates of change important in the analysis of data.

Integral calculus is the reverse of differential calculus. Integration is used to find the area under a curve (the product of the variables plotted on the X and Y axes). The area under a curve is approximated by dividing one of the variables into a number of very small rectangular bars under the curve **(Fig. 27.11B)**. Each bar is drawn so that equal areas lie above and below the curve and the average height of the bar is near its midpoint.

27.7 Graphical Differentiation

Graphical differentiation is used to determine the rate of change of two variables with respect to each other at any given point. **Figure 27.12** illustrates the preliminary construction of a derivative scale and pole point to be used to plot a derivative curve.

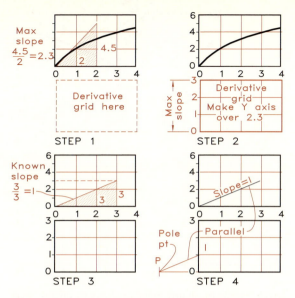

SCALES FOR DIFFERENTIATION

Figure 27.12 Scales for graphical differentiation:

Step 1 Estimate the maximum slope of the curve (here, 2.3) by drawing a line tangent to the curve where it is steepest.

Step 2 Draw the derivative grid with a maximum ordinate of 3.0 to accommodate the slope of 2.3.

Step 3 Find a known slope of 1 on the given grid. The slope has no relationship to the data curve.

Step 4 Draw a line from 1 on the Y axis of the derivative grid parallel to the slope of the triangle drawn in the given grid to locate the pole point on the extension of the X axis.

Figure 27.13 shows the graphical differentiation process. The maximum slope of the data curve is estimated to be slightly less than 12, so an ordinate scale long enough to accommodate the maximum slope is selected. To locate the pole point, a line is drawn from point 12 on the ordinate axis of the derivative grid parallel to the known slope on the given curve grid and the line is extended to the X axis.

Next, a series of chords is constructed on the given curve. The interval between 0 and 1, where the curve is steepest, is divided in half to obtain a more accurate plot. After other bars are found, a smooth curve is drawn through the top of them so that the area above and under the top of each bar is equal. The rate of change, $\Delta Y/\Delta X$, can be found for any value of X in the derivative graph.

Applications

The mechanical handling shuttle shown in **Fig. 27.14** converts rotational motion into linear motion. The drawing of the linkage shows the end positions of point P, which is the zero point for plotting travel versus degrees of revolution. Rotation is constant at one revolution every three seconds, so the degrees of revolution may be converted to time (**Fig. 27.15**). The drive crank, R1, is revolved at 30° intervals, and the distance that point P travels from its end position is plotted on the graph to give the distance–time relationship.

The ordinate scale of the derivative grid is scaled with an end value of 100 in./sec, or slightly larger than the estimated maximum slope of the curve. A slope of 40 is drawn on the given data grid. Pole point P is found by drawing a line from 40 on the derivative ordinate scale parallel to the slope of 40 in the given data graph to the extension of the X axis of the derivative graph.

Chords drawn on the curve approximate the slope at various points. Lines drawn from point P of the derivative scale are parallel to the chordal lines to the ordinate scale. These intersections on the Y axis are projected horizontally to their respective intervals to form vertical bars. A smooth curve is drawn through the tops of the bars to give an average of the bars. This curve is used to find the velocity of the shuttle in inches per second at any time interval.

The second derivative curve, acceleration versus time, is constructed in the same manner as the first derivative curve. Inspection of the first derivative curve reveals that the maximum slope is an estimated 200 in./sec/sec. An easily measured scale for the ordinate scale is chosen. A new

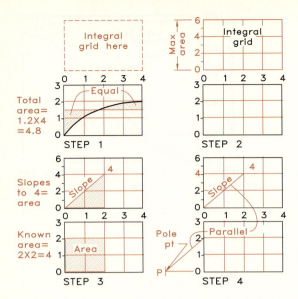

Figure 27.16 Scales for graphical integration:

Step 1 To determine the maximum value on the Y axis, draw a line to approximate the area under the given curve (4.8 square units here).

Step 2 Draw the integral with a Y axis of 6 to accommodate the maximum area.

Step 3 Find a known area of 4 on the given grid. Draw a slope from 0 to 4 on the integral grid directly above the known area to establish the integral.

Step 4 Draw a line from 2 on the Y axis of the given grid parallel to the slope line in the integral grid. Locate the pole point on the extension of the X axis.

at a rapid rate until the maximum velocity is attained at 90°, at which time deceleration begins and continues until the parts come to rest.

27.8 Graphical Integration

Graphical integration is used to determine the area (product of two variables) under a curve. For example, if the Y axis represented pounds and the X axis represented feet, the integral curve would give the product of the variables, foot-pounds, at any interval of feet along the X axis. **Figure 27.16** illustrates how the scales and pole point for graphical integration are determined.

In **Fig. 27.17**, the total area under the curve is estimated to be less than 80 units. Therefore the

maximum height of the Y axis on the integral curve is 80, drawn at a convenient scale. Pole point P is found by the steps shown in Fig. 27.16.

A series of vertical bars is constructed to approximate the areas under the curve. The narrower the bars, the more accurate will be the resulting plotted curve. The interval between 2 and 3 is divided into two bars to obtain more accuracy where the curve is sharpest. The tops of the bars are extended horizontally to the Y axis and these intersections are connected to point P.

Lines are drawn parallel to AP, BP, CP, DP, and EP in the integral grid to correspond to the respective intervals in the given grid. The intersection points of the chords are connected by a smooth curve—the integral curve—to give the cumulative product of the X and Y variables along the X axis.

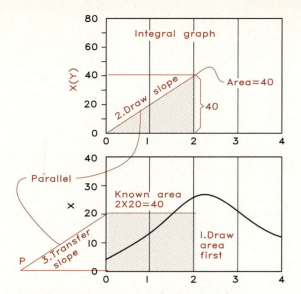

Figure 27.17 Performing graphical integration:
Required Plot the integral curve of the given data.

Step 1 Find pole point P by using the technique described in Fig. 27.16.

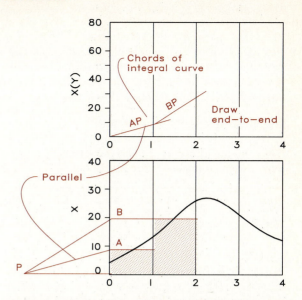

Step 2 Construct bars to approximate the areas under the curve. Project the heights of the bars to the Y axis and draw lines to the pole point. Draw sloping lines AP and BP at their respective intervals parallel to the lines drawn to P.

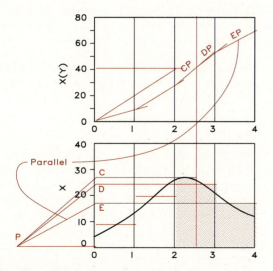

Step 3 Draw additional bars from 2 to 4 on the X axis. Project the heights of the bars to the Y axis and draw rays to P. Draw lines CP, DP, and EP at their respective intervals and parallel to their rays in the integral grid.

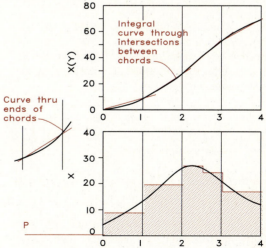

Step 4 The straight lines connected in the integral grid represent chords of the integral curve. Construct the integral curve to pass through the points where the chords intersect. An ordinate value on the integral curve represents the cumulative area under the given curve from zero to that point on the X axis.

Use size A sheets for your solutions to the following problems. For solutions involving mathematical calculations, show them on separate sheets if space is not available on the same sheet with the graphical solutions.

Empirical Equations—Logarithmic

1. Find the equation of the data shown in the following table. The empirical data compare input voltage, V, with input current in amperes, I, to a heat pump.

Y axis	V	0.8	1.3	1.75	1.85
X axis	I	20	30	40	45

2. Find the equation of the data presented in the following table. The empirical data give the relationship between peak allowable current in amperes, I, with the overload operating time in cycles at 60 cycles per second, C.

Y axis	I	2000	1840	1640	1480	1300	1200	1000
X axis	C	1	2	5	10	20	50	100

3. Find the equation of the data contained in the following table. The empirical data for a low-voltage circuit breaker used on a welding machine give the maximum loading during welding in amperes, rms, for the percentage of duty, pdc.

Y axis	rms	7500	5200	4400	3400	2300	1700
X axis	pdc	3	6	9	15	30	60

4. Construct a three-cycle by three-cycle logarithmic graph to find the equation of a machine's vibration displacement in mills (Y axis) and vibration frequency in cycles per minute, cpm (X axis). Data: 100 cpm, 0.80 mill; 400 cpm, 0.22 mill; 1000 cpm, 0.09 mill; 10,000 cpm, 0.009 mill; 50,000 cpm, 0.0017 mill.

5. Find the equation of the data shown in the following table that compares the velocities of air moving over a plane surface in feet per second, v, at different heights in inches, y, above the surface. Plot y values on the Y axis.

y	0.1	0.2	0.3	0.4	0.6	0.8	1.2	1.6	2.4	3.2
v	18.8	21.0	22.6	24.1	26.0	27.3	29.2	30.6	32.4	33.7

6. Find the equation of the data presented in the following table that shows the distance traveled in feet, s, at various times in seconds, t, of a test vehicle. Plot s on the Y axis and t on the X axis.

t	1	2	3	4	5	6
s	15.8	63.3	146.0	264.0	420.0	580.0

Empirical Equations—Linear

7. Construct a linear graph to determine the equation for the annual cost of a compressor in relation to the compressor's size in horsepower. Plot cost on the Y axis and compressor size on the X axis. Data: 0 hp, $0; 50 hp, $2100; 100 hp, $4500; 150 hp, $6700; 200 hp, $9000; 250 hp, $11,400. Write the equation for these data.

8. Construct a linear graph on which the X axis is the mat depth from 0 to 4 in. and the Y axis is tons per hour per foot of width from 0 to 70 for a conveyor traveling at a rate of 50 feet per minute. The conveyor actually is a moving shaker that screens particles of coal by size. Data: $X = 0$, $Y = 0$; $X = 1$, $Y = 13$; $X = 2$, $Y = 25$; $X = 3$, $Y = 38$; and $X = 4$, $Y = 50$.

9. Write the equation for the empirical data plotted in Fig. 27.8.

10. Plot the data contained in the following table on a linear graph and determine its equation. The empirical data show the deflection in centimeters of a spring, d, when it is loaded with different weights in kilograms, w. Plot w along the X axis and d along the Y axis.

w	0	1	2	3	4	5
d	0.45	1.10	1.45	2.03	2.38	3.09

11. Plot the data shown in the following table on a linear graph and determine the graph's equation. The empirical data show temperatures read from a

Fahrenheit scale thermometer, °F, and a Celsius scale thermometer, °C. Plot the °C values along the X axis and the °F values along the Y axis.

°C	−6.8	6.0	16.0	32.2	52.0	76.0
°F	20.0	43.0	60.8	90.0	125.8	169.0

Empirical Equations—Semilogarithmic

12. Construct a semilog graph of the following data to determine their equation. Make the Y axis a two-cycle log scale and the X axis a 10-unit linear scale. Plot the voltage, V, along the Y axis and time, t, in sixteenths of a second along the X axis to represent resistor voltage during capacitor charging. Data: 0 sec, 10 V; 2 sec, 6 V; 4 sec, 3.6 V; 6 sec, 2.2 V; 8 sec, 1.4 V; 10 sec, 0.8 V.

13. Write the equation for the data plotted in Fig. 27.10.

14. Construct a semilog graph of the following data to determine their equation. Make the Y axis a three-cycle log scale and the X axis a linear scale with values from 0 to 250. These data relate the reduction factor, R (Y axis), to the mass thickness per square foot MT (X axis), of a nuclear protection barrier. Data: $0MT$, $1.0R$; $100MT$, $0.9R$; $150MT$, $0.028R$; $200MT$, $0.009R$; $300MT$, $0.0011R$.

15. An engineering firm considering expansion is reviewing its past income as shown in the following table. Their years of operation are represented by x, and their annual income (in tens of thousands of dollars) by N. Plot x along the X axis and N along the Y axis and determine the equation for the data.

x	1	2	3	4	5	6	7	8	9	10
N	0.05	0.08	0.12	0.20	0.32	0.51	0.80	1.30	2.05	3.25

Empirical Equations—General Types

16–21. Plot the experimental data shown in Table 27.1 on a grid that allows the data to appear as straight-line curves. Determine the equations of the data.

Calculus—Graphical Differentiation

22. Plot the equation $Y = X^3/6$ as a rectangular graph. Graphically differentiate the curve to determine the first and second derivatives.

23. Plot the following equation on a graph and find the derivative curve of the data on a second graph placed below the first: $Y = 2X^2$.

24. Plot the following equation on a graph and find the derivative curve of the data on a second graph placed below the first: $4Y = 8 - X^2$.

Table 27.1

16	X	0	40	80	120	160	200	240	280		
	Y	4.0	7.0	9.8	12.5	15.3	17.2	21.0	24.0		
17	X	1	2	5	10	20	50	100	200	500	1000
	Y	1.5	2.4	3.3	6.0	9.0	15.0	23.0	24.0	60.0	85.0
18	X	1	5	10	50	100	500	1000			
	Y	3	10	19	70	110	400	700			
19	X	2	4	6	8	10	12	14			
	Y	6.5	14.0	32.0	75.0	115.0	320.0	710.0			
20	X	0	2	4	6	8	10	12	14		
	Y	20	34	53	96	115	270	430	730		
21	X	0	1	2	3	4	5	6	7	8	9	10
	Y	1.8	2.1	2.2	2.5	2.7	3.0	3.4	3.7	4.1	4.5	5.0

25. Plot the following equation on a graph and find the derivative curve of the data on a second graph placed below the first: $3Y = X^2 + 16$.

26. Plot the following equation on a graph and find the derivative curve of the data on a second graph placed below the first: $X = 3Y^2 - 5$.

Calculus—Graphical Integration

27. Plot the following equation on a graph and find the integral curve of the data on a second graph placed above the first: $Y = X^2$.

28. Plot the following equation on a graph and find the integral curve of the data on a second graph placed above the first: $Y = 9 - X^2$.

29. Plot the following equation on a graph and find the integral curve of the data on a second graph placed above the first: $Y = X$.

30. A plot plan shows that a tract of land is bounded by a lake front **(Fig. 27.18)**. By graphical integration, repre-

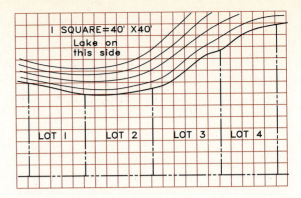

Figure 27.18 Problem 30. The tract of land shown here has been subdivided into four lots.

sent the cumulative area of the land (from left to right). What is the total area? What is the area of each lot?

28

Pipe Drafting

28.1 Introduction

An understanding of pipe drafting begins with knowing the types of pipe that are available. The commonly used types are steel pipe; cast-iron pipe; copper, brass, and bronze pipe and tubing; and plastic pipe.

The standards for the grades and weights for pipe and pipe fittings are specified by several organizations to ensure the uniformity of size and strength of interchangeable components. Among these many organizations are the American National Standards Institute (ANSI), the American Society for Test Materials (ASTM), the American Petroleum Institute (API), and the Manufacturers Standardization Society (MSS).

28.2 Welded and Seamless Steel Pipe

Traditionally, steel pipe has been specified in three weights: standard (STD), extra strong (XS), and double extra strong (XXS). These designations and their specifications are listed in the ANSI B 36.10 standards. However, additional designations for pipe, called **schedules**, have been introduced to provide the pipe designer with a wider selection of pipe for more applications.

The ten schedules of pipe are Schedules 10, 20, 30, 40, 60, 80, 100, 120, 140, and 160. The wall thicknesses of the pipes vary from the thinnest, in Schedule 10, to the thickest, in Schedule 160. The outside diameters are of a constant size for pipes of the same nominal size in all schedules.

Schedule designations correspond to STD, XS, and XXS specifications in some cases, as shown partially in **Table 28.1**. This table has been abbreviated from the ANSI B 36.10 tables by omitting some of the pipe sizes and schedules. The most often used schedules are 40, 80, and 120.

Pipes from the smallest size up to and including 12-in. pipes are specified by their inside diameter (ID), which means that the outside diameter (OD) is larger than the specified size. The inside diameters are the same size as the nominal sizes of the pipe for STD weight pipe. For XS and XXS pipe, the inside diameters are slightly different in

Table 28.1
Dimensions and Weights of Welded and Seamless Steel Pipe (ANSI B 36.10)

Inch Units				Identification		SI Units		
Inch Nominal Size	O.D. (in.)	Wall Thk. (in.)	Weight lbs/ft	*STD XS XXS	Sch. no.	O.D. (mm)	Wall Thk. (mm)	Weight kg/m
$1/_2$	0.84	0.11	0.85	STD	40	21.3	2.8	1.3
1	1.32	0.13	1.68	STD	40	33.4	3.4	2.5
1	1.3	0.18	2.17	XS	80	33.4	4.6	3.2
1	1.3	0.36	3.66	XXS		33.4	9.1	5.5
2	2.38	0.22	3.65	STD	40	60.3	3.9	5.4
2	2.38	0.22	5.02	XS	80	60.3	5.5	7.5
2	2.38	0.44	9.03	XXS		60.3	11.1	13.4
4	4.50	0.23	10.79	STD	40	114.3	6.0	16.1
4	4.50	0.34	14.98	XS	80	114.3	8.6	42.6
4	4.50	0.67	27.54	XXS		114.3	17.1	41.0
8	8.63	0.32	28.55	STD	40	219.1	8.2	42.6
8	8.63	0.50	43.39	XS	80	219.1	12.7	64.6
8	8.63	0.88	74.40	XXS		219.1	22.2	107.9
12	12.75	0.38	49.56	STD		323.0	9.5	67.9
12	12.75	0.50	65.42	XS		323.0	12.7	97.5
12	12.75	1.00	125.4	XXS	120	133.9	25.4	187.0
14	†14.00	0.38	54.57	STD	30	355.6	9.5	87.3
14	14.00	0.50	72.08	XS		355.6	12.7	107.4
18	18.00	0.38	70.59	STD		457	9.5	106.2
18	18.00	0.50	93.45	XS		457	12.7	139.2
24	24.00	0.38	94.62	STD	20	610	9.5	141.1
24	24.00	0.50	125.49	XS		610	12.7	187.1
30	30.00	0.38	118.65	STD		762	9.5	176.8
30	30.00	0.50	157.53	XS	20	762	12.7	234.7
40	40.00	0.38	158.70	STD		1016	9.5	236.5
40	40.00	0.50	210.90	XS		1016	12.7	314.2

*Standard (STD)

X-strong (XS)

XX-strong (XXS)

†Beginning with 14-in. DIA pipe, the nominal size represents the outside diameter (O.D.).

This table has been compressed by omitting many of the available pipe sizes. The nominal sizes of pipes that are listed in the complete table are: $1/_8$", $1/_4$", $3/_8$", $1/_2$", $3/_4$", 1", $11/_4$", $11/_2$", 2", $21/_2$", 3", $31/_2$", 4", 5", 6", 8", 10", 12", 14", 16", 18", 20", 22", ...(at 2" increments up to 60").

size from the nominal size. Beginning with the 14-in. diameter pipes, the nominal sizes represent the outside diameters of the pipe. The standard lengths for steel pipe are 20 ft and 40 ft.

Seamless steel (SMLS STL) pipe is a smooth pipe with no weld seams along its length. Welded pipe is formed into a cylinder and is butt-welded

(BW) at the seam, or it is joined with an electric resistance weld (ERW).

28.3 Cast-Iron Pipe

Cast-iron pipe is used for the transportation of liquids, water, gas, and sewage. When used as a sewage pipe, cast-iron pipe is referred to as "soil pipe." Cast-iron pipe is available in diameter sizes from 3 in. to 60 in. in standard lengths of 5 ft and 10 ft.

Cast iron is more brittle and more subject to cracking when loaded than is steel pipe. Therefore, cast-iron pipe should not be used where high pressures or weights will be applied to it.

28.4 Copper, Brass, and Bronze Piping

Copper, brass, and bronze are used in the manufacture piping and tubing for use in applications requiring high resistance to corrosive elements, such as acidic soils and chemicals transmitted through the pipes. Copper pipe is used when the pipes are placed within or under concrete slab foundations of buildings to ensure a resistance to corrosion. The standard length of pipes made of these nonferrous materials is 12 ft.

Tubing is a smaller-size pipe that can be easily bent when made of copper, brass, or bronze. The term **piping** refers to rigid pipes that are larger than tubes, usually in excess of 2 in. in diameter, and do not easily bend.

28.5 Miscellaneous Pipes

Other materials used in the manufacture of pipes are aluminum, asbestos-cement, concrete, polyvinyl chloride (PVC), and various other plastics. Each of these materials has special characteristics making it desirable or economical for certain applications. The method of designing and detailing piping systems by the pipe drafter is essentially the same regardless of the piping material used.

28.6 Pipe Joints

The basic connection in a pipe system is the joint where two straight sections of pipe fit together. Three types of joints are illustrated in **Fig. 28.1**: **screwed**, **welded**, and **flanged**.

Screwed joints are joined by pipe threads of the type covered in Chapter 10 and Appendix 10. Pipe threads are tapered at a ratio of 1 to 16 along the outside diameter (**Fig. 28.2**). As the

BASIC PIPE JOINTS

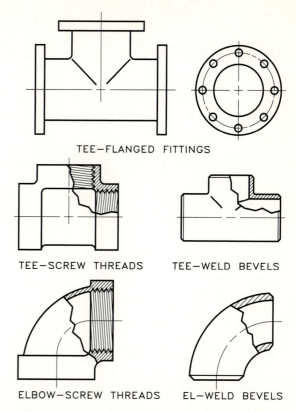

TEE—FLANGED FITTINGS

TEE—SCREW THREADS   TEE—WELD BEVELS

ELBOW—SCREW THREADS   EL—WELD BEVELS

Figure 28.1 The three basic types of joints are screwed, welded, and flanged joints.

pipes are screwed together, the threads bind to form a snug, locking fit. A cementing compound can be applied to the threads before joining to improve the seal.

Flanged joints, shown in **Fig. 28.3**, are welded to the straight sections of pipe, which are then bolted together around the perimeter of the flanges. Flanged joints form strong rigid joints that can withstand high pressure and permit disassembly of the joints when needed. Three types of flange faces are shown in **Fig. 28.4** and in Appendix 44.

PIPE THREAD SYMBOLS

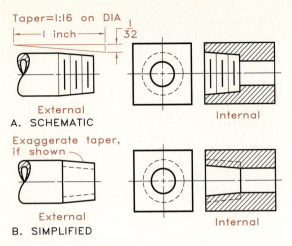

A. SCHEMATIC

External   Internal

B. SIMPLIFIED

External   Internal

Figure 28.2 A screwed pipe joint utilizes a pipe thread that binds tightly as they are screwed together.

FLANGED JOINTS

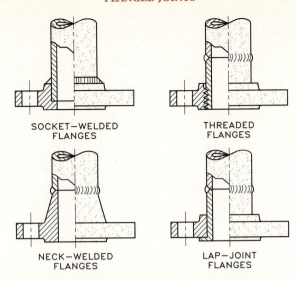

SOCKET—WELDED FLANGES   THREADED FLANGES

NECK—WELDED FLANGES   LAP—JOINT FLANGES

Figure 28.3 Types of flanged joints and the methods of attaching the flanges to the pipes are shown here.

TYPES OF FLANGE FACES

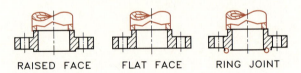

RAISED FACE   FLAT FACE   RING JOINT

Figure 28.4 Three types of flange faces are the raised face (RF), the flat face (FF), and the ring joint (RJ).

Welded joints are joined by welded seams around the perimeter of the pipe to form butt welds. Welded joints are used extensively in "big inch" pipelines that are used for transporting petroleum products cross-country.

Bell and spigot (B&S) joints are used to join cast-iron pipes (**Fig. 28.5**). The spigot is placed inside the bell, and the two are sealed with molten lead or a sealing ring that snaps into position to form a sealed joint.

Soldered and screwed joints are used to connect smaller pipes and tubes, especially nonferrous tubing. Screwed fittings are available to connect tubing as shown in **Fig. 28.6**.

28.7 Pipe Fittings

Pipe fittings are placed within a pipe system to join pipes at various angles, to transform the pipe diameter to a different size, or to control the flow and its direction within the system. Fittings are placed in the system using any of the previously covered joints. A pipe system can be drawn with **single-line** symbols or **double-line** symbols.

The fittings in **Fig. 28.7** are represented as singleline symbols with flanged, screwed, bell and spigot, weleded, and soldered joints. Most symbols have been shown as they would be drawn to appear in various orthographic views—top, front, and side views. These symbols have been extracted from ANSI Z32.2.3 standards.

544 • **CHAPTER 28 PIPE DRAFTING**

BELL & SPIGOT (B&S) JOINT

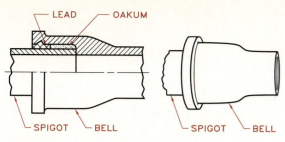

Figure 28.5 Bell and spigot (B&S) joints can be used to connect cast-iron pipes.

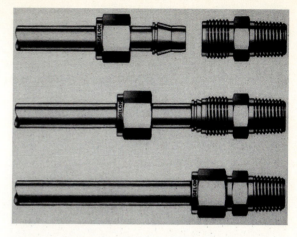

Figure 28.6 Screwed joints can be used to join small tubing. (Courtesy of Crawford Fitting Co.)

28.8 Screwed Fittings

A number of standard fittings with screwed fittings are shown in **Fig. 28.8** through **Fig. 28.11** as single-line and double-line symbols, by notes, and as isometric symbols for three-dimensional drawings as covered in Section 28.12. Double-line symbols are the more descriptive, since they are drawn to scale with double lines and appear most realistic. Single-line symbols are more symbolic since the pipe and fittings are drawn with single lines and schematic symbols.

Fittings are available in three weights—standard (STD), extra strong (XS), and double extra strong (XXS)—to match the standard weights of the pipes with which they will be connnected. Other weights of fittings are available, but these three weights are the most common.

A piping system of screwed fittings is shown in **Fig. 28.12** with double-line symbols in a single-line system to call attention to them. These fittings could just as well have been drawn using single-line symbols.

28.9 Flanged Fittings

Flanges are used to connect fittings into a piping system when heavy loads are supported in large pipes where pressures are great. Since flanges are expensive, other joining methods should be used where feasible. Flanges must be welded to straight pipe sections so they can be bolted together.

Examples of flanged fittings are drawn as double-line, single-line, and isometric symbols in **Figs. 28.13** and **28.14**. The elbow is commonly referred to as an "ell" and it is available in angles of turn of 90° and 45° in both short and long radii. The radius of a short-radius ell is equal to the diameter of the larger end. Long-radius (LR) ells have radii that are approximately 1.5 times the nominal diameter of the large end of the ell.

A table of dimensions for 125 lb and 250 lb cast-iron fittings is given in Appendixes 44 and 45. The dimensions of the fittings shown in both single- and double-line representations are extracted from actual sizes of these fittings when dimensions and sizes must be given.

28.10 Welded Fittings

Welding is used to join pipes and fittings for permanent, pressure-resistant joints. Examples of double-line, single-line, and isometric fittings con-

SINGLE-LINE FITTING SYMBOLS

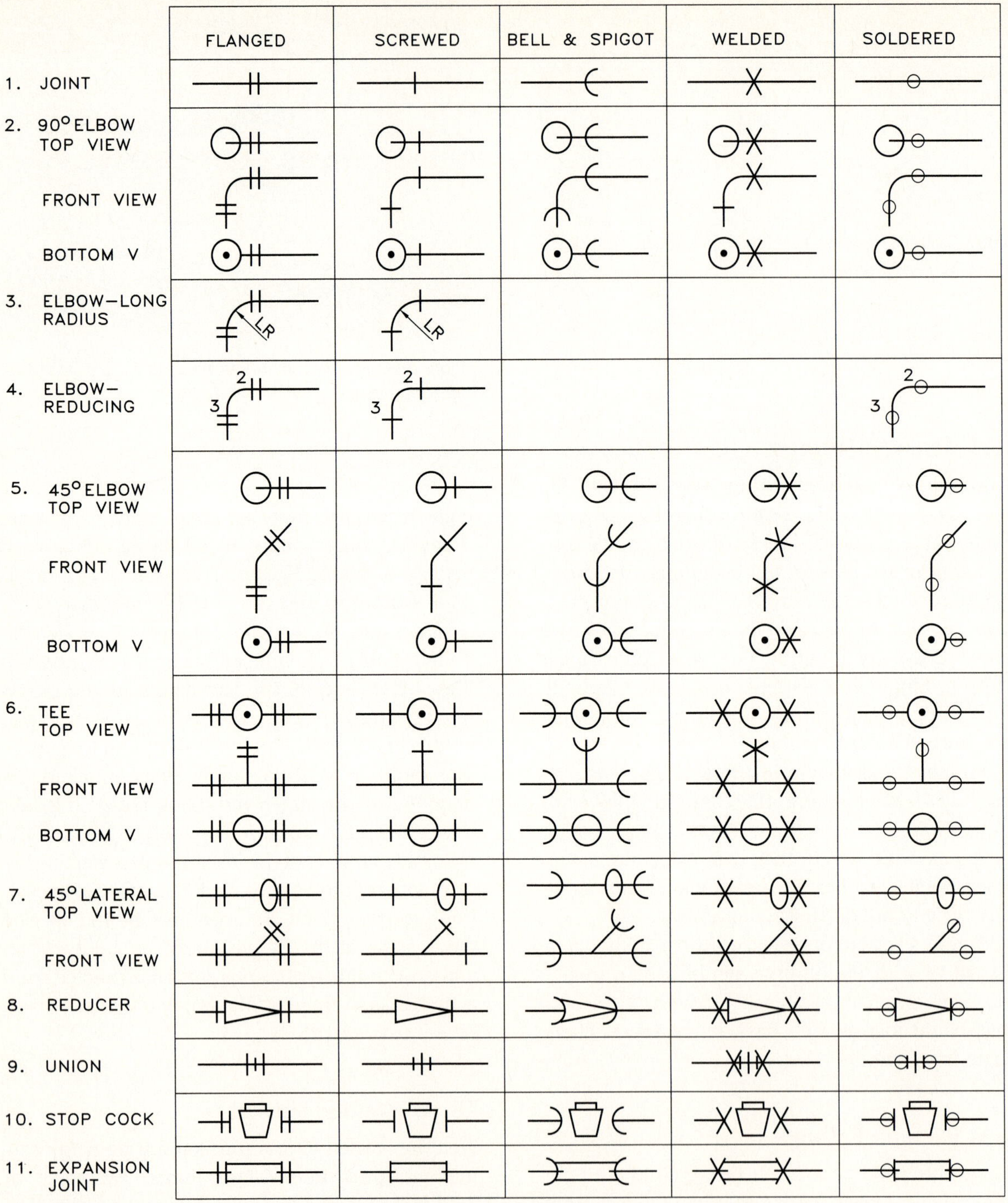

	FLANGED	SCREWED	BELL & SPIGOT	WELDED	SOLDERED
1. JOINT					
2. 90° ELBOW TOP VIEW					
FRONT VIEW					
BOTTOM V					
3. ELBOW—LONG RADIUS					
4. ELBOW—REDUCING					
5. 45° ELBOW TOP VIEW					
FRONT VIEW					
BOTTOM V					
6. TEE TOP VIEW					
FRONT VIEW					
BOTTOM V					
7. 45° LATERAL TOP VIEW					
FRONT VIEW					
8. REDUCER					
9. UNION					
10. STOP COCK					
11. EXPANSION JOINT					

Figure 28.7 These single-line pipe fitting symbols are extracted from the ANSI Z32.2.3 standards.

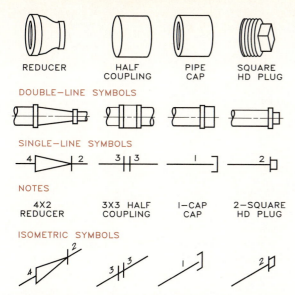

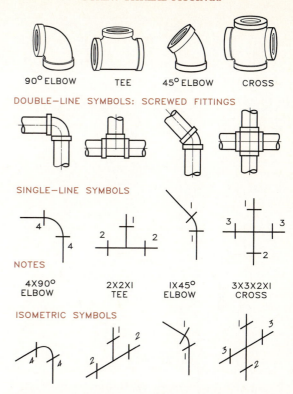

Figure 28.8 Examples of standard fittings for screwed connections are shown here. Nominal pipe sizes are indicated by numbers placed near the joints. When fittings are specified by note, the major flow direction is labeled first, with the branches labeled second. The large openings are noted to precede the smaller openings.

Figure 28.10 Further examples of standard fittings for screwed connections are shown here.

nected by welding are shown in **Figs. 28.15** and **28.16.** Fittings are available with beveled edges ready for welding.

The piping layout in **Fig. 28.17** illustrates a series of welded joints with a double-line drawing. The location of the welded joints has been dimensioned. Several flanged fittings have been welded into the system so the flanges to be used.

28.11 Valves

Valves are fittings used to regulate the flow within a pipeline or to turn off the flow completely. Valve types include **gate**, **globe**, **angle**, **check**, **safety**, **diaphragm**, **float**, and **relief** valves, to name a few. The three basic types—globe, gate, and check valves

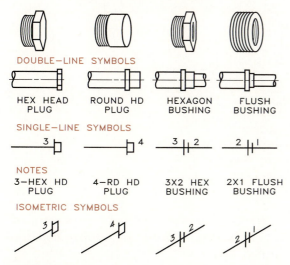

Figure 28.9 Examples of standard fittings for screwed connections are shown here.

SCREW-THREAD FITTINGS

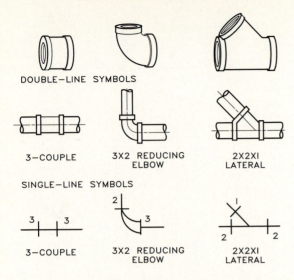

DOUBLE—LINE SYMBOLS

3—COUPLE   3X2 REDUCING ELBOW   2X2XI LATERAL

SINGLE—LINE SYMBOLS

3—COUPLE   3X2 REDUCING ELBOW   2X2XI LATERAL

Figure 28.11 Examples of standard fittings for screwed connections are shown here.

SINGLE-LINE PIPING SYSTEM

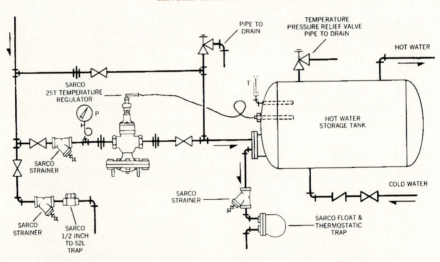

Figure 28.12 This is a single-line piping system with the major valves represented as double-line symbols. (Courtesy of Sarco, Inc.)

—are shown in **Fig. 28.18** using single-line and double-line symbols.

Gate valves are used to turn on or off the flow within a pipe and are not designed to regulate the degree of flow.

Globe valves are used not only to turn the flow on and off but also to regulate flow to a desired level.

Angle valves are types of globe valves that turn at 90° angles at bends in the piping system

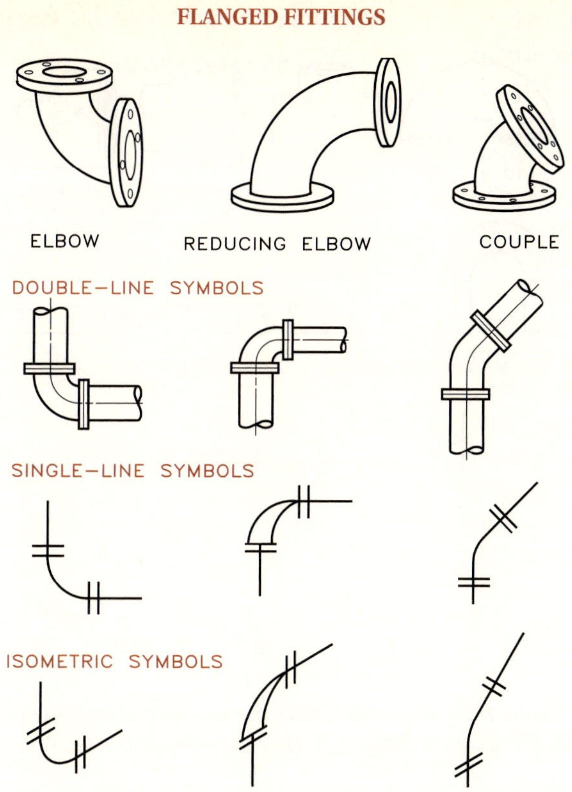

ELBOW   REDUCING ELBOW   COUPLE

DOUBLE—LINE SYMBOLS

SINGLE—LINE SYMBOLS

ISOMETRIC SYMBOLS

Figure 28.13 Examples of flanged fittings are shown here.

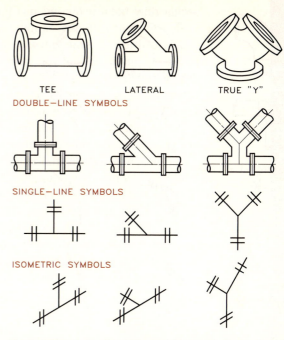

TEE   LATERAL   TRUE "Y"

DOUBLE—LINE SYMBOLS

SINGLE—LINE SYMBOLS

ISOMETRIC SYMBOLS

Figure 28.14 Examples of flanged fittings are shown here.

and have the same controlling features as the straight globe valves.

Check valves restrict the flow in the pipe to only one direction. A backward flow is prevented by either a movable piston or a swinging washer activated by a reverse in the flow. The single-line symbols for various types of valves are shown in **Fig. 28.19**.

28.12 Fittings in Orthographic Views

Fittings and valves must be shown from any view in orthographic projection. Two and three views of typical fittings are shown in **Fig. 28.7** and other figures as single-line screwed fittings. Observe the various views of the fittings and

notice how the direction of an elbow can be shown by a slight variation in the different views. The same general principles are used to represent joints as double-line drawings.

A piping system is shown in a single orthographic view in **Fig. 28.20,** where a combination of double-line and singleline symbols are drawn. Note that arrows are used to give the direction of flow in the system. Joints are screwed, welded, and flanged.

Horizontal elevation lines are given to dimension the heights of each horizontal pipe. Station 5 + 12 − 0-1/4" represents a distance of 500 feet plus 12' − 0-1/4", or 512' − 0-1/4" from the beginning station point of 0 + 00.

The dimensions in **Fig. 28.20** are measured from the centerlines of the pipes indicated by the **CL** symbols. In some cases, the elevations of the

ORTHOGRAPHIC AND ISOMETRIC DRAWINGS

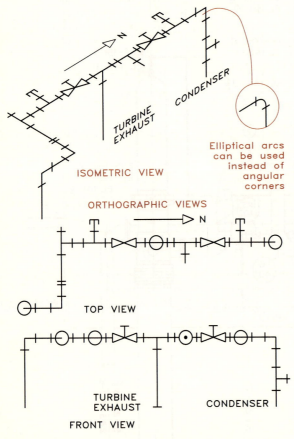

ISOMETRIC VIEW

Elliptical arcs can be used instead of angular corners

ORTHOGRAPHIC VIEWS

TOP VIEW

TURBINE EXHAUST   CONDENSER

FRONT VIEW

Figure 28.21 Top and front orthographic views are used as the basis for drawing a three-dimensional piping system using single-line symbols.

DEVELOPED PIPING DRAWING

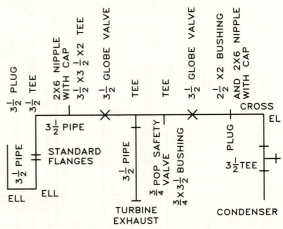

EXHAUST PIPING FOR A 25K STEAM TURBINE

Figure 28.22 The vertical pipes shown in Fig. 28.21 are revolved into the horizontal plane to form a developed drawing. The fittings and valves are noted on the sketch.

A DEVELOPED DRAWING

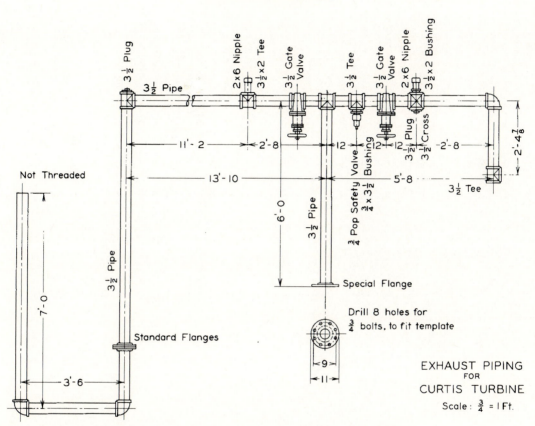

Figure 28.23 This finished developed drawing shows all of the components in the system true size with double-line symbols.

A SPOOL DRAWING

NO	QTY	DESCRIPTION	MATL
		PIPE	
1	1	8" X 18—2.5/8 SCH 40 SMLS STL OH	A–53
2	1	8" X 10—7.1/4" SCH 40 SMLS STL OH	A–53
3	1	8" X 1'—0 SCH 40 SMLS STL OH	A–53
4	1	8" X 0'—6.7/8 SCH 40 SMLS STL OH	A–53
5	1	8" X 0'—7 SCH SMLS STL OH	A–53
6	1	8" X 2'—6 SCH 40 SMLS STL OH	A–53
7	1	8" X 2'—1.1/2 SCH 40 SMLS STL OH	A–53
8	1	6" X 7'—5.7/8 SCH 40 SMLS STL OH	A–53
9	2	6" X 1'—1.7/8 SCH 40 SMLS STL OH	A–53
10	1	6" X 5'—2.1/8 SCH 40 SMLS STL OH	A–53
		FITTINGS	
11	3	8"—90 DEG LR ELL STD WT BW SMLS	A–53
12	1	8"—90 DEG LR ELL, LONG TANGENT	A–53
13	1	6"—90 DEG SR ELL STD BW SMLS	A–53
14	1	8" X 6" CONCENTRIC RED STD BW SMLS	A–53
15	1	8" X 6" RED ELL STD BW SMLS	A–53
16	2	8"—45 DEG LR ELL STD BW SMLS	A–53
		FLANGES	
17	5	8"—150 LBS RF FS WN	A–181
18	2	6"—150 LBS RF FS WN	A–181
19	2	6"—300 LBS RF FS WN	A–181
		VALVES	
20	2	8"—150 LBS CS FLG RF	47X
21	1	6"—150 LBS CS FLG RF GLOBE	143X
		OTHER	
22	48	3/4 DIA ASTM ALLOY STL STUD BOLTS	A–193
23	48	ASTM HVY HEX NUT, EACH BOLT	A–194
24	24	3/4 DIA ASTM ALLOY STL STUD BOLTS	A–193
25	24	ASTM HVY HEX NUT, EACH BOLT	A–194
26	1	FLUID RECORDER CONTROLLER	
27	1	8" SPEC BLIND	
28	5	8"—150 LBS SPIRAL WOUND 1/8" THK GASKET	304SS
29	4	6"—150 LBS SPIRAL WOUND 1/8" THK GASKET	304SS

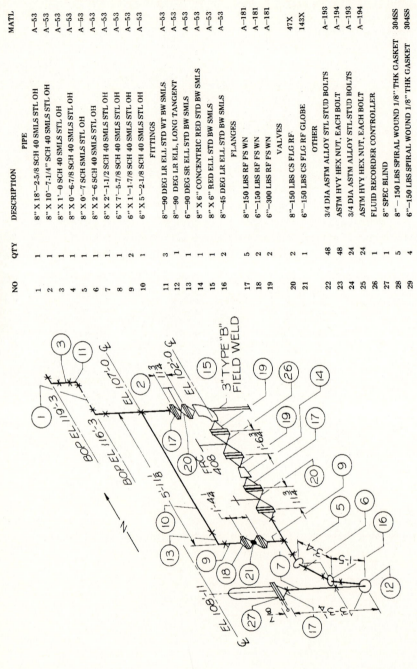

Figure 28.24 This dimensioned isometric pictorial is called a "spool drawing." It is sufficiently dimensioned and noted so that it can serve as a working drawing when used with the bill of materials.

Table 28.2

Standard Abbreviations Associated with Pipe Specifications

Abbr.	Definition	Abbr.	Definition	Abbr.	Definition
AVG	average	FS	forged steel	SPEC	specification
BC	bolt circle	FSS	forged stainless steel	SR	short radius
BE	beveled ends	FW	field weld	SS	stainless steel
BF	blind flange	GALV	galvanized	STD	standard
BM	bill of materials	GR	grade	STL	steel
BOP	bottom of pipe	ID	inside diameter	STM	steam
B&S	bell & spigot	INS	insulate	SW	socket weld
BWG	Birmingham wire gauge	IPS	iron pipe size	SWP	standard working pressure
CAS	cast alloy steel	LR	long radius	TC	test connection
CI	cast iron	LW	lap weld	TE	threaded ended
CO	clean out	MI	malleable iron	TEMP	temperature
CONC	concentric	MFG	manufacture	T&G	tongue & groove
CPLG	coupling	OD	outside diameter	TOS	top of steel
CS	carbon steel, cast steel	OH	open hearth	TYP	typical
DWG	drawing	PE	plain end—not beveled	VC	vitrified clay
ECC	eccentric	PR	pair	WE	weld end
EF	electric furnace	RED	reducer	WN	weld neck
EFW	electric fusion weld	RF	raised face	WB	welded bonnet
ELEV	elevation	RTG or RJ	ring type joint	WT	weight
EFW	electric resistance weld	SCH	schedule	XS	extra strong
FF	flat face	SCRD	screwed	XSS	double extra strong
FLG	flange	SMLS	seamless		
FOB	flat on bottom	SO	slip-on		

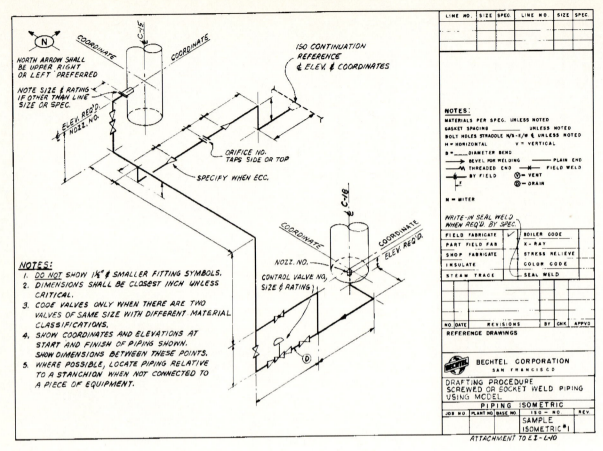

Figure 28.25 A suggested format for preparing spool drawings by the Bechtel Corp. is shown here. (Courtesy of the Bechtel Corp.)

Problems

1. On size A sheets (two fittings per sheet), draw five orthographic views of the fittings listed below. The views should include the front, top, bottom, left, and right views. Refer to **Fig. 28.7** through **Fig. 28.19** as guides in making these drawings. Using single-line symbols and a scale that makes full use of the space available, draw the following fittings with screwed joints: 90° ell, 45° ell, tee, lateral, cap-reducing ell, cross, concen-tric reducer, check valve, union, globe valve, gate valve, and bushing.

2. Repeat Problem 1, but draw the fittings as flanged fittings.

3. Repeat Problem 1, but draw the fittings as welded fittings.

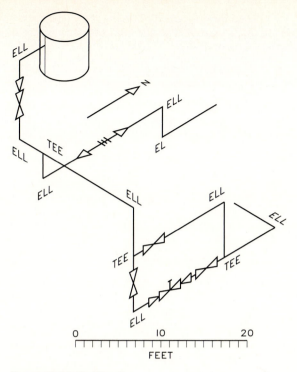

Figure 28.26 Problem 7.

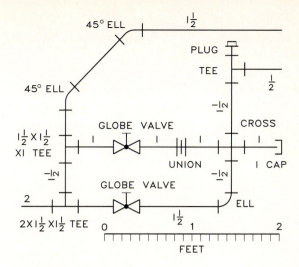

Figure 28.27 Problem 8.

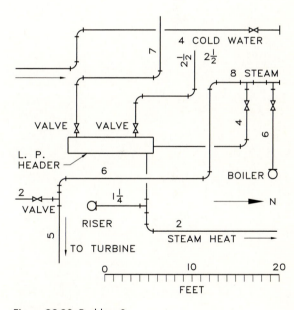

Figure 28.28 Problem 9.

4. Repeat Problem 1, but draw the fittings as double-line screwed fittings.

5. Repeat Problem 1, but draw the fittings as double-line flanged fittings.

6. Repeat Problem 1, but draw the fittings as double-line welded fittings.

7. Convert the single-line drawing in **Fig. 28.26** into a double-line pipe system that is scaled to fit on a size A sheet.

8. Convert the single-line pipe system in **Fig. 28.27** into a double-line drawing that will fit on a size A sheet, using the graphical scale.

9. Convert the single-line pipe system in **Fig. 28.28** into a double-line drawing that will fit on a size A sheet, using the graphical scale.

10. Repeat Problem 8, but draw with single-line symbols.

11. Convert the pipe system shown in isometric in **Fig. 28.26** into a double-line isometric drawing scaled to fit on a size B sheet.

12. Convert the pipe system given in **Fig. 28.21** into a two-view orthographic drawing using double-line symbols scaled to fit on a size A sheet.

13. Convert the isometric drawing of the pipe system in **Fig. 28.25** into a two-view orthographic drawing using single-line symbols scaled to fit on a size B sheet.

14. Convert the orthographic drawing of the pipe system in **Fig. 28.21** into a double-line isometric drawing scaled to fit on a size B sheet.

15. Convert the orthographic pipe system in **Fig. 28.12** into a single-line isometric drawing scaled to fit on a size B sheet. Estimate the dimensions.

16. Convert the orthographic pipe system in **Fig. 28.12** into a double-line orthographic view scaled to fit on a size B sheet.

29

Electric/Electronics Graphics

29.1 Introduction

Electric/electronics graphics is a specialty area of the field of technology. Electrical graphics is related to the transmission of electric power that is used in large quantities in homes and industry for lighting, heating, and equipment operation. **Electronics** graphics deals with circuits in which electronic components and transistors are employed to use power in much smaller quantities than in electrical applications. Examples of electronic equipment include radios, televisions, computers, and similar products.

Electronics drafters work from sketches and specifications developed by the engineer or electronics technologist. They prepare drawings for fabricating the circuit and bringing the product into being. This chapter will review the drafting practices necessary for the preparation of electronic diagrams.

A major portion of this chapter has been adapted from *ANSI Y14.15, Electrical and Electronics Diagrams,* the standards that regulate the graphics techniques used in this area. The

symbols used were adapted from *ANSI Y32.2, Graphic Symbols for Electrical and Electronics Diagrams.*

29.2 Types of Diagrams

Electronic circuits are classified and drawn in the format of one of the following types of diagrams:

1. Single-line diagrams,
2. Schematic diagrams, or
3. Connection diagrams.

The suggested line weights for drawing these types of diagrams are shown in **Fig. 29.1.**

Single-Line Diagrams
Single-line diagrams are drawn with single lines and symbols to show an electric circuit, or a system of circuits, and the parts and devices within it. A single line is used to represent both AC and DC systems as illustrated in **Fig. 29.2**. An example of a single-line diagram of an audio system is shown

RECOMMENDED LINE WEIGHTS

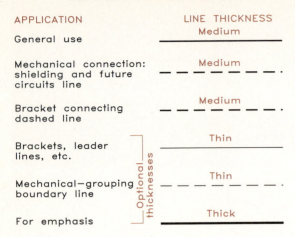

Figure 29.1 The recommended line weights for drawing electronics diagrams are shown here.

APPLICATION OF LINE WEIGHTS

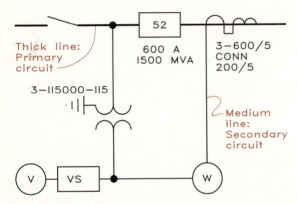

Figure 29.2 A portion of a single-line diagram illustrates the use of heavy lines to represent the primary circuits and medium lines to represent connections to the current and potential sources. (Courtesy of ANSI.)

in **Fig. 29.3**. Primary circuits are indicated by thick connecting lines, and medium lines are used to represent connections to the current and potential sources.

SINGLE-LINE DIAGRAM

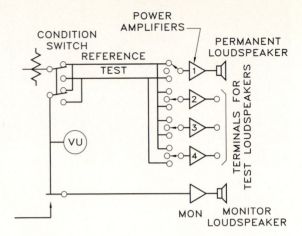

Figure 29.3 A typical single-line diagram for illustrating electronics and communications circuits is shown here.

Single-line diagrams show the connections of meters, major equipment, and instruments. In addition, ratings are often given to supplement the graphic symbols and provide such information as kilowatts, voltages, cycles and revolutions per minute, and generator ratings (**Fig. 29.4**).

Schematic Diagrams
Schematic diagrams use graphic symbols to show the electrical connections and functions of a specific circuit arrangement. A schematic diagram enables one to trace the circuit and its functions, but it does not show physical sizes, shapes, and locations of various components. The schematic diagram illustrated in **Fig. 29.5** can be referred to for many applications of the principles covered in this chapter.

Connection Diagrams
Connection diagrams show the connections and installations of the parts and devices of the system. In addition to showing the internal connections, external connections, or both, these

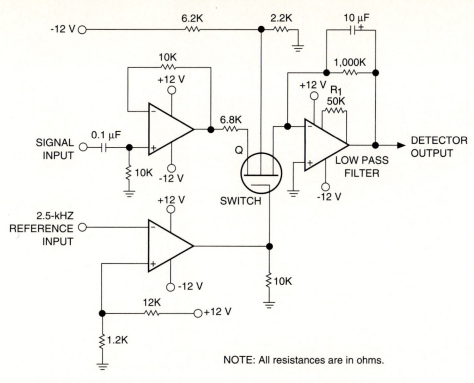

NOTE: All resistances are in ohms.

Figure 29.4 This single-line diagram illustrates a switching circuit complete with the notation of device designations. (Courtesy of NASA.)

diagrams show the physical arrangement of the parts. Connection diagrams can be described as installation diagrams such as the one shown in **Fig. 29.6**.

29.3 Schematic Diagram Connecting Symbols

The most basic symbols of a circuit are those used to represent connections of parts within the circuit. Connections, or junctions, are indicated by using either the "no dot" method (**Figure. 29.7A**) or small black dots as shown in **Fig. 29.7B**. The dots distinguish between connecting lines and those that simply pass over each other (**Fig. 29.7B**).

The use of dots to show connections is optional; it is preferable to omit them if clarity is not sacrificed. Also, it is preferred that connecting wires have single junctions wherever possible.

When the layout of a circuit does not permit the use of single junctions, and lines within the circuit must cross, then dots must be used to distinguish between crossing and connecting lines (**Figs. 29.7C** and **D**).

Interrupted paths are breaks in lines within a schematic diagram that are interrupted to conserve space when this can be done without confusion. For example, the circuit in **Fig. 29.8** has been interrupted, since the lines do not connect the left and the right sides of the circuit. Instead, the ends

A PARTIAL SCHEMATIC DIAGRAM

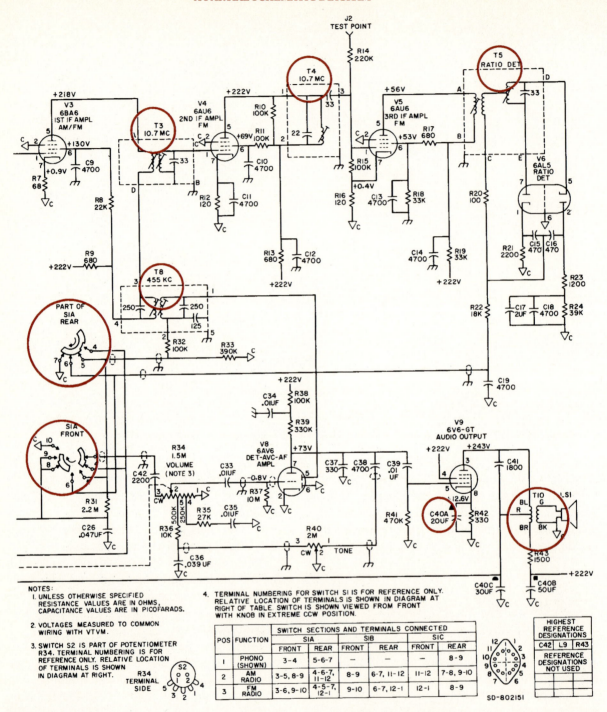

Figure 29.5 A portion of a typical schematic diagram of an AM/FM radio circuit with all parts of the system labeled is shown here. The title of a drawing of this type should specify that it is a schematic diagram and the type of circuit being presented. (Courtesy of ANSI.)

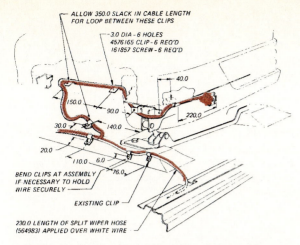

ALLOW 350.0 SLACK IN CABLE LENGTH
FOR LOOP BETWEEN THESE CLIPS

3.0 DIA - 6 HOLES
4576165 CLIP - 6 REQ'D
161857 SCREW - 6 REQ'D

40.0

150.0
90.0
220.0
30.0
140.0

20.0

110.0 6.0

BEND CLIPS AT ASSEMBLY
IF NECESSARY TO HOLD
WIRE SECURELY

76.0

EXISTING CLIP

230.0 LENGTH OF SPLIT WIPER HOSE
(564983) APPLIED OVER WHITE WIRE

Figure 29.6 This is a three-dimensional connection diagram that shows the circuit and its components with the necessary dimensions to explain how it is connected or installed. (Courtesy of the General Motors Corp.)

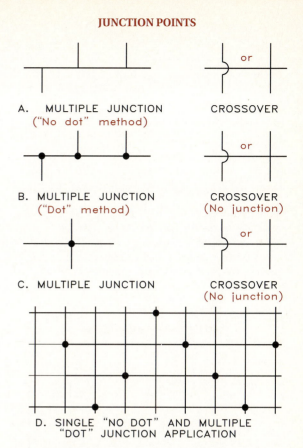

A. MULTIPLE JUNCTION ("No dot" method) CROSSOVER

B. MULTIPLE JUNCTION ("Dot" method) CROSSOVER (No junction)

C. MULTIPLE JUNCTION CROSSOVER (No junction)

D. SINGLE "NO DOT" AND MULTIPLE "DOT" JUNCTION APPLICATION

Figure 29.7 Connections should be shown with single-point junctions as shown at (A). Dots may be used to call attention to connections as shown at (B); and dots must be used when there are multiples of the type shown at (C).

of the lines are labeled to correspond to the matching notes at the other side of the interrupted circuit.

Occasionally, sets of lines in a horizontal or vertical direction will be interrupted (**Fig. 29.9**). Brackets will be used to interrupt the circuit and notes will be placed outside the brackets to indicate the destinations of the wires or their connections.

In some cases, a dashed line is used to connect brackets that interrupt circuits (**Fig. 29.10**). The dashed line should be drawn so that it will not be mistaken as a continuation of one of the lines within the bracket.

Mechanical linkages that are closely related to electronic functions may be shown as part of a schematic diagram (**Fig. 29.11**). An arrangement of this type helps clarify the relationship of the electronics circuit with the mechanical components.

29.4 Graphic Symbols

The electronics drafter must be familiar with the basic graphic symbols that are used to represent the parts and devices within electrical and electronics circuits. The symbols covered in this section (extracted from the *ANSI Y32.2* standard) are adequate for practically all diagrams. However, when a highly specialized part needs to be shown and a symbol for it is not provided in these standards, it is permissible for the drafter to develop his or her own symbol provided it is labeled and its meaning clearly conveyed.

INTERRUPTED CIRCUITS

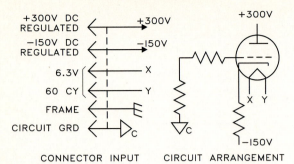

Figure 29.8 Circuits may be interrupted and connections not shown by lines if they are properly labeled to clarify their relationship to the removed portion of the circuit. The connections above are labeled to match those on the left and right sides of the illustration. (Courtesy of ANSI.)

THE USE OF BRACKETS

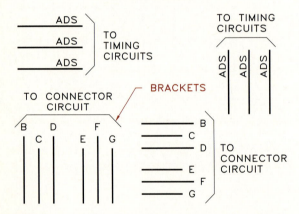

Figure 29.9 Brackets and notes may be used to specify the destinations of interrupted circuits, as shown in this illustration.

The symbols given in **Figs. 29.12–29.16** are drawn on a grid of 3-mm (0.13-in.) squares that have been reduced. The size of these square grids is equal to the letter height used on the drawing. It is general practice to size graphic symbols based on letter height, since text and numerals cannot be enlarged or reduced as easily as symbols with-

CONNECTIONS: INTERRUPTED CIRCUITS

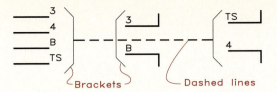

Figure 29.10 The connections of interrupted circuits can be indicated by using brackets and a dashed line in addition to labeling the lines. The dashed line should not be drawn to appear as an extension of one of the lines in the circuit.

MECHANICAL COMPONENTS

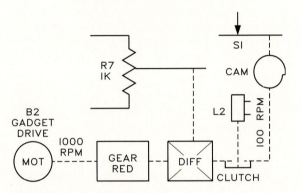

Figure 29.11 If mechanical functions are closely related to electrical functions, it may be desirable to link the mechanical components within the schematic diagram.

out affecting readability. Symbols may be drawn larger or smaller to fit the size of your layout provided the relative proportions of the symbols are kept about the same.

The symbols in **Figs. 29.12–29.16** are but a few of the more commonly used symbols. There are more than five hundred different symbols in the ANSI standards for variations of the basic electrical/electronics symbols.

Electronics symbols can be drawn with conventional drawing instruments by approximating

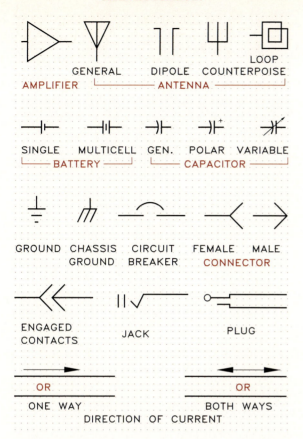

Figure 29.12 These graphic symbols within a schematic diagram are drawn on a 3-mm (0.125-in.) grid, which is the letter height used to label them. The suggested sizes of the symbols can be found by taking the dimensions from the grid to draw the symbols full size.

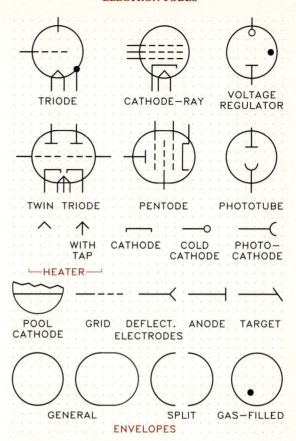

Figure 29.13 The upper six symbols are used to represent types of electron tubes. The interpretation of the parts that make up each symbol is given in the lower half of the figure.

the proportions of the symbols, and drafting templates of electronics symbols are available for hand-drawn drawings. Computer software is also available with predrawn symbols for drawing electronic circuits.

Most symbols can be noted to provide designations of their sizes or ratings when shown in a circuit diagram. The need for this additional infor-

mation depends on the requirements and the usage of the schematic diagrams.

The preparation of a schematic diagram begins with the drawing of a freehand sketch to show the circuit and the placement of its components (**Fig. 29.17A**). Sketching can be aided by using a printed grid to serve as guidelines. When the sketch is completed, an instrument drawing can be made by hand or by computer to show the components at a proper scale and reference designations added (**Fig. 29.17B**).

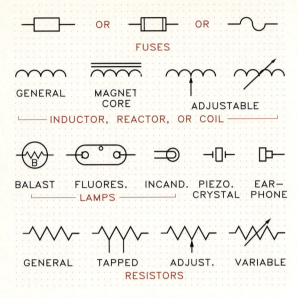

Figure 29.14 Graphics symbols of standard circuit components are drawn on a 3-mm grid.

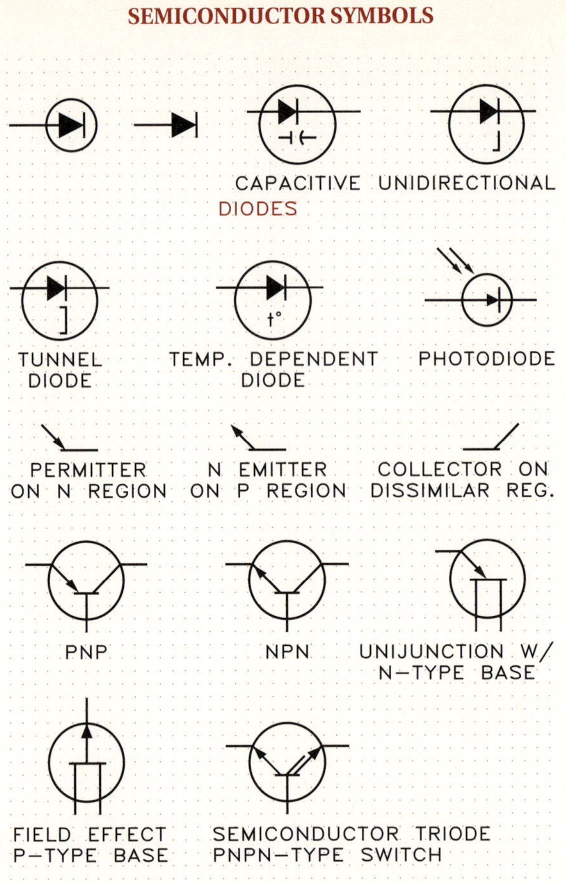

Figure 29.15 Graphics symbols for semiconductor devices and transistors are shown drawn on a 3-mm grid. The arrows in the middle of the figure illustrate the meanings of the arrows used in the transistor symbols shown below them.

29.5 Terminals

Terminals are the ends of devices that are attached in a circuit with connecting wires. Examples of devices with terminals that are specified in circuit diagrams are **switches**, **relays**, and **transformers**. The graphic symbol for a terminal is an open circle that is the same size as the solid circle used to indicate a connection.

Switches are used to turn a circuit on or off or to actuate a certain part of it while turning another part off. Examples of labeling switches are shown in **Fig. 29.5** where a table of notes is used to clarify the switching connections of the terminals.

When a group of parts is enclosed or shielded (drawn enclosed with dashed lines) and the terminal circles have been omitted, the terminal markings should be placed immediately outside the enclosure, as shown in **Fig. 29.5** at T3, T4, T5, and T8. The terminal identifications should be added to the graphic symbols that correspond to the actual physical markings that appear on or near the terminals of the part, such as 10.7 MC for transformer T3 in **Fig. 29.5.** Several examples of notes and symbols that explain the parts of a diagram are shown in **Figs. 29.18, 29.19,** and **29.20.**

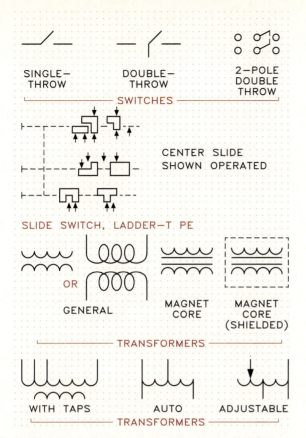

Figure 29.16 Graphics symbols for representing switches and transformers are drawn on a 3-mm grid.

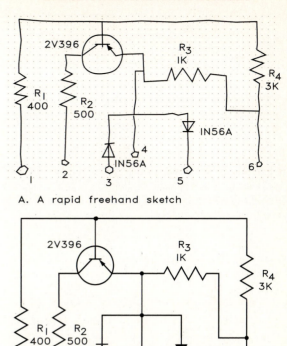

A. A rapid freehand sketch

B. An instrument drawing

Figure 29.17

A The circuit designer can make a freehand sketch of a circuit as a preliminary drawing.

B A final drawing is made using the proper symbols and line thicknesses.

Colored wires or symbols are often used to identify the various leads that connect to terminals. When colored wires need to be identified on a diagram, the colors are lettered on the drawing with abbreviations of colors, as was done for transformer T10 of **Fig. 29.5.** An example of the identification of a capacitor, C40A, that is labeled with geometric symbols is shown in **Fig. 29.5.**

Rotary terminals are used to regulate resistance in some circuits, and the direction of rota-

tion of the dial is indicated on the schematic diagram. The abbreviations CW (clockwise) or CCW (counterclockwise) are placed adjacent to the movable contact when it is in its extreme clockwise position, as shown in **Fig. 29.21A.** The movable contact has an arrow at its end.

If the device terminals are not marked, numbers may be used with the resistor symbol and the

METHOD OF LABELING TERMINALS

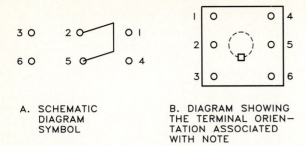

A. SCHEMATIC DIAGRAM SYMBOL

B. DIAGRAM SHOWING THE TERMINAL ORIENTATION ASSOCIATED WITH NOTE

Figure 29.18 A method of labeling the terminals of a toggle switch on a schematic diagram (left) and a diagram that illustrates the toggle switch when it is viewed from its rear (right) are shown here.

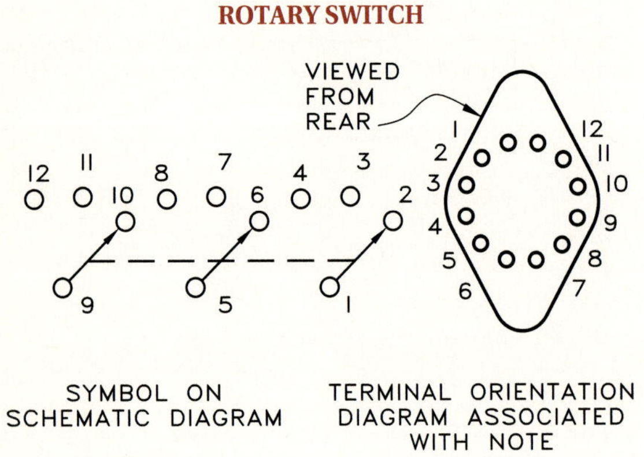

ROTARY SWITCH

SYMBOL ON SCHEMATIC DIAGRAM

TERMINAL ORIENTATION DIAGRAM ASSOCIATED WITH NOTE

Figure 29.19 A rotary switch as it would appear on a schematic diagram (left) and a diagram that shows the numbered terminals of the switch when viewed from its rear are shown here.

LEVER SWITCH PICTORIAL

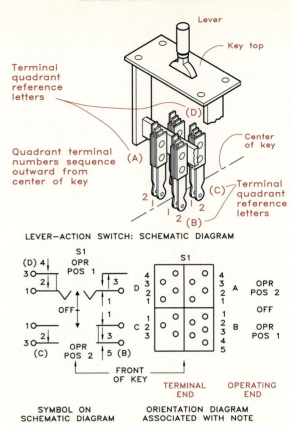

LEVER–ACTION SWITCH: SCHEMATIC DIAGRAM

SYMBOL ON SCHEMATIC DIAGRAM

ORIENTATION DIAGRAM ASSOCIATED WITH NOTE

Figure 29.20 An example of a typical lever switch as it would appear on a schematic diagram (left, Part A) and an orientation diagram that shows the numbered terminals of the switch when viewed from its operating end (right, Part A) are shown here. A pictorial of the lever switch and its four quadrants are given in Part B.

number 2 assigned to the adjustable contact (**Fig. 29.21B**). Other fixed taps may be sequentially numbered and added as shown in **Figure 29.21C**.

The position of a switch as it relates to the function of a circuit should be indicated on a schematic diagram. A method of showing functions of a variable switch is shown in **Fig. 29.22**. The arrow represents the movable end of the

switch that can be positioned to connect with several circuits. The different functional positions of the rotary switch are shown both by symbol and by table.

Another method of representing a rotary switch is shown in **Fig. 29.23** by symbol and by table. The tabular form is preferred due to the complexity of this particular switch. The dashes

ROTATION OF ROTARY SWITCHES

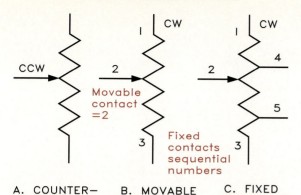

A. COUNTER-CLOCKWISE   B. MOVABLE CONTACT   C. FIXED CONTACTS

Figure 29.21 To indicate the direction of rotation of rotary switches, the abbreviations CW (clockwise) and CCW (counterclockwise) are placed near the movable contact (A). Numbers may be used to label resistor symbols and the number 2 assigned to the adjustable contact (B). Additional contacts may be labeled as shown at **C**.

COMPLEX SWITCHES

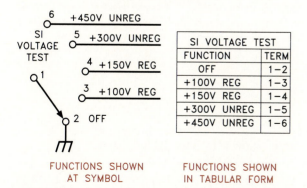

SI VOLTAGE TEST	
FUNCTION	TERM
OFF	1–2
+100V REG	1–3
+150V REG	1–4
+300V UNREG	1–5
+450V UNREG	1–6

FUNCTIONS SHOWN AT SYMBOL   FUNCTIONS SHOWN IN TABULAR FORM

Figure 29.22 For more complex switches, position-to-position function relations may be shown using symbols on the schematic diagram or by a table of values located elsewhere on the diagram. (Courtesy of ANSI.)

ROTARY SWITCH: BY SYMBOL AND TABLE

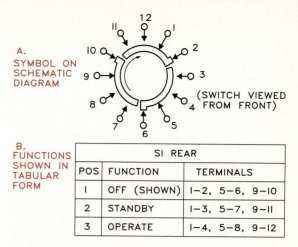

A. SYMBOL ON SCHEMATIC DIAGRAM

(SWITCH VIEWED FROM FRONT)

B. FUNCTIONS SHOWN IN TABULAR FORM

SI REAR		
POS	FUNCTION	TERMINALS
1	OFF (SHOWN)	1–2, 5–6, 9–10
2	STANDBY	1–3, 5–7, 9–11
3	OPERATE	1–4, 5–8, 9–12

Figure 29.23 A rotary switch may be shown on a schematic diagram with its terminals labeled graphically or its functions may be given in a table placed elsewhere on the drawing. Dashes between the numbers indicate linkage of the numbered terminals. For example, 1–2 means that terminals 1 and 2 are connected in the "off" position. (Courtesy of ANSI.)

between the numbers in the table indicate that the numbers have been connected. For example, when the switch is in position 2, the following terminals are connected: 1 and 3, 5 and 7, and 9 and 11. A table of this type is used at the bottom of **Fig. 29.5**.

Electron tubes have pins that fit into sockets that have terminals connecting into circuits. Pins are labeled with numbers placed outside the symbol used to represent the tube, as shown in **Fig. 29.24**, and are numbered in a clockwise direction with the tube viewed from its bottom.

29.6 Separation of Parts

In complex circuits, it is often advantageous to separate elements of a multielement part with portions of the graphic symbols drawn in different locations on the drawing. An example of this

PLACEMENT OF TUBE NUMBERS

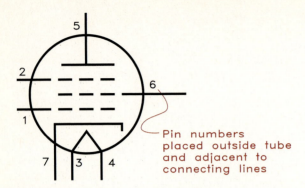

Figure 29.24 Tube pin numbers should be placed outside the tube envelope and adjacent to the connecting lines. (Courtesy of ANSI.)

A SUBDIVISION OF A CIRCUIT

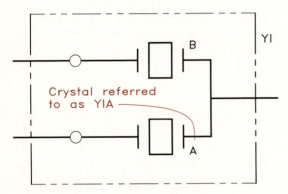

Figure 29.25 As subdivisions within the complete part, Crystals A and B are referred to as Y1A and Y1B.

ROTARY SWITCHES

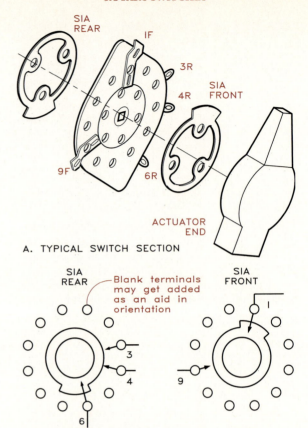

Figure 29.26 Parts of rotary switches are designated with suffix letters A, B, C, . . . and are referred to as S1A, S1B, S1C, ... The words FRONT and REAR are added to these designations when both sides of the switch are used.

method of separation is the switch labeled S1A FRONT and S1A REAR in Fig. 29.5. The switch is labeled S1 and the letters that follow, called suffixes, are used to designate different parts of the same switch. Suffix letters may also be used to label subdivisions of an enclosed unit that is made up of a series of internal parts, such as the crystal unit shown in **Fig. 29.25**. These crystals are referred to as Y1A and Y1B.

Rotary switches of the type shown in **Fig. 29.26** are designated as S1A, S1B, and so on. The suffix letters A, B, C, … are labeled in sequence beginning with the knob and working away from it. Each end of the various sections of the switch

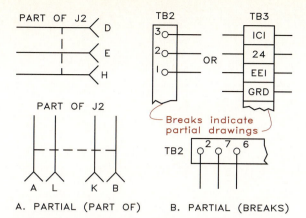

A. PARTIAL (PART OF)   B. PARTIAL (BREAKS)

Figure 29.27 If portions of connectors or terminal boards are functionally separated on a diagram, the words PART OF may precede the reference designation of that portion. Or conventional breaks can be used to indicate graphically that the part drawn is only a portion of the whole.

HIGHEST REFERENCE DESIGNATIONS	
R72	C40
REFERENCE DESIGNATIONS NOT USED	
R8, R10, R61	C12, C15, C17
R64, R70	C20, C22

Figure 29.28 Reference designations are used to identify parts of a circuit labeled numerically from left to right beginning at the upper left of the diagram. If parts are later deleted from the system, they should be listed in a table along with the highest reference number designations.

should be viewed from the same end. When both rear and front of the switches are used, the words FRONT and REAR are added to the designations.

Portions of items such as terminal boards, connectors, or rotary switches may be separated on a diagram. The words **PART OF** may precede the identification of the portion of the circuit of which it is a part, as shown in **Fig. 29.27**. A second method of showing a part of a system is to use conventional break lines, making the note **PART OF** unnecessary.

29.7 Reference Designations

A combination of letters and numbers that identify items on a schematic diagram are called **reference designations**. These designations are used to identify the components not only on the drawing, but in related documents that refer to them. Reference designations should be placed close to the symbols that represent the replaceable items of a circuit on a drawing. Items that are not separately

replaceable may be identified if it is considered necessary. Mounting devices for electron tubes, lamps, fuses, and the like are seldom identified on schematic diagrams.

It is standard practice to begin each reference designation with an uppercase letter that may be followed by a numeral with no hyphen between them. The number usually represents a portion of the part being represented. The lowest number of a designation should be assigned to begin at the upper left of the schematic diagram and proceed consecutively from left to right and top to bottom throughout the drawing.

Some of the standard abbreviations used to designate parts of an assembly are: amplifier—A, battery—BT, capacitor—C, connector—J, piezoelectric crystal—Y, fuse—F, electron tube—V, generator—G, rectifier—CR, resistor—R, transformer—T, and transistor—Q.

As the circuit is being designed, some of the numbered elements may be deleted from the circuit drawing. The numbered elements that remain should not be renumbered even though there is a missing element within the sequence of numbers used to label the parts. Instead, a table of the type shown in **Fig. 29.28** can be used to list the parts that have been omitted from the circuit. The

REFERENCE DESIGNATIONS

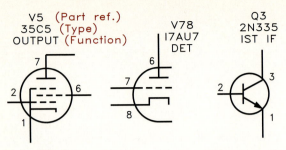

A. ELECTRON TUBES   B. TRANSISTOR

Figure 29.29 Three lines of notes can be used with electron tubes and transistors to specify reference designations, type designation, and function. This information should be located adjacent to the symbol, and preferably above it.

highest designations are also given in the table to ensure that all parts were considered.

Electron tubes and transistors are labeled not only with reference designations but with type designation and circuit function, as shown in **Fig. 29.29**. This information is labeled in three lines, such as V5/35C5/OUTPUT, which are located adjacent to the symbol.

29.8 Numerical Units of Function

Functional units such as the values of resistance, capacitance, inductance, and voltage should be specified with the fewest number of zeros by using the multipliers in **Fig. 29.30A** as prefixes. Examples using this method of expression are shown of **Figs. 29.30B** and **C**, where units of resistance and capacitance are given. Commas should be omitted when four-digit numbers are given (write one thousand as 1000, not as 1,000). You should recognize and use the lowercase or uppercase prefixes as indicated in **Fig. 29.30**.

A general note can be used where certain units are repeated on a drawing to reduce time and effort:

NUMERICAL MULTIPLIERS

A. MULTIPLIERS

MULTIPLIER	PREFIX	SYMBOL METHOD 1	METHOD 2
10^{12}	TERA	T	T
10^9	GIGA	G	G
10^6 (1,000,000)	MEGA	M	M
10^3 (1000)	KILO	k	K
10^{-3} (0.001)	MILLI	m	MILLI
10^{-6} (0.000,001)	MICRO	μ	U
10^{-9}	NANO	n	N
10^{-12}	PICO	p	P
10^{-13}	FEMTO	f	F
10^{-16}	ATTO	a	A

B. RESISTANCE

RANGE IN OHMS	EXPRESS AS	EXAMPLE
LESS THAN 1000	OHMS	0.031 470
1000 TO 99,999	OHMS OR KILOHMS	1800 15,853 10k
100,000 to 999,999	KILOHMS OR MEGOHMS	220k 0.22M
1,000,000 OR MORE	MEGOHMS	3.3M

C. CAPACITANCE

RANGE IN PICOFARADS	EXPRESS AS	EXAMPLE
LESS THAN 10,000	PICOFARADS	152.4pF 4700pF
10,000 OR MORE	MICROFARADS	0.015μF 30μF

Figure 29.30 A: Multipliers should be used to reduce the number of zeros in a number. Examples of expressing units of capacitance and resistance are shown at **B** and **C**.

UNLESS OTHERWISE SPECIFIED: RESISTANCE VALUES ARE IN OHMS. CAPACITANCE VALUES ARE IN MICROFARADS.

Or

CAPACITANCE VALUES ARE IN PICOFARADS.

METHODS OF LABELING RESISTANCE

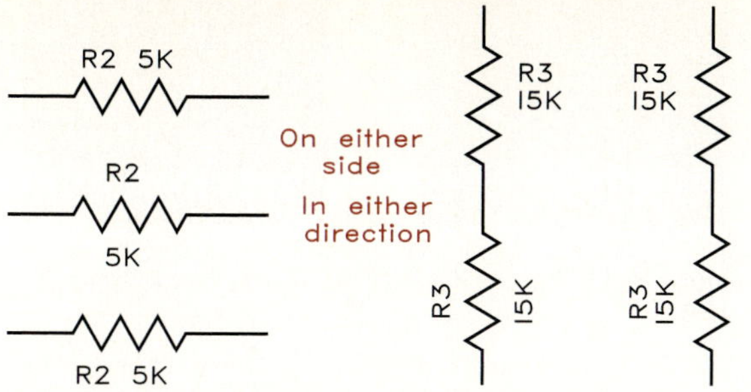

Figure 29.31 The units of resistance can be indicated on a schematic diagram by any of these arrangements.

A note for specifying capacitance values would be:

CAPACITANCE VALUES SHOWN AS NUMBERS EQUAL TO OR GREATER THAN UNITS ARE IN pF AND NUMBERS LESS THAN UNITY ARE IN μF.

Examples of the placement of the reference designations and the numerical values of resistors are shown in **Fig. 29.31**.

29.9 Functional Identification of Parts

The readability of a circuit is improved if parts are labeled to indicate their functions. Test points are labeled on drawings with the letters "TP" and their suffix numbers, such as TP1, TP2, and so forth. The sequence of the suffix numbers should be the same as the sequence of troubleshooting the circuit when it is defective. As an alternative, the test function can be indicated on the schematic diagram below the reference designation.

Additional information may be included on a schematic diagram to aid in the maintenance of the system:

DC resistance of windings and coils.

Critical input and output impedance values.

Wave shapes (voltage or current) at significant points.

Wiring requirements for critical ground points, shielding, pairing, etc.

Power or voltage ratings of parts.

Caution notation for electrical hazards at maintenance points.

Circuit voltage values at significant points (tube pins, test points, terminal boards, etc.).

Zones (grid system) on complex schematics.

Signal flow direction in main signal paths shall be emphasized.

29.10 Printed Circuits

Printed circuits are universally used for miniature electronic components and computer systems, mostly replacing the vacuum tube by a chip transistor the size of a pinhead. This smallness necessitates that drawings of printed circuits be drawn up to four times or more the size that the circuit will ultimately be printed. Drawings are usually made by computer in black India ink on acetate film and are then photographically reduced to the desired size. The circuit is "printed" onto an insulated board made of plastic or ceramics, and the devices within the circuit are connected and soldered.

The fabrication of a solid state logic technology (SLT) module is shown in **Fig. 29.32**. The tiny module (about one-half inch square) had its chip transistor positioned and attached in the last step of assembly before its encasement in a protective metal shell.

Some printed circuits are printed on both sides of the circuit board. This process requires two photographic negatives, as shown in **Fig. 29.33**, that are made from positive drawings (black lines on a white background). The drawing for each side can be made on separate sheets of acetate that are laid over each other when the second diagram is drawn. However, a more efficient method uses red and blue lines for making a single drawing from which two negatives are photographically made (**Fig. 29.34**). Filters are used on

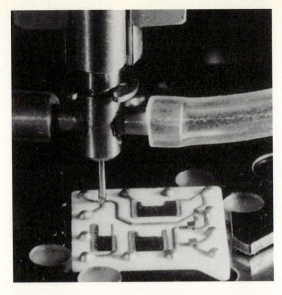

Figure 29.32 A chip is shown being attached to the one-half inch square SLT module at a rate of better than one per second. (Courtesy of IBM.)

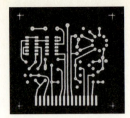 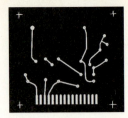

Figure 29.33 A printed circuit that is attached to both sides of the circuit board requires two circuit drawings, one for each side, that are photographically reduced and converted to negatives for printing. (Courtesy of Bishop Industries Corp.)

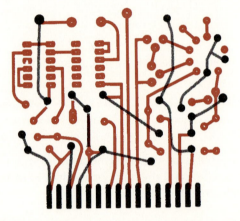

Figure 29.34 By using two colors, such as blue and red, one circuit drawing can be made, and two negatives made from the same drawing by using camera filters that screen out one of the colors with each shot. The circuits are then printed on each side of the board. (Courtesy of Bishop Industries Corp.)

the process camera, one to drop out the red for one negative and another filter for dropping out the blue for the second negative.

Printed circuits are usually coated with silicone varnish to prevent malfunction due to the collection of moisture or dust on the surface. They may also be enclosed in protective shells.

29.11 Shortcut Symbols

Several manufacturers produce preprinted symbols that can be used for "drawing" high-quality electronic circuits and printed circuits. The symbols are available on sheets or on tapes that can be burnished onto the surface of the drawing to form a permanent schematic diagram (**Fig. 29.35**).

The symbols can be connected with matching tape to represent wires between them instead of drawing the lines. Schematic diagrams made with these materials are of a very high quality and reproduce well when reduced in size for publication in specifications or in technical journals.

29.12 Installation Drawings

Many types of electric/electronic drawings are used to produce the finished installation, from the designer who visualized the system at the outset of the project to the contractor who builds it. Drawings are used to design the circuit, detail its parts for fabrication, specify the arrangement of the devices within the system, and instruct the contractor how to install the project.

A combination arrangement and wiring dia-

STICK-ON SYMBOLS

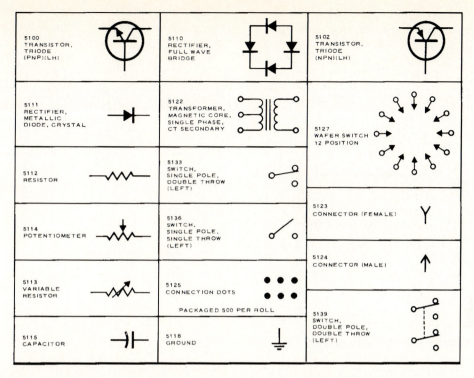

Figure 29.35 Stick-on symbols are available for laying out schematic diagrams with higher contrast and sharpness to improve their reproducibility for publication. (Courtesy of Bishop Industries Corp.)

INSTALLATION DRAWING

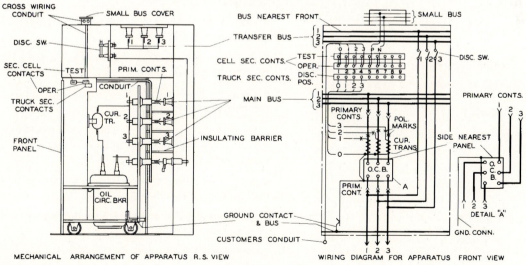

Figure 29.36 This drawing shows views of a metal-enclosed switchgear to describe the arrangement of the apparatus; it also gives the wiring diagram for the unit.

gram drawing is shown in **Fig. 29.36**, where the system is shown in a front and right-side view. The wiring diagram explains how the wires and components within the system are connected for the metal-encased switchgear. Bus bars are conductors for the primary circuits.

Problems

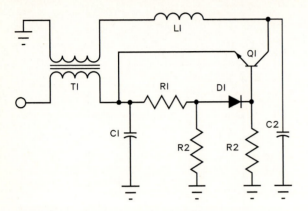

Figure 29.37 Problem 1: A low-pass inductive-input filter.

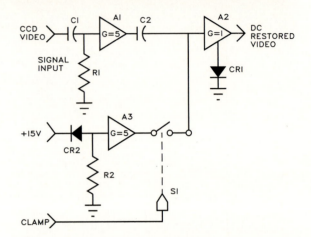

Figure 29.39 Problem 3: A temperature-compensating DC restorer circuit designed to condition the video circuit of a Fairchild area-image sensor. (Courtesy of NASA.)

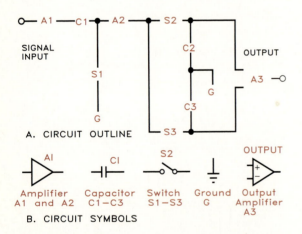

Figure 29.38 Problem 2: A quadruple sampling processor.

3. On a size A sheet, make a schematic diagram of the circuit shown in **Fig. 29.39**.

4. On a size A sheet, make a schematic diagram of the circuit shown in **Fig. 29.40**.

5. On a size A sheet, make a schematic diagram of the circuit shown in **Fig. 29.41**.

6. On a size B sheet, make a schematic diagram of the circuit shown in **Fig. 29.42**.

7. On a size C sheet, make a schematic diagram of the circuit shown in **Fig. 29.43**, and give a parts list of the type shown in **Fig. 29.45**.

8. On a size C sheet, make a schematic diagram of the circuit shown in **Fig. 29.44**.

9. On a size C sheet, make a schematic diagram of the circuit shown in **Fig. 29.45**.

10. On a size B sheet, make a schematic diagram of the circuit shown in **Fig. 29.4**.

1. On a size A sheet, make a schematic diagram of the circuit shown in **Fig. 29.37**.

2. On a size A sheet, make a schematic diagram of the circuit shown in **Fig. 29.38**. Insert the component symbols from B as specified in the circuit outline at A.

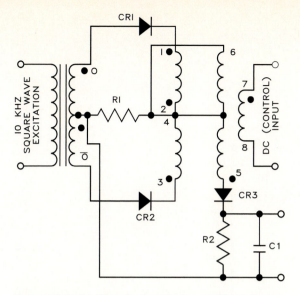

Figure 29.40 Problem 4: A magnetic-amplifier DC transducer. (Courtesy of NASA.)

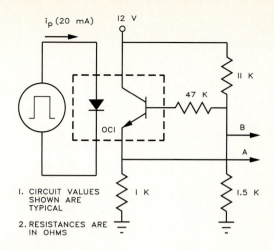

Figure 29.41 Problem 5: Linearly optically coupled isolator circuit.

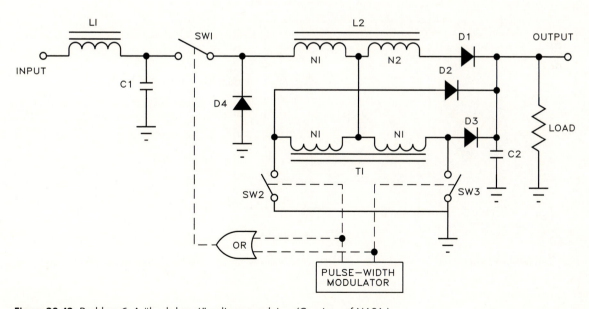

Figure 29.42 Problem 6: A "buck-boost" voltage regulator. (Courtesy of NASA.)

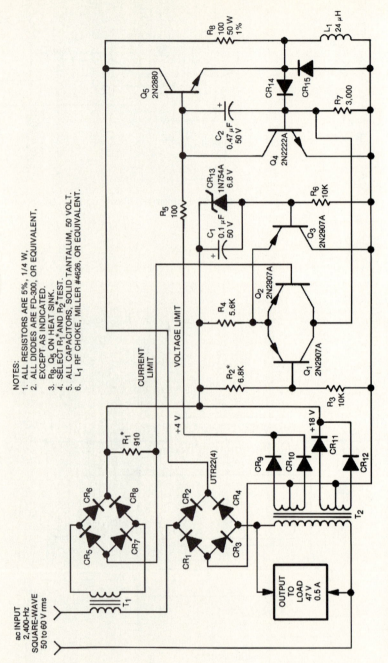

Figure 29.43 Problem 7: An overload protection circuit. (Courtesy of NASA.)

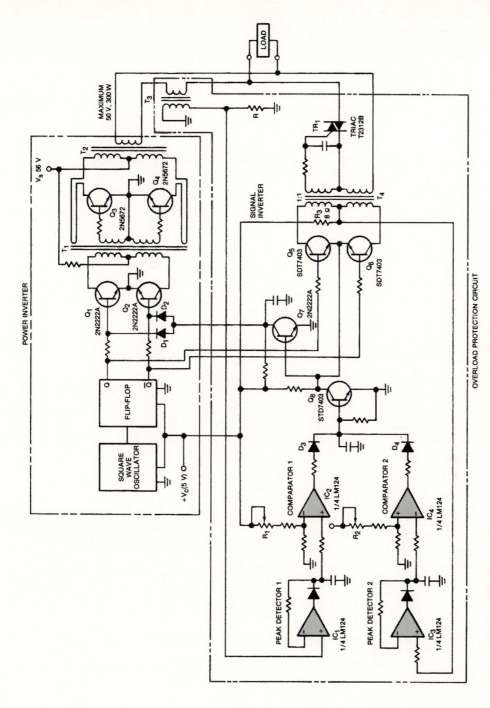

Figure 29.44 Problem 8: An alternating-current voltage/current limiter. (Courtesy of NASA.)

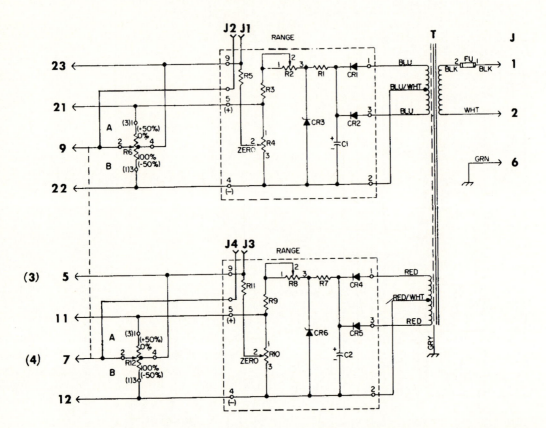

COMPONENT	DESCRIPTION	
CR1, CR2, CR3, CR4	DIODE	1N3193
CR3 & CR6	ZENER DIODE	24V 3W ±.5V TOL
R1 & R7	RESISTOR	560 Ω 5W 5%
R3 & R9	RESISTOR	56 Ω
R5 & R11	RESISTOR	2.7K 1/2W 5%
R2 & R8	TRIM POT	50 Ω
R4 & R10	TRIM POT	5K
R6 & R12	POT	500 Ω 2W DUAL
C1 & C2	CAPACITOR	60 MFD 60V
T	TRANSFORMER	
FU	FUSE	1 AMP
M	EDGEWISE METER	
J	CONNECTOR	
J1, J2, J3, J4	TEST JACK	

TYPE	R6 SCALE		M SCALE	
	A	B	BOTTOM	TOP
RS1100C	0%	100%	0%	100%
RS1110C	0%	100%	PER ENGINEERING DATA	
RS3100C	+50%	-50%	-50%	+50%
RS4100C	0%	100%	0%	100%
RS2120C	100%	0%	OMIT	
RS2100C	100%	0%	0%	100%

NOTE: OUTPUT WIRED TO TERMINALS 3 AND 4 ON
TYPES RS1100C, RS1110C, AND RS3100C.

OUTPUT WIRED TO TERMINALS 5 AND 7 ON
TYPES RS2100C, RS2120C, AND RS4100C.

Figure 29.45 Problem 9: A schematic diagram of a dual output manual station and its parts list.
(Courtesy of NASA.)

30

The Computer in Design and Graphics

30.1 Introduction

Computers are now widely used to produce graphics ranging from simple graphs to three-dimensional solid models of complex products. To be fully productive, engineering and technology students must become computer literate and familiar with the application of graphics software.

This chapter gives a brief overview of computer graphics. The major divisions covered here are computer terminology, hardware requirements, software, two-dimensional and three-dimensional drawing, and advanced applications.

30.2 Terminology of Computer-Aided Design

Computer-aided design (CAD) involves solving design problems with the help of computers: to make graphic images on a video display, print out these images on paper with a plotter or printer, analyze design data, and store design information

for easy retrieval. Many CAD systems perform these functions in an integrated manner, greatly increasing the designer's productivity.

Computer-aided design drafting (CADD), an offshoot of CAD, is the process of generating engineering drawings and other technical documents by computer and is more directly related to drafting than is CAD. The CADD user inputs data by keyboard and/or mouse to produce illustrations on the monitor screen that can be reproduced as paper copies with a plotter or printer.

Engineers generally agree that the computer does not change the nature of the design process but is a significant tool that improves efficiency and productivity. The designer and the CAD system may be described as a design team: The designer provides knowledge, creativity, and control; the computer generates accurate, easily modifiable graphics, performs complex design analysis at great speed, and stores and recalls design information.

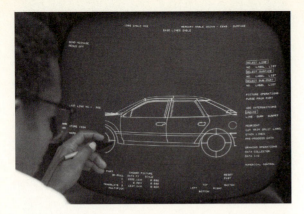

Figure 30.1 The Ford Taurus and Mercury Sable received more computer-aided design and engineering than any other car in the company's history. (Courtesy of Ford Motor Company.)

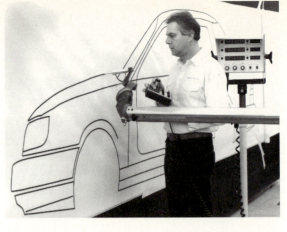

Figure 30.2 A scanning device records measurements from a life-size tape drawing of a new vehicle for storage in a computer and use for other design functions. (Courtesy of Ford Motor Company.)

Advantages of CAD and CADD

Depending on the nature of the problem and the sophistication of the computer system, computers offer the designer or drafter some or all of the following advantages.

1. **Easier creation and correction of drawings**. Working drawings may be created more quickly than by hand, and making changes and modifications is more efficient than correcting drawings made by hand.

2. **Better visualization of drawings**. Many systems allow different views of the same object to be displayed and 3D pictorials to be rotated on the CRT screen.

3. **Database of drawing aids**. Creation and maintenance of design databases (libraries of designs) permits storing designs and symbols for easy recall and application to the solution of new problems.

4. **Quick and convenient design analysis**. Because the computer offers ease of analysis, the designer can evaluate alternative designs, thereby considering more possibilities in less time.

5. **Simulation and testing of designs**. Some computer systems make possible the simulation of a product's operation, testing the design under a variety of conditions and stresses. Computer testing may improve on or replace construction of models and prototypes.

6. **Increased accuracy**. The computer is capable of producing drawings with more accuracy than is possible by hand. Many CAD systems are even capable of detecting errors and informing the user of them.

7. **Improved filing**. Drawings can be more conveniently filed, retrieved, and transmitted on disks and tapes.

Computer Graphics

Most graphical solutions that are possible with a pencil can be done on a computer—and usually more productively. Applications vary from 3D modeling and finite element analysis to 2D drawings and mathematical calculations.

Automobile bodies are designed at the computer, as shown in **Fig. 30.1**. A scanning device records measurements of the life-size tape draw-

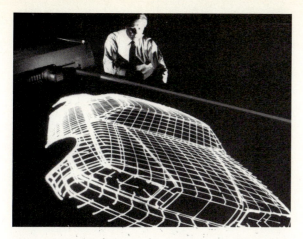

Figure 30.3 Design data stored in the computer's memory may be manipulated to obtain variations in body design of an automobile. (Courtesy of Ford Motor Company.)

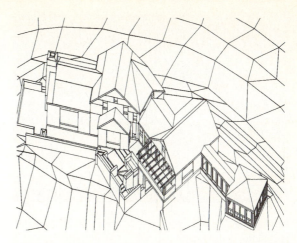

Figure 30.4 This perspective of a house and its site was produced with DynaPerspective® software as a 3D drawing.

ing of a new vehicle **(Fig. 30.2)**. Once recorded and stored in the computer, the data can be manipulated to form the 3D shape of the body style on the computer monitor from which 3D clay models are milled **(Fig. 30.3)**.

In **Fig. 30.4**, a perspective drawing of a site and a house was plotted using microcomputer software. This program lets the viewer be positioned at any height and location in the site, and even "walk through" the area by successively changing positions.

30.3 Computer-Aided Design/ Computer-Aided Manufacturing

An important extension of CAD is its application to manufacturing. **Computer-aided design/computer-aided manufacturing** (CAD/CAM) systems may be used to design a part or product, devise the essential production steps, and electronically communicate this information to and control the operation of manufacturing equipment, including robots **(Fig. 30.5)**. These systems offer many advantages over traditional design and manufacturing systems, including less design effort, more

Figure 30.5 This automatic welding system for Chrysler LeBaron GTS and Dodge Lancer car bodies uses computer-controlled robots for consistent welds of all components in the unitized body structure. This assembly plant also features energy-efficient electric robot welders that require low maintenance and provide a high degree of accuracy. (Courtesy of Chrysler Corporation.)

Figure 30.6 The Hewlett-Packard Vectra 486U computer, keyboard, and monitor provide unprecedented graphics and system performance for Microsoft Windows and the CAD environment. (Courtesy of Hewlett-Packard Company.)

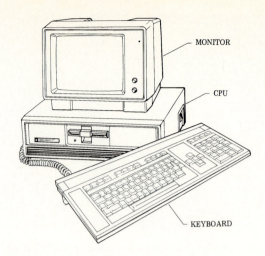

Figure 30.7 The basic components of a desktop computer system are the CPU, keyboard, and monitor (CRT).

efficient use of material, reduced lead time, greater accuracy, and improved inventory maintenance.

An extension of CAD/CAM is **computer-integrated manufacturing** (CIM), a computer or system of computers that coordinates all stages of manufacturing. It enables manufacturers to custom design and produce products efficiently and economically.

30.4 Hardware Systems

Computer-aided design systems have three major components: the **designer, hardware,** and **software**. Hardware comprises the physical components of a computer system, and software is the programmer's instructions to the computer. The hardware of a computer graphics system includes the **computer, monitor, terminal, input devices** (keyboard, digitizers, and light pens), and **output devices** (plotters and printers).

Computer

The computer receives input from the user, executes instructions, and produces output. A sequence of instructions called a **program** con-

trols the computer's activities. The part of the computer that follows the program's instructions is the **central processing unit** (CPU).

Mainframe computers are large, fast, powerful, and expensive. Smaller and less costly than mainframes, **minicomputers** are used by many businesses.

The smallest computers, **microcomputers**, are widely used for both personal and business applications **(Fig. 30.6)**. Advances in hardware technology and software capability, along with continually falling prices, have brought microcomputers into wide use for engineering graphics applications in industry, government, and education. Moreover, the microcomputer is no longer bound to the office; the user can take it into the field for on-site work.

Terminal

The terminal allows the user to communicate with the computer. It typically consists of a keyboard, a cathode-ray tube (monitor), and the interconnections between them and the computer **(Fig. 30.7)**.

The **keyboard** allows the user to communicate with the computer through a set of alphanumeric and function keys.

Figure 30.8 The digitizer tablet's set of coordinates correspond to points on the CRT screen. The user selects them by puck or stylus. (Courtesy of Compaq Computer Corporation.)

Figure 30.9 A light pen allows the user to modify drawings by touching the CRT screen with it. (Courtesy of Ford Motor Company.)

The **cathode-ray tube** (CRT) is a video display tube and screen that is phosphor-coated. An electron gun emits a beam that sweeps out rows of raster lines on the screen. Each raster line consists of dots called **pixels**. Turning pixels on and off generates images on the screen. A measure of the quality of a monitor is **resolution**, or the number of pixels per inch that can be produced on the screen. As the number of pixels per square inch on the screen increases, the quality of the graphics obtained improves.

Input Devices

The **digitizer** is a graphics input device that can communicate information from an image into the computer in digital form for display, storage, or modification. The user attaches a drawing to a digitizer tablet and "traces" it with a stylus to convert the picture to a digital format based on the x and y coordinates of individual points (**Fig. 30.8**).

The user may create or modify digitized pictures on a screen point-by-point with a **light pen**. The user touches the CRT screen with the light pen, telling the computer the position of the pen on the screen (**Fig. 30.9**).

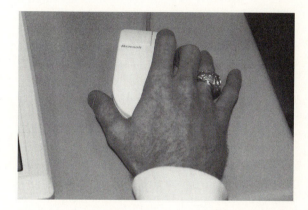

Figure 30.10 A mouse moves the cursor around a CRT screen, and the user executes commands or makes changes by pressing its buttons.

A **mouse** is a tabletop device that the user can move to position the cursor on the screen. With the mouse, the user can execute commands or change information on the screen (**Fig. 30.10**).

The **Spaceball**® enables the user to manipulate 3D objects on the screen (**Fig. 30.11**). By pushing, pulling, and twisting the ball, the user can move 3D images on the screen.

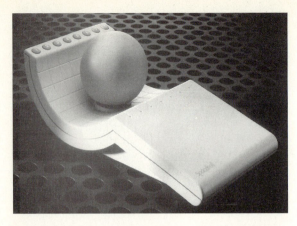

Figure 30.11 The user manipulates the Spaceball® digitizer to move an object in 3D space on the computer screen by pushing, pulling, and twisting it. (Courtesy of CalComp Corporation.)

Figure 30.12 The DesignMate® plotter is a pen plotter that can produce multicolored drawings that are accurate within 0.01 inch. (Courtesy of CalComp Corporation.)

Output Devices

The **plotter** is an output device directed by the computer to plot a drawing on paper or film with a pen in much the same manner as a drawing is made by hand. Three types of plotters are the **flatbed plotter**, **drum plotter**, and **sheet-fed plotter**. The paper of the flatbed plotter is attached to the bed and remains stationary while the pen moves about the paper in raised or lowered positions to produce the drawing. In the drum plotter, the paper is held between grit wheels and rolled back and forth over a rotating drum as the pen moves left or right along the drum (**Fig. 30.12**). The sheet-fed plotter holds the paper by grit wheels in a relatively flat position. The paper moves forward and backward and the pen moves right and left to plot the drawing (**Fig. 30.13**).

The **printer** transfers images to paper or film from the computer, but not with a pen. **An impact printer works like a typewriter, forming characters by striking typefaces against an inked ribbon and paper. Dot-matrix printers** are impact printers that have printheads composed of a rectangle (matrix) of pins that are raised or lowered to form characters. Dot-matrix printers are better than

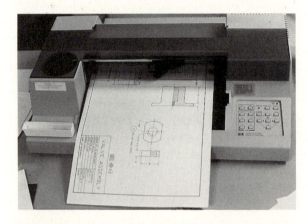

Figure 30.13 The Hewlett-Packard 7475 plotter produces pen-made drawings on size A and size B sheets.

impact printers for printing graphics, because their dot patterns correspond to lighted pixels on a CRT screen.

Nonimpact printers form characters by using ink sprays, laser beams, photography, or heat.

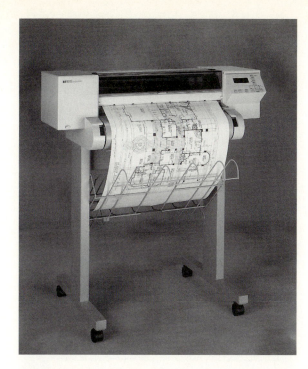

Figure 30.14 The PlotMaster® thermal transfer plotter/ printer produces fast, high-resolution color hard copy for computer-aided drawings. (Courtesy of CalComp Corporation.)

Figure 30.15 The Hewlett-Packard DesignJet 600® uses inkjet technology to make drawings with inkjet instead of pens. (Courtesy of Hewlett Packard Company.)

Figure 30.16 This view is from the engineering design graphics computer laboratories at Texas A&M University.

One example, the thermal transfer plotter, uses electrical fields to direct jets of ink to appropriate spots on the paper **(Fig. 30.14)**. Like the dot-matrix printer, the ink-jet printer forms a pattern of dots, thus limiting its accuracy and resolution. Multiple jet nozzles allow generation of multicolor graphics **(Fig. 30.15)**.

Laser printers give an excellent resolution of dense, accurately drawn lines in text and drawings, in color as well as in black and white. Although more costly than other types of printers, laser printers are being used in much greater numbers because of the quality of their output.

30.5 Introduction to Software

Most CAD software continues to improve over the previous versions and sell at lower prices,

giving more power to the user. This increased power requires a minimum of 4 MB of RAM, a 20 MB hard disk, and a 486 computer for most applications **(Fig. 30.16)**. The microcomputer market for computer graphics has been dominated by AutoCAD, which has been released in thirteen software versions since its introduction in 1982 **(Fig. 30.17)**.

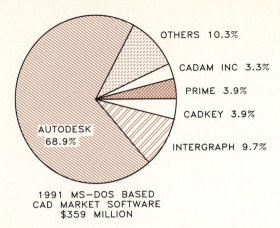

Figure 30.17 AutoCAD is used by almost 70 percent of the CAD market. (Courtesy of AutoDesk.)

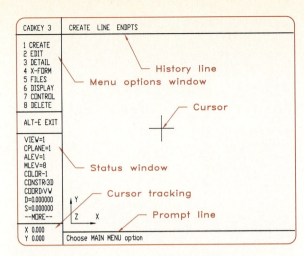

Figure 30.19 The working screen of CADKEY. (Courtesy of CADKEY.)

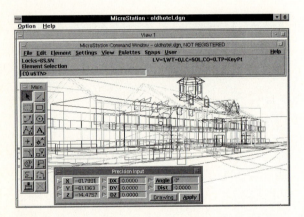

Figure 30.18 The working screen of MicroStation. (Courtesy of Intergraph.)

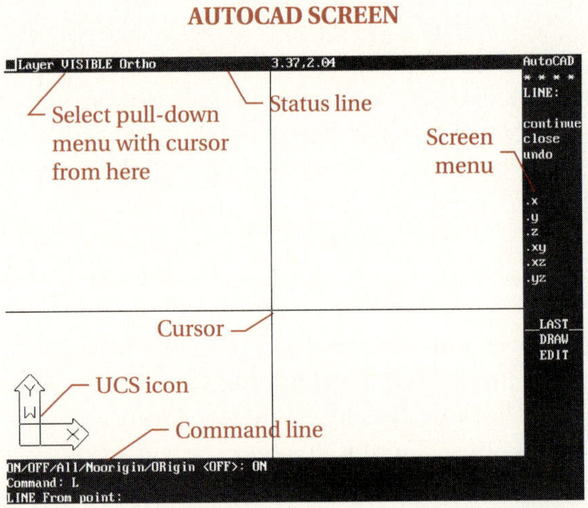

AUTOCAD SCREEN

Figure 30.20 After you boot up the system, the screen will appear ready for drawing.

Other graphics software are Intergraph's MicroStation, Prime's Medusula, CADKEY, and CADAM. Other software packages sharing the remainder of the market are Silver Screen and VersaCAdD. Other specialty packages include MegaCADD, DynaPerspective, 3D Studio AutoShade, and Mannequin® among many others.

Most graphics software packages share more similarities than differences; therefore your familiarity with one type of software is somewhat transferable to another version. Comparisons of the screens, as seen by the user, for MicroStation and CADKEY are shown in **Fig. 30.18** and **Fig. 30.19**,

MOUSE

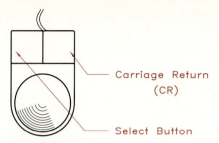

Figure 30.21 The left-hand button on the mouse is the select button, and the right-hand button is the carriage return (CR) button.

CREATING A NEW FILE

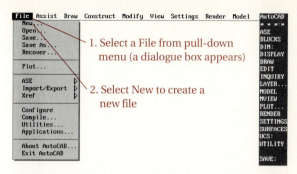

1. Select a File from pull-down menu (a dialogue box appears)

2. Select New to create a new file

Figure 30.22 To begin the procedure for creating a new file, select `File` and `New`.

CREATE NEW DRAWING BOX

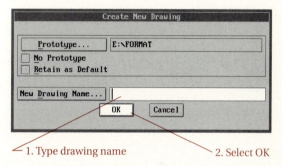

1. Type drawing name   2. Select OK

Figure 30.23 The `Create New Drawing` dialogue box lets you assign a prototype file (`E:\Format`) to a new file (`B:NEW-DWG`); press OK to proceed.

respectively. The AutoCAD screen is shown in **Fig. 30.20.**

Most of the examples that follow demonstrate how AutoCAD is used in a few of the more basic applications. Space does not permit more than a brief overview.

30.6 An Example Session

The following steps illustrate the techniques used at the beginning of a drawing session, how lines are drawn, and the printing of the drawing.

Much of your interaction with the computer will be by means of a **mouse (Fig. 30.21)**, but you may enter many commands more quickly at the keyboard after you learn the commands. Press the left button to "click on" to make a selection. In some cases a "double click" is needed.

Begin by turning the computer on and **booting up** the system by typing ACAD12 (or the command used by your system) to ready the screen for drawing **(Fig. 30.20)**. Move the **cursor** (the crosshairs controlled by the mouse) about the screen with your mouse, select items on the side menu, and try the pull-down menu.

To create a new **file** on a disk, place your formatted disk in its slot, pick FILES from the pull-down menu, and select NEW from the dialogue box

(Fig. 30.22). Then type the name of your new drawing, B:NEW-DWG, in the Edit box of the `Create New Drawing` dialogue box **(Fig. 30.23)**. The light at the B:drive where your disk is inserted will light up while a new file, B:NEW-DWG, is being saved.

Draw some lines on the screen just for fun **(Fig. 30.24)**. Move the cursor to the top bar to activate the pull-down menu and select DRAW, LINES, and SEGMENTS in succession to obtain the prompt From Point: in the COMMAND line at the bottom of

DRAWING WITH LINE

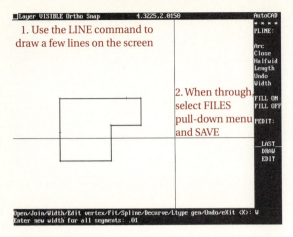

Figure 30.24 By selecting LINE from the side menu, you may produce lines on the screen by selecting points with the mouse.

SAVING A FILE

Figure 30.25 Select SAVE under FILE on the pull-down menu to save your drawing on a disk.

the screen. Select a point with the mouse by clicking the left button, move the cursor to a second point, and select other points. To disconnect the rubber band that stretches from the last endpoint, press the right button on your mouse, which is the same as the Carriage Return (CR) or Enter key. We use (CR) as the abbreviation for this key. Try drawing a circle and other shapes on the screen.

You may **repeat** a command by pressing (CR) (the right button) twice at the end of the previous command. For example, LINE appears in the command line at the bottom of the screen after you press (CR) twice, if that was the previous command used.

PLOTTING A FILE

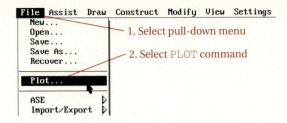

Figure 30.26 To prepare to plot a drawing, select PLOT from the FILE option of the pull-down menu.

PLOT CONFIGURATION

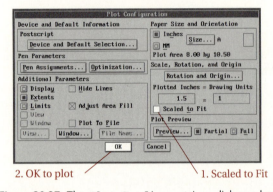

Figure 30.27 The Plot Configuration dialogue box will appear on the screen for plotting instructions. Select Scaled to Fit and OK to plot.

To **update** a drawing file, B:NEW-DWG, click on FILES from the pull-down menu and SAVE from its dialogue box **(Fig. 30.25)**. The command _QSAVE appears in the command line at the bottom of the screen, the light over drive B: blinks briefly, and the changes are added to B:NEW-DWG to update the file.

To **plot** a drawing, use the pull-down menu, then select FILES and PLOT from the dialogue boxes **(Fig. 30.26)** to fill the screen with the Plot Configuration dialogue box **(Fig. 30.27)**. Select only one setting, Scaled to Fit, to make the plotted drawing fill the sheet.

1. Load paper, lower lever
2. Pens: P.7 (slot 1); P.3 (slot 2)
3. Set for size A
4. Press P1 and P2

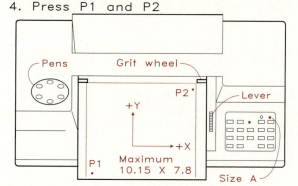

Figure 30.28 This Hewlett-Packard 7475A plotter is typical of those used to plot A and B sheet sizes.

Load a size A paper sheet in the plotter. If the plotter is a Hewlett-Packard 7475, it will plot both size A and size B sheets with ink pens. From the dialogue box, select the OK button to send the drawing data to the plotter (**Fig. 30.28**).

To end your first session with the computer, use the pull-down menu to select FILES and EXIT AUTOCAD from their dialogue boxes (**Fig. 30.29**) to return to the operating system.

30.7 Introduction to 2D Drawing

A two-dimensional (2D) drawing is one that shows only two dimensions, such as height and width, in a single view. The third dimension, depth in this case, must be shown in a separate view. Most documentation drawings from which projects are specified and constructed are 2D drawings.

The bicycle in **Fig. 30.30** is an example of a two-dimensional drawing. In this case, there is little need for a three-dimensional pictorial, since most of the bicycle's features lie in a single plane.

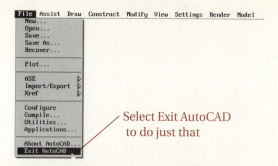

Select Exit AutoCAD to do just that

Figure 30.29 Select Exit AutoCAD from the File pull-down menu to exit AutoCAD.

Figure 30.30 This bicycle is drawn as a 2D drawing where only height and width are seen. (Courtesy of AutoDesk.)

The following sections will illustrate the methods of drawing, dimensioning, moving, zooming, and other fundamental operations. There are many more sophisticated commands that must be learned, but these examples will provide an overview.

30.8 Basic Operations and Commands

Using Dialogue Boxes

AutoCAD 12 has many **dialogue boxes** with names beginning with DD (DDLMODES, for exam-

OPENING A DRAWING

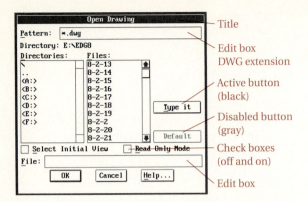

Title
Edit box
DWG extension
Active button
(black)
Disabled button
(gray)
Check boxes
(off and on)
Edit box

Figure 30.31 To open a saved drawing, select `Open` from the `File` pull-down menu, and the `Open Drawing` dialogue box will appear on the screen. You may select the file to be opened from the list or type its name into the `Edit Box`.

ple) that interact with you. You may use the `FILEDIA` command to turn off (zero = off and 1 = on) the dialogue boxes if you prefer not to use them. When a command on a menu is followed by three dots (...), it will respond with a dialogue box when selected; some dialogue boxes have subdialogue boxes.

The `Open Drawing` dialogue box shown in **Fig. 30.31** illustrates the features of a typical dialogue box. The title of a dialogue box appears at the top. The box contains a series of **buttons** from which you may select by using the cursor. The button with the darkest outline is the `Default` button, such as the `OK` button, and disabled buttons are shown in gray.

Check boxes are for toggling the options `On` (an `X` is shown) or `Off` (the box is empty). **Edit boxes** are long boxes into which you type a response, such as the name of file to be saved **(Fig. 30.31)**. **Radio buttons** are square boxes with squares inside them that you may turn on or off with the cursor.

Scroll bars allow you to move through the lists in some dialogue boxes **(Fig. 30.32)**. You may get

SCROLLING FILES

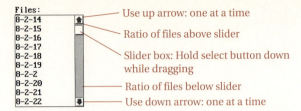

Use up arrow: one at a time
Ratio of files above slider
Slider box: Hold select button down while dragging
Ratio of files below slider
Use down arrow: one at a time

Figure 30.32 You may use `Scroll Bars` to scroll through a list of files by selecting the slider box while pressing the select button of the mouse. Directional arrows at each end move up or down the list one at a time.

SUBDIALOGUE BOXES

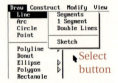

Select
button

Figure 30.33 Dialogue boxes followed by triangles will give action boxes for further selections.

subdialogue boxes with a command followed by a triangle **(Fig. 30.33)**. After selecting `LINE`, you must define its type in a second box. Use the `OK` button to accept and activate the selections made in the dialogue box.

`Control C` (press `Ctrl` and `C` at the same time) exits the current command and gives the `Command:` prompt at the bottom of the screen, indicating that the program is ready for a new command **(Fig. 30.34)**. `Control C` aborts a plot operation but does not take effect until the data have had time to exit the buffer.

Drawing Aids

You must become familiar with the drawing aids that are available. The `LIMITS` command establishes the size of the drawing area to be covered with dots when `GRID` is on. The `GRID` command

ABORTING A COMMAND

STEP 1   STEP 2

Figure 30.34 To abort the current operation, hold down the Ctrl button and press the C key.

UNITS CONTROL BOX

Figure 30.35 The Units Control dialogue box, under SETTINGS in the pull-down menu, lets you set the number of decimal places and the form of numbers and angles to the formats shown in Fig. 30.36.

sets the spacing of the dots within the LIMITS. A drawing that fills a size A sheet (11 × 8.5 inches) has a plotting area of about 10.1 × 7.8 inches (257 × 198 mm). The LIMITS command appears under SETTINGS of the pull-down and side menus:

```
Command: LIMITS (CR)

ON/OFF/<Lower left corner> <0.00,0.00>:
(CR) (Accept default value.)

Upper right corner <12.00,9.00>: 11,8.5
(CR)
```

You may reset LIMITS at any time while producing a drawing with these steps.

Use the UNITS command to set the format of numerals and their fractional parts. Selecting UNITS

DRAWING AIDS BOX

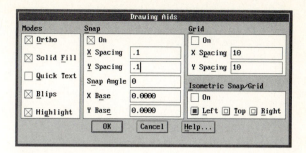

Figure 30.36 The Drawing Aids dialogue box is used to set Modes, Snap, and Grid.

under the pull-down heading, SETTINGS, gives the Units Control dialogue box (DDUNITS command) **(Fig. 30.35)**.

The Drawing Aids dialogue box (DDRMODES) appears under the SETTINGS heading of the pull-down menu, from which you may select the following aids **(Fig. 30.36)**.

Ortho The ORTHO mode forces all lines to be either horizontal or vertical (not angular). To set ORTHO, check its box (Fig. 30.36) by pressing function key F6, or by typing ORTHO and typing ON or OFF. When set to ON, ORTHO appears in the status line at the top of the screen.

Snap The SNAP mode forces the cursor to stop at points on an imaginary grid that you may set to any spacing. You may type the X and Y spacings of SNAP in the edit boxes of the pull-down dialogue box. Alternatively, you may begin from the side menu or the command line and type:

```
Command: SNAP (CR)

Snap spacing or ON/OFF/Aspect/ Rotate/
Style<0.25> .20
```

This response sets the SNAP grid to 0.20 unit. When on, SNAP appears in the status line at the top of the screen. You may toggle SNAP on and off by pressing F9.

FUNCTION KEYS

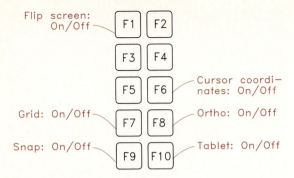

Figure 30.37 These function keys may be used to turn settings (Fig. 30.36) OFF or ON.

ALIASES (ABBREVIATIONS)

A	ARC	M	MOVE
C	CIRCLE	MS	MSPACE
CP	COPY	P	PAN
DV	DVIEW	PS	PSPACE
E	ERASE	PL	PLINE
L	LINE	R	REDRAW
LA	LAYER	Z	ZOOM

Figure 30.38 The ALIASES (abbreviations for commands) may be typed at the keyboard in their shortened form to speed up the entry process.

Function Keys **Figure 30.37** shows the function keys used to toggle ON and OFF several of the drawing aids described.

Help The HELP (?) dialogue box lists commands for which explanations are available. Press Ctrl C to abort the listing process and press F1 to return to the graphics mode. To obtain information on a command (LINE, for example), respond to the prompts as follows:

    Command: HELP (or ?) (CR)

    Command name (Return for list): LINE (CR)

Aliases The use of ALIASES (abbreviations of command names) increases typing speed. Note how much faster typing R instead of REDRAW is **(Fig. 30.38)**.

Grid Use GRID to fill the LIMITS area with the dot spacing assigned by typing values in the X and Y spacing boxes. Typing GRID and selecting the SNAP option sets the grid equal to the SNAP spacing.

Layers

You may name an almost infinite number of layers on which to draw and assign each a name, color, and line type. One layer, for example, may

be a layer named HIDDEN for drawing dashed lines in yellow.

Architects use separate copies of the same floor plan for different applications: dimensions, furniture arrangement, floor finishes, electrical details, and so on. Turning on the needed layers and turning off others allows use of the same basic plan for these applications.

Setting Layers The layers shown in the Layer Control dialogue box (DDLMODES) in **Fig. 30.39** are sufficient for most working drawings. Assigning different line types and colors to different layers distinguishes them from each other. The 0 (zero) layer is the default layer, which can be turned off but not deleted. Select LAYERS from the side menu and LAYER from the submenu and develop layers in the following manner.

New To create new layers, type NEW:

    Command: LAYER (CR)

    ?/Set/New/On/Off/Color/Ltype/

    Freeze/Thaw: NEW or N (CR)

    Layer name(s): VISIBLE,

    HIDDEN,CENTER,HATCH,DIMEN,

    CUT,WINDOW (CR)

Figure 30.39 shows the assignment of seven new layers by name, each having defaults of a white

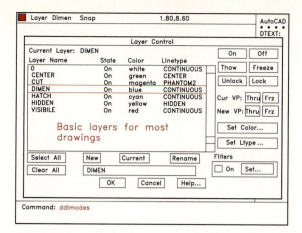

Figure 30.39 Set `Layers` by using the `Layer Control` dialogue box from `SETTINGS` in the pull-down menu. The layers shown here are sufficient for making most working drawings.

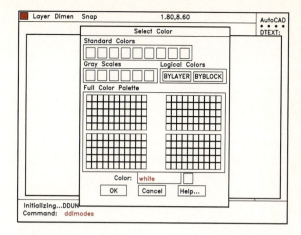

Figure 30.40 Use the `Select Color` dialogue box to assign colors to drawing layers by mouse or by typing in the `Edit Box`.

color and a continuous line type. You may assign new layers by using the dialogue box, typing a layer name in the edit box, or selecting `NEW` and then `OK`.

Color Set the `COLOR` of each layer as follows:

```
Command: LAYER

?/Set/New/On/Off/Color/Ltype/

Freeze/Thaw: COLOR or C (CR)

Color: RED (or 1) 1 (CR)

Layer name(s) for color 1

(red) <VISIBLE>: VISIBLE (CR)
```

You may also pick colors from the `Select Color` dialogue box (**Fig. 30.40**), obtained by selecting a layer from the `Layer Control` dialogue box and using the `Set Color` button (**Fig. 30.39**). Assign a color to each layer and use the `OK` button to save the settings. Note that the color red was assigned to the `VISIBLE` layer in Fig. 30.39, which could have been typed as `1` or `RED`.

Line Types Assign line types to layers as follows:

```
Command: LAYER (CR)

?/Set/New/On/Off/Color/Ltype/

Freeze/Thaw: Ltype (or L) (CR)

Linetype (or ?) <CONTINUOUS>: HIDDEN (CR)

Layer name(s) for linetype

HIDDEN <0>: HIDDEN (CR)
```

Of the twenty-five line types to pick from, the more common ones are `CONTINUOUS`, `HIDDEN`, and `CENTER`.

Set A layer must be `SET` for it to be the current layer and for you to be able to use it:

```
Command: LAYER (CR)

?/Set/New/On/Off/Ltype/Freeze/

Thaw: SET (or S) (CR)

New current layer <0>:VISIBLE (CR) (CR)
```

You may also set the current layer by selecting it from the dialogue box (Fig. 30.39) and then using the `Current` button.

DRAWING LINES

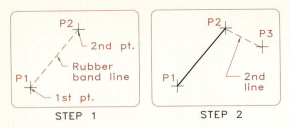

STEP 1　　　　　STEP 2

Figure 30.41 Drawing a LINE:

Step 1 Command: <u>LINE</u> or <u>L</u>

From point: <u>P1</u>

To point: <u>P2</u> (The line is drawn.)

Step 2 To point: <u>P3</u> (The line is drawn.)

((CR) to disengage the rubber band.)

On/Off Turn defined layers on or off with the ON/OFF command in the following manner:

    Command: <u>LAYER</u> (or <u>LA</u>) (CR)

    ?/Set/New/On/Off/Ltype/Freeze/

    Thaw: <u>ON</u> (or OFF)

    Layer name(s) to turn on: <u>VISIBLE</u>

    (or * for all layers)

    (Or <u>VISIBLE, HIDDEN, CENTER</u>, to turn

    these layers ON or OFF.) (CR)

Using Layers All layers may be on, but only the current layer can be drawn on. Selecting the question-mark option (?) of LAYER displays a list of the layers, their line types, colors, and on/off status. Press key F1 to change the screen back to the graphics editor. Obtain the Layer Control dialogue box to show the layers (**Fig. 30.39**) by selecting Layer Control under Settings of the pull-down menu.

Freeze and Thaw The Freeze and Thaw options under the LAYER command are similar to ON and OFF. When you FREEZE a layer, the program will ignore it until you THAW it. Therefore regeneration

LINE COMMAND FROM THE PULL-DOWN MENU

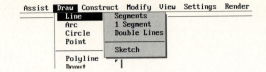

Figure 30.42 The LINE command appears under Draw on the pull-down menu. An action box offers four types of lines for use.

is much faster than using OFF. The current layer cannot be frozen.

LTSCALE Use LTSCALE to modify the length and spacing of noncontinuous lines, such as hidden lines. A large LTSCALE factor makes dashes and spaces longer and smaller factors do the opposite.

Save Layers The process of setting drawing aids takes time and effort, so you should save them by using the SAVE AS command under the FILE heading. You may save UNITS, GRID, SNAP, ORTHO, and other drawing aids as part of B:FORMAT for use as a PROTOTYPE having these settings. When you open B:FORMAT, it will have no drawings on it, but it will contain the layers and settings previously made and ready for making drawings.

30.9 Drawing Lines

You may draw a line by using the side menu, the keyboard, or the pull-down menu. If you use the side menu, select DRAW and LINE and respond to the command line, as shown in **Fig. 30.41**, to draw the lines by picking endpoints with the cursor and pressing the select button of the mouse (the left button). The current line will rubber band (stretch) from the last point and lines will be drawn in succession until you press (CR) or the right button of the mouse. If you use the pull-down menu, select DRAW, LINE, and SEGMENTS to begin drawing lines by using a dialogue box (**Fig. 30.42**). **Figure 30.43** compares absolute and polar coordinates.

LINES: 2D SPACE

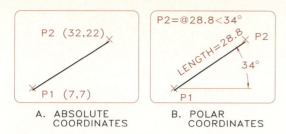

A. ABSOLUTE COORDINATES

B. POLAR COORDINATES

Figure 30.43

A Absolute coordinates may be typed to establish ends of a line.

B Polar coordinates are relative to the current point and are specified by a length and the angle, with the horizontal measured clockwise.

Absolute Cartesian Coordinates Type 3D coordinates in the form `2,3,1.5,` to give the coordinates of a point from the origin of `0,0,0.`

Polar Coordinates Type 2D coordinates as `3.6<56` to draw a line from `0,0,0` at an angle of 56° with the *X* axis in the *X*–*Y* plane.

30.10 Drawing Circles

Use the `CIRCLE` command from `DRAW` of the pull-down menu to draw circles with a center and radius, a center and diameter, or three points. You may drag a circle to its final size with the mouse **(Fig. 30.44)**.

30.11 Drawing Fillets and Rounds

You may draw fillets between two nonparallel lines by using the `FILLET` command. After generating the fillet, the command automatically trims the lines, as shown in **Fig. 30.45**.

Once you assign the radius, it remains in memory for drawing additional fillets. By setting the radius to 0, you can extend nonparallel lines to a perfect intersection.

DRAWING A CIRCLE

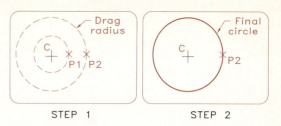

STEP 1

STEP 2

Figure 30.44 Using the `CIRCLE` command:

Step 1 Command: `CIRCLE` or `C` (CR)

`3P/2P/<Center point>:` `C` (with cursor)

`Diameter/<Radius>:`
(Drag radius to P1, and then to P2 to dynamically change it, if `DRAGMODE` is ON.)

Step 2 Select the final radius to draw the circle.

FILLET COMMAND

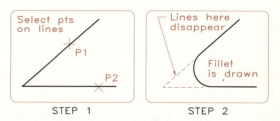

STEP 1

STEP 2

Figure 30.45 Using the `FILLET` command.

Step 1 Command: `FILLET` (CR)

`Polyline Radius/<Select two objects>:` `R` (CR)

`Enter fillet radius <0.0000>:` `1.5` (CR)
`Command:` (CR)

Step 2 `FILLET Polyline Radius/<Select two objects>:` `P1` and `P2`
(The fillet is drawn, and the lines trimmed.)

30.12 Text and Numerals

Use the `DTEXT` (dynamic text) and `TEXT` commands to insert text in a drawing. `DTEXT` displays the text on the screen as you type it. `DTEXT` begins by asking for the left starting point (the default) for the text line:

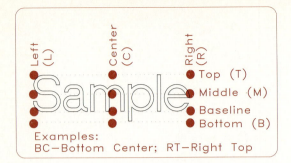

Figure 30.46 You may add text to a drawing by using any of the insertion points shown. For example, BC means the bottom center of a word or sentence that will be located at the cursor point.

```
Command: DTEXT

Justify/Style/<Start point>:
```

(Select point with cursor.)

```
Height <.18>: .125

Rotation angle <0>: (CR)

Text: TYPE WORDS
```

JUSTIFY prompts you for the insertion point for a string of text (**Fig. 30.46**).

    Figure 30.47 shows how to type multiple lines of text with DTEXT. It automatically spaces the lines when you press (CR). Fonts (styles of text) can be selected from the dialogue box shown in **Fig. 30.48.**

30.13 Zooming and Panning

To enlarge or reduce parts of a drawing, use the ZOOM command in the submenu under the DIS-PLAY menu. **Figure 30.49** shows the use of a ZOOM/WINDOW to select the portion to enlarge.

    The PAN command (**Fig. 30.50**) lets you pan the view across the screen. The first point you select is a handle for dragging the view of the drawing to its new view. The drawing is not being relocated; your view of it is being changed.

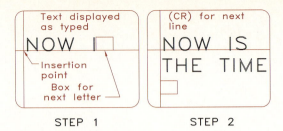

Figure 30.47 Inserting DTEXT:

Step 1 Command: DTEXT

Justify/Style/<Start point>: (Select point.)

Height <.18>: .125

Rotation angle <0>: (CR)

Text: NOW IS

Step 2 Press (CR) and box advances to next line of Text, THE TIME (CR). (Box spaces down with each (CR).)

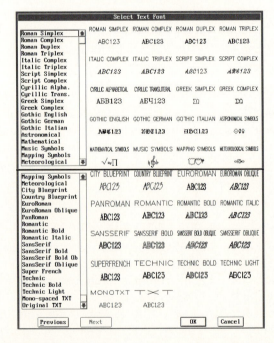

Figure 30.48 These fonts can be accessed under DRAW: TEXT: set style.

ZOOM COMMAND

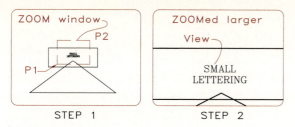

STEP 1 STEP 2

Figure 30.49 Using the ZOOM command:

Step 1 Command: ZOOM or Z (CR)

All/Center/Dynamic/Extents/Left/Previous/Vmax/

Window/<Scale(X/XP)>: W (CR) (Window is default.)

First corner: P1

Step 2 Other corner: P2

(The window is enlarged to fill the screen.)

PAN COMMAND

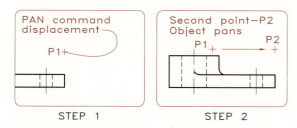

STEP 1 STEP 2

Figure 30.50 Using the PAN command:

Step 1 Command: PAN (CR)

Displacement: P1

Step 2 Second point: P2

(The view point is moved to new position.)

30.14 MOVE and COPY

The MOVE command is used to reposition a drawing **(Fig. 30.51)** and the COPY command to duplicate it. When copied, the drawing remains in its original position and the duplicate is located where specified. Applied identically, the COPY and MOVE commands let you drag drawings into posi-

MOVING: DRAGMODE ON

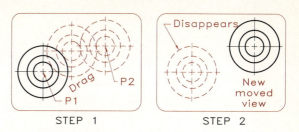

STEP 1 STEP 2

Figure 30.51 Using DRAGmode:

Step 1 Command: MOVE (CR)

Select objects: W (CR) (Window object.)

Base point or displacement: DRAG (CR)

Base point or displacement: P1 (Or X, Y distance.)

Second point of displacement: P2 (The drawing is DRAGged as the cursor is moved.)

Step 2 When moved to P2, press the Select button to draw the circle. If DRAGMODE is AUTO or On, dragging is automatic.

TYPES OF DIMENSIONS

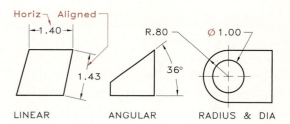

LINEAR   ANGULAR   RADIUS & DIA

Figure 30.52 These are common types of dimensions that appear on drawings.

tion. The COPY command has a MULTIPLE option for positioning multiple copies of drawings in different places.

30.15 Dimensioning

Figure 30.52 shows the types of dimensions that you may apply. Because measurements for dimensions are made from drawings on the screen, the

DIMENSIONING A LINE

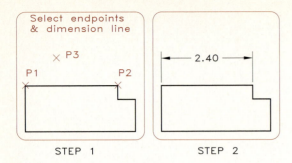

Figure 30.53 Dimensioning a line:
Step 1 `Command: DIM` (CR)

`Dim: HOR` (CR)

`First extension line origin or (CR) to select: P1`

`Second extension line origin: P2`

`Dimension line location: P3`

Step 2 Press (CR) and `2.40` appears at the command line. Press (CR) to accept `2.40`, or type a different value and press (CR).

DIMENSIONING ANGLES

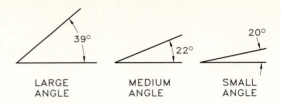

Figure 30.54 Angles may be dimensioned in any of these three formats using AutoCAD.

ANGULAR DIMENSION

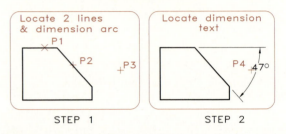

Figure 30.55 Using the `ANGULAR` command:
Step 1 `Command: DIM` (CR)

`Dim: ANGULAR` (CR)

`Select first line: P1`

`Second line: P2`

`Enter dimension line arc location: P3`

`Dimension text <47>:` (CR)

Step 2 `Enter text location: P4` or (CR)

---

drawings must be full size on the screen and scaled when plotted.

Before you can use dimensioning, you must set many variables. These include sizing arrowheads and numerals, specifying extension line offsets, assigning text fonts, and choosing units, to name a few.

Linear Dimensions

Begin dimensioning by selecting DRAW from the pull-down menu, picking DIMENSIONS, and specifying the type of dimension line, such as horizontal (**Fig. 30.53**). Prompts at the command line ask for the endpoints of the line. When you respond to the prompt, the program locates the dimension line and automatically produces the dimension.

Dimensioning Angles

Figure 30.54 shows variations for dimensioning angles based on the space available. Begin by selecting two lines of the angle and locate the dimension line arc (**Fig. 30.55**). Where space permits, center the dimension value in the arc between the arrows.

Leaders

When the LEADER command is used, you must know the circle's diameter and type it in to override that measurement (**Fig. 30.56**). LEADER does not measure radii or diameters.

DIAMETER BY LEADER

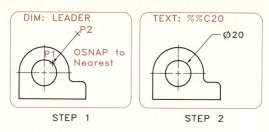

Figure 30.56 Using the LEADER option with OSNAP:
Step 1 Dim: <u>LEADER</u>

Leader start point: (OSNAP to NEAREST)

To point: <u>P2</u>

To point: (CR)

Step 2 Dimension text <1>: <u>%%C20</u> (CR)

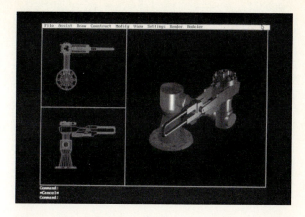

Figure 30.58 Multiple viewports can be used for making and displaying 2D and 3D drawings such as of this welding machine. (Courtesy of AutoDesk.)

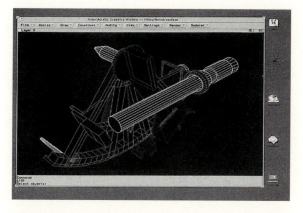

Figure 30.57 A three-dimensional (3D) pictorial of a sextant is shown here as a wire-diagram drawing. (Courtesy of AutoDesk.)

30.16 Introduction to 3D Graphics

The computer drawing of the sextant in **Fig. 30.57** is an example of a three-dimensional (3D) pictorial in which height, width, and depth can be seen in a single view. Unlike 2D drawings, a 3D drawing can be rotated on the screen so the object can be seen from any direction, and multiple views of it can be plotted. 3D drawings can be displayed as orthographic, axonometric, or perspective views.

A 3D drawing can be constructed by dividing the computer screen into different ports in which both 2D and 3D views of the object can be seen simultaneously. Top, front, and 3D views of the welding machine are shown in **Fig. 30.58.** A modification of a design feature in any viewport is automatically changed in all the other viewports. In this case, the 3D view has been rendered to remove the wire-diagram appearance. Separate or multiple views can be extracted and plotted from a 3D drawing such as the front view of the welding machine shown in **Fig. 30.59**.

Other software such as Design Board Professional, developed by MegaCADD, Inc., can be used for the development of 3D drawings. The CREATE mode **(Fig. 30.60)** provides a screen on which to create a perspective by drawing 3D shapes in plan view. The VIEW mode provides a screen on which to select a viewpoint and look at the orthographic views and see them in perspective **(Fig. 30.61)**.

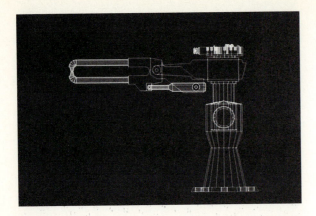

Figure 30.59 A 2D view of the welding machine in Fig. 30.58 can be selected for plotting as a single drawing. (Courtesy of AutoDesk.)

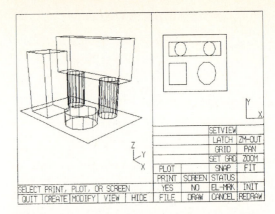

Figure 30.61 The VIEW screen of DBPro® shows the plan view of the model and its corresponding perspective view. You may change the viewpoint by selecting different observers' positions and target positions in the plan view.

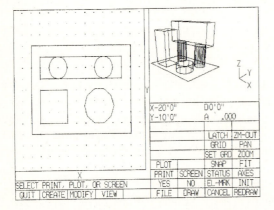

Figure 30.60 The CREATE screen of MegaCADD's Design Board Professional® enables you to create the orthographic views of a model that you want to convert to perspective views.

30.17 3D Drawing: Wire Diagrams

The method of making a wire-diagram drawing of a part and covering it with a skin (called a mesh) is demonstrated in the following steps. Once meshed, the part can be viewed from different angles as a solid, with its hidden lines suppressed. The process of applying meshes begins the construction of a 3D skeletal frame.

RULESURF Command RULESURF produces lines between two entities, which can be curves, arcs, polylines, lines, or points, even if one boundary is a point. Apply RULESURF to add faces between the circular ends, the parallel edges, and the arcs (**Fig. 30.62**).

TABSURF Command Apply TABSURF to tabulate a surface from a curve parallel and equal in length to a directional vector (**Fig. 30.63**). Select the circle first and the vector next to tabulate a cylinder with elements equal in length to the vector.

REVSURF Command Then use REVSURF to revolve a surface about an axis (**Fig. 30.64**), move it to 0,5,0, and add it to the hollow shell. Polylines, arcs, or circles may be revolved to form a surface of revolution, and SURFTAB1 controls its density.

EDGESURF Command Select four edges (boundary lines) that intersect to be spanned with a mesh by using EDGESURF (**Fig. 30.65**).

MESHES: RULESURF

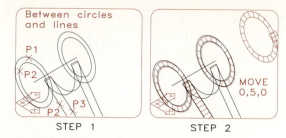

Figure 30.62 Applying the RULESURF command:
Step 1 Command: <u>RULESURF</u> (CR)

Select entity??: <u>P1</u>

Select entity??: <u>P2</u> (Circles are faced.)

Select entity??: <u>P3</u>

Select entity??: <u>P4</u> (Ends are faced.) (CR)

Step 2 Command: <u>MOVE</u> (CR)

Select objects? (Select faces) (CR)

Base point or displacement: <u>0,5,0</u> (CR)

(Faces are moved.)

MESHES: TABSURF

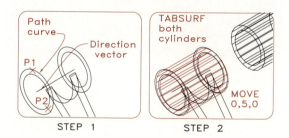

Figure 30.63 Using the TABSURF command:
Step 1 Command: <u>TABSURF</u>

Select path curve: <u>P1</u>

Select direction vector: <u>P2</u>

(The spacing between the tabulated vectors is determined by the SURFTAB1 variable.)

Step 2 Command: <u>MOVE</u> (CR)

Select objects? (Select faces) (CR)

Base point or displacement: <u>0,5,0</u> (CR)

(Faces are moved.)

MESHES: REVSURF

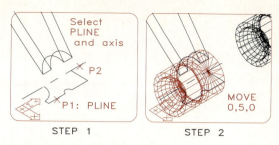

Figure 30.64 Applying the REVSURF command:
Step 1 Command: <u>REVSURF</u> (CR)

Select path of curve: <u>P1</u>

Select axis of revolution: <u>P2</u>

Start angle <0>: (CR)

Included angle (+=ccw,-=cw)<Full circle>: <u>360</u> (CR)

Step 2 Command: <u>MOVE</u> (CR)

Select objects? (Select faces) (CR)

Base point or displacement: <u>0,5,0</u> (CR)

(Faces are moved.)

Completion of the Connector **Figure 30.66** shows the beginning frame and two final views of the meshed connector, after we have applied the HIDE command. You may now obtain infinitely many views of the 3D connector drawing with the VIEWPOINT and DVIEW commands.

30.18 Introduction to Solid Modeling

Solid modeling is the technique of creating 3D solids from a combination of solid primitives—boxes, cylinders, spheres, and others—that can be added or subtracted from each other to form the final model. Unlike wire-diagram modeling, objects cannot be created on the screen that can-not actually be made

An exploded assembly of parts for a turbo is shown in **Fig. 30.67** as solid models. The parts of the turbo can be assembled and rendered with

MESHES: EDGESURF

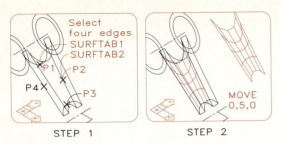

STEP 1   STEP 2

Figure 30.65 Utilizing the EDGESURF command:
Step 1 Command: <u>EDGESURF</u> (CR)

Select edge 1: <u>P1</u>

Select edge 2: <u>P2</u>

Select edge 3: <u>P3</u>

Select edge 4: <u>P4</u>

(Mesh is drawn in the boundary. System variables SURFTAB1 and SURFTAB2 determine the density of the mesh.)

Step 2 Command: <u>MOVE</u> (CR)

Select objects? (Select faces) (CR)

Base point or displacement: <u>0,5,0</u> (CR)

(Faces are moved.)

COMPLETED CONNECTOR 3D DRAWING

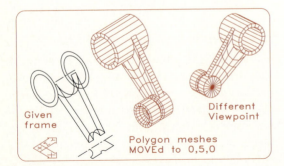

Figure 30.66 The given frame of the connector and the resulting 3D hollow shells from two viewpoints are shown here after use of the HIDE command.

Figure 30.67 Solid models of the parts of a turbo are shown here as an exploded assembly. (Courtesy of AutoDesk.)

Figure 30.68 The solid model of the turbo can be rendered with 3D Studio software. (Courtesy of AutoDesk.)

computer software, 3D Studio in this example (**Fig. 30.68**). The end result is a highly realistic 3D drawing shown in perspective.

30.19 An Example of Solid Modeling

Let's use the bracket shown in **Fig. 30.69** to produce a solid model. As shown in **Fig. 30.70**, first create the plan view of the base in the plane of the

BRACKET EXAMPLE

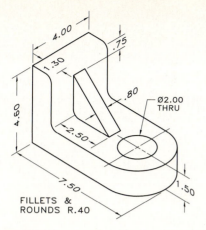

Figure 30.69 We use this bracket to demonstrate solid modeling in Figs. 30.70–30.76.

BRACKET: PART 1

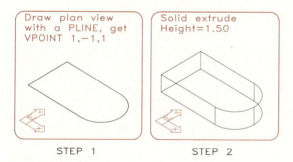

STEP 1   STEP 2

Figure 30.70 Bracket (SOLEXT command):
Step 1 Draw plan view of base of bracket with PLINE.

Command: <u>VPOINT</u> (CR)

Rotate/<Viewpoint>: <u>1,-1,1</u> (CR)

(Get isometric view of base.)

Step 2 Command: <u>SOLEXT</u> (CR)

(Select region's polylines and circles for extrusion.)

Select objects: <u>P1</u>

1 found

Select objects: (CR)

Height of extrusion: <u>1.50</u> (CR)

Extrusion taper angle <0>: (CR)

(Base is extruded to a 1.50 unit height.)

BRACKET: PART 2

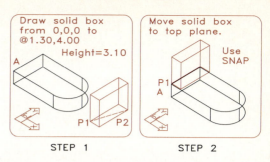

STEP 1   STEP 2

Figure 30.71 Bracket (SOLBOX command):
Step 1 Command: <u>SOLBOX</u> (CR)

Baseplane/Center/<Corner of box><0,0,0>: (CR)

Cube/Length/<Other corner>: <u>@1.30,4</u> (CR)

Height: <u>3.1</u> (CR) (Box is drawn.)

Step 2 (Set SNAP to END.)

Command: <u>MOVE</u> (CR)

Select objects: (Select box.)

Base point or displacement: <u>P1</u> (CR)

Second point of displacement: <u>A</u> (CR)

(Box is moved to base extrusion.)

XY icon as a PLINE and obtain an isometric view of it by VPOINT 1,-1,1. Then extrude the base to a height of 1.50 units.

Use SOLBOX to generate a box 1.30 × 4.00 × 3.10 units at a convenient location (**Fig. 30.71**) and then move P1 of the box to point A of the base. Use SOLWEDGE to draw a wedge conforming to the measurements of the bracket's rib (**Fig. 30.72**). Select and move the midpoint of a line on the wedge to the midpoint of the line on the upright box.

Next, create a cylinder with SOLCYL at a convenient position (**Fig. 30.73**) to represent the hole in the bracket. Then, move it to the center of the semicircular end of the base by using the Center option of OSNAP. **Figure 30.74** demonstrates how to use SOLSUB to subtract the hole from the base. Next, use SOLUNION to join the base, upright box, and wedge, making it a composite solid. Use

BRACKET: PART 3

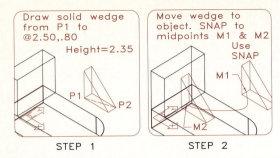

Figure 30.72 Bracket (SOLWEDGE command):
Step 1 Command: SOLWEDGE (CR)

Baseplane/<Corner of wedge>: P1 (CR)

Length/<Other corner>: @2.5,.8 (CR)

Height: 2.35 (CR) (Wedge is drawn.)

Step 2 (Set SNAP to MID.)

Command: MOVE (CR)

Select objects: (Select wedge.)

Base point or displacement: M1 (CR)

Second point of displacement: M2 (CR)

(Wedge is moved to midpoint of line.)

BRACKET: PART 4

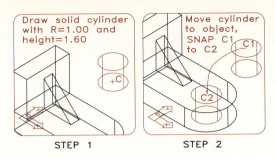

Figure 30.73 Bracket (SOCYL command):
Step 1 Command: SOLCYL or CYL (CR)

Elliptical/<Center point>: C (CR)

Diameter/<Radius>: 1.00 (CR)

Center of other end/<Height>: 1.60 (CR)

(Cylinder is drawn.)

Step 2 (Set SNAP to CENT.)

Command: MOVE (CR)

Select objects: (Select cylinder.)

Base point or displacement: P1 (CR)

Second point of displacement: P2 (CR)

(Cylinder is moved to center of arc.)

SOLFILL (**Fig. 30.75**) to select the edges to be filleted and rounded, specify a radius of 0.40 unit, and show fillets as wire diagrams. Finally, use SOLMESH to apply a mesh to the bracket and HIDE to suppress its hidden lines (**Fig. 30.76**). You may view the bracket with VPOINT or DVIEW from infinitely many viewpoints.

30.20 Advanced Applications

Computer graphics capabilities that were only ideas a decade ago are now realities in software form for today's applications. Perhaps the ultimate challenge in graphics has been the representation of the human figure. This has been achieved by HUMANCAD's Mannequin® software that can show men, women, and children of dif-

ferent nationalities of varying percentiles of size and weight in 2D and 3D drawings (**Fig. 30.77**). A similar application of the computer-represented man is shown in **Fig. 30.78.**

The computer, coupled with graphics software, can be used to depict designs as 2D and 3D images on the screen or on a sheet of paper. This same combination of hardware and software can be used to drive machining equipment to form the final parts with a minimum of worker interaction. **Figure 30.79** shows a computer-driven milling machine in the process of forming the prototype body of an automobile as a three-dimensional solid. Computer-driven robots are used to assemble and attach the components of automobiles on assembly lines not staffed with humans (**Fig. 30.80**).

BRACKET: PART 5

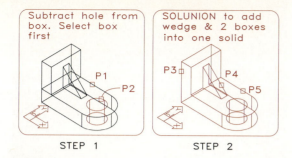

STEP 1   STEP 2

Figure 30.74 Bracket (SOLSUB and SOLUNION commands):

Step 1 Command: <u>SOLSUB</u>

Source objects...

Select objects: <u>P1</u>

Select objects: (CR)

1 solid selected.

Objects to subtract from them...

Select objects: <u>P2</u>

Select objects: (CR)

2 solids selected. (Hole is removed.)

Step 2 Command: <u>SOLUNION</u> (CR)

Select objects: <u>P3, P4, P5</u>

Select objects: (CR)

3 solids selected. (Bracket is unified.)

Also available is the multimedia approach, which combines images, sound, color, and motion. The images can be computer drawings, still photographs, or televised images in motion. When such images are combined, a Hollywood-type program can be developed to utilize a full range of sound, graphics, and motion.

Each upgrade of a software package brings with it more powerful applications at lower cost, giving us greater capabilities. We are challenged to be sufficiently creative so that we properly utilize the available capabilities. The future of computer applications appears ever widening and unlimited.

BRACKET: PART 6

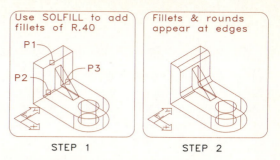

STEP 1   STEP 2

Figure 30.75 Bracket (SOLFILL command):

Step 1 Command: <u>SOLFILL</u>

Pick edges of solids to be filleted

(Press ENTER when done): <u>P1, P2, P3</u> (CR)

3 edges selected.

Step 2 Diameter/<Radius> of fillet<0.00>: <u>.40</u> (CR)

(Fillets and rounds are indicated on bracket.)

BRACKET: PART 7

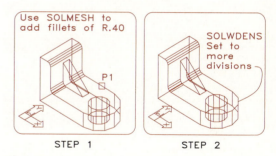

STEP 1   STEP 2

Figure 30.76 Bracket (SOLMESH and HIDE commands):

Step 1 Command: <u>SOLMESH</u> (CR)

Select solids to be meshed...

Select objects: <u>P1</u> (CR)

1 solid selected.

Surface meshing of current solid is completed.

Creating block for mesh representation...

Done.

Step 2 Command: <u>HIDE</u> (CR)

Regenerating drawing.

Hiding lines: done 100% (Visibility is shown.)

(SOLWDENS can be set from 1 to 12 to adjust the density of the 3D faces on curving surfaces.)

Figure 30.77 Human figures by MANNEQUIN® can be made to move and walk in orthographic, isometric, and perspective. (Courtesy of HUMANCAD.)

Figure 30.79 The computer and graphics software are used to form this three-dimensional automobile part prototype. (Courtesy of Chrysler Corporation.)

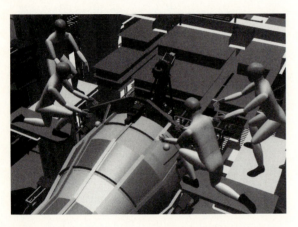

Figure 30.78 Humans working in space are represented by computer using Ergoman software. (Courtesy of Trilby Wallace, McDonald Douglas Space and Defense Systems.)

Figure 30.80 Automobiles are assembled and fabricated by computer-driven robots. (Courtesy of Ford Motor Company.)

Appendix Contents

APPENDIX 1 • Abbreviations (ANSI Z 32.13)

Word	Abbreviation	Word	Abbreviation	Word	Abbreviation
Allowance	ALLOW	Elevation	ELEV	Not to scale	NTS
Alloy	ALY	Equal	EQ	Number	NO.
Aluminum	AL	Estimate	EST	Octagon	OCT
Amount	AMT	Exterior	EXT	On center	OC
Anneal	ANL	Fahrenheit	F	Ounce	OZ
Approximate	APPROX	Feet	(') FT	Outside diameter	OD
Area	A	Feet per minute	FPM	Parallel	PAR.
Assembly	ASSY	Feet per second	FPS	Perpendicular	PERP
Auxiliary	AUX	Fillet	FIL	Piece	PC
Average	AVG	Fillister	FIL	Plastic	PLSTC
Babbitt	BAB	Finish	FIN.	Plate	PL
Between	BET.	Finish all over	FAO	Point	PT
Between centers	BC	Flat head	FH	Polish	POL
Bevel	BEV	Foot	(') FT	Pound	LB
Bill of material	B/M	Front	FR	Pounds per square inch	PSI
Both sides	BS	Gage	GA	Pressure	PRESS.
Bottom	BOT	Gallon	GAL	Production	PROD
Brass	BRS	Galvanize	GALV	Quarter	QTR
Brazing	BRZG	Galvanized iron	GI	Radius	R
Broach	BRO	General	GEN	Ream	RM
Bronze	BRZ	Gram	G	Rectangle	RECT
Cadmium plate	CD PL	Grind	GRD	Reference	REF
Cap screw	CAP SCR	Groove	GRV	Required	REQD
Case harden	CH	Hardware	HDW	Revise	REV
Cast iron	CI	Head	HD	Revolution	REV
Cast steel	CS	Heat treat	HT TR	Revolutions per minute	RPM
Casting	CSTG	Hexagon	HEX	Right	R
Center	CTR	Horizontal	HOR	Right hand	RH
Centerline	CL	Horsepower	HP	Rough	RGH
Center to center	C to C	Hot rolled steel	HRS	Screw	SCR
Centigrade	C	Hour	HR	Section	SECT
Centigram	CG	Hundredweight	CWT	Set screw	SS
Centimeter	cm	Inch	(") IN.	Shaft	SFT
Chamfer	CHAM	Inches per second	IPS	Slotted	SLOT.
Circle	CIR	Inside diameter	ID	Socket	SOC
Clockwise	CW	Interior	INT	Spherical	SPHER
Cold rolled steel	CRS	Iron	I	Spot faced	SF
Cotter	COT	Key	K	Spring	SPG
Counterclockwise	CCW	Kip (1000 lb)	K	Square	SQ
Counterbore	CBORE	Left	L	Station	STA
Counterdrill	CDRILL	Left hand	LH	Steel	STL
Counterpunch	CPUNCH	Length	LG	Symmetrical	SYM
Countersink	CSK	Light	LT	Taper	TPR
Cubic centimeter	cc	Machine	MACH	Temperature	TEMP
Cubic feet per minute	CFM	Malleable	MALL	Tension	TENS.
Cubic foot	CU FT	Manhole	MH	Thick	THK
Cubic inch	CU IN.	Manufacture	MFR	Thousand	M
Cylinder	CYL	Material	MATL	Thousand pound	KIP
Diagonal	DIAG	Maximum	MAX	Thread	THD
Diameter	DIA	Metal	MET.	Tolerance	TOL
Distance	DIST	Meter (Instrument or		Typical	TYP
Ditto	DO	measure of length)	M	Vertical	VERT
Down	DN	Miles	MI	Volume	VOL
Dozen	DOZ	Miles per gallon	MPG	Washer	WASH.
Drafting	DFTG	Miles per hour	MPH	Weight	WT
Drawing	DWG	Millimeter	MM	Width	W
Drill	DR	Minimum	MIN	Wrought iron	WI
Each	EA	Normal	NOR	Yard	YD

DECIMAL EQUIVALENTS—INCH-MILLIMETER CONVERSION TABLE

1/2	1/4	1/8	1/16	1/32	1/64	Decimals	Millimeters
					1	.015625	.396875
				1		.031250	.793750
					3	.046875	1.190625
			1			.062500	1.587500
					5	.078125	1.984375
				3		.093750	2.381250
					7	.109375	2.778125
		1				.125000	3.175000
					9	.140625	3.571875
				5		.156250	3.968750
					11	.171875	4.365625
			3			.187500	4.762500
					13	.203125	5.159375
				7		.218750	5.556250
					15	.234375	5.953125
	1					.250000	6.350000
					17	.265625	6.746875
				9		.281250	7.143750
					19	.296875	7.540625
			5			.312500	7.937500
					21	.328125	8.334375
				11		.343750	8.731250
					23	.359375	9.128125
		3				.375000	9.525000
					25	.390625	9.921875
				13		.406250	10.318750
					27	.421875	10.715625
			7			.437500	11.112500
					29	.453125	11.509375
				15		.468750	11.906250
					31	.484375	12.303125
1						.500000	12.700000

1/2	1/4	1/8	1/16	1/32	1/64	Decimals	Millimeters
					33	.515625	13.096875
				17		.531250	13.493750
					35	.546875	13.890625
			9			.562500	14.287500
					37	.578125	14.684375
				19		.593750	15.081250
					39	.609375	15.478125
		5				.625000	15.875000
					41	.640625	16.271875
				21		.656250	16.668750
					43	.671875	17.065625
			11			.687500	17.462500
					45	.703125	17.859375
				23		.718750	18.256250
					47	.734375	18.653125
	3					.750000	19.050000
					49	.765625	19.446875
				25		.781250	19.843750
					51	.796875	20.240625
			13			.812500	20.637500
					53	.828125	21.034375
				27		.843750	21.431250
					55	.859375	21.828125
		7				.875000	22.225000
					57	.890625	22.621875
				29		.906250	23.018750
					59	.921875	23.415625
			15			.937500	23.812500
					61	.953125	24.209375
				31		.968750	24.606250
					63	.984375	25.003125
2	4	8	16	32	64	1.000000	25.400000

LENGTH

1 millimeter (mm) = 0.03937 inch
1 centimeter (cm) = 0.39370 inch
1 meter (m) = 39.37008 inches
1 meter = 3.2808 feet
1 meter = 1.0936 yards
1 kilometer (km) = 0.6214 mile
1 inch = 25.4 millimeters (mm)
1 inch = 2.54 centimeters
1 foot = 304.8 millimeters
1 foot = 0.3048 meter
1 yard = 0.9144 meter
1 mile = 1.609 kilometers

DRY CAPACITY

1 cubic centimeter (cm3) = 0.061 cubic inch
1 liter = 0.0353 cubic foot
1 liter = 61.023 cubic inches
1 cubic meter (m3) = 35.315 cubic feet
1 cubic meter = 1.308 cubic yards
1 cubic inch = 16.38706 cubic centimeters
1 cubic foot = 0.02832 cubic meter
1 cubic foot = 28.317 liters
1 cubic yard = 0.7646 cubic meter

AREA

1 square millimeter = 0.00155 square inch
1 square centimeter = 0.155 square inch
1 square meter = 10.764 square feet
1 square meter = 1.196 square yards
1 square kilometer = 0.3861 square mile
1 square inch = 645.2 square millimeters
1 square inch = 6.452 square centimeters
1 square foot = 929 square centimeters
1 square foot = 0.0929 square meter
1 square yard = 0.836 square meter
1 square mile = 2.5899 square kilometers

LIQUID CAPACITY

1 liter = 1.0567 U.S. quarts
1 liter = 0.2642 U.S. gallon
1 liter = 0.2200 Imperial gallon
1 cubic meter = 264.2 U.S. gallons
1 cubic meter = 219.969 Imperial gallons
1 U.S. quart = 0.946 liter
1 Imperial quart = 1.136 liters
1 U.S. gallon = 3.785 liters
1 Imperial gallon = 4.546 liters

WEIGHT

1 gram (g) = 15.432 grains
1 gram = 0.03215 ounce troy
1 gram = 0.03527 ounce avoirdupois
1 kilogram (kg) = 35.274 ounces avoirdupois
1 kilogram = 2.2046 pounds
1000 kilograms = 1 metric ton (t)
1000 kilograms = 1.1023 tons of 2000 pounds
1000 kilograms = 0.9842 ton of 2240 pounds
1 ounce avoirdupois = 28.35 grams
1 ounce troy = 31.103 grams
1 pound = 453.6 grams
1 pound = 0.4536 kilogram
1 ton of 2240 pounds = 1016 kilograms
1 ton of 2240 pounds = 1.016 metric tons
1 grain = 0.0648 gram
1 metric ton = 0.9842 ton of 2240 pounds
1 metric ton = 2204.6 pounds

APPENDIX 4 • Logarithms of Numbers

N	0	1	2	3	4	5	6	7	8	9
1.0	.0000	.0043	.0086	.0128	.0170	.0212	.0253	.0294	.0334	.0374
1.1	.0414	.0453	.0492	.0531	.0569	.0607	.0645	.0682	.0719	.0755
1.2	.0792	.0828	.0864	.0899	.0934	.0969	.1004	.1038	.1072	.1106
1.3	.1139	.1173	.1206	.1239	.1271	.1303	.1335	.1367	.1399	.1430
1.4	.1461	.1492	.1523	.1553	.1584	.1614	.1644	.1673	.1703	.1732
1.5	.1761	.1790	.1818	.1847	.1875	.1903	.1931	.1959	.1987	.2014
1.6	.2041	.2068	.2095	.2122	.2148	.2175	.2201	.2227	.2253	.2279
1.7	.2304	.2330	.2355	.2380	.2405	.2430	.2455	.2480	.2504	.2529
1.8	.2553	.2577	.2601	.2625	.2648	.2672	.2695	.2718	.2742	.2765
1.9	.2788	.2810	.2833	.2856	.2878	.2900	.2923	.2945	.2967	.2989
2.0	.3010	.3032	.3054	.3075	.3096	.3118	.3139	.3160	.3181	.3201
2.1	.3222	.3243	.3263	.3284	.3304	.3324	.3345	.3365	.3385	.3404
2.2	.3424	.3444	.3464	.3483	.3502	.3522	.3541	.3560	.3579	.3598
2.3	.3617	.3636	.3655	.3674	.3692	.3711	.3729	.3747	.3766	.3784
2.4	.3802	.3820	.3838	.3856	.3874	.3892	.3909	.3927	.3945	.3962
2.5	.3979	.3997	.4014	.4031	.4048	.4065	.4082	.4099	.4116	.4133
2.6	.4150	.4166	.4183	.4200	.4216	.4232	.4249	.4265	.4281	.4298
2.7	.4314	.4330	.4346	.4362	.4378	.4393	.4409	.4425	.4440	.4456
2.8	.4472	.4487	.4502	.4518	.4533	.4548	.4564	.4579	.4594	.4609
2.9	.4624	.4639	.4654	.4669	.4683	.4698	.4713	.4728	.4742	.4757
3.0	.4771	.4786	.4800	.4814	.4829	.4843	.4857	.4871	.4886	.4900
3.1	.4914	.4928	.4942	.4955	.4969	.4983	.4997	.5011	.5024	.5038
3.2	.5051	.5065	.5079	.5092	.5105	.5119	.5132	.5145	.5159	.5172
3.3	.5185	.5198	.5211	.5224	.5237	.5250	.5263	.5276	.5289	.5302
3.4	.5315	.5328	.5340	.5353	.5366	.5378	.5391	.5403	.5416	.5428
3.5	.5441	.5453	.5465	.5478	.5490	.5502	.5514	.5527	.5539	.5551
3.6	.5563	.5575	.5587	.5599	.5611	.5623	.5635	.5647	.5658	.5670
3.7	.5682	.5694	.5705	.5717	.5729	.5740	.5752	.5763	.5775	.5786
3.8	.5798	.5809	.5821	.5832	.5843	.5855	.5866	.5877	.5888	.5899
3.9	.5911	.5922	.5933	.5944	.5955	.5966	.5977	.5988	.5999	.6010
4.0	.6021	.6031	.6042	.6053	.6064	.6075	.6085	.6096	.6107	.6117
4.1	.6128	.6138	.6149	.6160	.6170	.6180	.6191	.6201	.6212	.6222
4.2	.6232	.6243	.6253	.6263	.6274	.6284	.6294	.6304	.6314	.6325
4.3	.6335	.6345	.6355	.6365	.6375	.6385	.6395	.6405	.6415	.6425
4.4	.6435	.6444	.6454	.6464	.6474	.6484	.6493	.6503	.6513	.6522
4.5	.6532	.6542	.6551	.6561	.6571	.6580	.6590	.6599	.6609	.6618
4.6	.6628	.6637	.6646	.6656	.6665	.6675	.6684	.6693	.6702	.6712
4.7	.6721	.6730	.6739	.6749	.6758	.6767	.6776	.6785	.6794	.6803
4.8	.6812	.6821	.6830	.6839	.6848	.6857	.6866	.6875	.6884	.6893
4.9	.6902	.6911	.6920	.6928	.6937	.6946	.6955	.6964	.6972	.6981
5.0	.6990	.6998	.7007	.7016	.7024	.7033	.7042	.7050	.7059	.7067
5.1	.7076	.7084	.7093	.7101	.7110	.7118	.7126	.7135	.7143	.7152
5.2	.7160	.7168	.7177	.7185	.7193	.7202	.7210	.7218	.7226	.7235
5.3	.7243	.7251	.7259	.7267	.7275	.7284	.7292	.7300	.7308	7316
5.4	.7324	.7332	.7340	.7348	.7356	.7364	.7372	.7380	.7388	.7396
N	0	1	2	3	4	5	6	7	8	9

N	0	1	2	3	4	5	6	7	8	9
5.5	.7404	.7412	.7419	.7427	.7435	.7443	.7451	.7459	.7466	.7474
5.6	.7482	.7490	.7497	.7505	.7513	.7520	.7528	.7536	.7543	.7551
5.7	.7559	.7566	.7574	.7582	.7589	.7597	.7604	.7612	.7619	.7627
5.8	.7634	.7642	.7649	.7657	.7664	.7672	.7679	.7686	.7694	.7701
5.9	.7709	.7716	.7723	.7731	.7738	.7745	.7752	.7760	.7767	.7774
6.0	.7782	.7789	.7796	.7803	.7810	.7818	.7825	.7832	.7839	.7846
6.1	.7853	.7860	.7868	.7875	.7882	.7889	.7896	.7903	.7910	.7917
6.2	.7924	.7931	.7938	.7945	.7952	.7959	.7966	.7973	.7980	.7987
6.3	.7993	.8000	.8007	.8014	.8021	.8028	.8035	.8041	.8048	.8055
6.4	.8062	.8069	.8075	.8082	.8089	.8096	.8102	.8109	.8116	.8122
6.5	.8129	.8136	.8142	.8149	.8156	.8162	.8169	.8176	.8182	.8189
6.6	.8195	.8202	.8209	.8215	.8222	.8228	.8235	.8241	.8248	.8254
6.7	.8261	.8267	.8274	.8280	.8287	.8293	.8299	.8306	.8312	.8319
6.8	.8325	.8331	.8338	.8344	.8351	.8357	.8363	.8370	.8376	.8382
6.9	.8388	.8395	.8401	.8407	.8414	.8420	.8426	.8432	.8439	.8445
7.0	.8451	.8457	.8463	.8470	.8476	.8482	.8488	.8494	.8500	.8506
7.1	.8513	.8519	.8525	.8531	.8537	.8543	.8549	.8555	.8561	.8567
7.2	.8573	.8579	.8585	.8591	.8597	.8603	.8609	.8615	.8621	.8627
7.3	.8633	.8639	.8645	.8651	.8657	.8663	.8669	.8675	.8681	.8686
7.4	.8692	.8698	.8704	.8710	.8716	.8722	.8727	.8733	.8739	.8745
7.5	.8751	.8756	.8762	.8768	.8774	.8779	.8785	.8791	.8797	.8802
7.6	.8808	.8814	.8820	.8825	.8831	.8837	.8842	.8848	.8854	.8859
7.7	.8865	.8871	.8876	.8882	.8887	.8893	.8899	.8904	.8910	.8915
7.8	.8921	.8927	.8932	.8938	.8943	.8949	.8954	.8960	.8965	.8971
7.9	.8976	.8982	.8987	.8993	.8998	.9004	.9009	.9015	.9020	.9025
8.0	.9031	.9036	.9042	.9047	.9053	.9058	.9063	.9069	.9074	.9079
8.1	.9085	.9090	.9096	.9101	.9106	.9112	.9117	.9122	.9128	.9133
8.2	.9138	.9143	.9149	.9154	.9159	.9165	.9170	.9175	.9180	.9186
8.3	.9191	.9196	.9201	.9206	.9212	.9217	.9222	.9227	.9232	.9238
8.4	.9243	.9248	.9253	.9258	.9263	.9269	.9274	.9279	.9284	.9289
8.5	.9294	.9299	.9304	.9309	.9315	.9320	.9325	.9330	.9335	.9340
8.6	.9345	.9350	.9355	.9360	.9365	.9370	.9375	.9380	.9385	.9390
8.7	.9395	.9400	.9405	.9410	.9415	.9420	.9425	.9430	.9435	.9440
8.8	.9445	.9450	.9455	.9460	.9465	.9469	.9474	.9479	.9484	.9489
8.9	.9494	.9499	.9504	.9509	.9513	.9518	.9523	.9528	.9533	.9538
9.0	.9542	.9547	.9552	.9557	.9562	.9566	.9571	.9576	.9581	.9586
9.1	.9590	.9595	.9600	.9605	.9609	.9614	.9619	.9624	.9628	.9633
9.2	.9638	.9643	.9647	.9652	.9657	.9661	.9666	.9671	.9675	.9680
9.3	.9685	.9689	.9694	.9699	.9703	.9708	.9713	.9717	.9722	.9727
9.4	.9731	.9736	.9741	.9745	.9750	.9754	.9759	.9763	.9768	.9773
9.5	.9777	.9782	.9786	.9791	.9795	.9800	.9805	.9809	.9814	.9818
9.6	.9823	.9827	.9832	.9836	.9841	.9845	.9850	.9854	.9859	.9863
9.7	.9868	.9872	.9877	.9881	.9886	.9890	.9894	.9899	.9903	.9908
9.8	.9912	.9917	.9921	.9926	.9930	.9934	.9939	.9943	.9948	.9952
9.9	.9956	.9961	.9965	.9969	.9974	.9978	.9983	.9987	.9991	.9996
N	0	1	2	3	4	5	6	7	8	9

APPENDIX 5 • Trigonometric Functions

ANGLE in DEGREES	SINE	COSINE	TAN	COTAN	ANGLE in DEGREES
0	0.0000	1.0000	0.0000		90
1	.0175	.9998	.0175	57.290	89
2	.0349	.9994	.0349	28.636	88
3	.0523	.9986	.0524	19.081	87
4	.0698	.9976	.0699	14.301	86
5	.0872	.9962	.0875	11.430	85
6	.1045	.9945	.1051	9.5144	84
7	.1219	.9925	.1228	8.1443	83
8	.1392	.9903	.1405	7.1154	82
9	.1564	.9877	.1584	6.3138	81
10	.1736	.9848	.1763	5.6713	80
11	.1908	.9816	.1944	5.1446	79
12	.2079	.9781	.2126	4.7046	78
13	.2250	.9744	.2309	4.3315	77
14	.2419	.9703	.2493	4.0108	76
15	.2588	.9659	.2679	3.7321	75
16	.2756	.9613	.2867	3.4874	74
17	.2924	.9563	.3057	3.2709	73
18	.3090	.9511	.3249	3.0777	72
19	.3256	.9455	.3443	2.9042	71
20	.3420	.9397	.3640	2.7475	70
21	.3584	.9336	.3839	2.6051	69
22	.3746	.9272	.4040	2.4751	68
23	.3907	.9205	.4245	2.3559	67
24	.4067	.9135	.4452	2.2460	66
25	.4226	.9063	.4663	2.1445	65
26	.4384	.8988	.4877	2.0503	64
27	.4540	.8910	.5095	1.9626	63
28	.4695	.8829	.5317	1.8807	62
29	.4848	.8746	.5543	1.8040	61
30	.5000	.8660	.5774	1.7321	60
31	.5150	.8572	.6009	1.6643	59
32	.5299	.8480	.6249	1.6003	58
33	.5446	.8387	.6494	1.5399	57
34	.5592	.8290	.6745	1.4826	56
35	.5736	.8192	.7002	1.4281	55
36	.5878	.8090	.7265	1.3764	54
37	.6018	.7986	.7536	1.3270	53
38	.6157	.7880	.7813	1.2799	52
39	.6293	.7771	.8098	1.2349	51
40	.6428	.7660	.8391	1.1918	50
41	.6561	.7547	.8693	1.1504	49
42	.6691	.7431	.9004	1.1106	48
43	.6820	.7314	.9325	1.0724	47
44	.6947	.7193	.9657	1.0355	46
45	.7071	.7071	1.0000	1.0000	45

APPENDIX 6 • Screw Threads: American National and Unified (inches)

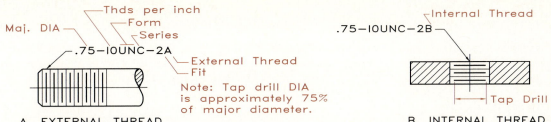

A. EXTERNAL THREAD

Note: Tap drill DIA is approximately 75% of major diameter.

B. INTERNAL THREAD

Nominal Diameter	Basic Diameter	Coarse NC & UNC		Fine NF & UNF		Extra Fine NEF/UNEF	
		Thds per In.	Tap Drill DIA	Thds per In.	Tap Drill DIA	Thds per In.	Tap Drill DIA
0	.060			80	.0469		
1	.073	64	No.53	72	No.53		
2	.086	56	No.50	64	No.50		
3	.099	48	No.47	56	No.45		
4	.112	40	No.43	48	No.42		
5	.125	40	No.38	44	No.37		
6	.138	32	No.36	40	No.33		
8	.164	32	No.29	36	No.29		
10	.190	24	No.25	32	No.21		
12	.216	24	No.16	28	No.14	32	No.13
1/4	.250	20	No.7	28	No.3	32	.2189
5/16	.3125	18	F	24	I	32	.2813
3/8	.375	16	.3125	24	Q	32	.3438
7/16	.4375	14	U	20	.3906	28	.4062
1/2	.500	13	.4219	20	.4531	28	.4688
9/16	.5625	12	.4844	18	.5156	24	.5156
5/8	.625	11	.5313	18	.5781	24	.5781
11/16	.6875	...	...	...	...	24	.6406
3/4	.750	10	.6563	16	.6875	20	.7031
13/16	.8125	...	...	...	...	20	.7656
7/8	.875	9	.7656	14	.8125	20	.8281
15/16	.9375	...	...	...	...	20	.8906

Nominal Diameter	Basic Diameter	Coarse NC & UNC		Fine NF & UNF		Extra Fine NEF/UNEF	
		Thds per In.	Tap Drill DIA	Thds per In.	Tap Drill DIA	Thds per In.	Tap Drill DIA
1	1.000	8	.875	12	.922	20	.953
1–1/16	1.063	...	...	...	...	18	1.000
1–1/8	1.125	7	.904	12	1.046	18	1.070
1–3/16	1.188	...	...	...	...	18	1.141
1–1/4	1.250	7	1.109	12	1,172	18	1.188
1–5/16	1.313	...	...	...	...	18	1.266
1–3/8	1.375	6	1.219	12	1.297	18	1.313
1–7/16	1.438	...	...	...	...	18	1.375
1–1/2	1.500	6	1.344	12	1.422	18	1.438
1–9/16	1.563	...	...	...	...	18	1.500
1–5/8	1.625	...	...	...	...	18	1.563
1–11/16	1.688	...	...	...	...	18	1.625
1–3/4	1.750	5	1.563	...	...	...	...
2	2.000	4.5	1.781	...	...	...	...
2–1/4	2.250	4.5	2.031	...	...	...	...
2–1/2	2.500	4	2.250	...	...	...	...
2–3/4	2.750	4	2.500	...	...	...	...
3	3.000	4	2.750	...	...	...	...
3–1/4	3.250	4	...	...	...	...	...
3–1/2	3.500	4	...	...	...	...	...
3–3/4	3.750	4	...	...	...	...	...
4	4.000	4	...	...	...	...	...

Source: ANSI/ASME B1.1–1989

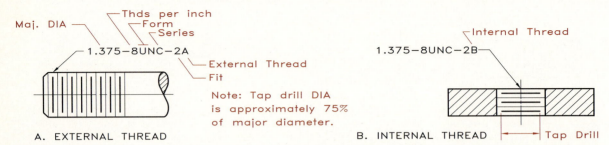

A. EXTERNAL THREAD

B. INTERNAL THREAD

Note: Tap drill DIA is approximately 75% of major diameter.

Nominal Diameter	8 Pitch 8N & 8UN		12 Pitch 12N & 12UN		16 Pitch 16N & 16UN		Nominal Diameter	8 Pitch 8N & 8UN		12 Pitch 12N & 12UN		16 Pitch 16N & 16UN	
	Thds per In.	Tap Drill DIA	Thds per In.	Tap Drill DIA	Thds per In.	Tap Drill DIA		Thds per In.	Tap Drill DIA	Thds per In.	Tap Drill DIA	Thds per In.	Tap Drill DIA
.500	...	...	12	.422	...	...	2.063	...	...	...	...	16	2.000
.563	...	...	12	.484	...	...	2.125	...	...	12	2.047	16	2.063
.625	...	...	12	.547	...	...	2.188	...	...	...	...	16	2.125
.688	...	...	12	.609	...	...	2.250	8	2.125	12	2.172	16	2.188
.750	...	...	12	.672	16	.688	2.313	...	...	...	...	16	2.250
.813	...	...	12	.734	16	.750	2.375	...	...	12	2.297	16	2.313
.875	...	...	12	.797	16	.813	2.438	...	...	...	...	16	2.375
.934	...	...	12	.859	16	.875	2.500	8	2.375	12	2.422	16	2.438
1.000	8	.875	12	.922	16	.938	2.625	...	...	12	2.547	16	2.563
1.063	...	...	12	.984	16	1.000	2.750	8	2.625	12	2.717	16	2.688
1.125	8	1.000	12	1.047	16	1.063	2.875	...	...	12	...	16	...
1.188	...	...	12	1.109	16	1.125	3.000	8	2.875	12	...	16	...
1.250	8	1.125	12	1.172	16	1.188	3.125	...	...	12	...	16	...
1.313	...	...	12	1.234	16	1.250	3.250	8	...	12	...	16	...
1.375	8	1.250	12	1.297	16	1.313	3.375	...	...	12	...	16	...
1.434	...	...	12	1.359	16	1.375	3.500	8	...	12	...	16	...
1.500	8	1.375	12	1.422	16	1.438	3.625	...	...	12	...	16	...
1.563	...	...	...	...	16	1.500	3.750	8	...	12	...	16	...
1.625	8	1.500	12	1.547	16	1.563	3.875	...	...	12	...	16	...
1.688	...	...	...	...	16	1.625	4.000	8	...	12	...	16	...
1.750	8	1.625	12	1.672	16	1.688	4.250	8	...	12	...	16	...
1.813	...	...	...	...	16	1.750	4.500	8	...	12	...	16	...
1.875	8	1.750	12	1.797	16	1.813	4.750	8	...	12	...	16	...
1.934	...	...	...	...	16	1.875	5.000	8	...	12	...	16	...
2.000	8	1.875	12	1.922	16	1.938	5.250	8	...	12	...	16	...

Source: ANSI/ASME B1.1—1989.

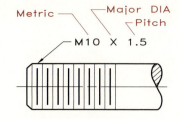

Metric — Major DIA
— Pitch
M10 X 1.5

A. EXTERNAL THREAD

Note: Tap drill DIA
is approximately 75%
of major diameter.

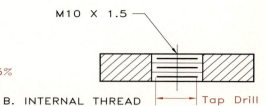

M10 X 1.5

B. INTERNAL THREAD — Tap Drill

COARSE		FINE		COARSE		FINE	
MAJ. DIA & THD PITCH	TAP DRILL	MAJ. DIA & THD PITCH	TAP DRILL	MAJ. DIA & THD PITCH	TAP DRILL	MAJ. DIA & THD PITCH	TAP DRILL
M1.6 X 0.35	1.25			M20 X 2.5	17.5	M20 X 1.5	18.5
M1.8 X 0.35	1.45			M22 X 2.5	19.5	M22 X 1.5	20.5
M2 X 0.4	1.6			M24 X 3	21.0	M24 X 2	22.0
M2.2 X 0.45	1.75			M27 X 3	24.0	M27 X 2	25.0
M2.5 X 0.45	2.05			M30 X 3.5	26.5	M30 X 2	28.0
M3 X 0.5	2.5			M33 X 3.5	29.5	M33 X 2	31.0
M3.5 X 0.6	2.9			M36 X 4	32.0	M36 X 3	33.0
M4 X 0.7	3.3			M39 X 4	35.0	M39 X 3	36.0
M4.5 X 0.75	3.75			M42 X 4.5	37.5	M42 X 3	39.0
M5 X 0.8	4.2			M45 X 4.5	40.5	M45 X 3	42.0
M6 X 1	5.0			M48 X 5	43.0	M48 X 3	45.0
M7 X 1	6.0			M52 X 5	47.0	M52 X 3	49.0
M8 X 1.25	6.8	M8 X 1	7.0	M56 X 5.5	50.5	M56 X 4	52.0
M9 X 1.25	7.75			M60 X 5.5	54.5	M60 X 4	56.0
M10 X 1.5	8.5	M10 X 1.25	8.75	M64 X 6	58.0	M64 X 4	60.0
M11 X 1.5	9.5			M68 X 6	62.0	M68 X 4	64.0
M12 X 1.75	10.3	M12 X 1.25	10.5	M72 X 6	66.0	M72 X 4	68.0
M14 X 2	12.0	M14 X 1.5	12.5	M80 X 6	74.0	M80 X 4	76.0
M16 X 2	14.0	M16 X 1.5	14.5	M90 X 6	84.0	M90 X 4	86.0
M18 X 2.5	15.5	M18 X 1.5	16.5	M100 X 6	94.0	M100 X 4	96.0

Source: ANSI/ASME B1.1—1989.

APPENDIX 9 • Square and Acme Threads

2.00−2.5 SQUARE

Typical thread note

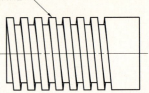

Dimensions are in inches.

Size	Size	Thds per inch	Size	Size	Thds per inch	Size	Size	Thds per inch
3/8	.375	12	1−1/8	1.125	4	3	3.000	1−1/2
7/16	.438	10	1−1/4	1.250	4	3−1/4	3.125	1−1/2
1/2	.500	10	1−1/2	1.500	3	3−1/2	3.500	1−1/3
9/16	.563	8	1−3/4	1.750	2−1/2	3−3/4	3.750	1−1/3
5/8	.625	8	2	2.000	2−1/2	4	4.000	1−1/3
3/4	.75	6	2−1/4	2.250	2	4−1/4	4.250	1−1/3
7/8	.875	5	2−1/2	2.500	2	4−1/2	4.500	1
1	1.000	5	2−3/4	2.750	2	Larger		1

APPENDIX 10 • American Standard Taper Pipe Threads (NPT)

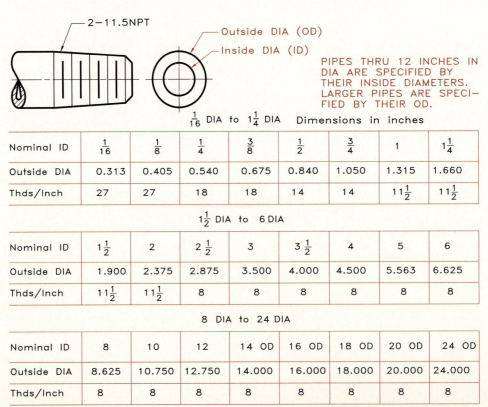

2−11.5NPT

Outside DIA (OD)

Inside DIA (ID)

PIPES THRU 12 INCHES IN DIA ARE SPECIFIED BY THEIR INSIDE DIAMETERS. LARGER PIPES ARE SPECIFIED BY THEIR OD.

$\frac{1}{16}$ DIA to $1\frac{1}{4}$ DIA   Dimensions in inches

Nominal ID	$\frac{1}{16}$	$\frac{1}{8}$	$\frac{1}{4}$	$\frac{3}{8}$	$\frac{1}{2}$	$\frac{3}{4}$	1	$1\frac{1}{4}$
Outside DIA	0.313	0.405	0.540	0.675	0.840	1.050	1.315	1.660
Thds/Inch	27	27	18	18	14	14	$11\frac{1}{2}$	$11\frac{1}{2}$

$1\frac{1}{2}$ DIA to 6 DIA

Nominal ID	$1\frac{1}{2}$	2	$2\frac{1}{2}$	3	$3\frac{1}{2}$	4	5	6
Outside DIA	1.900	2.375	2.875	3.500	4.000	4.500	5.563	6.625
Thds/Inch	$11\frac{1}{2}$	$11\frac{1}{2}$	8	8	8	8	8	8

8 DIA to 24 DIA

Nominal ID	8	10	12	14 OD	16 OD	18 OD	20 OD	24 OD
Outside DIA	8.625	10.750	12.750	14.000	16.000	18.000	20.000	24.000
Thds/Inch	8	8	8	8	8	8	8	8

Source: ANSI B2.1.

APPENDIX 11 • Square Bolts (inches)

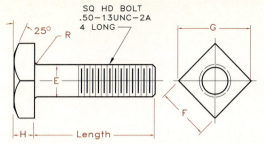

SQ HD BOLT
.50−13UNC−2A
4 LONG

STANDARD COMMERCIAL LENGTHS

*14 MEANS THAT LENGTHS ARE AVAILABLE
AT 1 INCH INCREMENTS UP 14 INCHES.

DIA	E Max.	F Max.	G Avg.	H Max.	R Max.
1/4	.250	.375	.530	.188	.031
5/16	.313	.500	.707	.220	.031
3/8	.375	.563	.795	.268	.031
7/16	.438	.625	.884	.316	.031
1/2	.500	.750	1.061	.348	.031
5/8	.625	.938	1.326	.444	.062

DIA	E Max.	F Max.	G Avg.	H Max.	R Max.
3/4	.750	1.125	1.591	.524	.062
7/8	.875	1.313	1.856	.620	.062
1	1.000	1.500	2.121	.684	.093
1−1/8	1.125	1.688	2.386	.780	.093
1−1/4	1.250	1.875	2.652	.876	.093
1−3/8	1.375	2.625	2.917	.940	.093
1−1/2	1.500	2.250	3.182	1.036	.093

APPENDIX 12 • Square Nuts

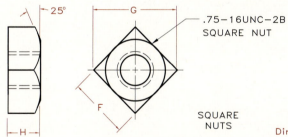

.75−16UNC−2B
SQUARE NUT

SQUARE NUTS

Dimensions are in inches.

DIA	DIA	F Max.	G Avg.	H Max.
1/4	.250	.438	.619	.235
5/16	.313	.563	.795	.283
3/8	.375	.625	.884	.346
7/16	.438	.750	1.061	.394
1/2	.500	.813	1.149	.458
5/8	.625	1.000	1.414	.569

DIA	DIA	F Max.	G Avg.	H Max.
3/4	.750	1.125	1.591	.680
7/8	.875	1.313	1.856	.792
1	1.000	1.500	2.121	.903
1−1/8	1.125	1.688	2.386	1.030
1−1/4	1.250	1.875	2.652	1.126
1−3/8	1.375	1.063	2.917	1.237
1−1/2	1.500	2.250	3.182	1.348

APPENDIX 13 • Hexagon Head Bolts

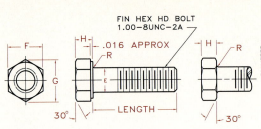

Dimensions are in inches.

DIA	E Max.	F Max.	G Avg.	H Max.	R Max.	DIA	E Max.	F Max.	G Avg.	H Max.	R Max.
1/4	.250	.438	.505	.163	.025	1-1/8	1.125	1.688	1.949	.718	.095
5/16	.313	.500	.577	.211	.025	1-1/4	1.250	1.875	2.165	.813	.095
3/8	.375	.563	.650	.243	.025	1-3/8	1.375	2.063	2.382	.878	.095
7/16	.438	.625	.722	.291	.025	1-1/2	1.500	2.250	2.598	.974	.095
1/2	.500	.750	.866	.323	.025	1-3/4	1.750	2.625	3.031	1.134	.095
9/16	.563	.812	.938	.371	.045	2	2.000	3.000	3.464	1.263	.095
5/8	.625	.938	1.083	.403	.045	2-1/4	2.250	3.375	3.897	1.423	.095
3/4	.750	1.125	1.299	.483	.045	2-1/2	2.500	3.750	4.330	1.583	.095
7/8	.875	1.313	1.516	.563	.065	2-3/4	2.750	4.125	4.763	1.744	.095
1	1.000	1.500	1.732	.627	.095	3	3.000	4.500	5.196	1.935	.095

APPENDIX 14 • Hex Nuts and Hex Jam Nuts

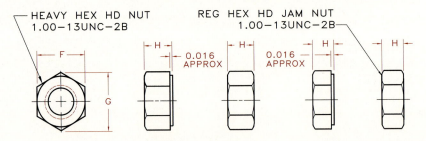

HEAVY HEX NUTS AND HEX JAM NUTS REGULAR HEX NUT HEX JAM NUT

MAJOR DIA		F Max.	G Avg.	H Max.	H Max.	MAJOR DIA		F Max.	G Avg.	H Max.	H Max.
1/4	.250	.438	.505	.226	.163	3/4	.750	1.125	1.299	.665	.446
5/16	.313	.500	.577	.273	.195	7/8	.875	1.313	1.516	.776	.510
3/8	.375	.563	.650	.337	.227	1	1.000	1.500	1.732	.887	.575
7/16	.438	.688	.794	.385	.260	1-1/8	1.125	1.688	1.949	.899	.639
1/2	.500	.750	.866	.448	.323	1-1/4	1.250	1.875	2.165	1.094	.751
9/16	.563	.875	1.010	.496	.324	1-3/8	1.375	2.063	2.382	1.206	.815
5/8	.625	.938	1.083	.559	.387	1-1/2	1.500	2.250	2.598	1.317	.880

APPENDIX 15 • Round Head Cap Screws

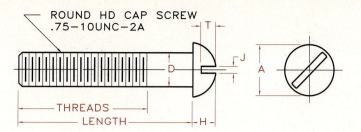

ROUND HD CAP SCREW
.75–10UNC–2A

THREADS

LENGTH

Dimensions are in inches.

STANDARD COMMERCIAL LENGTHS

OTHER LENGTHS AND DIAMETERS ARE AVAILABLE, BUT THESE ARE THE MORE STANDARD ONES.

DIA	D Max.	A Max.	H Avg.	J Max.	T Max.	DIA	D Max.	A Max.	H Avg.	J Max.	T Max.
1/4	.250	.437	.191	.075	.117	1/2	.500	.812	.354	.106	.218
5/16	.313	.562	.245	.084	.151	9/16	.563	.937	.409	.118	.252
3/8	.375	.625	.273	.094	.168	5/8	.625	1.000	.437	.133	.270
7/16	.438	.750	.328	.094	.202	3/4	.750	1.250	.546	.149	.338

APPENDIX 16 • Flat Head Cap Screws

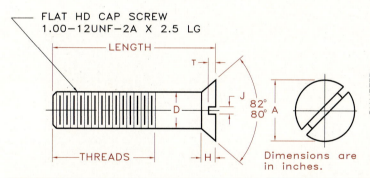

FLAT HD CAP SCREW
1.00–12UNF–2A X 2.5 LG

LENGTH

THREADS

82°
80°

Dimensions are in inches.

STANDARD COMMERCIAL LENGTHS

OTHER LENGTHS AND DIAMETERS ARE AVAILABLE, BUT THESE ARE THE MORE STANDARD ONES.

DIA	D Max.	A Max.	H Avg.	J Max.	T Max.	DIA	D Max.	A Max.	H Avg.	J Max.	T Max.
1/4	.250	.500	.140	.075	.068	3/4	.750	1.375	.352	.149	.171
5/16	.313	.625	.177	.084	.086	7/8	.875	1.625	.423	.167	.206
3/8	.375	.750	.210	.094	.103	1	1.000	1.875	.494	.188	.240
7/16	.438	.813	.210	.094	.103	1–1/8	1.125	2.062	.529	.196	.257
1/2	.500	.875	.210	.106	.103	1–1/4	1.250	2.312	.600	.211	.291
9/16	.563	1.000	.244	.118	.120	1–3/8	1.375	2.562	.665	.226	.326
5/8	.625	1.125	.281	.133	.137	1–1/2	1.500	2.812	.742	.258	.360

APPENDIX 17 • Fillister Head Cap Screws

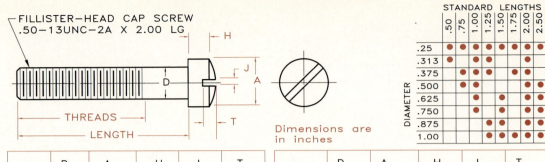

FILLISTER–HEAD CAP SCREW
.50–13UNC–2A X 2.00 LG

THREADS — LENGTH

Dimensions are in inches

DIA	D Max.	A Max.	H Avg.	J Max.	T Max.	DIA	D Max.	A Max.	H Avg.	J Max.	T Max.
1/4	.250	.375	.172	.075	.097	9/16	.563	.812	.375	.118	.213
5/16	.313	.437	.203	.084	.115	5/8	.625	.875	.422	.133	.239
3/8	.375	.562	.250	.094	.142	3/4	.750	1.000	.500	.149	.283
7/16	.438	.625	.297	.094	.168	7/8	.875	1.125	.594	.167	.334
1/2	.500	.750	.328	.106	.193	1	1.00	1.312	.656	.188	.371

Source: ANSI B18.6.2.

APPENDIX 18 • Flat Socket Head Cap Screws

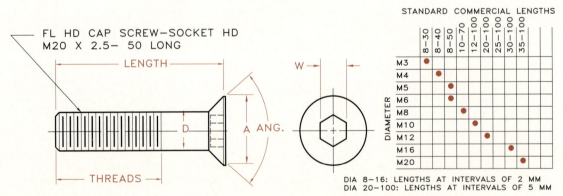

FL HD CAP SCREW–SOCKET HD
M20 X 2.5– 50 LONG

LENGTH — THREADS

DIA 8–16: LENGTHS AT INTERVALS OF 2 MM
DIA 20–100: LENGTHS AT INTERVALS OF 5 MM

Diameter mm	Inches	Pitch	A	Ang.	W	Diameter mm	Inches	Pitch	A	Ang.	W
M3	.118	.5	6	90	2	M10	.394	1.5	20	90	6
M4	.157	.7	8	90	2.5	M12	.472	1.75	24	90	8
M5	.197	.8	10	90	3	M14	.551	2	27	90	10
M6	.236	1	12	90	4	M16	.630	2	30	90	10
M8	.315	1.25	16	90	5	M20	.787	2.5	36	90	12

APPENDIX 19 • Socket Head Cap Screws

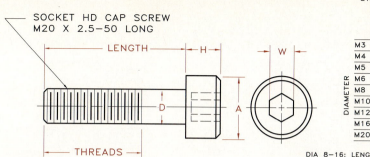

SOCKET HD CAP SCREW
M20 X 2.5—50 LONG

STANDARD COMMERCIAL LENGTHS

DIA 8–16: LENGTHS AT INTERVALS OF 2 MM
DIA 20–100: LENGTHS AT INTERVALS OF 5 MM

Diameter mm	Inches	Pitch	A	H	W	Diameter mm	Inches	Pitch	A	H	W
M3	.118	.5	6	3	2	M10	.394	1.5	20	10	8
M4	.157	.7	8	4	3	M12	.472	1.75	24	12	10
M5	.197	.8	10	5	4	M14	.551	2	27	14	12
M6	.236	1	12	6	6	M16	.630	2	30	16	14
M8	.315	1.25	16	8	6	M20	.787	2.5	36	20	17

APPENDIX 20 • Round Head Machine Screws

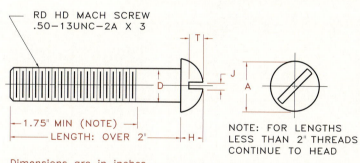

RD HD MACH SCREW
.50—13UNC—2A X 3

1.75" MIN (NOTE)
LENGTH: OVER 2"

NOTE: FOR LENGTHS LESS THAN 2" THREADS CONTINUE TO HEAD

STANDARD LENGTHS

OTHER LENGTHS AND DIAMETERS ARE AVAILABLE; THESE ARE THE MORE STANDARD ONES.

Dimensions are in inches.

DIA	D Max.	A Max.	H Avg.	J Max.	T Max.	DIA	D Max.	A Max.	H Avg.	J Max.	T Max.
0	.060	.113	.053	.023	.039	12	.216	.408	.153	.067	.096
1	.073	.138	.061	.026	.044	1/4	.250	.472	.175	.075	.109
2	.086	.162	.069	.031	.048	5/16	.313	.590	.216	.084	.132
3	.099	.187	.078	.035	.053	3/8	.375	.708	.256	.094	.155
4	.112	.211	.086	.039	.058	7/16	.438	.750	.328	.094	.196
5	.125	.236	.095	.043	.063	1/2	.500	.813	.355	.106	.211
6	.138	.260	.103	.048	.068	9/16	.563	.938	.410	.118	.242
8	.164	.309	.120	.054	.077	5/8	.625	1.000	.438	.133	.258
10	.190	.359	.137	.060	.087	3/4	.750	1.250	.547	.149	.320

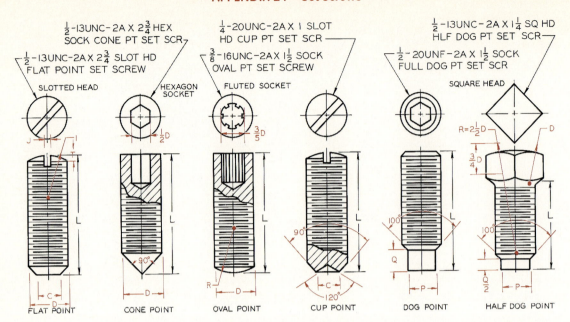

D	I	J	T	R	C		P		Q	q
	Radius of Headless Crown	Width of Slot	Depth of Slot	Oval Point Radius	Diameter of Cup and Flat Points		Diameter of Dog Point		Length of Dog Point	
Nominal Size					Max	Min	Max	Min	Full	Half
5 0.125	0.125	0.023	0.031	0.094	0.067	0.057	0.083	0.078	0.060	0.030
6 0.138	0.138	0.025	0.035	0.109	0.047	0.064	0.092	0.087	0.070	0.035
8 0.164	0.164	0.029	0.041	0.125	0.087	0.076	0.109	0.103	0.080	0.040
10 0.190	0.190	0.032	0.048	0.141	0.102	0.088	0.127	0.120	0.090	0.045
12 0.216	0.216	0.036	0.054	0.156	0.115	0.101	0.144	0.137	0.110	0.055
$\frac{1}{4}$ 0.250	0.250	0.045	0.063	0.188	0.132	0.118	0.156	0.149	0.125	0.063
$\frac{5}{16}$ 0.3125	0.313	0.051	0.076	0.234	0.172	0.156	0.203	0.195	0.156	0.078
$\frac{3}{8}$ 0.375	0.375	0.064	0.094	0.281	0.212	0.194	0.250	0.241	0.188	0.094
$\frac{7}{16}$ 0.4375	0.438	0.072	0.109	0.328	0.252	0.232	0.297	0.287	0.219	0.109
$\frac{1}{2}$ 0.500	0.500	0.081	0.125	0.375	0.291	0.270	0.344	0.344	0.250	0.125
$\frac{9}{16}$ 0.5625	0.563	0.091	0.141	0.422	0.332	0.309	0.391	0.379	0.281	0.140
$\frac{5}{8}$ 0.625	0.625	0.102	0.156	0.469	0.371	0.347	0.469	0.456	0.313	0.156
$\frac{3}{4}$ 0.750	0.750	0.129	0.188	0.563	0.450	0.425	0.563	0.549	0.375	0.188

Dimensions for the set screws shown in ANSI Fig. 18.44   (dimensions in inches)

Source: Courtesy of ANSI; B18.6.2.

APPENDIX 22 • Length of Thread Engagement Groups

Nominal Size Diam. Over	To and Incl	Pitch P	Group S To and Incl	Group N Over	Group N To and Incl	Group L Over
1.5	2.8	0.2	0.5	0.5	1.5	1.5
		0.25	0.6	0.6	1.9	1.9
		0.35	0.8	0.8	2.6	2.6
		0.4	1	1	3	3
		0.45	1.3	1.3	3.8	3.8
2.8	5.6	0.35	1	1	3	3
		0.5	1.5	1.5	4.5	4.5
		0.6	1.7	1.7	5	5
		0.7	2	2	6	6
		0.75	2.2	2.2	6.7	6.7
		0.8	2.5	2.5	7.5	7.5
5.6	11.2	0.75	2.4	2.4	7.1	7.1
		1	3	3	9	9
		1.25	4	4	12	12
		1.5	5	5	15	15
11.2	22.4	1	3.8	3.8	11	11
		1.25	4.5	4.5	13	13
		1.5	5.6	5.6	16	16
		1.75	6	6	18	18
		2	8	8	24	24
		2.5	10	10	30	30

Nominal Size Diam. Over	To and Incl	Pitch P	Group S To and Incl	Group N Over	Group N To and Incl	Group L Over
22.4	45	1	4	4	12	12
		1.5	6.3	6.3	19	19
		2	8.5	8.5	25	25
		3	12	12	36	36
		3.5	15	15	45	45
		4	18	18	53	53
		4.5	21	21	63	63
45	90	1.5	7.5	7.5	22	22
		2	9.5	9.5	28	28
		3	15	15	45	45
		4	19	19	56	56
		5	24	24	71	71
		5.5	28	28	85	85
		6	32	32	95	95
90	180	2	12	12	36	36
		3	18	18	53	53
		4	24	24	71	71
		6	36	36	106	106
180	355	3	20	20	60	60
		4	26	26	80	80
		6	40	40	118	118

All dimensions are given in millimeters. *Source:* Courtesy of ISO Standards.

APPENDIX 23 • Twist Drill Sizes

Letter Size Drills

Size	Inches	mm	Size	Inches	mm	Size	Inches	mm	Size	Inches	mm
A	0.234	5.944	H	0.266	6.756	O	0.316	8.026	V	0.377	9.576
B	0.238	6.045	I	0.272	6.909	P	0.323	8.204	W	0.386	9.804
C	0.242	6.147	J	0.277	7.036	Q	0.332	8.433	X	0.397	10.084
D	0.246	6.248	K	0.281	7.137	R	0.339	8.611	Y	0.404	10.262
E	0.250	6.350	L	0.290	7.366	S	0.348	8.839	Z	0.413	10.490
F	0.257	6.528	M	0.295	7.493	T	0.358	9.093			
G	0.261	6.629	N	0.302	7.601	U	0.368	9.347			

Source: Courtesy of General Motors Corporation.

Number Size Drills

Size	Inches	mm	Size	Inches	mm	Size	Inches	mm	Size	Inches	mm
1	0.2280	5.7912	21	0.1590	4.0386	41	0.0960	2.4384	61	0.0390	0.9906
2	0.2210	5.6134	22	0.1570	3.9878	42	0.0935	2.3622	62	0.0380	0.9652
3	0.2130	5.4102	23	0.1540	3.9116	43	0.0890	2.2606	63	0.0370	0.9398
4	0.2090	5.3086	24	0.1520	3.8608	44	0.0860	2.1844	64	0.0360	0.9144
5	0.2055	5.2197	25	0.1495	3.7973	45	0.0820	2.0828	65	0.0350	0.8890
6	0.2040	5.1816	26	0.1470	3.7338	46	0.0810	2.0574	66	0.0330	0.8382
7	0.2010	5.1054	27	0.1440	3.6576	47	0.0785	1.9812	67	0.0320	0.8128
8	0.1990	5.0800	28	0.1405	3.5560	48	0.0760	1.9304	68	0.0310	0.7874
9	0.1960	4.9784	29	0.1360	3.4544	49	0.0730	1.8542	69	0.0292	0.7417
10	0.1935	4.9149	30	0.1285	3.2639	50	0.0700	1.7780	70	0.0280	0.7112
11	0.1910	4.8514	31	0.1200	3.0480	51	0.0670	1.7018	71	0.0260	0.6604
12	0.1890	4.8006	32	0.1160	2.9464	52	0.0635	1.6129	72	0.0250	0.6350
13	0.1850	4.6990	33	0.1130	2.8702	53	0.0595	1.5113	73	0.0240	0.6096
14	0.1820	4.6228	34	0.1110	2.8194	54	0.0550	1.3970	74	0.0225	0.5715
15	0.1800	4.5720	35	0.1100	2.7940	55	0.0520	1.3208	75	0.0210	0.5334
16	0.1770	4.4958	36	0.1065	2.7051	56	0.0465	1.1684	76	0.0200	0.5080
17	0.1730	4.3942	37	0.1040	2.6416	57	0.0430	1.0922	77	0.0180	0.4572
18	0.1695	4.3053	38	0.1015	2.5781	58	0.0420	1.0668	78	0.0160	0.4064
19	0.1660	4.2164	39	0.0995	2.5273	59	0.0410	1.0414	79	0.0145	0.3638
20	0.1610	4.0894	40	0.0980	2.4892	60	0.0400	1.0160	80	0.0135	0.3429

Metric Drill Sizes   Preferred sizes are in color type. Decimal-inch equivalents are for reference only.

mm	in	mm	in.	mm	in.	mm	in.	mm	in.	mm	in.	mm	in.
.40	.0157	1.03	.0406	2.20	.0866	5.00	.1969	10.00	.3937	21.50	.8465	48.00	1.8898
.42	.0165	1.05	.0413	2.30	.0906	5.20	.2047	10.30	.4055	22.00	.8661	50.00	1.9685
.45	.0177	1.08	.0425	2.40	.0945	5.30	.2087	10.50	.4134	23.00	.9055	51.50	2.0276
.48	.0189	1.10	.0433	2.50	.0984	5.40	.2126	10.80	.4252	24.00	.9449	53.00	2.0866
.50	.0197	1.15	.0453	2.60	.1024	5.60	.2205	11.00	.4331	25.00	.9843	54.00	2.1260
.52	.0205	1.20	.0472	2.70	.1063	5.80	.2283	11.50	.4528	26.00	1.0236	56.00	2.2047
.55	.0217	1.25	.0492	2.80	.1102	6.00	.2362	12.00	.4724	27.00	1.0630	58.00	2.2835
.58	.0228	1.30	.0512	2.90	.1142	6.20	.2441	12.50	.4921	28.00	1.1024	60.00	2.3622
.60	.0236	1.35	.0531	3.00	.1181	6.30	.2480	13.00	.5118	29.00	1.1417		
.62	.0244	1.40	.0551	3.10	.1220	6.50	.2559	13.50	.5315	30.00	1.1811		
.65	.0256	1.45	.0571	3.20	.1260	6.70	.2638	14.00	.5512	31.00	1.2205		
.68	.0268	1.50	.0591	3.30	.1299	6.80	.2677	14.50	.5709	32.00	1.2598		
.70	.0276	1.55	.0610	3.40	.1339	6.90	.2717	15.00	.5906	33.00	1.2992		
.72	.0283	1.60	.0630	3.50	.1378	7.10	.2795	15.50	.6102	34.00	1.3386		
.75	.0295	1.65	.0650	3.60	.1417	7.30	.2874	16.00	.6299	35.00	1.3780		
.78	.0307	1.70	.0669	3.70	.1457	7.50	.2953	16.50	.6496	36.00	1.4173		
.80	.0315	1.75	.0689	3.80	.1496	7.80	.3071	17.00	.6693	37.00	1.4567		
.82	.0323	1.80	.0709	3.90	.1535	8.00	.3150	17.50	.6890	38.00	1.4961		
.85	.0335	1.85	.0728	4.00	.1575	8.20	.3228	18.00	.7087	39.00	1.5354		
.88	.0346	1.90	.0748	4.10	.1614	8.50	.3346	18.50	.7283	40.00	1.5748		
.90	.0354	1.95	.0768	4.20	.1654	8.80	.3465	19.00	.7480	41.00	1.6142		
.92	.0362	2.00	.0787	4.40	.1732	9.00	.3543	19.50	.7677	42.00	1.6535		
.95	.0374	2.05	.0807	4.50	.1772	9.20	.3622	20.00	.7874	43.50	1.7126		
.98	.0386	2.10	.0827	4.60	.1811	9.50	.3740	20.50	.8071	45.00	1.7717		
1.00	.0394	2.15	.0846	4.80	.1890	9.80	.3858	21.00	.8268	46.50	1.8307		

APPENDIX 24 • Cotter Pins: American National Standard

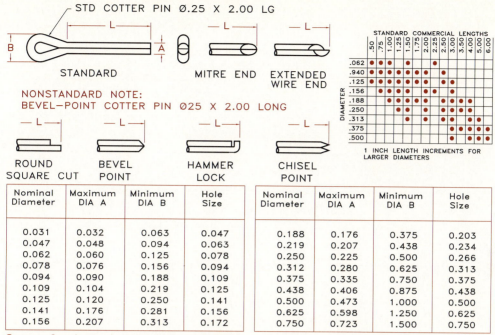

Nominal Diameter	Maximum DIA A	Minimum DIA B	Hole Size
0.031	0.032	0.063	0.047
0.047	0.048	0.094	0.063
0.062	0.060	0.125	0.078
0.078	0.076	0.156	0.094
0.094	0.090	0.188	0.109
0.109	0.104	0.219	0.125
0.125	0.120	0.250	0.141
0.141	0.176	0.281	0.156
0.156	0.207	0.313	0.172

Nominal Diameter	Maximum DIA A	Minimum DIA B	Hole Size
0.188	0.176	0.375	0.203
0.219	0.207	0.438	0.234
0.250	0.225	0.500	0.266
0.312	0.280	0.625	0.313
0.375	0.335	0.750	0.375
0.438	0.406	0.875	0.438
0.500	0.473	1.000	0.500
0.625	0.598	1.250	0.625
0.750	0.723	1.500	0.750

Source: Courtesy of ANSI: B18.8.1–1983.

APPENDIX 25 • Straight Pins

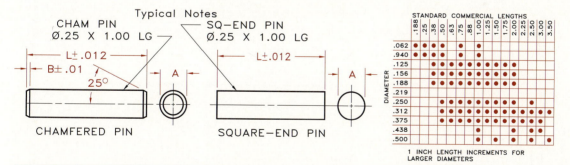

Nominal DIA	Diamter A		Chamfer B
	Max	Min	
0.062	0.0625	0.0605	0.015
0.094	0.0937	0.0917	0.015
0.109	0.1094	0.1074	0.015
0.125	0.1250	0.1230	0.015
0.156	0.1562	0.1542	0.015
0.188	0.1875	0.1855	0.015

Nominal DIA	Diamter A		Chamfer B
	Max	Min	
0.219	0.2187	0.2167	0.015
0.250	0.2500	0.2480	0.015
0.312	0.3125	0.3095	0.015
0.375	0.3750	0.3720	0.030
0.438	0.4345	0.4345	0.030
0.500	0.4970	0.4970	0.030

Source: ANSI: B5.20.

TYPICAL NOTE:
NO. 2 TAPER PIN—1.500 LG

L=Length

Number	7/0	6/0	5/0	4/0	3/0	2/0	0	1	2	3	4	5	6	7	8	9	10
Size (large end)	0.0625	0.0780	0.0940	0.1090	0.1250	0.1410	0.1560	0.1720	0.1930	0.2190	0.2500	0.2890	0.3410	0.4090	0.4920	0.5910	0.7060
Length, L																	
0.375	X	X															
0.500	X	X	X	X													
0.625	X	X	X	X	X	X	X										
0.750		X	X	X	X	X	X										
0.875					X	X	X	X	X								
1.000			X	X	X	X	X	X	X	X							
1.250					X	X	X	X	X	X	X	X					
1.500						X	X	X	X	X	X	X	X				
1.750							X	X	X	X	X	X	X	X			
2.000								X	X	X	X	X	X	X	X		
2.250									X	X	X	X	X	X	X	X	
2.500										X	X	X	X	X	X	X	
2.750										X	X	X	X	X	X	X	X
3.000													X	X	X	X	X
3.250													X	X	X	X	X
3.500													X	X	X	X	X
3.750															X	X	X
4.000															X	X	X
4.250															X	X	X
4.500															X	X	X
4.750																X	X
5.000																X	X
5.250																X	X
5.500																X	X
5.750																X	X
6.000																	X

All dimensions are given in inches.

Standard reamers are available for pins given above the line.

Pins Nos. 11 (size 0.8600), 12 (size 1.032), 13 (size 1.241), and 14 (1.523) are special sizes—hence their lengths are special.

To find small diameter of pin, multiply the length by 0.02083 and subtract the result from the large diameter.

Source: Courtesy of ANSI; B5.20–1958.

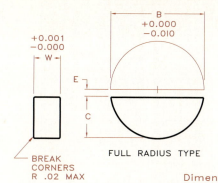

FULL RADIUS TYPE

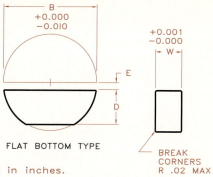

FLAT BOTTOM TYPE

BREAK CORNERS R .02 MAX

BREAK CORNERS R .02 MAX

Dimensions are in inches.

Key No.	W X B	C Max.	D Max.	E
204	1/16 X 1/2	.203	.194	.047
304	3/32 X 1/2	.203	.194	.047
404	1/8 X 1/2	.203	.194	.047
305	3/32 X 5/8	.250	.240	.063
405	1/8 X 5/8	.250	.240	.063
505	5/32 X 5/8	.250	.240	.063
406	1/8 X 3/4	.313	.303	.063

Key No.	W X B	C Max.	D Max.	E
506	5/32 X 3/4	.313	.303	.063
606	3/16 X 3/4	.313	.303	.063
507	5/32 X 7/8	.375	.365	.063
607	3/16 X 7/8	.375	.365	.063
807	1/4 X 7/8	.375	.365	.063
608	3/16 X 1	.438	.428	.063
609	3/16 X 1-1/8	.484	.475	.078

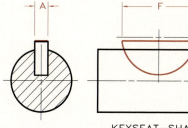

KEYSEAT—SHAFT

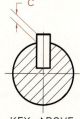

KEY ABOVE SHAFT

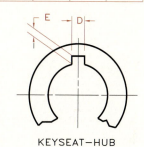

KEYSEAT—HUB

Key No.	A Min.	C +.005 −.000	F	D +.005 −.000	E +.005 −.000
204	.0615	.0312	.500	.0635	.0372
304	.0928	.0469	.500	.0948	.0529
404	.1240	.0625	.500	.1260	.0685
305	.0928	.0625	.625	.0948	.0529
405	.1240	.0469	.625	.1260	.0685
505	.1553	.0625	.625	.1573	.0841
406	.1240	.0781	.750	.1260	.0685

Key No.	A Min.	C +.005 −.000	F	D +.005 −.000	E +.005 −.000
506	.1553	.0781	.750	.1573	.0841
606	.1863	.0937	.750	.1885	.0997
507	.1553	.0781	.875	.1573	.0841
607	.1863	.0937	.875	.1885	.0997
807	.2487	.1250	.875	.2510	.1310
608	.1863	.3393	1.000	.1885	.0997
609	.1863	.3853	1.125	.1885	.0997

KEY SIZES VS. SHAFT SIZES

Shaft DIA	to .375	to .500	to .750	to 1.313	to 1.188	to 1.448	to 1.750	to 2.125	to 2.500
Key Nos.	204	304 305	404 405 406	505 506 507	606 607 608 609	807 808 809	810 811 812	1011 1012	1211 1212

APPENDIX 28 • Standard Keys and Keyways

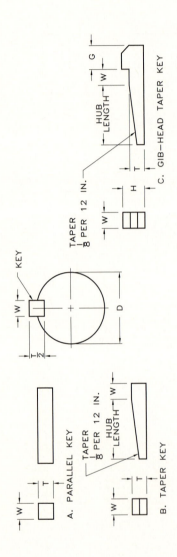

A. PARALLEL KEY
B. TAPER KEY — TAPER 1/8 PER 12 IN. — HUB LENGTH
C. GIB-HEAD TAPER KEY — TAPER 1/8 PER 12 IN. — HUB LENGTH

SPROCKET BORE (= SHAFT DIAM.) INCHES D	KEYWAY DIMENSIONS — INCHES				KEY DIMENSIONS — INCHES			GIB HEAD DIMENSIONS — INCHES				KEY TOLERANCES TAPER AND GIB HEAD	
	FOR SQUARE KEY		FOR FLAT KEY		SQUARE	FLAT	TOLERANCE ON W AND T (−)	SQUARE KEY		FLAT KEY		W (−)	T (+)
	WIDTH W	DEPTH T/2	WIDTH W	DEPTH T/2	WIDTH W × HEIGHT T	WIDTH W × HEIGHT T		H	G	H	G		
1/2 — 9/16	1/8	1/16	1/8	3/64	1/8 × 1/8	1/8 × 3/32	0.002	1/4	7/32	3/16	1/8	0.002	0.002
5/8 — 7/8	3/16	3/32	3/16	1/16	3/16 × 3/16	3/16 × 1/8	0.002	5/16	9/32	1/4	3/16	0.002	0.002
13/16 — 1 1/4	1/4	1/8	1/4	3/32	1/4 × 1/4	1/4 × 3/16	0.002	7/16	11/32	5/16	1/4	0.002	0.002
1 5/16 — 1 3/8	5/16	5/32	5/16	1/8	5/16 × 5/16	5/16 × 1/4	0.002	9/16	13/32	3/8	3/16	0.002	0.002
1 7/16 — 1 3/4	3/8	3/16	3/8	1/8	3/8 × 3/8	3/8 × 1/4	0.002	11/16	15/32	7/16	3/8	0.002	0.002
1 13/16 — 2 1/4	1/2	1/4	1/2	3/16	1/2 × 1/2	1/2 × 3/8	0.0025	7/8	19/32	5/8	1/2	0.0025	0.0025
2 5/16 — 2 3/4	5/8	5/16	5/8	7/32	5/8 × 5/8	5/8 × 7/16	0.0025	1 1/16	23/32	3/4	5/8	0.0025	0.0025
2 7/8 — 3 1/4	3/4	3/8	3/4	1/4	3/4 × 3/4	3/4 × 1/2	0.0025	1 1/4	7/8	7/8	3/4	0.0025	0.0025
3 3/8 — 3 3/4	7/8	7/16	7/8	5/16	7/8 × 7/8	7/8 × 5/8	0.003	1 1/4	1	1 1/16	7/8	0.003	0.003
3 7/8 — 4 1/2	1	1/2	1	3/8	1 × 1	1 × 3/4	0.003	1 3/4	1 3/16	1 1/4	1	0.003	0.003
4 3/4 — 5 1/2	1 1/4	5/8	1 1/4	7/16	1 1/4 × 1 1/4	1 1/4 × 7/8	0.003	2	1 7/16	1 1/2	1 1/4	0.003	0.003
5 3/4 — 7 3/8	1 1/2	3/4	1 1/2	1/2	1 1/2 × 1 1/2	1 1/2 × 1	0.003	2 1/2	1 3/4	1 3/4	1 1/2	0.003	0.003
7 1/2 — 9 7/8	1 3/4	7/8	..	..	1 3/4 × 1 3/4	.. × ..	0.004	3	2	..	..	0.004	0.004
10 — 12 1/2	2	1	..	..	2 × 2	.. × ..	0.004	3 1/2	2 3/8	..	..	0.004	0.004

Standard Keyway Tolerances: Straight Keyway — Width (W) + .005 / − .000   Depth (T/2) + .010 / − .000
Taper Keyway — Width (W) + .005 / − .000   Depth (T/2) + .000 / − .010

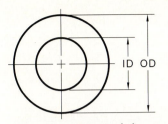

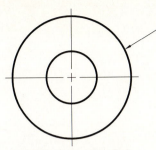

.938 X 2.25 X .165
TYPE A PLAIN WASHER

Dimensioned
Washer

In Screw Size Column
N= Narrow washer
W= Wide washer

Narrow Washer (N)
TYPE A PLAIN WASHERS

WIDE WASHER (W)

SCREW SIZE	ID SIZE	OD SIZE	THICK-NESS	SCREW SIZE	ID SIZE	OD SIZE	THICK-NESS
0.138	0.156	0.375	0.049	0.875 N	0.938	1.750	0.134
0.164	0.188	0.438	0.049	0.875 W	0.938	2.250	0.165
0.190	0.219	0.500	0.049	1.000 N	1.062	2.000	0.134
0.188	0.250	0.562	0.049	1.000 W	1.062	2.500	0.165
0.216	0.250	0.562	0.065	1.125 N	1.250	2.250	0.134
0.250 N	0.281	0.625	0.065	1.125 W	1.250	2.750	0.165
0.250 W	0.312	0.734	0.065	1.250 N	1.375	2.500	0.165
0.312 N	0.344	0.688	0.065	1.250 W	1.375	3.000	0.165
0.312 W	0.375	0.875	0.083	1.375 N	1.500	2.750	0.165
0.375 N	0.406	0.812	0.065	1.375 W	1.500	3.250	0.180
0.375 W	0.438	1.000	0.083	1.500 N	1.625	3.000	0.165
0.438 N	0.469	0.922	0.065	1.500 W	1.625	3.500	0.180
0.438 W	0.500	1.250	0.083	1.625	1.750	3.750	0.180
0.500 N	0.531	1.062	0.095	1.750	1.875	4.000	0.180
0.500 W	0.562	1.375	0.109	1.875	2.000	4.250	0.180
0.562 N	0.594	1.156	0.095	2.000	2.125	4.500	0.180
0.562 W	0.594	1.469	0.109	2.250	2.375	4.750	0.220
0.625 N	0.625	1.312	0.095	2.500	2.625	5.000	0.238
0.625 N	0.625	1.750	0.134	2.750	2.875	5.250	0.259
0.750 W	0.812	1.469	0.134	3.000	3.125	5.500	0.284
0.750 W	0.812	2.000	0.148				

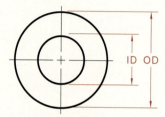

FLAT WASHERS
DIN 9021

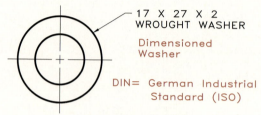

17 X 27 X 2
WROUGHT WASHER

Dimensioned
Washer

DIN= German Industrial
Standard (ISO)

WROUGHT WASHERS
DIN 433

SCREW SIZE	ID SIZE	OD SIZE	THICK-NESS	SCREW SIZE	ID SIZE	OD SIZE	THICK-NESS
3	3.2	9	0.8	2.6	2.8	5.5	0.5
4	4.3	12	1	3	3.2	6	0.5
5	5.3	15	1.5	4	4.3	8	0.5
6	6.4	18	1.5	5	5.3	10	1.0
8	8.4	25	2	6	6.4	11	1.5
10	10.5	30	2.5	8	8.4	15	1.5
12	13	40	3	10	10.5	18	1.5
14	15	45	3	12	13	20	2.0
16	17	50	3	14	15	25	2.0
18	19	56	4	16	17	27	2.0
20	21	60	4	18	19	30	2.5
				20	21	33	2.5

APPENDIX 31 • Regular Helical Spring Lock Washers (inches)

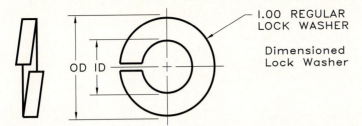

1.00 REGULAR LOCK WASHER

Dimensioned Lock Washer

SCREW SIZE	ID SIZE	OD SIZE	THICK-NESS	SCREW SIZE	ID SIZE	OD SIZE	THICK-NESS
0.164	0.168	0.175	0.040	0.812	0.826	1.367	0.203
0.190	0.194	0.202	0.047	0.875	0.890	1.464	0.219
0.216	0.221	0.229	0.056	0.938	0.954	1.560	0.234
0.250	0.255	0.263	0.062	1.000	1.017	1.661	0.250
0.312	0.318	0.328	0.078	1.062	1.080	1.756	0.266
0.375	0.382	0.393	0.094	1.125	1.144	1.853	0.281
0.438	0.446	0.459	0.109	1.188	1.208	1.950	0.297
0.500	0.509	0.523	0.125	1.250	1.271	2.045	0.312
0.562	0.572	0.587	0.141	1.312	1.334	2.141	0.328
0.625	0.636	0.653	0.156	1.375	1.398	2.239	0.344
0.688	0.700	0.718	0.172	1.438	1.462	2.334	0.359
0.750	0.763	0.783	0.188	1.500	1.525	2.430	0.375

METRIC LOCK WASHERS—DIN 127 (Millimeters)

SCREW SIZE	ID SIZE	OD SIZE	THICK-NESS	SCREW SIZE	ID SIZE	OD SIZE	THICK-NESS
4	4.1	7.1	0.9	22	22.5	34.5	4
5	5.1	8.7	1.2	24	24.5	38.5	5
6	6.1	11.1	1.6	27	27.5	41.5	5
8	8.2	12.1	1.6	30	30.5	46.5	6
10	10.2	14.2	2	33	33.5	53.5	6
12	12.1	17.2	2.2	36	36.5	56.5	6
14	14.2	20.2	2.5	39	39.5	59.5	6
16	16.2	23.2	3	42	42.5	66.5	7
18	18.2	26.2	3.5	45	45.5	69.5	7
20	20.2	28.2	3.5	48	49	73	7

APPENDIX 32 • American Standard Running and Sliding Fits (hole basis)

Limits are in thousandths of an inch.
Limits for hole and shaft are applied algebraically to the basic size to obtain the limits of size for the parts.
Data in bold face are in accordance with ABC agreements.
Symbols H5, g5, etc., are Hole and Shaft designations used in ABC System.

Nominal Size Range Inches (Over – To)	Class RC 1 Limits of Clearance	Hole H5	Shaft g4	Class RC 2 Limits of Clearance	Hole H6	Shaft g5	Class RC 3 Limits of Clearance	Hole H7	Shaft f6	Class RC 4 Limits of Clearance	Hole H8	Shaft f7
0 – 0.12	0.1 / 0.45	+0.2 / 0	−0.1 / −0.25	0.1 / 0.55	+0.25 / 0	−0.1 / −0.3	0.3 / 0.95	+0.4 / 0	−0.3 / −0.55	0.3 / 1.3	+0.6 / 0	−0.3 / −0.7
0.12 – 0.24	0.15 / 0.5	+0.2 / 0	−0.15 / −0.3	0.15 / 0.65	+0.3 / 0	−0.15 / −0.35	0.4 / 1.12	+0.5 / 0	−0.4 / −0.7	0.4 / 1.6	+0.7 / 0	−0.4 / −0.9
0.24 – 0.40	0.2 / 0.6	0.25 / 0	−0.2 / −0.35	0.2 / 0.85	+0.4 / 0	−0.2 / −0.45	0.5 / 1.5	+0.6 / 0	−0.5 / −0.9	0.5 / 2.0	+0.9 / 0	−0.5 / −1.1
0.40 – 0.71	0.25 / 0.75	+0.3 / 0	−0.25 / −0.45	0.25 / 0.95	+0.4 / 0	−0.25 / −0.55	0.6 / 1.7	+0.7 / 0	−0.6 / −1.0	0.6 / 2.3	+1.0 / 0	−0.6 / −1.3
0.71 – 1.19	0.3 / 0.95	+0.4 / 0	−0.3 / −0.55	0.3 / 1.2	+0.5 / 0	−0.3 / −0.7	0.8 / 2.1	+0.8 / 0	−0.8 / −1.3	0.8 / 2.8	+1.2 / 0	−0.8 / −1.6
1.19 – 1.97	0.4 / 1.1	+0.4 / 0	−0.4 / −0.7	0.4 / 1.4	+0.6 / 0	−0.4 / −0.8	1.0 / 2.6	+1.0 / 0	−1.0 / −1.6	1.0 / 3.6	+1.6 / 0	−1.0 / −2.0
1.97 – 3.15	0.4 / 1.2	+0.5 / 0	−0.4 / −0.7	0.4 / 1.6	+0.7 / 0	−0.4 / −0.9	1.2 / 3.1	+1.2 / 0	−1.2 / −1.9	1.2 / 4.2	+1.8 / 0	−1.2 / −2.4
3.15 – 4.73	0.5 / 1.5	+0.6 / 0	−0.5 / −0.9	0.5 / 2.0	+0.9 / 0	−0.5 / −1.1	1.4 / 3.7	+1.4 / 0	−1.4 / −2.3	1.4 / 5.0	+2.2 / 0	−1.4 / −2.8
4.73 – 7.09	0.6 / 1.8	+0.7 / 0	−0.6 / −1.1	0.6 / 2.3	+1.0 / 0	−0.6 / −1.3	1.6 / 4.2	+1.6 / 0	−1.6 / −2.6	1.6 / 5.7	+2.5 / 0	−1.6 / −3.2
7.09 – 9.85	0.6 / 2.0	+0.8 / 0	−0.6 / −1.2	0.6 / 2.6	+1.2 / 0	−0.6 / −1.4	2.0 / 5.0	+1.8 / 0	−2.0 / −3.2	2.0 / 6.6	+2.8 / 0	−2.0 / −3.8
9.85 – 12.41	0.8 / 2.3	+0.9 / 0	−0.8 / −1.4	0.8 / 2.9	+1.2 / 0	−0.8 / −1.7	2.5 / 5.7	+2.0 / 0	−2.5 / −3.7	2.5 / 7.5	+3.0 / 0	−2.5 / −4.5
12.41 – 15.75	1.0 / 2.7	+1.0 / 0	−1.0 / −1.7	1.0 / 3.4	+1.4 / 0	−1.0 / −2.0	3.0 / 6.6	+ / 0	−3.0 / −4.4	3.0 / 8.7	+3.5 / 0	−3.0 / −5.2
15.75 – 19.69	1.2 / 3.0	+1.0 / 0	−1.2 / −2.0	1.2 / 3.8	+1.6 / 0	−1.2 / −2.2	4.0 / 8.1	+1.6 / 0	−4.0 / −5.6	4.0 / 10.5	+4.0 / 0	−4.0 / −6.5
19.69 – 30.09	1.6 / 3.7	+1.2 / 0	−1.6 / −2.5	1.6 / 4.8	+2.0 / 0	−1.6 / −2.8	5.0 / 10.0	+3.0 / 0	−5.0 / −7.0	5.0 / 13.0	+5.0 / 0	−5.0 / −8.0
30.09 – 41.49	2.0 / 4.6	+1.6 / 0	−2.0 / −3.0	2.0 / 6.1	+2.5 / 0	−2.0 / −3.6	6.0 / 12.5	+4.0 / 0	−6.0 / −8.5	6.0 / 16.0	+6.0 / 0	−6.0 / −10.0
41.49 – 56.19	2.5 / 5.7	+2.0 / 0	−2.5 / −3.7	2.5 / 7.5	+3.0 / 0	−2.5 / −4.5	8.0 / 16.0	+5.0 / 0	−8.0 / −11.0	8.0 / 21.0	+8.0 / 0	−8.0 / −13.0
56.19 – 76.39	3.0 / 7.1	+2.5 / 0	−3.0 / −4.6	3.0 / 9.5	+4.0 / 0	−3.0 / −5.5	10.0 / 20.0	+6.0 / 0	−10.0 / −14.0	10.0 / 26.0	+10.0 / 0	−10.0 / −16.0
76.39 – 100.9	4.0 / 9.0	+3.0 / 0	−4.0 / −6.0	4.0 / 12.0	+5.0 / 0	−4.0 / −7.0	12.0 / 25.0	+8.0 / 0	−12.0 / −17.0	12.0 / 32.0	+12.0 / 0	−12.0 / −20.0
100.9 – 131.9	5.0 / 11.5	+4.0 / 0	−5.0 / −7.5	5.0 / 15.0	+6.0 / 0	−5.0 / −9.0	16.0 / 32.0	+10.0 / 0	−16.0 / −22.0	16.0 / 36.0	+16.0 / 0	−16.0 / −26.0
131.9 – 171.9	6.0 / 14.0	+5.0 / 0	−6.0 / −9.0	6.0 / 19.0	+8.0 / 0	−6.0 / −11.0	18.0 / 38.0	+8.0 / 0	−18.0 / −26.0	18.0 / 50.0	+20.0 / 0	−18.0 / −30.0
171.9 – 200	8.0 / 18.0	+6.0 / 0	−8.0 / −12.0	8.0 / 22.0	+10.0 / 0	−8.0 / −12.0	22.0 / 48.0	+16.0 / 0	−22.0 / −32.0	22.0 / 63.0	+25.0 / 0	−22.0 / −38.0

Source: Courtesy of USASI; B4.1–1955.

Class RC 5			Class RC 6			Class RC 7			Class RC 8			Class RC 9			Nominal Size Range Inches	
Limits of Clearance	Hole H8	Shaft e7	Limits of Clearance	Hole H9	Shaft e8	Limits of Clearance	Hole H9	Shaft d8	Limits of Clearance	Hole H10	Shaft c9	Limits of Clearance	Hole H11	Shaft	Over	To
0.6 / 1.6	+0.6 / −0	−0.6 / −1.0	0.6 / 2.2	+1.0 / −0	−0.6 / −1.2	1.0 / 2.6	+1.0 / 0	−1.0 / −1.6	2.5 / 5.1	+1.6 / 0	−2.5 / −3.5	4.0 / 8.1	+2.5 / 0	−4.0 / −5.6	0	0.12
0.8 / 2.0	+0.7 / −0	−0.8 / −1.3	0.8 / 2.7	+1.2 / −0	−0.8 / −1.5	1.2 / 3.1	+1.2 / 0	−1.2 / −1.9	2.8 / 5.8	+1.8 / 0	−2.8 / −4.0	4.5 / 9.0	+3.0 / 0	−4.5 / −6.0	0.12	0.24
1.0 / 2.5	+0.9 / −0	−1.0 / −1.6	1.0 / 3.3	+1.4 / −0	−1.0 / −1.9	1.6 / 3.9	+1.4 / 0	−1.6 / −2.5	3.0 / 6.6	+2.2 / 0	−3.0 / −4.4	5.0 / 10.7	+3.5 / 0	−5.0 / −7.2	0.24	0.40
1.2 / 2.9	+1.0 / −0	−1.2 / −1.9	1.2 / 3.8	+1.6 / −0	−1.2 / −2.2	2.0 / 4.6	+1.6 / 0	−2.0 / −3.0	3.5 / 7.9	+2.8 / 0	−3.5 / −5.1	6.0 / 12.8	+4.0 / −0	−6.0 / −8.8	0.40	0.71
1.6 / 3.6	+1.2 / −0	−1.6 / −2.4	1.6 / 4.8	+2.0 / −0	−1.6 / −2.8	2.5 / 5.7	+2.0 / 0	−2.5 / −3.7	4.5 / 10.0	+3.5 / 0	−4.5 / −6.5	7.0 / 15.5	+5.0 / 0	−7.0 / −10.5	0.71	1.19
2.0 / 4.6	+1.6 / −0	−2.0 / −3.0	2.0 / 6.1	+2.5 / −0	−2.0 / −3.6	3.0 / 7.1	+2.5 / 0	−3.0 / −4.6	5.0 / 11.5	+4.0 / 0	−5.0 / −7.5	8.0 / 18.0	+6.0 / 0	−8.0 / −12.0	1.19	1.97
2.5 / 5.5	+1.8 / −0	−2.5 / −3.7	2.5 / 7.3	+3.0 / −0	−2.5 / −4.3	4.0 / 8.8	+3.0 / 0	−4.0 / −5.8	6.0 / 13.5	+4.5 / 0	−6.0 / −9.0	9.0 / 20.5	+7.0 / 0	−9.0 / −13.5	1.97	3.15
3.0 / 6.6	+2.2 / −0	−3.0 / −4.4	3.0 / 8.7	+3.5 / −0	−3.0 / −5.2	5.0 / 10.7	+3.5 / 0	−5.0 / −7.2	7.0 / 15.5	+5.0 / 0	−7.0 / −10.5	10.0 / 24.0	+9.0 / 0	−10.0 / −15.0	3.15	4.73
3.5 / 7.6	+2.5 / −0	−3.5 / −5.1	3.5 / 10.0	+4.0 / −0	−3.5 / −6.0	6.0 / 12.5	+4.0 / 0	−6.0 / −8.5	8.0 / 18.0	+6.0 / 0	−8.0 / −12.0	12.0 / 28.0	+10.0 / 0	−12.0 / −18.0	4.73	7.09
4.0 / 8.6	+2.8 / −0	−4.0 / −5.8	4.0 / 11.3	+4.5 / 0	−4.0 / −6.8	7.0 / 14.3	+4.5 / 0	−7.0 / −9.8	10.0 / 21.5	+7.0 / 0	−10.0 / −14.5	15.0 / 34.0	+12.0 / 0	−15.0 / −22.0	7.09	9.85
5.0 / 10.0	+3.0 / 0	−5.0 / −7.0	5.0 / 13.0	+5.0 / 0	−5.0 / −8.0	8.0 / 16.0	+5.0 / 0	−8.0 / −11.0	12.0 / 25.0	+8.0 / 0	−12.0 / −17.0	18.0 / 38.0	+12.0 / 0	−18.0 / −26.0	9.85	12.41
6.0 / 11.7	+3.5 / 0	−6.0 / −8.2	6.0 / 15.5	+6.0 / 0	−6.0 / −9.5	10.0 / 19.5	+6.0 / 0	−10.0 / −13.5	14.0 / 29.0	+9.0 / 0	−14.0 / −20.0	22.0 / 45.0	+14.0 / 0	−22.0 / −31.0	12.41	15.75
8.0 / 14.5	+4.0 / 0	−8.0 / −10.5	8.0 / 18.0	+6.0 / 0	−8.0 / −12.0	12.0 / 22.0	+6.0 / 0	−12.0 / −16.0	16.0 / 32.0	+10.0 / 0	−16.0 / −22.0	25.0 / 51.0	+16.0 / 0	−25.0 / −35.0	15.75	19.69
10.0 / 18.0	+5.0 / 0	−10.0 / −13.0	10.0 / 23.0	+8.0 / 0	−10.0 / −15.0	16.0 / 29.0	+8.0 / 0	−16.0 / −21.0	20.0 / 40.0	+12.0 / 0	−20.0 / −28.0	30.0 / 62.0	+20.0 / 0	−30.0 / −42.0	19.69	30.09
12.0 / 22.0	+6.0 / 0	−12.0 / −16.0	12.0 / 28.0	+10.0 / 0	−12.0 / −18.0	20.0 / 36.0	+10.0 / 0	−20.0 / −26.0	25.0 / 51.0	+16.0 / 0	−25.0 / −35.0	40.0 / 81.0	+25.0 / 0	−40.0 / −56.0	30.09	41.49
16.0 / 29.0	+8.0 / 0	−16.0 / −21.0	16.0 / 36.0	+12.0 / 0	−16.0 / −24.0	25.0 / 45.0	+12.0 / 0	−25.0 / −33.0	30.0 / 62.0	+20.0 / 0	−30.0 / −42.0	50.0 / 100	+30.0 / 0	−50.0 / −70.0	41.49	56.19
20.0 / 36.0	+10.0 / 0	−20.0 / −26.0	20.0 / 46.0	+16.0 / 0	−20.0 / −30.0	30.0 / 56.0	+16.0 / 0	−30.0 / −40.0	40.0 / 81.0	+25.0 / 0	−40.0 / −56.0	60.0 / 125	+40.0 / 0	−60.0 / −85.0	56.19	76.39
25.0 / 45.0	+12.0 / 0	−25.0 / −33.0	25.0 / 57.0	+20.0 / 0	−25.0 / −37.0	40.0 / 72.0	+20.0 / 0	−40.0 / −52.0	50.0 / 100	+30.0 / 0	−50.0 / −70.0	80.0 / 160	+50.0 / 0	−80.0 / −110	76.39	100.9
30.0 / 56.0	+16.0 / 0	−30.0 / −40.0	30.0 / 71.0	+25.0 / 0	−30.0 / −46.0	50.0 / 91.0	+25.0 / 0	−50.0 / −66.0	60.0 / 125	+40.0 / 0	−60.0 / −85.0	100 / 200	+60.0 / 0	−100 / −140	100.9	131.9
35.0 / 67.0	+20.0 / 0	−35.0 / −47.0	35.0 / 85.0	+30.0 / 0	−35.0 / −55.0	60.0 / 110.0	+30.0 / 0	−60.0 / −80.0	80.0 / 160	+50.0 / 0	−80.0 / −110	130 / 260	+80.0 / 0	−130 / −180	131.9	171.9
45.0 / 86.0	+25.0 / 0	−45.0 / −61.0	45.0 / 110.0	+40.0 / 0	−45.0 / −70.0	80.0 / 145.0	+40.0 / 0	−80.0 / −105.0	100 / 200	+60.0 / 0	−100 / −140	150 / 310	+100 / 0	−150 / −210	171.9	200

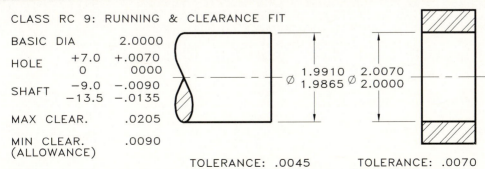

CLASS RC 9: RUNNING & CLEARANCE FIT

BASIC DIA   2.0000

HOLE   +7.0   +.0070
                 0   0000

SHAFT   −9.0   −.0090
             −13.5   −.0135

MAX CLEAR.   .0205

MIN CLEAR. (ALLOWANCE)   .0090

Ø 1.9910 / 1.9865   Ø 2.0070 / 2.0000

TOLERANCE: .0045   TOLERANCE: .0070

APPENDIX 33 • American Standard Clearance Locational Fits (hole basis)

Limits are in thousandths of an inch.
Limits for hole and shaft are applied algebraically to the basic size to obtain the limits of size for the parts.
Data in bold face are in accordance with ABC agreements.
Symbols H9,f8, etc., are Hole and Shaft designations used in ABC System.

Nominal Size Range Inches Over	To	Class LC 1 Limits of Clearance	Hole H6	Shaft h5	Class LC 2 Limits of Clearance	Hole H7	Shaft h6	Class LC 3 Limits of Clearance	Hole H8	Shaft h7	Class LC 4 Limits of Clearance	Hole H10	Shaft h9	Class LC 5 Limits of Clearance	Hole H7	Shaft g6
0 −	0.12	0 / 0.45	+0.25 / −0	+0 / −0.2	0 / 0.65	+0.4 / −0	+0 / −0.25	0 / 1	+0.6 / −0	+0 / −0.4	0 / 2.6	+1.6 / −0	+0 / −1.0	0.1 / 0.75	+0.4 / −0	−0.1 / −0.35
0.12−	0.24	0 / 0.5	+0.3 / −0	+0 / −0.2	0 / 0.8	+0.5 / −0	+0 / −0.3	0 / 1.2	+0.7 / −0	+0 / −0.5	0 / 3.0	+1.8 / −0	+0 / −1.2	0.15 / 0.95	+0.5 / −0	−0.15 / −0.45
0.24−	0.40	0 / 0.65	+0.4 / −0	+0 / −0.25	0 / 1.0	+0.6 / −0	+0 / −0.4	0 / 1.5	+0.9 / −0	+0 / −0.6	0 / 3.6	+2.2 / −0	+0 / −1.4	0.2 / 1.2	+0.6 / −0	−0.2 / −0.6
0.40−	0.71	0 / 0.7	+0.4 / −0	+0 / −0.3	0 / 1.1	+0.7 / −0	+0 / −0.4	0 / 1.7	+1.0 / −0	+0 / −0.7	0 / 4.4	+2.8 / −0	+0 / −1.6	0.25 / 1.35	+0.7 / −0	−0.25 / −0.65
0.71−	1.19	0 / 0.9	+0.5 / −0	+0 / −0.4	0 / 1.3	+0.8 / −0	+0 / −0.5	0 / 2	+1.2 / −0	+0 / −0.8	0 / 5.5	+3.5 / −0	+0 / −2.0	0.3 / 1.6	+0.8 / −0	−0.3 / −0.8
1.19−	1.97	0 / 1.0	+0.6 / −0	+0 / −0.4	0 / 1.6	+1.0 / −0	+0 / −0.6	0 / 2.6	+1.6 / −0	+0 / −1	0 / 6.5	+4.0 / −0	+0 / −2.5	0.4 / 2.0	+1.0 / −0	−0.4 / −1.0
1.97−	3.15	0 / 1.2	+0.7 / −0	+0 / −0.5	0 / 1.9	+1.2 / −0	+0 / −0.7	0 / 3	+1.8 / −0	+0 / −1.2	0 / 7.5	+4.5 / −0	+0 / −3	0.4 / 2.3	+1.2 / −0	−0.4 / −1.1
3.15−	4.73	0 / 1.5	+0.9 / −0	+0 / −0.6	0 / 2.3	+1.4 / −0	+0 / −0.9	0 / 3.6	+2.2 / −0	+0 / −1.4	0 / 8.5	+5.0 / −0	+0 / −3.5	0.5 / 2.8	+1.4 / −0	−0.5 / −1.4
4.73−	7.09	0 / 1.7	+1.0 / −0	+0 / −0.7	0 / 2.6	+1.6 / −0	+0 / −1.0	0 / 4.1	+2.5 / −0	+0 / −1.6	0 / 10	+6.0 / −0	+0 / −4	0.6 / 3.2	+1.6 / −0	−0.6 / −1.6
7.09−	9.85	0 / 2.0	+1.2 / −0	+0 / −0.8	0 / 3.0	+1.8 / −0	+0 / −1.2	0 / 4.6	+2.8 / −0	+0 / −1.8	0 / 11.5	+7.0 / −0	+0 / −4.5	0.6 / 3.6	+1.8 / −0	−0.6 / −1.8
9.85−	12.41	0 / 2.1	+1.2 / −0	+0 / −0.9	0 / 3.2	+2.0 / −0	+0 / −1.2	0 / 5	+3.0 / −0	+0 / −2.0	0 / 13	+8.0 / −0	+0 / −5	0.7 / 3.9	+2.0 / −0	−0.7 / −1.9
12.41−	15.75	0 / 2.4	+1.4 / −0	+0 / −1.0	0 / 3.6	+2.2 / −0	+0 / −1.4	0 / 5.7	+3.5 / −0	+0 / −2.2	0 / 15	+9.0 / −0	+0 / −6	0.7 / 4.3	+2.2 / −0	−0.7 / −2.1
15.75−	19.69	0 / 2.6	+1.6 / −0	+0 / −1.0	0 / 4.1	+2.5 / −0	+0 / −1.6	0 / 6.5	+4 / −0	+0 / −2.5	0 / 16	+10.0 / −0	+0 / −6	0.8 / 4.9	+2.5 / −0	−0.8 / −2.4
19.69−	30.09	0 / 3.2	+2.0 / −0	+0 / −1.2	0 / 5.0	+3 / −0	+0 / −2	0 / 8	+5 / −0	+0 / −3	0 / 20	+12.0 / −0	+0 / −8	0.9 / 5.9	+3.0 / −0	−0.9 / −2.9
30.09−	41.49	0 / 4.1	+2.5 / −0	+0 / −1.6	0 / 6.5	+4 / −0	+0 / −2.5	0 / 10	+6 / −0	+0 / −4	0 / 26	+16.0 / −0	+0 / −10	1.0 / 7.5	+4.0 / −0	−1.0 / −3.5
41.49−	56.19	0 / 5.0	+3.0 / −0	+0 / −2.0	0 / 8.0	+5 / −0	+0 / −3	0 / 13	+8 / −0	+0 / −5	0 / 32	+20.0 / −0	+0 / −12	1.2 / 9.2	+5.0 / −0	−1.2 / −4.2
56.19−	76.39	0 / 6.5	+4.0 / −0	+0 / −2.5	0 / 10	+6 / −0	+0 / −4	0 / 16	+10 / −0	+0 / −6	0 / 41	+25.0 / −0	+0 / −16	1.2 / 11.2	+6.0 / −0	−1.2 / −5.2
76.39−	100.9	0 / 8.0	+5.0 / −0	+0 / −3.0	0 / 13	+8 / −0	+0 / −5	0 / 20	+12 / −0	+0 / −8	0 / 50	+30.0 / −0	+0 / −20	1.4 / 14.4	+8.0 / −0	−1.4 / −6.4
100.9 −	131.9	0 / 10.0	+6.0 / −0	+0 / −4.0	0 / 16	+10 / −0	+0 / −6	0 / 26	+16 / −0	+0 / −10	0 / 65	+40.0 / −0	+0 / −25	1.6 / 17.6	+10.0 / −0	−1.6 / −7.6
131.9 −	171.9	0 / 13.0	+8.0 / −0	+0 / −5.0	0 / 20	+12 / −0	+0 / −8	0 / 32	+20 / −0	+0 / −12	0 / 8	+50.0 / −0	+0 / −30	1.8 / 21.8	+12.0 / −0	−1.8 / −9.8
171.9 −	200	0 / 16.0	+10.0 / −0	+0 / −6.0	0 / 26	+16 / −0	+0 / −10	0 / 41	+25 / −0	+0 / −16	0 / 100	+60.0 / −0	+0 / −40	1.8 / 27.8	+16.0 / −0	−1.8 / −11.8

Source: Courtesy of USASI; B4.1–1955.

Class LC 6			Class LC 7			Class LC 8			Class LC 9			Class LC 10			Class LC 11			Nominal Size Range Inches	
Limits of Clearance	Standard Limits		Limits of Clearance	Standard Limits		Limits of Clearance	Standard Limits		Limits of Clearance	Standard Limits		Limits of Clearance	Standard Limits		Limits of Clearance	Standard Limits			
	Hole H9	Shaft f8		Hole H10	Shaft e9		Hole H10	Shaft d9		Hole H11	Shaft c10		Hole H12	Shaft		Hole H13	Shaft	Over	To
0.3 / 1.9	+1.0 / 0	−0.3 / −0.9	0.6 / 3.2	+1.6 / 0	−0.6 / −1.6	1.0 / 3.6	+1.6 / 0	−1.0 / −2.0	2.5 / 6.6	+2.5 / 0	−2.5 / −4.1	4 / 12	+4 / 0	−4 / −8	5 / 17	+6 / 0	−5 / −11	0	0.12
0.4 / 2.3	+1.2 / 0	−0.4 / −1.1	0.8 / 3.8	+1.8 / 0	−0.8 / −2.0	1.2 / 4.2	+1.8 / 0	−1.2 / −2.4	2.8 / 7.6	+3.0 / 0	−2.8 / −4.6	4.5 / 14.5	+5 / 0	−4.5 / −9.5	6 / 20	+7 / 0	−6 / −13	0.12	0.24
0.5 / 2.8	+1.4 / 0	−0.5 / −1.4	1.0 / 4.6	+2.2 / 0	−1.0 / −2.4	1.6 / 5.2	+2.2 / 0	−1.6 / −3.0	3.0 / 8.7	+3.5 / 0	−3.0 / −5.2	5 / 17	+6 / 0	−5 / −11	7 / 25	+9 / 0	−7 / −16	0.24	0.40
0.6 / 3.2	+1.6 / 0	−0.6 / −1.6	1.2 / 5.6	+2.8 / 0	−1.2 / −2.8	2.0 / 6.4	+2.8 / 0	−2.0 / −3.6	3.5 / 10.3	+4.0 / 0	−3.5 / −6.3	6 / 20	+7 / 0	−6 / −13	8 / 28	+10 / 0	−8 / −18	0.40	0.71
0.8 / 4.0	+2.0 / 0	−0.8 / −2.0	1.6 / 7.1	+3.5 / 0	−1.6 / −3.6	2.5 / 8.0	+3.5 / 0	−2.5 / −4.5	4.5 / 13.0	+5.0 / 0	−4.5 / −8.0	7 / 23	+8 / 0	−7 / −15	10 / 34	+12 / 0	−10 / −22	0.71	1.19
1.0 / 5.1	+2.5 / 0	−1.0 / −2.6	2.0 / 8.5	+4.0 / 0	−2.0 / −4.5	3.0 / 9.5	+4.0 / 0	−3.0 / −5.5	5 / 15	+6 / 0	−5 / −9	8 / 28	+10 / 0	−8 / −18	12 / 44	+16 / 0	−12 / −28	1.19	1.97
1.2 / 6.0	+3.0 / 0	−1.2 / −3.0	2.5 / 10.0	+4.5 / 0	−2.5 / −5.5	4.0 / 11.5	+4.5 / 0	−4.0 / −7.0	6 / 17.5	+7 / 0	−6 / −10.5	10 / 34	+12 / 0	−10 / −22	14 / 50	+18 / 0	−14 / −32	1.97	3.15
1.4 / 7.1	+3.5 / 0	−1.4 / −3.6	3.0 / 11.5	+5.0 / 0	−3.0 / −6.5	5.0 / 13.5	+5.0 / 0	−5.0 / −8.5	7 / 21	+9 / 0	−7 / −12	11 / 39	+14 / 0	−11 / −25	16 / 60	+22 / 0	−16 / −38	3.15	4.73
1.6 / 8.1	+4.0 / 0	−1.6 / −4.1	3.5 / 13.5	+6.0 / 0	−3.5 / −7.5	6 / 16	+6 / 0	−6 / −10	8 / 24	+10 / 0	−8 / −14	12 / 44	+16 / 0	−12 / −28	18 / 68	+25 / 0	−18 / −43	4.73	7.09
2.0 / 9.3	+4.5 / 0	−2.0 / −4.8	4.0 / 15.5	+7.0 / 0	−4.0 / −8.5	7 / 18.5	+7 / 0	−7 / −11.5	10 / 29	+12 / 0	−10 / −17	16 / 52	+18 / 0	−16 / −34	22 / 78	+28 / 0	−22 / −50	7.09	9.85
2.2 / 10.2	+5.0 / 0	−2.2 / −5.2	4.5 / 17.5	+8.0 / 0	−4.5 / −9.5	7 / 20	+8 / 0	−7 / −12	12 / 32	+12 / 0	−12 / −20	20 / 60	+20 / 0	−20 / −40	28 / 88	+30 / 0	−28 / −58	9.85	12.41
2.5 / 12.0	+6.0 / 0	−2.5 / −6.0	5.0 / 20.0	+9.0 / 0	−5 / −11	8 / 23	+9 / 0	−8 / −14	14 / 37	+14 / 0	−14 / −23	22 / 66	+22 / 0	−22 / −44	30 / 100	+35 / 0	−30 / −65	12.41	15.75
2.8 / 12.8	+6.0 / 0	−2.8 / −6.8	5.0 / 21.0	+10.0 / 0	−5 / −11	9 / 25	+10 / 0	−9 / −15	16 / 42	+16 / 0	−16 / −26	25 / 75	+25 / 0	−25 / −50	35 / 115	+40 / 0	−35 / −75	15.75	19.69
3.0 / 16.0	+8.0 / 0	−3.0 / −8.0	6.0 / 26.0	+12.0 / 0	−6 / −14	10 / 30	+12 / 0	−10 / −18	18 / 50	+20 / 0	−18 / −30	28 / 88	+30 / 0	−28 / −58	40 / 140	+50 / 0	−40 / −90	19.69	30.09
3.5 / 19.5	+10.0 / 0	−3.5 / −9.5	7.0 / 33.0	+16.0 / 0	−7 / −17	12 / 38	+16 / 0	−12 / −22	20 / 61	+25 / 0	−20 / −36	30 / 110	+40 / 0	−30 / −70	45 / 165	+60 / 0	−45 / −105	30.09	41.49
4.0 / 24.0	+12.0 / 0	−4.0 / −12.0	8.0 / 40.0	+20.0 / 0	−8 / −20	14 / 46	+20 / 0	−14 / −26	25 / 75	+30 / 0	−25 / −45	40 / 140	+50 / 0	−40 / −90	60 / 220	+80 / 0	−60 / −140	41.49	56.19
4.5 / 30.5	+16.0 / 0	−4.5 / −14.5	9.0 / 50.0	+25.0 / 0	−9 / −25	16 / 57	+25 / 0	−16 / −32	30 / 95	+40 / 0	−30 / −55	50 / 170	+60 / 0	−50 / −110	70 / 270	+100 / 0	−70 / −170	56.19	76.39
5.0 / 37.0	+20.0 / 0	−5 / −17	10.0 / 60.0	+30.0 / 0	−10 / −30	18 / 68	+30 / 0	−18 / −38	35 / 115	+50 / 0	−35 / −65	50 / 210	+80 / 0	−50 / −130	80 / 330	+125 / 0	−80 / −205	76.39	100.9
6.0 / 47.0	+25.0 / 0	−6 / −22	12.0 / 67.0	+40.0 / 0	−12 / −27	20 / 85	+40 / 0	−20 / −45	40 / 140	+60 / 0	−40 / −80	60 / 260	+100 / 0	−60 / −160	90 / 410	+160 / 0	−90 / −250	100.9	131.9
7.0 / 57.0	+30.0 / 0	−7 / −27	14.0 / 94.0	+50.0 / 0	−14 / −44	25 / 105	+50 / 0	−25 / −55	50 / 180	+80 / 0	−50 / −100	80 / 330	+125 / 0	−80 / −205	100 / 500	+200 / 0	−100 / −300	131.9	171.9
7.0 / 72.0	+40.0 / 0	−7 / −32	14.0 / 114.0	+60.0 / 0	−14 / −54	25 / 125	+60 / 0	−25 / −65	50 / 210	+100 / 0	−50 / −110	90 / 410	+160 / 0	−90 / −250	125 / 625	+250 / 0	−125 / −375	171.9	200

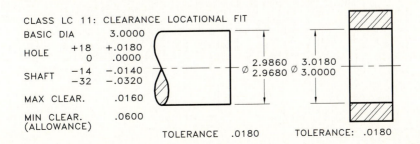

CLASS LC 11: CLEARANCE LOCATIONAL FIT

BASIC DIA	3.0000	
HOLE	+18 / 0	+.0180 / .0000
SHAFT	−14 / −32	−.0140 / −.0320
MAX CLEAR.		.0160
MIN CLEAR. (ALLOWANCE)		.0600

∅ 2.9860 / 2.9680   ∅ 3.0180 / 3.0000

TOLERANCE .0180   TOLERANCE: .0180

APPENDIX 34 • American Standard Transition Locational Fits (hole basis)

Limits are in thousandths of an inch.

Limits for hole and shaft are applied algebraically to the basic size to obtain the limits of size for the mating parts.

Data in bold face are in accordance with ABC agreements.

"Fit" represents the maximum interference (minus values) and the maximum clearance (plus values).

Symbols H7, js6, etc., are Hole and Shaft designations used in ABC System.

Nominal Size Range Inches Over	To	Class LT 1 Fit	Hole H7	Shaft js6	Class LT 2 Fit	Hole H8	Shaft js7	Class LT 3 Fit	Hole H7	Shaft k6	Class LT 4 Fit	Hole H8	Shaft k7	Class LT 5 Fit	Hole H7	Shaft n6	Class LT 6 Fit	Hole H7	Shaft n7
0	0.12	−0.10 / +0.50	+0.4 / −0	+0.10 / −0.10	−0.2 / +0.8	+0.6 / −0	+0.2 / −0.2							−0.5 / +0.15	+0.4 / −0	+0.5 / +0.25	−0.65 / +0.15	+0.4 / −0	+0.65 / +0.25
0.12	0.24	−0.15 / +0.65	+0.5 / −0	+0.15 / −0.15	−0.25 / +0.95	+0.7 / −0	+0.25 / −0.25							−0.6 / +0.2	+0.5 / −0	+0.6 / +0.3	−0.8 / +0.2	+0.5 / −0	+0.8 / +0.3
0.24	0.40	−0.2 / +0.8	+0.6 / −0	+0.2 / −0.2	−0.3 / +1.2	+0.9 / −0	+0.3 / −0.3	−0.5 / +0.5	+0.6 / −0	+0.5 / +0.1	−0.7 / +0.8	+0.9 / −0	+0.7 / +0.1	−0.8 / +0.2	+0.6 / −0	+0.8 / +0.4	−1.0 / +0.2	+0.6 / −0	+1.0 / +0.4
0.40	0.71	−0.2 / +0.9	+0.7 / −0	+0.2 / −0.2	−0.35 / +1.35	+1.0 / −0	+0.35 / −0.35	−0.5 / +0.6	+0.7 / −0	+0.5 / +0.1	−0.8 / +0.9	+1.0 / −0	+0.8 / +0.1	−0.9 / +0.2	+0.7 / −0	+0.9 / +0.5	−1.2 / +0.2	+0.7 / −0	+1.2 / +0.5
0.71	1.19	−0.25 / +1.05	+0.8 / −0	+0.25 / −0.25	−0.4 / +1.6	+1.2 / −0	+0.4 / −0.4	−0.6 / +0.7	+0.8 / −0	+0.6 / +0.1	−0.9 / +1.1	+1.2 / −0	+0.9 / +0.1	−1.1 / +0.2	+0.8 / −0	+1.1 / +0.6	−1.4 / +0.2	+0.8 / −0	+1.4 / +0.6
1.19	1.97	−0.3 / +1.3	+1.0 / −0	+0.3 / −0.3	−0.5 / +2.1	+1.6 / −0	+0.5 / −0.5	−0.7 / +0.9	+1.0 / −0	+0.7 / +0.1	−1.1 / +1.5	+1.6 / −0	+1.1 / +0.1	−1.3 / +0.3	+1.0 / −0	+1.3 / +0.7	−1.7 / +0.3	+1.0 / −0	+1.7 / +0.7
1.97	3.15	−0.3 / +1.5	+1.2 / −0	+0.3 / −0.3	−0.6 / +2.4	+1.8 / −0	+0.6 / −0.6	−0.8 / +1.1	+1.2 / −0	+0.8 / +0.1	−1.3 / +1.7	+1.8 / −0	+1.3 / +0.1	−1.5 / +0.4	+1.2 / −0	+1.5 / +0.8	−2.0 / +0.4	+1.2 / −0	+2.0 / +0.8
3.15	4.73	−0.4 / +1.8	+1.4 / −0	+0.4 / −0.4	−0.7 / +2.9	+2.2 / −0	+0.7 / −0.7	−1.0 / +1.3	+1.4 / −0	+1.0 / +0.1	−1.5 / +2.1	+2.2 / −0	+1.5 / +0.1	−1.9 / +0.4	+1.4 / −0	+1.9 / +1.0	−2.4 / +0.4	+1.4 / −0	+2.4 / +1.0
4.73	7.09	−0.5 / +2.1	+1.6 / −0	+0.5 / −0.5	−0.8 / +3.3	+2.5 / −0	+0.8 / −0.8	−1.1 / +1.5	+1.6 / −0	+1.1 / +0.1	−1.7 / +2.4	+2.5 / −0	+1.7 / +0.1	−2.2 / +0.4	+1.6 / −0	+2.2 / +1.2	−2.8 / +0.4	+1.6 / −0	+2.8 / +1.2
7.09	9.85	−0.6 / +2.4	+1.8 / −0	+0.6 / −0.6	−0.9 / +3.7	+2.8 / −0	+0.9 / −0.9	−1.4 / +1.6	+1.8 / −0	+1.4 / +0.2	−2.0 / +2.6	+2.8 / −0	+2.0 / +0.2	−2.6 / +0.4	+1.8 / −0	+2.6 / +1.4	−3.2 / +0.4	+1.8 / −0	+3.2 / +1.4
9.85	12.41	−0.6 / +2.6	+2.0 / −0	+0.6 / −0.6	−1.0 / +4.0	+3.0 / −0	+1.0 / −1.0	−1.4 / +1.8	+2.0 / −0	+1.4 / +0.2	−2.2 / +2.8	+3.0 / −0	+2.2 / +0.2	−2.6 / +0.6	+2.0 / −0	+2.6 / +1.4	−3.4 / +0.6	+2.0 / −0	+3.4 / +1.4
12.41	15.75	−0.7 / +2.9	+2.2 / −0	+0.7 / −0.7	−1.0 / +4.5	+3.5 / −0	+1.0 / −1.0	−1.6 / +2.0	+2.2 / −0	+1.6 / +0.2	−2.4 / +3.3	+3.5 / −0	+2.4 / +0.2	−3.0 / +0.6	+2.2 / −0	+3.0 / +1.6	−3.8 / +0.6	+2.2 / −0	+3.8 / +1.6
15.75	19.69	−0.8 / +3.3	+2.5 / −0	+0.8 / −0.8	−1.2 / +5.2	+4.0 / −0	+1.2 / −1.2	−1.8 / +2.3	+2.5 / −0	+1.8 / +0.2	−2.7 / +3.8	+4.0 / −0	+2.7 / +0.2	−3.4 / +0.7	+2.5 / −0	+3.4 / +1.8	−4.3 / +0.7	+2.5 / −0	+4.3 / +1.8

Source: Courtesy of ANSI; B4.1–1955.

APPENDIX 35 • American Standard Interference Locational Fits (hole basis)

Limits are in thousandths of an inch.
Limits for hole and shaft are applied algebraically to the
basic size to obtain the limits of size for the parts.
Data in bold face are in accordance with ABC agreements,
Symbols H7, p6, etc., are Hole and Shaft designations
used in ABC System.

Nominal Size Range Inches		Class LN 1			Class LN 2			Class LN 3		
		Limits of Interference	Standard Limits		Limits of Interference	Standard Limits		Limits of Interference	Standard Limits	
Over	To		Hole H6	Shaft n5		Hole H7	Shaft p6		Hole H7	Shaft r6
0 – 0.12		0 / 0.45	+ 0.25 / – 0	+0.45 / +0.25	0 / 0.65	+ 0.4 / – 0	+ 0.65 / + 0.4	0.1 / 0.75	+ 0.4 / – 0	+ 0.75 / + 0.5
0.12 – 0.24		0 / 0.5	+ 0.3 / – 0	+0.5 / +0.3	0 / 0.8	+ 0.5 / – 0	+ 0.8 / + 0.5	0.1 / 0.9	+ 0.5 / 0	+ 0.9 / + 0.6
0.24 – 0.40		0 / 0.65	+ 0.4 / – 0	+0.65 / +0.4	0 / 1.0	+ 0.6 / – 0	+ 1.0 / + 0.6	0.2 / 1.2	+ 0.6 / – 0	+ 1.2 / + 0.8
0.40 – 0.71		0 / 0.8	+ 0.4 / – 0	+0.8 / +0.4	0 / 1.1	+ 0.7 / – 0	+ 1.1 / + 0.7	0.3 / 1.4	+ 0.7 / – 0	+ 1.4 / + 1.0
0.71 – 1.19		0 / 1.0	+ 0.5 / – 0	+1.0 / +0.5	0 / 1.3	+ 0.8 / – 0	+ 1.3 / + 0.8	0.4 / 1.7	+ 0.8 / – 0	+ 1.7 / + 1.2
1.19 – 1.97		0 / 1.1	+ 0.6 / – 0	+1.1 / +0.6	0 / 1.6	+ 1.0 / – 0	+ 1.6 / + 1.0	0.4 / 2.0	+ 1.0 / – 0	+ 2.0 / + 1.4
1.97 – 3.15		0.1 / 1.3	+ 0.7 / – 0	+1.3 / + 0.7	0.2 / 2.1	+ 1.2 / – 0	+ 2.1 / + 1.4	0.4 / 2.3	+ 1.2 / – 0	+ 2.3 / + 1.6
3.15 – 4.73		0.1 / 1.6	+ 0.9 / – 0	+1.6 / +1.0	0.2 / 2.5	+ 1.4 / – 0	+ 2.5 / + 1.6	0.6 / 2.9	+ 1.4 / – 0	+ 2.9 / + 2.0
4.73 – 7.09		0.2 / 1.9	+ 1.0 / – 0	+1.9 / +1.2	0.2 / 2.8	+ 1.6 / – 0	+ 2.8 / + 1.8	0.9 / 3.5	+ 1.6 / – 0	+ 3.5 / + 2.5
7.09 – 9.85		0.2 / 2.2	+ 1.2 / – 0	+2.2 / +1.4	0.2 / 3.2	+ 1.8 / – 0	+ 3.2 / + 2.0	1.2 / 4.2	+ 1.8 / – 0	+ 4.2 / + 3.0
9.85 – 12.41		0.2 / 2.3	+ 1.2 / – 0	+2.3 / +1.4	0.2 / 3.4	+ 2.0 / – 0	+ 3.4 / + 2.2	1.5 / 4.7	+ 2.0 / – 0	+ 4.7 / + 3.5
12.41 – 15.75		0.2 / 2.6	+ 1.4 / – 0	+2.6 / +1.6	0.3 / 3.9	+ 2.2 / – 0	+ 3.9 / + 2.5	2.3 / 5.9	+ 2.2 / – 0	+ 5.9 / + 4.5
15.75 – 19.69		0.2 / 2.8	+ 1.6 / – 0	+2.8 / +1.8	0.3 / 4.4	+ 2.5 / – 0	+ 4.4 / + 2.8	2.5 / 6.6	+ 2.5 / – 0	+ 6.6 / + 5.0
19.69 – 30.09			+ 2.0 / – 0		0.5 / 5.5	+ 3 / – 0	+ 5.5 / + 3.5	4 / 9	+ 3 / – 0	+ 9 / + 7
30.09 – 41.49			+ 2.5 / – 0		0.5 / 7.0	+ 4 / – 0	+ 7.0 / + 4.5	5 / 11.5	+ 4 / – 0	+11.5 / + 9
41.49 – 56.19			+ 3.0 / – 0		1 / 9	+ 5 / – 0	+ 9 / + 6	7 / 15	+ 5 / – 0	+15 / +12
56.19 – 76.39			+ 4.0 / – 0		1 / 11	+ 6 / – 0	+11 / + 7	10 / 20	+ 6 / – 0	+20 / +16
76.39 – 100.9			+ 5.0 / – 0		1 / 14	+ 8 / – 0	+14 / + 9	12 / 25	+ 8 / – 0	+25 / +20
100.9 – 131.9			+ 6.0 / – 0		2 / 18	+10 / – 0	+18 / +12	15 / 31	+10 / – 0	+31 / +25
131.9 – 171.9			+ 8.0 / – 0		4 / 24	+12 / – 0	+24 / +16	18 / 38	+12 / – 0	+38 / +30
171.9 – 200			+10.0 / – 0		4 / 30	+16 / – 0	+30 / +20	24 / 50	+16 / – 0	+50 / +40

Source: Courtesy of ANSI; B4.1–1955.

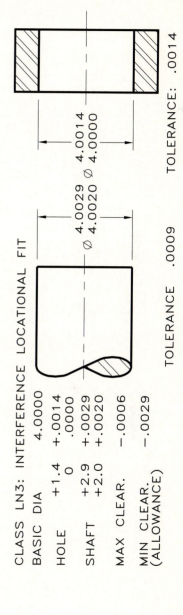

CLASS LN3: INTERFERENCE LOCATIONAL FIT

TOLERANCE: .0014

TOLERANCE .0009

BASIC DIA	4.0000
HOLE	+.0014 / .0000
SHAFT	+.0029 / +.0020
MAX CLEAR.	–.0006
MIN CLEAR. (ALLOWANCE)	–.0029

	+1.4 / 0
	+2.9 / +2.0
	–.0006
	–.0029

Ø 4.0014 / Ø 4.0000

Ø 4.0029 / Ø 4.0020

APPENDIX 36 • American Standard Force and Shrink Fits (hole basis)

Limits are in thousandths of an inch.
Limits for hole and shaft are applied algebraically to the basic size to obtain the limits of size for the parts.
Data in bold face are in accordance with ABC agreements.
Symbols H7, s6, etc., are Hole and Shaft designations used in ABC System.

Nominal Size Range Inches (Over — To)	Class FN 1 Limits of Interference	Class FN 1 Hole H6	Class FN 1 Shaft	Class FN 2 Limits of Interference	Class FN 2 Hole H7	Class FN 2 Shaft s6	Class FN 3 Limits of Interference	Class FN 3 Hole H7	Class FN 3 Shaft t6	Class FN 4 Limits of Interference	Class FN 4 Hole H7	Class FN 4 Shaft u6	Class FN 5 Limits of Interference	Class FN 5 Hole H8	Class FN 5 Shaft x7
0 — 0.12	0.05 0.5	+0.25 − 0	+ 0.5 + 0.3	0.2 0.85	+0.4 − 0	+ 0.85 + 0.6				0.3 0.95	+0.4 − 0	+ 0.95 + 0.7	0.3 1.3	+0.6 − 0	+ 1.3 + 0.9
0.12 — 0.24	0.1 0.6	+0.3 − 0	+ 0.6 + 0.4	0.2 1.0	+0.5 − 0	+ 1.0 + 0.7				0.4 1.2	+0.5 − 0	+ 1.2 + 0.9	0.5 1.7	+0.7 − 0	+ 1.7 + 1.2
0.24 — 0.40	0.1 0.75	+0.4 − 0	+ 0.75 + 0.5	0.4 1.4	+0.6 − 0	+ 1.4 + 1.0				0.6 1.6	+0.6 − 0	+ 1.6 + 1.2	0.5 2.0	+0.9 − 0	+ 2.0 + 1.4
0.40 — 0.56	0.1 0.8	−0.4 − 0	+ 0.8 + 0.5	0.5 1.6	+0.7 − 0	+ 1.6 + 1.2				0.7 1.8	+ 0.7 − 0	+ 1.8 + 1.4	0.6 2.3	+ 1.0 − 0	+ 2.3 + 1.6
0.56 — 0.71	0.2 0.9	+0.4 − 0	+ 0.9 + 0.6	0.5 1.6	+0.7 − 0	+ 1.6 + 1.2				0.7 1.8	+ 0.7 − 0	+ 1.8 + 1.4	0.8 2.5	+ 1.0 − 0	+ 2.5 + 1.8
0.71 — 0.95	0.2 1.1	+0.5 − 0	+ 1.1 + 0.7	0.6 1.9	+0.8 − 0	+ 1.9 + 1.4				0.8 2.1	+ 0.8 − 0	+ 2.1 + 1.6	1.0 3.0	+ 1.2 − 0	+ 3.0 + 2.2
0.95 — 1.19	0.3 1.2	+0.5 − 0	+ 1.2 + 0.8	0.6 1.9	+0.8 − 0	+ 1.9 + 1.4	0.8 2.1	+0.8 − 0	+ 2.1 + 1.6	1.0 2.3	+0.8 − 0	+ 2.3 + 1.8	1.3 3.3	+ 1.2 − 0	+ 3.3 + 2.5
1.19 — 1.58	0.3 1.3	+0.6 − 0	+ 1.3 + 0.9	0.8 2.4	+1.0 − 0	+ 2.4 + 1.8	1.0 2.6	+1.0 − 0	+ 2.6 + 2.0	1.5 3.1	+1.0 − 0	+ 3.1 + 2.5	1.4 4.0	+ 1.6 − 0	+ 4.0 + 3.0
1.58 — 1.97	0.4 1.4	+0.6 − 0	+ 1.4 + 1.0	0.8 2.4	+1.0 − 0	+ 2.4 + 1.8	1.2 2.8	+1.0 − 0	+ 2.8 + 2.2	1.8 3.4	+1.0 − 0	+ 3.4 + 2.8	2.4 5.0	+ 1.6 − 0	+ 5.0 + 4.0
1.97 — 2.56	0.6 1.8	+0.7 − 0	+ 1.8 + 1.3	0.8 2.7	+1.2 − 0	+ 2.7 + 2.0	1.3 3.2	+1.2 − 0	+ 3.2 + 2.5	2.3 4.2	+1.2 − 0	+ 4.2 + 3.5	3.2 6.2	+ 1.8 − 0	+ 6.2 + 5.0
2.56 — 3.15	0.7 1.9	+0.7 − 0	+ 1.9 + 1.4	1.0 2.9	+1.2 − 0	+ 2.9 + 2.2	1.8 3.7	+1.2 − 0	+ 3.7 + 3.0	2.8 4.7	+1.2 − 0	+ 4.7 + 4.0	4.2 7.2	+ 1.8 − 0	+ 7.2 + 6.0
3.15 — 3.94	0.9 2.4	+0.9 − 0	+ 2.4 + 1.8	1.4 3.7	+1.4 − 0	+ 3.7 + 2.8	2.1 4.4	+1.4 − 0	+ 4.4 + 3.5	3.6 5.9	+1.4 − 0	+ 5.9 + 5.0	4.8 8.4	+ 2.2 − 0	+ 8.4 + 7.0
3.94 — 4.73	1.1 2.6	+0.9 − 0	+ 2.6 + 2.0	1.6 3.9	+1.4 − 0	+ 3.9 + 3.0	2.6 4.9	+1.4 − 0	+ 4.9 + 4.0	4.6 6.9	+1.4 − 0	+ 6.9 + 6.0	5.8 9.4	+ 2.2 − 0	+ 9.4 + 8.0
4.73 — 5.52	1.2 2.9	+1.0 − 0	+ 2.9 + 2.2	1.9 4.5	+1.6 − 0	+ 4.5 + 3.5	3.4 6.0	+1.6 − 0	+ 6.0 + 5.0	5.4 8.0	+1.6 − 0	+ 8.0 + 7.0	7.5 11.6	+ 2.5 − 0	+11.6 +10.0
5.52 — 6.30	1.5 3.2	+1.0 − 0	+ 3.2 + 2.5	2.4 5.0	+1.6 − 0	+ 5.0 + 4.0	3.4 6.0	+1.6 − 0	+ 6.0 + 5.0	5.4 8.0	+1.6 − 0	+ 8.0 + 7.0	9.5 13.6	+ 2.5 − 0	+13.6 +12.0
6.30 — 7.09	1.8 3.5	+1.0 − 0	+ 3.5 + 2.8	2.9 5.5	+1.6 − 0	+ 5.5 + 4.5	4.4 7.0	+1.6 − 0	+ 7.0 + 6.0	6.4 9.0	+1.6 − 0	+ 9.0 + 8.0	9.5 13.6	+ 2.5 − 0	+13.6 +12.0
7.09 — 7.88	1.8 3.8	+1.2 − 0	+ 3.8 + 3.0	3.2 6.2	+1.8 − 0	+ 6.2 + 5.0	5.2 8.2	+1.8 − 0	+ 8.2 + 7.0	7.2 10.2	+1.8 − 0	+10.2 + 9.0	11.2 15.8	+ 2.8 − 0	+15.8 +14.0
7.88 — 8.86	2.3 4.3	+1.2 − 0	+ 4.3 + 3.5	3.2 6.2	+1.8 − 0	+ 6.2 + 5.0	5.2 8.2	+1.8 − 0	+ 8.2 + 7.0	8.2 11.2	+1.8 − 0	+11.2 +10.0	13.2 17.8	+ 2.8 − 0	+17.8 +16.0
8.86 — 9.85	2.3 4.3	+1.2 − 0	+ 4.3 + 3.5	4.2 7.2	+1.8 − 0	+ 7.2 + 6.0	6.2 9.2	+1.8 − 0	+ 9.2 + 8.0	10.2 13.2	+1.8 − 0	+13.2 +12.0	13.2 17.8	+ 2.8 − 0	+17.8 +16.0
9.85 — 11.03	2.8 4.9	+1.2 − 0	+ 4.9 + 4.0	4.0 7.2	+2.0 − 0	+ 7.2 + 6.0	7.0 10.2	+2.0 − 0	+10.2 + 9.0	10.0 13.2	+2.0 − 0	+13.2 +12.0	15.0 20.0	+ 3.0 − 0	+20.0 +18.0
11.03 — 12.41	2.8 4.9	+1.2 − 0	+ 4.9 + 4.0	5.0 8.2	+2.0 − 0	+ 8.2 + 7.0	7.0 10.2	+2.0 − 0	+10.2 + 9.0	12.0 15.2	+2.0 − 0	+15.2 +14.0	17.0 22.0	+ 3.0 − 0	+22.0 +20.0
12.41 — 13.98	3.1 5.5	+1.4 − 0	+ 5.5 + 4.5	5.8 9.4	+2.2 − 0	+ 9.4 + 8.0	7.8 11.4	+2.2 − 0	+11.4 +10.0	13.8 17.4	+2.2 − 0	+17.4 +16.0	18.5 24.2	+ 3.5 + 0	+24.2 +22.0
13.98 — 15.75	3.6 6.1	+1.4 − 0	+ 6.1 + 5.0	5.8 9.4	+2.2 − 0	+ 9.4 + 8.0	9.8 13.4	+2.2 − 0	+13.4 +12.0	15.8 19.4	+2.2 − 0	+19.4 +18.0	21.5 27.2	+ 3.5 − 0	+27.2 +25.0
15.75 — 17.72	4.4 7.0	+1.6 − 0	+ 7.0 + 6.0	6.5 10.6	+2.5 − 0	+10.6 + 9.0	9.5 13.6	+2.5 − 0	+13.6 +12.0	17.5 21.6	+2.5 − 0	+21.6 +20.0	24.0 30.5	+ 4.0 − 0	+30.5 +28.0
17.72 — 19.69	4.4 7.0	+1.6 − 0	+ 7.0 + 6.0	7.5 11.6	+2.5 − 0	+11.6 +10.0	11.5 15.6	+2.5 − 0	+15.6 +14.0	19.5 23.6	+2.5 − 0	+23.6 +22.0	26.0 32.5	+ 4.0 − 0	+32.5 +30.0

Source: Courtesy of ANSI; B4.1-1955.

APPENDIX 37 • The International Tolerance Grades (ANSI B4.2)

The international tolerance grades (ANSI B4.2)

Basic sizes		Tolerance grades[3]																		
Over	Up to and including	IT01	IT0	IT1	IT2	IT3	IT4	IT5	IT6	IT7	IT8	IT9	IT10	IT11	IT12	IT13	IT14	IT15	IT16
0	3	0.0003	0.0005	0.0008	0.0012	0.002	0.003	0.004	0.006	0.010	0.014	0.025	0.040	0.060	0.100	0.140	0.250	0.400	0.600
3	6	0.0004	0.0006	0.001	0.0015	0.0025	0.004	0.005	0.008	0.012	0.018	0.030	0.048	0.075	0.120	0.180	0.300	0.480	0.750
6	10	0.0004	0.0006	0.001	0.0015	0.0025	0.004	0.006	0.009	0.015	0.022	0.036	0.058	0.090	0.150	0.220	0.360	0.580	0.900
10	18	0.0005	0.0008	0.0012	0.002	0.003	0.005	0.008	0.011	0.018	0.027	0.043	0.070	0.110	0.180	0.270	0.430	0.700	1.100
18	30	0.0006	0.001	0.0015	0.0025	0.004	0.006	0.009	0.013	0.021	0.033	0.052	0.084	0.130	0.210	0.330	0.520	0.840	1.300
30	50	0.0006	0.001	0.0015	0.0025	0.004	0.007	0.011	0.016	0.025	0.039	0.062	0.100	0.160	0.250	0.390	0.620	1.000	1.600
50	80	0.0008	0.0012	0.002	0.003	0.005	0.008	0.013	0.019	0.030	0.046	0.074	0.120	0.190	0.300	0.460	0.740	1.200	1.900
80	120	0.001	0.0015	0.0025	0.004	0.006	0.010	0.015	0.022	0.035	0.054	0.087	0.140	0.220	0.350	0.540	0.870	1.400	2.200
120	180	0.0012	0.002	0.0035	0.005	0.008	0.012	0.018	0.025	0.040	0.063	0.100	0.160	0.250	0.400	0.630	1.000	1.600	2.500
180	250	0.002	0.003	0.0045	0.007	0.010	0.014	0.020	0.029	0.046	0.072	0.115	0.185	0.290	0.460	0.720	1.150	1.850	2.900
250	315	0.0025	0.004	0.006	0.008	0.012	0.016	0.023	0.032	0.052	0.081	0.130	0.210	0.320	0.520	0.810	1.300	2.100	3.200
315	400	0.003	0.005	0.007	0.009	0.013	0.018	0.025	0.036	0.057	0.089	0.140	0.230	0.360	0.570	0.890	1.400	2.300	3.600
400	500	0.004	0.006	0.008	0.010	0.015	0.020	0.027	0.040	0.063	0.097	0.155	0.250	0.400	0.630	0.970	1.550	2.500	4.000
500	630	0.0045	0.006	0.009	0.011	0.016	0.022	0.030	0.044	0.070	0.110	0.175	0.280	0.440	0.700	1.100	1.750	2.800	4.400
630	800	0.005	0.007	0.010	0.013	0.018	0.025	0.035	0.050	0.080	0.125	0.200	0.320	0.500	0.800	1.250	2.000	3.200	5.000
800	1000	0.0055	0.008	0.011	0.015	0.021	0.029	0.040	0.056	0.090	0.140	0.230	0.360	0.560	0.900	1.400	2.300	3.600	5.600
1000	1250	0.0065	0.009	0.013	0.018	0.024	0.034	0.046	0.066	0.105	0.165	0.260	0.420	0.660	1.050	1.650	2.600	4.200	6.600
1250	1600	0.008	0.011	0.015	0.021	0.029	0.040	0.054	0.078	0.125	0.195	0.310	0.500	0.780	1.250	1.950	3.100	5.000	7.800
1600	2000	0.009	0.013	0.018	0.025	0.035	0.048	0.065	0.092	0.150	0.230	0.370	0.600	0.920	1.500	2.300	3.700	6.000	9.200
2000	2500	0.011	0.015	0.022	0.030	0.041	0.057	0.077	0.110	0.175	0.280	0.440	0.700	1.100	1.750	2.800	4.400	7.000	11.000
2500	3150	0.013	0.018	0.026	0.036	0.050	0.069	0.093	0.135	0.210	0.330	0.540	0.860	1.350	2.100	3.300	5.400	8.600	13.500

[3] IT Values for tolerance grades larger than IT16 can be calculated by using the following formulas:
IT17 = IT12 × 10; IT18 = IT13 × 10; etc.

APPENDIX 38 • Preferred Hole Basis Clearance Fits—Cylindrical Fits (ANSI B4.2)

Dimensions in mm.

BASIC SIZE		LOOSE RUNNING Hole H11	Shaft c11	Fit	FREE RUNNING Hole H9	Shaft d9	Fit	CLOSE RUNNING Hole H8	Shaft f7	Fit	SLIDING Hole H7	Shaft g6	Fit	LOCATIONAL CLEARANCE Hole H7	Shaft h6	Fit
1	MAX	1.060	0.940	0.180	1.025	0.980	0.070	1.014	0.994	0.030	1.010	0.998	0.018	1.010	1.000	0.016
	MIN	1.000	0.880	0.060	1.000	0.955	0.020	1.000	0.984	0.006	1.000	0.992	0.002	1.000	0.994	0.000
1.2	MAX	1.260	1.140	0.180	1.225	1.180	0.070	1.214	1.194	0.030	1.210	1.198	0.018	1.210	1.200	0.016
	MIN	1.200	1.080	0.060	1.200	1.155	0.020	1.200	1.184	0.006	1.200	1.192	0.002	1.200	1.194	0.000
1.6	MAX	1.660	1.540	0.180	1.625	1.580	0.070	1.614	1.594	0.030	1.610	1.598	0.018	1.610	1.600	0.016
	MIN	1.600	1.480	0.060	1.600	1.555	0.020	1.600	1.584	0.006	1.600	1.592	0.002	1.600	1.594	0.000
2	MAX	2.060	1.940	0.180	2.025	1.980	0.070	2.014	1.994	0.030	2.010	1.998	0.018	2.010	2.000	0.016
	MIN	2.000	1.880	0.060	2.000	1.955	0.020	2.000	1.984	0.006	2.000	1.992	0.002	2.000	1.994	0.000
2.5	MAX	2.560	2.440	0.180	2.525	2.480	0.070	2.514	2.494	0.030	2.510	2.498	0.018	2.510	2.500	0.016
	MIN	2.500	2.380	0.060	2.500	2.455	0.020	2.500	2.484	0.006	2.500	2.492	0.002	2.500	2.494	0.000
3	MAX	3.060	2.940	0.180	3.025	2.980	0.070	3.014	2.994	0.030	3.010	2.998	0.018	3.010	3.000	0.016
	MIN	3.000	2.880	0.060	3.000	2.955	0.020	3.000	2.984	0.006	3.000	2.992	0.002	3.000	2.994	0.000
4	MAX	4.075	3.930	0.220	4.030	3.970	0.090	4.018	3.990	0.040	4.012	3.996	0.024	4.012	4.000	0.020
	MIN	4.000	3.855	0.070	4.000	3.940	0.030	4.000	3.978	0.010	4.000	3.988	0.004	4.000	3.992	0.000
5	MAX	5.075	4.930	0.220	5.030	4.970	0.090	5.018	4.990	0.040	5.012	4.996	0.024	5.012	5.000	0.020
	MIN	5.000	4.855	0.070	5.000	4.940	0.030	5.000	4.978	0.010	5.000	4.988	0.004	5.000	4.992	0.000
6	MAX	6.075	5.930	0.220	6.030	5.970	0.090	6.018	5.990	0.040	6.012	5.996	0.024	6.012	6.000	0.020
	MIN	6.000	5.855	0.070	6.000	5.940	0.030	6.000	5.978	0.010	6.000	5.988	0.004	6.000	5.992	0.000
8	MAX	8.090	7.920	0.260	8.036	7.960	0.112	8.022	7.987	0.050	8.015	7.995	0.029	8.015	8.000	0.024
	MIN	8.000	7.830	0.080	8.000	7.924	0.040	8.000	7.972	0.013	8.000	7.986	0.005	8.000	7.991	0.000
10	MAX	10.090	9.920	0.260	10.036	9.960	0.112	10.022	9.987	0.050	10.015	9.995	0.029	10.015	10.000	0.024
	MIN	10.000	9.830	0.080	10.000	9.924	0.040	10.000	9.972	0.013	10.000	9.986	0.005	10.000	9.991	0.000
12	MAX	12.110	11.905	0.315	12.043	11.950	0.136	12.027	11.984	0.061	12.018	11.994	0.035	12.018	12.000	0.029
	MIN	12.000	11.795	0.095	12.000	11.907	0.050	12.000	11.966	0.016	12.000	11.983	0.006	12.000	11.989	0.000
16	MAX	16.110	15.905	0.315	16.043	15.950	0.136	16.027	15.984	0.061	16.018	15.994	0.035	16.018	16.000	0.029
	MIN	16.000	15.795	0.095	16.000	15.907	0.050	16.000	15.966	0.016	16.000	15.983	0.006	16.000	15.989	0.000
20	MAX	20.130	19.890	0.370	20.052	19.935	0.169	20.033	19.980	0.074	20.021	19.993	0.041	20.021	20.000	0.034
	MIN	20.000	19.760	0.110	20.000	19.883	0.065	20.000	19.959	0.020	20.000	19.980	0.007	20.000	19.987	0.000
25	MAX	25.130	24.890	0.370	25.052	24.935	0.169	25.033	24.980	0.074	25.021	24.993	0.041	25.021	25.000	0.034
	MIN	25.000	24.760	0.110	25.000	24.883	0.065	25.000	24.959	0.020	25.000	24.980	0.007	25.000	24.987	0.000
30	MAX	30.130	29.890	0.370	30.052	29.935	0.169	30.033	29.980	0.074	30.021	29.993	0.041	30.021	30.000	0.034
	MIN	30.000	29.760	0.110	30.000	29.883	0.065	30.000	29.959	0.020	30.000	29.980	0.007	30.000	29.987	0.000

Source: American National Standard Preferred Metric Limits and Fits, ANSI B4.2 — 1978.

Dimensions in mm.

BASIC SIZE		LOOSE RUNNING Hole H11	Shaft c11	Fit	FREE RUNNING Hole H9	Shaft d9	Fit	CLOSE RUNNING Hole H8	Shaft f7	Fit	SLIDING Hole H7	Shaft g6	Fit	LOCATIONAL CLEARANCE Hole H7	Shaft h6	Fit
40	MAX	40.160	39.880	0.440	40.062	39.920	0.204	40.039	39.975	0.089	40.025	39.991	0.050	40.025	40.000	0.041
	MIN	40.000	39.720	0.120	40.000	39.858	0.080	40.000	39.950	0.025	40.000	39.975	0.009	40.000	39.984	0.000
50	MAX	50.160	49.870	0.450	50.062	49.920	0.204	50.039	49.975	0.089	50.025	49.991	0.050	50.025	50.000	0.041
	MIN	50.000	49.710	0.130	50.000	49.858	0.080	50.000	49.950	0.025	50.000	49.975	0.009	50.000	49.984	0.000
60	MAX	60.190	59.860	0.520	60.074	59.900	0.248	60.046	59.970	0.106	60.030	59.990	0.059	60.030	60.000	0.049
	MIN	60.000	59.670	0.140	60.000	59.826	0.100	60.000	59.940	0.030	60.000	59.971	0.010	60.000	59.981	0.000
80	MAX	80.190	79.850	0.530	80.074	79.900	0.248	80.046	79.970	0.106	80.030	79.990	0.059	80.030	80.000	0.049
	MIN	80.000	79.660	0.150	80.000	79.826	0.100	80.000	79.940	0.030	80.000	79.971	0.010	80.000	79.981	0.000
100	MAX	100.220	99.830	0.610	100.087	99.880	0.294	100.054	99.964	0.125	100.035	99.988	0.069	100.035	100.000	0.057
	MIN	100.000	99.610	0.170	100.000	99.793	0.120	100.000	99.929	0.036	100.000	99.966	0.012	100.000	99.978	0.000
120	MAX	120.220	119.820	0.620	120.087	119.880	0.294	120.054	119.964	0.125	120.035	119.988	0.069	120.035	120.000	0.057
	MIN	120.000	119.600	0.180	120.000	119.793	0.120	120.000	119.929	0.036	120.000	119.966	0.012	120.000	119.978	0.000
160	MAX	160.250	159.790	0.710	160.100	159.855	0.345	160.063	159.957	0.146	160.040	159.986	0.079	160.040	160.000	0.065
	MIN	160.000	159.540	0.210	160.000	159.755	0.145	160.000	159.917	0.043	160.000	159.961	0.014	160.000	159.975	0.000
200	MAX	200.290	199.760	0.820	200.115	199.830	0.400	200.072	199.950	0.168	200.046	199.985	0.090	200.046	200.000	0.075
	MIN	200.000	199.470	0.240	200.000	199.715	0.170	200.000	199.904	0.050	200.000	199.956	0.015	200.000	199.971	0.000
250	MAX	250.290	249.720	0.860	250.115	249.830	0.400	250.072	249.950	0.168	250.046	249.985	0.090	250.046	250.000	0.075
	MIN	250.000	249.430	0.280	250.000	249.715	0.170	250.000	249.904	0.050	250.000	249.956	0.015	250.000	249.971	0.000
300	MAX	300.320	299.670	0.970	300.130	299.810	0.450	300.081	299.944	0.189	300.052	299.983	0.101	300.052	300.000	0.084
	MIN	300.000	299.350	0.330	300.000	299.680	0.190	300.000	299.892	0.056	300.000	299.951	0.017	300.000	299.968	0.000
400	MAX	400.360	399.600	1.120	400.140	399.790	0.490	400.089	399.938	0.208	400.057	399.982	0.111	400.057	400.000	0.093
	MIN	400.000	399.240	0.400	400.000	399.650	0.210	400.000	399.881	0.062	400.000	399.946	0.018	400.000	399.964	0.000
500	MAX	500.400	499.520	1.280	500.155	499.770	0.540	500.097	499.932	0.228	500.063	499.980	0.123	500.063	500.000	0.103
	MIN	500.000	499.120	0.480	500.000	499.615	0.230	500.000	499.869	0.068	500.000	499.940	0.020	500.000	499.960	0.000

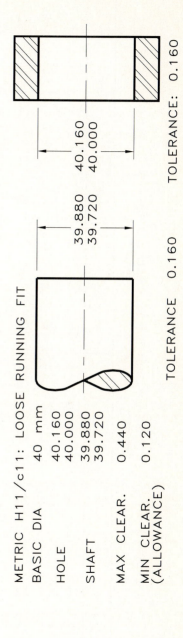

METRIC H11/c11: LOOSE RUNNING FIT

BASIC DIA   40 mm

HOLE   40.160
                   40.000

SHAFT   39.880
                   39.720

MAX CLEAR.   0.440

MIN CLEAR.   0.120
(ALLOWANCE)

40.160
40.000

39.880
39.720

TOLERANCE 0.160   TOLERANCE: 0.160

APPENDIX 39 • Preferred Hole Basis Transition and Interference Fits—Cylindrical Fits (ANSI B4.2)

Dimensions in mm.

BASIC SIZE		LOCATIONAL TRANSN. Hole H7	Shaft k6	Fit	LOCATIONAL TRANSN. Hole H7	Shaft n6	Fit	LOCATIONAL INTERF. Hole H7	Shaft p6	Fit	MEDIUM DRIVE Hole H7	Shaft s6	Fit	FORCE Hole H7	Shaft u6	Fit
1	MAX	1.010	1.006	0.010	1.010	1.010	0.006	1.010	1.012	0.004	1.010	1.020	-0.004	1.010	1.024	-0.008
	MIN	1.000	1.000	-0.006	1.000	1.004	-0.010	1.000	1.006	-0.012	1.000	1.014	-0.020	1.000	1.018	-0.024
1.2	MAX	1.210	1.206	0.010	1.210	1.210	0.006	1.210	1.212	0.004	1.210	1.220	-0.004	1.210	1.224	-0.008
	MIN	1.200	1.200	-0.006	1.200	1.204	-0.010	1.200	1.206	-0.012	1.200	1.214	-0.020	1.200	1.218	-0.024
1.6	MAX	1.610	1.606	0.010	1.610	1.610	0.006	1.610	1.612	0.004	1.610	1.620	-0.004	1.610	1.624	-0.008
	MIN	1.600	1.600	-0.006	1.600	1.604	-0.010	1.600	1.606	-0.012	1.600	1.614	-0.020	1.600	1.618	-0.024
2	MAX	2.010	2.006	0.010	2.010	2.010	0.006	2.010	2.010	0.004	2.010	2.020	-0.004	2.010	2.024	-0.008
	MIN	2.000	2.000	-0.006	2.000	2.004	-0.010	2.000	2.006	-0.012	2.000	2.014	-0.020	2.000	2.018	-0.024
2.5	MAX	2.510	2.506	0.010	2.510	2.510	0.006	2.510	2.512	0.004	2.510	2.520	-0.004	2.510	2.524	-0.008
	MIN	2.500	2.500	-0.006	2.500	2.504	-0.010	2.500	2.506	-0.012	2.500	2.514	-0.020	2.500	2.518	-0.024
3	MAX	3.010	3.006	0.010	3.010	3.010	0.006	3.010	3.012	0.004	3.010	3.020	-0.004	3.010	3.024	-0.008
	MIN	3.000	3.000	-0.006	3.000	3.004	-0.010	3.000	3.006	-0.012	3.000	3.014	-0.020	3.000	3.018	-0.024
4	MAX	4.012	4.009	0.011	4.012	4.016	0.004	4.012	4.020	0.000	4.012	4.027	-0.007	4.012	4.031	-0.011
	MIN	4.000	4.001	-0.009	4.000	4.008	-0.016	4.000	4.012	-0.020	4.000	4.019	-0.027	4.000	4.023	-0.031
5	MAX	5.012	5.009	0.011	5.012	5.016	0.004	5.012	5.020	0.000	5.012	5.027	-0.007	5.012	5.031	-0.011
	MIN	5.000	5.001	-0.009	5.000	5.008	-0.016	5.000	5.012	-0.020	5.000	5.019	-0.027	5.000	5.023	-0.031
6	MAX	6.012	6.009	0.011	6.012	6.016	0.004	6.012	6.020	0.000	6.012	6.027	-0.007	6.012	6.031	-0.011
	MIN	6.000	6.001	-0.009	6.000	6.008	-0.016	6.000	6.012	-0.020	6.000	6.019	-0.027	6.000	6.023	-0.031
8	MAX	8.015	8.010	0.014	8.015	8.019	0.005	8.015	8.024	0.000	8.015	8.032	-0.008	8.015	8.037	-0.013
	MIN	8.000	8.001	-0.010	8.000	8.010	-0.019	8.000	8.015	-0.024	8.000	8.023	-0.032	8.000	8.028	-0.037
10	MAX	10.015	10.010	0.014	10.015	10.019	0.005	10.015	10.024	0.000	10.015	10.032	-0.008	10.015	10.037	-0.013
	MIN	10.000	10.001	-0.010	10.000	10.010	-0.019	10.000	10.015	-0.024	10.000	10.023	-0.032	10.000	10.028	-0.037
12	MAX	12.018	12.012	0.017	12.018	12.023	0.006	12.018	12.029	0.000	12.018	12.039	-0.010	12.018	12.044	-0.015
	MIN	12.000	12.001	-0.012	12.000	12.012	-0.023	12.000	12.018	-0.029	12.000	12.028	-0.039	12.000	12.033	-0.044
16	MAX	16.018	16.012	0.017	16.018	16.023	0.006	16.018	16.029	0.000	16.018	16.039	-0.010	16.018	16.044	-0.015
	MIN	16.000	16.001	-0.012	16.000	16.012	-0.023	16.000	16.018	-0.029	16.000	16.028	-0.039	16.000	16.033	-0.044
20	MAX	20.021	20.015	0.019	20.021	20.028	0.006	20.021	20.035	-0.001	20.021	20.048	-0.014	20.021	20.054	-0.020
	MIN	20.000	20.002	-0.015	20.000	20.015	-0.028	20.000	20.022	-0.035	20.000	20.035	-0.048	20.000	20.041	-0.054
25	MAX	25.021	25.015	0.019	25.021	25.028	0.006	25.021	25.035	-0.001	25.021	25.048	-0.014	25.021	25.061	-0.027
	MIN	25.000	25.002	-0.015	25.000	25.015	-0.028	25.000	25.022	-0.035	25.000	25.035	-0.048	25.000	25.048	-0.061
30	MAX	30.021	30.015	0.019	30.021	30.028	0.006	30.021	30.035	-0.001	30.021	30.048	-0.014	30.021	30.061	-0.027
	MIN	30.000	30.002	-0.015	30.000	30.015	-0.028	30.000	30.022	-0.035	30.000	30.035	-0.048	30.000	30.048	-0.061

Source: American National Standard Preferred Metric Limit and Fits, ANSI B4.2 —1978.

APPENDIX 39 • (continued)

Dimensions in mm.

BASIC SIZE		LOCATIONAL TRANSN. Hole H7	Shaft k6	Fit	LOCATIONAL TRANSN. Hole H7	Shaft n6	Fit	LOCATIONAL INTERF. Hole H7	Shaft p6	Fit	MEDIUM DRIVE Hole H7	Shaft s6	Fit	FORCE Hole H7	Shaft u6	Fit
40	MAX	40.025	40.018	0.023	40.025	40.033	0.008	40.025	40.042	-0.001	40.025	40.059	-0.018	40.025	40.076	-0.035
	MIN	40.000	40.002	-0.018	40.000	40.017	-0.033	40.000	40.026	-0.042	40.000	40.043	-0.059	40.000	40.060	-0.076
50	MAX	50.025	50.018	0.023	50.025	50.033	0.008	50.025	50.042	-0.001	50.025	50.059	-0.018	50.025	50.086	-0.045
	MIN	50.000	50.002	-0.018	50.000	50.017	-0.033	50.000	50.026	-0.042	50.000	50.043	-0.059	50.000	50.070	-0.086
60	MAX	60.030	60.021	0.028	60.030	60.039	0.010	60.030	60.051	-0.002	60.030	60.072	-0.023	60.030	60.106	-0.057
	MIN	60.000	60.002	-0.021	60.000	60.020	-0.039	60.000	60.032	-0.051	60.000	60.053	-0.072	60.000	60.087	-0.106
80	MAX	80.030	80.021	0.028	80.030	80.039	0.010	80.030	80.051	-0.002	80.030	80.078	-0.029	80.030	80.121	-0.072
	MIN	80.000	80.002	-0.021	80.000	80.020	-0.039	80.000	80.032	-0.051	80.000	80.059	-0.078	80.000	80.102	-0.121
100	MAX	100.035	100.025	0.032	100.035	100.045	0.012	100.035	100.059	-0.002	100.035	100.093	-0.036	100.035	100.146	-0.089
	MIN	100.000	100.003	-0.025	100.000	100.023	-0.045	100.000	100.037	-0.059	100.000	100.071	-0.093	100.000	100.124	-0.146
120	MAX	120.035	120.025	0.032	120.035	120.045	0.012	120.035	120.059	-0.002	120.035	120.101	-0.044	120.035	120.166	-0.109
	MIN	120.000	120.003	-0.025	120.000	120.023	-0.045	120.000	120.037	-0.059	120.000	120.079	-0.101	120.000	120.144	-0.166
160	MAX	160.040	160.028	0.037	160.040	160.052	0.013	160.040	160.068	-0.003	160.040	160.125	-0.060	160.040	160.215	-0.150
	MIN	160.000	160.003	-0.028	160.000	160.027	-0.052	160.000	160.043	-0.068	160.000	160.100	-0.125	160.000	160.190	-0.215
200	MAX	200.046	200.033	0.042	200.046	200.060	0.015	200.046	200.079	-0.004	200.046	200.151	-0.076	200.046	200.265	-0.190
	MIN	200.000	200.004	-0.033	200.000	200.031	-0.060	200.000	200.050	-0.079	200.000	200.122	-0.151	200.000	200.236	-0.265
250	MAX	250.046	250.033	0.042	250.046	250.060	0.015	250.046	250.079	-0.004	250.046	250.169	-0.094	250.046	250.313	-0.238
	MIN	250.000	250.004	-0.033	250.000	250.031	-0.060	250.000	250.050	-0.079	250.000	250.140	-0.169	250.000	250.284	-0.313
300	MAX	300.052	300.036	0.048	300.052	300.066	0.018	300.052	300.088	-0.004	300.052	300.202	-0.118	300.052	300.382	-0.298
	MIN	300.000	300.004	-0.036	300.000	300.034	-0.066	300.000	300.056	-0.088	300.000	300.170	-0.202	300.000	300.350	-0.382
400	MAX	400.057	400.040	0.053	400.057	400.073	0.020	400.057	400.098	-0.005	400.057	400.244	-0.151	400.057	400.471	-0.378
	MIN	400.000	400.004	-0.040	400.000	400.037	-0.073	400.000	400.062	-0.098	400.000	400.208	-0.244	400.000	400.435	-0.471
500	MAX	500.063	500.045	0.058	500.063	500.080	0.023	500.063	500.108	-0.005	500.063	500.292	-0.189	500.063	500.580	-0.477
	MIN	500.000	500.005	-0.045	500.000	500.040	-0.080	500.000	500.068	-0.108	500.000	500.252	-0.292	500.000	500.540	-0.580

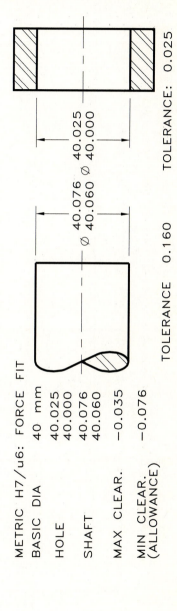

METRIC H7/u6: FORCE FIT

BASIC DIA	40 mm
HOLE	40.025 / 40.000
SHAFT	40.076 / 40.060
MAX CLEAR.	-0.035
MIN CLEAR. (ALLOWANCE)	-0.076

Ø 40.076 / Ø 40.060   Ø 40.025 / Ø 40.000

TOLERANCE 0.160   TOLERANCE 0.025   TOLERANCE: 0.025

APPENDIX 40 • Preferred Shaft Basis Clearance Fits—Cylindrical Fits (ANSI B4.2)

Dimensions in mm.

BASIC SIZE		LOOSE RUNNING			FREE RUNNING			CLOSE RUNNING			SLIDING			LOCATIONAL CLEARANCE		
		Hole C11	Shaft h11	Fit	Hole D9	Shaft h9	Fit	Hole F8	Shaft h7	Fit	Hole G7	Shaft h6	Fit	Hole H7	Shaft h6	Fit
1	MAX	1.120	1.000	0.180	1.045	1.000	0.070	1.020	1.000	0.030	1.012	1.000	0.018	1.010	1.000	0.016
	MIN	1.060	0.940	0.060	1.020	0.975	0.020	1.006	0.990	0.006	1.002	0.994	0.002	1.000	0.994	0.000
1.2	MAX	1.320	1.200	0.180	1.245	1.200	0.070	1.220	1.200	0.030	1.212	1.200	0.018	1.210	1.200	0.016
	MIN	1.260	1.140	0.060	1.220	1.175	0.020	1.206	1.190	0.006	1.202	1.194	0.002	1.200	1.194	0.000
1.6	MAX	1.720	1.600	0.180	1.645	1.600	0.070	1.620	1.600	0.030	1.612	1.600	0.018	1.610	1.600	0.016
	MIN	1.660	1.540	0.060	1.620	1.575	0.020	1.606	1.590	0.006	1.602	1.594	0.002	1.600	1.594	0.000
2	MAX	2.120	2.000	0.180	2.045	2.000	0.070	2.020	2.000	0.030	2.012	2.000	0.018	2.010	2.000	0.016
	MIN	2.060	1.940	0.060	2.020	1.975	0.020	2.006	1.990	0.006	2.002	1.994	0.002	2.000	1.994	0.000
2.5	MAX	2.620	2.500	0.180	2.545	2.500	0.070	2.520	2.500	0.030	2.512	2.500	0.018	2.510	2.500	0.016
	MIN	2.560	2.440	0.060	2.520	2.475	0.020	2.506	2.490	0.006	2.502	2.494	0.002	2.500	2.494	0.000
3	MAX	3.120	3.000	0.180	3.045	3.000	0.070	3.020	3.000	0.030	3.012	3.000	0.018	3.010	3.000	0.016
	MIN	3.060	2.940	0.060	3.020	2.975	0.020	3.006	2.990	0.006	3.002	2.994	0.002	3.000	2.994	0.000
4	MAX	4.145	4.000	0.220	4.060	4.000	0.090	4.028	4.000	0.040	4.016	4.000	0.024	4.012	4.000	0.020
	MIN	4.070	3.925	0.070	4.030	3.970	0.030	4.010	3.988	0.010	4.004	3.992	0.004	4.000	3.992	0.000
5	MAX	5.145	5.000	0.220	5.060	5.000	0.090	5.028	5.000	0.040	5.016	5.000	0.024	5.012	5.000	0.020
	MIN	5.070	4.925	0.070	5.030	4.970	0.030	5.010	4.988	0.010	5.004	4.992	0.004	5.000	4.992	0.000
6	MAX	6.145	6.000	0.220	6.060	6.000	0.090	6.028	6.000	0.040	6.016	6.000	0.024	6.012	6.000	0.020
	MIN	6.070	5.925	0.070	6.030	5.970	0.030	6.010	5.988	0.010	6.004	5.992	0.004	6.000	5.992	0.000
8	MAX	8.170	8.000	0.260	8.076	8.000	0.112	8.035	8.000	0.050	8.020	8.000	0.029	8.015	8.000	0.024
	MIN	8.080	7.910	0.080	8.040	7.964	0.040	8.013	7.985	0.013	8.005	7.991	0.005	8.000	7.991	0.000
10	MAX	10.170	10.000	0.260	10.076	10.000	0.112	10.035	10.000	0.050	10.020	10.000	0.029	10.015	10.000	0.024
	MIN	10.080	9.910	0.080	10.040	9.964	0.040	10.013	9.985	0.013	10.005	9.991	0.005	10.000	9.991	0.000
12	MAX	12.205	12.000	0.315	12.093	12.000	0.136	12.043	12.000	0.061	12.024	12.000	0.035	12.018	12.000	0.029
	MIN	12.095	11.890	0.095	12.050	11.957	0.050	12.016	11.982	0.016	12.006	11.989	0.006	12.000	11.989	0.000
16	MAX	16.205	16.000	0.315	16.093	16.000	0.136	16.043	16.000	0.061	16.024	16.000	0.035	16.018	16.000	0.029
	MIN	16.095	15.890	0.095	16.050	15.957	0.050	16.016	15.982	0.016	16.006	15.989	0.006	16.000	15.989	0.000
20	MAX	20.240	20.000	0.370	20.117	20.000	0.169	20.053	20.000	0.074	20.028	20.000	0.041	20.021	20.000	0.034
	MIN	20.110	19.870	0.110	20.065	19.948	0.065	20.020	19.979	0.020	20.007	19.987	0.007	20.000	19.987	0.000
25	MAX	25.240	25.000	0.370	25.117	25.000	0.169	25.053	25.000	0.074	25.028	25.000	0.041	25.021	25.000	0.034
	MIN	25.110	24.870	0.110	25.065	24.948	0.065	25.020	24.979	0.020	25.007	24.987	0.007	25.000	24.987	0.000
30	MAX	30.240	30.000	0.370	30.117	30.000	0.169	30.053	30.000	0.074	30.028	30.000	0.041	30.021	30.000	0.034
	MIN	30.110	29.870	0.110	30.065	29.948	0.065	30.020	29.979	0.020	30.007	29.987	0.007	30.000	29.987	0.000

Source: American National Standard Preferred Metric Limits and Fits, ANSI B4.2 — 1978.

APPENDIX 40 • (continued)

Dimensions in mm.

BASIC SIZE		LOOSE RUNNING Hole C11	Shaft h11	Fit	FREE RUNNING Hole D9	Shaft h9	Fit	CLOSE RUNNING Hole F8	Shaft h7	Fit	SLIDING Hole G7	Shaft h6	Fit	LOCATIONAL CLEARANCE Hole H7	Shaft h6	Fit
40	MAX	40.280	40.000	0.440	40.142	40.000	0.204	40.064	40.000	0.089	40.034	40.000	0.050	40.025	40.000	0.041
	MIN	40.120	39.840	0.120	40.080	39.938	0.080	40.025	39.975	0.025	40.009	39.984	0.009	40.000	39.984	0.000
50	MAX	50.290	50.000	0.450	50.142	50.000	0.204	50.064	50.000	0.089	50.034	50.000	0.050	50.025	50.000	0.041
	MIN	50.130	49.840	0.130	50.080	49.938	0.080	50.025	49.975	0.025	50.009	49.984	0.009	50.000	49.984	0.000
60	MAX	60.330	60.000	0.520	60.174	60.000	0.248	60.076	60.000	0.106	60.040	60.000	0.059	60.030	60.000	0.049
	MIN	60.140	59.810	0.140	60.100	59.926	0.100	60.030	59.970	0.030	60.010	59.981	0.010	60.000	59.981	0.000
80	MAX	80.340	80.000	0.530	80.174	80.000	0.248	80.076	80.000	0.106	80.040	80.000	0.059	80.030	80.000	0.049
	MIN	80.150	79.810	0.150	80.100	79.926	0.100	80.030	79.970	0.030	80.010	79.981	0.010	80.000	79.981	0.000
100	MAX	100.390	100.000	0.610	100.207	100.000	0.294	100.090	100.000	0.125	100.047	100.000	0.069	100.035	100.000	0.057
	MIN	100.170	99.780	0.170	100.120	99.913	0.120	100.036	99.965	0.036	100.012	99.978	0.012	100.000	99.978	0.000
120	MAX	120.400	120.000	0.620	120.207	120.000	0.294	120.090	120.000	0.125	120.047	120.000	0.069	120.035	120.000	0.057
	MIN	120.180	119.780	0.180	120.120	119.913	0.120	120.036	119.965	0.036	120.012	119.978	0.012	120.000	119.978	0.000
160	MAX	160.460	160.000	0.710	160.245	160.000	0.345	160.106	160.000	0.146	160.054	160.000	0.079	160.040	160.000	0.065
	MIN	160.210	159.750	0.210	160.145	159.900	0.145	160.043	159.960	0.043	160.014	159.975	0.014	160.000	159.975	0.000
200	MAX	200.530	200.000	0.820	200.285	200.000	0.400	200.122	200.000	0.168	200.061	200.000	0.090	200.046	200.000	0.075
	MIN	200.240	199.710	0.240	200.170	199.885	0.170	200.050	199.954	0.050	200.015	199.971	0.015	200.000	199.971	0.000
250	MAX	250.570	250.000	0.860	250.285	250.000	0.400	250.122	250.000	0.168	250.061	250.000	0.090	250.046	250.000	0.075
	MIN	250.280	249.710	0.280	250.170	249.885	0.170	250.050	249.954	0.050	250.015	249.971	0.015	250.000	249.971	0.000
300	MAX	300.650	300.000	0.970	300.320	300.000	0.450	300.137	300.000	0.189	300.069	300.000	0.101	300.052	300.000	0.084
	MIN	300.330	299.680	0.330	300.190	299.870	0.190	300.056	299.948	0.056	300.017	299.968	0.017	300.000	299.968	0.000
400	MAX	400.760	400.000	1.120	400.350	400.000	0.490	400.151	400.000	0.208	400.075	400.000	0.111	400.057	400.000	0.093
	MIN	400.400	399.640	0.400	400.210	399.860	0.210	400.062	399.943	0.062	400.018	399.964	0.018	400.000	399.964	0.000
500	MAX	500.880	500.000	1.280	500.385	500.000	0.540	500.165	500.000	0.228	500.083	500.000	0.123	500.063	500.000	0.103
	MIN	500.480	499.600	0.480	500.230	499.845	0.230	500.068	499.937	0.068	500.020	499.960	0.020	500.000	499.960	0.000

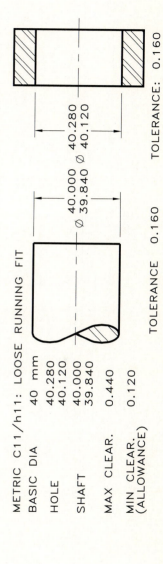

METRIC C11/h11: LOOSE RUNNING FIT

BASIC DIA	40 mm
HOLE	40.280 / 40.120
SHAFT	40.000 / 39.840
MAX CLEAR.	0.440
MIN CLEAR. (ALLOWANCE)	0.120

TOLERANCE 0.160 TOLERANCE: 0.160

APPENDIX 41 • Preferred Shaft Basis Transition and Interference Fits—Cylindrical Fits (ANSI B4.2)

Dimensions in mm.

BASIC SIZE		LOCATIONAL TRANSN. Hole K7	Shaft h6	Fit	LOCATIONAL TRANSN. Hole N7	Shaft h6	Fit	LOCATIONAL INTERF. Hole P7	Shaft h6	Fit	MEDIUM DRIVE Hole S7	Shaft h6	Fit	FORCE Hole U7	Shaft h6	Fit
1	MAX	1.000	1.000	0.006	0.996	1.000	0.002	0.994	1.000	0.000	0.986	1.000	-0.008	0.982	1.000	-0.012
	MIN	0.990	0.994	-0.010	0.986	0.994	-0.014	0.984	0.994	-0.016	0.976	0.994	-0.024	0.972	0.994	-0.028
1.2	MAX	1.200	1.200	0.006	1.196	1.200	0.002	1.194	1.200	0.000	1.186	1.200	-0.008	1.182	1.200	-0.012
	MIN	1.190	1.194	-0.010	1.186	1.194	-0.014	1.184	1.194	-0.016	1.176	1.194	-0.024	1.172	1.194	-0.028
1.6	MAX	1.600	1.600	0.006	1.596	1.600	0.002	1.594	1.600	0.000	1.586	1.600	-0.008	1.582	1.600	-0.012
	MIN	1.590	1.594	-0.010	1.586	1.594	-0.014	1.584	1.594	-0.016	1.576	1.594	-0.024	1.572	1.594	-0.028
2	MAX	2.000	2.000	0.006	1.996	2.000	0.002	1.994	2.000	0.000	1.986	2.000	-0.008	1.982	2.000	-0.012
	MIN	1.990	1.994	-0.010	1.986	1.994	-0.014	1.984	1.994	-0.016	1.976	1.994	-0.024	1.972	1.994	-0.028
2.5	MAX	2.500	2.500	0.006	2.496	2.500	0.002	2.494	2.500	0.000	2.486	2.500	-0.008	2.482	2.500	-0.012
	MIN	2.490	2.494	-0.010	2.486	2.494	-0.014	2.484	2.494	-0.016	2.476	2.494	-0.024	2.472	2.494	-0.028
3	MAX	3.000	3.000	0.006	2.996	3.000	0.002	2.994	3.000	0.000	2.986	3.000	-0.008	2.982	3.000	-0.012
	MIN	2.990	2.994	-0.010	2.986	2.994	-0.014	2.984	2.994	-0.016	2.976	2.994	-0.024	2.972	2.994	-0.028
4	MAX	4.003	4.000	0.011	3.996	4.000	0.004	3.992	4.000	0.000	3.985	4.000	-0.007	3.981	4.000	-0.011
	MIN	3.991	3.992	-0.009	3.984	3.992	-0.016	3.980	3.992	-0.020	3.973	3.992	-0.027	3.969	3.992	-0.031
5	MAX	5.003	5.000	0.011	4.996	5.000	0.004	4.992	5.000	0.000	4.985	5.000	-0.007	4.981	5.000	-0.011
	MIN	4.991	4.992	-0.009	4.984	4.992	-0.016	4.980	4.992	-0.020	4.973	4.992	-0.027	4.969	4.992	-0.031
6	MAX	6.003	6.000	0.011	5.996	6.000	0.004	5.992	6.000	0.000	5.985	6.000	-0.007	5.981	6.000	-0.011
	MIN	5.991	5.992	-0.009	5.984	5.992	-0.016	5.980	5.992	-0.020	5.973	5.992	-0.027	5.969	5.992	-0.031
8	MAX	8.005	8.000	0.014	7.996	8.000	0.005	7.991	8.000	0.000	7.983	8.000	-0.008	7.978	8.000	-0.013
	MIN	7.990	7.991	-0.010	7.981	7.991	-0.019	7.976	7.991	-0.024	7.968	7.991	-0.032	7.963	7.991	-0.037
10	MAX	10.005	10.000	0.014	9.996	10.000	0.005	9.991	10.000	0.000	9.983	10.000	-0.008	9.978	10.000	-0.013
	MIN	9.990	9.991	-0.010	9.981	9.991	-0.019	9.976	9.991	-0.024	9.968	9.991	-0.032	9.963	9.991	-0.037
12	MAX	12.006	12.000	0.017	11.995	12.000	0.006	11.989	12.000	0.000	11.979	12.000	-0.010	11.974	12.000	-0.015
	MIN	11.988	11.989	-0.012	11.977	11.989	-0.023	11.971	11.989	-0.029	11.961	11.989	-0.039	11.956	11.989	-0.044
16	MAX	16.006	16.000	0.017	15.995	16.000	0.006	15.989	16.000	0.000	15.979	16.000	-0.010	15.974	16.000	-0.015
	MIN	15.988	15.989	-0.012	15.977	15.989	-0.023	15.971	15.989	-0.029	15.961	15.989	-0.039	15.956	15.989	-0.044
20	MAX	20.006	20.000	0.019	19.993	20.000	0.006	19.986	20.000	-0.001	19.973	20.000	-0.014	19.967	20.000	-0.020
	MIN	19.985	19.987	-0.015	19.972	19.987	-0.028	19.965	19.987	-0.035	19.952	19.987	-0.048	19.946	19.987	-0.054
25	MAX	25.006	25.000	0.019	24.993	25.000	0.006	24.986	25.000	-0.001	24.973	25.000	-0.014	24.960	25.000	-0.027
	MIN	24.985	24.987	-0.015	24.972	24.987	-0.028	24.965	24.987	-0.035	24.952	24.987	-0.048	24.939	24.987	-0.061
30	MAX	30.006	30.000	0.019	29.993	30.000	0.006	29.986	30.000	-0.001	29.973	30.000	-0.014	29.960	30.000	-0.027
	MIN	29.985	29.987	-0.015	29.972	29.987	-0.028	29.965	29.987	-0.035	29.952	29.987	-0.048	29.939	29.987	-0.061

Source: American National Standard Preferred Metric Limits and Fits, ANSI B4.2 — 1978.

Dimensions in mm.

BASIC SIZE		LOCATIONAL TRANSN. Hole K7	Shaft h6	Fit	LOCATIONAL TRANSN. Hole N7	Shaft h6	Fit	LOCATIONAL INTERF. Hole P7	Shaft h6	Fit	MEDIUM DRIVE Hole S7	Shaft h6	Fit	FORCE Hole U7	Shaft h6	Fit
40	MAX	40.007	40.000	0.023	39.992	40.000	0.008	39.983	40.000	-0.001	39.966	40.000	-0.018	39.949	40.000	-0.035
	MIN	39.982	39.984	-0.018	39.967	39.984	-0.033	39.958	39.984	-0.042	39.941	39.984	-0.059	39.924	39.984	-0.076
50	MAX	50.007	50.000	0.023	49.992	50.000	0.008	49.983	50.000	-0.001	49.966	50.000	-0.018	49.939	50.000	-0.045
	MIN	49.982	49.984	-0.018	49.967	49.984	-0.033	49.958	49.984	-0.042	49.941	49.984	-0.059	49.914	49.984	-0.086
60	MAX	60.009	60.000	0.028	59.991	60.000	0.010	59.979	60.000	-0.002	59.958	60.000	-0.023	59.924	60.000	-0.057
	MIN	59.979	59.981	-0.021	59.961	59.981	-0.039	59.949	59.981	-0.051	59.928	59.981	-0.072	59.894	59.981	-0.106
80	MAX	80.009	80.000	0.028	79.991	80.000	0.010	79.979	80.000	-0.002	79.952	80.000	-0.029	79.909	80.000	-0.072
	MIN	79.979	79.981	-0.021	79.961	79.981	-0.039	79.949	79.981	-0.051	79.922	79.981	-0.078	79.879	79.981	-0.121
100	MAX	100.010	100.000	0.032	99.990	100.000	0.012	99.976	100.000	-0.002	99.942	100.000	-0.036	99.889	100.000	-0.089
	MIN	99.975	99.978	-0.025	99.955	99.978	-0.045	99.941	99.978	-0.059	99.907	99.978	-0.093	99.854	99.978	-0.146
120	MAX	120.010	120.000	0.032	119.990	120.000	0.012	119.976	120.000	-0.002	119.934	120.000	-0.044	119.869	120.000	-0.109
	MIN	119.975	119.978	-0.025	119.955	119.978	-0.045	119.941	119.978	-0.059	119.899	119.978	-0.101	119.834	119.978	-0.166
160	MAX	160.012	160.000	0.037	159.988	160.000	0.013	159.972	160.000	-0.003	159.915	160.000	-0.060	159.825	160.000	-0.150
	MIN	159.972	159.975	-0.028	159.948	159.975	-0.052	159.932	159.975	-0.068	159.875	159.975	-0.125	159.785	159.975	-0.215
200	MAX	200.013	200.000	0.042	199.986	200.000	0.015	199.967	200.000	-0.004	199.895	200.000	-0.076	199.781	200.000	-0.190
	MIN	199.967	199.971	-0.033	199.940	199.971	-0.060	199.921	199.971	-0.079	199.849	199.971	-0.151	199.735	199.971	-0.265
250	MAX	250.013	250.000	0.042	249.986	250.000	0.015	249.967	250.000	-0.004	249.877	250.000	-0.094	249.733	250.000	-0.238
	MIN	249.967	249.971	-0.033	249.940	249.971	-0.060	249.921	249.971	-0.079	249.831	249.971	-0.169	249.687	249.971	-0.313
300	MAX	300.016	300.000	0.048	299.986	300.000	0.018	299.964	300.000	-0.004	299.850	300.000	-0.118	299.670	300.000	-0.298
	MIN	299.964	299.968	-0.036	299.934	299.968	-0.066	299.912	299.968	-0.088	299.798	299.968	-0.202	299.618	299.968	-0.382
400	MAX	400.017	400.000	0.053	399.984	400.000	0.020	399.959	400.000	-0.005	399.813	400.000	-0.151	399.586	400.000	-0.378
	MIN	399.960	399.964	-0.040	399.927	399.964	-0.073	399.902	399.964	-0.098	399.756	399.964	-0.244	399.529	399.964	-0.471
500	MAX	500.018	500.000	0.058	499.983	500.000	0.023	499.955	500.000	-0.005	499.771	500.000	-0.189	499.483	500.000	-0.477
	MIN	499.955	499.960	-0.045	499.920	499.960	-0.080	499.892	499.960	-0.108	499.708	499.960	-0.292	499.420	499.960	-0.580

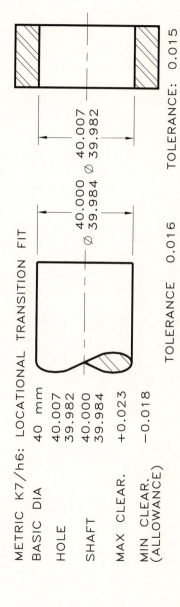

METRIC K7/h6: LOCATIONAL TRANSITION FIT

BASIC DIA   40 mm

HOLE   40.007
                   39.982

SHAFT   40.000
                   39.984

MAX CLEAR.   +0.023

MIN CLEAR.   -0.018
(ALLOWANCE)

Ø 40.000 Ø 39.984   Ø 40.007 Ø 39.982

TOLERANCE   0.016   TOLERANCE: 0.015

APPENDIX 42 • Hole Sizes for Nonpreferred Diameters (millimeters)

Basic Size	C11	D9	F8	G7	H7	H8	H9	H11	K7	N7	P7	S7	U7
OVER 0 TO 3	+0.120	+0.045	+0.020	+0.012	+0.010	+0.014	+0.025	+0.060	0.000	−0.004	−0.006	−0.014	−0.018
	+0.060	+0.020	+0.006	+0.002	0.000	0.000	0.000	0.000	−0.010	−0.014	−0.016	−0.024	−0.028
OVER 3 TO 6	+0.145	+0.060	+0.028	+0.016	+0.012	+0.018	+0.030	+0.075	+0.003	−0.004	−0.008	−0.015	−0.019
	+0.070	+0.030	+0.010	+0.004	0.000	0.000	0.000	0.000	−0.009	−0.016	−0.020	−0.027	−0.031
OVER 6 TO 10	+0.170	+0.076	+0.035	+0.020	+0.015	+0.022	+0.036	+0.090	+0.005	−0.004	−0.009	−0.017	−0.022
	+0.080	+0.040	+0.013	+0.005	0.000	0.000	0.000	0.000	−0.010	−0.019	−0.024	−0.032	−0.037
OVER 10 TO 14	+0.205	+0.093	+0.043	+0.024	+0.018	+0.027	+0.043	+0.110	+0.006	−0.005	−0.011	−0.021	−0.026
	+0.095	+0.050	+0.016	+0.006	0.000	0.000	0.000	0.000	−0.012	−0.023	−0.029	−0.039	−0.044
OVER 14 TO 18	+0.205	+0.093	+0.043	+0.024	+0.018	+0.027	+0.043	+0.110	+0.006	−0.005	−0.011	−0.021	−0.026
	+0.095	+0.050	+0.016	+0.006	0.000	0.000	0.000	0.000	−0.012	−0.023	−0.029	−0.039	−0.044
OVER 18 TO 24	+0.240	+0.117	+0.053	+0.028	+0.021	+0.033	+0.052	+0.130	+0.006	−0.007	−0.014	−0.027	−0.033
	+0.110	+0.065	+0.020	+0.007	0.000	0.000	0.000	0.000	−0.015	−0.028	−0.035	−0.048	−0.054
OVER 24 TO 30	+0.240	+0.117	+0.053	+0.028	+0.021	+0.033	+0.052	+0.130	+0.006	−0.007	−0.014	−0.027	−0.040
	+0.110	+0.065	+0.020	+0.007	0.000	0.000	0.000	0.000	−0.015	−0.028	−0.035	−0.048	−0.061
OVER 30 TO 40	+0.280	+0.142	+0.064	+0.034	+0.025	+0.039	+0.062	+0.160	+0.007	−0.008	−0.017	−0.034	−0.051
	+0.120	+0.080	+0.025	+0.009	0.000	0.000	0.000	0.000	−0.018	−0.033	−0.042	−0.059	−0.076
OVER 40 TO 50	+0.290	+0.142	+0.064	+0.034	+0.025	+0.039	+0.062	+0.160	+0.007	−0.008	−0.017	−0.034	−0.061
	+0.130	+0.080	+0.025	+0.009	0.000	0.000	0.000	0.000	−0.018	−0.033	−0.042	−0.059	−0.086
OVER 50 TO 65	+0.330	+0.174	+0.076	+0.040	+0.030	+0.046	+0.074	+0.190	+0.009	−0.009	−0.021	−0.042	−0.076
	+0.140	+0.100	+0.030	+0.010	0.000	0.000	0.000	0.000	−0.021	−0.039	−0.051	−0.072	−0.106
OVER 65 TO 80	+0.340	+0.174	+0.076	+0.040	+0.030	+0.046	+0.074	+0.190	+0.009	−0.009	−0.021	−0.048	−0.091
	+0.150	+0.100	+0.030	+0.010	0.000	0.000	0.000	0.000	−0.021	−0.039	−0.051	−0.078	−0.121
OVER 80 TO 100	+0.390	+0.207	+0.090	+0.047	+0.035	+0.054	+0.087	+0.220	+0.010	−0.010	−0.024	−0.058	−0.111
	+0.170	+0.120	+0.036	+0.012	0.000	0.000	0.000	0.000	−0.025	−0.045	−0.059	−0.093	−0.146

Basic Size	c11	d9	f8	g7	h7	h8	h9	h11	k7	n7	p7	s7	u7
OVER 100 TO 120	+0.400 +0.180	+0.207 +0.120	+0.090 +0.036	+0.047 +0.012	+0.035 0.000	+0.054 0.000	+0.087 0.000	+0.220 0.000	+0.010 −0.025	−0.010 −0.045	−0.024 −0.059	−0.066 −0.101	−0.131 −0.166
OVER 120 TO 140	+0.450 +0.200	+0.245 +0.145	+0.106 +0.043	+0.054 +0.014	+0.040 0.000	+0.063 0.000	+0.100 0.000	+0.250 0.000	+0.012 −0.028	−0.012 −0.052	−0.028 −0.068	−0.077 −0.117	−0.155 −0.195
OVER 140 TO 160	+0.460 +0.210	+0.245 +0.145	+0.106 +0.043	+0.054 +0.014	+0.040 0.000	+0.063 0.000	+0.100 0.000	+0.250 0.000	+0.012 −0.028	−0.012 −0.052	−0.028 −0.068	−0.085 −0.125	−0.175 −0.215
OVER 160 TO 180	+0.480 +0.230	+0.245 +0.145	+0.106 +0.043	+0.054 +0.014	+0.040 0.000	+0.063 0.000	+0.100 0.000	+0.250 0.000	+0.012 −0.028	−0.012 −0.052	−0.028 −0.068	−0.093 −0.133	−0.195 −0.235
OVER 180 TO 200	+0.530 +0.240	+0.285 +0.170	+0.122 +0.050	+0.061 +0.015	+0.046 0.000	+0.072 0.000	+0.115 0.000	+0.290 0.000	−0.013 −0.033	−0.014 −0.060	−0.033 −0.079	−0.105 −0.151	−0.219 −0.265
OVER 200 TO 225	+0.550 +0.260	+0.285 +0.170	+0.122 +0.050	+0.061 +0.015	+0.046 0.000	+0.072 0.000	+0.115 0.000	+0.290 0.000	+0.013 −0.033	−0.014 −0.060	−0.033 −0.079	−0.113 −0.159	−0.241 −0.287
OVER 225 TO 250	+0.570 +0.280	+0.285 +0.170	+0.122 +0.050	+0.061 +0.015	+0.046 0.000	+0.072 0.000	+0.115 0.000	+0.290 0.000	+0.013 −0.033	−0.014 −0.060	−0.033 −0.079	−0.123 −0.169	−0.267 −0.313
OVER 250 TO 280	+0.620 +0.300	+0.320 +0.190	+0.137 +0.056	+0.069 +0.017	+0.052 0.000	+0.081 0.000	+0.130 0.000	+0.320 0.000	+0.016 −0.036	−0.014 −0.066	−0.036 −0.088	−0.138 −0.190	−0.295 −0.347
OVER 280 TO 315	+0.650 +0.330	+0.320 +0.190	+0.137 +0.056	+0.069 0.017	+0.052 0.000	+0.081 0.000	+0.130 0.000	+0.320 0.000	+0.016 −0.036	−0.014 −0.066	−0.036 −0.088	−0.150 −0.202	−0.330 −0.382
OVER 315 TO 355	+0.720 +0.360	+0.350 +0.210	+0.151 +0.062	+0.075 +0.018	+0.057 0.000	+0.089 0.000	+0.140 0.000	+0.360 0.000	+0.017 −0.040	−0.016 −0.073	−0.041 −0.058	−0.169 −0.226	−0.369 −0.426
OVER 355 TO 400	+0.760 +0.400	+0.350 +0.210	+0.151 +0.062	+0.075 +0.018	+0.057 0.000	+0.089 0.000	+0.140 0.000	+0.360 0.000	+0.017 −0.040	−0.016 −0.073	−0.041 −0.058	−0.187 −0.244	−0.414 −0.471
OVER 400 TO 450	+0.840 +0.440	+0.385 +0.230	+0.165 +0.068	+0.083 +0.020	+0.063 0.000	+0.097 0.000	+0.155 0.000	+0.400 0.000	+0.018 −0.045	−0.017 −0.080	−0.045 −0.108	−0.209 −0.272	−0.467 −0.530
OVER 450 TO 500	+0.880 +0.480	+0.385 +0.230	+0.165 +0.068	+0.083 +0.020	+0.063 0.000	+0.097 0.000	+0.155 0.000	+0.400 0.000	+0.018 −0.045	−0.017 −0.080	−0.045 −0.108	−0.229 −0.292	−0.517 −0.580

APPENDIX 43 • Shaft Sizes for Nonpreferred Diameters (millimeters)

Basic Size	c11	d9	f7	g6	h6	h7	h9	h11	k6	n6	p6	s6	u6
OVER 0 TO 3	−0.060 / −0.120	−0.020 / −0.045	−0.006 / −0.016	−0.002 / −0.008	0.000 / −0.006	0.000 / −0.010	0.000 / −0.025	0.000 / −0.060	+0.006 / 0.000	+0.010 / +0.004	+0.012 / +0.006	+0.020 / +0.014	+0.024 / +0.018
OVER 3 TO 6	−0.070 / −0.145	−0.030 / −0.060	−0.010 / −0.022	−0.004 / −0.012	0.000 / −0.008	0.000 / −0.012	0.000 / −0.030	0.000 / −0.075	+0.009 / +0.001	+0.016 / +0.008	+0.020 / +0.012	+0.027 / +0.019	+0.031 / +0.023
OVER 6 TO 10	−0.080 / −0.170	−0.040 / −0.076	−0.013 / −0.028	−0.005 / −0.014	0.000 / −0.009	0.000 / −0.015	0.000 / −0.036	0.000 / −0.090	+0.010 / +0.001	+0.019 / +0.010	+0.024 / +0.015	+0.032 / +0.023	+0.037 / +0.028
OVER 10 TO 14	−0.095 / −0.205	−0.050 / −0.093	−0.016 / −0.034	−0.006 / −0.017	0.000 / −0.011	0.000 / −0.018	0.000 / −0.043	0.000 / −0.110	+0.012 / +0.001	+0.023 / +0.012	+0.029 / +0.018	+0.039 / +0.028	+0.044 / +0.033
OVER 14 TO 18	−0.095 / −0.205	−0.050 / −0.093	−0.016 / −0.034	−0.006 / −0.017	0.000 / −0.011	0.000 / −0.018	0.000 / −0.043	0.000 / −0.110	+0.012 / +0.001	+0.023 / +0.012	+0.029 / +0.018	+0.039 / +0.028	+0.044 / +0.033
OVER 18 TO 24	−0.110 / −0.240	−0.065 / −0.117	−0.020 / −0.041	−0.007 / −0.020	0.000 / −0.013	0.000 / −0.021	0.000 / −0.052	0.000 / −0.130	+0.015 / +0.002	+0.028 / +0.015	+0.035 / +0.022	+0.048 / +0.035	+0.054 / +0.041
OVER 24 TO 30	−0.110 / −0.240	−0.065 / −0.117	−0.020 / −0.041	−0.007 / −0.020	0.000 / −0.013	0.000 / −0.021	0.000 / −0.052	0.000 / −0.130	+0.015 / +0.002	+0.028 / +0.015	+0.035 / +0.022	+0.048 / +0.035	+0.061 / +0.048
OVER 30 TO 40	−0.120 / −0.280	−0.080 / −0.142	−0.025 / −0.050	−0.009 / −0.025	0.000 / −0.016	0.000 / −0.025	0.000 / −0.062	0.000 / −0.160	+0.018 / +0.002	+0.033 / +0.017	+0.042 / +0.026	+0.059 / +0.043	+0.076 / +0.060
OVER 40 TO 50	−0.130 / −0.290	−0.080 / −0.142	−0.025 / −0.050	−0.009 / −0.025	0.000 / −0.016	0.000 / −0.025	0.000 / −0.062	0.000 / −0.160	+0.018 / +0.002	+0.033 / +0.017	+0.042 / +0.026	+0.059 / +0.043	+0.086 / +0.070
OVER 50 TO 65	−0.140 / −0.330	−0.100 / −0.174	−0.030 / −0.060	−0.010 / −0.029	0.000 / −0.019	0.000 / −0.030	0.000 / −0.074	0.000 / −0.190	+0.021 / +0.002	+0.039 / +0.020	+0.051 / −0.032	+0.072 / +0.053	+0.106 / +0.087
OVER 65 TO 80	−0.150 / −0.340	−0.100 / −0.174	−0.030 / −0.060	−0.010 / −0.029	0.000 / −0.019	0.000 / −0.030	0.000 / −0.074	0.000 / −0.190	+0.021 / +0.002	+0.039 / +0.020	+0.051 / +0.032	+0.078 / +0.059	+0.121 / +0.102
OVER 80 TO 100	−0.170 / −0.390	−0.120 / −0.207	−0.036 / −0.071	−0.012 / −0.034	0.000 / −0.022	0.000 / −0.035	0.000 / −0.087	0.000 / −0.220	+0.025 / +0.003	+0.045 / +0.023	+0.059 / +0.037	+0.093 / +0.071	+0.146 / +0.124

Basic Size	c11	d9	f7	g6	h6	h7	h9	h11	k6	n6	p6	s6	u6
OVER 100 TO 120	−0.180 −0.400	−0.120 −0.207	−0.036 −0.071	−0.012 −0.034	0.000 −0.022	0.000 −0.035	0.000 −0.087	0.000 −0.220	+0.025 +0.003	+0.045 +0.023	+0.059 +0.037	+0.101 +0.079	+0.166 +0.144
OVER 120 TO 140	−0.200 −0.450	−0.145 −0.245	−0.043 −0.083	−0.014 −0.039	0.000 −0.025	0.000 −0.040	0.000 −0.100	0.000 −0.250	+0.028 +0.003	+0.052 +0.027	+0.068 +0.043	+0.117 +0.092	+0.195 +0.170
OVER 140 TO 160	−0.210 −0.460	−0.145 −0.245	−0.043 −0.083	−0.014 −0.039	0.000 −0.025	0.000 −0.040	0.000 −0.100	0.000 −0.250	+0.028 +0.003	+0.052 +0.027	+0.068 +0.043	+0.125 +0.100	+0.215 +0.190
OVER 160 TO 180	−0.230 −0.480	−0.145 −0.245	−0.043 −0.083	−0.014 −0.039	0.000 −0.025	0.000 −0.040	0.000 −0.100	0.000 −0.250	+0.028 +0.003	+0.052 +0.027	+0.068 +0.043	+0.133 +0.108	+0.235 +0.210
OVER 180 TO 200	−0.240 −0.530	−0.170 −0.285	−0.050 −0.096	−0.015 −0.044	0.000 −0.029	0.000 −0.046	0.000 −0.115	0.000 −0.290	+0.033 +0.004	+0.060 +0.031	+0.079 +0.050	+0.151 +0.122	+0.265 +0.236
OVER 200 TO 225	−0.260 −0.550	−0.170 −0.285	−0.050 −0.096	−0.015 −0.044	0.000 −0.029	0.000 −0.046	0.000 −0.115	0.000 −0.290	+0.033 +0.004	+0.060 +0.031	+0.079 +0.050	+0.159 +0.130	+0.287 +0.258
OVER 225 TO 250	−0.280 −0.570	−0.170 −0.285	−0.050 −0.096	−0.015 −0.044	0.000 −0.029	0.000 −0.046	0.000 −0.115	0.000 −0.290	+0.033 +0.004	+0.060 +0.031	+0.079 +0.050	+0.169 +0.140	+0.313 +0.284
OVER 250 TO 280	−0.300 −0.620	−0.190 −0.320	−0.056 −0.108	−0.017 −0.049	0.000 −0.032	0.000 −0.052	0.000 −0.130	0.000 −0.320	+0.036 +0.004	+0.066 +0.034	+0.088 +0.056	+0.190 +0.158	+0.347 +0.315
OVER 280 TO 315	−0.330 −0.650	−0.190 −0.320	−0.056 −0.108	−0.017 −0.049	0.000 −0.032	0.000 −0.052	0.000 −0.130	0.000 −0.320	+0.036 +0.004	+0.066 +0.034	+0.088 +0.056	+0.202 +0.170	+0.382 +0.350
OVER 315 TO 355	−0.360 −0.720	−0.210 −0.350	−0.062 −0.119	−0.018 −0.054	0.000 −0.036	0.000 −0.057	0.000 −0.140	0.000 −0.360	+0.040 +0.004	+0.073 +0.037	+0.098 +0.062	+0.226 +0.190	+0.426 +0.390
OVER 355 TO 400	−0.400 −0.760	−0.210 −0.350	−0.062 −0.119	−0.018 −0.054	0.000 −0.036	0.000 −0.057	0.000 −0.140	0.000 −0.360	+0.040 +0.004	+0.073 +0.037	+0.098 +0.062	+0.244 +0.208	+0.471 +0.435
OVER 400 TO 450	−0.440 −0.840	−0.230 −0.385	−0.068 −0.131	−0.020 −0.060	0.000 −0.040	0.000 −0.063	0.000 −0.155	0.000 −0.400	+0.045 +0.005	+0.080 +0.040	+0.108 +0.068	+0.272 +0.232	+0.530 +0.490
OVER 450 TO 500	−0.480 −0.880	−0.230 −0.385	−0.068 −0.131	−0.020 −0.060	0.000 −0.040	0.000 −0.063	0.000 −0.155	0.000 −0.400	+0.045 +0.005	+0.080 +0.040	+0.108 +0.068	+0.292 +0.252	+0.580 +0.540

APPENDIX 44 • American National Standard 125-lb Cast Iron Screwed Fittings (inches)

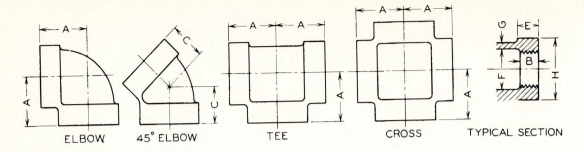

ELBOW   45° ELBOW   TEE   CROSS   TYPICAL SECTION

Nominal Pipe Size	A	C	B Min	E Min	F Min	F Max	G Min	H Min
¼	0.81	0.73	0.32	0.38	0.540	0.584	0.110	0.93
⅜	0.95	0.80	0.36	0.44	0.675	0.719	0.120	1.12
½	1.12	0.88	0.43	0.50	0.840	0.897	0.130	1.34
¾	1.31	0.98	0.50	0.56	1.050	1.107	0.155	1.63
1	1.50	1.12	0.58	0.62	1.315	1.385	0.170	1.95
1¼	1.75	1.29	0.67	0.69	1.660	1.730	0.185	2.39
1½	1.94	1.43	0.70	0.75	1.900	1.970	0.200	2.68
2	2.25	1.68	0.75	0.84	2.375	2.445	0.220	3.28
2½	2.70	1.95	0.92	0.94	2.875	2.975	0.240	3.86
3	3.08	2.17	0.98	1.00	3.500	3.600	0.260	4.62
3½	3.42	2.39	1.03	1.06	4.000	4.100	0.280	5.20
4	3.79	2.61	1.08	1.12	4.500	4.600	0.310	5.79
5	4.50	3.05	1.18	1.18	5.563	5.663	0.380	7.05
6	5.13	3.46	1.28	1.28	6.625	6.725	0.430	8.28
8	6.56	4.28	1.47	1.47	8.625	8.725	0.550	10.63
10	8.08	5.16	1.68	1.68	10.750	10.850	0.690	13.12
12	9.50	5.97	1.88	1.88	12.750	12.850	0.800	15.47
14 O.D.	10.40	—	2.00	2.00	14.000	14.100	0.880	16.94
16 O.D.	11.82	—	2.20	2.20	16.000	16.100	1.000	19.30

Source: Extracted from American National Standards, "Cast-Iron Screwed Fittings, 125-and 250-lb" (ANSI B16.4), with the permission of the publisher, The American Society of Mechanical Engineers.

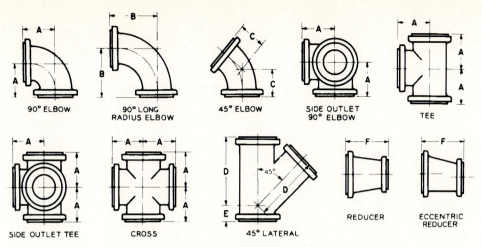

90° ELBOW   90° LONG RADIUS ELBOW   45° ELBOW   SIDE OUTLET 90° ELBOW   TEE

SIDE OUTLET TEE   CROSS   45° LATERAL   REDUCER   ECCENTRIC REDUCER

Dimensions of 250-lb Cast Iron Flanged Fittings

	Flanges			Fittings		Straight					
Nominal Pipe Size	Dia of Flange	Thickness of Flange (Min)	Dia of Raised Face	Inside Dia of Fittings (Min)	Wall Thickness	Center to Face 90 Deg Elbow Tees, Crosses and True "Y"	Center to Face 90 Deg Long Radius Elbow	Center to Face 45 Deg Elbow	Center to Face Lateral	Short Center to Face True "Y" and Lateral	Face to Face Reducer
						A	B	C	D	E	F
1	$4\frac{7}{8}$	$\frac{11}{16}$	$2\frac{11}{16}$	1	$\frac{7}{16}$	4	5	2	$6\frac{1}{2}$	2	....
$1\frac{1}{4}$	$5\frac{1}{4}$	$\frac{3}{4}$	$3\frac{1}{16}$	$1\frac{1}{4}$	$\frac{7}{16}$	$4\frac{1}{4}$	$5\frac{1}{2}$	$2\frac{1}{2}$	$7\frac{1}{4}$	$2\frac{1}{4}$	....
$1\frac{1}{2}$	$6\frac{1}{8}$	$\frac{13}{16}$	$3\frac{9}{16}$	$1\frac{1}{2}$	$\frac{7}{16}$	$4\frac{1}{2}$	6	$2\frac{3}{4}$	$8\frac{1}{2}$	$2\frac{1}{2}$	....
2	$6\frac{1}{2}$	$\frac{7}{8}$	$4\frac{3}{16}$	2	$\frac{7}{16}$	5	$6\frac{1}{2}$	3	9	$2\frac{1}{2}$	5
$2\frac{1}{2}$	$7\frac{1}{2}$	1	$4\frac{15}{16}$	$2\frac{1}{2}$	$\frac{1}{2}$	$5\frac{1}{2}$	7	$3\frac{1}{2}$	$10\frac{1}{2}$	$2\frac{1}{2}$	$5\frac{1}{2}$
3	$8\frac{1}{4}$	$1\frac{1}{8}$	$5\frac{11}{16}$	3	$\frac{9}{16}$	6	$7\frac{3}{4}$	$3\frac{1}{2}$	11	3	6
$3\frac{1}{2}$	9	$1\frac{3}{16}$	$6\frac{5}{16}$	$3\frac{1}{2}$	$\frac{9}{16}$	$6\frac{1}{2}$	$8\frac{1}{2}$	4	$12\frac{1}{2}$	3	$6\frac{1}{2}$
4	10	$1\frac{1}{4}$	$6\frac{15}{16}$	4	$\frac{5}{8}$	7	9	$4\frac{1}{2}$	$13\frac{1}{2}$	3	7
5	11	$1\frac{3}{8}$	$8\frac{5}{16}$	5	$\frac{11}{16}$	8	$10\frac{1}{4}$	5	15	$3\frac{1}{2}$	8
6	$12\frac{1}{2}$	$1\frac{7}{16}$	$9\frac{11}{16}$	6	$\frac{3}{4}$	$8\frac{1}{2}$	$11\frac{1}{2}$	$5\frac{1}{2}$	$17\frac{1}{2}$	4	9
8	15	$1\frac{5}{8}$	$11\frac{15}{16}$	8	$\frac{13}{16}$	10	14	6	$20\frac{1}{2}$	5	11
10	$17\frac{1}{2}$	$1\frac{7}{8}$	$14\frac{1}{16}$	10	$\frac{15}{16}$	$11\frac{1}{2}$	$16\frac{1}{2}$	7	24	$5\frac{1}{2}$	12
12	$20\frac{1}{2}$	2	$16\frac{7}{16}$	12	1	13	19	8	$27\frac{1}{2}$	6	14
14	23	$2\frac{1}{8}$	$18\frac{15}{16}$	$13\frac{1}{4}$	$1\frac{1}{8}$	15	$21\frac{1}{2}$	$8\frac{1}{2}$	31	$6\frac{1}{2}$	16
16	$25\frac{1}{2}$	$2\frac{1}{4}$	$21\frac{1}{16}$	$15\frac{1}{4}$	$1\frac{1}{4}$	$16\frac{1}{2}$	24	$9\frac{1}{2}$	$34\frac{1}{2}$	$7\frac{1}{2}$	18
18	28	$2\frac{3}{8}$	$23\frac{5}{16}$	17	$1\frac{3}{8}$	18	$26\frac{1}{2}$	10	$37\frac{1}{2}$	8	19
20	$30\frac{1}{2}$	$2\frac{1}{2}$	$25\frac{9}{16}$	19	$1\frac{1}{2}$	$19\frac{1}{2}$	29	$10\frac{1}{2}$	$40\frac{1}{2}$	$8\frac{1}{2}$	20
24	36	$2\frac{3}{4}$	$30\frac{5}{16}$	23	$1\frac{5}{8}$	$22\frac{1}{2}$	34	12	$47\frac{1}{2}$	10	24
30	43	3	$37\frac{3}{16}$	29	2	$27\frac{1}{2}$	$41\frac{1}{2}$	15	....	....	30

Source: Courtesy of ANSI; B16.1-1967.

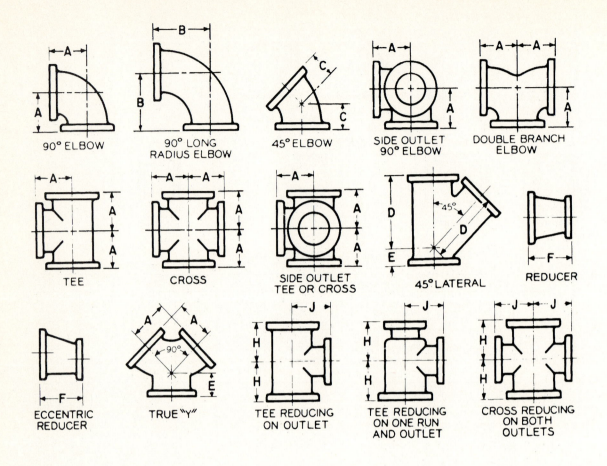

90° ELBOW

90° LONG RADIUS ELBOW

45° ELBOW

SIDE OUTLET 90° ELBOW

DOUBLE BRANCH ELBOW

TEE

CROSS

SIDE OUTLET TEE OR CROSS

45° LATERAL

REDUCER

ECCENTRIC REDUCER

TRUE "Y"

TEE REDUCING ON OUTLET

TEE REDUCING ON ONE RUN AND OUTLET

CROSS REDUCING ON BOTH OUTLETS

APPENDIX 46 • (continued)

Nominal Pipe Size	Flanges: Dia of Flange	Flanges: Thickness of Flange (Min)	General: Inside Dia of Flange Fittings	General: Wall Thickness	Straight Fittings: Center to Face 90 deg Elbow Tees, Crosses True "Y" and Double Branch Elbow A	Center to Face 90 deg Long Radius El-bow B	Center to Face 45 deg Elbow C	Center to Face Lateral D	Short Center to Face True "Y" and Lateral E	Face to Face Reducer F	Reducing Fittings (Short Body Patterns), Tees and Crosses: Size of Outlet and Smaller	Center to Face Run H	Center to Face Outlet or Side Outlet J
1	4 1/4	7/16	1	5/16	3 1/2	5	1 3/4	5 3/4	1 3/4	. . .	All reducing tees and crosses, sizes 16 in. and smaller, shall have same center to face dimensions as straight size fittings, corresponding to the size of the largest opening.		
1 1/4	4 5/8	1/2	1 1/4	5/16	3 3/4	5 1/2	2	6 1/4	1 3/4	. . .			
1 1/2	5	9/16	1 1/2	5/16	4	6	2 1/4	7	2				
2	6	5/8	2	5/16	4 1/2	6 1/2	2 1/2	8	2 1/2	5			
2 1/2	7	11/16	2 1/2	5/16	5	7	3	9 1/2	2 1/2	5 1/2			
3	7 1/2	3/4	3	3/8	5 1/2	7 3/4	3	10	3	6			
3 1/2	8 1/2	13/16	3 1/2	7/16	6	8 1/2	3 1/2	11 1/2	3	6 1/2			
4	9	15/16	4	1/2	6 1/2	9	4	12	3	7			
5	10	15/16	5	1/2	7 1/2	10 1/4	4 1/2	13 1/2	3 1/2	8			
6	11	1	6	9/16	8	11 1/2	5	14 1/2	3 1/2	9			
8	13 1/2	1 1/8	8	5/8	9	14	5 1/2	17 1/2	4 1/2	11			
10	16	1 3/16	10	3/4	11	16 1/2	6 1/2	20 1/2	5	12			
12	19	1 1/4	12	13/16	12	19	7 1/2	24 1/2	5 1/2	14			
14	21	1 3/8	14	7/8	14	21 1/2	7 1/2	27	6	16			
16	23 1/2	1 7/16	16	1	15	24	8	30	6 1/2	18			
18	25	1 9/16	18	1 1/16	16 1/2	26 1/2	8 1/2	32	7	19	12	13	15 1/2
20	27 1/2	1 11/16	20	1 1/8	18	29	9 1/2	35	8	20	14	14	17
24	32	1 7/8	24	1 1/4	22	34	11	40 1/2	9	24	16	15	19
30	38 3/4	2 1/8	30	1 7/16	25	41 1/2	15	49	10	30	20	18	23
36	46	2 3/8	36	1 5/8	28*	49	18	. . .	. . .	36	24	20	26
42	53	2 5/8	42	1 13/16	31*	56 1/2	21	. . .	. . .	42	24	23	30
48	59 1/2	2 3/4	48	2	34*	64	24	. . .	. . .	48	30	26	34

Source: Courtesy of ANSI; B16.1-1967.

UNITED STATES SYSTEM

LINEAR MEASURE

Inches	Feet	Yards	Rods	Furlongs	Miles
1.0 =	.08333 =	.02778 =	.0050505 =	.00012626 =	.00001578
12.0 =	1.0 =	.33333 =	.0606061 =	.00151515 =	.00018939
36.0 =	3.0 =	1.0 =	.1818182 =	.00454545 =	.00056818
198.0 =	16.5 =	5.5 =	1.0 =	.025 =	.003125
7920.0 =	660.0 =	220.0 =	40.0 =	1.0 =	.125
63360.0 =	5280.0 =	1760.0 =	320.0 =	8.0 =	1.0

SQUARE AND LAND MEASURE

Sq. Inches	Square Feet	Square Yards	Sq. Rods	Acres	Sq. Miles
1.0 =	.006944 =	.000772			
144.0 =	1.0 =	.111111			
1296.0 =	9.0 =	1.0 =	.03306 =	.000207	
39204.0 =	272.25 =	30.25 =	1.0 =	.00625 =	.0000098
	43560.0 =	4840.0 =	160.0 =	1.0 =	.0015625
		3097600.0 =	102400.0 =	640.0 =	1.0

AVOIRDUPOIS WEIGHTS

Grains	Drams	Ounces	Pounds	Tons
1.0 =	.03657 =	.002286 =	.000143 =	.0000000714
27.34375 =	1.0 =	.0625 =	.003906 =	.00000195
437.5 =	16.0 =	1.0 =	.0625 =	.00003125
7000.0 =	256.0 =	16.0 =	1.0 =	.0005
14000000.0 =	512000.0 =	32000.0 =	2000.0 =	1.0

DRY MEASURE

Pints	Quarts	Pecks	Cubic Feet	Bushels
1.0 =	.5 =	.0625 =	.01945 =	.01563
2.0 =	1.0 =	.125 =	.03891 =	.03125
16.0 =	8.0 =	1.0 =	.31112 =	.25
51.42627 =	25.71314 =	3.21414 =	1.0 =	.80354
64.0 =	32.0 =	4.0 =	1.2445 =	1.0

LIQUID MEASURE

Gills	Pints	Quarts	U. S. Gallons	Cubic Feet
1.0 =	.25 =	.125 =	.03125 =	.00418
4.0 =	1.0 =	.5 =	.125 =	.01671
8.0 =	2.0 =	1.0 =	.250 =	.03342
32.0 =	8.0 =	4.0 =	1.0 =	.1337
			7.48052 =	1.0

METRIC SYSTEM

UNITS

Length—Meter : Mass—Gram : Capacity—Liter
for pure water at 4°C. (39.2°F.)
1 cubic decimeter or 1 liter = 1 kilogram

1000 Milli {meters (mm), grams (mg), liters (ml)} = 100 Centi {meters (cm), grams (cg), liters (cl)} = 10 Deci {meters (dm), grams (dg), liters (dl)} = 1 {meter, gram, liter}

1000 {meters, grams, liters} = 100 Deka {meters (dkm), grams (dkg), liters (dkl)} = 10 Hecto {meters (hm), grams (hg), liters (hl)} = 1 Kilo {meter (km), gram (kg), liter (kl)}

1 Metric Ton   = 1000 Kilograms
100 Square Meters   = 1 Are
100 Ares   = 1 Hectare
100 Hectares   = 1 Square Kilometer

DECIMAL EQUIVALENTS — INCH-MILLIMETER CONVERSION TABLE

1/2	1/4	1/8	1/16	1/32	1/64	Decimals	Millimeters
				1	1	.015625	.396875
					3	.031250	.793750
			1		3	.046875	1.190625
						.062500	1.587500
				3	5	.078125	1.984375
					7	.093750	2.381250
						.109375	2.778125
		1				.125000	3.175000
				5	9	.140625	3.571875
					11	.156250	3.968750
			3			.171875	4.365625
						.187500	4.762500
				7	13	.203125	5.159375
					15	.218750	5.556250
						.234375	5.953125
	1					.250000	6.350000
				9	17	.265625	6.746875
			5		19	.281250	7.143750
						.296875	7.540625
						.312500	7.937500
				11	21	.328125	8.334375
					23	.343750	8.731250
						.359375	9.128125
		3				.375000	9.525000
				13	25	.390625	9.921875
					27	.406250	10.318750
			7			.421875	10.715625
						.437500	11.112500
				15	29	.453125	11.509375
					31	.468750	11.906250
						.484375	12.303125
1						.500000	12.700000

1/2	1/4	1/8	1/16	1/32	1/64	Decimals	Millimeters
				17	33	.515625	13.096875
					35	.531250	13.493750
			9			.546875	13.890625
						.562500	14.287500
				19	37	.578125	14.684375
					39	.593750	15.081250
						.609375	15.478125
		5				.625000	15.875000
				21	41	.640625	16.271875
					43	.656250	16.668750
			11			.671875	17.065625
						.687500	17.462500
				23	45	.703125	17.859375
					47	.718750	18.256250
						.734375	18.653125
	3					.750000	19.050000
				25	49	.765625	19.446875
			13		51	.781250	19.843750
						.796875	20.240625
						.812500	20.637500
				27	53	.828125	21.034375
					55	.843750	21.431250
						.859375	21.828125
		7				.875000	22.225000
				29	57	.890625	22.621875
					59	.906250	23.018750
			15			.921875	23.415625
						.937500	23.812500
				31	61	.953125	24.209375
					63	.968750	24.606250
			16	32	64	.984375	25.003125
	4	8				1.000000	25.400000

WIRE AND SHEET METAL GAGES
IN DECIMALS OF AN INCH

Name of Gage	United States Standard Gage*		The United States Steel Wire Gage	American or Brown & Sharpe Wire Gage	New Birmingham Standard Sheet & Hoop Gage	British Imperial or English Legal Standard Wire Gage	Birmingham or Stubs Iron Wire Gage	Name of Gage
Principal Use	Uncoated Steel Sheets and Light Plates		Steel Wire except Music Wire	Non-Ferrous Sheets and Wire	Iron and Steel Sheets and Hoops	Wire	Strips, Bands, Hoops and Wire	Principal Use
Gage No.	Weight Oz. per Sq. Ft.	Approx. Thickness Inches	Thickness, Inches					Gage No.
7/0's			.4900		.6666	.500		7/0's
6/0's			.4615	.5800	.625	.464		6/0's
5/0's			.4305	.5165	.5883	.432	.500	5/0's
4/0's			.3938	.4600	.5416	.400	.454	4/0's
3/0's			.3625	.4096	.500	.372	.425	3/0's
2/0's			.3310	.3648	.4452	.348	.380	2/0's
0			.3065	.3249	.3964	.324	.340	0
1			.2830	.2893	.3532	.300	.300	1
2			.2625	.2576	.3147	.276	.284	2
3	160	.2391	.2437	.2294	.2804	.252	.259	3
4	150	.2242	.2253	.2043	.250	.232	.238	4
5	140	.2092	.2070	.1819	.2225	.212	.220	5
6	130	.1943	.1920	.1620	.1981	.192	.203	6
7	120	.1793	.1770	.1443	.1764	.176	.180	7
8	110	.1644	.1620	.1285	.1570	.160	.165	8
9	100	.1495	.1483	.1144	.1398	.144	.148	9
10	90	.1345	.1350	.1019	.1250	.128	.134	10
11	80	.1196	.1205	.0907	.1113	.116	.120	11
12	70	.1046	.1055	.0808	.0991	.104	.109	12
13	60	.0897	.0915	.0720	.0882	.092	.095	13
14	50	0747	.0800	.0641	.0785	.080	.083	14
15	45	.0673	.0720	.0571	.0699	.072	.072	15
16	40	.0598	.0625	.0508	.0625	.064	.065	16
17	36	.0538	.0540	.0453	.0556	.056	.058	17
18	32	.0478	.0475	.0403	.0495	.048	.049	18
19	28	.0418	.0410	.0359	.0440	.040	.042	19
20	24	.0359	.0348	.0320	.0392	.036	.035	20
21	22	.0329	.0318	.0285	.0349	.032	.032	21
22	20	.0299	.0286	.0253	.0313	.028	.028	22
23	18	.0269	.0258	.0226	.0278	.024	.025	23
24	16	.0239	.0230	.0201	.0248	.022	.022	24
25	14	.0209	.0204	.0179	.0220	.020	.020	25
26	12	.0179	.0181	.0159	.0196	.018	.018	26
27	11	.0164	.0173	.0142	.0175	.0164	.016	27
28	10	.0149	.0162	.0126	.0156	.0148	.014	28
29	9	.0135	.0150	.0113	.0139	.0136	.013	29
30	8	.0120	.0140	.0100	.0123	.0124	.012	30
31	7	.0105	.0132	.0089	.0110	.0116	.010	31
32	6.5	.0097	.0128	.0080	.0098	.0108	.009	32
33	6	.0090	.0118	.0071	.0087	.0100	.008	33
34	5.5	.0082	.0104	.0063	.0077	.0092	.007	34
35	5	.0075	.0095	.0056	.0069	.0084	.005	35
36	4.5	.0067	.0090	.0050	.0061	.0076	.004	36
37	4.25	.0064	.0085	.0045	.0054	.0068		37
38	4	.0060	.0080	.0040	.0048	.0060		38
39			.0075	.0035	.0043	.0052		39
40			.0070	.0031	.0039	.0048		40

* U. S. Standard Gage is officially a weight gage, in oz. per sq. ft. as tabulated. The Approx. Thickness shown is the "Manufacturers' Standard" of the American Iron and Steel Institute, based on steel as weighing 501.81 lbs. per cu. ft. (489.6 true weight plus 2.5 percent for average over-run in area and thickness). The A.I.S.I. standard nomenclature for flat rolled carbon steel is as follows:

Widths, Inches	Thicknesses, Inch							
	0.2500 and thicker	0.2499 to 0.2031	0.2030 to 0.1875	0.1874 to 0.0568	0.0567 to 0.0344	0.0343 to 0.0255	0.0254 to 0.0142	0.0141 and thinner
To 3½ incl.	Bar	Bar	Strip	Strip	Strip	Strip	Sheet	Sheet
Over 3½ to 6 incl.	Bar	Bar	Strip	Strip	Strip	Sheet	Sheet	Sheet
" 6 to 12 "	Plate	Strip	Strip	Strip	Sheet	Sheet	Sheet	Sheet
" 12 to 32 "	Plate	Sheet	Sheet	Sheet	Sheet	Sheet	Sheet	Black Plate
" 32 to 48 "	Plate	Sheet	Sheet	Sheet	Sheet	Sheet	Sheet	Sheet
" 48	Plate	Plate	Plate	Sheet	Sheet	Sheet	Sheet	—

Index